Multiple Perspectives of Entrepreneurship:

Text, Readings, and Cases

Daniel F. Jennings
Baylor University

COLLEGE DIVISION South-Western Publishing Co.

Cincinnati Ohio

Sponsoring Editor: Randy G. Haubner
Production Editor: Mark Sears
Production House: Books By Design, Inc.
Internal Design: Russell Schneck
Cover Design: Lotus Wittkopf
Cover Photographer: © Tim Davis/Allstock
Marketing Manager: Scott Person

GV60AA
Copyright © 1994
by SOUTH-WESTERN PUBLISHING CO.
Cincinnati, Ohio

I(T)P
International Thomson Publishing

South-Western Publishing Co. is an ITP Company. The ITP trademark is used under license.

2 3 4 5 6 7 MT 9 8 7 6 5 4

Printed in the United States of America

Library of Congress Cataloging-in-Publication Data

Jennings, Daniel F.
    Multiple perspectives of entrepreneurship : text, readings, and cases / Daniel F. Jennings
        p.   cm.
    Based on the author's thesis (doctoral)--Texas A&M.
    ISBN 0-538-81090-4
    1. Entrepreneurship. 2. Entrepreneurship--Case studies.
I. Title.
HB 615.J453 1993
338'.04--dc20   93-36592
                                                         CIP

To Kay, who could have written this but instead became an entrepreneur, and to the late John Reynolds, who encouraged me to study entrepreneurship.

ABOUT THE
AUTHOR

Dr. Daniel F. Jennings has published over 100 articles in academic and practitioner journals and recently authored six textbooks in management theory and business simulations. His research has been published in such journals as the *Strategic Management Journal, Journal of Management, Journal of Business Venturing* and *Entrepreneurship Theory and Practice* and has been described in both the *Wall Street Journal* and *New York Times*.

Professor Jennings was given the 1988 Outstanding Research Award by the Hankamer School of Business, Baylor University, and received a Best Paper Award from the Stern Center of Entrepreneurship, New York University, for a conceptual paper on corporate entrepreneurship.

Dr. Jennings is active in numerous academic associations including the Academy of Management, Southern Management Association, Southwest Academy of Management, and Southwest Case Research Association. He was elected to the Board of Governors of the Southern Management Association for 1992–1994 and elected secretary of the Southwest Case Research Association in 1993.

Dr. Jennings is the W. A. Mays Professor of Entrepreneurship and Strategic Management in the Department of Management at Baylor University. He received a B.S. degree in Industrial Engineering (with honors) from the University of Tennessee and an M.B.A. from Northeast Louisiana University.

After twenty years of experience as an industrial engineer, corporate planner, plant manager, and operations manager with forest products and chemical firms in the U.S. and South America, he earned a Ph.D. degree in Strategic Management from Texas A&M University. Professor Jennings is a registered professional engineer and has taught in several professional development programs as well as performed consulting assignments for a variety of firms and labor unions.

PREFACE

Multiple Perspectives of Entrepreneurship: Text, Readings, and Cases emerged from my doctoral dissertation, which was completed at Texas A&M University. The focus of this dissertation was on the relationship between strategic management and corporate entrepreneurship. During the development of the literature review for my dissertation, I learned that several schools of thought had developed that described the notion of entrepreneurship. These entrepreneurial "schools of thought," however, existed in different academic areas: economics, management, and psychology, to name a few. Interestingly, these broad areas contained a number of subareas. For example, in the management literature, the concept of entrepreneurship is covered in strategic management, organization behavior, organization theory, small business, production operations, and, of course, in "entrepreneurship" courses. I also learned that individuals from one academic field rarely acknowledge the work of scholars from other academic fields when entrepreneurship is involved. It seemed that Peter Kilby's (1971) statement of entrepreneurial researchers was true. Kilby, after having reviewed research activities in entrepreneurship, stated that each researcher in entrepreneurship appears to have developed his or her own definition without building on the works of others. Kilby described these definitional attempts as being similar to hunting the heffalump. Unfortunately, even today, the search for the source of dynamic entrepreneurial performance has much in common with hunting the heffalump. (The reader is directed to Exhibit 8.5, page 130, for Kilby's description of the heffalump.)

The purpose of this text is to present three different schools of entrepreneurial thought as three distinct modules or perspectives. These include (1) the notion of corporate entrepreneurship, (2) entrepreneurship as an economic function, and (3) behavioral factors and psychological traits of entrepreneurs. Each module presents theories of each perspective, and cases are provided as a possible approach toward integrating theory with the actual practices of entrepreneurial activity.

Acknowledgments

Many people played an important part in the creation of this textbook. This is my chance to say thank you.

A number of busy scholars took substantial time to provide informative, thoughtful suggestions. Their names and affiliations are: Humberto Barreto, Wabash College; Jeffrey Bracker, University of Louisville; John Butler, University of Washington; Steven Gardner, Baylor University; Jerome Katz, St. Louis University; Albert N. Link, University of North Carolina–Greensboro; Tracey Miller, Dordt College; Theodore Schultz, Nobel Laureate–University of Chicago; Shaker Zahra, Georgia State University.

A number of excellent cases have been provided by case authors. They include: Stephen Barndt, Pacific Lutheran University; Jeffrey Bracker, University of Louisville; Scott Bruce, Sam Houston State University; Keith Crow, Sam Houston State University; Jeffrey Harrison, Clemson University; Raymond Kinnunen, Northeastern University; R. Dean Lewis, Sam Houston State University; Carla Litvany, Rollins College; James Molloy, Jr., Northeastern University; James Prichard, Sam Houston State University; Allie J. Quinn, Dartmouth College; James Brian Quinn, Dartmouth College; Paul Reed,

Sam Houston State University; John Seeger, Bentley College; Carolyn Silliman, Clemson University; Natalie Tabb Taylor, Babson College; J. Barry Teare, Sam Houston State University; Julian Vincze, Rollins College; Wendy Vittori, Northeastern University; Shaker Zahra, Georgia State University.

The people from South-Western Publishing provided valuable assistance, including acquiring editor Randy Haubner, production editor Mark Sears, and editorial assistant Pamela Meisman. Herb Nolan of Books By Design is thanked for his copy editing and other valuable suggestions.

Don Edwards, Chairman of the Management Department, and Richard Scott, Dean of the Hankamer School of Business at Baylor University, are thanked for providing the setting and atmosphere in which this book could be written.

The efforts of Sandy Tighe and Ranjit Thorat in preparing this manuscript are certainly appreciated.

Finally, this textbook is dedicated to my wife, Kay Cothran Jennings, who could have written this but instead became an entrepreneur, and to my dissertation chairman, the late John Reynolds, who encouraged me to study entrepreneurship.

Daniel F. Jennings
Baylor University

CONTENTS

CASES

Introduction

Robert Sobel and David Sicilia have written that Americans have fallen in love with the French noun *entrepreneur* and have described how numerous seminars are being conducted at various business schools in an attempt to uncover the clues as how to best isolate and distill entrepreneurship and then infuse it into modern corporations.[1]

An important question is, what is the relationship between entrepreneurship and corporate revitalization? A beginning point, perhaps, is integrating theory with practice. In any endeavor, theory and practice should be integrated. Why? For the reason that without practice, any particular field takes on a tremendous ideological burden because idea systems can obscure certain items.[2] This argument considers that a particular theory is applicable to some specific situation. For example, all the elements of the theoretical sciences of human action are implied in the hard core of *praxis,* or practice.[3] Proponents of this school of thought suggest that no action can be devised and ventured on without definite ideas concerning the relationship between cause and effect.[4] Imre Lakatos stated that praxis is "the general and formal science of human action, involving all human endeavors in their infinite multiplicity and variety and all individual actions with all their accidental, special, and particular implications."[5] Lakatos also described how theories can be developed and tested through the use of a "research program." According to Lakatos:

> A research program is a set of theories bound together by a common logical foundation and consists of a theoretical hard core, a protective belt of auxiliary assumptions and observational theories, and a positive heuristic. The theoretical hard core consists of statements that are regarded by the scientist working in a research program as

beyond dispute and can be of a metaphysical nature. The protective belt consists of auxiliary assumptions and observational theories. It is the part of the research program that can be modified when observations are not consistent with those predicted by the theory. The positive heuristic consists of a set of guidelines on how to develop the research program. The negative heuristic prohibits refutations from being directed at the hard core of the research program.[6]

What happens, however, when the "theoretical hard core" is missing? What if the "protective belt of auxiliary assumptions, observational theories, and [the] positive heuristic" also are missing? When these situations occur, theory development and theory testing are extremely difficult, to say the least. Unfortunately these conditions affect the concept of entrepreneurship. For example, most of the so-called theories in the field of entrepreneurship have evolved from anecdotal stories. Many organizational-science researchers have argued that entrepreneurial research lacks this "theoretical hard core" and is fragmented.[7] Furthermore, many researchers have asserted that certain aspects of entrepreneurship are multidimensional.[8]

Organizational-science researchers, however, have attempted to solve these theoretical problems. In developing various theories, these researchers have indicated that there are at least three schools of thought regarding entrepreneurship. These include (1) the notion of corporate entrepreneurship, (2) entrepreneurship as an economic function, and (3) behavioral factors and psychological traits of entrepreneurs.

The purpose of this text is to present these three different schools of entrepreneurial thought as three distinct modules or perspectives. Each module (1) presents theories of each perspective and then (2) provides cases as a possible approach toward integrating theory with the actual practices of entrepreneurial activity. This text is not a how-to book about entrepreneurship—we offer no solutions on how to start a business, prepare business plans, or obtain finances.

A word of caution is offered, however. The theory modules are neat and tidy, offering a few conceptual ideas, while the cases contain a wide variety of issues. The reader should not push too far in attempting to link particular cases with certain modules; each case should be analyzed on its own merits. However, as Quinn, Mintzberg, and Waters reveal, when a case and specific readings connect, powerful learning can take place in the form of clarification or revelation.[9] I hope the readers of this text will have those experiences.

Quinn, Mintzberg, and Waters have provided some insights toward using particular theories to understand the issues of a case by quoting Von Clausewitz, a great military theorist:

All the theory can do is to give the artist or soldier points of reference and standards of evaluation . . . with the ultimate purpose not of telling him how to act but of developing his judgment.[10]

THEORY MODULES

A variety of published articles were reviewed in the development of the theory perspective for each of the three modules. Some of the articles are presented in their original form, while in others the key message of the reading has been extracted to provide a brief and concise view. In addition, certain articles have been summarized. I hope this cutting and summarizing have not destroyed the original richness. My apologies are offered to both the reader and the affected authors, but I believe this process is worthwhile.

Several of my own works are included in this text. They are presented not because of my own biases but to illustrate certain issues.

THE CASES

The cases are presented to provide specifics so the reader can relate practice with theoretical perspectives. Granted, cases are not the real world, but they do provide aspects of organizational realities that can be used conveniently in a classroom.

The case method is a Socratic teaching method designed to assist students in focusing on the core problem or problems developed in the case and is the most common technique used in teaching business policy and strategic management courses. In reality there is no such thing as "the" case method, because nearly every instructor uses his or her own variation.

The cases in this text are not intended to be examples of good or bad entrepreneurial practices, nor do they provide examples of concepts from a particular reading. Rather these cases are discussion vehicles for applying concepts developed from this course and from the reader's own experiences.

There is no "correct" answer for any case. The reader should look for issues that develop—to do that requires an understanding of the situation. Two sets of issues usually emerge. The first deals with why did "it" happen in a particular way, and what are the strong and weak features of what happened? The second set of issues involves what should be done next? What are the major alternatives? Which alternative should be chosen and why?

A few questions are included at the end of each case as discussion guides to assist students in organizing their thoughts about the case. Different professors, however, may conduct their classes in different fashions.

Most of these cases can be used at a number of different times during the course. Their actual positioning in the text is only as a convenience to students and professors. Naturally the final case selection depends on the professor's teaching style and the particular students involved.

ORGANIZATION OF THE BOOK

As stated earlier, this text contains three distinct modules based on the different schools of entrepreneurial thought. The first module, "Economic Theory and Entrepreneurship," describes the beginning of the entrepreneur in economic thought and continues with the viewpoints of certain early English and American economists together with those of the German school. We further discuss the disappearance of the entrepreneur from economic thought and describe a renewed interest in entrepreneurship by economists.

The second module, "Behavioral Aspects of Entrepreneurs," focuses on the individual and considers the variety of psychological and personality factors that entrepreneurs supposedly possess. This module concludes with an interesting perspective regarding whether entrepreneurs really are different from nonentrepreneurs. The third module, "Corporate Entrepreneurship," begins with an overview of corporate entrepreneurship and then considers factors that either foster or impede entrepreneurship at an organizational level of analysis as well as corporate venturing processes. Differences between corporate entrepreneurship and intrapreneurship are explored. Major factors contributing to the success or failure of the venturing activity are considered. Finally the textbook concludes with a discussion of entrepreneurship in the future.

Following is a review of the text, chapter by chapter.

Chapter 2, Problems in Defining Entrepreneurship

Before the three distinct modules are presented, various definitions of entrepreneurship are described in Chapter 2. Included is an article by Murray Low and Ian MacMillan that describes past research activities in the area of entrepreneurship together with future challenges.

Module 1, Entrepreneurship and Economic Theory

The first module contains Chapters 3 through 7 and describes the economic theory school of thought regarding the notion of entrepreneurship.

Chapter 3, Overview of Entrepreneurship and Economic Theory

Chapter 3 traces the development of the science of economics and outlines a variety of functional roles played by the entrepreneur in economic thought together with a taxonomy of entrepreneurial theories. It also examines how economists have investigated the relationship between innovation and firm size with entrepreneurial activity.

Chapter 4, The Beginning of Entrepreneurship

Chapter 4 details how entrepreneurship began in economic thought by presenting concepts developed by two individuals living in France, Richard Cantillon and Jean-Baptiste Say. The chapter concludes with excerpts from George Koolman's article that describes Say's conception of the entrepreneur's role and why Say's theories were not widely accepted.

Chapter 5, Early English and American Economists, the German School, and Entrepreneurship

Chapter 5 focuses on how early English and American economists and those from the German school considered the entrepreneur in economic thought. The early English economists include Francis Edgeworth and Alfred Marshall. The early American economists include Frederick Hawley, John Bates Clark, Irving Fisher, and Frank Knight. Economists from the German school include Ludwig Von Mises and Joseph Schumpeter. The chapter concludes with an excerpted article by Charles Tuttle regarding the function of the entrepreneur.

Chapter 6, Disappearance of the Entrepreneur from Economic Thought

Despite the fact that entrepreneurship had its beginnings in economic thought, entrepreneurship no longer plays a major role in orthodox economic theory. Chapter 6 contains two excerpted articles, one by William Baumol and one by Humberto Barreto, that describe the disappearance of the entrepreneur from economic thought.

Chapter 7, Renewed Interest in Entrepreneurship by Economists

Chapter 7 describes the renewed interest in entrepreneurship by economists. The first section of this chapter discusses how several economists have identified a number of situations where modern theory is inappropriate in dealing with certain market conditions. The second section describes the Austrian school of economic thought and presents the viewpoint of Israel Kirzner, who is critical of modern economic theory because it leaves no room for purposeful human action. The third section contains Theodore Schultz's concept of entrepreneurship, which involves the theory of human capital. The chapter concludes with an article by Theodore Schultz on entrepreneurship and human capital.

Module 2, Behavioral Aspects of Entrepreneurs

The second module contains Chapters 8 through 10 and describes the behavioral theory school of thought regarding the notion of entrepreneurship.

Chapter 8, Overview of Behavioral Aspects of Entrepreneurs

Chapter 8 traces the historical development of the behavioral aspects of entrepreneurship first described by Max Weber and includes the contributions of Everett Hagen; the team of Orvis Collins, David Moore, and Darab Unwalla; David McClelland; and Peter Kilby. The chapter concludes with two articles, one written jointly by James Carland, Frank Hoy, William Boulton, and Jo Ann Carland and the other written by William Gartner.

Chapter 9, Key Psychological and Personality Factors Relating to Entrepreneurs

Chapter 9 describes a variety of psychological and personality factors associated with entrepreneurship and notes that no pattern of traits has been discovered that distinguishes successful entrepreneurs from nonentrepreneurs. Dysfunctional aspects of the entrepreneur's personality are discussed from the perspective that while certain personality traits allow an entrepreneur to be creative, these same traits can be destructive for an organization. The chapter concludes with an article by Daniel Jennings and Carl Zeithaml that provides insights into research involving locus of control.

Chapter 10, Are Entrepreneurs Really Different from Nonentrepreneurs?

Chapter 10 describes the lack of research support for the argument that individual differences exist between entrepreneurs and nonentrepreneurs. The notion of individual differences is discussed, and two research studies regarding the individual differences between entrepreneurs and nonentrepreneurs are reviewed. The chapter concludes with Nobel laureate Theodore Schultz's argument in which he states that "the notion that entrepreneurs are only entrepreneurs is pure fiction."

Module 3, Corporate Entrepreneurship

The third module contains Chapters 11 through 14 and describes various aspects of the notion of corporate entrepreneurship.

Chapter 11, Overview of Corporate Entrepreneurship

Chapter 11 distinguishes between the dominant, independent-minded, owner-manager as an entrepreneur and the entrepreneurial activities of the firm. The relationships between entrepreneurship and organizational innovation and organizational size are described from the organizational-science researcher's perspective.

Chapter 12, Organizational Factors That Affect Corporate Entrepreneurship

Chapter 12 describes processes of corporate entrepreneurship at an organizational level of analysis. The concept of corporate entrepreneurship as multidimensional is explained. The differences between entrepreneurial and nonentrepreneurial organizations with respect to certain variables are presented through discussion of an article by Danny Miller and Peter Friesen. An article by Daniel Jennings and James Lumpkin functionally models corporate entrepreneurship using an objective definition and empirically tests certain hypotheses.

Chapter 13, Corporate Venturing

Chapter 13 describes conceptual approaches used by organizational-science researchers in their study of corporate venturing and contains excerpts from three articles. The first article, by Robert Burgelman, reports the findings of a field study of the internal venturing activities of a diversified major firm. From this study Burgelman develops a process model of internal corporate venturing and describes the factors involved in successful internal corporate ventures. The second article, by Daniel F. Jennings, suggests that contextual factors affect venturing activities and develops a framework based on a technological process model for studying venturing using an analysis of contextual factors. The third article, also by Robert Burgelman, describes how internal corporate ventures can be better managed.

Chapter 14, Intrapreneurship

Chapter 14 explains the differences between entrepreneurs and intrapreneurs, and includes excerpts from three articles. The first article, by Richard Nielsen, Michael Peters, and Robert Hisrich, explains the conceptual foundations for an intrapreneurship strategy and develops a distinction between corporate entrepreneurship and intrapreneurship. The second article, by Erik Rule and Donald Irwin, describes how top managers can encourage and foster intrapreneurship within an organizational setting. The third article, by Marsha Sinetar, describes two types of entrepreneurs that exist in organizations and how creative personalities and creative thinking can cause chaos in a well-oiled organizational process. Sinetar demonstrates how management can identify and cultivate creative talent while still maintaining the orderly functions of the company.

Chapter 15, Entrepreneurship in the Future

Chapter 15 describes how entrepreneurship is related to underdeveloped countries. It then discusses how entrepreneurship can flourish in large organizations, trends for creating small entrepreneurial businesses, and the implications for future research activities. The chapter concludes with Robert Reich's discussion of the "new entrepreneurs."

ENDNOTES

1. R. Sobel and D. Sicilia, *The Entrepreneurs* (New York: Houghton Mifflin, 1986).
2. A. Giddens, *Central Problems in Social Theory: Action, Structure and Contradiction in Social Analysis* (Berkeley, Calif.: University of California Press, 1979).
3. Ibid.
4. L. Boland, "Testability in Economic Science," *South African Journal of Economics* 45 (1977): 93–105.
5. I. Lakatos, "The Methodology of Scientific Research Programs," in *Philosophical Papers*, ed. J. Worrall and G. Currie (Cambridge: Cambridge University Press, 1978).
6. Ibid., 92–94.
7. M. Low and I. MacMillan, "Entrepreneurship: Past Research and Future Challenges," *Journal of Management* 14 (1988).
8. This concept is discussed in greater detail in Chapter 3.
9. J. B. Quinn, H. Mintzberg, and R. James, *The Strategy Process* (Englewood Cliffs, N.J.: Prentice-Hall, 1988).
10. C. Von Clausewitz, *On War*, trans. M. Howard and P. Paret (Princeton, N.J.: Princeton University Press, 1976). Von Clausewitz's quotation is further expanded by J. B. Quinn, *Strategies for Change: Logical Incrementalism* (Homewood, Ill.: Richard D. Irwin, 1980).
11. Most textbooks on strategic management and business policy contain a section on approaches to analyzing a "strategic management" case. The following texts capture the essence of these approaches: J. M. Higgins and J. W. Vincze, *Strategic Management: Text And Cases*, 5th ed. (New York: Dryden, 1993), and A. A. Thompson, Jr. and A. J. Strickland, III, *Strategic Management: Concepts and Cases*, 6th ed. (Homewood, Ill: Richard D. Irwin, 1992). An excellent text for instructors on how to teach using cases is C. R. Christensen with A. J. Hansen, *Teaching and the Case Method* (Boston: Harvard Business School Publishing Division, 1987).

CHAPTER 2

Problems in Defining Entrepreneurship

We begin this textbook by exploring why definitions are perceived as being important. In the strict sense a definition provides a set of terms synonymous with the term defined, so they are mutually replaceable. The definition formulates the conditions that are both necessary and sufficient for the applicability of the term defined. Definitions are also useful in developing paradigms, because most paradigms are not capable of definition in the strict sense.[1] A paradigm is a set of beliefs, values, and techniques that are shared by members of a given community.[2] The word *community* is used here as a collective term to describe whole sets of individuals whose disposition is to study and investigate certain phenomena. Paradigms may not mirror reality, but they perform a service in our dealings with reality. For example, they specify something with which a real situation or action is compared and surveyed for formulating clearly significant components to deal with internal vagueness. Ordinary vagueness is external, that is, it concerns the difficulty of deciding whether something belongs to a designated classification. Internal vagueness provides an instrument for conceptual clarification. For example, new terms can be introduced to yield more homogeneous subclasses. Absolute terms can be replaced by comparatives. Defining conditions can be treated in such a manner that a term may be expected to apply in one respect but not in another.[3] Researchers use paradigms to develop theories and operational definitions in explaining various phenomena.[4]

As early as 1971 Kilby stated that each researcher in entrepreneurship appears to have developed his or her own definition without building on the works of others.[5] The focus of this text is not on a single definition of entrepreneurship but rather on multiple perspectives or paradigms. Our argument is that the field of entrepreneurship needs multiple paradigms that are different because entrepreneurial research serves a variety of purposes. For example, the perspective regarding the effects of organizational factors such as structure and control on entrepreneurial activities is quite different from a perspective on the relationship between entrepreneurial activities and a psychological characteristic such as locus of control. To argue that only one of these perspectives describes entrepreneurship certainly limits our understanding.

An important question, however, is whether multiple perspectives or paradigms really provide additional insights or just create unnecessary confusion. Certain researchers have argued for a single paradigm while others have made a case for multiple paradigms. For example, an argument for a single paradigm has been offered by Bygrave:

> Just consider the field of physics. Some of the leading physicists believe they are close to the "Theory of Everything." Stephen Hawking, one of the most brilliant theoretical physicists, wrote, "I still believe there are grounds for the ultimate laws of nature." Physics has reached this remarkable stage less than a hundred years after the electron was discovered by J. J. Thomson, less than seventy-five years after Rutherford conceived the nucleus and Bohr conceived the atom, and less than fifty years after the first meson was discovered. Soon after each of those discoveries, physicists were specializing in atomic, nuclear, and elementary particle physics. They knew which paradigm they were working in. Regrettably, we entrepreneurship scholars are still confused about which paradigm we are working in. Schumpeter introduced the modern concept of the entrepreneur at about the same time that Rutherford introduced the modern concept of the nucleus. Yet while nuclear physicists have essentially solved the puzzle of the structure of the nucleus, we entrepreneurship scholars are still bickering over a working definition of entrepreneurship. What is worse is that we are continually shifting the boundary of the paradigm.[6]

The advantages of multiple paradigms have been argued by a number of philosophy of science scholars. For example, Kaplan noted:

> It is dangerous to repress one cognitive style for another. In doing so, we confuse mature emancipation with adolescent rebellion. The dangers are not in working with multiple paradigms, but in working with too few, and those too much alike, and above all, in belittling any efforts to work with anything else.[7]

Furthermore, while Bygrave argues for an empirical boundary for the concept of entrepreneurship, an interesting argument has been advanced by Morgan that describes the advantages of "unboundness." Morgan argues that concepts, like metaphors, are most valuable when gaps exist between descriptive reality and the concept; that is, when the operational definition of the concept does not capture all the details present in the objective world. Morgan believes that new insights and scientific progress occur when some falsehood exists in the concept or metaphor, giving rise to new imagery and previously unrecognized alternatives.[8]

Despite these arguments regarding a single or multiple paradigms, the term *entrepreneur* appeals to a variety of individuals who aspire to the freedom, wealth, and independence that an entrepreneur supposedly enjoys. Chief executives of large companies continually state that their firms must become entrepreneurial. We can also see evidences of entrepreneurial activities. For example, the number of annual new business incorporations has doubled in the last ten years, and many of these new companies have raised large sums of money in public capital markets.

An increased interest in entrepreneurship as an academic discipline also is being exhibited in many business schools. As an example, Vesper and McMullan indicate that while twenty years ago only a half-dozen colleges and universities were offering courses in entrepreneurship, now more than three hundred schools offer courses in entrepreneurship and faculty members in nearly one hundred schools are conducting some type of research on entrepreneurship.[9]

In spite of this growth in academia and a continued interest by practicing managers, existing definitional problems of entrepreneurship pose a major threat for research activities. A clearer understanding of the notion of entrepreneurship will provide important answers to how practicing managers can utilize the concepts of entrepreneurship.

The following section contains some of the definitions that have been used to describe entrepreneurship. Finally this chapter closes with an article by Murray Low and Ian MacMillan that describes how definitional problems affect entrepreneurial research and offers suggestions for future entrepreneurial research activities.

EXISTING DEFINITIONS OF ENTREPRENEURSHIP

The word *entrepreneur* is derived from the French verb *entreprendre*, which means to undertake. During the early sixteenth century, Frenchmen who organized and managed military and exploration expeditions were referred to as entrepreneurs.[10]

Later, in 1934, Joseph Schumpeter argued that innovation develops from entrepreneurship. Schumpeter stated that entrepreneurs "may also be capitalists, managers, or inventors, but as entrepreneurs they provide a recombination of preexisting factors of production where the outcome of this recombination cannot be clearly predicted."[11] In 1947 Schumpeter stated that it took an individual who possessed the unusual traits and will to "found a private kingdom, a drive to overcome obstacles, a joy in creating, and satisfaction in exercising one's ingenuity" to become an entrepreneur.[12]

While unresolved differences exist in defining entrepreneurship, there is agreement that entrepreneurship entails some part of the administrative decision-making function in organizations.[13] There are differences in emphasis, however. Schumpeter argued that innovation should be the criterion of entrepreneurship. In Schumpeter's view a manager becomes an entrepreneur only while making a creative response to market forces.[14] Another view of entrepreneurship was developed by Cole, who argued that entrepreneurship can be equated with the continuing general activities of managers.[15]

Several researchers have attempted to make a distinction between the entrepreneur and others. For example, Brockhaus defined an entrepreneur as a major owner and manager of a business venture who is not employed elsewhere.[16] Carland, Hoy, Boulton, and Carland stated that the difference between an entrepreneur and the owner of a small business is that the entrepreneur is interested in expanding the business.[17]

A few definitions of entrepreneurship are so broad that they appear to include any human attempt to try something new.[18] VanderWerf and Brush in their review of twenty-five definitions for entrepreneurship indicated that entrepreneurship has been defined as a business activity consisting of some "intersection" of the following behaviors:[19]

- *Creation*—the establishment of a new business unit
- *General management*—the managerial direction of or resource allocation for a business
- *Innovation*—the commercial exploitation of some new product, process, market, material, or organization
- *Risk bearance*—the acceptance of uncommonly high risk from the potential losses or failure of a business unit
- *Performance intention*—the intent to realize high levels of growth and/or profit through a business unit

Interestingly there is disagreement concerning risk taking in defining entrepreneurs. For example, Richard Cantillon writing in the eighteenth century considered an entrepreneur to be a "bearer of uninsurable risk." While a number of present-day researchers have equated entrepreneurship with risk taking, others argue that risking one's capital is not intrinsic to the entrepreneurial function.[20] Kallenberg suggests that disagreements resulting from the role of risk taking in defining an entrepreneur occur in how the context of entrepreneurship is considered by a particular researcher.[21]

Stevenson considers entrepreneurship to be a continuum: at one extreme he identifies a "promoter—the type who says, I can make it happen." At the opposite extreme is the "trustee—who says I must guard what I have." Stevenson suggests that (1) the entrepreneur is not identical to the promoter but occupies a range on the promoter end of the spectrum and (2) an administrator or manager of a business occupies a range on the trustee end of the spectrum. Stevenson utilizes his "continuum" by developing a paradigm that includes the following five dimensions of business activity: strategic orientation, commitment to opportunity, commitment of resources, control of resources, and management structure.[22] Exhibit 2.1 summarizes Stevenson's five dimensions into one chart.

The Entrepreneurship Division of the Academy of Management has developed the following domain statement to guide entrepreneurial research:

EXHIBIT 2.1 Stevenson's Entrepreneurial Continuum

Pressures toward the Promoter	Promoter	Key Business Dimension	Trustee	Pressures toward the Trustee
Diminishing opportunity streams Rapidly changing: Technology Consumer economics Social values Political rules	Driven by perception of opportunity	**Strategic orientation** ←——→ Entrepreneurial ←——→ Administrative	Driven by resources currently controlled	Social contracts Performance measurement criteria Planning systems and cycles
Action orientation Short decision windows Risk management Limited decision constituencies	Revolutionary with short duration	**Commitment to opportunity** ←——→ Entrepreneurial ←——→ Administrative	Evolutionary of long duration	Acknowledgement of multiple constituencies Negotiation of strategy Risk reduction Management of fit
Lack of predictable resource needs Lack of long-term control Social needs for more opportunity per resource unit International pressure for more efficient resource use	Multistaged with minimal exposure at each stage	**Commitment of resources** ←——→ Entrepreneurial ←——→ Administrative	Single-staged with complete commitment upon decision	Personal risk reduction Incentive compensation Managerial turnover Capital allocation systems Formal planning systems
Increased resource specialization Long resource life compared to need Risk of obsolescence Risk inherent in any new venture Inflexibility of permanent commitment to resources	Episodic use or rent of required resources	**Control of resources** ←——→ Entrepreneurial ←——→ Administrative	Ownership or employment of required resources	Power, status, and financial rewards Coordination Efficiency measures Inertia and cost of change Industry structures
Coordination of key noncontrolled resources Challenge to legitimacy of owner's control Employees' desire for independence	Flat with multiple informal networks	**Management structure** ←——→ Entrepreneurial ←——→ Administrative	Formalized hierarchy	Need for clearly defined authority and responsibility Organizational culture Reward systems Management theory

Source: Adapted from H. H. Stevenson, M. J. Roberts, and H. I Grousbeck, *New Business Ventures and the Entrepreneur,* 3rd ed. (Homewood, Ill.: Richard D. Irwin, 1989), 18–19.

Specific domain: the creation and management of new businesses, small businesses and family businesses, and the characteristics and special problems of entrepreneurs. Major topics include: new venture ideas and strategies; ecological influences on venture capital and venture teams; self-employment; the owner-manager; and the relationship between entrepreneurship and economic development.[23]

This domain statement relates to a specific group of people working in the area of entrepreneurship and leaves out many persons in other fields who conduct research in entrepreneurship.

A number of researchers now consider entrepreneurship to be a multidimensional concept. There is disagreement, however, regarding what dimensions should be included in defining entrepreneurs.[24] Module 1 of this text, "Entrepreneurship and Economic Theory," describes how the entrepreneur has been defined in the economics literature.

After reading the article by Low and MacMillan, you should have a better understanding of the state of research activity in entrepreneurship.

ARTICLE 2.1   ENTREPRENEURSHIP: PAST RESEARCH AND FUTURE CHALLENGES
by Murray Low and Ian MacMillan

The past decade has witnessed a significant rise in popular enthusiasm for entrepreneurs and entrepreneurship. This enthusiasm has been matched in the academic arena, resulting in a significant increase in the amount of research effort being devoted to the subject. This increased attention seems justified given the growing evidence that new firm creation is a critical driving force of economic growth, creating hundreds of thousands of new jobs (Birch, 1979; Birley, 1987; Reynolds, 1987), as well as enhancing federal and local tax revenues, boosting exports, and generally increasing national productivity (*President's Commission Report*, 1984).

As a body of literature develops, it is useful to stop occasionally, take inventory of the work that has been done, and identify new directions and challenges for the future. This reflective process is essential in order to derive the maximum benefit from future research.

The organizing theme of this paper consists of six key specification decisions that we feel researchers need to address as they begin to assemble a research program in the area of entrepreneurship. These design specification decisions are interrelated, and cannot be made independently. These include: **Purpose**—what is the specific as well as larger purpose of the study? **Theoretical perspective**—what is the theoretical perspective adopted? **Focus**—on what specific phenomena shall the investigation be focused? **Level of analysis**—what level or levels of analysis will be considered? **Time frame**—what length of time frame will be considered? **Methodology**—what methodology will be adopted?

Past entrepreneurship research will be reviewed within the context of these six design dimensions. This organizing structure is meant to complement previous reviews that have been organized around subject categories or units of analysis. Readers who have limited familiarity with the entrepreneurship literature or those interested in specific topics may find it useful to refer to these previous comprehensive works.

Finally, since our intention is to provide a critical review, we wish to preface our remarks by acknowledging a debt to those who have pioneered the study of entrepreneurship. Although hindsight makes it easy to identify the shortcomings of early studies, it is important to recognize that these works were necessary first steps in the exploration of the entrepreneurship phenomenon.

Decision 1: Specification of Purpose

Entrepreneurship is a multifacted phenomenon that cuts across many disciplinary boundaries. Studies falling under the rubric of "entrepreneurship" have pursued a wide range of purposes and objectives, asked different questions, and adopted different units of analysis, theoretical perspectives, and methodologies. This diversity is reflected in the many and varied definitions of entrepreneurship.

The problem with these definitions is that though each captures an aspect of entrepreneurship, none captures the whole picture. The phenomenon of entrepreneurship is intertwined with a complex set of contiguous and overlapping constructs such as management of change, innovation, technological and environmental turbulence, new product development, small business management, individualism, and industry evolution. Furthermore, the phenomenon can be productively investigated from disciplines as varied as economics, sociology, finance, history, psychology, and anthropology, each of which uses its own concepts and operates within its own terms of reference. Indeed, it seems likely that the desire for common definitions and a clearly defined area of inquiry will remain unfulfilled in the foreseeable future.[a]

However, because of the range of approaches available for entrepreneurship research, some common ground is needed upon which to synthesize the insights of diverse approaches of inquiry. At the broadest level, there is a need for an overall, common purpose that will forge some unity among entrepreneurship researchers.

In the spirit of the challenge to define an overall, common purpose, we suggest that entrepreneurship be defined as the "creation of new enterprise" and propose the following: that entrepreneurship research seek to *explain and facilitate the role of new enterprise in furthering economic progress*. This fundamental purpose,

---

[a] It can be argued that the term *entrepreneurship* is too imprecise a concept to be of much use to researchers. In this respect, it is interesting to make comparison with the term *leadership*. Pfeffer (1977) argues that the concept of leadership is so broad that its usefulness is called to question. "Apparently there are few meaningful distinctions between leadership and other concepts of social influence. Thus, an understanding of the phenomenon subsumed under the rubric of leadership may not require the construct of leadership." It seems the same argument could be made about the construct of entrepreneurship.

or one like it, is wide in scope yet still delineates a constrained area of inquiry within which multidisciplinary research programs may be built.[b]

In the past, much of the entrepreneurship research has either lacked clarity of purpose or the specified purpose was of little consequence. Many early works were of the "census taking" type—confined largely to documenting and reporting the occurrence of entrepreneurs or their personality characteristics, with little attempt to uncover causal relationships or to explore implications for practice. Many of these studies left the reader wondering what the authors really hoped to achieve. The failure to clearly specify the purpose of the research combined with the lack of common ground for synthesizing research findings has hindered the advancement of the field. To address this problem, we suggest not only that the specific purpose of a study be explicitly stated at the outset, but that the field will best advance if this more specific purpose is explicitly linked to a generally accepted overall purpose such as "explaining and facilitating the role of new enterprise in furthering economic progress."

Decision 2: Specification of Theoretical Perspective

After the specification of purpose, the next important decision is the specification of theoretical perspective. Much of the entrepreneurship research to date has implicitly assumed a "strategic adaptation" perspective. A strategic adaptation perspective suggests that the key to entrepreneurial success lies in the decisions of the individual entrepreneurs who identify opportunities, develop strategies, assemble resources and take initiatives. Recently, this perspective has been challenged by theorists who adopt a "population ecology" perspective, which suggests that individual goal-driven behavior is largely irrelevant and that environmental selection procedures are the most powerful determining factors.

The Strategic Adaptation Perspective

Authors that adopt a strategic adaptation perspective usually start by identifying key success factors that enhance the chances of survival, identifying key failure factors, and an entry strategy.

The most advanced strategic adaptation entrepreneurship research has come from researchers who have tried to capture the expertise of the venture capital

---

[b] In this context, it is appropriate for us to explicitly raise our point of view regarding the outcomes of entrepreneurial effort. A comprehensive research program cannot confine itself solely to studies of entrepreneurial success. This is for two reasons. First, the venture's failure may be the result of established competitors' reactions to the entry of the new firm. If this competitive response enhances the industry's overall competitiveness, then economic progress has still been achieved, even if the venture fails. Second, failure is an important source of learning, and even though a specific venture may fail, the people involved may have developed skills and knowledge that will lead to future entrepreneurial success (Maidique & Zirger, 1985).

community. The assumption here is that people who make profits from assessing new venture proposals will have developed expertise in distinguishing between winning and losing ventures. In the review of these studies it became clear that entrepreneurial firms are too diverse to permit simple generalization (Gartner, 1985a). Some researchers have dealt with this complexity by adopting a *contingency approach* that seeks to identify major contingent variables that significantly shape entrepreneurial outcomes. Sandberg and Hofer (1987), who also collected data via the venture capital route, have developed and tested a contingency model for predicting venture performance based upon characteristics of the entrepreneur, the structure of the industry being entered, the venture strategy, and the interactive effects of these three factors. Although their findings are based on a small sample and can be challenged on statistical grounds, their results are nevertheless suggestive: the entrepreneur's characteristics appear to have little effect on venture performance, whereas the interaction between industry structure and strategy appear to be strongly associated with performance. By using theory and inductive arguments to develop and test hypotheses that consider the interaction of personal, environmental, and strategic variables on performance, Sandberg and Hofer take the research on strategic adaptation an important step forward. Hopefully future studies of this type will follow.

Another emerging stream of strategy research seeks to determine what repeatedly successful entrepreneurs have learned through experience. More recently, the notion that there is much to be learned by studying repeatedly successful entrepreneurs was advocated by an individual who has himself started over thirty new businesses over a ten-year period (Executive Forum, 1986). He contends that study of one-shot entrepreneurs will inevitably focus on problems and obstacles that may simply be a product of inexperience. His argument is that only multiple entrepreneurs can provide the base for a theory of entrepreneurship since only they have developed an "experience curve."

A review of the strategic adaptation literature shows that progress is being made. The strategy conceptualizations have advanced from rather static, overly generalized "key success factor" models to contingency models that consider a range of variables under varied circumstances and take into account the learning effect of past efforts. In spite of this progress, it is still surprising that so little work has been done in the area of entrepreneurship strategy. There are very few good empirical studies, and those that exist are limited by small sample sizes.

Whether it is explicitly stated or not, the dominant assumption of the strategy oriented literature is that success is primarily dependent upon the entrepreneur's ability to develop and execute effective strategies. The literature that adopts a population ecology perspective offers a different point of view and will be discussed next.

The Population Ecology Perspective

Hannan and Freeman's 1977 article entitled "The Population Ecology of Organizations" was a provocative piece that challenged many assumptions held by organizational researchers. The authors argued that most management theory overemphasizes the capacity of an organization to adapt to a changing environment. In contrast, they viewed inertia as a dominant organizational characteristic. Employing a biological analogy, they suggested that those organizations that are well adapted to their environment will survive, and those that are not will die. Through this selection mechanism, the environment will determine the characteristics of populations of organizations. The essence of the argument is that chance variations in organizational forms that are adaptive are selected *for* whereas nonadaptive forms are selected *against*.

Perhaps the best articulation of the application of ecological thinking to entrepreneurship lies in the work of Greenfield and Strickon (1986). They argued that contemporary paradigms in social science research and thought have become static and therefore incapable of explaining dynamic social processes. As an alternative, they proposed a new paradigm that has its origins in Darwinian biology:

> With respect to entrepreneurship this means that we are no longer looking for a transcendent type—the analogue of the immutable species—but instead recognize existing diversity of behavior within specific populations, which at its extremes encompasses innovation and novelty. What is called entrepreneurship, from this point of view, is actually one segment of an otherwise seamless variability.

Population ecology theory has significantly matured in recent years, developing from a simplistic and deterministic biological metaphor into a rich theoretical framework capable of incorporating other theoretical perspectives.

Strategic adaptation and population ecology perspectives are not irreconcilable. One promising opportunity for combining the insights of these perspectives lies in the study of industry evolution, or the "community" level of analysis, as it has been labeled by the ecologists (Astley, 1985; Carroll, 1984). A good example is the work of Tushman and Anderson (1986), who studied three different industries and observed that technology evolves "through periods of incremental change punctuated by technological breakthroughs." They defined technological breakthroughs in Schumpeterian terms: "Major technological innovations represent technical advances so significant that no increase in scale, efficiency, or design can make older technologies competitive with the new technology." They added an interesting dimension by distinguishing between two fundamentally different types of technological discontinuity: competence-enhancing and competence-destroying. A competence-enhancing technological shift builds upon existing know-how (replacement of mechanical typewriters by electric), whereas with a competence-destroying shift, existing know-how is largely irrelevant (replacement of steam-engines by diesel locomotives).

Tushman and Anderson found that competence-destroying technological discontinuities favor the entrance of new firms into an industry because of the inability of established competitors to exploit the new technology. Competence-enhancing discontinuities, on the other hand, work to the long-run advantage of established firms who can use their resources and market position to incorporate the new technology. Thus the entrepreneurial firm that enters an industry via incremental change or via the introduction of a new competence-enhancing technology is in far greater peril from existing competitors than one that enters via the introduction of competence-destroying technology.

This is an example of how the ecological perspective can provide valuable insight that can lead to more effective strategy formulation: an aggressive entry strategy is more likely to succeed under conditions of a competence-destroying discontinuity than under conditions of a competence-enhancing discontinuity, where competitors are in a strong position to retaliate.

Our review of the population ecology literature leads us to the following comment regarding future entrepreneurship research: In the past, much of the entrepreneurship research has implicitly assumed a strategic adaptation perspective. The application of ecological thinking to entrepreneurship has challenged many previously held assumptions, increased our understanding of the entrepreneurial process, and demonstrated the significant benefits of theory driven research. Ideally, the example of population ecology will encourage the exploration of other theoretical perspectives that have the potential to provide insight into the entrepreneurship phenomenon.

Whether the strategic adaptation, population ecology, or some other perspective or combination of perspectives is pursued, it is clear that the field will be better served in the future if the issue of theoretical perspective is addressed directly and unstated assumptions are avoided. Theory can then be tested and elaborated, and from this, *informed* knowledge can be developed to aid the academic and the practitioner alike.

In the next section, on focus, we pursue a second, related set of issues by examining the trend toward more contextual and process-oriented research.

Decision 3: Specification of Focus

While some researchers have used personality traits and psychological theories to study entrepreneurs, definitional and methodological problems such as non-comparable samples, bias toward successful entrepreneurs, and the possibility that observed entrepreneurial traits are the *product* of entrepreneurial experience, it is difficult to interpret the results. At a more fundamental level, it can be argued that the wide variations among entrepreneurs make any attempt to develop a standard psychological profile futile.

Demographic studies of entrepreneurship suffer from some of the same problems as the psychological/personality literature. Most of the empirical work that examines the demographic characteristics of entrepreneurs suffers from small sample sizes, non-comparability of samples, and static term of reference. The most comprehensive study to date is by Cooper and Dunkelberg (1987). They collected broadly based data on 890 entrepreneurs and contrasted their findings with earlier research using smaller samples. They confirmed that entrepreneurs tend to be better educated, come from families where the parents owned a business, start firms related to their previous work, and locate where they are already living and working. In other ways, however, the entrepreneurs in their sample were less different than previous research has indicated, "being no more likely to be of foreign-stock and not being particularly likely to leave school early or to drift from job to job" than the general population. Cooper and Dunkelberg concluded that diversity seems to be a central characteristic of their sample. This is our conclusion as well: being innovators and idiosyncratic, entrepreneurs tend to defy aggregation. They tend to reside at the tails of population distributions, and though they may be expected to differ from the mean, the nature of these differences is not predictable. It seems that any attempt to profile the typical entrepreneur is inherently futile.

More useful are recent psychological studies that focus on the entrepreneur within an organizational context. Schein (1983) examined the role of the founder in creating organizational culture. According to Schein, entrepreneurs "typically . . . have strong assumptions about the nature of the world, the role their organizations will play in that world, the nature of human nature, truth, relationships, time and space." Schein examined the process by which the assumptions and theories of the founders interacted with the organization's own experiences to determine culture. Kets de Vries (1985) focused on dysfunctional entrepreneurial personality characteristics by examining the negative repercussions of need for control, sense of distrust, desire for applause, and psychological coping mechanisms demonstrated by some entrepreneurs. This article was the result of studies done in collaboration with Miller that sought to link executive personality with strategy and organizational structure (Kets de Vries & Miller, 1984, 1986). Kets de Vries and Miller developed a typology of pathological organizations, and their most recent work examined culture as the link between personality and strategy.

The work done by Schein and by Kets de Vries and Miller is important because it does not focus simply on the psychology of the entrepreneur, but focuses instead on the relationship between the entrepreneur and the organization and on the *process* by which individual characteristics affect organizational outcomes. The focus of these most recent psychological studies is clearly more contextual and process-oriented than the earlier work.

Social-Cultural Theories

One of the earliest and best known attempts to link entrepreneurship to the larger social context was Weber's classic work "The Protestant Ethic and the Spirit of Capitalism" (1930). Weber argued that the rise of Protestantism encouraged hard work, thrift, and striving for material advancement, which in turn gave rise to capitalism. Although the causal effects of the Protestant ethic on the development of capitalism have since been hotly contested, it does seem clear that the rise of Protestantism swept away many institutional obstacles that were preventing the development of capitalism. Our conclusion is that there must be congruence between ideological constructs and economic behavior if entrepreneurship is to flourish.

The tendency of certain cultures to produce entrepreneurs has made it intuitively appealing to view culture as a determinant of entrepreneurship. Hagen (1960) explained entrepreneurial behavior as a means by which disadvantaged minorities seek to alter the status quo. Some examples are the Dissenters in England, the Protestants in France, the Samurai in Japan, the Jews in many countries, and the Parsees in India (Greenfield & Strickon, 1981). This perspective is continued today in the work of Brenner (1987), who argued that it is those groups that have lost or face the prospect of losing social status that are driven to take entrepreneurial risks. Although there may be some validity to these assertions, some contradictory evidence does exist (Shapero & Sokol, 1982). The recent entrepreneurial proliferation associated with Silicon Valley (Stanford and Berkeley graduates) and Route 128 (Harvard and MIT graduates) demonstrates that not all entrepreneurs come from disadvantaged backgrounds. The best that can be said with confidence is that *in some cases* entrepreneurship is a response to lack of social mobility through other channels.

Studies in the 1960s by Cochran (1965) and Alexander (1967) recognized the complex economic, social, and psychological factors that impact the entrepreneurial process. However, it was Glade (1967) that really set the stage for the types of contextual models currently advocated. Glade viewed the entrepreneur as a decision maker operating within a specific social and cultural setting. He termed this setting an "opportunity structure," implying both the perception and existence of an opportunity combined with the availability of resources: "Integral features of any given situation are both an 'objective' structure of economic opportunity and a structure of differential advantage in the capacity of the system's participants to perceive and act upon such opportunities."

More recently, Vesper (1983), Martin (1984), and Shapero and Sokol (1982) all developed models of venture initiation that build upon this idea. The Shapero and Sokol model is perhaps the most sophisticated model of entrepreneurial event formation in the Glade tradition. It identifies life-path changes, perceptions of desirability, and perceptions of feasibility as variables leading to new company formation. Their model considers the interaction of many situational cultural factors and provides a dynamic framework that captures the range of positive pulls and negative displacements leading to the start-up of a business.

Network Theories

Recent studies that have examined "networks" are more refined attempts to place the entrepreneur within a social context. Birley (1985) studied the role of networks in the founding of new firms by sampling 160 firms in Indiana. She differentiated between two kinds of networks: informal (family, friends, business) and formal (banks, accountants, lawyers, SBA) and found that entrepreneurs rely heavily on the informal network, but seldom tap into the formal network. MacMillan (1983) argued that there is a distinct manipulative aspect of networks. In a small sample longitudinal study he identified the critical role played by deliberate network building in the launch of eight start-ups.

The importance of networks has been reflected in a growing interest in "incubators." An incubator may be a formally organized facility offering laboratory and office space, support services, technical and business consulting services, and contact with other entrepreneurs (Smilor & Gill, 1986), or may simply be the organization where the entrepreneur worked prior to launching a venture. The most famous example of a firm acting as an incubator for entrepreneurial spinoffs is Fairchild, which spawned at least 35 companies (Vesper, 1983). Studies of such incubator organizations have shown that high-tech entrepreneurs tend to locate themselves in the same area as their previous employer and develop products that are closely related to their prior organizations (Cooper, 1986).

The understanding of networks was further advanced by Aldrich and Zimmer (1986), who viewed the entrepreneurial process as embedded in a shifting network of continuing social relations that facilitate and constrain "linkages between aspiring entrepreneurs, resources and opportunities." They contended that new business formation is part of an evolutionary process of "variation, selection, retention, and diffusion and the struggle for existence." Though recognizing that individuals are intentional or purposeful in their actions, they argued that the growing evidence of cognitive limits on human behavior and the "powerful influence of social factors on cognitions and information processing" means that one cannot attribute new business formation to individual acts. For Aldrich and Zimmer, the entrepreneurial process takes on meaning only in the context of the broader social processes that they described.

These recent studies demonstrate how the focus of entrepreneurship research has progressed to become more contextual and process-oriented. Several authors have suggested frameworks for capturing this contextual complexity. Gartner (1985a) suggested a conceptual framework for describing the phenomenon of new venture creation that identified the similarities and differences between ventures. His framework "integrates four major perspectives in entrepreneurship characteristics of the individual(s) who start the venture, the organization which they create, the environment surrounding the new venture, and the process by which the new venture is started." Carsrud, Olm, and Eddy (1986) suggested a similar model, one that examines the interaction between psychological, personal/demographic, organizational, and situation/environmental variables on the venture creation process.

Decision 4: Specification of Level of Analysis

Given our earlier comments about the general purpose of entrepreneurship research, it follows that we are interested in *all* entrepreneurial phenomena that impact economic progress. This means we may be concerned with the fate of the individual entrepreneur, the progress of an entire industry, or the impact of that industry on society as a whole. Thus researchers may choose among five levels of analysis: individual, group, organizational, industry, and societal levels. Most of the research to date has been at a single level of analysis. However, two recent studies illustrate just how much can be gained by attempting a richer, albeit more difficult multi-level research design.

The first is a study by Van de Ven, Hudson, and Schroeder (1984) that examined the start-up of fourteen educational software companies. The firms were divided into high and low performers based on a composite measure of success. Key variables from three different levels of analysis were examined for their impact on success. The three levels are entrepreneurial (characteristics of the founding individual), organizational (planning and initial development processes of the firm), and ecological (industry as a whole).

The Van de Ven et al. study is exemplary in its use of the literature to identify key variables for investigation at each level of analysis. At the entrepreneurial level, the authors concluded that success was related to education and experience, internal locus of control and risk reduction, a broad and clear business idea, and personal investment. At the organizational level, success was positively related to planning activities (although ironically, spending time on a detailed business plan seemed to result in poorer performance), small-scale start-up, incremental expansion, single person command, and active involvement of top management and board members in decision making. At the ecological level, the study suggested that assistance from a corporate sponsor in the form of equity capital, training, or guaranteed contracts was actually maladaptive, and that firms competing for contracts on an independent basis advance more quickly, at least over the short run.

Aldrich and Auster (1986) provide a second example of multi-level research design. They built upon Stinchcombe's work and argued that the "strengths of large, old organizations are often the weaknesses of small, new organizations and vice versa." For smaller and newer organizations they looked at various strategies such as franchising, long-term contracts, and mergers and acquisitions, to overcome the liabilities of newness and smallness. For larger and older organizations, they examined strategies of franchising, mergers and acquisitions, subcontracting, and corporate venturing to overcome the liabilities of oldness and largeness. The connection between different levels of analysis was made through the observation that adaptive strategies at the organizational level result in new "forms" at the industry level that improve the viability of whole populations of organizations.

The relationships between phenomena that can be observed at different levels of analysis are important not just for academics, but for both practitioners and public policy makers as well. From the entrepreneur's perspective, the success of the individual enterprise will be affected by factors that can only be observed at different levels of analysis. To miss any one of these perspectives increases the probability that key factors will be overlooked, and that unanticipated events will take the entrepreneur by surprise. From the public policy maker's perspective, the insights generated by multi-level studies have the potential to improve targeting of government efforts to encourage successful entrepreneurship.

The two studies discussed above demonstrate that each level of analysis provides unique insight and that the synthesis of these insights yields a richer understanding than that possible from the perspective of a single level of analysis. The challenge for entrepreneurship research is to increase the incorporation of multiple levels of analysis into future research designs.

Decision 5: Specification of Time Frame

A key building block for understanding the pattern of new business formation is the notion that start-ups move through predictable stages. The fact that this pattern can only be observed through wide time frame research is the key thrust of this section. Other issues related to longitudinal research will be discussed in the final section on methodology.

Most of the studies that focus on stages in the start-up of an enterprise are variations on a theme. Although typically arranging the stages in natural order, most theorists note that the stages need not be strictly sequential, nor can they be dealt with in isolation. One of the more detailed works (Swayne & Tucker, 1973) listed 57 steps in three overall stages of concept, planning and implementation. A recent review by Gartner (1985a) of the work of eight researchers identified six common actions undertaken in the entrepreneurial process: locating a business opportunity, accumulating resources, marketing products and services, producing the product, building an organization, and responding to government and society. Stevenson et al. (1985) identified five steps in the start-up: evaluating the opportunity, developing the business concept, assessing required resources, acquiring needed resources, and managing and harvesting the business.

Block and MacMillan (1985) focused on the planning for a launch and suggested that there are critical milestones in a start-up. They argued that a new venture is an experiment with implicit hypotheses of assumptions about the relations among product, market, and competition that can only be tested through experience. Block and MacMillan suggested that go/no-go or redirection decisions be made at each of ten milestones, based upon emerging information that becomes available as each milestone is reached.

From the point of view of advancing theory, studies that merely document the stages of a start-up are of questionable value. However, identifying the major tasks that need to be accomplished during the launch of a venture has practical value; furthermore, the notion that a start-up moves through discrete stages is an insight that must be incorporated into any theory of new venture creation.

Although the above researchers focus on the stages of start-up, other researchers use still longer time frames and focus on major stages of growth in fully launched organizations. Greiner (1972) identified five distinguishable phases of development, each characterized by "evolutionary" periods of relative calm followed by "revolutionary" periods of management crisis and realignment. This approach was furthered by Churchill and Lewis (1983) and Hambrick and Crozier (1985) and bears similarity to the "life-cycle" work of Kimberly and Miles (1980). These works go beyond the start-up phase and demonstrate that different management and strategic issues become paramount at different stages of development. Robinson and Pearce (1986) took the analysis one step further with a comprehensive study of the relation between venture performance at different stages of development and the attention given to strategic and operational decisions. They showed that as the firm evolves, each state calls for emphasis on different strategic activities.

Short time frame studies are simpler to design and easier to execute but clearly lack the richness of insight that results from studying a phenomenon over a longer time period. For entrepreneurship research this is extremely important, since new firms are extremely fragile and experience many changes within short periods of time. Often the seeds of future problems are sown in the early stages. Only wide time frame studies will allow us to study the development problems faced by new firms and to pursue the objective of causal inference.

Decision 6: Specification of Methodology

As entrepreneurship emerges as a recognized area of inquiry, the quality and usefulness of the theory that is developed will be tied to the ability of researchers to identify patterns of causality. Early efforts in entrepreneurship research were understandably exploratory case studies or cross sectional statistical studies of the "census-taking" type. However, if such exploratory studies are successful, they should be followed by more systematic studies that subject a priori hypotheses to formal testing and work toward the development of theory.

Unfortunately, the progress toward a priori hypothesis testing has been slow. The current standard appears to be data collection and a posteriori statistical testing. Still, there has been some progress in terms of building upon previous research and designing more rigorous studies. For example, in measuring the contribution of entrepreneurship to economic progress, Birley (1987) and Reynolds (1987) built upon the earlier work of Birch (1979), with their analyses characterized by much greater precision. In Reynolds' case, he used regression and discriminant analyses to distinguish between factors related to the social contribution of new firms and factors related to their survival. A further example is Khan (1987), whose study of the effectiveness of venture capital decision making went beyond simple additive regression approaches (MacMillan et al., 1987) and employed non-compensatory decision modeling.

The goal of establishing causal linkages among variables means that more longitudinal work is necessary. Longitudinal studies are inevitably more difficult and expensive than cross sectional studies, but the benefits are considerable. Two good examples of longitudinal studies are Hambrick and Crozier's (1985) examination of the difficulties of managing rapid growth firms, and Tushman, Virany, and Romanelli's (1985) study of a cohort of minicomputer firms over a protracted time period. Following a group of firms over time is expensive and time consuming, but it is important to recognize that only such large scale cross sectional *and* longitudinal studies can start to provide us with enough confidence about causality to provide the basis for theoretical model-building and experimental research.

To date the attempts to develop formal methods have been limited. Baumol (1982) developed a theoretical model describing the influences that determine the supply of entrepreneurship and its influence on economic growth. Kihlstrom and Laffont (1979) proposed an entrepreneurship-based theory of competitive equilibrium by building upon Knight's (1921) concept of risk. Casson (1982) developed an economic theory of entrepreneurship within the neoclassical framework. These attempts at formal model building hold promise, but pale compared to the sophistication of the models used in other fields. Until progress is made in the development of rigorous models of the entrepreneurial process, our ability to generate theory will be severely circumscribed.

If attempts at formal model building have been limited, attempts at experimentation have been rare. Worthy of note are two studies—the use of simulation techniques to study venture capital investment effectiveness by Stevenson, Muzycka, and Timmons (1987) and the experimental study by Kourilsky (1980) that examined the entrepreneurial behavior of children in a simulated economy. The lack of experimental research is a further indication of slow progress in developing entrepreneurship theory.

It is interesting to note that the studies cited above stem from a variety of disciplinary backgrounds: Hambrick and Crozier from strategy; Reynolds from sociology; Kourilsky from education; Kihlstrom and Laffont, Baumol, and Casson from economics. Other disciplines that have contributed to the study of entrepreneurship include anthropology (Owens, 1978), marketing (Dickson & Giglierano, 1986), psychology (Brockhaus, 1982), history (Cochran, 1965), finance (Huntsman & Hoban, 1980), and political science (Gatewood, Hoy, & Spindler, 1984). This diversity of approaches and methods is to be encouraged, for entrepreneurship is as varied as it is elusive, and the range of research methods should match the complexity of the phoneomenon under study.

Our review of the literature leads us to suggest that there is a need to pursue causality more aggressively. The field must move to the stage where exploratory case analyses or cross sectional census-taking studies that are not theory driven and do not test hypotheses are no longer acceptable.

Implications for Entrepreneurs

This review has focused on issues of research design and is primarily targeted at an academic audience. This approach reflects the belief that useful knowledge for practice will only result from the pursuit of rigorous research and the development of entrepreneurship theory. For those who do not share this view, there is no shortage of anecdotal "how to" books to which they may refer.

Even though this review has focused on research design issues, several important implications for practice have been raised. At the most general level, the design issues raised in this paper can serve as criteria for sifting through the vast amount of popular and academic literature dealing with entrepreneurship. In much of this literature the practitioner is advised to look out for the same inappropriate generalizations and misleading assumptions about causality that we caution academics to beware.

Although past attempts to stereotype entrepreneurs based upon psychological and cultural characteristics have been discredited, recent work suggests that entrepreneurs' personalities do have important influences on the organizations they create (Kets de Vries, 1985; Schein, 1983). The behaviors and values of the entrepreneur interact with the experiences of the unfolding organization to imprint its culture. In turn, organizational culture has important implications for the performance. Entrepreneurs are encouraged to be aware of how their behavior shapes the emerging culture. We by no means suggest that entrepreneurs try to change their personalities, but it may be possible for them to be alert for and avoid behaviors that have dysfunctional organizational consequences.

The literature makes it clear that opportunities do not drop from the sky. Opportunities are created within and among existing organizations as a product of ongoing networks of relationships and exchanges. Opportunities come most frequently to people located at advantageous positions within networks. Furthermore, exploiting an opportunity requires certain resources (human resources, capital, marketing and technical information, sales etc.). The same types of network relationships and contacts needed to identify opportunities are also necessary to obtain the resources required to exploit opportunities. Aspiring entrepreneurs are advised to evaluate and map their current networks. Doing so is the first step toward building an effective network, an activity that is too important to be left to chance.

It is also clear from the literature that there are no magic formulae for success. Each venture will have its own key success factors, any one of which will be sufficient to kill the venture if overlooked. Some important items for consideration are the following: Is there an established market for the product? Is the market defensible? If the strategy appropriate for the industry structure?

Although planning is important, spending too much time on a detailed business plan can be counterproductive. And though assistance from a corporate sponsor is usually thought to be helpful, evidence suggests that firms competing for contracts on an independent basis advance more quickly (Van de Ven et al., 1984). For technologically innovative ventures, it is important to establish whether the innovation can easily be adopted by established competitors (Tushman & Anderson, 1986). If so, a long-range objective might be to be acquired by an existing firm. If not, an aggressive share-building strategy might be most appropriate.

The ecology literature suggests that success is also a matter of chance, and that one needs some luck. This is true, but it is also possible to shape luck—by building networks, by exercising parsimony of investment, by seeking competitively insulated niches, by moving incrementally, and by continually monitoring performance. This approach conserves resources, heightens awareness of developing trends, and maintains the flexibility needed to quickly respond to new opportunities.

Finally, start-ups move through distinct phases, with different management and strategic issues paramount in each phase. Effort must be taken to ensure that resources are spent on the areas most critical to the firm's success, given its stage of development. And care must be exercised to think through how short-term actions might be planting the seeds of future problems.

Summary and Recommendations

We have reviewed the literature in the context of the challenges faced when designing an entrepreneurship research program. In the course of this review, we came to the conclusions that are summarized in Exhibit 2.2 and discussed in greater detail below:

1. Purpose. There is a need for future research programs to include a clear statement of purpose. Furthermore, we appeal to researchers to link the specific purpose of their study to the more fundamental purpose we have proposed: to explain and facilitate the role of new enterprise in furthering economic progress. It is hoped that by linking to this overall purpose, a wide variety of research activities can be brought into a broad but unifying arena.

EXHIBIT 2.2   Overview of Entrepreneurship: Past Research and Future Challenges

Research Design Decisions	Past Research	Model Research and Future Challenges
Specification of purpose	Little clarity, descriptive, lack of unity	Clearly stated, explanatory, further economic progress
Specification of theoretical perspective	Weak theory development, implicitly assuming strategic choice	Theory driven, clearly stated assumptions, variety of theoretical perspectives
Specification of focus	Focus on personality or cultural determinants	Focus on entrepreneurial process in social context
Specification of level of analysis	Primarily single level of analysis	Multiple levels of analysis
Specification of time frame	Narrow time frame	Wide time frame

2. Theoretical perspective. In the past, much of the entrepreneurship literature has implicitly assumed a strategic adaptation perspective. The
insights resulting from recent work using the population ecology perspective have challenged some of these assumptions and demonstrated
the benefits of theory driven research. We suggest that future research
should examine and clearly state theoretical assumptions and that additional theoretical perspectives should be explored.

3. Focus. Recently, there has been a trend toward more contextual and
process-oriented research. This is an important advancement and moves
the field closer to a position of being able to explain rather than merely
document the entrepreneurial phenomenon. Future research should continue this trend.

4. Level of analysis. There has been a welcome initiation of studies that
examined more than one of the individual, group, organization, industry, and society levels of analysis. Such multilevel studies provide a
much richer understanding of the entrepreneurial phenomenon and
should therefore be encouraged in future research programs.

5. Time frame. It appears that greater insights can be obtained from studies
which employ wide time frames than from studies employing cross sectional "snapshots." A push towards longer time frame studies is desirable, particularly since it is becoming clear that different strategic issues
become important as firm and industry evolve.

6. Methodology. There has been disappointingly slow progress in research
that addresses issues of causality, perhaps reflecting the elusiveness of
the entrepreneurial phenomenon. Recent years have seen only limited
examples of research designs that develop a priori hypotheses.
Consequently, formal modeling and experimental research have lacked a
foundation for development. On the positive side, the incidence of studies that are both cross sectional and longitudinal is on the rise.

In closing we wish to be realistic. Clearly it is unrealistic to expect that future
research designs will incorporate all the qualities we have suggested. Very few
researchers have sufficient resources to design and execute projects that are theory driven, choose a contextual and process-oriented focus, adopt multiple levels
of analysis, and employ wide time frames. Indeed, although we have been arguing that entrepreneurship research needs to move in a particular direction, we
accept the fact that there are unavoidable tradeoffs in research and that there is
no single best approach (McGrath, 1964; Weick, 1979). However, we do suggest
that more meaningful and insightful results will be forthcoming if researchers
consider these design issues and eschew research program designs in which all
of the easy design alternatives are selected.

Source: This article was originally published in the *Journal of Management,* 14(2), 1988. Reprinted with
deletions with permission of the authors and the *Journal of Management.*

ENDNOTES

1. The discussion of the term *definition* and how it relates to the development of para-digms was adapted from A. Kaplan, "What Good Is 'Truth'?" *Journal of Philosophy and Phenomenological Research* 15 (1954): 151–70.

2. T. Kuhn, *The Structure of Scientific Revolutions*, 2nd ed. (Chicago: University of Chicago Press, 1970).

3. This concept regarding the openness of meaning was adapted from A. Kaplan, "Definition and Specification of Meaning," *Journal of Philosophy* 43 (1946): 80–104.

4. An expanded discussion on the nature of paradigms is developed by Max Weber in *The Methodology of the Social Sciences* (New York: Harper and Row, 1949).

5. P. Kilby, *Entrepreneurship and Economic Development* (New York: Free Press, 1971).

6. W. Bygrave, "Micro-, Macro-, and Corporate Entrepreneurs: Can They All Fit in the Same Paradigm?" (Paper presented at the National Academy of Management, Washington, D.C., 1989).

7. A. Kaplan, *The Conduct of Inquiry: Methodology for Behavioral Science* (New York: Chandler-Harper and Row, 1963).

8. G. Morgan, "Paradigms, Metaphors, and Puzzle Solving in Organization Theory," *Administrative Science Quarterly* 25 (1980): 605–22.

9. K. Vesper and W. E. McMullan, "Entrepreneurship: Today Courses, Tomorrow Degrees?" *Entrepreneurship Theory and Practice* 13 (Fall 1988), 7–14.

10. B. Ellis, *Entrepreneurship in Rough Seas* (Nashville: Vanderbilt University Press, 1975).

11. J. Schumpeter, *The Theory of Economic Development* (Cambridge: Harvard University Press, 1934).

12. J. Schumpeter, "The Creative Response In Economic History," *Journal of Economic History* 7 (1947): 149–59.

13. T. Cochran, "Entrepreneurship," in *International Encyclopedia of the Social Sciences*, ed. D. L. Sills (New York: Free Press, 1968) 87–91.

14. Schumpeter, "The Creative Response," 154.

15. A. Cole, "Entrepreneurship as an Area of Research," *Journal of Economic History* 2 (1942), 118–26.

16. R. Brockhaus, Sr., "Risk Taking Propensity of Entrepreneurs," *Academy of Management Journal* 23 (1980), 509–20.

17. J. Carland et al, "Differentiating Entrepreneurs from Small Business Owners: A Conceptualization," *Academy of Management Review* 9 (1984), 354–59.

18. A. Shapero, "Entrepreneurship and Economic Development," *Entrepreneurship and Enterprise Development: A Worldwide Perspective* (Milwaukee: Proceedings of Project ISEED, 1975) and J. Timmons, "Growing Up Big: Entrepreneurship and the Creation of High Potential Ventures," in *The Art and Science of Entrepreneurship*, ed. D. Sexton and R. Smilor (Cambridge, Mass.: Ballinger, 1986) 211–22.

19. P. VanderWerf and C. Brush, "Toward Agreement on the Focus of Entrepreneurship Research: Progress Without Definition." (Paper presented at the National Academy of Management, Washington, D.C., 1989).

20. R. Cantillon, *Essai sur la Nature du Commerce en General* (London: Fletcher Gyles, 1755), trans. and ed. H. Higgs (London: MacMillan, 1931).

21. A. Kallenberg, "Defining Entrepreneurship," in *Advances in the Study of Entrepre-neurship, Innovation, and Economic Growth*, ed. G. Libecap (Greenwich, Conn.: JAI Press, 1986) 158–61.

22. H. Stevenson, M. Roberts, and H. I. Grousbeck, *New Business Ventures and the Entrepreneur,* 2nd ed. (Homewood, Ill: Richard D. Irwin, 1985).

23. The domain statement for the Entrepreneurship Division of the Academy of Management is presented in the Academy of Management's "1990 Call for Papers."

24. These researchers are identified in S. Zahra, "A Canonical Analysis of Corporate Entrepreneurship Antecedents and Impact on Performance," *Proceedings of the National Academy of Management* 46 (1986): 71–75, and also in S. Zahra, "Predictors and Financial Outcomes of Corporate Entrepreneurship: An Exploratory Study," *Journal of Business Venturing* 6 (1991): 259–85.

Entrepreneurship and Economic Theory

Overview of Entrepreneurship and Economic Theory

T his chapter, together with Chapters 4, 5, 6, and 7, describes the economic theory school of thought regarding the notion of entrepreneurship. Chapter 3 begins by tracing the development of the science of economics and outlines a variety of functional roles played by the entrepreneur in economic thought together with a taxonomy of entrepreneurial theories.

Later in this book, we indicate that certain organizational science researchers have suggested an existing relationship between organizational innovation and corporate entrepreneurship; a section in Chapter 11 describes organizational innovation. Researchers in the area of economics also have studied innovation, and a section in Chapter 3 examines those studies. Chapter 3 concludes with a discussion of how economists have investigated the relationship between firm size and entrepreneurial activity. Chapter 4 details how entrepreneurship began in economic thought and contains an article by George Koolman regarding French economist Jean-Baptiste Say's conception of the role of the entrepreneur. Chapter 5 focuses on how early English and American economists and those from the German school considered the entrepreneur in economic thought and contains an article by Charles Tuttle regarding the function of the entrepreneur.

Despite the fact that entrepreneurship had its beginnings in economic thought, entrepreneurship no longer plays a major role in orthodox economic theory. Chapter 6 contains two articles, one by William Baumol and one by Humberto Barreto, that describe the disappearance of the entrepreneur from economic thought. Chapter 7 examines the renewed interest in entrepreneurship by economists.

We are now ready to begin Chapter 3 and to consider the historical development of economic thought.

DEVELOPMENT OF ECONOMIC THOUGHT

Scott stated that the science of economics can be traced to two schools of thought, one contributed by philosophers and the other by "men of affairs." According to Scott, the philosophical school dates back to the ancient Greeks—Aristotle, Plato, and the Stoics and the Epicureans—and progresses to the Roman Jurists and such modern philosophers as Grotius, Hobbes, Locke, Hume, and Hutcheson (Adam Smith's teacher).

Scott argued that the "men of affairs" school of thought is more difficult to trace because their school consisted of the thinking and writing of businessmen, legislators, and other individuals connected with government. These people were stimulated by economic problems and solutions often were crude, naive, and lacking in the systematic approach used by the philosophers. These "men of affairs," however, often developed an interpretation of their contemporary lives that was frequently "keen and illuminating."[1]

During the latter part of the eighteenth century, these two schools of thought were coalesced by Adam Smith in his *Wealth of Nations,* and economics emerged as a distinct and independent discipline.

An interesting aspect of economic thought is the method used by economists to develop various theories. The following section describes several methodological approaches used in the development of economic theory and how those approaches have affected the role of the entrepreneur in economic thought.

DEVELOPMENT OF ECONOMIC THEORY

Theory development in economics can be grouped into several methodologies: analytical or theoretical, historical research and statistical investigation, and mathematical economics.[2]

Proponents of the analytical-theoretical approach argue that economics can be deduced from fundamental axioms that are so generally true that they are self-evident. The main approach that economists from the analytical-theoretical school use to test or falsify an economic theory would be to analyze the deductive process by which the economic theory was derived.[3] Many noteworthy economists belong to this tradition, including John Cairnes, Frank Knight, and Lionel Robbins.[4]

An important subset of analytical-theoretical economic theory development is methodological subjectivism used by the Austrian school of economic thought. Methodological subjectivism is the doctrine that maintains that there is some introspective knowledge or some knowledge gained by common experience that legitimately may be used in assessing the merits of hypotheses, theories, or research programs in the social sciences. Members of the Austrian school—

Ludwig Von Mises, Friedrich Hayek, Murray Rothbard, and Israel Kirzner—use methodological subjectivism as a prescriptive methodology derived from a number of well-developed epistemological systems.[5] Chapter 10 discusses in greater detail how Kirzner views the role of the entrepreneur in economic thought.

Historical research and statistical investigations should not be considered as substitutes for sound economic theory but as complementary to it. This methodological approach allows the economists to put "content" into highly abstract theories. For example, the provision of averages and aggregates together with their movements can add a great deal to what can be inferred from abstract theories. This methodology does not suggest, however, that economics is purely statistics. As Knight stated, "If statistical magnitudes and correlations are to be understood and intelligently used, they must be understood by weaving them into the general structure of our knowledge and relating them to other things we know."[6] Economists using this approach include Nikolai Kondratieff, Wolfram Fischer, Simon Kuznets, and Robert Solow.[7]

The use of mathematics in economic theory development allows the economist to bring together, into a single comprehensive picture, a variety of complex, interdependent variables. Knight stated that the value of mathematical economics is that it "forcibly reminds the inquirer that a change in practically any economic variable has direct or indirect effects on innumerable other magnitudes, thus preventing him from fatally oversimplifying concepts of economic cause and effect."[8] A French economist, A. A. Cournot, was the first to successfully develop a mathematical treatment of economic principles. Others include Leon Walras, Vilfredo Pareto, Alfred Marshall, Arthur Pigou, and Wassily Leontief.[9]

The entrepreneur is well described by economists using the analytical-theoretical methodology. However, in mathematical economics the entrepreneur is omitted and usually becomes a residual along with the effects of other hard-to-define terms such as *institutional organization*.[10]

FUNCTIONAL ROLES AND TAXONOMIES OF THE ENTREPRENEUR IN ECONOMIC THOUGHT

In economic thought, there is no generally accepted theory of entrepreneurship.[11] Economists, however, have characterized the entrepreneur in a variety of ways.[12] For example, Barreto has detailed six functional roles of the entrepreneur in economic thought, while Hebert and Link have described three intellectual taxonomies of entrepreneurial theories.

Barreto's Functional Roles

Humberto Barreto's functional roles are based on the entrepreneur's function in the productive process as an active agent, carrying out specific tasks.[13] These functional roles and the economic theorist responsible for developing each role are as follows:

Functional Role	Theorist
Speculator	Richard Cantillon
Coordinator	Jean-Baptiste Say
Product owner	Frederick Hawley
Innovator	Joseph Schumpeter
Decision maker	Frank Knight
Arbitrageur	Israel Kirzner

Each of these functional roles and its theorist are described in greater detail in subsequent chapters: Cantillon and Say in Chapter 7, Hawley, Schumpeter, and Knight in Chapter 8, and Kirzner in Chapter 10.

In developing these functional roles, Barreto stated, "The work of every theorist who has subscribed to a particular view of entrepreneurship is not reviewed . . . . Instead, only a representative work is chosen and examined."[14] Interestingly Hebert and Link have identified "at least" twelve distinct entrepreneurial roles in the economic literature:[15]

- Assumer of the risk associated with uncertainty
- Supplier of financial capital
- Innovator
- Decision maker
- Industrial leader
- Manager or superintendent
- Organizer and coordinator of economic resources
- Owner of an enterprise
- Employer of factors of production
- Contractor
- Arbitrageur
- Allocator of resources among alternatives used

Hebert and Link's Taxonomy of Entrepreneurial Theories

Robert Hebert and Albert Link argued that contemporary economic theory recognizes the entrepreneur as an independent factor of production "on a more-or-less equal footing with land, labor, and capital."[16] Hebert and Link developed a distinction between the manager and the entrepreneur and considered only dynamic theories where "the entrepreneur becomes a robust figure" in developing their three taxonomies of entrepreneurial theories. Each taxonomy begins with Richard Cantillon and includes the following:

Taxonomy	Theorist
German tradition	Johann von Thunen and Joseph Schumpeter
Chicago tradition	Frank Knight and Theodore Schultz
Austrian tradition	Ludwin Von Mises and Israel Kirzner

Graphically the taxonomy presented by Hebert and Link is shown in Exhibit 3.1.

EXHIBIT   3.1

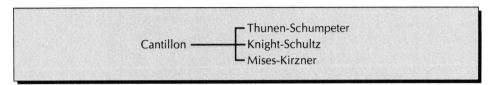

Source: R. F. Hebert and A. N. Link, "In Search of the Meaning of Entrepreneurship," *Small Business Economics* 1 (1989): 41. Used with permission of the editor of *Small Business Economics* and the authors; reprinted with permission of Kluwer Academic Publisher.

Each economist's theory is described in greater detail in subsequent chapters: Thunen and Schumpeter's theories in Chapter 7, Knight in Chapter 8, and Schultz, Mises, and Kirzner in Chapter 10.

Certainly other writers have developed works that have described the entrepreneur in a setting using economic thought. For example, Mark Casson integrated what he called the "functional approach" and the "indicative approach." According to Casson, a functional approach is "that an entrepreneur is what an entrepreneur does," while the indicative approach "provides a description by which he may be recognized."[17]

INNOVATION AND ECONOMIC THOUGHT

In Chapter 11 we will discuss that in the organizational-science literature a number of researchers have linked various aspects of entrepreneurship with types of innovation at both individual and organizational levels of analysis. While a number of economists consider the entrepreneur to be an innovator, very few studies in economics have investigated the relationship between entrepreneurship and innovation. Instead, researchers in economics have tended to examine how various factors such as firm size and market structure have influenced innovation. These researchers have investigated the notion of innovation from a technological progress model. This particular model is described in greater detail in the Jennings article that appears in Chapter 13.

Economists have also researched the effects of monopoly power on innovation. For instance, Galbraith posited that high barriers to entry and high concentration tend to promote innovation. He viewed lack of rivalry as increasing profits, which would provide more funds for risky research and development (R&D) projects. Innovators would be protected from those that might "steal" their ideas.[18] Williamson argued, however, that the relative innovative performance of leading firms is greater where competition exists and concentration is lower.[19]

Schumpeter claimed that the monopoly firm would have a greater demand for innovative activity than would the competitive firm, since it can profit from the innovation as a result of its market power.[20] Arrow first demonstrated that this demand argument is incorrect, and Hu substantiated Arrow's argument.[21]

FIRM SIZE AND ENTREPRENEURIAL ACTIVITY

In studying firm size and how it relates to innovative activity, a number of researchers have investigated the "Schumpeterian hypothesis." This hypothesis is based on Schumpeter's argument that economic growth occurs through a process of "creative destruction" where the old industrial structure—its product, its process, or its organization—is continually changed by "new" innovative industrial activity. According to Schumpeter, large firm size is essential to the success of such innovative activity. Larger firms can provide economies of scale in production and innovation which make available sufficient resources necessary for successful completion of this process.[22] Mansfield and his associates investigated firm size and innovation using the measures of inputs (R&D money and personnel) and outputs (number of patents) and reported that no significant evidence existed to indicate that R&D intensity, relative to firm size, increased beyond medium-sized firms and that "inventive output" did not match measured input.[23]

Two overviews of research regarding firm size and innovation have been reported. One overview surveyed these studies and concluded that the statistical evidence supporting Schumpeter's hypothesis is, in general, "wanting."[24] The other overview suggested that the most favorable industrial environment for rapid technological innovation would be to have a majority of medium-sized firms bounded on one side by a "horde" of small technology-oriented firms "bubbling over with bright new ideas" and on the other by a few larger companies with the resources to undertake "exceptionally ambitious" developments.[25]

Following these overviews, other researchers have argued that the existing empirical literature regarding innovative activity is not a test of Schumpeter's hypothesis. These researchers suggested that it is incorrect to measure innovative activity, as described by Schumpeter, by some absolute index, like R&D expenditures to firm size or market concentration.[26]

Link suggested that innovative activity should be viewed as an entrepreneurial process because the process notion of innovation is "clear from Schumpeter's discussion of creative destruction wherein the entrepreneur is continually creating the disequilibria from equilibrium states"[27] and used both Kirzner's and Schultz's definitions of entrepreneurship, which stress perception of disequilibria and then adjustment to an equilibrium.[28] Link then formulated an empirical test of Schumpeter's hypothesis by testing whether rate of return to R&D is a function of firm size and reported that "efficient innovative activity, as measured by rate of return to R&D expenditures, is a function of firm size. The estimated rate of return in the larger size grouping is significantly greater than in smaller firms."[29]

ENDNOTES

1. W. A. Scott, *The Development of Economics* (New York: D. Appleton-Century, 1933). Scott's view is supported by A. Gray, *The Development of Economic Doctrine*, 2nd ed. (London: Longman, 1980), and S. T. Lowry, *The Archaeology of Economic Ideas* (Durham, N.C.: Duke University Press, 1987).

2. F. H. Knight, *On the History and Method of Economics: Selected Essays* (Chicago: University of Chicago Press, 1956).

3. M. L. Blaug, *The Methodology of Economics: Or How Economists Explain* (Cambridge: Cambridge University Press, 1980).

4. Ibid.

5. L. V. Mises, *Human Action* (New Haven, Conn: Yale University Press, 1949).

6. Knight, *Selected Essays*.

7. Blaug, *The Methodology of Economics*.

8. Knight, *Selected Essays*.

9. Ibid.

10. P. Kilby, *Entrepreneurship and Economic Development* (New York: Free Press, 1971).

11. M. Casson, *The Entrepreneur: An Economic Theory* (Totowa, N.J.: Barnes and Noble, 1982).

12. R. F. Hebert and A. N. Link, *The Entrepreneur: Mainstream Views and Radical Critiques*, 2nd ed. (New York: Praeger, 1988).

13. H. Barreto, *The Entrepreneur in Microeconomic Theory: Disappearance and Explanation* (London: Routledge, 1989).

14. Ibid.

15. R. F. Hebert and A. N. Link, "In Search of the Meaning of Entrepreneurship," *Small Business Economics* 1 (1989): 39–49.

16. Ibid.

17. Casson, The *Entrepreneur*.

18. J. K. Galbraith, *American Capitalism* (Boston: Houghton Mifflin, 1956).

19. O. E. Williamson, *Markets and Hierarchies* (New York: The Free Press, 1975).

20. J. A. Schumpeter, *Capitalism, Socialism, and Democracy*, 3rd ed. (New York: Harper and Bros., 1950).

21. K. J. Arrow, "Economic Welfare and the Allocation of Resources for Invention," *National Bureau of Economic Research* (1962): 13–22; S. C. Hu, "On the Incentive to Invent: A Clarificatory Note," *Journal of Law and Economics* 16 (1973): 169–77.

22. Schumpeter, *Capitalism, Socialism, and Democracy*.

23. E. Mansfield et al., *The Production and Application of New Industrial Technology* (New York: Norton, 1977).

24. M. I. Kamien and N. L. Schwartz, "Market Structure and Innovation: A Survey," *Journal of Economic Literature* 13 (1975): 1–37.

25. F. M. Scherer, *Industrial Market Structure and Economic Performance*, 2nd ed. (Chicago: Rand McNally, 1972).

26. J. W. Markham, "Rates of Return from Industrial Research and Development," *American Economic Review—Papers and Proceedings* 55 (1965): 323–32; F. M. Fisher and P. Tamin, "Returns to Scale in Research and Development: What Does the Schumpeterian Hypothesis Imply?" *Journal of Political Economy* 81 (1973): 56–70.

27. A. N. Link, "Firm Size and Efficient Entrepreneurial Activity: A Reformulation of the Schumpeter Hypothesis," *Journal of Political Economy* 88 (1980): 771–83.

28. I. M. Kirzner, *Competition and Entrepreneurship* (Chicago: University of Chicago Press, 1973); T. W. Schultz, "The Value of the Ability to Deal with Disequilibria," *Journal of Economic Literature* 13 (9175): 827–46.

29. Link, "Firm Size and Efficient Entrepreneurial Activity."

CHAPTER 4

The Beginning of Entrepreneurship

T he word *entrepreneur* is derived from the French verb *entreprendre*, which means to undertake. In this chapter we describe how the notion of entrepreneurship began in economic thought by reviewing concepts developed by two individuals who lived in France, Richard Cantillon and Jean-Baptiste Say. We conclude the chapter with an article by George Koolman, who provides additional insights into Say's concept of the entrepreneur's role.

RICHARD CANTILLON

Richard Cantillon, described by his associates as a cosmopolitan, was an Irishman with a Spanish name who became a successful banker in France during the early eighteenth century. During that time governmental control of economic affairs was falling into disuse in France. Free-trade doctrines were emerging. It was in France, of course, that the phrase *laissez faire* (meaning that government should intervene as little as possible in the direction of economic affairs) originated in the first half of the eighteenth century.

Cantillon moved from Ireland to Paris following the death of Louis XIV, in 1715. Shortly after his arrival in Paris Cantillon associated with a group of speculators who invested in various ventures and became quite wealthy.

During this same period a number of French intellectuals began to produce noteworthy writings on economic subjects. Included in this material was Cantillon's essay entitled "Essay on the Nature of Commerce." It was originally written in English and published in England between 1730 and 1734. The essay, or a portion of it, was subsequently translated by the author himself for use by a French friend and published in 1755 in French and titled "Essai sur la Nature du Commerce en General." The English version was lost but the French translation was widely circulated throughout the eighteenth century and was extremely influential many years after Cantillon's death in 1734. Over time the manuscript was neglected but was rediscovered by William Stanley Jevons, an English economist and philosopher, in 1881. The French version of Cantillon's work was translated into English and edited in 1931 by Henry Higgs.

In his essay Cantillon wrote that land is the source of all wealth and recognized three types of economic actors: (1) landowners who are financially independent, (2) entrepreneurs who engage in market exchanges at their own risk in order to make a profit, and (3) hired people who avoid active decision making in order to secure contractual guaranties of stable income. Cantillon's entrepreneurs did not initiate change, nor were they innovators. Instead, he used a risk theory of profit as a means to identify entrepreneurship. For example, Cantillon wrote that the role of his entrepreneur was to transact purchases at certain prices and sales at uncertain ones.[1]

Cantillon's function of the entrepreneur has been described as follows:

> By tracing the various exchanges which are made as the product reaches the customer, Cantillon repeatedly points out the distinguishing feature of entrepreneurship—the uncertain return. Wholesalers buy (from carriers) at a certain price and sell (to retailers) at an uncertain price. Retailers buy (from wholesalers) at a certain price and sell (to consumers) at an uncertain price. Farmers, carriers, wholesalers, and retailers are all entrepreneurs.[2]

Social standing was not a characteristic of Cantillon's notion of entrepreneurship. In fact he identified beggars and robbers as entrepreneurs, provided they earned an uncertain income.[3]

Barreto described Cantillon's contribution toward the development of a theory of entrepreneurship as follows:

> Cantillon's entrepreneur is a crucial part of the market system, buying at a fixed price and selling at an uncertain one. The willingness to do this allows exchange to take place. Furthermore, the responsiveness to profit opportunities drives the market toward equilibrium. Cantillon's distribution theory focuses entirely on the type of income earned. Receipt of an uncertain return is the identifying feature of the entrepreneur. By the middle of the 18th century, Richard Cantillon had presented the first theory of entrepreneurship—casting the entrepreneur as a speculator in an uncertain environment.[4]

JEAN-BAPTISTE SAY

Jean-Baptiste Say, both a journalist and a cotton manufacturer, was a pioneer in the mechanization of the French textile industry. In the early nineteenth century

Say introduced the "new" English economic ideas of Adam Smith at several French and other European universities. He was well known in the "enlightened" circles of his time and was considered to be "excessively liberal." Say was more than a mere popularizer of Smith's work, however. He developed some clear-cut views of his own and extended Smith's work by emphasizing the role of the entrepreneur.

Say's famous law of markets (Say's law) became widely accepted as a statement of the eternal ability of market forces to produce equilibrium of production and demand. Say's major work, *A Treatise on Political Economy*, published in 1803, presented an analysis of the production and distribution of products in a competitive market system, with a dominant role assigned to the entrepreneur as coordinator. There were five editions of the *Treatise* during Say's lifetime. A fourth edition, translated by C. R. Prinsep in 1845 had a much greater influence in the United States than in Great Britain. A second book, *Cours Complet d'Economie Politique Pratique*, which was first published in 1828 and which had three editions, described the "applications" of the entrepreneur as a coordinator.[5]

Several economists have mentioned the lack of initiative in Say's colleagues in integrating his entrepreneurial notions into economic thought, for example:

> Ricardo failed entirely to pursue Say's suggestion that the entrepreneur is distinguishable from the other agents of production. Smith could not have done so because his work preceded Say's, but Say had formalized the term entrepreneur and given it definition some 14 years before Ricardo's *Principles* appeared . . . It is noteworthy that in the correspondence between Say and Ricardo, neither the nature nor role of the entrepreneur is once mentioned, the usual discussion focusing instead on the topic of value.[6]

In developing his theory of entrepreneurship, Say visualized three agents of production: (1) land and other natural agents that contribute to it, (2) capital, and (3) human industry. Say further separated human industry into the functions of the scientist, the entrepreneur, and the workman. Say did not consider that the three functions of human industry are equally important. According to Say, while the scientist (the theory developer) and the workman (who provides execution) are important in the production process, it is the entrepreneur who drives the productive process by applying theory and directing execution. Say argued that in agriculture, manufacturing, or commercial industry, some actor must command the necessary resources and organize the productive process: coordination, supervision, and decision making are functions performed by the entrepreneur. In other words, after seeing an economic opportunity, Say's entrepreneur had to estimate demand and then supply that demand. They secured raw materials, organized and trained a work force, and at the same time found customers.[7]

Say also provided insights regarding barriers to entry facing the prospective entrepreneur, the entrepreneur's income, and distinguishing between the entrepreneur and the capitalist.

Barriers to Entry Facing the Prospective Entrepreneur

Say argued that productive services receive payment according to the laws of supply and demand. The limits of supply are, in essence, barriers to entry and include the necessary finances to fund the entrepreneurial endeavor. The entrepreneur must already be rich or have the ability to borrow capital based on connections. Entrepreneurs must also be solvent, intelligent, prudent, and honest, and be "regular" in their work habits. Say also indicated that the entrepreneur must possess moral qualities, judgment, perseverance, and a knowledge of the world. Say suggested that the "lack of these requisites shuts out a great many competitors." Finally, Say indicated that "sheer bad luck" is a final limit to the available supply of entrepreneurship.[8]

The Entrepreneur's Income

The entrepreneur's income is a function of financial resources, connections, personal qualities, and sheer luck.[9] Say noted that the entrepreneur obtains income in the following manner:

> The entrepreneur hires the factors of production (knowledge, labor capital, and natural agents) and remunerates them for their efforts (wages, interest, and rents) from the sale of the product. The residual is the entrepreneur's return, in equilibrium, exactly equal to the entrepreneur's wage determined by the forces of supply and demand. If, after the entrepreneur pays himself the market wage, a surplus still remains—"the producers of this kind of product become more numerous and their competition will cause the price of the product to fall." If revenues cannot cover costs, "he loses, if he has anything to lose: or if he has nothing, those lose who have given him their confidence."[10]

Furthermore, a degree of uncertainty exists for Say's entrepreneurs. For example, they must choose between endeavors, estimate demand, produce the product, locate customers, and maintain order and efficiency. Say did not emphasize the aspect of uncertainty, but noted that entrepreneurs could lose their fortunes and their reputations without any fault of their own in any adventure.[11]

Distinguishing between the Entrepreneur and the Capitalist

According to Koolman, Say's entrepreneur's income "consisted of a wage for the work of coordination and supervision but also included interest payments for capital and supplied a premium for risk taking. This analysis allows him to correctly distinguish between entrepreneur and capitalist."[12]

In summary, Say portrayed his entrepreneur as the driving force in producing goods and services with coordination being the key function. Other roles included decision making and risk bearing. Barreto stated that "although Say's ideas on entrepreneurship went largely unnoticed by the English classicals, his influence can be seen in the work of future economists such as Leon Walras and Joseph Schumpeter."[13]

The following article by George Koolman provides some insights into Say's concept of the entrepreneur's role.

ARTICLE 4.1	SAY'S CONCEPTION OF THE ROLE OF THE ENTREPRENEUR

SAY'S CONCEPTION OF THE ROLE OF THE ENTREPRENEUR
by George Koolman

It is true that Say's law of markets has been subjected to fairly intense scrutiny by economists, largely as being a theoretical construction of "classical economics"; it is only very recently that its historical origins have been closely examined. Little or nothing has been made of Say's contribution to the theory of the entrepreneur. It is the purpose of this paper to attempt in some small measure to correct the gross neglect that Say has suffered in all the various histories of economic thought.

Say's Concept of the Entrepreneur and the Nature of His Functions

Say made a tri-partite division of the functions to be found in any process of production: effort, knowledge and the "applications" of the entrepreneur. Knowledge of how to do something was considered a necessary but not a sufficient condition for production. The really important step was the application of this knowledge to a specific end. For this purpose an entrepreneur was needed. In this way, for Say the entrepreneur became the principal agent of production. Other operations were certainly indispensable, but it was the entrepreneur who gave effect to them and conferred value on them. For positive activity the entrepreneur would have to command the necessary resources and organize their appropriate activities. Say argued that although a country might be deficient in the supply of "knowledge," this was not a serious matter since "men of science" had an over-riding interest in the diffusion of their knowledge and hence knowledge could be obtained from abroad if necessary. But this was not the case with the "other two operations of industry," for "there is no way of dispensing with . . . the art of applying the knowledge of man to the supply of his wants . . . and the skill of execution . . . so that a country well stocked with intelligent merchants, manufacturers and agriculturalists has more powerful means of attaining prosperity, than one devoted chiefly to the pursuit of the arts and sciences." He then argued that the commercial success of Britain and her great wealth were due to the "wonderful practical skill of her adventurers in the useful application of knowledge" and to the laboring skills of her workmen.

Say's division of functions was essentially analytic since he recognized that the three functions could be combined in one person. Consequently the entrepreneur was not necessarily a member of a distinct social class: he was the performer of a distinct economic function. The exact specification of this function was elaborated by Say in the successive editions of the *Treatise on Political Economy* and in his other writings. To draw a picture of the entrepreneur as Say saw him therefore requires considerable care, and it depends upon a collation of his views taken from a number of different sources. Some points, however, are sufficiently well established to require little elaboration. Thus in Say's schema it is shown how the entrepreneur hired the services of the other productive agents, land, labour and, in most cases capital, in return for the payment of rent, wages and interest, and how he combined them in order to meet the demands of final consumers. In this way, entrepreneurs were pure intermediaries in the productive process. They established claims on those productive services which they considered necessary for the production of the commodities the demand for which they were attempting to satisfy. The demand by the entrepreneurs was seen as one of the forces which operated to determine the value of productive services. On the other hand, the supply of the various productive services was determined by a variety of motives. The entrepreneur, therefore, occupied a central role in the economy. He was the linchpin, holding together landlord and capitalist, technician and labourer, producer and consumer. He was the organizer of production, and in that capacity the intermediary between all the agents of production, and between all these and the final consumers; he was the centre of a web of relationships, and was able to profit from his knowledge and the ignorance of others. Say's schema was much more revealing than that of his predecessors, the Physiocrats, who had conceived of the process of exchange as one based on socio-economic classes rather than on individuals.

The entrepreneur was occupied both on the demand and the supply sides of the market equation. On the demand side, "he is called upon to estimate, with tolerable accuracy, the importance of the specific product, the probable amount of demand," whilst on the supply side his concern was with the means of production: "at one time he must employ a great number of hands; at another, buy or order the raw material, collect labourers . . . and give at all times a rigid attention to order and economy." However, the entrepreneurial function was something more than "the art of superintendence and administration," although at one point Say seems to be asserting that this is all there is to it; for he goes on to make clear that there are risks and uncertainties attendant on the process of production and that these limit the supply of successful enterprise. Hence Say is misinterpreted when, as historians have done in the past, stress is placed on the identification of the coordinating activity of entrepreneurs as being his sole contribution to the theory of the entrepreneur. In any enterprise activity "there is an abundance of obstacles to be surmounted, of anxieties to be repressed, of misfortunes to be repaired, and of expedients to be devised . . . [and] there is always a degree of risk attending such undertakings." The entrepreneur, as the provider of capital, was at risk to the extent of his capital commitment, but also his reputation was at stake in the success or failure of his enterprise. The same argument was used elsewhere by Say. Some risk accompanied every industrial enterprise, and even an able entrepreneur might lose the capital he has committed, and to a certain extent his reputation for trustworthiness. Say went on to write that the entrepreneur benefits from his own knowledge by creating on his own account, at his own risk, and for his own profit a product that will have value in the market.

Besides giving a general picture of the large-scale entrepreneur, Say also analysed the role of the person working on his own account. "When a workman carries on an enterprise on his own account, as the knifegrinder in the streets, he is both workman and undertaker." Here it was argued that the productive services were acquired by the entrepreneur under contract—he purchased or hired them—and he used them in his own productive enterprise and became the owner of the finished products. In this way production was undertaken by the entrepreneur at his own behest and at his own risk. This view of the entrepreneur as the sole trader, owning and organizing a business, was a description of the most typical business unit at the time when he was writing.

Say devoted considerable space to the qualities a successful entrepreneur would display. The prime quality was that of judgment. The entrepreneur was continually having to estimate the needs of the market and the means by which they could be met. In this connection the practical knowledge and the laboring skills necessarily associated with production was inessential to the entrepreneur; what he had to possess was an unerring market sense, or else he was likely to produce at great expense something that was valueless.

Say reasoned that in the same line of activity some entrepreneurs would have this essential quality and would be successful, whilst others would not and would be ruined. In addition, since the entrepreneur was placed in a position of uncertainty, it was essential that he should be firm of purpose, act with constancy and generally possess that "judicious courage which can envisage all manner of risks and an imperturbable sang-froid which permits one to use all means of escaping them."

Say's most notable achievement in his treatment of the entrepreneur was the explicit distinction he introduced between the supply-of-capital function and the enterprise function. This was a considerable step forward as is clear when one considers the views on this subject of his predecessors, Turgot and Garnier, and the almost total identification of the entrepreneur and the capitalist by his English contemporaries. To Say it was essential to make this distinction, since in his view it was the entrepreneur who was the active agent in production, and who from his pivotal position in the productive process exercised the most important influence on the distribution of wealth. This was not the role of the capitalist, nor, for that matter, that of the landowner, or of the labourer. Say admitted that while the entrepreneur would necessarily employ capital, it was not sufficient for him just to possess these talents and judgment which characterized his industry, for these had to be exercised upon something. In other words, besides these necessary qualities the entrepreneur had to possess "the materials on which he would employ his industry, and the indispensable instruments to carry it into effect." All these things have a value previously acquired, and this value is called capital. In most cases the entrepreneur would employ his own capital, for he would rarely be able to borrow the whole of his funds from "strangers." Clearly the fact that it was necessary for the entrepreneur to possess the necessary qualities for the execution of his functions and that it was "commonly requisite for the adventurer himself to provide the necessary funds" served to "shut out a great many competitors." Capital funds, however, might not be provided by the entrepreneur himself. But whether or not the enterprise was self-financed was irrelevant to the exercise of the entrepreneurial activity of profit-making. The difficulty facing the entrepreneur was different from that facing the capitalist, for the entrepreneur had to produce commodities the value of which would cover the cost of production, including the cost of the capital employed. From the moment the commodity was worth as much as it cost to produce, its production became advantageous, for it paid for all the costs of the productive services.

There are weaknesses in Say's treatment of the role of the entrepreneur. There is, for instance, very little investigation of the possible relationship between the activities of the entrepreneur and the processes of capital accumulation and investment; and there is little insistence on the innovating role of the entrepreneur. However, although the entrepreneur was seen primarily in his role of co-ordinator, Say did not envisage his activity solely as a superior form of labor effort; for he did acknowledge that the income of the entrepreneur might also be derived from the exploitation of an innovation. Say argued that new methods of working must be introduced, and that, if the entrepreneur was not the first in the field as an inventor, then the inventions of others should be copied as quickly as possible. In speaking of the "man of science" Say wrote: "Sometimes a manufacturer discovers a process, calculated either to introduce a new product, to increase the beauty of an old one, or to produce with greater economy . . ." and then the entrepreneur would gain a monopoly profit for the short period during which the innovation remained a secret. That this was desirable was implicit in Say's argument, since it ensured that economic progress would be more rapid and more diversified than otherwise. It was also clear that the inventor need not be the person to exploit the invention, for this was seen to be a task more appropriate to the entrepreneur.

Say's Neglect

In contrast to Say, his English contemporaries, the "school of Ricardo," almost completely neglected the entrepreneur. Their engine of analysis, articulated on the basis of the interactions of capitalists, landowners and labourers conceived largely as macro-economic groups, found no place for a distinction either between profits and interest or between entrepreneurs and capitalists; and it provided no scope for an anlysis of the behaviour and constitution of business units. Only later did these subjects begin to receive due recognition at the hands of Ricardian critics, clearly prompted by the writings of Say.

The English classical writers were largely uninterested in Say whom they regarded primarily as a popularizer of Adam Smith.

Why was it that Say was able to write so intelligently about the entrepreneur whilst the acknowledged leaders of economic thought neglected the concept?

It has been said that Say's work "grew from purely French sources, if we consider Cantillon as a French economist. It is the Cantillon-Turgot tradition which he carried on and from which he could have developed . . . all the main features of his analysis. . . ." Further, it is generally agreed that the first systematic conception of the role of the entrepreneur is to be found in Richard Cantillon's *Essai*, with its distinction between those whose incomes are uncertain. In Cantillon's view the active groups in society could:

> be divided into two classes, Undertakers and Hired People; and . . . all the Undertakers are as it were on unfixed wages and the others on wages fixed so long as they receive them though their functions and ranks may be very unequal. The general who has his pay, the Courtier his pension and the Domestic servant who has wages all fall into this last class. All the rest are Undertakers, whether they set up with a capital to conduct their enterprise, or are Undertakers of their own labour without capital, and they may be regarded as living at uncertainty. . . .

To what extent would it be valid to infer that Say was influenced by the work of Cantillon whereas his English contemporaries were not? For Cantillon an entrepreneur was not a capitalist first and foremost, nor was he necessarily an employer. He might be either of these; but essentially he was an undertaker in uncertainty, and a key figure on the economic scene, because "the circulation and exchange of goods and merchandize as well as their production are carried on . . . by Undertakers, and at a risk." The crucial distinction Cantillon made was between those who were prepared to accept uncertainty and those who contracted out of it for fixed rates of return. But this was not the kind of analysis offered by Say. Certainly Say spoke of risk and uncertainty, but Cantillon's sharp distinction was not made by him. In fact there is no overt indication that Say directly knew Cantillon's work.

Smith, on the other hand, referred directly to Cantillon's *Essai*, and it was plagiarized by both Postlethwayt and Harris. It must have been as well known to English writers as it was to Say, who would probably have learnt of it from the works of Quesnay and the other Physiocrats, as well as from Turgot or from Garnier. But the original Cantillon formulation was lost sight of in Physiocratic writings. And there is no textual evidence of any connecting links between what Cantillon wrote on the nature of the entrepreneur and what Say wrote. Cantillon made no reference to the entrepreneur as the planner and organizer of a productive enterprise or as a supervisor of the agents of production. In these respects Say's ideas were much closer to those of the Physiocrats, in particular to those of the Abbe Baudeau and Turgot, who had included these elements in their expositions. However, Say was generally opposed to Physiocratic ideas, and this opposition manifested itself in the development of a subjective theory of value. It is doubtful, therefore, whether his own formulations can be traced directly to his predecessors. As his own ideas developed, Say was most concerned about the need to distinguish enterprise and capital as separate elements in the productive process—a distinction which his English contemporaries were quite unable to make. The differences, then, between his own ideas and those of his predecessors and contemporaries were sufficiently marked for us to regard his ideas as markedly original.

Say, himself, offered several reasons why English economists neglected his work. First, he argued that English writers had an insufficiently sophisticated terminology with this deficiency being traceable to a linguistic poverty. Secondly, the English had no word equivalent to the French word "entrepreneur." Thirdly, Say referred to the state of English law. During Say's time, in English law, a capitalist was not simply a creditor who received a fixed interest on his capital, but a capitalist was also described as an active partner who shared in the gains and losses of an undertaking.

It is doubtful whether Say's explanations can carry the weight he placed upon them. A writer's ability to expound his ideas may be impaired by linguistic deficiencies, deficiencies in his conceptual apparatus, or by institutional forms which blur underlying functional relationships; but neither of these considerations can explain the almost total lack of comment in English classical political economy on the nature of business enterprise. Much more important is the focus from which the problem is approached. A different conceptual apparatus is required for a microscopic than for a telescopic analysis of economic connections. Here it can be argued that, taking as the starting-point Smith's *Wealth of Nations*, Ricardian analysis looked for a more fruitful interpretation of economic phenomena in terms of macroeconomic connections, whilst Say sought for enlightenment more in microeconomic connections. It can be argued also that Say's personal experience was such as to lead him in this direction. He was working in England in the early 1790s as the manager of an assurance company when he came across the *Wealth of Nations*. Later, after the publication of the first edition of the *Traite*, the financial proposals of which met with official disapproval and caused his dismissal from the Tribunate, he established a cotton factory at Maubuisson, which he later transferred to Aulchy-les-Moines in the Pas-de-Calais. He was a practising enterpreneur, and in the course of his operations he faced and overcame numerous difficulties, including unco-operative workers, a hostile environment and adverse natural conditions.

Clearly Say's treatment of the entrepreneur has deficiencies. Its central preoccupation was with the static role of the entrepreneur organizing resources necessary to satisfy market demands. There was no appreciation of the entrepreneur acting on his environment; consequently the calculations in which the Sayian enterpreneur was likely to be involved were all in response to exogenous variables. It is not surprising, therefore, to find only limited mention of innovation, although in a number of places the analysis was extended to introduce the principle of economic change and the consequent elements of uncertainty. In retrospect it is right to emphasize these elements wherever they appear, though for Say, perhaps, at the time, they remained more in the nature of suggestions without the consequences being worked out. However, this would be to judge Say in terms of the results of an analysis which did not develop until nearly a century later. Judged by the standards of his own age, Say's ideas were highly sophisticated, and, for a static analysis, completely adequate. Undoubtedly he had a marked effect on the development of thought of a number of English writers who adopted some of his terminology and his analytic approach to business units; and none of the neo-classical writers half-a-century later was to advance beyond the position he had developed.

Source: This article excerpted from George Koolman, "Say's Conception of the Role of the Entrepreneur," *Economica* 38 (1971): 269–86. Used by permission of *Economica*.

ENDNOTES

1. Information pertaining to Cantillon was developed from W. A. Scott, *The Development of Economics* (New York: Appleton, Century, 1933); F. H. Knight, *On the History and Method of Economics: Selected Essays* (Chicago: University of Chicago Press, 1956); H. W. Spiegel, *The Growth of Economic Thought* (Durham, N.C.: Duke University Press, 1983); M. Blaug and P. Sturges (eds.), *Who's Who in Economics: A Biographical Dictionary of Major Economists 1700–1981* (Cambridge: MIT Press, 1983).
2. H. Barreto, *The Entrepreneur in Microeconomic Theory: Disappearance and Explanation* (London: Routledge, 1989).
3. Ibid.
4. Ibid.
5. Information pertaining to Say was developed from Scott, *The Development of Economics*; Knight, *Selected Essays*; Spiegel, *The Growth of Economic Thought*; Blaug and Sturges, *Who's Who in Economics*.
6. R. F. Hebert and A. N. Link, *The Entrepreneur: Mainstream Views and Radical Critiques*, 2nd ed. (New York: Praeger, 1988).
7. Spiegel, *The Growth of Economic Thought*.
8. Barreto, *The Entrepreneur in Microeconomic Theory*.
9. Ibid.
10. Ibid.
11. Ibid.
12. G. Koolman, "Say's Conception of the Role of the Entrepreneur," *Economica* 38 (1971): 269–86.
13. Barreto, *The Entrepreneur in Microeconomic Theory*.

Early English and American Economists, the German School, and Entrepreneurship

T he first section of this chapter briefly discusses how economic thought evolved from Adam Smith's *Wealth of Nations,* published in 1776, until the neoclassical era of economic thought, which ended in the 1930s.[1] During this period the entrepreneur remained a central figure in economic thought. However, economists in the neoclassical era did not always agree on the entrepreneur's specific function.

During the neoclassical era, the concepts of two English economists—Francis Edgeworth and Alfred Marshall—and four American economists—Frederick Hawley, John Bates Clark, Irving Fisher, and Frank Knight—summarized the various viewpoints regarding the entrepreneur's specific function.[2] The concepts of these six economists are presented in the second section of this chapter.

The German school of entrepreneurship,[3] developed near the end of the neoclassical era, is discussed in the third section of this chapter.

The fourth section summarizes the variety of functions performed by the entrepreneur as described by early English and American economists as well as those economists of the German school. Finally the chapter concludes with an article by Charles Tuttle describing his concept of the entrepreneur's function, which he wrote near the end of the neoclassical era.

ECONOMIC THOUGHT FROM SMITH'S *WEALTH OF NATIONS* TO THE NEOCLASSICAL ERA

Following the publication in 1776 of Adam Smith's classic work, *Wealth of Nations*,[a] in which he "resolved the chaos of competition and the welter of buying and selling into an orderly system of economic cooperation where a nation's wants are supplied and its wealth increased under individual freedom,"[4] a variety of economists attempted to explain the theory of value, or why goods exchange at particular ratios. Modern economists explain value theory today by using microeconomic theory (the theory of the firm). Classical economists,[b] however, used a theory of distribution in which the total product was divided into three shares: wages of labor, profits of capital, and rent of land. Later, French economists, following Say's logic,[c] argued that a fourth share, the entrepreneur, existed.[5]

Knight described the classical economic approach as follows:

> The classical theory of value stressed chiefly the tendency for the prices of goods produced and sold under competitive conditions to be proportionate to the respective costs of producing them. However, costs meant not only the money outlays of the entrepreneurs, but the "real" costs, human sacrifice or pain.[6]

During the classical economic period, in addition to Adam Smith, two other economists are noted for their contributions: David Ricardo and John Stuart Mill.[7] Ricardo's contribution was his "law of rents," which was based on the observation that the differing fertility of land yielded unequal profits to the capital and labor applied to it.[8] John Stuart Mill published a transitional summary of then-current economic thought and provided a comprehensive analysis of money, international trade, dynamics of distribution, and the role of government in economic life.[9] Mill's *Principles of Political Economy*, published in 1848, became the leading economic textbook in the English-speaking world for the rest of the nineteenth century.[10]

During the latter part of the nineteenth century, critics objected to various aspects of classical economic thought. For example, certain economists disliked the notion of laissez faire, preferring an ordered society. Others argued that long-run analyses tended to overlook how normal economic life is interrupted by unemployment and depressions. Still others suggested that economics is a historical categorization that can be explained by a study of concrete facts of the particular situation.

---

[a] In essence Adam Smith theorized that competition and the forces of the marketplace constituted an "invisible hand" that if left unfettered could create a wondrous machine for the creation of riches and a rising standard of living.

[b] The classical economic period existed from 1776 to 1870.

[c] Say's logic was described in Chapter 2.

Over time the circle of dissenters widened and the era of neoclassical economic thought emerged and existed from 1870 to the early 1930s.[11] From 1870 to 1914 marginalism and equilibrium concepts were introduced and discussed by a number of economists. From 1914 until the 1930s marginalism concepts generally were accepted, and economists focused on equilibrium analysis.[12]

During the neoclassical era of economic thought, the entrepreneur remained a central figure in the explanation of distribution. However, economists in this period did not always agree on the entrepreneur's specific function in the theory of distribution.

The following sections summarize the concepts developed by two English and four American economists to describe a variety of functions performed by the entrepreneur.

EARLY ENGLISH ECONOMISTS

Francis Edgeworth (1845–1926)

Francis Edgeworth was a professor of political economics at All Souls College, Oxford University, whose work is still noted for its precedents in mathematical and statistical analyses.[13] While Edgeworth never presented a theory of entrepreneurship, he is noted for his disagreement with Leon Walras over the role of the entrepreneur in general equilibrium.[14]

Walras, a Frenchman and economist on the faculty at the University of Lausanne, was influenced by Say's concept of the entrepreneur. Walras considered the entrepreneur to be a coordinator and arbitrageur. Walras did not attempt to describe the entrepreneur's role in a disequilibrium situation but focused, instead, on a general equilibrium environment. Walras described the entrepreneur as being "profitless" in general equilibrium.

Edgeworth argued against Walras's "profitless" view of the entrepreneur by stating that a positive stream of income, called profit, existed and accrued to the entrepreneur.[15]

Edgeworth's viewpoint of the entrepreneurial function is as follows:

> Edgeworth distinguished between "factors of production which are articles of exchange" and factors, namely entrepreneurship, which are not traded. The entrepreneur performs necessary functions, coordination and arbitrage, but his work is such that it cannot be rewarded analogously to other factor returns because supply and demand curves for entrepreneurship do not exist.... For Edgeworth, the entrepreneur as coordinator, combining factors of production, and as middleman, connecting product and factor markets never disappears, even in general equilibrium. He is rewarded for his productive services by a return called profit, which, likewise, never disappears and is not a function of marginal productivity.... The key to Edgeworth's argument lies in his refusal to admit that a market for entrepreneurship exists. This separates the entrepreneur from the other factors not on the production, but on the distribution side. Edgeworth believed that the entrepreneur was somehow

special or different. Therefore he argued against the simple elimination, a la Walras, of the entrepreneur from the explanatory scheme.[16]

In summary Edgeworth argued that the entrepreneur was a coordinator and middleman that never disappeared, even in general equilibrium. This viewpoint was the opposite of Walras' perspective.

Alfred Marshall (1842–1924)

Alfred Marshall, a professor of political economics at Cambridge University, was the dominant figure in British economics during the late nineteenth and early twentieth centuries. He was considered one of the ablest mathematicians of his time and an eclectic theorist, drawing a variety of ideas together in an attempt to describe the total picture of economic thought. The publication of his *Principles of Economics* in 1890 contained a partial equilibrium analysis and controlled neoclassical thought.[17]

Marshall never precisely stated the entrepreneur's function but instead described a variety of entrepreneurial roles, including the following:

> As uncertainty bearers and coordinators undertaking the chief risks of the business and controlling its general direction. . . . As cost minimizers obtaining better results with a given expenditure or equal results with a less expenditure. . . . As an innovator by trying new techniques and different ideas. . . . As responsible for the growth and decline of firms. . . . On the production side, Marshall's entrepreneur performs several tasks: directing production, applying the principle of substitution, trying new techniques and bearing uncertainty. Through these varied functions, the Marshallian entrepreneur induces progress and is responsible for the rise and decline of firms. . . . On the distribution side, the entrepreneur pays the factors according to their respective marginal productivities keeping the residual (gross profits) for himself. . . . Gross profits contain interest, wages of management, and a premium for risk bearing. . . . Entrepreneurs with exceptional talents will receive additional income as a "rent of ability" which is often the largest share.[18]

In summary Marshall's theory was the dominant neoclassical perspective for forty years. His partial equilibrium analysis focused on particular markets and firms where the entrepreneur played a key role in neoclassical economic thought regarding the market system.

EARLY AMERICAN ECONOMISTS

Frederick Hawley (1843–1929)

Frederick Hawley, a graduate of Williams College, was a businessman who published a number of articles on the significance of the entrepreneur in major economic journals, including the *Quarterly Journal of Economics* and *American Economic Review*.[19]

While Hawley accepted that land, labor, and capital were the three factors of orthodox production theory, he argued that a fourth factor, "enterprise," was missing. The enterprise factor was not considered to be a productive factor but instead a motivating force.[20]

Hawley's enterpriser, or entrepreneur, made the decision regarding what product or service was to be produced and answered to no one except consumers. The entrepreneur was responsible for the gain or loss of his endeavors. He received profits—an uncertain residual income—as a "return for bearing the attendant risks and responsibilities."[21]

John Bates Clark (1847–1938)

John Bates Clark was a professor of economics at Smith College, Amherst College, and Columbia University. Early in his career he was a critic of capitalism, but while at Columbia he shifted his intellectual position toward a support for capitalism. Clark was involved in "lively" controversies with several of his contemporaries.[22] One such controversy involved Hawley's description of the entrepreneur. The Hawley-Clark debate dominated entrepreneurial investigations by American economists during the early neoclassical era.[23]

Clark analyzed static and dynamic economies rather than taking Hawley's approach of distinguishing between certain and uncertain states.[24] Clark's argument has been described as follows:

> In a static economy, characterized by perfect competition, the entrepreneur disappears.... The Clarkian entrepreneur is an arbitrageur in a dynamic economy.... The essence of entrepreneurship is not superintendence or management but preparing a special coordinating function.... The Clarkian entrepreneur is not a factor of production, not an uncertainty bearer, and not a capitalist. He performs a purely mercantile function, paying for the elements of a product and then selling the product.... The fundamental difference between Clark and Hawley is that Clark's entrepreneur is not an uncertainty bearer.[25]

In summary Clark offered a different view of entrepreneurship than the one presented by Hawley. For example, Clark's entrepreneur was an arbitrageur, while Hawley's entrepreneur was an uncertainty bearer.[d] Furthermore, Clark focused on a dynamic environment, while Hawley considered an uncertain environment.

Irving Fisher (1867–1947)

Irving Fisher was a professor of economics at Yale University. He is considered to be one of the greatest and most colorful American economists. Fisher made

---

[d] For the notion of uncertainty bearer in economic thought, the entrepreneur is the bearer of uncertainty. Without the entrepreneur, production could not take place in an uncertain environment.

major contributions to mathematical economics, capital theory, monetary theory, and statistics. He also made a fortune from the invention of a card index system.[26]

Fisher's work on the entrepreneur's function focused on problems created by an uncertain environment, and his entrepreneur counterbalanced the paralyzing effects of randomness.[27] Fisher's entrepreneur is described as follows:

> Employees avoid chance while employers are willing to assume risks. . . . The entrepreneur bears uncertainty. One of his chief functions is to make forecasts, to decide what to do based on subjective expectation. The entrepreneur needs no capital, but, typically, he is a capitalist as well as an undertaker. . . . The entrepreneur, once he has made his forecast, acts upon it by hiring and combining factors of production, providing leadership and judgment. . . . After payment of guaranteed wages and other input prices, the entrepreneur gains the residual profit. In theory, profits and wages should be roughly equal. However, in reality profits are often much higher than wages. The actual magnitude of profits depends on chance and entrepreneurial ability. Though large profits may seem unjust to the layman, they are a necessary result of the efficient working of the market system. Profits are a reward and a return for accurate forecasting and superior ability.[28]

In summary Fisher's entrepreneur reduced the randomness of uncertainty by making forecasts using subjective speculation and received a special income—profit—for his efforts. The importance and distinctiveness of Fisher's entrepreneur are due to his role as profit receiver.

Frank Knight (1885–1972)

Frank Knight was a professor of economics at the University of Iowa and later at the University of Chicago. He agreed with many economists of his time that land, labor, and capital combined to make a product and that the price system allocated resources to their most productive uses. The price system also determined which products would be produced. In such a system pure profit is nonexistent in a state of general equilibrium. Each factor received a fixed rate of return based on the values of their marginal product. The prevailing reasoning was that any deviation in the equality of revenues and costs led to an instant adjustment. Knight was aware of the Hawley-Clark debate regarding the concept of uncertainty.[29]

Knight's contribution was his distinction between the notions of risk and uncertainty. He defined risk as a random event with a known distribution. Uncertainty was considered to be randomness where the distribution of probabilities was completely unknown.[30] In essence Knight's argument regarding uncertainty was a critique against Hawley's theory of risk and profits. To Knight, randomness was not critical. For example, if the chances of an event occurring are known, then they can be determined. Knight argued that managers in dealing with randomness can calculate expected values and receive fixed returns. In that situation pure profit is nonexistent.

Knight posited, however, that the notion of uncertainty changes the system. Decisions made under the conditions of uncertainty, according to Knight, are based on ignorance or opinion rather than knowledge. Knight theorized that some agent must take responsibility for making decisions where uncertainty exists. Knight's agent was the entrepreneur, who acts as a decision maker in an uncertain environment.

Knight considered that his entrepreneur replaced one of the functions of the price system—what products are produced.[31] In performing this function of determining consumers' wants and directing production toward perceived wants, the entrepreneur faces the presence of uncertainty. Knight stated that the "following factors of entrepreneurship" enabled the entrepreneur to deal with uncertainty: "foresight and executive capacity, the knowledge of one's own powers, a disposition to trust them in action, and a knowledge of other men's powers and judgment."[32]

Knight stated that the entrepreneur received a profit based on the following:

> [T]he character of the entrepreneur's profit is based on an income which is ordinary contractual income received for services (wages) or earned by property belonging to him (rent) and a differential element. . . . [T]he differential element is the difference between the market price of the productive agencies employed by the entrepreneur and the amount which he has to guarantee to secure various services and materials to produce the product or service.[33]

To Knight, then, profit is the residual, if any, left for the entrepreneur after he pays out the contractual incomes agreed on for the factor he hires. Knight identified the entrepreneur as being ultimately in control of the venture, ultimately responsible for all receipts and all outlays, and thus subject to the uncertainty that surrounds the amount and the difference between them. Knight did not view profits as compensation for dealing with uncertainty but considered them to be the uncertainty-based differences between the anticipated value of resource services and their actual value.[34] The profits of any particular entrepreneur depended on his or her own ability and good luck as well as on the general level of initiative and ability in the market.[35]

THE GERMAN SCHOOL

Chapter 3 presented the German School of entrepreneurship as part of Hebert and Link's taxonomy of entrepreneurship. These researchers indicated that Johann von Thunen and Joseph Schumpeter were two theorists from the German tradition. The following section describes the viewpoints of Thunen and Schumpeter with respect to entrepreneurship.

Johann von Thunen (1783–1850)

Johann von Thunen was a German landowner and farmer whose work in economics was little appreciated in his own time but which has since been reevaluated as one of the outstanding early contributions to economics. Thunen developed an abstract model referred to as the "isolated state," which he used to develop theories of rent, location, wages, and interest. His ideas were built on the meticulous accumulation of data from farming experiments on his estate. Thunen expressed his ideas verbally, arithmetically, and algebraically, making extensive use of calculus. He developed an "exact theory of marginal productivity" and applied the theory to questions of production and distribution.[36]

Thunen did not attempt to define what role the entrepreneur played in his theories. Interestingly Hebert and Link state that

> the lines of connection between Cantillon, Thunen, and Schumpeter are not as straightforward as the graphic suggests. These connections are tenuous. We base the linkages here more on expository convenience than on historical fact. There is a certain logic of affiliation between Thunen and Schumpeter in that they shared a common language and intellectual heritage. But the connection between Thunen and Cantillon is somewhat contrived on the basis of a common emphasis rather than direct intellectual lineage.[37]

Kauder, however, reported that Thunen's work significantly influenced Eugen Von Bohm-Bawerk, who was Schumpeter's teacher.[38]

Joseph Schumpeter (1883–1950)

Joseph Schumpeter, a professor of economics at Bonn University from 1925 to 1932 and at Harvard University from 1932 to 1950, was highly regarded as a teacher and historian of economics.[39]

Although Schumpeter studied under Bohm-Bawerk, considered to be a great figure of the Austrian school,[40] he did not slavishly imitate the concepts of the Austrian school.[41] Instead Schumpeter combined Bohm-Bawerk's ideas with those of Menger and Wiser, both members of the Austrian school, together with the ideas of Marx, Weber, and Walras. Schumpeter melded concepts from these various individuals "into something uniquely his own."[42]

Chapter 2 noted that Schumpeter argued that innovation develops from entrepreneurship and that it takes an individual who possesses the unusual traits and will to "found a private kingdom, a drive to overcome obstacles, a joy in creating, and satisfaction in exercising one's ingenuity" to become an entrepreneur.[43]

Unlike Say's theories, Schumpeter's concept of the entrepreneur was widely recognized and discussed.[44] Schumpeter agreed with Walras's general equilibrium concept of a static market system where goods and productive services are exchanged between producers and sellers. However, Schumpeter argued that the market system has a tendency toward change and that the entrepreneur plays a crucial role in this market system change.[45]

Many classical economists had problems in dealing with the notion that goods may require two economic periods for their consumption or that current productive power can be exchanged for future consumption goods. Schumpeter addressed this concern by developing a "dynamic circular flow" concept[e] which stated the following:

> The circular flow is a self-perpetuating mechanism. Individual businesses are places where products are made and revenues are divided amongst the productive services. The necessary requirements for production, in the ultimate sense, are directed labor, land, and directing labor (which serves to combine the other two). The key is that the function of directing labor is performed in every period mechanically as it were, of its own accord, without requiring a personal element distinguishable from superintendence and similar things.[47]

In essence distribution of income is based on "marginal utility (product value) and marginal productivity considerations."[48]

Schumpeter introduced his concept of economic development in his circular flow model as follows:

> The concept of economic development covers the following five cases: (1) the introduction of a new good—that is one with which consumers are not yet familiar—or of a new quality of a good. (2) The introduction of a new method of production, that is one not yet tested by experience in the branch of manufacture concerned, which need by no means be founded upon a discovery scientifically new, and can also exist in a new way of handling a commodity commercially. (3) The opening of a new market, that is a market into which the particular branch of manufacture of the country in question has not previously entered, whether or not this market has existed before. (4) The conquest of a new source of supply of raw materials or half-manufactured goods, again irrespective of whether this source already exists or whether it has first to be created. (5) The carrying out of the new organization of an industry, like the creation of a monopoly position or the breaking up of a monopoly position.[49]

Schumpeter's theory of economic development was based on "new combinations," or innovation. For example, Schumpeter considered economic development to be the development of a new good, a new method of production, new markets, new sources of raw material, or a new organizational form. Schumpeter did not define his notion of new combinations in terms of slight incremental change, but as "radical, discontinuous breaks from the past."[50]

In Schumpeter's free market system, the entrepreneur implements these new combinations—"he is the key figure and champion of any economic development."[51] Furthermore, Schumpeter noted that "established firms do not typically engage in change nor does innovation occur by acquiring idle productive factors. Currently employed factors must be induced away from their present employment."[52]

---

[e] A detailed discussion of Schumpeter's circular flow concept is beyond the scope of this chapter. For an expanded discussion see H. Barreto, *The Entrepreneur in Microeconomic Theory: Disappearance and Explanation* (London: Routledge, 1989), 36–47, and J. A. Schumpeter, *The Theory of Economic Development* (Cambridge: Harvard University Press, 1934), 77–86.

In a later work Schumpeter described the process of developing new combinations as "creative destruction" which he argued is the essence of economic development.[53]

Following is a summary of Schumpeter's entrepreneur:

> Schumpeter's entrepreneur is the functional agent who carries out new combinations. He breaks out of established patterns, thereby disrupting the circular flow. This process of creative destruction is the means by which an economy develops. The key lies, not in decision making, per se, but in decision making that results in new combinations (new goods, different productive processes and the like). In carrying out new combinations the entrepreneur generates profits—a surplus of receipts over outlays. Under a free market system, he reaps this excess—paying the remaining factors their respective value of the marginal products. . . . Schumpeter wanted to find the cause of systematic, endogenous change in market economies. In the process of explaining the business cycle, Schumpeter found an entire theory of economic development. At the core of the Schumpeterian explanatory scheme lies the entrepreneur—inducing change and reactions from imitators. A single agent, the entrepreneur, is the key element in Schumpeter's theory of economic development.[54]

Exhibit 5.1 summarizes the concepts of entrepreneurial functions developed by the economists discussed in this chapter.

This chapter concludes with an article written by Charles Tuttle near the end of the neoclassical era of economic thought. In the article Tuttle reviews the economic literature and argues that the entrepreneur should be considered the owner of a business.

ARTICLE 5.1 **THE ENTREPRENEUR AS A BUSINESS OWNER**
by Charles Tuttle

In the analysis of the employer's place in production and distribution, the distinctions of practical life should serve as a guide to scientific truth. Business men have long distinguished, though in a loose and general manner, between employer and workman, between employer and capitalist, and between employer and landowner, on the one hand, and, on the other, between profit and wages, between profit and interest on a money loan, and between profit and the rent of instruments. There appears, therefore, to be ample justification for a strong presumption that these distractions have a scientific basis. It should accordingly be the economist's first task to find that basis. A scientific analysis of the varied relations which the employer actually sustains to business would appear to be prerequisite to a scientific theory of profit. The traditional method reverses this process. From the time of Turgot and Adam Smith to the present, economists have been vainly trying to formulate a theory of profit without a definite conception of the basic function upon which such a theory must logically rest.

EXHIBIT 5.1   Summary of Entrepreneurial Functions Described by Early English, American, and German School Economists

Economist	Concept of Entrepreneurial Function
Francis Edgeworth	Entrepreneur is a coordinator and middleman that never disappears, even in general equilibrium.
Alfred Marshall	Entrepreneur is a business leader and head of the firm—innovating, coordinating, responding to profit signals, and bearing risk.
Frederick Hawley	Entrepreneur is an owner or enterpriser who makes decisions regarding what product or service is to be produced and is also the bearer of uncertainty.
John Bates Clark	Entrepreneur is not an uncertainty bearer but an arbitrageur who shifts resources toward their most profitable uses.
Irving Fisher	Entrepreneur is a bearer of uncertainty who reduces the randomness of uncertainty by making forecasts and deciding what to do based on subjective speculation. His role as profit receiver makes him an important and distinct economic agent.
Frank Knight	Entrepreneur is a decision maker in an uncertain environment. In that role he determines consumers' wants and secures various services and materials to produce the product or service. Profits received are not for dealing with uncertainty but are the uncertainty-based differences between the anticipated value of resource services and their actual value.
Joseph Schumpeter	Entrepreneur is an innovator who carries out new combinations of economic development, which are new goods, a new method of production, new markets, new sources of raw material, or a new organizational form.

It is the purpose of this paper to sketch the gradual emergence and final differentiation in economic literature of the function of ownership of the business, viewed as an organized unit, as the distinctive function of the entrepreneur.

By the close of the eighteenth century, capital had come to be recognized as an essential factor of production, and occupied, in proportion to labor, a relatively more important place than hitherto in the business unit. In the absence of credit facilities, which would render the borrowing and loaning of capital easy, business was rapidly passing into the hands of the capitalists, who alone possessed the large amount of capital which for efficient production was then required for combination with land and labor in the business unit. The independent artisans, their shops and tools now obsolescent, and, in Turgot's quaint phrase, "having nothing but their arms," had become a wage-earning class, placing their human energy at the disposal of capitalist employers, who alone could build factories and equip them with power-driven machines. The business unit was still relatively small, and was owned by capitalists, or landowners, who also organized the business and managed it as a going concern. One could scarcely expect under such conditions that economic writers of that period would differentiate the composite function of capitalist-employer, or landlord-employer, into specifically distinct economic functions, and analyze their general income into specifically distinct functional shares. The economist is dependent upon objective realities to awaken his consciousness of the idea.

Originally land ownership and the cultivation of the land were linked together. Before private property in land was recognized by law, "a man could retain the ownership of a field only in the way he had acquired it and by continuing to cultivate it," as Turgot expresses it. It was private property in land that made the differentiation of the proprietor of the land from the cultivator of it—the farmer—practically possible, and the separation actually took place. The ownership of an agricultural business, which had long been united with the ownership of land, became now completely divorced from it. The rich farmer was regarded no longer as a landowner, or even, as Quesnay puts it, "as a laborer who himself tills the soil, but as an entrepreneur who manages and makes his business profitable by his intelligence and wealth." Obviously Quesnay has in mind a capitalist farmer who owns and manages an agricultural business on land owned by another, and is the first economist, to the writer's knowledge, to apply the term "entrepreneur" to the independent owner of a business. The landowner is thus enabled to live without work on the "revenue" which the farmer turns over to him for the usance of his land. It is interesting to note that Turgot calls the landowners the "disposable class."

Turgot carries the analysis a step farther, and, for the first time perhaps in economic literature, clearly differentiates the ownership of capital as a separate economic function in business. He was enabled to do this by his conception of capital. The capitalist, as the owner of an accumulated fund of value is represented by Turgot as having to choose between two alternatives; either personally to invest his capital, or to loan it to another. If he accepts the first alternative and decides himself to invest his capital, he still has to choose between land, as a form of investment, and business. If he purchases land, he is then both capitalist and landowner. If, however, he becomes an entrepreneur, he immediately invests his capital in the different kinds of goods required for his particular business, and he is then both capitalist and entrepreneur. As capitalist he is owner of the accumulated fund of value which he, as entrepreneur, invests; and as entrepreneur he owns the specific goods in which he invests it. If, however, the capitalist accepts the other alternative and decides to loan his capital in the form of money, he remains capitalist only; for he surrenders his capital to another for investment in goods to be selected and owned by the borrower. Again, if the capitalist desires to have an income without labor on his own part he possesses, according to Turgot, two alternatives: he may either "purchase lands" or become a "lender of money." In either case he would belong to the so-called "disposable class," so far as his person is concerned.

It appears that the capitalist who becomes entrepreneur is bound, like the wage-earning laborer, to "a particular labor." As entrepreneur he invests capital and employs laborers in all sorts of enterprises—agricultural, manufactural, and commercial—and is actively engaged in making his business yield him each year, "besides the interest on his capital,"

> a profit to recompense him for his care, his labor, his talents and his risks, and to furnish him in addition with that wherewith he may replace the annual wear and tear of his advances,—which he is obliged to convert from the very first into effects which are susceptible of change, and which are, moreover, exposed to every kind of accident.

With Turgot, then, the ownership of capital is a qualification for becoming entrepreneur, but the two functions are distinct. Turgot's entrepreneur is an employer who invests capital in a business which he owns, organizes, and manages. Turgot, however, does not place the emphasis upon the ownership of the business; for, had he done so, he would have put the entrepreneur in the "disposable class" as one who, like the landowner and the capitalist "lender of money," secures an income without labor. He expressly says the opposite of this, and seems to take business ownership as a matter of course, or as a mere incident. He does put the emphasis, rather, if the writer has correctly interpreted him, upon labor, which binds the entrepreneur, like the wage-earning workman, "to a particular labor." Turgot's entrepreneur, then, is an independent organizer and manager of a business.

It remained for Adam Smith to take the next step in the differentiation of the function of the entrepreneur. The function of the "undertaker" is, to the writer's knowledge, nowhere in the *Wealth of Nations* directly discussed; even the term rarely occurs. It is only by implication from the discussion of "profits of stock" that one is able to construct the great Scotchman's conception of the function to which profit attaches. Early in his great work, however, Adam Smith takes direct issue with the view, which we have described as clearly Turgot's, that organizing and directive labor is the determining element in the function with which profit is associated.

It is evident that Adam Smith eliminated from the function which entitles a man to profit the very element upon which Turgot had placed especial stress; and in so doing he made a distinct contribution to the cause of sound theory. Human labor logically comprises labor of every "particular sort"; and its share of the product, in logical consistency, should be called wages.

But, while clearing up the error into which Turgot had fallen, Adam Smith, unfortunately, falls into an error from which acquaintance with Turgot's analysis should have saved him. He evidently confounds production goods and capital, and consequently "profits of stock" and interest. In so doing, through the influence of his great name, he gave the cause of sound theory a serious backset. To make clear, then, Adam Smith's notion of the function which entitles a person to profit, it is necessary at this point to recall his conception of capital.

In an earlier article, the writer has shown that Adam Smith sidetracked the Turgot capital concept, and substituted therefor a brand-new one which we may appropriately call the "Adam Smith concept." He characterizes an accumulated stock of concrete goods, exclusive of land and natural agents, from which a man expects to derive a revenue, as "capital." Only a portion of this stock of goods is represented as employed "in setting to work industrious people," and supplying them with "materials and subsistence in order to make a profit by the sale of their work." It is this portion which is pertinent to our inquiry. In representing, therefore, the ownership of "capital" as the essential element to which profit attaches, Adam Smith explicitly means the ownership of the so-called "artificial" production goods employed in a business, as distinguished from consumption goods. The very phrase "profits of stock" seemingly indicates this. Here it should be observed that in this specific point Adam Smith is in accord with Turgot. Adam Smith's failure, however, consciously to distinguish between capital and production goods rendered it impossible for him to differentiate, as Turgot had done, the ownership of capital from the ownership of a business. To him the two ownerships were essentially one and "profits of stock" was but another name for interest.

Yet Adam Smith did, *intuitively*, recognize the accumulated fund of value invested in his accumulated stock of production goods as a distinct element, and its ownership as a distinct mode by which the individual may participate in production. He says:

> Whoever derives his revenue from a fund which is his own, must draw it either from his labor, from his stock, or from his land. The revenue derived from labor is called wages. That derived from stock, by the person who manages or employs it, is called profit. That derived from it by the person who does not employ it himself, but lends it to another, is called the interest or the use of money. It is the compensation which the borrower pays to the lender, for the profit which he has an opportunity of making by the use of the money. Part of that profit naturally belongs to the borrower, who runs the risk and takes the trouble of employing it; and part to the lender, who affords him the opportunity of making this profit. . . . The revenue which proceeds altogether from land, is called rent, and belongs to the landlord. The revenue of the farmer is derived partly from his labor, and partly from his stock. To him, land is only the instrument which enables him to earn the wages of this labor, and to make the profits of this stock.

It is evident that Adam Smith, here, recognizes interest as "the compensation which the borrower [the employer] pays to the lender [the capitalist] for the profit which he [the employer] has an opportunity of making by the use of the money [the capital]." And, strange as it may seem, he regards interest as an important element in profit; for he says later:

> It may be laid down as a maxim, that wherever a great deal can be made by the use of money, a great deal will commonly be given for the use of it; and that wherever little can be made by it, less will commonly be given for it.

The logical conclusion must be that, should borrowing and loaning cease, interest would vanish, and "profits of stock" would alone remain as the share of the capitalist employer. It seems but a fair inference that, had Adam Smith made consciously the distinction between "stock" and money-to-lend, which he seemingly made intuitively, he would have grasped the capital concept of the great Frenchman, and would have distinguished, as did the latter, between capital as an accumulated fund of value, expressible in money, and the accumulated stock of concrete "artificial" production goods in which the employer invests it. He would, then, have recognized consciously that the capitalist owns and loans capital, while the employer, whether he be capitalist or borrower, owns and employs "stock" (production goods); that the capitalist, as such, is entitled to the earnings of capital, while the employer, as such, receives profit by virtue of the ownership of the buildings, machines, apparatus, and materials ("stock") in which he invests capital. He must then have recognized that profit and interest as "altogether different," and "regulated by quite different principles." The failure of Adam Smith consciously to differentiate the function of the capitalist from that of the undertaker must be attributed to the prevailing business practice with which he was familiar. In England, at this time, the ownership of capital was prerequisite to becoming the independent head of a business; the same was true in France. Yet while Turgot stressed labor as the essential element in the function of the entrepreneur, Adam Smith, with stronger emphasis, identified that function with the ownership of "capital"; and both took the ownership of the business, as a going concern, as a matter of course.

After the publication of the *Wealth of Nations*, Adam Smith's version of the entrepreneur became traditional in England. A capitalist employer—and independent farmer, manufacturer, or merchant—conveniently poses as residuary legatee in all discussions of distribution. "Profit," or "profit of stock," becomes a sort of blanket term, which expands or contracts, as though by magic, exactly to cover the residue of the joint product after all claims against it have been met. To ascertain the amount of "profit" becomes, therefore, a simple matter of subtraction. However, when inquiry was directed toward the determination of the rate of "profit," there was difficulty. In attempting to solve this problem, Adam Smith admitted that the employer acts in different capacities; that he owns stock, that he labors, that he incurs "hazard," that he may, or may not, own the money with which the stock was purchased. It was his opinion that, in ascertaining the rate of "profit," attention must be given to all of these variable elements. Consequently there is frequent discussion among his followers as to whether this particular item, or that, should be called "profit," just as there is as to whether this particular concrete good, or that, should be called "capital." In all this discussion the fundamental importance of the ownership of the business unit is successfully camouflaged; while in the business world the development of credit facilities and the incorporation of joint-stock companies are creating distinctions in law prior to their discovery by the economists. No further evidence is needed to show how utterly impossible it is for one who holds the Adam Smith capital concept to differentiate the capitalist function from that of the entrepreneur. This view is expressed with unmistakable clearness by Professor Edgeworth, who writes, when he reaches the point, in his analysis of the parties to distribution, for distinguishing the capitalist from the entrepreneur: "To determine at what point the capitalist ends and the entrepreneur begins, appears to defy analysis."

French writers generally, it may be observed, follow the example of Turgot, and emphasize the personal capacities and activities of the entrepreneur in organizing and directing the business. Even Jean Baptiste Say who became the continental interpreter of the *Wealth of Nations*, represents the personal entrepreneur as the pivot of the whole system of production and distribution, and accordingly magnifies and perpetuates the Turgot view. It seems fitting, therefore, to call the Turgot version of the entrepreneur the French version; while early German economists, it should be noted, were perhaps evenly divided in their adherence to the English and the French views of the function.

It is obvious that John Stuart Mill must have been acquainted with the French as well as with the English version of the function of the entrepreneur; yet we find in his *Principles of Political Economy*, published in 1848, no fresh analysis of the problem. He retains the classical phrase "profits of capital or stock," and describes the activities of the capitalist employer which reveal his relationship to the different elements in "profits." To Mill he is first a "capitalist"—"the person who advances the expenses of production—who, from funds in his possession, pays the wages of the laborers, or supports them during the work; who supplies the requisite buildings, materials, and tools or machines; and to whom, by the usual terms of the contract, the produce belongs, to be disposed of at his pleasure." He is also a business owner; for he "embarks in business on his own account," and "exposes his capital to some and in many cases to very great danger of partial or total loss." He is also a worker; for this same person is represented as devoting to the business "his time and labor"; as "the control of the operations of industry usually belongs to the person who supplies the whole or the greatest part of the funds by which they are carried on, and who, according to the ordinary arrangement, is either alone interested, or is the person most interested (at least directly), in the result." "To exercise this control with efficiency," he continues, "if the concern is large and complicated, requires great assiduity, and other, no ordinary skill. This assiduity and skill must be remunerated." Accordingly, "the three parts into which profit may be considered as resolving itself, may be described respectively as interest, insurance, and wages of superintendence." It was apparently Mill's intention to combine in the capitalist employer, with equally distributed emphasis, all of the functions which had hitherto been attributed to him. The ownership of the business has no especial significance to Mill, but rather seems to be taken as a mere incident of the ownership of capital. Profit, as Mill conceived it, cannot be determined by a definite law; its only unity rests in the fact that a single person received it. It is obvious, however, that the law of interest and the law of wages are not identical. If ownership of the business unit is the distinctive element in the varied relationships which the employer sustains to business, it is certain that Mill did not make the discovery. Had he done so, he would have found that wages and interest are altogether different from profit and are, each, "regulated by quite different principles."

While Mill's version of the entrepreneur's composite function was apparently adopted by Alfred Marshall and by J. Shield Nicholson, among others, it is not surprising that Henry George, with blunt straightforwardness, should deny to "profit," and, by implication, to the entrepreneur, any distinctive place whatever in distribution. He says:

Of the three parts into which profits are divided by political economists—namely, compensation for risk, wages of superintendence, and return for the use of capital—the latter falls under the term interest, which includes all the returns for the use of capital, and excludes everything else; wages of superintendence falls under the term wages, which includes all returns for human exertion, and excludes everything else; and compensation for risk has no place whatever, as risk is eliminated when all the transactions of a community are taken together.

It may be added that Henry George expresses substantially the position taken by Roscher, avoids altogether the use of the term "profit," and represents the entrepreneur as a managerial laborer who owns and directs the business on his own responsibility. His income, besides interest and rent, he describes as a "wage" which constitutes no exception to the general use of wages, the only difference being that it is never the direct result of bargaining. We thus find the founder of the German historical school of political economy to be an exponent of the Turgot version of the entrepreneur.

On account of the prominence which the French version of the entrepreneur has been given by American text-writers, it seems advisable to give it more than a passing notice. To the late Francis A. Walker, the entrepreneur is pre-eminently a "master," a "technical organizer," a "commander of the armies of industry." In his *Political Economy,* published in 1884, Walker gives the following graphic description of the problems confronting the so-called "entrepreneur":

When, however, the hand-loom gives way to the power-loom; when the giant factory absorbs a thousand petty shops; when many persons, of all degrees of skills and strength, are joined in labor, all contributing to a result which perhaps not one of them understands perfectly or at all; when machinery is introduced which deals with the gauzy fabric more delicately than the human hand, and crushes stone and iron with more than the force of lightning; when costly materials require to be brought from the four quarters of the globe, and the products are distributed by the agencies of commerce through every land; when fashion enters, demanding incessant changes in form or substance to meet the caprices of the market, the master becomes a necessity of the situation. The work he is called on to perform is not alone to enforce discipline through the body of laborers thus brought under one roof; not alone to organize these parts into a whole and keep every part in its place, at its proper work; not alone to furnish technical skill, and exercise a general care of the vast property involved; but beyond these and far more than these, to assume the responsibilities of production, to decide what shall be made, after what patterns, in what quantities, and at what times; to whom the product shall be sold, at what prices, and on what terms of payment.

The problems here so vividly described are clearly problems of organization and direction. They make their appeal for the highest types of economic labor. Walker is at least logical in describing the nature of the function to which, in his judgment, profit attaches, before he discusses profit as a separate share in distribution. He has really given us, however, a classification of the workers in modern industry into two groups, which separate the organizing and directive laborers from those who are organized and directed. Those in one group are called "entrepreneurs," and receive "profit"; while those in the other are "laborers" merely, and receive "wages." Walker's so-called theory of profit, then, proves to be in reality a theory of wages for managerial laborers; while his theory of wages applies to the laborers in the other group. It may be added that either theory would serve equally well to explain the shares of the members of the other group. Accordingly, Walker has virtually given us what would appear to be two interchangeable theories of wages. A discussion of these theories does not come within the scope of this paper; they are here mentioned merely to emphasize the fact that organizing and directive labor cannot be made a distinctive function by giving it a distinctive name. The writer would not be understood, however, as at all minimizing the tremendous importance of organizing and directive labor in modern industry. Organization naturally implies a distinction between the organizer and the organized, between directive and directed labor; and each is perhaps equally essential to the other. But it is believed that economic labor logically includes all human labor in industry, and that its share of the joint product should be called wages. It is further the writer's judgment that clearness of analysis would be served by the conscious recognition by economists of this fact. It should be noted, also, that the function of ownership of the business unit receives no attention in Walker's analysis.

Among the American exponents of the French version of the entrepreneur mention should be made of Professors Seager and Fetter, who, like Walker, characterize the so-called "entrepreneur" as an organizing and directive laborer. Unlike the latter, however, these writers comprise under the term profit elements which cannot properly be ascribed to labor. Professor Seager differentiates "profits" into three portions, namely, first, "wages of management," which "are governed by the same law that controls wages generally and that for this reason require no separate treatment"; second, "net or competitive profits," which are directly ascribed to the frequent changes occurring in actual industrial society; and third, "monopoly profits," which exist "when one firm or a combination of firms secures such a control over the supply that it may regulate the price." From this it appears that the function of directive labor—his so-called "entrepreneur" function—entitles the "captain of industry" to wages; while some other function, not specifically emphasized, but at least recognized, entitles his "entrepreneur" to profit.

Professor Fetter, on the other hand, describes the "enterprizer" as "the man who gives his name and energies to the launching and guiding of a business," and then explicitly states with all the emphasis of a paragraph heading: "Typical economic profits are thus a species of wages but are marked by peculiar features." He closes his discussion with the statement: "Profits are the share, or income, of the enterprizer for his skill in directing industry and in assuming the risks. Despite the complex influences, they are determined by his contribution to industry essentially as is the value of any skilled service." According to Professor Fetter's express statement, therefore, the "enterprizer function" and "profits," as he conceives them, are not logically entitled to a distinctive and co-ordinate place in production and distribution. In a later chapter, however, another sort of "profits," what he calls "monopoly profits," is described. Professor Fetter here shifts his emphasis, perhaps unconsciously; but he explicitly states that the "profits of monopoly" "appear to be due not to the services of the enterprizer in increasing production, but to his success in limiting it"—a limitation born of "ownership and control." Here, there appears to be an unconscious reference to a distinctive economic function, and to a distinctive share in distribution.

In the contention that "organizing and directive labor" is labor and, therefore, does not constitute an adequate basis on which to construct a theory of profit, the writer finds himself in accord with a decided trend in current opinion. Professor Taussig, in answer to the question, "Where do business profits cease and mere wages begin?" says:

> Probably the best plan for the exposition of distribution at large is to follow the tradition of describing all reward for exertion as wages. . . . Certainly for most purposes of classification, we should not be consistent if we drew the line between wages and not wages according to the bare independence of the workmen. The cobbler who works alone in his petty shop gets in the main a return for labor as much as the workman in the shoe factory.

Professor Taussig goes on to make a distinction of great *practical* moment, when he says:

> The independent worker gets a primary and not a derivative share of the total income of society . . . he is dependent on no fixed bargain for the money income which will serve him to procure a share in society's real income of consumable goods. Herein his situation differs essentially from that of the hired laborer. . . . The hired laborer gets his money income as the result of a bargain by which he sells his working power for a space. The independent workman gets his money income directly from the sale of what he makes.

It should be kept in mind, however, that the present article is written from a theoretical point of view. In economic distribution bargaining and contract have no place. For us the primary question, therefore, is not, What does the laborer actually get? but, rather, What is the product of his labor? and what is he economically entitled to? According to this view, the independent laborer and the hired workman stand on the same footing. Professor Carver expresses his position as follows: "If wages are the earnings of all labor, they must, of course, include the earnings of the independent worker, whether he runs a small shop where he works alone, or a large establishment where hundreds are working for stipulated wages under him." Professor John Bates Clark explicitly says of the function of the entrepreneur: "The function in itself includes no working." Professor Flux says: "The distributive share known as profits, then, has, in practice, had the remuneration of the services of management cut out of it." It would seem scarcely necessary to multiply illustrations. The general trend of economic opinion had been indicated.

Professor Mithoff justly claims for German economists the credit for inaugurating the movement to differentiate entrepreneur's profit as a distinctive functional share in distribution. The earliest suggestion of such a differentiation is credited to Hufeland, 1807; a fuller expression of it to Riedel, 1839, and von Thunen, 1842; and its complete accomplishment to Mangoldt, 1855. Mangoldt's concept of the function of the entrepreneur is, therefore, of great importance in our inquiry.

Mangoldt makes it clear, at the outset, that his investigation is concerned only with businesses which produce for the market. He explains that a business of this sort necessarily involves more or less uncertainty of success, and that the responsibility for its success or failure rests upon its owner. Such a business he calls an enterprise, and to its responsible owner he applies the term "entrepreneur." The entrepreneur is, accordingly, the responsible owner of an enterprise. He explains, at considerable length, that the ownership of capital is not essential to the conception. Further, in a criticism of the views of Hermann and Riedel, Mangoldt takes exception to the proposition that certain kinds of labor—organizing and directive labor—are inseparable from the conception of the entrepreneur, and expresses himself as follows: "All that is inseparable from the conception of the entrepreneur is, on the one hand, the mere receiving of the product of the enterprise, and, on the other, the responsibility for whatever losses occur." This is perhaps what Professor Clark means when he speaks of the entrepreneur as one "who simply extends the aegis of his civil rights over the elements of a product and then withdraws it, in order that the product may pass into other hands. The *entrepreneur* or *assumer* is he who takes upon himself the responsibility of ownership." Mangoldt evidently places the emphasis upon the element which, to the present writer, is the distinctive function of the entrepreneur; and yet he was not able to differentiate it altogether from organizing and directive labor and capital-owning. This inconsistency is not revealed until he turns to the analysis of the several elements of profit which the entrepreneur receives as his share. Here it becomes evident that the function of responsible ownership does not serve, solely, as the basis of profit. If one were to construct Mangoldt's conception of the entrepreneur function, by the implications involved in the elements of profit ascribed to it, the function would obviously comprise, besides the responsible ownership of the business, a modicum of organizing and directive labor, as well as of capital-owning. Yet Mangoldt, in giving us the conception of the responsible ownership of the business as the distinctive function of the entrepreneur, and in emphasizing its importance as a basis for profit, in the writer's judgment, made a notable contribution to the cause of sound theory. After the publication of his monograph, economists could no longer consider the function as a mere incident to some other function, or ignore it altogether, as had been the case hitherto. On the contrary, many economists have come to recognize the responsible ownership of the business unit as the predominant element, if not the only one, in the function of the entrepreneur—notably Mithoff and Cohn, in Germany, and John Bates Clark, F. M. Taylor, and A. S. Johnson in America; while others, still clinging to a broader view of the function, give this specific element unmistakable recognition.

To Professor John Bates Clark, pre-eminently, belongs the credit for giving the function of the entrepreneur, as a distinctive function, a permanent place in economic theory. He views the problem of distribution as "primarily functional rather than personal." Accordingly, he conceives of a person's income as composed of "the incomes attaching to the functions he performs." Professor Clark, therefore, considered it essential, in working out his theory of distribution, to distinguish clearly between the different functions through which men draw an income from the product of socialized industry. Unfortunately, however, in his earlier writing he employed the term "entrepreneur" in the broad sense of an employer who organizes and directs a business which he personally owns. Accordingly, his entrepreneur is at this time a person of several functions, which, to be sure, are carefully distinguished. Upon one function, that of the ownership of the business, he places unmistakable emphasis as the distinctive one; for he says: "Pure profit is the return of simple ownership. It is free from all admixture of wages and interest." Here he clearly connects the distinctive share with the distinctive function; but he fails to restrict specifically the personal entrepreneur, as such, to the performance of the distinctive function. This defect in his analysis, however, he remedies in an article published six years later. Here Professor Clark uses the term entrepreneur, as he says:

> in the unusually strict sense, to designate the man who co-ordinates labor and capital, without in his own proper capacity furnishing either of them. . . . In performing this one function he contributes to industry nothing but relations. . . . He connects labor and capital with each other in his own establishment.

Here, it should be observed, Professor Clark restricts the personal entrepreneur, as such, to the performance of a distinctive function; but he describes the specific function in terms not used before. It is now characterized, not as "simple business ownership," but as the "co-ordination of labor and capital" in a business. The question naturally arises whether Professor Clark is here describing a different function as that of the entrepreneur, or is characterizing the "function of simple business ownership" in different and perhaps more analytical terms. It is the writer's judgment that the latter is the correct answer; but he recognizes that the terms are susceptible of an entirely different construction. This striking characterization of the entrepreneur's function as that of "co-ordination of the factors of production" appears again, after an interval of seven years, in Professor Clark's volume *The Distribution of Wealth*. In this work, which contains his complete theory, published in 1899, Professor Clark describes the entrepreneur's function as "purely co-ordinating work," and adds: "The function in itself includes no working and no owning of capital; it consists entirely in the establishing and maintaining of efficient relations between the agents of production." And finally in Professor Clark's latest work, *Essentials of Economic Theory* (1907), the entrepreneur's function is again described as "a special co-ordinating function which is not labor," "but is essential for rendering labor and capital productive." After stating that the "function is quite distinct from the work of the superintendent or manager of a business," he speaks of it as "the function of hiring both labor and capital and getting whatever their joint product is worth above the cost of the elements which enter into it."

It is true that we commonly speak of the business owner, as such, as hiring both labor and capital, as placing labor and capital in effective relations to each other, and as doing everything in fact that is done; and yet he does no work. However, there is no doubt that the "co-ordination of the factors of production" calls for labor of the highest type—that of organization and direction. All that the entrepreneur, in his true capacity, does is to choose and hire the organizing and directive worker, who creates the organized business unit by placing the factors of production in effective relations to each other, and directs it as a going concern—and all in the name of the entrepreneur who owns it. This is also Professor Clark's view, as he clearly shows in his illustration of "how a man can be an entrepreneur only." A. S. Johnson, who was evidently influenced by Professor Clark's analysis, confirms the writer's interpretation. He speaks of the entrepreneur as "the man who performs the function of combining labor and capital for the exploitation of an opportunity," and then adds, by way of explaining his connection with the business: "He lends it his name, he assumes legal responsibility for the conduct of the business, and he reserves to himself the ultimate power of approving or vetoing proposals made by his staff. These are the only functions that the enterpriser must necessarily retain." All of these matters are obviously involved in the function of business ownership. With this view Professor F. M. Taylor is seemingly in accord, when he writes: "The peculiar function of the entrepreneur must surely be found in something which he only can do."

The student of economic theory can but regret Professor Clark's failure to retain in all his writing his earliest characterization of the entrepreneur's specific function as that of "simple business ownership." The function, thus characterized, clearly involves no labor, no capital-owning, and no land-owning, and is the distinctive function to which profit attaches.

Source: This article excerpted from Charles Tuttle, "The Entrepreneur Function in Economic Literature," *Journal of Political Economy* 35 (1927): 501–21. Used by permission of the *Journal of Political Economy*.

ENDNOTES

1. Dates for these periods of economic thought were developed from E. K. Hunt, *History of Economic Thought: A Critical Perspective* (Belmont, Calif.: Wadsworth Publishing Company, 1979), and H. W. Spiegel, *The Growth of Economic Thought* (Durham, N.C.: Duke University Press, 1983).
2. H. Barreto, *The Entrepreneur in Microeconomic Theory: Disappearance and Explanation* (London: Routledge, 1989).
3. The German School of entrepreneurship is discussed in Chapter 6 and is part of a taxonomy of entrepreneurship developed in R. F. Hebert and A. N. Link, "In Search of the Meaning of Entrepreneurship," *Small Business Economics* 1 (1989): 39–49.
4. F. H. Knight, *On the History and Method of Economics: Selected Essays* (Chicago: University of Chicago Press, 1956), 8.
5. Knight, *Selected Essays*, 11.
6. Ibid., 12.
7. W. A. Scott, *The Development of Economics* (New York: D. Appleton-Century, 1933), 4.

8. Ibid., 114.

9. Ibid., 152.

10. V. W. Bladen, "Mill, John Stuart: Economic Considerations," in vol. 10 of *International Encyclopedia of the Social Sciences*, ed. D. L. Sills (New York: Free Press, 1968), 114–19.

11. Hunt, *History of Economic Thought*, 18; Spiegel, *The Growth of Economic Thought*, 53.

12. Ibid.

13. J. M. Keynes, "Francis Ysidro Edgeworth," in *Essays in Biography* (New York: Macmillan, 1972).

14. Barreto, *The Entrepreneur in Microeconomic Theory*.

15. Ibid., 86.

16. Ibid., 87–88.

17. J. M. Keynes, "Alfred Marshall," in *Essays in Biography* (New York: Macmillan, 1972).

18. Barreto, *The Entrepreneur In Microeconomic Theory*, 91–92.

19. K. W. Bigelow, "Hawley, Frederick Barnard," in vol. 7 of *Encyclopaedia of the Social Sciences*, ed. E. R. A. Seligman and A. Johnson (New York: Macmillan, 1935).

20. Barreto, *The Entrepreneur in Microeconomic Theory*, 58–59.

21. Ibid., 61.

22. J. M. Clark, "Clark, John Bates," in vol. 2 of *International Encyclopedia of the Social Sciences*, ed. D. L. Sills (New York: Free Press, 1968).

23. J. M. Clark, *John Bates Clark: A Memorial* (New York: Columbia University Press, 1938).

24. J. B. Clark, *Essentials of Economic Theory* (New York: Macmillan, 1922).

25. Barreto, *The Entrepreneur in Microeconomic Theory*, 96–98.

26. M. Allais, "Fisher, Irving," in vol. 5 of *International Encyclopedia of the Social Sciences*, ed. D. L. Sills (New York: Free Press, 1968).

27. Barreto, *The Entrepreneur in Microeconomic Theory*, 93.

28. Ibid., 74.

29. J. M. Buchanan, "Knight, Frank Hyneman," in vol. 8 of *International Encyclopedia of the Social Sciences*, ed. D. L. Sills (New York: Free Press, 1968).

30. F. H. Knight, "Profit," in *Readings in the Theory of Income Distribution*, ed. W. Fellner and B. Haley (New York: Blakson, 1949).

31. F. H. Knight, *Risk, Uncertainty and Profit* (Boston: Houghton Mifflin, 1921).

32. Ibid., 277–78.

33. Ibid., 279–81.

34. J. F. Weston, "Profit as the Payment for the Function of Uncertainty-Bearing," *Journal of Business* 22 (1949): 106–18.

35. Knight, *Risk, Uncertainty and Profit*, 272.

36. A. H. Leigh, "Thunen, Johann Heinrich von." in vol. 16 of *International Encyclopedia of the Social Sciences*, ed. D. L. Sills (New York: Free Press, 1968).

37. Hebert and Link, *In Search of the Meaning of Entrepreneurship*, 41.

38. E. Kauder, "Bohm-Bawerk, Eugen Von," in vol. 2 of *International Encyclopedia of the Social Sciences*, ed. D. L. Sills (New York: Free Press, 1968).

39. W. F. Stolper, "Schumpeter, Joseph Alois," in vol. 14 of *International Encyclopedia of the Social Sciences*, ed. D. L. Sills (New York: Free Press, 1968).

40. J. A. Schumpeter, "Eugen Von Bohm-Bawerk," in *Ten Great Economists from Marx to Keynes* (Oxford: Oxford University Press, 1951).

41. S. E. Harris, *Schumpeter: Social Scientist* (Cambridge: Harvard University Press, 1951).

42. Hebert and Link, *In Search of the Meaning of Entrepreneurship*, 43.

43. J. A. Schumpeter, "The Creative Response in Economic History," in vol. 7 of *Journal of Economic History* (1947), 149–59.

44. E. R. Schneider, *Joseph A. Schumpeter,* trans. W. E. Kuhn (Lincoln, Neb.: Bureau of Business Research, 1975), 17.

45. J. A. Schumpeter, *The Theory of Economic Development* (Cambridge: Harvard University Press, 1934).

46. Ibid., 45.

47. Barreto, *The Entrepreneur in Microeconomic Theory,* 42.

48. Ibid.

49. Schumpeter, *Economic Development,* 66–67.

50. Ibid., 77.

51. Ibid., 85.

52. Ibid., 86.

53. J. A. Schumpeter, *Capitalism, Socialism, and Democracy,* 3rd ed. (New York: Harper and Row), 1950.

54. Barreto, *The Entrepreneur in Microeconomic Theory,* 52.

CHAPTER 6

Disappearance of the Entrepreneur from Economic Thought

Despite the fact that entrepreneurship had its beginnings in economic thought, it no longer plays a major role in orthodox economic theory. For example, Barreto reported that in 1934 Nicholas Kaldor discussed the entrepreneur as a coordinator in an attempt to demonstrate a long-run inconsistency in the theory of cost.[1, 2] Later, in 1937, Ronald Coase equated the entrepreneur with the firm in his argument that transaction costs were the firm's reason for existence.[3] Beyond 1937 the entrepreneur seemed to disappear from orthodox economic theory. As Barreto states, "The fruitful theories of innovation, uncertainty bearing, coordination, and arbitrage were downplayed or totally neglected. In this sense, the entrepreneur had 'disappeared' from microeconomic theory."[4]

The first section of this chapter briefly describes how the modern economic theory of the firm evolved. The second section offers a variety of explanations regarding why the entrepreneur has disappeared from microeconomic theory. The chapter concludes with two articles that offer explanations for the entrepreneur's disappearance. The first article, by William Baumol, attempts to explain why economic theory has failed to develop a formal analysis of entrepreneurship and why economics is unlikely to do so in the foreseeable future. The second article, by Humberto Barreto, describes why various functions played by the entrepreneur in economic thought are no longer accepted in the modern theory of the firm. Barreto also explains how the concept of internal consistency has created the motivation to neglect the entrepreneur in modern microeconomic theory.

DEVELOPMENT OF THE MODERN ECONOMIC THEORY OF THE FIRM

Barreto states that the modern economic theory of the firm is best described by integrating the concepts of the isoquant, output, and factor market sides into a cohesive whole. According to Barreto,

> The factor market side had the earliest roots—classical economists placed "diminishing returns" at the center of their analysis. Johann von Thunen precisely formulated the maximization conditions in 1826. Wickstead and Wicksell polished and presented the graphical and mathematical expositions. The output side was marked by the neglected insight of Augustin Cournot in 1838. He was "reborn" in the Marshallian analysis. The modern presentation of the "cost curves" was given by Harrod and Viner in the early 1930s. W. E. Johnson simply borrowed the indifference analysis from consumer theory (originally formulated by Edgeworth and Fisher) to solve the firm's isoquant side problem.

> The pieces were all laid out—all that remained was for someone to tie them together. This process was hindered greatly in the case of Walras, Bowley, and Hicks because of a fundamental misunderstanding. The cost function defines the minimum cost of producing any given output. It is true that for a firm to maximize profit, it must produce this chosen rate of output in a least cost manner. But this is very different from saying the optimal output is that which can be produced at the minimum point of the average cost curve. The modern reader has no trouble understanding this distinction—it seems so very commonsense. But to those initially grappling with the various facets of the theory it was an impassable obstacle.

> The work of Joan Robinson focused attention on the ties between the factor market and output sides. The introduction of the marginal revenue curve forced all to realize marginal considerations determine optimal choices. From there, any one of several economists can be considered as having synthesized the parts into their present, logically coherent whole. This was achieved in the late 1930s. By the middle of the twentieth century, an understanding of the interrelation between the three facets had spread throughout the discipline. With the exception of Ronald Shephard's research in duality theory, nothing new has been added. Once synthesized, the theory of the firm has remained virtually unchanged—one of the pillars of the orthodox theory of value.

> Not only did the entrepreneur disappear as the theory of the firm was integrated into a consistent whole; but as fast as he departed, the theory of the firm entered. The theory of the firm came in a rush and the entrepreneur was rejected, simultaneously, just as quickly.[5]

EXPLANATIONS FOR THE ENTREPRENEUR'S DISAPPEARANCE

Hebert and Link reported that the omission of the entrepreneur from the center of economic analysis can be attributed to Adam Smith, who replaced the entrepreneur with the capitalist in his writings.[6] A number of economists have suggested that the disappearance of the entrepreneur from orthodox economic thought can be traced to Keynesian economics. For example, Kilby noted that Keynesian economics is concerned with aggregate demand. In the Keynesian analysis, there is no reason to expect that automatic forces will act in the economy to ensure full employment following a period of adjustment.[7] Keynesian economists believed that massive infusions of government spending will be required to ensure full employment. The disciples of Keynes argued that entrepreneurship would be forthcoming only so long as total spending is maintained at a sufficiently high level in the private or public sector to produce full employment.[8]

Certain economists note that the entrepreneur was excluded from economic analysis when economists began using mathematics:

> Mathematics introduced greater precision to economics, and thereby promised to increase the power of economics to *predict*. Yet it was a two-edged sword. Its sharp edge cut through the tangled confusion of real-world complexity, making economics more tractable and accelerating its theoretic advance. But its blunt edge hacked away one of the fundamental forces of economic life—the entrepreneur. Because there was not and is not a satisfactory mathematics to deal with the dynamics of economic life, economic analysis evolved by concentrating on comparative statics and the entrepreneur took on a purely passive, even useless, role.[9]

Orthodox microeconomic theory is a perfectly interlocking, self-contained model:

> Production theory is composed of three mutually consistent characterizations of the firm's optimization problem—the isoquant, output, and factor market sides. Distribution theory directly results from solving the factor market side maximization problem. Furthermore, in conjunction with consumer theory, the orthodox theory of value is formed. Thus, modern microeconomic theory is a set of consistent, nested models; a series of pieces which fit perfectly together.

> Any attempt to introduce the entrepreneur into this theoretical structure destroys the internal consistency of the model. The fundamental problem lies in the ability to compromise the consistency requirement. The choice is an "either-or" proposition—there is no happy medium. The corner solution which modern microtheorists have chosen is consistency and, for this reason, the entrepreneur has been removed from the orthodox explanatory scheme.[10]

ARTICLE 6.1   **ENTREPRENEURSHIP IN ECONOMIC THEORY**
by William Baumol

The entrepreneur is at the same time one of the most intriguing and one of the most elusive characters in the cast that constitutes the subject of economic analysis. He has long been recognized as the apex of the hierarchy that determines the behavior of the firm and thereby bears a heavy responsibility for the vitality of the free enterprise society. In the writings of the classical economist his appearance was frequent, though he remained a shadowy entity without clearly defined form and function. Only Schumpeter and, to some degree, Professor Knight succeeded in infusing him with life and in assigning to him a specific area of activity to any extent commensurate with his acknowledged importance.

In more recent years, while the facts have apparently underscored the significance of his role, he has at the same time virtually disappeared from the theoretical literature. And, as we will see, while some recent theoretical writings seem at first glance to offer a convenient place for an analysis of his activities, closer inspection indicates that on this score matters have not really improved substantially.

This paper will undertake to examine three major matters. First, I will review briefly the grounds on which entrepreneurship should concern us. Second, I will seek to explain why economic theory has failed to develop an illuminating formal analysis of entrepreneurship and I shall conclude that it is unlikely to do so for the foreseeable future. Finally, I shall argue that theory can say a great deal that is highly relevant to the subject of entrepreneurship even if it fails to provide a rigorous analysis of the behavior of the entrepreneur or of the supply of entrepreneurship.

Before proceeding with the discussion I would like to make a distinction that is somewhat artificial but nevertheless important. It is necessary for us to differentiate between the entrepreneurial and the managerial functions. We may define the manager to be the individual who oversees the ongoing efficiency of continuing processes. It is his task to see that available processes and techniques are combined in proportions appropriate for current output levels and for the future outputs that are already in prospect. He sees to it that inputs are not wasted, that schedules and contracts are met, he makes routine pricing and advertising outlay decisions, etc., etc. In sum, he takes charge of the activities and decisions encompassed in our traditional models.

The preceding description is not intended to denigrate the importance of managerial activity or to imply that it is without significant difficulties. Carl Kaysen has remarked that in practice most firms no doubt find themselves in a position well inside their production possibility loci and one of their most challenging tasks is to find ways of approaching those loci more closely; i.e., of increasing their efficiency even within the limits of known technology. This is presumably part of the job of the manager who is constantly on the lookout for means to save a little here and to squeeze a bit more there. But for many purposes the standard models would appear to provide an adequate description of the functions of the manager. Given an arrangement which calculation, experience, or judgment indicate to constitute a reasonable approximation to the current optimum, it is the manager's task to see that this arrangement is in fact instituted to a reasonable degree of approximation.

The entrepreneur (whether or not he in fact also doubles as a manager) has a different function. It is his job to locate new ideas and to put them into effect. He must lead, perhaps even inspire; he cannot allow things to get into a rut and for him today's practice is never good enough for tomorrow. In short, he is the Schumpeterian innovator and some more. He is the individual who exercises what in the business literature is called "leadership." And it is he who is virtually absent from the received theory of the firm.

I. On the Significance of the Entrepreneur

If we are interested in explaining what Haavelmo has described as the "really big dissimilarities in economic life," we must be prepared to concern ourselves with entrepreneurship. For the really big differences are most usually those that correspond to historical developments over long periods of time or to the comparative states of various economies, notably those of the developed and the underdeveloped areas.

It has long been recognized that the entrepreneurial function is a vital component in the process of economic growth. Recent empirical evidence and the lessons of experience both seem to confirm this view. For example, some empirical studies on the nature of the production function have concluded that capital accumulation and expansion of the labor force leave unexplained a very substantial proportion of the historical growth of the nation's output. Thus, in a well-known paper, Solow has suggested on the basis of American data for the period 1909–49 that "gross output per man-hour doubled over the interval, with $87\frac{1}{2}$ percent of the increase attributable to technical change and the remaining $12\frac{1}{2}$ percent to increase in the use of capital." But any such innovation, whether it is purely technological or it consists in a modification in the way in which an industry is organized, will require entrepreneurial initiative in its introduction. Thus we are led to suspect that by ignoring the entrepreneur we are prevented from accounting fully for a very substantial proportion of our historic growth.

Those who have concerned themselves with development policy have apparently been driven to similar conclusions. If we seek to explain the success of those economies which have managed to grow significantly with those that have remained relatively stagnant, we find it difficult to do so without taking into consideration differences in the availability of entrepreneurial talent and in the motivational mechanism which drives them on. A substantial proportion of the energies of those who design plans to stimulate development has been devoted to the provision of means whereby entrepreneurs can be trained and encouraged.

The entrepreneur is present in institutional and applied discussions of a number of other economic areas. For example, his absence is sometimes cited as a significant source of the difficulties of a declining industry, and a balance-of-payments crisis is sometimes discussed in similar terms. Thus both macro problems and micro problems offer a substantial place for him in their analysis. Whether or not he is assigned the starring role he would appear in practice to be no minor character.

II. The Entrepreneur in Formal Models

Contrast all this with the entrepreneur's place in the formal theory. Look for him in the index of some of the most noted of recent writings on value theory, in neo-classical or activity analysis models of the firm. The references are scanty and more often they are totally absent. The theoretical firm is entrepreneurless—the Prince of Denmark has been expunged from the discussion of *Hamlet*.

It is not difficult to explain his absence. Consider the nature of the model of the firm. In its simplest form (and in this respect we shall see that the more complex and more sophisticated models are no better) the theoretical firm must choose among alternative values for a small number of rather well-defined variables: price, output, perhaps advertising outlay. In making this choice management is taken to consider the costs and revenues associated with each candidate set of values, as described by the relevant functional relationships, equations, and inequalities. Explicitly or implicitly the firm is then taken to perform a mathematical calculation which yields optimal (i.e., profit maximizing) values for all of its decision variables and it is these values which the theory assumes to be chosen—which are taken to constitute the business decision. There matters rest, forever or until exogenous forces lead to an autonomous change in the environment. Until there is such a shift in one of the relationships that define the problem, the firm is taken to replicate precisely its previous decisions, day after day, year after year.

Obviously, the entrepreneur has been read out of the model. There is no room for enterprise or initiative. The management group becomes a passive calculator that reacts mechanically to changes imposed on it by fortuitous external developments over which it does not exert, and does not even attempt to exert, any influence. One hears of no clever ruses, ingenious schemes, brilliant innovations, of no charisma or of any of the other stuff of which outstanding entrepreneurship is made; one does not hear of them because there is no way in which they can fit into the model.

It must be understood clearly that what I have been saying constitutes no criticism, not even an attempt to reprove mildly the neoclassical model of the firm. I think that model does what it was designed to do and does it well. Like any respectable analysis, one hopes that it will be modified, amended, and improved with time. But not because it cannot handle an issue for which it is irrelevant. The model is essentially an instrument of optimality analysis of well-defined problems, and it is precisely such (very real and important) problems which need no entrepreneur for their solution.

Some readers may suspect that I am subtly putting forward as more appropriate candidates for the job some alternative models of the firm with which I have to some degree been associated. But this is certainly not my intention, because it seems clear to me that these models are no better for the purpose than the most hidebound of conventional constructs. For example, consider what Oliver Williamson has described as the "managerial discretion models," in which the businessman is taken to maximize the number of persons he employs, or sales, or still another objective distinct from profits. True, this businessman has (somewhere outside the confines of the model) made a choice which was no mere matter of calculation. He has decided, in at least some sense, to assign priority to some goal other than profit. But having made this choice he becomes, no less than the profit maximizer, a calculating robot, a programmed mechanical component in the automatic system that constitutes the firm. He makes and enforces the maximizing decision and in this the choice of maximand makes no difference.

Nor can the "practical pertinence" of the decision variables make the difference in carving out a place for the entrepreneur. Maximization models have recently been developed in which, instead of prices and outputs, the decision variables are the firm's real investment program, or its financial mix (the proportion of equity and debt in its funding), or the attributes of a new product to be launched by the company. These decisions seem to smell more of the ingredients of entrepreneurship. But though the models may be powerful and serve their objective well, they take us not a whit further in the analysis of entrepreneurship, for their calculations are again mechanistic and automatic and call for no display of entrepreneurial initiative.

Finally, it must be understood that the timeless nature of these models has nothing to do with the problem. Professor Evans long ago developed a model in which the firm considered the consequence of its decisions for the time path of prices and where the calculus of variations served as his instrument of analysis. In one of my own models the firm was taken to choose not a stationary, once-and-for-all output level, but selected instead an optimal growth rate. None of these alternatives helps matters. In all these models, automaton maximizers the businessmen are and automaton maximizers they remain.

And this shows us why our body of theory, as it has developed, offers us no promise of being able to deal effectively with a description and analysis of the entrepreneurial function. For maximization and minimization have constituted the foundation of our theory, and as a result of this very fact the theory is deprived of the ability to provide an analysis of entrepreneurship. The terminology of game theory has been extremely suggestive; the willingness of the behaviorists to break away from traditional formulations has been encouraging; but I see no real breakthroughs in this area even on the distant horizon. At most I hope for more brilliant observations and descriptive insights such as those provided by Schumpeter and more recently by Leibenstein, but I foresee for the immediate future no more formal, manipulatable engine of calculation and analysis.

III. On the Supply of Entrepreneurship

There is yet another reason why a marriage between theory and policy is not easily arranged in this area. In its discussions of inputs our formal analysis deals, by and large, with the way in which these inputs are used, and tells us relatively little about where they come from. In our growth models, for example, the behavior of the labor supply exerts a critical influence on the economy's expansion path. But the determination of the growth of the labor force itself is generally taken to be an exogenous matter. Similarly, in a neo-classical or a programming analysis of production one investigates how inputs should be used in the production process, but one assumes that their supply is somehow determined outside the system. Thus even if we were to develop a model which were successful in advancing the theory of entrepreneurship to the level of sophistication of our treatment of other inputs, we would have defined more effectively the entrepreneurial role, but we would have added relatively little in our understanding the determinants of the level of output of entrepreneurship.

From the point of view of policy, however, the priorities would seem to be reversed. The first order of business in an economy which exhibits very little business drive is presumably to induce the appearance of increased supplies of entrepreneurial skills which would then be let loose upon the area's industry. The policy-maker thus is interested primarily in what determines the supply of entrepreneurship and in the means that can be used to expand it.

But there is reason to suppose that these issues are to a very considerable extent matters of social psychology, of social arrangements, of cultural developments and the like. And perhaps this is why many of the recent discussions of the theory of entrepreneurship have been contributed by the sociologists and the psychologists. This may then be no fortuitous development. The very nature of the more pressing issues relating to entrepreneurship may invite more directly the attention of the practitioners of disciplines other than theoretical economics.

IV. A Place for Theory and Entrepreneurship

Given these difficulties besetting any attempt to construct a relevant economic theory in the area, I can offer only one suggestion for a theoretical approach to entrepreneurship, but one which I think is not without promise. We may not be able to analyze in detail the supply of entrepreneurship, the entrepreneur's strategy choices, his attitudes to risk, or the sources of his ideas. But one can hope to examine fruitfully what can be done to encourage his activity. Here an analogy is illuminating. The Keynesian analysis really bypasses the issue of expectations which is surely at the heart of the investment decision and yet the model succeeds in coming to grips with some means that can stimulate investment. In the same way one can undertake to grapple, assisted by theoretical instruments, with the policies that encourage entrepreneurship.

This can be done by considering not the means which the entrepreneur employs or the process whereby he arrives at his decisions but by examining instead the determinants of the payoff to his activity. In his operations he must bear risks, never mind just how he does this, but let the theory consider how the marginal costs of his risk bearing can be reduced. He employs the results of work in research and development; very well, let us investigate what means make it easier, economically, to undertake R and D. Theoretical analysis of the effects of alternative tax arrangements, for example, should shed some light on these matters. The role of the structure of interest rates is no doubt also pertinent and we do have a powerful body of literature which treats of these matters. On all of these fronts analysis is well advanced and it is no heroic exercise to imagine rather complex and probing theoretical formulations capable of shedding light upon them.

It should be recognized, moreover, that such a theoretical analysis can be of enormous significance for policy. In a growth-conscious world I remain convinced that encouragement of the entrepreneur is the key to the stimulation of growth. The view that this must await the slow and undependable process of change in social and psychological climate is a counsel of despair for which there is little justification. Such a conclusion is analogous to an argument that all we can do to reduce spending in an inflationary period is to hope for a revival of the Protestant ethic and the attendant acceptance by the general public of the virtues of thrift! Surely we have learned to do better than that, in effect by producing a movement along the relevant functional paths rather than undertaking the more heroic task involved in shifting the relationships. This is precisely why I have just advocated more careful study of the rewards of entrepeneurship. Without awaiting a change in the entrepreneurial drive exhibited in our society, we can try to learn how one can stimulate the volume and intensity of entrepreneurial activity, thus making the most of what is permitted by current mores and attitudes. If the theory succeeds in no more than showing us something about how that can be done, it will have accomplished very much indeed.

Source: This article excerpted from William Baumol, "Entrepreneurship in Economic Theory," *American Economic Review* 58 (1968): 64–71. Used by permission of the *American Economic Review*.

ARTICLE 6.2   **THE RATIONALE AND MOTIVATION FOR THE ENTREPRENEUR'S DISAPPEARANCE**
by Humberto Barreto

The foundation of the modern theory of the firm, its basic axioms, consists of the following three fundamental concepts: the production function, the logic of rational choice, and perfect information. These three postulates form the core of the model and, most importantly, are responsible for the removal of the entrepreneur from modern microeconomics. The key lies in the unyielding nature of these axioms; they effectively prevent the entrepreneur from playing a role in orthodox microeconomics.

The first section of this paper examines the three fundamental assumptions in the modern theory of the firm. The second section describes how the three postulates of the modern theory have effectively removed the entrepreneur as innovator, uncertainty-bearer, coordinator, and arbitrageur from the modern theory of the firm. A third section describes why the theoretical core of modern microeconomic theory is so restrictive that it prevents the introduction of the entrepreneur.

The Theoretical Core

As is the case with any theoretical structure, a set of axioms (in the mathematical sense) are needed to provide a basis and starting point for further theoretical work. This section examines the axioms upon which the modern theory of the firm rests. Importantly, these fundamental postulates cannot be compromised; any factor that yields the slightest disagreement necessitates the rejection of the postulates or the factor in question.

By axiom or postulate we do not mean simply any condition or restriction. Microeconomic theorists often discuss, for example, convexity conditions, market power, and the degree of factor mobility. These assumptions, although indispensable to the correct working of the model, are strictly secondary.

In this section, the three fundamental assumptions in the modern theory of the firm are examined.

The Production Function

The first fundamental building block or postulate in the modern theory of the firm is the production function. Much analysis and debate centers on the properties of the production function. The goal is to minimize the necessary assumptions of the production function in order to achieve greater generality. Our interest lies, however, not with the properties of the production function, but with the production function itself. The 'well-behaved' nature of the function is irrelevant—it is the use of a production relationship per se that is our main concern.

A production function describes the maximum output that can be generated from any given combination of inputs. Thus the production function presents the set of all technologically efficient production possibilities. Three important results flow from the use of the production function in the modern theory of the firm.

First, the production technology explicitly states not only the quantities of each factor necessary to make a given level of output, but also the type and function of each factor necessary to produce a given product. The production function gives the firm a complete and exact understanding of its input-output possibilities. Not only raw materials and manual labor are included, but also managers, supervisors, and decision-makers—every single factor necessary for production is explicitly designated. Each of these factors is involved in the production process in a particular, given way; that is, the function of each factor is tightly and precisely defined.

Second, use of the production function in the modern theory of the firm implies that every product has a given production relationship. All products are made by an explicitly given technological input-output relationship. At any point in time, the existing possibilities for output are known and given by a production function that corresponds to each product.

Finally, the use of the production function presents the firm, on the output and factor market sides, with an objective function to maximize. Profits are defined as revenues minus costs and revenues are, of course, product price times output. The production function tells the firm the output it can expect from any given combination of inputs. On the isoquant side, the production function provides a needed constraint in the optimization problem; minimize the cost of producing a given (by the production function) level of output. The elements in the production function, the output and factor levels, are the endogenous variables in each of the three optimization problems that comprise the modern theory of the firm.

Thus the production function is a crucial part of the modern theory of the firm. By exactly describing the firm's input-output possibilities, production function states the quantities and types of each factor necessary for production and the range of products available to the economy. In addition, the production relationship forms a key part of the firm's three optimization problems.

The Logic of Rational Choice

The second fundamental postulate inherent in the modern theory of the firm involves rational choice. Specifically, the theory assumes that the firm rationally pursues its objectives—cost minimization and profit maximization. This axiom drives the model; the firm is exclusively engaged in solving the problem of how much output to produce and what types and quantities of factors to hire.

During the 1930s, orthodox microeconomic theory adopted Robbins' definition of economics: 'Economics is the science which studies human behavior as a relationship between ends and scarce means which have alternative uses.' The modern theory of the firm, itself the foundation of modern microeconomics, naturally incorporates optimization into its framework. The firm, given its ends (the twin behavioral assumptions of cost minimization and profit maximization), applies the logic of rational choice; it chooses the optimal levels of the endogenous variables given its exogenous variables and constraints.

Applying the logic of rational choice has two crucial implications. First, it completely focuses the analysis on the endogenous variables. Once a problem is set up, the key is to find optimum levels of the choice variables, and other considerations are irrelevant. Second, an optimization problem, in order to have a solution, must be close-ended, that is, it must contain all relevant information. For the modern theory of the firm, this means that the firm's production, output demand, and input supply functions must be known and given. By viewing the firm in an ends-means framework, the modern theory of the firm focuses exclusively on solving the firm's optimization problems. The firm is best characterized as a "black box," or given production function, and the focus of attention is centered on the endogenous variables.

Perfect Information

The final fundamental postulate in the modern theory of the firm is the assumption of perfect information or perfect knowledge. It is often criticized as the most unrealistic and restrictive theoretical assumption in the model, yet it cannot be relaxed.

For the modern theory of the firm, the perfect information assumption implies that each firm is completely aware of all considerations affecting its decisions. The firm is aware of its own product's production function, and that of every other commodity. It knows the quality and price of every product and factor of production. Furthermore, it knows these things, not only in the present, but also in the future.

Assuming perfect knowledge enables the firm to solve its optimization problem. It must have complete information about the production function, relevant prices, and any constraints. The perfect knowledge assumption guarantees these conditions are met. Without perfect information, the logic of rational choice, the application of the equimarginal principle, would be empty and useless.

Special mention should be made that the choice variables need not be deterministic; stochastic endogenous variables are permitted as long as their probability distributions are known. Thus Knight's distinction between risk and uncertainty is relevant here. The modern theory of the firm encounters no problems with risk, but it cannot operate in an environment characterized by true (or Knightian) uncertainty. The knowns must be known, either deterministically or probabilistically, for the logic of rational choice to function.

Therefore perfect knowledge is the third fundamental assumption of the modern theory of the firm. It guarantees that all information necessary for the solution of the firm's optimization problem is available. Without it, the theory would collapse.

To summarize in this section, we have presented three fundamental postulates of the modern theory of the firm: the production function, the logic of rational choice, and perfect information. Although further refinements and restrictions are needed to round out the model, these three assumptions form the core of the theory.

The production function is the backbone of the modern theory of the firm. It allows the firm to be viewed as an array of input-output possibilities. The logic of rational choice is the driving force in the theory. It provides the firm with objectives (typically, cost minimization and profit maximization) and endows the firm with the ability to strive rationally for its given goals. The final assumption, perfect information, ensures that all necessary data for the application of the ends-means framework are available.

These three assumptions form the foundation of the modern theory of the firm. Additional assumptions (market structure, production function restrictions, and the like) are added to generate "testable predictions" through comparative static exercises. However, the broad outline of the theoretical structure is entirely captured within the three fundamental axioms discussed in this section.

The following section shows how the assumptions discussed in the previous section prevent the introduction of the entrepreneur in any of the four functional roles of innovator, uncertainty-bearer, coordinator, and arbitrageur.

Exclusion of the Entrepreneur as Innovator

Innovation is one of the more commonly accepted roles the entrepreneur has played in the history of economic thought. Schumpeter, of course, had one of the most appealing theories of the entrepreneur as innovator or creator of new combinations. In this role, the entrepreneur became the engine of the capitalist process.

For the modern theory of the firm, however, the entrepreneur as innovator is ruled out by the production function and the logic of rational choice. The production function presents the firm with an array of input-output possibilities. All possible outputs and their technologically efficient means of production are given by the production function. The logic of rational choice transforms the firm into an entity where choices are made in an environment of known parameters and objectives.

In the modern theory of the firm, the production relationship contains all of the endogenous variables. The production function manifests inself in the theory of the firm through the isoquant, the cost function, and the marginal (and average) factor productivity schedules. The logic of rational choice has the optimizing agent choose the factor uses that minimize cost, the output that maximizes profit, and the factor uses that maximize profit.

There is no orthodox theory of innovation within modern microeconomic theory because any such theory would clash with the modern theory of the firm's theoretical core. Of course, there can be innovation in terms of an exogenous shift in the production function, but a genuine theory of innovation focusing on the entrepreneur as creating internal change (*a la* Schumpeter) is incompatible with the modern theory of the firm.

New products are ruled out because the list of production functions and their corresponding products must be given and known in order for the logic of rational choice to allow the optimal values of the endogenous variables to be determined. Similarly, new production techniques involving cheaper or better methods of production are impossible given the fact that the production function establishes technologically efficient means of production. It is defined as the maximum output that can be obtained from any given combination of inputs.

Opening new markets, finding new sources of supply, or presenting new organizational forms are means of innovation that conflict with the logic of rational choice. All of the options have to be available to the decision-makers and their consequences must be known. The word "new" is simply not allowed and, for this reason, innovation is simply beyond the scope of the analysis.

Any attempt to introduce innovation will cause the theory to collapse. Schumpeter noted that entrepreneurship, the generation of new combinations, could not exist within calculating personalities. There had to be an element of non-rational, instinctive decision-making. But it is precisely this element which crashes headfirst against the postulate of the ends-means framework. Innovation essentially implies that an agent has rejected the known means and is searching for something new, but this activity cannot be explained by the modern theory of the firm. Furthermore, it cannot be allowed to co-exist for it directly contradicts the logic of rational choice. Thus the entrepreneur as innovator cannot be an explanatory element within an orthodox microeconomics that accepts the modern theory of the firm.

Exclusion of the Entrepreneur as Uncertainty-Bearer

A great deal of research into entrepreneurship has been done under the banner of uncertainty. For example, Cantillon's spectulator, Hawley's responsible owner, and Knight's responsible decision-maker are examples of theories placing emphasis on the entrepreneur's role in an uncertain environment. In each case, the entrepreneur acted as a buffer against the debilitating effects of an uncertain environment.

It is easy to see, however, that no such role need be played in the modern theory of the firm. The entrepreneur as uncertainty-bearer is removed by the assumption of perfect information. The firm exists in a world in which it has all necessary information, in which its expectations are exactly fulfilled. In such an environment, the optimizing agent can choose the optimum values of the endogenous variables.

The postulates of the logic of rational choice and perfect information straightforwardly remove any need for an entrepreneur as uncertainty-bearer. Since there is no uncertainty, such a function is superfluous.

Sometimes, attempts to incorporate uncertainty are characterized by the introduction of a random variable (for example, a random output demand function). As noted in the previous section, however, the randomness is limited to the case of risk, in which the probability distributions of all random variables are known. By optimizing expected values, the problem is essentially the same as in a world characterized by perfect knowledge. Davidson sees this point clearly.

> Replacing the concept of certainty by the concept of a known probability distribution merely replaces the assumption of perfect foreknowledge by the assumption that economic agents possess actuarial knowledge. In such a situation actuarial costs and benefits can be calculated, and the economic agent can act as if he possessed absolute foreknowledge.

Not only is the entrepreneur as uncertainty-bearer superfluous, but the attempt to introduce such an agent would sound the death knell for the modern theory of the firm. Clearly, a truly uncertain environment (in the Knightian sense) would spell the end of the logic of rational choice. Radical uncertainty prevents the application of any optimization technique or rational, calculating solution algorithm; subjective opinion and intuition are the only decision-making rules. Perfect information is a necessary part of the modern theory of the firm. Without it, problems facing the firm could not be cast and solved in an optimization framework. With it, however, the entrepreneur as uncertainty-bearer is needless.

Exclusion of the Entrepreneur as Coordinator

That the introduction of the entrepreneur as innovator or uncertainty-bearer is incompatible with the assumptions inherent in the modern theory of the firm does not seem controversial. Neoclassical economists rarely, if ever, claim to include these entrepreneurial roles in the theory of the firm.

The entrepreneur as coordinator and arbitrageur, however, is another matter. Neoclassicals often describe the theory of the firm headed by an entrepreneur as decision-maker, coordinating or arbitraging. We will show that, like innovation and uncertainty-bearing, these functions are unnecessary, given the postulates that form the theoretical core of the modern theory of the firm.

"Coordination" is used in microeconomic theory in two senses: as a necessary function in production and as a decision-making activity. The first definition is simply another factor of production. Managers and supervisors, just as other types of labor and raw materials, are needed in production; they are factors x_i and x_j in the input vector. There is no entrepreneurial activity involved in such a task.

The latter definition is more widely used. In this sense, the entrepreneur as coordinator is defined as the agent who chooses and arranges the quantities of inputs hired:

> A firm is a technical unit in which commodities are produced. Its entrepreneur (owner and manager) decides how much of and how one or more commodities will be produced, and gains the profit or bears the loss which results from his decision.

But both tasks, arranging and choosing, are completely determined by the givens and objectives facing the optimizing agent. By giving the optimizer a production function, applying the logic of rational choice (including providing relevant givens and the two behavioral objectives of cost minimization and profit maximization), and perfect information, the problem is solved. In no real sense has any decision-making been exercised.

For example, on the isoquant side, the optimizing agent is said to determine "how one or more commodities will be produced," but cost minimization immediately makes clear his only possible arrangement. In Exhibit 6.1 there is no "choice" between input combinations A, B, and C, given that the objective is to minimize cost. The optimizing agent must choose point B; there is no "arranging" to be done.

For the same reason, "deciding how much . . . will be produced" involves no real decision-making. The optimizing agent must choose that quantity which maximizes profit; any other rate of output must be rejected.

It is a misuse of the word to argue the optimizing agent "chooses" the levels and arrangement of the factors of production and output. The constraints so circumscribe the optimizer that only one true option is possible. Clearly, the lack of a viable alternative removes any notion of entrepreneurship as coordination, in the decision-making sense of the term, from the theory of the firm. True coordination, choosing and arranging the factors of production, requires the possibility of real error.

EXHIBIT 6.1   "Choosing" on the Isoquant Side

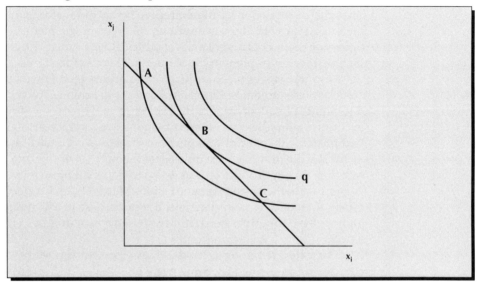

Thus, for example, Say's entrepreneur as coordinator was a special factor due to the presence of imperfect knowledge and an uncertain environment. Decision-making, combining, and supervising factors, involved choice among viable alternatives. The modern theory of the firm reduces coordination to, in Knight's terms, "routine management" or, as Schumpeter said, "mere management". No real choice and therefore no real entrepreneurial activity is needed. Kay argues that the entrepreneur, in orthodox theory, is reduced to a mere computer:

> The assumption of rationality and the existence of marginalist profit-maximising rules couched in the perfect knowledge assumption, ensures that the entrepreneur has no real discretion over questions of resource allocation. . . . These same assumptions result in the treatment of the entrepreneur as an automaton.

To allow the entrepreneur as coordinator to play a role, the theory must loosen its grip, easing the constraints in order to provide a true choice in decision-making. The modern theory of the firm, however, can allow for no such complications. Any attempt to introduce the possibility of error would require ambiguity in one of the initial givens (production function, behavioral assumptions, or perfect information), destroying the optimizing structure of the model.

Once again, an entrepreneurial function has come face to face with an axiom in the modern theory of the firm and lost. The entrepreneur as coordinator is barred from the modern theory of the firm by the logic of rational choice and perfect information. There can be neither real choice nor real decision-making in the modern theory of the firm and therefore no entrepreneur as coordinator.

Exclusion of the Entrepreneur as Arbitrageur

An entrepreneurial role often cited in the modern theory of the firm is that of arbitrageur. Once again, we will argue that, in fact, there are no real arbitrage opportunities in the theory and thus no need for the entrepreneur as arbitrageur. Furthermore, the introduction of such an element is blocked by the postulates in the theoretical core.

In orthodox microeconomic theory, the entrepreneur, as the head of the firm, is supposedly an arbitrageur by virtue of his responsiveness to profit opportunities. In any industry where excess profits (defined as price greater than average cost) exist, firms enter, setting off a chain of events that eliminates the surplus. The reverse, exit in the face of loss, works much the same way. The entrepreneur is therefore the equilibrating agent, the means by which the economy reaches a long-run, general equilibrium.

This story is intuitively appealing, but false; seemingly consistent, but not. The only reason that a nonzero profit situation can ever arise in modern microeconomic theory (given free entry and exit) is due to factor immobility. Fixed factors of production prevent a firm from exiting when price falls below average cost and prevents existing firms from moving into excess profit markets. In time, as firms face long-run planning horizons (where all factors are variable), they move out of loss situations into excess profit industries. These adjustments continue until there are no excess profit markets—a long-run general equilibrium.

There is no need for any notions of arbitrage in this process. Time (removing the fixed factor constraint), free movement, and the profit-maximization objective will guarantee a long-run general equilibrium. No special entrepreneurial role need be played for the system to reach a position of rest.

The essence of arbitrage is reaction to ignorance. For some reason, a profitable situation is not being acted upon, resulting in an arbitrage opportunity. It is very much a disequilibrium phenomenon, for example, to have a price such that quantity demanded is greater than quantity supplied, leaving a profit opportunity.

The firm in modern microeconomic theory is constantly in some sort of equilibrium. When in equilibrium, it maximizes profit, leaving no tendency for change. If excess profits exist at this point, it is not by virtue of a missed opportunity or a disequilibrium situation. Nonzero profit may exist, but only because of a binding constraint (for example, factor fixity), not because a Kirznerian entrepreneur failed to be alert to a profit opportunity. In fact, every agent in the modern theory of the firm knows where excess profits exist and is prevented from moving there only because of some constraint. Once all constraints are removed, profit will automatically disappear. No arbitrageur is needed.

Once again, the introduction of an entrepreneur as arbitrageur is not only unnecessary, but would require changing axioms in the theoretical core. Thus, for example, Kirzner's entrepreneur as arbitrageur was alert to profit opportunities in the Austrian disequilibrium environment. He had the capacity to learn, to adjust in the face of new information, to realize errors are being made that will, when corrected, yield profit.

The modern theory of the firm has no room for such ideas. Even in firm equilibrium, if nonzero profits exist, it is certainly not due to inequality between quantities demanded and supplied. Neither are profits due to firms operating at non-profit maximizing levels of output because of some "error" in choosing the level of output. Nonzero profit is only due to some kind of constraint, which will in time automatically correct itself.

The modern theory of the firm is a system guided by the logic of rational choice and aided by the assumption of perfect information. The modern orthodox explanation of market equilibrium is self-contained. Within this environment, entrepreneurs as arbitrageurs are simply redundant because some sort of equilibrium is always automatically reached. General equilibrium mechanically follows firm equilibrium as soon as the factor fixity constraint is removed. Furthermore, any attempt to include an entrepreneur as arbitrageur threatens the theoretical core that forms the heart of the modern theory of the firm.

To summarize, this section has shown that the entrepreneur, in any of his four fundamental roles, is not and cannot be a part of the modern theory of the firm. There is no innovation; the production function is given and the logic of rational choice demands that choices be made in an ends-means framework. There is no uncertainty-bearing; the present and future are known with absolute precision (or, what amounts to the same thing, all probability distributions are known) because there is perfect information. There is no coordination; "choice" is exactly determined by the constraints and objectives. And, finally, there is no arbitrage; perfect information and the logic of rational choice ensure that all profit opportunities will be seized as soon as possible. Excess profits exist only because the factor fixity constraint makes adjustments impossible.

Furthermore, we have shown that any attempts to introduce entrepre-neurial considerations directly collide with one or more of the three postulates found in the theoretical core of the modern theory of the firm. The confrontation between the basic axioms and the entrepreneur leaves two possibilities; to accept the entrepreneur and reject the modern theory of the firm, or to reject the entrepreneur and maintain allegiance to the modern theory of the firm. The history of economic thought clearly shows the choice that was made.

It is important to note that the word "entrepreneur" may be used by a modern microeconomic theorist, but only as one of many, equally important, factors of production. For the modern theory of the firm, entrepreneurship as innovation, true uncertainty-bearing, coordination, or arbitrage is absolutely superfluous—and to force the entrepreneur into the theory is absolutely devastating.

The following section describes why the theoretical core of modern microeconomic theory is so restrictive that it prevents the introduction of the entrepreneur.

Consistency over Entrepreneurship

The aim of the modern theory of the firm is to present a determinate and consistent model of the market system. This is accomplished admirably with the essential help of its theoretical core. The requirement of internal consistency within a theoretical structure is indispensable—compromise is impossible.

With the integration of the isoquant, output, and factor market sides, the modern theory of the firm was born. The theory fits together in a consistent framework. In one interlocking system, the theory explains the supply curve on the output side, demand curves on the input side, and income distribution.

However, in achieving a perfect fit among the various facets, the theory found no use for the entrepreneur. The model only requires a production function, the logic of rational choice, and perfect information. Using optimization techniques, the theory itself shows what and how much factor use will minimize cost and maximize profit. In the modern microeconomic theory of production and cost, no place exists for an active entrepreneurial function. In the orthodox firm, the entrepreneur plays an essentially sterile role, choosing the optimum values of the endogenous variables.

Significantly, not only is entrepreneurship unnecessary, but it threatens the interlocking structure that is the hallmark of the modern theory of the firm. Thus it is not a question of redundancy, but one of mutual exclusivity; the entrepreneur and consistency cannot co-exist.

Why can't the entrepreneur as innovator be incorporated into the modern theory of the firm? Because the production function exactly describes every possible input-output relationship; because the logic of rational choice requires that the ends and means be known and given. The introduction of innovation requires relaxing these core assumptions, but this, in turn, is impossible; the consistent, interlocking nature of the theory would be destroyed.

Why can't the entrepreneur as uncertainty-bearer be incorporated into the modern theory of the firm? Because perfect information, a fundamental assumption, guarantees every agent's expectations will be exactly fulfilled. The introduction of uncertainty requires relaxing this assumption, but this, in turn, would prevent the application of the logic of rational choice. Decision-making would not have some real meaning, but the resulting destruction of the consistent framework of the theory is unacceptable.

Why can't the entrepreneur as coordinator be incorporated into the modern theory of the firm? Because perfect information and the logic of rational choice exactly determine the only viable alternative. True coordination requires relaxing these assumptions, but the immediate consequence, the breakdown of the model, is too costly.

Why can't the entrepreneur as arbitrageur be incorporated into the modern theory of the firm? Because perfect information prevents the introduction of ignorance, a requirement for arbitrage. Once again, relaxing this assumption in order to allow arbitrage has too high a cost—the removal of a crucial attribute, consistency, from the theory.

In every case, the entrepreneur is prevented from playing a role by the modern theory of the firm's theoretical core. The three basic axioms are arranged the way they are so as to guarantee an internally consistent framework. This is one of the most appealing features of the model and a basic defense against attack.

When the pieces of the firm were integrated, consistency was recognized as the key attribute. The perfect fit could not be disturbed. Any attempt at the introduction of an entrepreneurial role causes inconsistency. And, in general, inconsistency is a charge from which it is impossible to recover. For this reason, the entrepreneur was elevated to a meaningless role, that of optimizing agent.

In fact, the human element, in general, is of no consequence in modern orthodox theory. Georgescu-Roegen explicitly points to the "special pride" economists take in creating a consistent, interlocking system:

> Standard economics takes special pride in operating with a man-less picture. As Pareto overtly claimed, once we have determined the means at the disposal of the individual and obtained a "photograph of his tastes . . . the individual may disappear." The individual is thus reduced to a mere subscript in the ophelimity function. The logic is perfect: man is not an economic agent simply because there is no economic process. There is only a jigsaw puzzle of fitting given means to given ends, which requires a computer not an agent.

The modern theory of the firm is entirely self-contained; it is a perfectly consistent system, given its assumptions. The presentation of the theory by its founders focused on this powerful and attractive property.

Samuelson, for example, clearly understood the crucial attribute of interrelatedness. He believed logical coherence to be an important element and one that should be explicitly presented:

> Economic theory as taught in the textbooks has often tended to become segmentalized into loosely integrated compartments, such as production, value, and distribution. There are, no doubt, pedagogical advantages in such a treatment and yet something of the *essential unity and interdependence* of economic forces is lost in so doing. A case in point is the conventional assuming of a cost curve for each firm and the working out of its optimum output with respect to its demand conditions. Only later is the problem of the purchase of factors of production by the firm investigated, and often its connection with the previous process is not brought out.

Samuelson rails against those who assume linearly homogenous production functions and non-constant average and marginal cost curves: "It is indicative of the lack of integration mentioned above that many writers assume U-shaped cost curves in the same breadth with homogeneity of the product function."

Carlson, whose *Study on the Pure Theory of Production* is essentially his doctoral dissertation at the University of Chicago, is also very aware of the advantage a theory has when it can claim a harmonious interrelationship among its constituent parts:

> Although economists have long recognized the main relationships of the theory of production, these relationships have not been co-ordinated in a single body of theory—except in such works as those of Frisch and Schneider—but have been scattered in isolated fragments throughout cost theory, capital and interest theory and the theory of distribution. To bring together and co-ordinate in one *consistent* scheme the different relationships of the theory of production has been the main purpose of this essay.

There is no doubt that the founders of the modern theory of the firm were aware of the powerful property of consistency. As an integrated whole, the modern theory of the firm presents a logically perfect, self-contained explanation of production, cost, and distribution. In conjunction with the theory of consumer behavior, the orthodox theory of value is, similarly, a consistent, deterministic system. Nothing can disturb this perfect system, not even the entrepreneur, for the entire structure comes and goes as one. Pieces cannot be broken off, reorganized, and then reinserted. If a change is to be made, the whole structure must be torn down and then rebuilt. It is this tight, interlocking attribute which, initially, made the theory so appealing and which, today, accounts for its resistance to change. Improvement can be made in one of the nested sub-groups of the overall theory, but the cost of tearing down the rest of the edifice is what makes any such change problematic.

Source: This article excerpted from Humberto Barreto, *The Entrepreneur in Microeconomic Theory: Disappearance and Explanation* (London: Routledge, 1989), 103–17; 131–36. Used by permission of Routledge and the author.

ENDNOTES

1. H. Barreto, *The Entrepreneur in Microeconomic Theory: Disappearance and Explanation* (London: Routledge, 1989), 110.
2. N. Kaldor, "The Equilibrium of the Firm," *Economic Journal*, 44 (1934): 60–76.
3. R. H. Coase, "The Nature of the Firm," *Economica* 4 (New Series, 1937): 386–405.
4. Barreto, *The Entrepreneur in Microeconomic Theory*, 157.
5. Ibid., 152–54.
6. R. F. Hebert and A. N. Link, *The Entrepreneur: Mainstream Views and Radical Critiques*, 2nd ed. (New York: Praeger, 1988).
7. P. Kilby, *Entrepreneurship and Economic Development* (New York: Free Press, 1971).
8. A. H. Hansen, *Business Cycles and National Income* (New York: Norton, 1964).
9. R. F. Herbert and A. N. Link, "In Search of the Meaning of Entrepreneurship," *Small Business Economics* 1 (1989): 48.
10. Barreto, *The Entrepreneur in Microeconomic Theory*, 2–3.

7

Renewed Interest in Entrepreneurship by Economists

I n Chapter 6 we learned that entrepreneurship no longer plays a major role in orthodox economic theory. Several economists, however, have identified a number of situations where modern theory is inappropriate in dealing with certain market conditions. In addition, another school of economic thought—the Austrian School—has made entrepreneurship a focal point.

The first section of this chapter discusses how these various viewpoints differ from modern theory. The second section describes the Austrian school of economic thought and presents the views of Israel Kirzner, who is critical of modern theory because it leaves no room for purposeful human action. The third section contains Theodore Schultz's concept of entrepreneurship, which involves the theory of human capital. The chapter concludes with Theodore Schultz's article on entrepreneurship and human capital.

INAPPROPRIATENESS OF THE MODERN THEORY

A number of economists have stated that the modern theory of firm is not adept at

> . . . dealing with those aspects of entrepreneurship that through innovations in organizations and technology, seek to shift cost curves. Nor are they well suited to aspects

of entrepreneurship that seek to shift demand curves or to create new products for which demand curves previously did not exist at all. In short, although the modern approach can help us understand the factors that determine the equilibrium price of toothpaste, they are of little use in explaining the sudden appearance of toothpaste pumps as a replacement for tubes.[1]

Furthermore, other economists have developed streams of literature that deal with the inappropriateness of two of the building blocks of the modern theory ("the logic of rational choice" and "perfect information") in describing certain market conditions. For example, Almarin Phillips has noted that a market where buyers and sellers need only knowledge of market price to determine the quantities of a good or service they are willing to sell or buy is quite different from the markets in which venture capitalists operate.[2] Venture capital markets involve the study of financial intermediaries who finance high-risk, innovative economic activities.

The following brief discussion examines the inappropriateness of the modern theory's building blocks of rational choice and perfect information.

Rational Choice

Rational choice is identical to normative models of decision making that involve an all-knowing individual who optimizes in light of myriad facts. Richard Cyert and James March developed the notion of "limited search," which stemmed from the limits of human cognitive powers.[3] Cyert and March suggested that the decision maker is not concerned with the whole problem in all its complexity, but always with parts of the problem and with solutions that are familiar or near at hand. Herbert Simon's concept of bounded rationality also referred to finite human information-processing abilities.[4]

Bounded rationality is an appropriate concept for characterizing the extent to which economic actors have limited understanding of the marketplace. On the one hand, a vast amount of information exists in the environment of every market. On the other hand, economic actors do not, and cannot, comprehend every element of a market's environment. Oliver Williamson commented:

> Bounded rationality means that actors in the market place are unable to obtain accurate information fully and certainly, even with expenditures of time and money, and are dealing in complex circumstances such that, even with more complete data, optimizing behavior is difficult either to define or, if defined, still difficult to achieve. Under those circumstances, transactions, if they occur, occur with incomplete and possibly inaccurate information. Further, repeated transactions yield learning—learning about what is relevant and what is not, which actions to avoid and which to repeat, and so forth.[5]

Perfect Information

Perfect information, or perfect knowledge, implies that each firm is completely aware of considerations that affect its decisions. The firm is aware of its own product's production function and that of every other commodity. It knows the quality and price of every product and factor of production. Furthermore, it knows these things, not only in the present, but also in the future.

Nobel laureate Friedrich von Hayek stated, however, that knowledge of the economic problem faced by society "does not exist in concentrated or integrated form, but solely as the dispersed bits of incomplete and frequently contradictory knowledge which all separate individuals possess."[6] Hayek argued that society's economic problem involves securing the best use of resources "known to any members of society, for ends whose relative importance only these individuals know. Or, to put it briefly, it is a problem of the utilization of knowledge not given to anyone in its totality."[7]

Hayek's argument is described as follows:

> Suppose, says Hayek, that a major new use for tin arises. It may be in manufacturing, electronics, medicine—it doesn't matter. Also, it is important for understanding the role of markets that the exact nature of the new use does not matter. All that tin users really need to know is that the opportunity cost of using tin has gone up—that is, that some can now be more profitably used elsewhere—and as a consequence, they must economize on tin. The great majority of them need not know what the new use is but that there is some new, more urgent use. If only some of them know the nature of the new use and switch resources over to it, and if the people who are aware of the resulting gap in turn fill it from still other sources, the effect will spread rapidly. It will influence the uses not only of tin but of its substitutes, substitutes for the substitutes, the supply of all things made of tin, the supply of all things made of its substitutes, and so on. All of this will happen with the great majority of those involved unaware of the exact cause of the original disturbance. . . . Prices are an efficient means of communicating this information because they allow each tin user to concentrate on the details of the work at hand while giving just enough information about opportunity costs to guide decisions in the right direction. As Hayek puts it, "The whole acts as one market not because their limited individual fields of vision sufficiently overlap so that through many intermediaries the relevant information is communicated to all."[8]

Williamson also offered the following comment regarding perfect information:

> Different economic actors have different information. The information available to the buyer is different from that of the seller, and different people within the selling firm have different skills and knowledge. Information transfer designed to reduce the degree of impactedness or information asymmetry is again costly and imperfect. Further, there is a "paradox of information" that limits the efficiency of market exchanges of information: buyers become more willing to pay for information as they better realize what they are to buy, but then have it and need not pay! And sellers, after conveying information to one buyer, are no less able to sell the same thing to another.[9]

A number of economists also have implied that the core of economic theory does not encompass all types of economic activity. Accordingly this core is being extended and applied in new ways to new problems to analyze aspects of economic activities that heretofore have been neglected.[10]

THE AUSTRIAN SCHOOL AND ISRAEL KIRZNER

As mentioned in Chapter 3, Hebert and Link's taxonomies of entrepreneurial theories contained the Austrian tradition and included Ludwig Von Mises, Israel Kirzner, and other theorists.[11] This section reviews the work of Mises and Kirzner.

Mises (1881–1973), who held faculty positions in economics at the University of Vienna, the Graduate Institute of International Studies, and later at New York University, has been called the founding father of the "new" Austrian school of economic thought.[12] Mises is noted for developing the particular methodology known as praxeology, which is a cornerstone of the new, or modern, Austrian school. Using this approach, Mises argued that individual choices and purposive human action can be considered as the *a priori* foundation of valid economic reasoning. According to Mises, economics

> . . . is the collection and systematic arrangement of all the data of experience concerning human action. It deals with the concrete content of human action. It studies all human endeavors in their infinite multiplicity and variety and all individual actions with all their accidental, special and particular implications. It scrutinizes the ideas guiding acting man and the outcome of the actions performed. It embraces every aspect of human activities. It is on the one hand, general history, and on the other hand the history of various narrow fields. . . . Economic history, descriptive economics, and economic statistics are, of course, history.[13]

Mises emphasized the importance of entrepreneurship in a market economy.[a] For example, Mises stated, "[E]ntrepreneur means acting man in regard to the changes occurring in the data of the market."[14] Mises also stated that there is an entrepreneurial element present in all human action.[15]

Based on relating his work on human action with entrepreneurship, Mises stated:

> The term entrepreneur as used by catalectic theory means: acting man exclusively seen from the uncertainty inherent in every action. In using this term one must never forget that every action is embedded in the flux of time and therefore involves a speculation. The capitalist, the landowners, and the laborers are by necessity speculators. So is the consumer in providing for anticipated future needs. There's many a slip twixt cup and lip.[16]

---

[a] A complete discussion of the modern Austrian economics perspective of a market economy is beyond the scope of this text. In addition to Mises, the theories of three other economists provide the methodological foundation of modern Austrian economics: Murray Rothbard, Friedrich von Hayek, and Ludwig Lachman. While the theories of Mises, Rothbard, Hayek, and Lachman contain diverse elements, their similarities outweigh their differences.

Kirzner perhaps provides the best description of the Misesian view of entrepreneurship as follows:

> Profit opportunities arise when the prices of products on the product markets are not adjusted to the prices of resource services on the factor markets. In other words, "something" is being sold at different prices in two markets, as a result of imperfect communication between the markets. This "something," it is true, is sold in different physical forms in the two markets: in the factor market it appears as a bundle of inputs, and in the product market it appears as a consumption good. But economically we still have the "same" thing being sold at different prices, because the input bundle contains all that is technologically required (and no more than is required) to yield the product. The entrepreneur notices this price discrepancy before others do. What distinguishes this situation from the usual arbitrage case is that input purchases precede output sales; at the time of the production decision the product prices do not yet exist except as anticipations. The entrepreneur guesses that future product prices will not be fully adjusted to today's input prices.[17]

While Mises discussed the importance of the entrepreneur in a market economy, he did not attempt to develop a theory of entrepreneurship. The Austrian economist who developed such a theory was Israel Kirzner.

Israel Kirzner, professor of economics at New York University, originally developed a theory of entrepreneurship that contained three concepts. The first concept is that of an *alertness* by individuals to gain pure profits. This entrepreneurial process is the force that generates the market process and determines its direction. Second, using Hayek's concept of an equilibrating force, the entrepreneur, by *arbitraging markets,* creates a greater consistency or compatibility of plans. Errors can occur in the market process but result from individuals overlooking opportunities to gain pure profit by not being sufficiently alert. Third, Kirzner regarded the *ownership of physical resources to be totally distinct from the entrepreneurial process.* Kirzner excluded time and uncertainty from his original theory.[18]

Kirzner's original theory of entrepreneurship was based on Mises's concept of human action and Mises's argument that there is an entrepreneurial element present in all human action. Kirzner considered that this entrepreneurial element involves an alertness to perceive Mises's "ends-means" framework, where maximizing behavior occurs. According to Kirzner,

> Human action, in the sense developed by Mises, involves courses of action taken by the human being "to remove uneasiness" and to make himself "better off." Being broader than the notion of economizing, the concept of human action does not restrict analysis of the decision to the allocation problem posed by the juxtaposition of scarce means and multiple ends. The decision, in the framework of the human action approach, is not arrived at merely by mechanical computation of the solution to the maximization problem implicit in the configuration of the given ends and means. It reflects not merely the manipulation of given means to correspond faithfully with a hierarchy of given ends, but also the *very perception of the ends-means framework,* within

which allocation and economizing is to take place . . . Mises's *homo agens* . . . is endowed not only with the propensity to pursue goals efficiently, once ends and means are clearly identified, but also with the drive and alertness to identify which ends to strive for and which means are available.[19]

Kirzner altered his original theory of entrepreneurship in response to criticism that time and uncertainty are important consequences in human decision making. For example, a theory that "ignores uncertainty cannot explain entrepreneurial losses, only entrepreneurial gains."[20]

Kirzner's modified theory retains the basics of the original theory while distinguishing between entrepreneurship in single-period market decisions and in multiple periods involving time and uncertainty. Entrepreneurship in the single period involves gaining pure profit by arbitraging markets. Entrepreneurship in multiple periods involves gaining pure profit by speculative insights of "time-to-come" that "pushes aside to some extent the swirling fogs of uncertainty, permitting meaningful action."[21]

While Kirzner's modified theory involves arbitrage and speculation, both theories describe entrepreneurship as bringing about a greater mutual consistency in market transactions.[22]

Kirzner's theory of entrepreneurship provides two primary explanations for the superiority of spontaneous order generated by unhampered markets.[23] According to one researcher,

> First, Kirzner's theory of entrepreneurship indicates how a market process arises and why. . . . He explains how the unhampered market process can bring about a degree of consistency or mutual compatibility between market participants' plans. In this respect, Kirzner's theory of entrepreneurship explains the observed tendency for prices of homogenous goods or assets to converge to a common level. Secondly, by emphasizing the importance of entrepreneurial alertness and perception, by supporting Mises's contention that the entrepreneur-promoter is the driving force of the market economy, Kirzner's theory of entrepreneurship implies that the institutional arrangement which allows and encourages individuals to use their entrepreneurial ability to the greatest extent is the institutional arrangement which produces superior results.[24]

ENTREPRENEURSHIP AND HUMAN CAPITAL

Nobel laureate Theodore Schultz, professor of economics at Iowa State University and later at the University of Chicago, has developed a theory of entrepreneurship based on his concept of human capital. Certain aspects of Schultz's theory of entrepreneurship are described in this section, and Schultz's article describing the relationship between entrepreneurship and human capital follows.

Schultz offered two contributions in developing his theory of entrepreneurship. First, he defined entrepreneurship as "the ability to deal with disequilibria."[25] According to Schultz,

> Individuals in many different walks of life engage in optimizing behavior, which entails reallocating resources to regain equilibrium. All of them are in this respect entrepreneurs.[26]

Second, Schultz reported that a number of studies have produced evidence that education affects people's ability to perceive and react to disequilibria.[27]

Schultz argued that entrepreneurial ability is useful and can be considered to be an identifiable marginal product. For example, Schultz reported that entrepreneurial activity is a differential return to ability:

> My argument is that disequilibria are inevitable in a dynamic economy. These disequilibria cannot be eliminated by law, by public policy, and surely not by rhetoric. A modern dynamic economy would fall apart were it not for the entrepreneurial actions of a wide array of human agents who reallocate their resources and thereby bring their part of the economy back into equilibrium. Every entrepreneurial decision to reallocate resources entails risk. What entrepreneurs do has an economic value. This value accrues to them . . . as a reward for their entrepreneurial performance. The reward is earned. Although this reward for the entrepreneurship of most human agents is small, in the aggregate in a dynamic economy it accounts for a substantial part of the increases in national income. The concealment of this part of national income implies that entrepreneurs have not received their due in economics.[28]

Schultz criticized the standard concept and treatment of entrepreneurs used by others in the following four areas: (1) the concept is restricted to businessmen, (2) it does not take into account the differences in allocative abilities among entrepreneurs, (3) the supply of entrepreneurship is not treated as a scarce resource, and (4) there is no need for entrepreneurship in general equilibrium theory.[29]

Schultz defended the notion of equilibrium in economic analysis as follows:

> Unless we develop equilibrating models, the function of this particular ability (entrepreneurship) cannot be analyzed. Within such models, the function of entrepreneurship would be much extended and the supply of entrepreneurial ability would be treated as a scarce resource.[30]

Schultz stated that whenever the term *entrepreneur* appears in the theoretical core of economics, it is "confined to businessmen, thus it excludes laborers who are reallocating their labor services, and it excludes housewives, students, and consumers who are also in the act of reallocating their resource (consisting, to be sure, largely of their own time)."[31]

Schultz's theory of entrepreneurship differed from Schumpeter's concept in a number of ways. For example, Schultz argued that Schumpeter's analysis was restricted to one subset of entrepreneurs—"captains of industry who carry out large combinations of the means of production," while investments made by families and individuals in their own human capital also create favorable changes in economic conditions. Furthermore, according to Schultz, (1) technological advances are pervasive in a modernizing economy, and (2) most of the changes in economic conditions that enhance productivity and that originate from within the economy are not in Schumpeter's analytical domain. For example, while "research and development" is a major source for developing both lower costs and new production techniques, many small, self-employed entrepreneurs do not engage in either basic or applied research.[32]

Schultz also addressed the affects of risk and uncertainty on entrepreneurial profits. According to Schultz,

> The concept of risk is clear and cogent; so is the concept of true uncertainty. But the concept of "uncertainty" that is not true uncertainty is neither clear nor cogent. The probabilities of some types of risk can be reckoned; but the probabilities of true uncertainty are indeterminate. Risk and true uncertainty are frequently joined when entrepreneurs deal with an economic disequilibrium. The risk component is a cost whatever its probability and regardless how it may be insured. The true uncertainty component, however, is not a cost. It results in a windfall profit or loss.[33]

Schultz argued that risk and uncertainty occur jointly when an entrepreneur analyzes a venture. For example, the entrepreneur who is involved in the construction of a new type of manufacturing (or industrial) facility that requires years of construction before completion experiences various risks during construction. These risks and expenditures, according to Schultz, are contractual costs. The true uncertainty of the project, as defined by Schultz, is the precise output of the new plant and the selling price of the product. Schultz argued that this output quantity and the selling price cannot be known until the plant has been completed and is in operation, which will not occur until years after the commitment to build has been made.[34]

Schultz stated that an important aspect of an analysis of entrepreneurship is the demand for and the supply of entrepreneurs. According to Schultz:

> The demand for entrepreneurship has several distinctive characteristics. It often emerges somewhat abruptly, it is transitory, and it is specific to each type of change in economic conditions.... What an entrepreneur expects to earn for his allocative effort is the incentive that motivates his actions. The quantity and quality attributes of the incentives are the essential elements of the demand for entrepreneurship; namely, the amount of the incentive and the transitory nature of the incentive. The expectations of entrepreneurs are critical in determining the demand for their allocative ability. Changes in economic conditions that create the incentives and the expectations are either favorable or unfavorable, that is, expected earnings are positive or negative. When they are negative action is taken to reduce expected losses in earnings and wealth.[35]

Schultz discussed the supply of entrepreneurs as follows:

In accounting terms, the aggregate supply of entrepreneurship is the sum of how many adults are actually and potentially active entrepreneurs, of the quality of their generic abilities and of their acquired abilities. The supply is large in terms of numbers and the supply is widely distributed throughout the adult population at any given time. The quality of the supply is enhanced over time by investment in various forms of human capital. The economic attributes of the short term supply correspond to that of other factors of production. . . . The supply can be enhanced by means of investment in acquired abilities.[36]

The following article by Schultz relates investments in human capital with entrepreneurship. Interestingly other economists also have argued the relationship of investments in human capital (employee training, general education, and health care costs) to increased productivity and entrepreneurial activity.[37]

| ARTICLE 7.1 | **THE VALUE OF THE ABILITY TO DEAL WITH DISEQUILIBRIA**
by Theodore Schultz

I am indebted to C. Arnold Anderson, Gary S. Becker, Mary Jean Bowman, Issac Ehrlich, Richard B. Freeman, Wallace Huffman, D. Gale Johnson, Lawrence W. Kenny, Donald N. McCloskey, Jacob Mincer, Marc Nerlove, Lawrence S. Olson, George Psacharopoulous, and Margaret Reid for their comments on an earlier draft. I am grateful to the Ford Foundation and NIE for their grants supporting my studies of the increasing value of human time, of which this is a part.

No matter what part of a modern economy is being investigated, we observe that many people are consciously reallocating their resources in response to changes in economic conditions. How efficient they are in their responses is in no small part determined by their "allocative ability." The ability to reallocate is not restricted to entrepreneurs who are engaged in business. People who supply labor services for hire or who are self-employed are reallocating their services in response to changes in the value of the work they do. So are housewives in devoting their time in combination with purchased goods and services in household production. Students likewise are reallocating their own time along with the educational services they purchase as they respond to changes in expected earnings along with changes in the value of the personal satisfactions they expect to derive from their education. Consumption opportunities are also changing, and inasmuch as pure consumption entails time, here too people are reallocating their own time in response to changing opportunities.

The main purpose of this study is to explore how education and experience influence the efficiency of human beings to perceive, to interpret correctly, and to undertake action that will appropriately reallocate their resources. The central questions to keep in mind are: To what extent are these allocative abilities acquired? Are education and experience measurable sources of these abilities?

What factors determine the economic value of the stocks of such abilities that various individuals possess? The starting point is the concept that the behavior of human beings is governed by the criterion of optimization under constraints that are specific to the circumstances confronting each person. I assume that there is a competitive factor market that encompasses the aggregate of individual decisions and that the terms of trade are being adjusted to bring these decisions of individuals into a mutually consistent relationship, in the sense that supply tends to equal demand. With respect to the particular abilities under consideration, I assume that the demand for them is determined by the events that give rise to the observed disequilibria and that the supply is one of the components of human capital.

My plan is to investigate the following topics: (1) the concepts of human abilities, (2) the equilibrating activities of individuals to regain equilibrium, (3) the idea of the stationary state, (4) two economic states compared, (5) extending the role of entrepreneurship, (6) the elements of a theory, and (7) an interpretation of a substantial amount of evidence.

I. Concepts of Human Abilities

Our knowledge of a person's abilities consists of inferences drawn from his performance. An ability is thus perceived as the competence and efficiency with which particular acts are performed. What a person does we shall treat as a service, and we shall consider only those services that are deemed to be both useful and scarce, which implies that they have some economic value. The service attributed to any ability has a time dimension, that is, a certain amount is accomplished *per* hour or day, in a year, or over a lifetime.

There are various classes of abilities: they include the ability: (1) to learn, (2) to do useful work, (3) to play, (4) to create something, and (5) specifically for the purpose at hand, to deal with economic disequilibria. Since what is done can be observed, it is convenient to assume that the observed performance is related to a specific ability. Although these various classes undoubtedly overlap and interact, it is useful to proceed with qualifications as if each class has a special set of attributes. There comes a point, however, at which this reductionist approach is misleading for it postulates the separability of abilities; whereas normal human beings possess hierarchies of integration among abilities.[b]

Much attention is given in our schools to the testing of aptitudes and intelligence: I.Q. tests, for example, are designed to predict school-performance. There are tests to ascertain verbal and quantitative abilities, presumably to predict performance in education. Partly to limit the supply and partly to assure standards

---

[b] The controversy in biology between those who argue for reductionism, the essence of which is the belief that all of life can be reduced to fundamental laws of physics and chemistry, and those who argue for hierarchies and integration in biological systems is instructive on this basic issue.

of performance, professional associations promote tests to determine who is "qualified" to practice law or medicine. The limitations and misuses of these various tests aside, their usefulness in determining economic performance is very limited.[c] Obviously, these tests are not designed for that purpose. Economists are still hard pressed in explaining the wide variance in the earnings profile of people over their lifetime. The role of differences in abilities is yet in large part unknown. Virtually no attention has been given to the role of abilities with respect to the time spent and the satisfactions obtained from engaging in play, in creative activity, and in pure consumption, in spite of the fact that time is valuable and its economic value has been rising secularly and markedly in high income countries. Although changing economic conditions are pervasive in a modern economy, the efficiency with which people adjust to these changes has not yet become a part of standard economics. One of the reasons why this is so, arises out of the analytical neglect of the equilibrating activities of human agents.

II. Equilibrating Activities to Regain Equilibrium

Determining precisely what people do who are not in equilibrium is not one of the notable achievements of economics. What people do is, in general, concealed in the assumption that their optimizing behavior is such that they regain equilibrium instantaneously. However, it is unlikely that they would be able to do this in fact; but more important, even if they were able, it would not normally be economic for them to make all of the required reallocations of their resources instantaneously. Thus, regaining equilibrium takes time, and how people proceed over time depends on their efficiency in responding to any given disequilibrium and on the costs and returns of the sequence of adjustments available to them. The analytical core of general equilibrium theory is not designed to analyze the specific actions and performances of people who are engaged in these equilibrating activities.

Our closely reasoned general economic equilibrium [Arrow, 1974] rests on two basic concepts: (1) the human being is an optimizing agent whose behavior is governed by constraints that are in part peculiar to him, and (2) the market provides the auction at which all individual offers are acknowledged and the terms of trade are established for equalizing supply and demand. General equilibrium theory yields many meaningful implications [Arrow, 1974] that are useful in

---

[c] In ascertaining the value of an ability that is embodied in a person, both the psychologist and the economist are dependent upon observable acts which are assumed to be the effects of the ability being analyzed. The psychologist may thus look for cognitive ability, the knowing activity of the mind by means of which a person becomes aware of events and the manner in which he perceives them. I am looking for the ability to perceive and interpret correctly economic events, which may be a particular type of "cognitive ability."

organizing economic knowledge, and more important, in guiding economic analyses. Although it is used predominantly to explain market-oriented activities, it can be extended to encompass various non-market activities, as it has been in analyzing household production, investment in education and in other types of human capital, as well as in examining the sorting and mating behavior leading to marriage and fertility, and the time and purchased services that parents invest in their children. In all of these applications, theory is an essential analytical device, a method, or an approach, in studying aspects of economic behavior. It is, however, a serious mistake not to distinguish between the analytical properties of the theory and the fact that human beings are not always in equilibrium and the further fact that they do not regain equilibrium instantaneously.

Instead of extending parts of general equilibrium theory to analysis of the optimizing equilibrating behavior of individuals, it is all too convenient to treat the observable state of an economy, whatever its apparent disarray, as if it were nevertheless in a state of equilibrium. Using this approach, the economy is deemed to be in equilibrium each and every day regardless of changing economic conditions. To make it so, all that is required is to assume that the costs of information and of transactions are such as to provide the conditions that are required for an economic equilibrium. The usefulness of the concepts of search for information and of transaction costs is not in doubt, but when they are applied as indicated, they merely conceal the disequilibrium that persists into the next day and for more days to come.

What we want to analyze are the various equilibrating processes that are observable activities of people, especially of people living in an economy characterized by high incomes and by continuing modernization. It is true that some of the adjustments to secular changes in relative prices of factors and products have been on the agenda of economists. The role of lags in economic adjustments has, in fact, received much attention. Many sophisticated econometric studies using lags have been published. The achievements of these studies are cogently evaluated by Marc Nerlove [1972, 1974]. They concentrate primarily on the problems of statistical inference, although there are some extensions of economic theory to explain the equilibrating activities that are revealed by such lags.

The approach of this paper is to extend the concept of entrepreneurship. I shall postulate a supply function of entrepreneurs that takes into account their abilities to deal with disequilibria. Before turning to this approach, I shall comment on the perceived realities of the stationary state, on two very different economic states, and on the inadequacy of the received treatment of entrepreneurship.

III. The Idea of a Stationary State

A stationary state implies zero growth, and it also implies that the economic value of allocative abilities would be zero. If the supply of resources and the demand for their services were to remain constant long enough, the economy would arrive at a stationary state with no economic disequilibria. Currently, long-standing unsettled social issues are being raised once again in evaluating the economic growth of our modernizing economy. Doubts about the ultimate value of economic growth are persuasive and are multiplying. Zero economic growth, coupled with zero population growth, is viewed by many as a condition of an ideal society. It could be that birth and death rates are tending toward a population equilibrium [T. W. Schultz, 1974]. However, with reference to zero economic growth, the rank and file of people *act* as if they prefer the increasing range of choices and opportunities that they obtain from positive economic growth. I am not implying that they are unconcerned about some of the more obvious social losses entailed in modern growth.

The economist is far from successful in reconciling the views of the articulate intellectuals with the revealed preferences of people generally. The economist wants to be accepted as an intellectual, but he knows that the preferences of people are fundamental to his analytical work. Even if he had the courage, it would be cynical and less than candid for him to assert that intellectuals typically are biased by living in a sheltered, affluent enclave. But regardless of the facts on this point, an economy is supposed to serve the preferences of people, not the particular preferences of economists.

The idea of economic progress predates the theoretical work of the early English economists, who were not, however, of one mind about the value of what was then called the "progressive state." For Adam Smith, "the progressive state is in reality the cheerful and hearty state . . ." while "the stationary state is dull." Ricardo concurred [Robbins, 1930]. John Stuart Mill, in contemplating the progressive changes in the economy, was "not satisfied with merely tracing the laws of movement." Akin to some of the current protest, he too was troubled by the ultimate purpose of these "progressive" movements. He maintained that rich and prosperous countries could derive real advantages from the stationary state. (See Mill as edited by Ashley [1926].)d For these countries to forego such advantages meant paying too high a price for further improvements in the productive arts and for the additional accumulations of capital.e Marshall, in turn, disagreed sharply with his eminent predecessor by saying, "But indeed a perfect adjust-

---

d Mill puts it thusly, "I am inclined to believe that it [stationary state] would be, on the whole, a considerable improvement on our present condition. I confess I am not charmed with the idea of life held out by those who think that the normal state of human beings is that of struggling to get on; that the trampling, crunching, elbowing, and treading on each other's heels, which form the existing type of social life, are the most desirable lot of human kind, or anything but the disagreeable symptoms of one of the phases of industrial progress" [1926, p. 748].

e Among the "advantages" of the idea of the stationary state, Mill did not anticipate that "general equilibrium theory" would become the analytical core of economics and that it would postulate that economic conditions were given. Robbins [1930, p. 202] makes the point that the first paragraph of Book IV of Mill's *Principles of Political Economy* opened the door for many ambiguities by his "adding a theory of motion to our theory of equilibrium, the dynamics of political economy to the statics." Robbins [1935] continued to hold fast to equilibrium theory and expressed the belief that it cannot be extended to cope with economic development.

ment is inconceivable. Perhaps even it is undesirable. For after all man is the end of production; and perfectly stable business would be likely to produce men who were little better than machines" [Marshall, 1919].

Judging from the economic behavior of "ordinary" people before and since the time of Mill, they prefer an economy with "progressive changes." Moreover, since Mill's time modern economics has developed specialized sectors, the purpose of which is to improve the productive arts. The accumulation of capital has gone on apace. We have created an economy that is organized to produce this type of "progress." Such is the economic reality we shall investigate and try to explain.

IV. Two Economic States Compared

Once an economy arrives at an equilibrium and if henceforth the supply of resources and the demand for their services remain constant, custom could fix rents, wages, and the interest rate, and the economy would continue to be efficient.[f] They could be efficient prices in the sense that no appreciable stresses and strains would arise as long as economic conditions remained unchanged.

It may be helpful to compare the realized over-all efficiency under two very different sets of conditions. A simple comparison between traditional and modern agricultural conditions highlights the difference. Let me state the inference that emerges before elaborating on the underlying circumstances or on the implications they have for applications of theory. The basic inference is that farm people under traditional conditions are closer to an economic optimum, given the resources that are available to them than are "modern" farm people in view of the new and better possibilities that are constantly crowding in on the latter. I use the term "farm people" advisedly because in this context it is not only farm production that matters, but also household production and the investment in human capital by farm people. Farm people in India, say before the green revolution, were closer to an optimum use of the resources at their disposal than the farm people, say, of Iowa, have been since the early thirties in view of the many complex changes in resources and associated opportunities with which they have been dealing.

The reasoning underlying this inference can be stated simply. Farm people who have lived for generations with essentially the same resources tend to approximate the economic equilibrium of the stationary state. When the productive arts remain virtually constant over many years, farm people know from long experience what their own effort can get out of the land and equipment. In allocating the resources at their disposal, in choosing a combination of crops, in deciding on how and when to cultivate, plant, water, and harvest, and what

---

[f] There are studies by anthropologists of isolated "primitive" communities that show that the rewards to the factors of production are fixed by custom.

combination of tools to use with draft animals and simple field equipment—these choices and decisions all embody a fine regard for marginal costs and returns. These farm people also know from experience the value of their household production possibilities; in allocating their own time along with material goods within the domain of the household, they too are finely attuned to marginal costs and returns. Furthermore, children acquire the skills that are worthwhile from their parents as children have for generations under circumstances where formal schooling has little economic value. This simplified economic picture of traditional farm life, which includes knowing how to live with variations in weather, strongly implies a high level of general economic efficiency.[8] It also implies that there is, for all practical purposes, no premium for the human ability to deal with secular economic changes.

For contrast, I now look at farm people who live in a modernizing economy. Here they deal with a sequence of changes in economic conditions, which are in general not of their own making because they originate mainly out of the activities of people other than farm people. For this reason Schumpeter's theory of economic development is far from sufficient to explain most of these changes. The changes are nevertheless endogenous for the reason that I stressed at the outset. They have their origin predominantly in the useful contributions that flow from organized agricultural research and from improvements in the inputs that farm people purchase and use in agricultural and household production. Accordingly, the *demand* for the ability to deal with the new and better production possibilities is in large part determined by organized agricultural research and by the nonfarm firms that produce the inputs that farm people purchase. Furthermore, it takes time to reallocate resources in arriving at a new equilibrium. Moreover, additional changes occur even before the reallocation called for by the preceding change has been completed. Hence, the implication is that "full efficiency" is kept beyond the reach of farm people.

V. Extending the Role of Entrepreneurship

Whether or not economic growth is deemed to be "progress," it is a process beset with various classes of disequilibria. In response, individuals in many different walks of life engage in optimizing behavior, which entails reallocating resources to regain equilibrium. All of them are in this respect entrepreneurs. But the standard concept and treatment of entrepreneurs will not suffice for the following reasons: (1) the concept is restricted to businessmen, (2) it does not take into account the differences in allocative abilities among entrepreneurs, (3) the supply

---

8 This is the foundation of my analysis of the allocative efficiency of farm people in traditional agriculture in *transforming traditional agriculture* [1964]. As a matter of historical fact, however, it would be rare indeed to discover a situation and a period during which farm people were in "perfect" equilibrium for reasons that I noted with care in the 1964 book.

of entrepreneurship is not treated as a scarce resource, and (4) there is no need for entrepreneurship in general equilibrium theory.

The concept of the entrepreneur rarely appears in the theoretical core of economics. When it does, it is confined to businessmen, thus it excludes laborers who are reallocating their labor services, and it excludes housewives, students, and consumers who are also in the act of reallocating their resources (consisting, to be sure, largely of their own time). In standard theory, it is hard to find a treatment of the supply of entrepreneurship. An exception is Gary S. Becker's "supply curve of entrepreneurial capacity" [1971]. When entrepreneurs appear in economic analysis, the role attributed to them as businessmen is confined to dealing with risk and uncertainty. The rewards, however, for performing this role are not allowed in general equilibrium theory, for it implies a "zero profit" for this role. In fact, it is obvious that every equilibrating activity entails elements of risk and uncertainty, and it is also obvious that individuals improve their economic position, and in this sense rewards accrue to them as a consequence of their regaining equilibrium.

Although the entrepreneur is a stranger in general equilibrium theory, he has been around for a long time in parts of our economic literature. The entrepreneur appears early in the writings of French economists [Hoselitz, 1951], but they are only descriptively at home in the work of the early English economists, and it is their work that has become the core of received theory. In Schumpeter's theory of economic development, the role of the entrepreneur is confined to those who engage in activities motivated by profits in the market sector [1911]. What they do is, however, only a part of the story because households and individuals both within and outside of the market sector are also present. The entrepreneur as seen by Schumpeter *creates* developmental disequilibria; but his function is not extended to deal successfully with all manner of other disequilibria as they occur within the economic system. In his approach, the mainspring of development consists of the "creative and innovative responses" of the entrepreneur. Edwin F. Gay, Arthur H. Cole, and Leland H. Jenks followed this lead in their endeavor, among other things, to distinguish between the managerial and entrepreneurial functions. But their studies appear not to have been successful, according to Thomas C. Cochran [1968], in extending received theory. Although, as already noted, the business entrepreneur is only one of many classes of people who are engaged in equilibrating processes, it is inexplicable that Schumpeter's contribution has not become an integral part of received theory.

Israel M. Kirzner presents a perceptive analysis of the state of economic theory with respect to the entrepreneur [1973]. He sees clearly the omission of the entrepreneur in received equilibrium theory, but he persists in holding fast to the zero profit concept in that theory and, as a consequence, fails to see the economic rewards that accrue to those who bring about the equilibrating process.

It bears repeating that the standard economic concept of the function of laborers does not include their role as entrepreneurs in allocating their own time and their ability to do this successfully under changing economic conditions. Similarly, the entrepreneurial role and ability of housewives in managing household production and of mature students deciding how to invest in themselves, are omitted in most economic studies.

The human capital approach in analyzing the useful abilities of people represents a marked advance in that it specifies the various skills of people and specifies the manner in which the skills are acquired. At the outset, this approach was restricted empirically to individuals who enter the labor market (where data on earnings could be had). The more recent developments of a theory of the allocation of time[h] and of the household production function have extended the analysis to determine the economic value of the human abilities in this large and long neglected nonmarket sector. This broadened approach is proving useful also in analyzing the capabilities of human beings to do work for hire, or for themselves, or to carry out household activities, or to use their own time in investing in themselves.[i]

VI. Elements of a Theory

In analyzing the equilibrating activities of people, we postulate that there are economic incentives to reallocate resources, that people respond to these incentives to the best of their ability, and that the difference in their performance is a measure of the difference among people with respect to the particular type of ability that is required. In accordance with this postulate, there is a type of ability that is useful and whose value is some function of the demand for and the supply of that ability. This particular ability, as noted at the outset, represents the competence of people to perceive a given disequilibrium and to evaluate its attributes properly in determining whether it is worthwhile to act, and if it is worthwhile, people respond by reallocating their resources. The realized gains[j] from such reallocations are the observable rewards.

The expected gains are the economic incentives to enter upon these equilibrating activities. Since the gains that are realized represent an improvement in income, it obviously is not the "zero profit" result derived from general instantaneous adjustments in equilibrium theory. These gains are exemplified by the profitability of the adoption of hybrid corn [Griliches, 1957, 1960]. In household production, it is exemplified by the gain in utility from using the sewing machine over hand sewing. It is also evident in the gains in income that laborers derive

---

[h] Notably beginning with Becker's paper, "A Theory of the Allocation of Time" [1965].

[i] I have sketched the economic logic of the effects of increases in the value of time upon pure consumption, the plausibility that improvements in the technical arts are of little or no avail in economizing on time in consumption, and the implication that the time required in consumption may hold the key to the upper limit of material economic growth in "The High Value of Human Time: Population Equilibrium" [1974].

[j] For people to have gains from their resource allocations does not imply that they are necessarily better off than they were prior to the disequilibrium, but it does imply that their economic position has been improved relative to what it would be if they had stayed in disequilibrium.

from geographical migration to better jobs, and by the improvement in earnings that students realize by adjusting their studies to changes in the markets for college educated personnel.

The demand for the services of these abilities is determined by the characteristics of the disequilibrium. Accordingly, the demand is some function of the particular economic disequilibrium under investigation. For a given disequilibrium there may be a demand schedule in the sense that the incentive to act is high at the outset and as resources are reallocated the incentive to make further adjustments declines.[k]

In searching for the factors that determine the various classes of disequilibria and in ascertaining their respective incentives for resource reallocation, there are strong reasons for distinguishing between the disequilibria that firms, households, and individuals (laborers, students) face. The incentive associated with an advance in knowledge pertaining to nutrition, for example, is easier to perceive and to act upon in feeding poultry and livestock than it is in rearranging the diet pattern in a household. Young people facing the need to change the investment they make in themselves are confronted by a much more complex set of future rewards than most firms are required to reckon with when they alter their investment in structures and equipment.

The supply of services from these abilities depends upon the stock of a particular form of human capital at any point in time and on the costs and the rate at which the stock can be increased in response to the rewards derived from the services of these abilities. The amount of such human capital may be small *per* person, but it is never zero. Regardless of how poor people are, how long they have lived under "stationary" conditions, how limited their experience, and how much they lack in literacy, they are neither indifferent to, nor wholly unresponsive to, opportunities to improve their economic lot.[l] The supply of the services from these abilities in a particular area (sector) can be augmented by the immigration of individuals with a relatively large component of these abilities who

---

[k] The part of this demand schedule that matters in analyzing observable behavior lies substantially above a zero gain because if it were very small the incentive that directs the equilibrating process would become too weak to warrant proceeding to the perfect equilibrium point. The disequilibrium associated with the event of hybrid corn is instructive. It became available in the early thirties and it spread rapidly through the Corn Belt. There were marked geographic differences, however, in the rate at which hybrid corn was adopted. These differences in the rate of adoption were a consequence of the wide differences in the profitability from the increases in yield that could be obtained from the available hybrid seed. In Iowa in five years the percentage of the total acreage planted with hybrid seed increased from 10 to over 90 percent, whereas in Wisconsin during the same period it reached the 60 percent level. (See Griliches [1957; 1960].)

[l] Although they may be relatively slow in perceiving and in taking the appropriate action, their performance in response to strong incentives leaves little room for doubt that there is a component of this ability in the most disadvantaged of the world's population. The fairly rapid adoption of new, highly productive, wheat varieties by the small, financially poor, uneducated farmers of India, associated with the green revolution, is strong evidence of this point.

move in response to incentives created by the disequilibrium. A case in point is the response in parts of North India to the high profitability of the new wheat varieties where no small number of well-qualified nonfarm people sought entry into farming. The existing stock of these abilities can be complemented (made more effective) by various forms of extension activities. Over a longer span of time, if the incentives persist, the supply can and will be increased by learning from experience the art of dealing with changing economic conditions and by making investments in this form of human capital by training and schooling.

The effects of education in this connection can be tested empirically, and it is proving to be a strong explanatory variable. It is important to find out what features of education augment the supply of the services from these abilities. The presumption is that education—even primary schooling—enhances the ability of students to perceive new classes of problems, to clarify such problems, and to learn ways of solving them. Although the problem-solving abilities that students acquire pertain to classroom work, the abilities that are developed by this work seem to have general properties that contribute measurably to their performance as economic agents in perceiving and solving the problems that arise as a consequence of economic changes.

VII. Interpreting the Evidence

We begin by limiting the implications to the optimizing behavior of individuals, followed by a comment on difficulties inherent in the data, and then turn to insights derived from some general observations and from specific studies.

Limiting the Implications

We are not searching for evidence to explain why disequilibria occur. Instead, given a disequilibrium, we are concerned with the ensuing behavior that is induced by the incentive to reallocate resources. Over time this stock of allocative abilities can be enhanced by various means. Our analysis, however, will be restricted to the existing stock of such human capital, although we shall point out that students also differ in their allocative ability, which in turn affects their efficiency as they invest in education.

The hypotheses that are most readily subject to empirical analysis are that the effects of education and of experience are positive and important in their contribution to the rate at which resources are reallocated. Education in fact has both an income and a price effect. The earnings of individuals tend to rise with their education, and as their earnings increase, the value of their time rises, the consequences of which are revealed as price effects.

Difficulties

Risk and uncertainty are ever present in the optimizing behavior here under consideration. How much of the observed difference in responses is a consequence of the difference in risk and uncertainty (including the difference in preferences to bear them) is very difficult to determine. The allocative efficiency attributed to education presumably affects the costs of searching for information. But the data are as a rule too crude to analyze this interaction. There is no easy way of identifying and measuring the incentives to reallocate resources that are strictly a consequence of a particular disequilibrium, although some progress has been made on this score. For small firms, i.e., farms and households, and for individuals who are laborers or who are students investing in themselves, it is less difficult to get usable data than it is for large complex firms. However, studies by Edwin Mansfield et al. of the research and innovation behavior of the modern corporation find that the difference in education influences the ability of corporate executives in this context [1971]. The specific studies to which I shall refer are restricted mainly to small firms. Finis Welch in a pioneering study of the role of education in modern agricultural production presents estimates of the "worker effects" and of the "allocative effects" attributed to education [1970]. In economics, however, there is no decisive test.

General Observations

Historically, the economic development of agriculture is replete with examples of the positive effects of education on economic performance of farmers. Although there is as a rule both a worker effect and an allocative effect, it seems fairly obvious that a substantial part of the successful performance is a consequence of the ability associated with education to deal with changes in economic conditions. The marked difference in the economic performance between the second generation California farmers of Japanese and those of Mexican heritage is in considerable part explained by a difference in education. Among the European immigrants who entered U.S. agriculture, those who had been lowly peasants or hired farm workers and who had little schooling were in general less successful during the first generation than immigrants in settlements that consisted of a complete community of people with a relatively high average level of education, for example, the settlements of the Dutch in parts of Iowa. Very rapid modernization of U.S. agriculture following World War II has more than halved the number of farms. In the ensuing competition to survive and remain in agriculture, the effects of education on the ability to cope with changes in agricultural production are strongly positive in determining who has been able to survive (see G. S. Tolley [1970]).

Similarly, in Brazil there is the impressive agricultural success of the Japanese immigrants who entered with more education and with more experience in dealing with agricultural modernization than most Brazilian farmers. The performance of the Huguenots in Canada and those who became farmers in the United States also exemplifies the positive effects of education. In the rapid development of agriculture in Israel, occidental immigrant Jews have been much more successful than the oriental Jews; here too, the difference in education appears to be a strong explanatory factor (see Ezra Sadan, Chaba Nachmias, and Gideon Bar-Lev [1974]).

We have had and continue to have a vast amount of internal migration by members of the labor force who have been adjusting to changes in job opportunities. Here, too, in terms of economic performance, those with 16 years of education are more successful than those with 12 years, and the latter do better on this score than those with 8 years of schooling. The difference in ability to deal with these job disequilibria is apparently related to education.

Specific Studies

[*Professor Schultz's discussion of a variety of studies supporting his argument is omitted from this version.*]

In Summary

There is enough evidence to give validity to the hypothesis that the ability to deal successfully with economic disequilibria is enhanced by education and that this ability is one of the major benefits of education accruing to people privately in a modernizing economy. We see it in the equilibrating performance of housewives, laborers, students, and farmers. There is no reason to suppose that it is not important in the case of businessmen, although as yet the necessary evidence is lacking. Unless we develop equilibrating models, the function of this particular ability can not be analyzed. Within such models, the function of entrepreneurship would be much extended and the supply of entrepreneurial ability would be treated as a scarce resource.

There are many unsettled questions. Is it the cognitive ability as perceived by psychologists that accounts for what we attribute to education? If it is, what are the sources of the differences in cognitive ability? Is it a general ability in the sense that it is revealed in many different types of human performance? Since the supply of it is a scarce resource that can be augmented, what is the supply response to increases in its economic value? In this study we have taken the first step on what appears to be a long new road.

Source: This article excerpted from Theodore Schultz, "The Value of the Ability to Deal with Disequilibria," *Journal of Economic Literature* 13 (1975): 827–46. Used by permission of the *Journal of Economic Literature*.

ENDNOTES

1. E. G. Dolan and D. E. Lindsey, "Entrepreneurship and the Market Process," in *Economics*, 5th ed. (New York: Dryden Press, 1988), 676.
2. A. Phillips, "Theory and the Analysis of Financial Markets," in *Advances in the Study of Entrepreneurship, Innovation, and Economic Growth*, ed. G. D. Libecap (Greenwich, Conn.: JAI Press, 1986), 80.
3. R. Cyert and J. March, *A Behavioral Theory of the Firm* (New York: Prentice-Hall, 1970).

4. H. A. Simon, *Administrative Behavior* (New York: Macmillan, 1947).

5. O. E. Williamson, *Markets and Hierarchies* (New York: The Free Press, 1975), 84 .

6. F. A. von Hayek, "The Use of Knowledge in Society," *American Economic Review* 35 (1945): 519–30.

7. Ibid., 520.

8. Dolan and Lindsey, "Entrepreneurship and the Market Process," 678.

9. Williamson, "Markets and Hierarchies," 87.

10. Examples include G. J. Stigler, "The Economics of Information," *Journal of Political Economy* 69 (1961): 213–25; J. F. Muth, "Rational Expectations and the Theory of Price Movements," *Econometrica* 29 (1961): 315–24; L. K. Gilbreath, *Red Capitalism: An Analysis of the Navajo Economy* (Norman, Okla.: University of Oklahoma Press, 1973); G. S. Becker, *Economic Theory* (New York: Alfred Knopf, 1971); G. S. Becker, *The Economics of Discrimination* (Chicago: University of Chicago Press, 1971); G. S. Becker, *Human Capital*, 2nd ed. (Chicago: University of Chicago Press, 1975); G. S. Becker, *The Economic Approach to Human Behavior* (Chicago: University of Chicago Press, 1976); T. W. Schultz, *Investing in People* (Berkeley, Calif.: University of California Press, 1980); R. E. Lucas, Jr., *Studies in Business-Cycle Theory* (Cambridge: MIT Press, 1982); S. Rosan, "Specialization and Human Capital," *Journal of Labor Economics* 1 (1983): 43–49; C. A. Kent, "The Rediscovery of the Entrepreneur," in *The Environment for Entrepreneurship*, ed. C. A. Kent (Lexington, Mass.: Lexington Books, 1984).

11. R. F. Hebert and A. N. Link, "In Search of the Meaning of Entrepreneurship," *Small Business Economics* 1 (1989): 39–49.

12. S. C. Littlechild, *The Fallacy of the Mixed Economy* (San Francisco: Cato Institute, 1979). Littlechild notes that while the "new" school differs from the old Austrian school of economics of Menger, Bohm-Bawerk, and Wieser it shares and has developed many of the insights of the old school.

13. L. V. Mises, *Human Action* (Chicago: Henry Regnery, 1966), 30.

14. Ibid., 254.

15. Ibid., 255.

16. Ibid., 253.

17. I. M. Kirzner, *Competition and Entrepreneurship* (Chicago: University of Chicago Press, 1973), 85–86.

18. Kirzner's original theory of entrepreneurship appeared in I. M. Kirzner, *Competition and Entrepreneurship* (Chicago: University of Chicago Press, 1973), and later advanced in I. M. Kirzner, *Perception Opportunity and Profit* (Chicago: University of Chicago Press, 1979).

19. Kirzner, *Competition and Entrepreneurship*, 33–34.

20. Hebert and Link, "In Search of the Meaning of Entrepreneurship," 47.

21. I. M. Kirzner, "Uncertainty, Discovery, and Human Actions: A Study of the Entrepreneurial Profile in the Missian System," in *Method, Process and Austrian Economics*, ed. I. M. Kirzner (Lexington, Mass.: Lexington Books, 1982): 139–59.

22. Ibid., 155.

23. For a detailed discussion of the modern Austrian school of economics approach to efficient markets, see E. G. Dolan, "Austrian Economics as Extraordinary Science," in *The Foundations of Modern Austrian Economics*, ed. E. G. Dolan (Kansas City, Mo.: Sheed and Ward, 1976); G. P. O'Driscoll, Jr., "Rational Expectations, Politics and Stagflation," in *Time, Uncertainty and Disequilibrium*, ed. M. J. Rizzo (Lexington, Mass.: Lexington Books, 1979); and R. Fryeman, "Toward an Understanding of Market Processes: Individual Expectations, Learning, and Convergence to Rational Expectations," *American Economic Review* 72 (1982): 652–68.

24. C. G. Hulbert, "Choice and Market Processes: An Austrian Analysis" (Ph.D. diss., University of Nebraska, 1986), 79–80.
25. T. W. Schultz, "The Value of the Ability to Deal with Disequilibria," *Journal of Economic Literature* 13 (1975): 831.
26. Ibid., 833.
27. Ibid., 839–42.
28. T. W. Schultz, "Investment in Entrepreneurial Ability," *Scandinavian Journal of Economics* 82 (1980): 443.
29. Schultz, "The Value of the Ability to Deal with Disequilibria," 832.
30. Ibid., 843.
31. Ibid., 835.
32. T. W. Schultz, *Restoring Economic Equilibrium: Human Capital in the Modernizing Economy* (London: Basil Blackwell, 1990), 212–20.
33. Ibid., 33.
34. Ibid., 34.
35. Ibid., 86–88.
36. Ibid., 89–91.
37. For an expanded discussion see Commission on Workforce Quality and Labor Market Efficiency, *Investing in People* (Washington, D. C.: GPO, 1989), 2–15; L. Thurow, *Head to Head: The Coming Economic Battle among Japan, Europe, and America* (New York: William Morrow and Company, 1992), 273–79; D. F. Jennings, *Effective Supervision: Frontline Management for the '90s.* (St. Paul: West Publishing, 1993), 96–98.

Behavioral Aspects of Entrepreneurs

8

Overview of Behavioral Aspects of Entrepreneurs

T his module, which consists of Chapters 8, 9, and 10, describes the behavioral school of thought regarding the notion of entrepreneurship. Chapter 8 begins by tracing the historical development of the behavioral aspects of entrepreneurship first described by Max Weber and includes the contributions of Everett Hagen; the team of Orvis Collins, David Moore, and Darab Unwalla; David McClelland; and Peter Kilby. Because the research activities of the behavioral aspects regarding entrepreneurship have been criticized, a research issues section is provided in Chapter 8. This chapter also contains two articles, one written jointly by James Carland, Frank Hoy, William Boulton, and JoAnn Carland and one by William Gartner. Chapter 9 describes a variety of psychological and personality factors associated with entrepreneurship and closes with an article by Daniel Jennings and Carl Zeithaml. Chapter 10 presents the argument of whether entrepreneurs are different from nonentrepreneurs.

DEVELOPMENT OF BEHAVIORAL ASPECTS OF ENTREPRENEURSHIP

This section reviews the contributions of Max Weber; Everett Hagen; the team of Orvis Collins, David Moore, and Darab Unwalla; David McClelland; and Peter Kilby.

Max Weber

The German sociologist Max Weber was perhaps the first theorist to indicate that ideological values lead directly to entrepreneurial behavior.[1] Weber, in explaining why capitalism has been successful in Western civilizations but less so in other civilizations, developed a multidimensional model of economic and social conditions. An important social aspect of Weber's model was the "Protestant work ethic," which demanded a life of good works and the avoidance of spontaneous, impulsive, self-enjoyment. This belief in a life of good works produced an intensive exertion in occupational pursuits. According to Weber, the Protestant work ethic became the driving force behind entrepreneurial activities and behaviors.[2] Exhibit 8-1 describes Weber's causal chain that leads to capitalism. Interestingly, nearly fifteen years later, Weber stated that the Protestant work ethic provided entrepreneurs with a clear conscience in their ruthless exploitation of workers through capitalism because ecclesiastical discipline controlled the workers' lives.[3]

While Weber attempted to develop a multidimensional theory for sociology, many sociologists have argued that his model is an inconsistency rather than a

EXHIBIT 8.1 The Weberian Causal Chain Leading to Capitalism

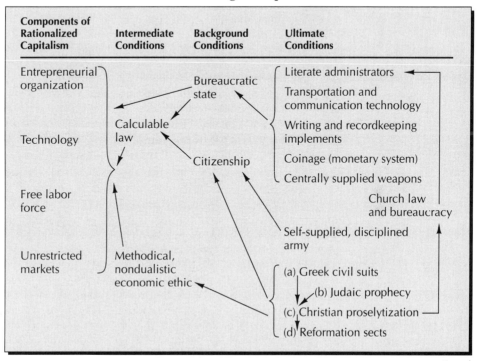

continued

EXHIBIT 8.1 *continued*

Entrepreneurial organization. All means of production must be privately owned and controlled by entrepreneurs. These entrepreneurs make decisions regarding the acquisition and use of land, buildings, machinery, and materials with maximum efficiency. Property rights are represented by commercial instruments that are negotiable in a stock market.

Technology. Mechanization to reduce production costs. Weber did not view technology as the key to economic transformation because mechanization is feasible only with mass production, which is worthless without a large-scale market for specific products.

Free labor force. Labor must have the freedom to move about to any work in response to demand conditions.

Unrestricted markets. Noneconomic restrictions on the movement of goods or of any factor of production must be minimized.

At the intermediate causal level, two components exist—one "legal" and the other "ethical"—as follows:

Calculable law. Laws must be "calculable" in general terms applicable to all persons and administered in such a manner to make the enforcement of economic contracts and rights highly predictable.

Methodical, nondualistic economic ethic. Nearly all premodern societies have two different and divergent sets of ethical beliefs and practices. One set involves an "internal ethic" that addresses rules of fairness, status, and tradition for members of a particular society. The prohibition on usury and the avoidance of gain from transactions within the community are an example of an internal ethic of charity, which existed in medieval Europe. The other set involves an "external ethic" for dealing with outsiders in which cheating, price gouging, and loans at exorbitant rates of interest are the norm. Both forms of ethics are a barrier to capitalism. For example, the internal ethic prevents the making of loans and conducting transactions for commercial gain. The external ethic makes trading relations too episodic and distrustful. A nondualistic economic ethic through innumerable daily repetitions of making loans available regularly and promoting the buying and selling of all services and commodities makes possible the massive economic transactions needed for capitalism.

At the background causal level, two components exist—a bureaucratic state and citizenship—as follows:

Bureaucratic state. The bureaucratic state is a crucial background for the legal and institutional underpinnings of capitalism. Specialized professional administrations are employed to manage and laws are made and applied by full-time professional jurists. A bureaucratic state provides the basis for a reliable system of banking, investment, property rights, and contracts through a rational and universally applied system of law courts.

Citizenship. Entrepreneurs emerge from the population of citizens as well as workers, jurists, administrators, and other professionals. Entrepreneurial activities and behaviors are reinforced by the religious foundations of Calvinism. Through the teachings of John Calvin, individuals are instructed that (1) God does not exist for man, but men for God; (2) originally man was pure and made in the image of God but has fallen from

continued

EXHIBIT   8.1   *concluded*

this state through his own voluntary act; (3) man can be saved only through the unmerited grace of God, as mediated to him through Christ; (4) man can do nothing to promote his own salvation, and no amount of good works can further it; (5) those predestined for salvation will be saved, since it is impossible for the elect to fall away from grace; (6) life should be not only one good work but many good works; and (7) man can prove his faith by engaging in worldly activity through an ethic for honest, hard work rather than the pursuit of self-pleasures.

Source: Adapted from R. Collins, *Max Weber: A Skeleton Key* (Beverly Hills, Calif.: Sage Publications, 1986) 83–94; M. Weber, *The Protestant Ethic and the Spirit of Capitalism*, trans. T. Parsons (New York: Charles Scribner's Sons, 1930), 112–26. Adapted by permission of Macmillan Publishing Co.

true synthesis and that his writings are schizophrenic. However, Weber's work influenced a number of individuals involved in social phenomenology, organization theory, conflict sociology, and economic growth theory.[4] As mentioned in Chapter 2, Schumpeter was familiar with and influenced by Weber's work.

Despite Weber's theory of entrepreneurial behavior, little if any research was conducted on the behavioral and psychological traits of entrepreneurs by organizational science researchers until Schumpeter argued in 1947 that entrepreneurs were individuals who possessed certain traits.[5] For example, Schumpeter noted that "it took an individual who possessed the unusual traits and will to found a private kingdom, a drive to overcome obstacles, a joy in creating, and satisfaction in exercising one's ingenuity to become an entrepreneur."[6] Research using the individual as the level of analysis began in an attempt to determine what these unusual traits are and how they are formed.

Orvis Collins, David Moore, and Darab Unwalla

The research team of Orvis Collins, David Moore, and Darab Unwalla, which was associated with the Bureau of Business and Economic Research at Michigan State University, interviewed 150 entrepreneurs involved in "light manufacturing" who owned businesses ranging in age from two to seventeen years. They concluded that entrepreneurs are driven by unresolved Oedipal problems.[7] Exhibit 8.2 describes the characteristics observed by Collins, Moore, and Unwalla.

Interestingly a recent study, which is depicted in Exhibit 8.3, indicates that present-day Japanese businessmen also experience Oedipal problems.

Generally the study by Collins, Moore, and Unwalla was not widely noticed by practitioners or cited by many researchers. However, a book by Collins and Moore that was published in 1970 was widely read by practicing managers and appears in many literature reviews.[8]

David McClelland

David McClelland, sponsored by the Center of Entrepreneurial Studies at Harvard University, linked Protestantism, the need for achievement (nAch), and

EXHIBIT 8.2 Key Characteristics of Entrepreneurs

1. Experiences difficult relations with authority. (The symbolic mother figure—the company—must not be dominated by a strong father.)
2. Is unable to perform well in the employment of others. (Success on the job brings on anxiety produced by a subconscious fear of invoking the jealous wrath of his father.)
3. Is comfortable only when "in charge" (His own company—symbolic mistress—allows him to act out his needs without incurring the wrath of jealous male authorities.)
4. Is uncomfortable with partnerships. (His business—symbolic "bad seductive mother"—must not be shared with a partner.)
5. Is able to accept failure and rise again. (The business—"bad mother"—helps him demonstrate his maleness. This is immoral and leads to anxiety. The need for punishment may bring on business failure, which results in relief from anxiety, thus producing successful comebacks.)

Source: Adapted from O. F. Collins, D. G. Moore, and D. B. Unwalla, *The Enterprising Man* (East Lansing, Mich.: Michigan State University Press, 1964); N. E. G. Robbins, "Entrepreneurial Assessment: Characteristics Which Differentiate Entrepreneurs, Intrapreneurs, and Managers" (Ph.D. diss., University of Minnesota, 1986).

EXHIBIT 8.3 The Oedipus Complex and Japanese Men

A mother and son live together in unhealthy intimacy, leading to violence and—sometimes—incest. Together, they bully father who dreads coming home from work.

It may sound like some Oedipal stage drama, a bit overwrought at that. But it's a daily tragedy endured by a small but growing number of Japanese families who psychiatrists say are paying a price for the country's economic miracle.

Millions of men became "economic animals" in Japan's postwar production fever, forsaking home life for unrelenting devotion to work. The resulting alienation between them and their families has sometimes had traumatic consequences.

One of the more bizarre outcomes was portrayed earlier this year in a book called *Father Can't Come Home Anymore!* The author, psychiatrist Toru Sekiya, runs a Tokyo clinic and night shelter for "salary men" who are terrified of returning to a home where they feel unwelcome.

"For many husbands, the home is just a place to sleep. It's always the company, the company . . .," Mr. Sekiya says in a recent interview. "In Europe and America, families have a personal life together when the husbands get home that's unrelated to work. You don't have that as much in Japan."

"In the United States, marriages start with the husband and wife," says Mr. Sekiya. "But in Japan, without a child, the husband and wife do not exist as a relationship."

However distant emotionally, that relationship worked well enough during Japan's high-growth 1950s and 1960s, when rebuilding the war-torn country was a national mission and pay increases and promotions were plentiful.

continued

EXHIBIT 8.3 *concluded*

> The workaholic dad was a family's pride and joy, even if he wasn't there. To a Japanese wife, a husband who came home from work promptly at 6 p.m. was as much a neighborhood embarrassment as a husband with a taste for late-night carousing might be to an American wife.
>
> Since the oil shocks of the 1970s, however, the Japanese economy has grown at a slower pace. Competition for a relatively static number of managerial posts has intensified. At the same time, outlandish land prices and other high costs have made life a round of struggles for many middle-management salary men.
>
> Exacerbating the situation, wives who traditionally have controlled the family budget are growing more independent. In the last 10 years, they have begun to establish their own separate bank accounts, Mr. Sekiya says.
>
> "The relationship between wife and husband has become a 'cold war,' with the wife and son in alliance against the father," Mr. Sekiya says.
>
> Ironically, the pressures on the haggard husband have grown only worse since the government has pushed Japanese to spend more leisure time on weekends, the doctors say. To many workaholic Japanese, that simply means more hours in the office on weekdays.
>
> Because authorities consider family-related trouble to be a "private matter," there has been little official effort to gauge the depth of the problem.
>
> Nonetheless, family problems such as home-avoidance syndrome have become so severe that they've made their way into several primetime television dramas. One recently portrayed a harried father who found solace only by drinking with the homeless in a park.

Source: "Workaholic Men in Japan Find They Can't Go Home At All," *Dallas Morning News,* 25 February 1991, C1.

economic development by hypothesizing that a psychological motive derived from family socialization intervened between Weber's Protestant work ethic and entrepreneurial behavior. McClelland argued that family socialization consisting mainly of child-rearing practices that stressed standards of excellence, maternal warmth, self-reliance, and low father dominance contributes to the development of nAch. McClelland further concluded that nAch is the key for entrepreneurial success.[9]

In developing a measure for nAch, McClelland believed that fantasy is the best way to assess motives and used the Thematic Apperception Test (TAT). The TAT requires subjects to write imaginative stories in response to a set of pictures. The stories are then content-analyzed for achievement imagery to obtain an nAch score.[10] By performing correlation studies in the laboratory, McClelland concluded that individuals with a high nAch, as determined by the TAT, tend to exhibit the following behavioral traits:

- Personal responsibility is taken for finding solutions to problems.
- Moderate achievement goals are set, and calculated risks are taken.
- Concrete feedback regarding performance is desired.[11]

While McClelland's research influenced a large number of subsequent researchers to use nAch as a distinguishing entrepreneurial behavioral characteristic, a definite link between achievement motivation and entrepreneurial success has not yet been established.[12] Furthermore, McClelland's research has been criticized by psychologists for his measurement of nAch, by economists for his analysis of economic development, and by researchers in entrepreneurship for his definition of *entrepreneur*.[13]

Everett Hagen

Everett Hagen, an economics professor at the Massachusetts Institute of Technology, developed a well-respected theory of social change that describes how economic growth begins.[14] Hagen argued that value systems different from those of the mainstream of society lead to unconventional patterns of behavior. In certain instances entrepreneurship becomes one of those unconventional patterns.

Hagen conceptualized that a society creates certain traditional values from its child-rearing practices. A particular segment of the population without those values tends to experience a deterioration in status, which causes a psychosocial disequilibrium leading to situations of (1) being rejected by society and (2) the development of low self-esteem. Anger and anxiety follow, and eventually the individual retreats from most normal behavior patterns. This period is an unstable state and may trigger certain personality transformations. For example, because old patterns of social behavior are not accepted, together with the fact that an individual's social group is not respected, the individual must find new, innovative modes of behavior in order to integrate with society. This innovative behavior may be manifested in creative, entrepreneurial activity. For example, members of a minority group may experience discriminatory treatment that prevents them from obtaining an established, higher status-bearing role in society. As a consequence, members of that minority group may have no other choice but to do something new—something that has not been done before.[15] According to Hagen, four types of events, which are described in Exhibit 8.4, can produce the process of status withdrawal that also may lead to creative, entrepreneurial activity.[16]

Peter Kilby

Peter Kilby, an economics professor at Wesleyan University, edited a text containing sixteen articles written by a variety of authors from the fields of economics, sociology, and psychology. These articles related entrepreneurship to the process of economic development and growth.[17] Following is a summary of the articles that appear in Kilby's text: (1) McClelland's research was criticized for his measurement of nAch and economic growth;[18] (2) Hagen's concept of how an individual's value system affects economic growth was well received;[19] (3) research seeking to develop personality profiles of the entrepreneur was criticized while research to study the behaviors and activities of entrepreneurs was

8.4 A Typology of Withdrawal Events That May Lead to Creative, Entrepreneurial Behavior

According to Hagen, a group of individuals within a society feels frustrated and humiliated when they experience one of the following types of status withdrawal. This frustration and humiliation cause a conflict within individuals that alters their home life in such a manner that the personalities of future generations are affected. At first, a retreatist personality is created, which eventually gives way to an innovative personality, which leads to creative, entrepreneurial activities.

Withdrawal Event	Description
Displacement by force	One group replaces another as the "controller" of a social order. The top elite may be displaced by force by either a rival group within the society or by an invasion from abroad.
Denigration of valued symbols	Contempt, scorn, or some other form of psychological ostracism is manifested by a high-prestige group toward a subordinate group because of distaste for some element in the role of the subordinate group.
Inconsistency of status symbols	As a society develops economically, certain members become financiers and have great economic power. The elite of the society then find it advantageous to go to the financiers for financial aid. While the financiers have an important status symbol—economic power—they are denied other elements of social recognition. The elites, who have become supplicants, economically cling to other claims of social superiority, and social discrimination continues. As a result both groups (the elites and the financiers) become frustrated. The financiers are denied the social status that traditionally has belonged to individuals of their economic position, while the elite are denied exclusive possession of the economic status that used to be part of the bundle of status symbols setting them apart. Accordingly neither group feels that its position is fully respected.
Nonacceptance in a new society	When a group migrates to a new society, their way of doing things is alien and is not accorded recognition.

Source: Adapted from E. E. Hagen, *On the Theory of Social Change* (Homewood, Ill.: Dorsey Press, 1962), 187–93.

encouraged;[20] (4) Schumpeter's dynamic model of entrepreneurship was considered superior to Weber's ideal-type static model for describing the relationship between entrepreneurship and economic growth;[21] (5) Weber's perspective was expanded to include cultural values, role expectations, and social sanctions as determining factors in entrepreneurial behavior;[22] and (6) a framework for fostering entrepreneuring in underdeveloped countries was suggested. The framework argues that, first, the overall environmental setting must provide stability and an adequate level of reward for private business initiative. Second, a well-functioning system of price signals that accurately reflects society's economic needs is required. Third, positive programs are needed to aid the emerging entrepreneur to upgrade critical skills, increase access to important technological and market knowledge, and benefit from better-quality, less-expensive factor inputs by means of improved institutional arrangements.[23] Kilby, after having reviewed research activities in entrepreneurship, stated that each researcher in entrepreneurship appears to have developed his or her own definition without building on the works of others. Kilby described these definitional attempts, which are depicted in Exhibit 8.5, as being similar to hunting the heffalump.[24]

RESEARCH ISSUES

Research relating the notion of entrepreneurship to behavioral aspects has been plagued with a number of problems. These problems include definitions regarding entrepreneurship, theory development, measurement of psychological concepts, methodological determinism, data-analytic techniques, and sample selection and sample size. Following is a brief discussion of five of these six problem areas. (Definitional problems regarding entrepreneurship were discussed in the preceding section and in Chapter 1.)

Theory Development

According to Kuhn, scientific inquiry begins with a paradigm that defines a set of problems for a community of scholars.[25] Each problem area is sufficiently novel to attract adherents; each problem area is open-ended to leave much to resolve; and each problem area is acknowledged as the foundation for further research. The shared paradigm is the basis for defining key research issues. A community of scholars emerges dedicated to research programs that articulate and specify the paradigm. A common language emerges, as do accepted modes and protocols of investigation. Progress is measured in terms of solved intellectual problems, the resolution of ambiguities in the paradigm, and increased precision.[26] Theory development in the behavioral perspective area of entrepreneurship,

EXHIBIT 8.5   Hunting the Heffalump

The search for the source of dynamic entrepreneurial performance has much in common with hunting the Heffalump. The Heffalump is a rather large and very important animal. He has been hunted by many individuals using various ingenious trapping devices, but no one so far has succeeded in capturing him. All who claim to have caught sight of him report that he is enormous, but they disagree on his particularities. Not having explored his current habitat with sufficient care, some hunters have used as bait their own favorite dishes and have then tried to persuade people that what they caught was a Heffalump. However, very few are convinced, and the search goes on.

Source: Peter Kilby, *Entrepreneurship and Economic Development* (New York: Free Press, 1971), 1. Kilby stated that he developed the notion of the Heffalump from A. A. Milne's *Winnie-the-Pooh* and *The House at Pooh Corner*.

however, has not followed Kuhn's approach. Instead, theory has consisted mainly of anecdotal stories represented by normative or "how to" publications.[27]

Measurement of Psychological Concepts

Certain difficulties are inherent in the measuring of psychological concepts or constructs. Exhibit 8.6 describes the meaning of a construct and how it relates to scientific inquiry. Many research studies that involve the relationship between entrepreneurship and psychological constructs have inadequate construct validities and reliabilities (see Exhibit 8.6 for an explanation of these terms), or the researcher has failed to report these measures.[28]

A major problem in measuring a psychological construct is that visual references do not exist for many of the constructs. Exhibit 8.7 provides an example of this problem.

Methodological Determinism

Methodological determinism is a situation in which the methodological tools available determine the ways that researchers think and develop their theories and research questions. For example, Kaplan noted that when the only tool that an individual possesses is a hammer it is surprising how many objects appear to be a nail.[29]

EXHIBIT 8.6   Constructs and Scientific Inquiry

Researchers use theories in an attempt to explain phenomena. These theories consist of concepts or constructs. For example, both need for achievement and locus of control are psychological constructs. A construct is defined in terms of other constructs by *conceptual definitions*. The definition may take the form of an equation that precisely expresses the particular construct, such as the equation in physics that states that energy equals the mass of an object times the speed of light squared ($E = mc^2$). Alternatively the relationship may be only imprecisely stated, which is typically the case in social science research. An *operational definition* describes how the construct is to be measured and specifies the activities that the researcher must complete in order to assign a value to the construct.

Certain statistical techniques can be utilized to determine whether the operational definition actually measures the construct of interest. For example, *construct validity* is a statistical form that tells the researcher what is being measured. Another statistical form, *reliability*, informs the researcher how consistent his or her research activities have been in measuring the construct of interest.

Source: Adapted from G. A. Churchill, Jr., *Marketing Research: Methodological Foundations* (New York: Dryden Press, 1987). For a more detailed discussion of construct validity and reliability measures, see J. P. Peter and G. A. Churchill, Jr., "The Relationship among Research Design Choices and Psychometric Properties of Rating Scales: A Meta Analysis," *Journal of Marketing Research* 23 (1986): 1–10.

8.7   Measuring Psychological Constructs

Consider the following measurement procedure. Dale has brown eyes while Paul has blue eyes; therefore, Dale is taller than Paul. You would probably reply that "the color of a person's eyes has nothing to do with their height and you have not correctly measured the height of Dale and Paul." Perhaps a better procedure for measuring height would be to use a yardstick or to stand Dale and Paul side by side and compare their height. What if I measured both Dale and Paul by asking them how tall they are? You probably would not have an objection unless I reported that Dale was taller while your observation indicated that Paul was the taller.

The interesting thing about most psychological constructs is that visual comparisons cannot be relied upon to either confirm or refute a measure. The researcher cannot see a personality characteristic such as opportunism or a behavioral characteristic such as locus of control. Their magnitude, however, must be inferred from the researcher's measurement. The ability to assess certain characteristics relies heavily on an understanding of measurement, measurement error, and the notions of construct validity and reliability.

Source: Adapted from W. S. Torgerson, *Theory and Methods of Scaling* (New York: John Wiley, 1958), 1–11.

Data-Analytic Techniques

The data-analytic techniques employed in the majority of entrepreneurship–behavioral perspective studies consist of only univariate and bivariate statistics. We are not suggesting that one data-analytic technique is superior to another. For example, in descriptive or exploratory studies, univariate statistics (means, modes, percentages, or standard deviations) may be sufficient. However, if the interrelationship of two or more variables is the object of interest, then a multivariate analysis may be in order. For example, changes in the knowledge of leadership were improved when researchers switched from using simple correlational techniques to the use of structural modeling techniques, such as LISREL.[30] In essence, a more appropriate data analysis may yield what Kuhn has described as the intersection between theory building and theory testing.[31]

Sample Selection and Size

A criticism of research involving the behavioral aspects of entrepreneurship is whether researchers are studying the same phenomena because of the wide diversity of individuals selected as study participants. For example, participants have included third graders participating in simulated economies, university students with high expectations of starting their own businesses, nonbusiness and business majors in universities, farmers in India, managers of branch banks, sales managers, franchise operators, chain motel operators, real estate brokers, and individuals who have started businesses.[32] Furthermore, one researcher reported that in a survey of sixty-three studies involving behavioral aspects and entrepreneurship, thirty-four (54 percent) employed samples of fewer than thirty subjects.[33] In essence, the wide disparity of study participants and small sample sizes tend to make study findings and their generalizability suspect.

*   *   *   *

This chapter concludes with two articles. The first article, written by James Carland, Frank Hoy, William Boulton, and JoAnn Carland, establishes a conceptual framework for the differentiation of entrepreneurs from small business owners. The second article, written by William Gartner, states that while the article written by Carland et al. was intended to achieve a greater precision in defining *entrepreneurship* those authors actually increased the ambiguity in what is already a definitional dilemma. Gartner argues that the article by Carland et al. focuses on the trait approach, which has been unfruitful. Gartner suggests that behavioral approaches will be more productive for future research in entrepreneurship and posits that the primary phenomenon of entrepreneurship is the creation of organizations, that is, the process by which organizations come into existence.

ARTICLE 8.1 **DIFFERENTIATING ENTREPRENEURS FROM SMALL BUSINESS OWNERS: A CONCEPTUALIZATION**
by James Carland, Frank Hoy, William Boulton, and JoAnn Carland

Schumpeter (1934) was among the first to identify the entrepreneur as an entity worthy of study, distinct from business owners and managers. He described entrepreneurs as individuals whose function was to carry out new combinations of means of production. To Schumpeter, this function was fundamental to economic development. Entrepreneurs, therefore, warranted study independent of capitalists and business managers. Today there continues to be an implicit assumption that the entrepreneur contributes disproportionately to the economy of a nation, yet little has been done to isolate this individual for further analysis. Extending the theory of Schumpeter, who argued that an entrepreneur was distinguishable both by type and by conduct, two conceptualizations are proposed in this paper: one for differentiating entrepreneurs from small business owner/managers and the second for differentiating entrepreneurial ventures from small businesses.

Entrepreneurship: The Contribution

Because the definition of entrepreneurship denotes the creation of some combination that did not previously exist, entrepreneurship often is equated with small business ownership and management. The small business sector has received attention in the economic and management literature because of its significance to the economy. The Small Business Administration (U.S. Government Printing Office, 1982) has compiled a list of statistics that dramatically demonstrate the impact of small business on the nation's economy:

1. There are 14.7 million businesses in the United States, of which 3.2 million are farms.

2. Approximately 99.7 percent of these businesses are considered small by the SBA's size standards for loan applicants.

3. The small businesses identified above account for: 38 percent of the gross national product; 44 percent of the gross business product; and 47 percent of total U.S. business employment.

4. The small business sector identified above accounted for the vast majority of the net new jobs created by business between 1969 and 1976.

Although there is no uniform definition of a small firm, the statistics above relate to businesses that fall within SBA guidelines as being small. The Small Business Act states that "a small business concern shall be deemed to be one which is independently owned and operated and which is not dominant in its field of operation" (U.S. Small Business Administration, 1978).

As the SBA statistics demonstrate, small business research is justified because of sheer numbers. It must be noted that small firms are treated as a separate sector, not because they are cohesive and homogeneous, but because there are certain common management limitations due to extremely limited resources as compared with the "deep pockets" or resources of larger corporate organizations. Research often is directed toward the implications of public policy developments or the impact of environmental variables on the small business sector (Chilton & Weidenbaum, 1982; Coodman, 1981; Legler & Hoy, 1982; Robinson, 1982).

Although small business is a significant segment of the American economy, the entrepreneurial portion of that segment may wield a disproportionate influence. If entrepreneurship can be viewed as incorporating innovation and growth, the most fertile ground for management research may be entrepreneurs and entrepreneurial ventures. Entrepreneurship has been found to extend beyond small businesses: some large corporations have been described as engaging in entrepreneurial behavior (Ronstadt, 1982; Schollhammer, 1982; Shils, 1982). Additionally, a person who owns an enterprise is not necessarily an entrepreneur (Martin, 1982). Clearly, an overlap exists of entrepreneurship with the small business sector. The concern of this paper is: If entrepreneurs exist as entities distinct from small and large organizations and if entrepreneurial activity is a fundamental contributor to economic development, on what bases may entrepreneurs be separated from nonentrepreneurial managers in order for the phenomenon of entrepreneurship to be studied and understood?

Literature Review: The "Entrepreneur"

One of the earliest definitions of an entrepreneur was that of Cantillon (circa 1700) who described the individual as a rational decision maker who assumed the risk and provided management for the firm (Kilby, 1971). Schumpeter (1934) credited Mill (1848) with bringing the term into general use among economists.

Mill, also, believed that the key factor in distinguishing a manager from an entrepreneur was the bearing of risk. Schumpeter, however, countered that risk bearing was inherent in ownership and that entrepreneurs, the combiners, were not necessarily owners; therefore, the risk-bearing propensity would not be a trait. Martin (1982) believes that capital risk is a function of the investor. Further, Brockhaus (1980) cast doubt on the validity of the risk-taking propensity as an entrepreneurial characteristic with his descriptive work. Brockhaus found no statistical difference in the risk preference patterns of a group of entrepreneurs and a group of managers. It should be noted that Brockhaus used the establishment of a business as the criterion for inclusion of the participants in the entrepreneur group. Omitting business ownership as a designation of entrepreneurship permits both the inclusion of corporate entrepreneurs and the elimination of the risk-bearing characteristic. However, many writers have asserted and continue to assert that risk bearing is a prime factor in the entrepreneurial character and function (McClelland, 1961; Palmer, 1971; Timmons, 1978; Welsh & White, 1981).

Numerous normative and descriptive studies have supported various sets of personality characteristics of entrepreneurship. For example, Brockhaus (1982) has presented an excellent historic overview of the definitions of entrepreneurs. Perhaps the most important factor from a societal perspective is the characteristic of innovation. Schumpeter (1934) believed that innovation was the central characteristic of the entrepreneurial endeavor. His emphasis on this point is revealed in his declaration that one behaves as an entrepreneur only when carrying out innovations. McClelland (1961) stated that energetic and/or novel instrumental activity was a key factor in entrepreneurial activity. Martin (1982) stressed that entrepreneurial creativity is different from literary or artistic creativity in that the entrepreneur does not innovate by creating ideas but by exploiting the value of ideas. [Exhibit 8.8] displays a sampling of entrepreneurial characteristics appearing in the literature.

The characteristics listed in [Exhibit 8.8] represent attitudes and behaviors that may be manifested by entrepreneurs. Demographic characteristics such as birth order, sex, or marital status have been examined in certain of the studies cited and in various other investigations (Vaught & Hoy, 1981). They have been excluded from the present conceptualization because of the inability of a prospective entrepreneur to alter those variables in order to increase his/her probability of success.

Schein's (1974) work on career anchors clarifies some of the differences in individual approaches to careers. In studying M.I.T. graduates' careers, he found that five types of job directions were prevalent. He described these as career anchors that included managerial competence, technical/functional competence, security need, independence need, and creativity. The entrepreneurs made up his creative group.

> The group concerned with creativity is the most interesting in that it contains the entrepreneurs. Four of these men are successful in that they have been able to launch enterprises which have succeeded and have brought to their founders either fame or fortune or both. The kinds of activities vary greatly—but they all have in common

that they are clear extensions of the person and his identity is heavily involved in the vehicle which is created (1974, p. 19).

It is difficult to sketch a profile of an entrepreneur from the attitudinal and behavioral characteristics listed in [Exhibit 8.8]. It may be more appropriate to accept Vesper's (1980) view of a continuum along which several "types" of entrepreneurs exist. The question then becomes: Which characteristics and what level

EXHIBIT 8.8   Characteristics of Entrepreneurs

Date	Author(s)	Characteristic(s)	Normative	Empirical
1848	Mill	Riskbearing	x	
1917	Weber	Source of formal authority	x	
1934	Schumpeter	Innovation, initiative	x	
1954	Sutton	Desire for responsibility	x	
1959	Hartman	Source of formal authority	x	
1961	McClelland	Risk taking, need for achievement		x
1963	Davids	Ambition; desire for independence; responsibility; self-confidence		x
1964	Pickle	Drive/mental; human relations; communication ability; technical knowledge		x
1971	Palmer	Risk measurement		x
1971	Hornaday & Aboud	Need for achievement; autonomy; aggression; power; recognition; innovative/independent		x
1973	Winter	Need for power	x	
1974	Borland	Internal locus of control		x
1974	Liles	Need for achievement		x
1977	Gasse	Personal value orientation		x
1978	Timmons	Drive/self-confidence; goal oriented; moderated risk taker; internal locus of control; creativity/innovation	x	x
1980	Sexton	Energetic/ambitious; positive reaction to setbacks		x
1981	Welsh & White	Need to control; responsibility seeker; self-confidence/drive; challenge taker; moderate risk taker		x
1982	Dunkelberg & Cooper	Growth oriented; independence oriented; craftsman oriented		x

of intensity do the entrepreneurs possess at various points on the continuum? Vesper described the entrepreneur as an individual but implied that he or she could be found working with others in larger organizations. His first type, the "Solo Self-Employed Individual," is essentially what is treated here as the small business owner/operator, but not truly an entrepreneur in the Schumpeterian sense because a new combination is not created.

A major obstacle preventing the attribution of characteristics to entrepreneurs in firms along Vesper's continuum is the great diversity of sources from which the authors cited in [Exhibit 8.8] derived the identified characteristics. Those citations that are indicated in [Exhibit 8.8] as normative are generally anecdotal, describing either the authors' personal impressions or conclusions drawn from reading the works of others. The empirical studies draw from quite diverse samples. McClelland's (1961) entrepreneurs were in fact business executives representing various functional specialities: general management, sales and marketing, finance, engineering, and personnel. Senior marketing managers were found to have the highest need for achievement. More frequently, samples of small business owners are chosen for study (Hornaday & Aboud, 1971; Pickle, 1964). The assumption underlying these selections is that the entrepreneur was the individual who brought the resources together and initiated the venture. Successful entrepreneurs are defined as those whose enterprises have survived some period of time, perhaps two years. The question then is: Are the characteristics listed in [Exhibit 8.8] those of entrepreneurs, of small business owners, or of some mixture that may or may not be capable of demonstrating the entrepreneurial function of economic development?

The Entrepreneurial Venture

A considerable body of literature has been built up treating the stages of organizational development (Vozikis, 1979). This growth-orientation, in and of itself, would represent an entrepreneurial characteristic to some scholars (Dunkelberg & Cooper, 1982). Yet, as Vesper (1980) has pointed out in his continuum of venture types, many business owners never intend for their businesses to grow beyond what they consider to be a controllable size. It is necessary to go beyond the notion of corporate life cycles and stages to conceive of an entrepreneurial venture.

Glueck (1980) distinguished between entrepreneurial ventures and what he termed family business ventures by focusing on strategic practices. Strategic management in Glueck's family business must emphasize preferences and need of the family as opposed to those of the business. When in conflict, the needs of the family will override those of the business. Glueck cited the oft observed family business strategies to remain independent and to provide outlets for family investment and careers for family members as an example of conflict. In contrast, an entrepreneurial strategist would opt for pursuit of growth and maintenance of the firm's distinctive competence through obtaining the best personnel available. Glueck's distinction is that strategic practices oriented toward the best interests of the firm are observed in entrepreneurial ventures.

An entrepreneurial venture can be identified by the strategic behavior of the firms. Schumpeter (1934) suggested that five categories of behavior can be observed that are characteristic of an entrepreneurial venture. These categories, listed below, are supported by Vesper (1980) and can be used as the basis for classification criteria.

1. Introduction of new goods
2. Introduction of new methods of production
3. Opening of new markets
4. Opening of new sources of supply
5. Industrial reorganization

Because of the ambiguity of criterion 4, it is not employed in this study. If any one of the remaining four criteria is observed in a firm's strategic actions, then that firm can be classified as an entrepreneurial venture. These criteria do permit the classification of a new small traditional firm as entrepreneurial if that firm represents an original entry into a market. Again, the determining factor would be whether organizational activity in any of the four criteria resulted in a new combination, indicating innovative behavior. Additionally, these criteria permit medium and large firms to be classified either as entrepreneurial ventures themselves or as the instigators of entrepreneurial ventures.

Schumpeter's criteria represent evidence of innovative strategies or innovative strategic postures. The criteria also emphasize the behavior of a firm consistent with its own best interests. This perspective is congruent with the development and pursuit of a distinctive competence prescribed by Vesper (1980) as a requirement for an entrepreneurial venture.

A Conceptual Distinction Between Small Business and Entrepreneurship

From the foregoing discussion, it can be seen that, although there is considerable overlap between small business and entrepreneurship, the concepts are not the same. All new ventures are not entrepreneurial in nature. Entrepreneurial firms may begin at any size level, but key on growth over time. Some new small firms may grow, but many will remain small businesses for their organizational lifetimes.

The critical factor proposed here to distinguish entrepreneurs from nonentrepreneurial managers and, in particular, small business owners is innovation. The entrepreneur is characterized by a preference for creating activity, manifested by some innovative combination of resources for profit. Drawing further on the characteristics outlined in [Exhibit 8.8], it is suggested that analyses of prospective entrepreneurial characteristics examine such traits as need for achievement (perhaps more appropriately labeled goal-orientation), internal locus of control, need for independence, need for responsibility, and need for power. Although a risk-taking propensity is mentioned frequently in the literature, Schumpeter noted that it is inherent in ownership rather than entrepreneurship. Further,

Brockhaus (1980) supported Schumpeter with empirical results demonstrating that risk-taking behavior cannot be used as a distinguishing characteristic of entrepreneurship.

From this analysis, it is suggested that many published studies may be misleading in their conclusions. Economic theorists propose that the entrepreneur is essential to economic development (Schumpeter, 1934; Williams, 1981). Yet studies of entrepreneurship neglect to distinguish adequately between entrepreneurs and other business managers, primarily small business owners. Erroneous descriptions of entrepreneurs can jeopardize investigations in a variety of ways. Specifically, analyses of how entrepreneurs make their fundamental contributions to economic development cannot draw sound conclusions if the case studies are not entrepreneurial.

To guide future studies, the following definitions are proposed to distinguish among the entities discussed in the paper.

Small business venture: A small business venture is any business that is independently owned and operated, not dominant in its field, and does not engage in any new marketing or innovative practices.

Entrepreneurial venture: An entrepreneurial venture is one that engages in at least one of Schumpeter's four categories of behavior: that is, the principal goals of an entrepreneurial venture are profitability and growth and the business is characterized by innovative strategic practices.

Small business owner: A small business owner is an individual who establishes and manages a business for the principal purpose of furthering personal goals. The business must be the primary source of income and will consume the majority of one's time and resources. The owner perceives the business as an extension of his or her personality, intricately bound with family needs and desires.

Entrepreneur: An entrepreneur is an individual who establishes and manages a business for the principal purposes of profit and growth. The entrepreneur is characterized principally by innovative behavior and will employ strategic management practices in the business.

Source: This article excerpted from J. Carland, F. Hoy, W. Boulton, and J. Carland, "Differentiating Entrepreneurs from Small Business Owners: A Conceptualization," *Academy of Management Review* 9 (1984): 354–59. Used by permission of the authors and the *Academy of Management Review*.

ARTICLE 8.2 **"WHO IS AN ENTREPRENEUR?" IS THE WRONG QUESTION**
by William B. Gartner

My own personal experience was that for ten years we ran a research center in entrepreneurial history, for ten years we tried to define the entrepreneur. We never succeeded. Each of us had some notion of it—what he thought was, for his purposes, a useful definition. And I don't think you're going to get farther than that. (Cole, 1969)

How can we know the dancer from the dance? (Yeats, 1956)

Arthur Cole's words have taken on the deeper tones of prophecy. Recent reviews of the entrepreneurship literature have found few changes in this dilemma in the sixteen years since Cole's statement. Brockhaus and Horwitz's (1985) review of the psychology of the entrepreneur concluded that "The literature appears to support the argument that there is no generic definition of the entrepreneur, or if there is we do not have the psychological instruments to discover it at this time. Most of the attempts to distinguish between entrepreneurs and small business owners or managers have discovered no significant differentiating features." Other scholars have concurred that a common definition of the entrepreneur remains elusive (Carsrud, Olm, & Edy, 1985; Sexton & Smilor, 1985; Wortman, 1985).

Cole's early doubts about whether the entrepreneur could be defined have not stopped researchers from attempting to do so. Much research in the entrepreneurship field has focused on the person of the entrepreneur, asking the question, Why do certain individuals start firms when others, under similar conditions, do not? Asking *why* has led us to answering with *who*: Why did X start a venture? Because X has a certain inner quality or qualities. This focus can be identified in any research which seeks to identify traits that differentiate entrepreneurs from nonentrepreneurs: need for achievement (Komives, 1972; McClelland, 1961; McClelland & Winter, 1969), locus of control (Brockhaus, 1980a; Brockhaus & Nord, 1979; Hull, Bosley, & Udell, 1982; Liles, 1974), risk taking (Brockhaus, 1980b; Hull, Bosley, & Udell, 1982; Liles, 1974; Mancuso, 1975; Palmer, 1971), values (DeCarlo & Lyons, 1979; Hornaday & Aboud, 1971; Hull, Bosley, & Udell, 1980; Komives, 1972), age (Cooper, 1973; Howell, 1972; Mayer & Goldstein, 1961) are but a few examples. X starts a venture because of qualities that made X who (s)he is. Entrepreneurship research has long asked, "Who is an entrepreneur?"

I believe the attempt to answer the question "Who is an entrepreneur?" which focuses on the traits and personality characteristics of entrepreneurs, will neither lead us to a definition of the entrepreneur nor help us to understand the phenomenon of entrepreneurship. This search for characteristics and traits of the entrepreneur is labeled in this article as the trait approach. In this approach the entrepreneur is the basic unit of analysis and the entrepreneur's traits and characteristics are the key to explaining entrepreneurship as a phenomenon, since the entrepreneur "causes" entrepreneurship. The purpose of the first part of this article is to look at research based on the trait view of entrepreneurship and to show that this view alone is inadequate to explain the phenomenon of entrepreneurship. Another approach is needed to help us refocus our thoughts on entrepreneurship. That approach—the behavioral approach—will be presented and the two approaches will be compared and contrasted.

The Trait Approach

In the trait approach the entrepreneur is assumed to be a particular personality type, a fixed state of existence, a describable species that one might find a picture of in a field guide, and the point of much entrepreneurship research has been to enumerate a set of characteristics describing this entity known as the entrepreneur. One indication of the tenacity of this point of view—i.e., once an entrepreneur, always an entrepreneur, since an entrepreneur is a personality type, a state of being that doesn't go away—can be seen in the selection of samples of "entrepreneurs" in many well-regarded research studies [Exhibit 8.9]. In many studies "entrepreneurs" are sampled many years after having started their firms. Hornaday and Aboud (1971), for example, chose to study individuals who headed firms. These "entrepreneurs" were interviewed anywhere from two to sixteen years after start-up. Is the owner/manager of an ongoing firm two or ten or even fifteen years after start-up an entrepreneur? If this individual is included in a sample of entrepreneurs, what does that imply about the researcher's definition of the entrepreneur, and what will the resulting data reflect?

[Exhibit 8.9] is an attempt to organize concisely much of the major literature on the entrepreneur and entrepreneurship. It represents a succumbing to the grand temptation that haunts many writers and researchers in the entrepreneurship field: if we could just systematically go back and extract, categorize, and organize what has already been discovered about the entrepreneur, we will return with the pieces of a puzzle which we can then fit together into the big picture, and the entrepreneur will appear defined on the page. [Exhibit 8.9] is most emphatically not the big picture. Instead [Exhibit 8.9] shows:

(1) that many (and often vague) definitions of the entrepreneur have been used (in many studies the entrepreneur is never defined);

(2) there are few studies that employ the same definition;

(3) that lack of basic agreement as to "who an entrepreneur is" has led to the selection of samples of "entrepreneurs" that are hardly homogeneous. This lack of homogeneity occurs not only among the various samples listed, but actually *within* single samples. For many of the samples it could be said that variation *within* the sample is more significant, i.e., it could tell us more than variation between the sample and the general population.

(4) that a startling number of traits and characteristics have been attributed to the entrepreneur, and a "psychological profile" of the entrepreneur assembled from these studies would portray someone larger than life, full of contradictions, and, conversely, someone so full of traits that (s)he would have to be a sort of generic "Everyman."

Behavioral and Trait Approaches to Entrepreneurship

I think the study of the entrepreneur is actually one step removed from the primary phenomenon of entrepreneurship—the creation of organizations, the process by which new organizations come into existence (Vesper, 1982). This behavioral approach views the creation of an organization as a contextual event, the outcome of many influences. The entrepreneur is part of the complex process of new venture creation. This approach to the study of entrepreneurship treats the organization as the primary level of analysis and the individual is viewed in

EXHIBIT   8.9   Definitions, Samples, and Characteristics of Entrepreneurs

Author(s)	Type*	Definition	Sample	Characteristics
Brockhaus (1980)	E	. . . an entrepreneur is defined as a major owner and manager of a business venture not employed elsewhere. (p. 510)	31 individuals who, within the three months prior to the study, had ceased working for their employers and at the time of the study owned as well as managed business ventures. These businesses (type unspecified) were licensed by St. Louis County Missouri during the months of August and September 1975.	Risk-taking propensity
Cole (1959)	N	. . . the purposeful activity (including an integrated sequence of decision) of an individual or group of individuals, undertaken to initiate, maintain, or aggrandize a profit-oriented business unit for the production or distribution of economic goods and services. (p. 7)		
Collins and Moore (1970)	E	We distinguish between organization builders who create new and independent firms and those who perform entrepreneurial functions within already established organizations. Perhaps we are, after all, thinking of the entrepreneur in the way Schumpeter viewed him: "everyone is an entrepreneur only when he actually 'carries out new combinations,' and loses that character as soon as he has built up his business." (p. 10)	Owners of 110 Michigan manufacturing firms established between 1945 and 1958 with 20 or more employees. Interviews were from 2 to 16 years after start-up.	Parents' occupation, education, previous job satisfaction, social attitudes
Cooper and Dunkelberg (1981)	E	This paper reports upon what we believe to be the largest and most varied sample of entrepreneurs studied to date. The findings are from a survey of 1805 owner-managers.	1805 members of National Federation of Independent Business, all types of industries/businesses started pre-1941 to 1979	Parents, immigrants, education, number of previous jobs, age

continued

* (N) Normative, (E) Empirical

EXHIBIT   8.9   *continued*

Author(s)	Type	Definition	Sample	Characteristics
Davids (1963)	E	Founders of new businesses (p. 3)	521 owners of firms in Georgia and Texas. Firms were 1 to 10 years old, in manufacturing, retail, wholesale, construction and service.	Education, number of children, religious, sports and club affiliations
DeCarlo and Lyons (1979)	E	None given	Random selection of 122 individuals from a pooled listing of female entrepreneurs drawn from the business and manufacturing directories of several Mid-Atlantic states, from directories of women business owners, and from directories of minority-owned firms.	Age, marriage rate, education, previous entrepreneurial effort, regimentation, means of starting, achievement, autonomy, aggression, independence, leadership, support, conformity
Draheim (1972)	E	Entrepreneurship—the act of founding a new company where none existed before. Entrepreneur is the person and entrepreneurs are the small group of persons who are new company founders. The term is also used to indicate that the founders have some significant ownership stake in the business (they are not only employees) and that their intention is for the business to grow and prosper beyond the self-employment stage. (p. 1)	Survey of other studies on technical companies from Buffalo (42), Palo Alto (265) and Twin Cities (90).	Credibility, fear of losing job, prior work experience, "track record," degree of "state of the art technology"
Durand (1975)	E	None given	27 male and 8 female participants from the black community of a large Midwestern metropolitan area. All 35 were either owners or operators of businesses (type and age unspecified) or were seriously considering entering business at the conclusion of the course (p.79)	Achievement motivation, locus of control, training

continued

<u>EXHIBIT</u> 8.9   *continued*

Author(s)	Type	Definition	Sample	Characteristics
Ely and Hess (1937)	N	The person or group of persons who assume the task and responsibility of combining the factors of production into a business organization and keeping this organization in operation . . . he commands the industrial forces, and upon him rests the responsibility for their success or failure. (p. 113)		
Gomolka (1977)	E	None given	A nationwide mail questionnaire completed by the owners of minority business organizations. 644 sampled, 220 usable responses. All types of industries/businesses. Mean age of business was 16.1 years.	Sex, age, ethnicity, education, parents' work and social background
Gould (1969)	E	None given	119 boys attending high school in Seattle, Washington who had juvenile court records (p. 712)	Delinquent associations, perception of opportunity, social class, achievement motivation
Hartman (1959)	N	A distinction between manager and entrepreneur in terms of their relationship to formal authority in the industrial organization. . . . The entrepreneur may justify his formal authority independently or he may describe it as delegated from others, notably from the stockholders. But within the organization he alone is the source of all formal authority. Management is defined residually as "not being the source of all authority." The borderline between the entrepreneur and the manager is thus relatively precise. (p. 450–51)		

continued

EXHIBIT   8.9   *continued*

Author(s)	Type	Definition	Sample	Characteristics
Hisrich and O'Brien (1981)	E	None given	21 female entrepreneurs in greater Boston area in service and construction businesses	Self discipline and perseverance, desire to succeed, action orientation, goal orientation, energy level
Hornaday and Aboud (1971)	E	The "successful entrepreneur" was defined as a man or woman who started a business where there was none before, who had at least 8 employees and who had been established for at least 5 years.	60 entrepreneurs from East Coast in manufacturing, sales, and service businesses. No industry specified.	Need for achievement, autonomy, aggression, recognition, independence leadership, regimentation, family background, power, innovative tendencies
Hornaday and Bunker (1970)	E	. . . the "successful" entrepreneur was an individual who had started a business, building it where no previous business had been functioning, and continuing for a period of at least 5 years to the present profit-making structure . . . with 15 or more employees. (p. 50)	20 individuals from Boston area. Manufacturing and service businesses at least 5 years old.	Need for achievement, intelligence, creativity, energy level, taking initiative, self-reliance, leadership, desire for money, recognition desire, accomplishment drive, power, affiliation, tolerance of uncertainty
Howell (1972)	E	Entrepreneurship—the act of founding a new company where none existed before. Entrepreneur is the person and entrepreneurs are the small group of persons who are new company founders. The term is also used to indicate that the founders have some significant ownership stake in the business (they are not only employees) and that their intention is for the business to grow and prosper beyond the self-employment stage. (p. 1)	12 founders of semi-conductor companies in Palo Alto area. Average age of companies was 5 years.	Age, marital status, outside activities, educational level, number of previous jobs, previous job pushes, influences

continued

$\overline{\text{E X H I B I T}}$ 8.9 *continued*

Author(s)	Type	Definition	Sample	Characteristics
Hull, Bosley, and Udell (1980)	E	A person who organizes and manages a business undertaking assuming the risk for the sake of profit. For present purposes, this standard definition will be extended to include those individuals who purchase or inherit an existing business with the intention of (and effort toward) expanding it. (p. 11)	57 owners or partial owners of business (type and age unspecified). 31 of the 57 had helped create the business or had been involved with the creating of a business in the past.	Interest in "money or fame," social desirability, task preferences, locus of control, risk propensity, creativity, achievement
Lachman (1980)	E	The entrepreneur is perceived as a person who uses a new combination of production factors to produce the first brand in an industry.	29 males who started at least one new enterprise in Israel which was the first in the industry. (Type and age not specified).	Age, years in Israel, education, father's occupation, achievement motivation, achievement orientation
Lavington (1922)	N	In modern times the entrepreneur assumes many forms. He may be a private business man, a partnership, a joint stock company, a cooperative society, a municipality or similar body. (p. 19)		
Leibenstein (1968)	N	By routine entrepreneurship we mean the activities involved in coordinating and carrying on a well-established, going concern in which the parts of the production function in use (and likely alternatives to current use) are well known and which operates in well established and clearly defined markets. By N-entrepreneurship we mean the activities necessary to create or carry on an enterprise where not all the markets are well established or clearly defined and/or in which the relevant parts of the production function are not completely known. (p. 73)		

continued

EXHIBIT 8.9 *continued*

Author(s)	Type	Definition	Sample	Characteristics
Liles (1974)	N	We have examined the entrepreneur who is involved in substantial ventures and have considered what we found in light of traditional thinking that he is a special type of individual—somehow an unusual and uncommon man—a man apart. It probably is true that very successful entrepreneurs *become* men apart. But, at the beginning, when they make the decision to start an entrepreneurial career, they are in most respects very much like many other ambitious, striving individuals. (p. 14)		
Litzinger (1965)	E	The distinction is drawn between "entrepreneurs" who are goal and action oriented as contrasted to "managers" who carry out policies and procedures in achieving the goals. . . . Owners of mom and pop motels appear as the entrepreneurial type who have invested their own capital and operate a business. (p. 268)	15 mom and pop owner-operators of motels (age unspecified) in Northern Arizona along Highway 66.	Risk preference, independence, leadership, recognition, support, conformity, benevolence, structure, consideration
McClelland (1961)	E	. . . someone who exercises some control over the means of production and produces more than he can consume in order to sell (or exchange) it for individual (or household) income. . . . In practice such people turned out to be traders, independent artisans and firm operators (p. 65)	Middle level managers from Harvard and MIT executive programs, General Electric unit managers, managers from Turkey, Italy, Poland, Indian mechanics.	Achievement, optimism, affiliation, power, conscientiousness, asceticism, belief in achieved status, market morality
Mescon and Montanari (1981)	E	Entrepreneurs are, by definition, founders of new businesses.	31 real estate brokers who owned and operated their own firms in north central region of the United States. Age of firms not specified.	Achievement, autonomy, dominance, endurance, order, locus of control

continued

$\overline{\text{EXHIBIT}}$ 8.9 *continued*

Author(s)	Type	Definition	Sample	Characteristics
Palmer (1971)	N	. . . the entrepreneurial function involves primarily risk measurement and risk taking within a business organization. Furthermore, the successful entrepreneur is that individual who can correctly interpret the risk situation and then determine policies which will minimize the risk involved. . . . Thus, the individual who can correctly measure the risk situation, but is unable to minimize the risk, would not be defined as an entrepreneur. (p. 38)		
Say (1816)	N	The agent who unites all means of production and who finds in the value of the products . . . the re-establishment of the entire capital he employs, and the value of the wages, the interest and the rent which he pays, as well as the profits belonging to himself. (p. 28–29)		
Schrage (1965)	E	None given	22 R&D companies, less than 10 years old, in service, consulting, and manufacturing.	Veridical perception, achievement motivation, power motivation, awareness of impaired performance under tension
Schumpeter (1934)	N	. . . entrepreneurship, as defined, essentially, consists in doing things that are not generally done in the ordinary course of business routine, it is essentially a phenomenon that comes under the wider aspect of leadership. (p. 254)		
Stauss (1944)	N	This paper is an argument to advance the proposition that the *firm* is the *entrepreneur.*		

continued

EXHIBIT   8.9   *concluded*

Author(s)	Type	Definition	Sample	Characteristics
Thorne and Ball (1981)	E	None given	51 founders of smaller manufacturing firms and firms servicing these companies. Average age of business was 11 years.	Age, number of previous ventures, education, family background
Wainer and Rubin (1969)	E	The entrepreneur in McClelland's scheme is "the man who organizes the firm (the business unit) and/or increases its productive capacity." (p. 178)	51 technically based service and manufacturing companies that were spinoffs from MIT. 4–10 years old.	Achievement, power, affiliation
Welsch and Young (1982)	E	None given	53 owners of small businesses. Average size of 10 full time employees and 4 part time employees. All types of industries and businesses. (No age given.)	Locus of control, Machiavellianism, self-esteem, risk taking, openness to innovation, rigidity, government regulation, economic optimism

terms of activities undertaken to enable the organization to come into existence (Gartner, 1985). The personality characteristics of the entrepreneur are ancillary to the entrepreneur's behaviors. Research on the entrepreneur should focus on what the entrepreneur does and not who the entrepreneur is.

This behavioral view of entrepreneurship is not new. Many authors have asked as their primary question, "How does an organization come into existence?" (Hebert & Link, 1982; Shapero & Sokol, 1982). Arthur Cole, for example, taking a behavioral viewpoint, quoted Say (1816) and defined the entrepreneur as an economic agent who:

> unites all means of production—the labor of the one, the capital or the land of the others—and who finds in the value of the products which result from their employment the reconstitution of the entire capital that he utilizes, and the value of the wages, the interest, and the rent which he pays, as well as the profits belonging to himself. (Cole, 1946, p. 3)

This view places the entrepreneur within the process of new venture creation, performing a series of actions that result in the creation of an organization. However, after setting out admirably to define the entrepreneur according to a behavioral orientation, Cole immediately falls back to the "who is an entrepreneur" approach, and we are once more involved with traits and characteristics:

> This person, this entrepreneur, *must have special personal qualities*: . . . (from Say) judgment, perseverance, and a knowledge of the world as well as of business. (p. 3, emphasis added)

Although the behavioral view of entrepreneurship is not new, it seems that it has always been a difficult view to maintain (Peterson, 1981). As we have seen, the entrepreneur has long seemed to many researchers to be a special person whose qualities need to be investigated. In 1980 Van de Ven issued a warning to entrepreneurship researchers not to be tempted into studies of traits and characteristics:

> Researchers wedded to the conception of entrepreneurship for studying the creation of organizations can learn much from the history of research on leadership. Like the studies of entrepreneurship, this research began by investigating the traits and personality characteristics of leaders. However, no empirical evidence was found to support the expectation that there are a finite number of characteristics or traits of leaders and that these traits differentiate successful from unsuccessful leaders. More recently, research into leadership has apparently made some progress by focusing on the behavior of leaders (that is, on what they do instead of what they are) and by determining what situational factors or conditions moderate the effects of their behavior and performance. (p. 86)

Jenks (1950) and Kilby (1971) have also strongly criticized research which seeks to develop personality profiles of the entrepreneur; both have encouraged researchers to study the behaviors and activities of entrepreneurs. In empirical research, certain researchers (Brockhaus, 1980; Brockhaus & Nord, 1979; Sexton & Kent, 1981) have found that when certain psychological traits are carefully evaluated, it is not possible to differentiate entrepreneurs from managers or from the general population based on the entrepreneur's supposed possession of such traits.

The trait approach to entrepreneurship research is understandably persistent. Entrepreneurs often *do* seem like special people who achieve things that most of us do not achieve. These achievements, we think must be based on some special inner quality. It is difficult *not* to think this way. But let us try to step outside this way of thinking. We can illustrate this point with a story. What if the United States suddenly found itself unable to field a team of baseball players that could win in world competition? One response to such a problem might be to do research on baseball players to learn "Who is a baseball player?," so that individuals with baseball playing propensity could be selected from the population. Such studies might determine that, on average, baseball players weigh 185 pounds, are six feet tall, and most of them can bench press over 250 pounds. We could probably develop a very good personality profile of the baseball player. Based on upbringing and experience we could document a baseball player's locus of control, need for achievement, tolerance of ambiguity, and other characteristics that we thought must make for good baseball playing. We could then recruit individuals with this set of characteristics and feel confident once again in our competitive edge. Yet, this type of research simply ignores the obvious—that is, the baseball player, in fact, plays baseball. Baseball involves a set of behaviors—running, pitching, throwing, catching, hitting, sliding, etc.—that baseball players exhibit. To be a baseball player means that an individual is behaving as a baseball player. A baseball player is not something one is, it is something one does, and the definition of a baseball player cannot stray far from this obvious fact without getting into difficulty.

This might be said about any occupation—manager, welder, doctor, butcher. How can we know the baseball player from the game? How can we know the entrepreneur from starting an organization?

While this baseball metaphor might help to make the difference between behavioral and trait viewpoints very clear and keep it clear, this clarity is not so easily achieved in real life empirical research, and researchers' viewpoints become cloudy and out of focus. Behavioral and trait issues merge and conclusions are vague and don't really tell us anything.

An Example of the Trait Viewpoint

An article by Carland, Hoy, Boulton, and Carland (1984), "Differentiating Entrepreneurs from Small Business Owners: A Conceptualization" is, I believe, a good recent example of research which continues in the long tradition of "if-we-can-just-find-out-who-the-entrepreneur-is-then-we'll-know-what-entrepreneur-ship-is." By singling out this article I do not mean to imply that it is any better or worse than the myriad of other entrepreneurship articles that take the trait approach. I have chosen it because it is the first review article on entrepreneurship to appear in a major journal since 1977, and after such a long hiatus, my reaction was to focus hard on the offering.

As noted above, the central issue in trait approach research is to distinguish entrepreneurs from other populations of individuals. And, indeed, the Carland et al. article begins by rearticulating the perpetual dilemma of entrepreneurship researchers:

> If entrepreneurs exist as entities distinct from small and large organizations and if entrepreneurial activity is a fundamental contributor to economic development, *on what bases may entrepreneurs be separated from nonentrepreneurial managers in order for the phenomenon of entrepreneurship to be studied and understood?* (p. 355—emphasis added)

Carland et al. do recognize that the owner/manager of the ten- or fifteen-year-old firm is not necessarily engaged in entrepreneurship, and therefore these "small business owners," as Carland et al. call them, should not be included in a sample of entrepreneurs. However, when it comes to distinguishing between the entrepreneur and the small business owner, it can be shown that Carland et al. are hindered by trait views, by focusing on the entrepreneur and who (s)he is as the primary level of analysis. After a selective review of the literature, the paper concludes with some definitions which attempt to distinguish the entrepreneur from the small business owner:

> Entrepreneur: An entrepreneur is an individual who establishes and manages a business for the principal purposes of profit and growth. The entrepreneur is characterized principally by innovative behavior and will employ strategic management practices in the business.

Small business owner: A small business owner is an individual who establishes and manages a business for the principal purpose of furthering personal goals. The business must be the primary source of income and will consume the majority of one's time and resources. The owner perceives the business as an extension of his or her personality, intricately bound with family needs and desires. (p. 358)

From the previous discussion, focusing on the intentionality of the individual in order to determine whether that individual is an entrepreneur is just another variation on the trait theme, and requires us to investigate the psychology of the entrepreneur and establish a psychological profile of the entrepreneurial entity. Furthermore, even if we take the definitions at face value, we are immediately aware that the definitions raise more questions than they answer. If by definition a small business owner establishes a business to further personal goals and an entrepreneur establishes a business for profit and growth, then what do we do with the individual whose personal goal is to establish a business for profit and growth? (Are the goals of profit and growth to be considered impersonal goals?) How do we distinguish personal goals from goals of profit and growth? Are we not, then, embroiled in another dilemma of distinguishing? When you define small business owners as having a business which is their primary source of income and will consume the majority of their time, do you not thereby imply that entrepreneurs start organizations that will *not* be their primary source of income, and will *not* occupy the majority of their time and resources? (Are we to assume that the entrepreneurs are off spending the majority of their time pursuing personal goals, which, by definition, cannot be related to their organizations?) If small business owners perceive the business as an extension of their personalities, intricately bound with family needs and desires, as opposed to entrepreneurs who do not perceive their firms in this way, then isn't this definition of small business likely to include such family run organizations as Marriott, Best, and Nordstrom, leaders of their industries in both profits and growth? To suggest that entrepreneurial start-ups are not intricately bound up with the personality of the founders is to suggest that organizations such as Apple, Hewlett-Packard, Lotus, and Microsoft are not entrepreneurial.

The last part of the Carland et al. entrepreneurial definition ties the state of being an entrepreneur to innovative behavior and strategic management practices. Carland et al. use a Schumpeterian definition of innovative behavior (p. 357) which identifies five innovative strategic postures: (1) introduction of new goods, (2) introduction of new methods of production, (3) opening of new markets (4) opening of new sources of supply, and (5) industrial reorganization. Correlating entrepreneurship with innovation, although it is intuitively appealing, and seems to take more of a behavioral viewpoint, leads to the problem of identifying which firms in an industry are the innovative ones. Would the first entrant in an industry be considered the entrepreneurial firm, while all subsequent entrants would be small businesses? How are we to determine the degree of difference between one product and another similar product which constitutes innovation? Do new methods of manufacturing/marketing/distributing the product count as innovative, and, again, what is the degree of difference between the truly innovative and the not so innovative? Among the fifty or so personal computer manufacturing companies, e.g., Compaq, Columbia, Leading Edge, Intertec, ACT Ltd., Polo Microsystems, Tava, Stearns Computer, Wyse Technology, Microcraft, Electro Design, STM Electronics, MAD Computer, Seequa Computer, GRiD Systems, Bytec-Comterm, Seattle Computer, Durango Systems, Otrona Advance Systems, which are the innovators, which are the small businesses? Correlating innovation with entrepreneurship implies that almost all firms in an industry which sell to similar customer groups would be considered small businesses. The Carland et al. definitions, while intending to achieve greater precision, actually increase the ambiguity in what is already a definitional dilemma. Operationalizing these definitions—pinpointing who is an entrepreneur—becomes more and more difficult as Van de Ven (1980) warned.

Carland et al. discuss some past research studies in order to identify and list many characteristics that have been attributed to entrepreneurs. As I mentioned earlier, this is the grand temptation. Entrepreneurship research has reached such a point of accumulation of data that the Carland et al. attempt to sort out past research according to characteristics studied and to list these characteristics in a table ([Exhibit 8.8]: Characteristics of Entrepreneurs) certainly might seem like the most effective way to proceed in attempting to reach a definition of who is an entrepreneur (although it is hoped that my own table [Exhibit 8.9] has shown that such a mega-table is not the answer). On setting up the table, however, it becomes immediately clear, as Carland et al. admit, that the studies which investigated these characteristics and attributed them to entrepreneurs were not all empirical, and more importantly, as Carland et al. point out, the research samples were by no means homogeneous. As discussed earlier, the authors of these past studies usually did not provide important information regarding their samples; e.g., what type of industry or type of firm was studied. The past studies usually made broad generalizations in defining an entrepreneur, and the samples, therefore, included executives, managers, salespeople, and small business persons. Once Carland et al. set up the table and recognized difficulties with it, we are left wondering about the relevance of including [Exhibit 8.8] in a paper whose main purpose is to distinguish entrepreneurs from small business owners.[a] Carland et al. end the discussion of [Exhibit 8.8] with this question:

---

[a] Carland et al. attempt to make sense of the wide range of characteristics attributed to entrepreneurs in their [Exhibit 8.8] by stating that Vesper's view (1980) (that several types of entrepreneurs exist) may be an appropriate view, and by implying that different entrepreneurs may possess different characteristics, thus accounting for the wide range of them in their table. However, Carland et al. quickly undercut Vesper's notion of entrepreneurial types by calling Vesper's typology "a continuum along which several 'types' of entrepreneurs exist," and then insisting that the entrepreneurs along the continuum differ, not merely by possessing different characteristics, but by displaying different *degrees of intensity* of the set of characteristics which makes a person an entrepreneur. We are back to making fine distinctions and measuring imponderables. Vesper's notion of entrepreneurial types is reduced by Carland et al. to a caste system, with the most entrepreneurial entrepreneurs (the purest types) at the furthest end of the continuum. This is another illustration of the extremes to which the trait view may take us: the entrepreneur is an entity like an accordion file who can be more full or less full of entrepreneurial "stuff."

Are the characteristics listed in [Exhibit 8.8] those of entrepreneurs, of small business owners, or of some mixture that may or may not be capable of demonstrating the entrepreneurial function of economic development?

By ending the discussion in this way they view [Exhibit 8.8] as worthless. In the Carland et al. attempt to distinguish the entrepreneur from the small business owner do we come any closer to a definition of the entrepreneur or to an understanding of entrepreneurship? I hope I have shown the Carland et al. article is a good example of where we end up when, with every good intention, we ask the wrong question. Who is an entrepreneur? is the wrong question.

Entrepreneurship is the Creation of Organizations

Organization creation (Vesper, 1982), I believe, separates entrepreneurship from other disciplines. Studies of psychological characteristics of entrepreneurs, sociological explanations of entrepreneurial cultures, economic and demographic explanations of entrepreneurial locations, etc., all such investigations in the entrepreneurship field actually begin with the creation of new organizations. *Entrepreneurship is the creation of new organizations.* The purpose of this paper is not to substitute one highly specific entrepreneurial definition for another. "Entrepreneurship is the creation of new organizations" is not offered as a definition, but rather it is an attempt to change a long held and tenacious viewpoint in the entrepreneurship field. If we are to understand the phenomenon of entrepreneurship in order to encourage its growth, then we need to focus on the process by which new organizations are created. This may seem like a simple refinement of focus (i.e., look at what the entrepreneur does, not who the entrepreneur is), but it is actually a rather thoroughgoing change in our orientation. From this perspective, other issues in the field might be seen with new clarity.

An example of such an issue: if entrepreneurship is behavioral, then it can be seen that these behaviors cease once organization creation is over. One of the problems in the entrepreneurship field is deciding when entrepreneurship ends (Vesper, 1980). (Actually, the Carland et al. attempt to distinguish entrepreneurs from small business owners might be approached more fruitfully if looked at from the behavioral perspective of entrepreneurship ending.) The organization can live on past its creation stage to such possible stages as growth, maturity, or decline (Greiner, 1972; Steinmetz, 1969). From the process viewpoint, the individual who creates the organization as the entrepreneur takes on other roles at each stage—innovator, manager, small business owner, division vice-president, etc. Entrepreneurs, like baseball players, are identified by a set of behaviors which link them to organization creation. Managers, small business owners, etc., are also identified by their behaviors. As long as we adhere to the behavioral approach and view entrepreneurship as something one does and not who one is, then we can more effectively avoid the Carland et al.–type definitional dilemmas. But once we are tempted to view the entrepreneur, the manager, the small business owner, etc., as states of being, we become embroiled in trying to pin down their inner qualities and intentions. This approach may not completely resolve the question of when entrepreneurship ends, but it makes us look at the organization, rather than the person, for our answer. Entrepreneurship ends when the creation stage of the organization ends.

Implications for Research on the Entrepreneur

Reorientation toward a behavioral approach to entrepreneurship begins by asking the primary question, "How do organizations come into existence?" We should think of entrepreneurs in regard to the role they play in enabling organizations to come into existence (Jenks, 1950; Kilby, 1971; Peterson, 1981; Van de Ven, 1980). The focus will be on research questions that ask (among other things) what individuals do to enable organizations to come into existence, rather than on traits and characteristics of these individuals.

Entrepreneurship research should follow the path of research taken in managerial behaviors (Mintzberg, 1973). The issues that Mintzberg articulated regarding managers are the issues which also confront entrepreneurship. Substitute the word entrepreneur for manager, and entrepreneurial for managerial in Mintzberg's statement of the purpose of his study:

> We must be able to answer a number of specific questions before we can expect managerial training and management science to have any real impact on practice:
>
> What kinds of activities does the manager perform? What kinds of information does he process? With whom must he work? Where? How frequently?
>
> What are the distinguishing characteristics of managerial work? What is of interest about the media the manager uses, the activities he prefers to engage in, the flow of these activities during the workday, his use of time, the pressures of the job?
>
> What basic roles can be inferred from the study of the manager's activities? What roles does the manager perform in moving information, in making decisions, in dealing with people?
>
> What variations exist among managerial jobs? To what extent can basic differences be attributed to the situation, the incumbent, the job, the organization, and the environment?
>
> To what extent is management a science? To what extent is the manager's work programmed (that is, repetitive, systematic and predictable)? To what extent is it programmable? To what extent can the management scientist "re-program" managerial work? (Mintzberg, 1973: 3)

I believe that research on entrepreneurial behaviors must be based on field work similar to Mintzberg's study of managerial work. Researchers must observe entrepreneurs in the process of creating organizations. This work must be described in detail and the activities systematized and classified. Knowledge of entrepreneurial behaviors is dependent on field work.

The results of this field work should also be able to answer additional questions. What are the specific organization creation skills that an entrepreneur needs to know (Palmer, 1971)? If we've given up the perspective that tells us that an entrepreneur is born with these skills and abilities, then we must ask how are these skills acquired? Some research suggests that entrepreneurial skills are "learn-as-you-go" (Collins & Moore, 1970; Gartner, 1984). Entrepreneurs who have started one organization seem to be more successful and more efficient in the start-up of their second and third organizations (Vesper, 1980). If this is usually true, then what expertise, what special knowledge do these entrepreneurs gain from doing their first start-up? One skill they might learn is how to identify and evaluate problems. A new organization is confronted by many problems, and some problems are more important than others. It would seem that the more successful entrepreneurs develop expertise in judging which problems need immediate attention (Hoad & Rosko, 1964; Lamont, 1972).

The process of team formation needs to be studied (Timmons, 1979). How and why do individuals enter a new venture? How do they claim ownership of a new idea, organization, etc.? How is *esprit de corps* generated? How do individuals convince themselves that entering a new organization will benefit them (Kidder, 1981)?

All new ventures need some type of support, e.g., financial, legal, marketing, technological. This assistance can be obtained in many ways. In internal start-ups the entrepreneur has to convince senior management to provide support (Schollhammer, 1982). What is the political process—the strategies—that the entrepreneur undertakes to gain internal assistance? Is this any different than the process undertaken by independent entrepreneurs to persuade venture capitalists to invest in their ventures? In either case, we need to make this process more efficient and successful because it appears that few new venture plans gain support. The importance of business plans to the process of obtaining venture capital and support needs to be studied (Roberts, 1983). What are the features of successful business plans?

Conclusion

How do we know the dancer from the dance? When we view entrepreneurship from a behavioral perspective we do not artificially separate dancer from dance, we do not attempt to fashion a reassuring simplicity. The behavioral approach challenges us to develop research questions, methodologies and techniques that will do justice to the complexity of entrepreneurship (Gartner, 1985). The creation of an organization is a very complicated and intricate process, influenced by many factors and influencing us even as we look at it. The entrepreneur is not a fixed state of existence, rather entrepreneurship is a role that individuals undertake to create organizations.

Source: This article excerpted from W. B. Gartner, "'Who Is An Entrepreneur?' Is the Wrong Question," *Entrepreneurship Theory and Practice* 13 (1989): 47–64. Used by permission of the author and *Entrepreneurship Theory and Practice*.

ENDNOTES

1. R. Collins, *Max Weber: A Skeleton Key* (Beverly Hills, Calif.: Sage Publications, 1986).
2. M. Weber, *The Protestant Ethic and the Spirit of Capitalism*, trans. T. Parsons (New York: Charles Scribner's Sons, 1930). Weber's original essay was titled *Die Protestantische Ethik und der Geist des Kapitalismus* and was published in 1904 in a leading German sociological journal, *Archiv fur Sozialwissenschaft und Sozialpolitik*, XX.
3. M. Weber, *General Economic History*, trans. F. H. Knight (New York: Macmillan, 1923). Weber first presented this argument in a lecture at the University of Heidelberg in 1919. The ecclesiastical discipline that Weber refers to is described under "Citizenship" in Exhibit 8.1 of this text.
4. J. C. Alexander, *Theoretical Logic in Sociology: Weber's Classical Attempt at Theoretical Synthesis* (Berkeley, Calif.: University of California Press, 1983).
5. D. F. Jennings, "A Process Model of Organizational Entrepreneurship, Strategic Actions, and Performance" (Ph.D. diss., Texas A&M University, 1986).
6. J. A. Schumpeter, "The Creative Response in Economic History," *Journal of Economic History* 7 (1947): 149–59.
7. O. F. Collins, D. G. Moore, and D. B. Unwalla, *The Enterprising Man* (East Lansing, Mich.: Michigan State University Press, 1964).
8. O. F. Collins and D. G. Moore, *The Organization Makers: A Behavioral Study of Independent Entrepreneurs* (New York: Meredith Press, 1970).
9. D. C. McClelland, *The Achieving Society* (Princeton, N.J.: Van Nostrand, 1961); D. C. McClelland, "Achievement and Entrepreneurship: A Longitudinal Study," *Journal of Personality and Social Psychology* 1 (1965): 389–92.
10. B. R. Johnson, "Toward a Multidimensional Model of Entrepreneurship: The Case of Achievement Motivation and the Entrepreneur," *Entrepreneurship Theory and Practice* 14 (1990): 39–54.
11. D. C. McClelland, "Business Drive and National Achievement," *Harvard Business Review* 40 (1962): 99–112.
12. W. B. Gartner, "A Conceptual Framework for Describing the Phenomenon of New Venture Creation," *Academy of Management Review* 10 (1985): 696–706; R. H. Brockhaus and P. S. Horwitz, "The Psychology of the Entrepreneur," in *The Art and Science of Entrepreneurship*, ed. D. L. Sexton and R. W. Smilor (Cambridge, Mass.: Ballinger, 1986), 25–48.
13. E. Klinger, "Fantasy Need Achievement as a Motivational Construct," *Psychological Bulletin* 66 (1980): 108–16; S. P. Schatz, "n Achievement and Economic Growth: A Critical Appraisal," in *Entrepreneurship and Economic Development*, ed. P. Kilby (New York: Free Press, 1971), 183–90; Johnson, "Toward A Multidimensional Model of Entrepreneurship." Klinger discusses the low predictive validity of the TAT, together with McClelland's research design problems; Schatz argues that McClelland employed a biased data selection and utilized faulty analysis in an interpretation of economic growth; Johnson notes that while McClelland considered entrepreneurs to be the owner/managers of new or small ventures, commissioned salesmen, management consultants, and executives in large companies were also included in the research sample.
14. J. H. Kunkel, "Psychological Factors in the Analysis of Economic Development." *Journal of Social Issues* 19 (1963): 68–87.
15. E. E. Hagen, *On the Theory of Social Change* (Homewood, Ill.: Dorsey Press, 1962).
16. Ibid.
17. P. Kilby, ed., *Entrepreneurship and Economic Development* (New York: Free Press, 1971).

Notes 18-23 are articles developed from a text edited by P. Kilby, *Entrepreneurship and Economic Development* (New York: Free Press, 1971).

18. Schatz, "n Achievement and Economic Growth," 183–89.
19. J. H. Kunkel, "Values and Behavior in Economic Development," in *Entrepreneurship and Economic Development,* ed. P. Kilby (New York: Free Press, 1971), 151–82.
20. F. W. Young, "A Macrosociological Interpretation of Entrepreneurship," in *Entrepreneurship and Economic Development,* ed. P. Kilby (New York: Free Press, 1971), 139–50.
21. R. Macdonald, "Schumpeter and Max Weber: Central Visions and Social Theories," in *Entrepreneurship and Economic Development,* ed. P. Kilby (New York: Free Press, 1971), 71–94.
22. T. C. Cochran, "The Entrepreneur in Economic Change," in *Entrepreneurship and Economic Development,* ed. P. Kilby (New York: Free Press, 1971), 95–108.
23. E. Staley and R. Morse, "Developing Entrepreneurship: Elements for a Program," in *Entrepreneurship and Economic Development,* ed. P. Kilby (New York: Free Press, 1971), 357–84.
24. Kilby, *Entrepreneurship and Economic Development.*
25. T. Kuhn, *The Structure of Scientific Revolutions,* 2nd ed. (Chicago: University of Chicago Press, 1970).
26. R. L. Daft and A. Y. Lewin, "Can Organization Studies Begin to Break Out of the Normal Science Straitjacket? An Editorial Essay," *Organization Science* 1 (1990): 1–9.
27. W. L. Paulin, R. E. Coffey, and M. E. Spaulding, "Entrepreneurship Research: Methods and Directions," in *Encyclopedia of Entrepreneurship,* ed. C. A. Kent et al. (Englewood Cliffs, N.J.: Prentice-Hall, 1982); T. M. Begley and D. P. Boyd, "Psychological Characteristics Associated with Performance in Entrepreneurial Firms and Smaller Businesses," *Journal of Business Venturing* 2 (1987): 79–93.
28. A number of studies have described this problem. See, for instance: D. L. Hull, J. J. Bosley, and G. G. Udell, "Renewing the Hunt for the Heffalump: Identifying Potential Entrepreneurs by Personality Characteristics," *Journal of Small Business* 18 (1980): 1–18; F. Hoy and J. W. Carland, Jr., "Differentiating Between Entrepreneurs and Small Business Owners in New Venture Formation," *Frontiers of Entrepreneurial Research* 3 (1983): 180–91; D. L. Sexton and N. B. Bowman, "Comparative Entrepreneurship Characteristics of Students: Preliminary Results," *Frontiers of Entrepreneurial Research* 3 (1983): 213–32.
29. A. Kaplan, *The Conduct of Inquiry: Methodology for Behavioral Science* (New York: Chandler-Harper and Row, 1964).
30. For a detailed account of the study describing leadership, see L. J. Williams and P. M. Podsakoff, "Longitudinal Field Methods for Studying Reciprocal Relationships in Organizational Behavior Research: Toward Improved Causal Analysis," in *Research in Organizational Behavior,* ed. L. L. Cummings and B. M. Staw, vol. 11 (Greenwich, Conn.: JAI Press, 1989), 247–92. For an explanation of LISREL (linear structural relationships), see K. G. Joreskog and D. Sorbom, *LISREL V User's Guide* (Chicago: International Educational Services, 1983), and K. G . Joreskog and D. Sorbom, *LISREL VI: Analysis of Linear Structural Relationships by Maximum Likelihood, Instrumental Variables, and Least Square Method* (Uppsala, Sweden: University of Uppsala, 1984).
31. Kuhn, *The Structure of Scientific Revolutions.*
32. N. E. G. Robbins, "Entrepreneurial Assessment: Characteristics Which Differentiate Entrepreneurs, Intrapreneurs, and Managers" (Ph.D. diss., University of Minnesota, 1986).
33. Ibid.

Key Psychological
and Personality Factors
Relating to Entrepreneurs

As noted in Chapter 8, a considerable amount of research on entrepreneurship has focused on determining the psychological and personality factors of successful entrepreneurs.[1] A compelling rationale for these studies has been that if characteristics unique to successful entrepreneurs could be discovered it would be possible to encourage individuals with those characteristics to become entrepreneurs and discourage individuals without those characteristics from becoming entrepreneurs, thus increasing the number of new-venture creations.[2]

Unfortunately, the objective of this research has not been achieved. There appears to be no discoverable pattern of traits that distinguish successful entrepreneurs from nonentrepreneurs.[3]

Despite this lack of empirical research support, the purpose of this chapter is to describe a variety of psychological and personality factors associated with entrepreneurship. The chapter concludes with an article by Daniel Jennings and Carl Zeithaml, who provide insights into research involving one of those factors, locus of control.

PSYCHOLOGICAL FACTORS

The psychological factors that tend to be most associated with entrepreneurs are as follows:

- *Need for achievement (nAch).* McClelland reported that nAch is high in individuals who start their own businesses. These individuals tend to set challenging but attainable goals, and they require frequent and timely feedback about performance.[4]

- *Locus of control.* An individual's belief that his or her destiny is controlled either from within or by external events is referred to as the locus of control. Most entrepreneurs have been described as having an internal locus of control—they believe they have control over events that affect their success—while individuals with an external locus of control believe that events beyond their control determine their fate.[5]

- *Propensity for risk.* Entrepreneurs are reported to accept the risk inherent in starting a new venture and are willing to risk money, security, reputation, and status.[6]

- *Tolerance for ambiguity.* Entrepreneurs are reported to be able to deal effectively, without experiencing psychological discomfort or threat, with a situation or information that is vague, incomplete, unstructured, uncertain, or unclear. The uncertainty-bearing role[7] of the entrepreneur also has been viewed as an ambiguity-bearing role, which is necessary because of the ambiguities surrounding either the creation or the managing of a business.[8]

PERSONALITY FACTORS

The personality factors that most often are related to entrepreneurship are as follows:

- *Self-confidence* is the ability to do without constant approval and recognition from others. Entrepreneurship reportedly involves specific self-confidence in the ability to master the problems associated with starting a new venture.[9]

- *Opportunism.* Entrepreneurs are reported to be characterized as having competencies in discerning and acting on opportunities.[10] The opportunistic entrepreneur tends to seek and to plan for the growth of the venture.[11]

- *Ambition* is the earnest desire for some type of achievement or distinction. An energetic and ambitious individual is believed to be more willing to devote the time and effort needed to create an entrepreneurial venture.[12]

DESTRUCTIVE ASPECTS OF THE ENTREPRENEUR'S PERSONALITY

As stated earlier, most researchers tend to consider the preceding psychological and personality factors as a form of creative energy that allows the entrepreneur to start and implement a successful venture. However, this same creative energy has desires and needs behind it that if let loose can wreak havoc in an organization. For example, while entrepreneurs somehow know how to lead an organization and give it momentum, some entrepreneurs are difficult to work with because they have personality quirks. These quirks include need for control, sense of distrust, desire for applause, and scapegoating.[13] Exhibit 9.1 describes these destructive traits in greater detail.

Being aware of the "dark side" of entrepreneurs can allow executives and venture capitalists to keep in mind that entrepreneurs' personality quirks may have been responsible for their drive and energy and are important factors in making them successful. Instead of fighting these idiosyncrasies, managers should regard developing them as a challenge.[14]

The following article, written by Daniel Jennings and Carl Zeithaml, reviews a number of locus of control studies and argues that a more sophisticated, multi-dimensional approach should be utilized in measuring locus of control and that a scale designed specifically for entrepreneurs may be appropriate.

EXHIBIT   9.1   Destructive Traits of the Entrepreneur's Personality

A "dark side" exists within the creative drive of successful entrepreneurs. Personality quirks may make some entrepreneurs difficult people to work with. Following are descriptions of four destructive traits that some entrepreneurs may possess.

Need for Control

Occasionally the preoccupation with a need for control affects the ability of some entrepreneurs to take direction or to give it appropriately to others. These entrepreneurs find it difficult to work with others in structured situations unless they created the structure and the work is done on their terms.

Sense of Distrust

Some entrepreneurs have a strong distrust for the world around them and live in fear of being victimized. They want to be ready when disaster strikes and continually scan the environment for something to confirm their fears. This type of behavior has its constructive side: the entrepreneur is alert to moves of competitors, suppliers, customers, or government that will affect the industry. This type of vigilance, however, can cause the entrepreneur to lose any sense of proportion. By focusing on certain trouble spots and ignoring others, these entrepreneurs may blow up trivial things and lose sight of the reality of the situation.

A need for control assisted by a strong sense of distrust can cause serious organizational problems. For example, individuals within the organization stop acting independently, and political gamesmanship becomes rampant. These entrepreneurs may interpret harmless acts as threats to their control and see them as warranting destructive counteractions.

Desire for Applause

Some entrepreneurs have an overriding concern to be heard and recognized and to be seen as heroes. They need to show others that they cannot be ignored. These entrepreneurs may build monuments—huge office buildings, imposing factories, or plush offices—as symbols of their success.

continued

concluded

Scapegoating

Most individuals tend to project their discomforts and fears onto others. A threat becomes more manageable when it is scapegoated, that is, attributed to someone else or to an event. If this tendency to scapegoat becomes exaggerated and the predominant reaction to stressful situations, then it can be problematic.

Entrepreneurs who practice scapegoating refuse to see what they do not like and blame others. This type of thinking contributes to political infighting, denial of responsibility, and isolation.

Source: Adapted from M. E. R. Kets de Vries, "The Dark Side of Entrepreneurship," *Harvard Business Review* 63 (1985): 160–67.

ARTICLE 9.1   **LOCUS OF CONTROL: A REVIEW AND DIRECTIONS FOR ENTREPRENEURIAL RESEARCH**
by Daniel Jennings and Carl Zeithaml

Current economic conditions have caused a rethinking of the managerial and organizational factors related to growth and superior performance. The academic and popular press have begun to emphasize the importance of entrepreneurial activity both in terms of individual organizations and within larger corporate settings. As a result, research on entrepreneurs and their organizations should receive increased attention and critical analysis.

Much of this research has focused on the characteristics of entrepreneurs and individual differences related to success. Locus of control has been one of the key constructs included in many of these studies. Locus of control is a complex individual phenomenon which is concerned with determining the effects of an individual's perception of control. "Internals" believe that they can determine their own fate within limits, while "externals" believe outside forces determine their fate. Although Lefcourt (1981) points out that the history of psychology is replete with examples of constructs which experience brief prominence and then disappear, locus of control has occupied a central position in personality research for almost twenty years.

The endurance and perceived research value of this construct, coupled with the existing entrepreneurial studies where it has been included, indicate that locus of control may play an increasingly prominent role in future research on entrepreneurs. The purpose of this paper, therefore, is to review the development of locus of control and to suggest potential directions for the use of this construct in entrepreneurial research. The paper is divided into five sections: (1) background and assessment techniques, (2) general locus of control studies, (3) locus of control studies in organizational and managerial settings, (4) locus of control in entrepreneurial research, and (5) research implications and discussion. Our intent is to stimulate conceptual and empirical growth with respect to locus of control and its application to research on entrepreneurs.

Background and Assessment Techniques

Psychologists have long dealt with studies of perceived control and its effect within certain situations (Milgram, 1963; Mowrer & Veck, 1968). Rotter (1966) extended this tradition with major contributions to the understanding and assessment of the locus of control construct, advancing the premise that locus of control could be viewed as an internal-external characteristic. Consistent with this position, he developed a questionnaire based on previous work (James, 1957; Phares, 1955) containing 23 forced choice and six filler items to determine internal versus external locus of control.

However, various authors (Hersch & Schiebe, 1967; DuCette, Wolk, & Soucar, 1972) questioned the validity of Rotter's unidimensional I-E Concept and called for a multi-dimensional view of the construct implying that Rotter's scale may be too simplistic. Subsequently, Reid and Ware (1974) developed a 45 item forced choice questionnaire composed of three factors: self-control, social systems control, and fatalism. Levenson (1973) presented a three subscale version of Rotter's I-E scale, internal, chance, and powerful others, and suggested that it is possible for all three dimensions to coexist independently within individuals. Despite these refinements and the praise which has accompanied them (Lefcourt, 1979), virtually all of the studies examining locus of control and entrepreneurs have employed the Rotter scale.

General Locus of Control Studies

Exhibit 9.2 contains a selected review of studies using locus of control in a variety of topic areas. Furthermore, Blass (1977) and Lefcourt (1981) have described significant studies using locus of control within a social learning framework. Although the reader may review Exhibit 9.2 for specific findings, several summary points are relevant to the topic of interest in this paper.

First, from a measurement standpoint, many researchers in psychology and psychiatry report that locus of control has many dimensions, and that a multidimensional construct should be used. Many studies in these disciplines have used Levenson's multidimensional model as opposed to Rotter's unidimensional I-E approach. It is interesting to note that several researchers have also developed their own locus of control instruments for their specific topics of interest.

Second, in many different situations involving life stress events, life cycle changes, psychological adjustment, cognitive ability, achievement, performance, and health, internals tend to adjust faster, to achieve more, and to do well in creative problem solving situations. Psychiatrists report that having an external locus of control is a hindrance to coping with challenges and tends to be associated with negative feelings.

Finally, there is strong evidence that locus of control can be altered deliberately, and that the shift was toward greater internality. This has important impli-

EXHIBIT   9.2   Locus of Control Research Within the Social Learning Framework

Topic: Health Problems

Author (Date)	Construct Utilized*	Findings
1. Seeman & Evans (1966)	R	Hospital patients with internal locus of control knew more about their condition, questioned doctors more, were not satisfied with information being received.
2. DuCette (1974)	L	Confirmed findings of Seeman & Evans studying diabetics.
3. Cromwell (1977)	L	Confirmed findings of Seeman & Evans studying heart patients.
4. Dabbs & Kirscht (1971)	R	Internal college students took steps to control their health by scheduling medical and dental checkups, exercising, and controlling their diet.
5. Strickland (1973)	R	Internals were more interested in health control measures than externals, confirming Dabbs & Kirscht.
6. Devito, et al. (1979)	L	
7. Achterberg, et al. (1977)	L	Internals with cancer believed that their bodies could fight the disease and outlived their predicted life expectancies.
8. Greber (1979)	L	
9. Wallston et al. (1976)	HLC	Developed health-related locus of control construct.
10. Wallston et al. (1978)	MHLC	Developed HLC into multidimensional construct.
11. Wallston et al. (1976)	HLC	Confirmed Seeman & Evans findings using HLC construct.
12. Kaplan (1976)	MHLC	Internals had greater satisfaction with self managed weight reduction program rather than one directed by a therapist.
13. Kaplan & Cowles (1978)	MHLC	Internals were more successful in reducing smoking than externals.
14. Saltzer (1979)	MHLC	Internals more concerned about appearance and took action to lose weight.
15. Carnahan (1979)	MHLC	The MHLC was a useless construct in predicting dental behavior.
16. Shadish (1979)	MHLC	Concerned individuals with severe spinal cord injuries; internals were able to adjust better after their accident than externals.
17. Hersch & Scheibe (1967)	R	Externals tend to experience more anxiety about their ability to recover from illness than do internals.
18. Powell & Vega (1973)	L	
19. Duke & Nowicki (1979)	MHLC	

* Construct abbreviations:

  R=Rotter construct
  L=Levenson construct
  HLC=Health-related locus of control construct
  MHLC=Multidimensional HLC construct
  W=Weiner construct
  I&L=Ickes and Layden construct
  R&Z=Reid and Ziegler construct

continued

EXHIBIT   9.2   *continued*

Topic: Life Cycle Changes

Author (Date)	Construct Utilized	Findings
1. Lao (1974) 2. Ryckman & Malikioski (1975)	R L	While family life and career success can affect life cycle stability, internals believed they have the power to affect change from youth to adulthood and this belief does not change with age.
3. Penk (1969) 4. Nowicki & Strickland (1973) 5. Gruen et al. (1974)	R R L	Reported an increasing internality with age among children from grades eight through twelve.
6. Reinsch (1979)	L	There was no decrease in internality nor increase in externality with age.
7. McArthur (1970) 8. Kaplan & Moore (1972)	R R	Students who became draft susceptible tended to become more external than students whose draft status was not affected. Kaplan and Moore could not replicate McArthur's findings.

Topic: Psychological Adjustment

Author (Date)	Construct Utilized	Findings
1. Shybut (1968) 2. Cash & Stock (1973) 3. Levenson (1973) 4. Lefcourt (1976) 5. Martin (1979) 6. Morelli et al. (1979)	R R L L L L	Mental patients having neuroses, paranoia, and schizophrenia tended to be externals.

Topic: Alcoholism

Author (Date)	Construct Utilized	Findings
1. Palmer (1971) 2. Butts & Chotlos (1973) 3. Nowicki & Hopper (1974) 4. Krampin & Nispel (1978)	R R R L	Alcoholic patients were externals.
5. Goss & Morosko (1970) 6. Gozali & Sloan (1971)	R R	Alcoholic patients were internals.
7. Donovan & O'Leary (1975)	L	No difference in locus of control between alcoholics and non-alcoholics.
8. Donovan & O'Leary (1978)	—	Reviewed previous studies, concluding that a multidimensional approach is needed.
9. Oziel & Obitz (1975)	R	Successfully treated alcoholics increased their internality.

continued

<u>EXHIBIT</u>   9.2   *continued*

Topic: Cognitive Ability

Author (Date)	Construct Utilized	Findings
1. Sherman et al. (1973)	L	Dogmatic individuals tended to be external.
2. Seeman & Evans (1974)	L	Externally-oriented hospital patients scored lower on an objective test about their illness.
3. Beck (1979)	L	Undergraduate college students who did well in creative problem solving tended to be more internal.
4. Christensen et al. (1979)	L	Internals tended to evaluate their job performance consistent with appraisals made by their supervisors.

Topic: Achievement

Author (Date)	Construct Utilized	Findings
1. Prociuk & Breen (1974)	L	Internals tended to have better study habits and higher grade point averages.
2. Lefcourt (1981)	—	Called for research using a multidimensional construct.

Topic: Occupational Choices

Author (Date)	Construct Utilized	Findings
1. Ryckman & Malikioski (1974)	L	Professionals and students tended to be internals; workers were externals.
2. Rupkey (1978)	R&L	Studied entrepreneurs and nonentrepreneurs. Both scales revealed that entrepreneurs had an internal locus of control, felt in control, but had an appreciation of the fact that others exercise authority.
3. Scanlan (1979)	L	Studied two types of entrepreneurs—those interested in growth and those who were small business owners. Both types scored relatively the same as the internals.

Topic: Social-Political Involvement

Author (Date)	Construct Utilized	Findings
1. Evans & Alexander (1970) 2. Blanchard & Scarboro (1972) 3. Gootnick (1974)	R	No relationship between activism and locus of control.
4. Gore & Rotter (1966) 5. Strickland (1968)	R	Black civil rights activists tended to be internals.
6. Ransford (1973) 7. Sanger & Alker (1974)	L	White feminist activists were more externally-oriented than control groups.
8. Trigg et al. (1976)	L	Internals were more involved in anti-pollution activities.

continued

EXHIBIT 9.2 *continued*

Topic: Success and Failure Attributes

Author (Date)	Construct Utilized	Findings
1. Weiner (1974)	W	Modified Levenson scale; stable versus unstable conditions rather than locus of control produced expectancy shifts.
2. Fontaine et al. (1979)	W	Supported Weiner's conclusions.
3. Ickes & Layden (1978)	I&L	Developed 9 category construct; internals adjusted aspirations downward after failure; externals performed better on an avoidance task after exposure to uncontrollable outcomes.

Topic: Performance

Author (Date)	Construct Utilized	Findings
1. Davis & Davis (1972)	R	Externals rationalized failure rather than considering their performance or ability.
2. Dies (1968)	R	Externals failed more than internals where individuals strive for rewards or achieve positive outcomes in various tests.
3. Gilmor & Minton (1974)	L	
4. Joe (1974)	L	
5. Krovetz (1974)	L	
6. Lefcourt et al. (1975)	L	
7. Scrull & Karabenick (1975)	R	
8. Karabenick & Scrull (1978)	L	
9. Levine & Uleman (1979)	R&L	
10. Wright et al. (1980)	L	
11. Hochreich (1975)	R	No difference in success or failure characteristics between internals or externals.
12. Luginbuhl et al. (1976)	L	
13. Gregory (1978)	R	
14. Lloyd & Chang (1979)	L	

Topic: Adjustments to the Aging Process

Author (Date)	Construct Utilized	Findings
1. Harris (1975)	L	Internals make the best adjustments to the problems of aging.
2. Reid & Ziegler (1975)	Modified L	
3. Karl et al. (1978)	R&Z	

Topic: Attempts to Change Locus of Control

Author (Date)	Construct Utilized	Findings
1. Singer (1967)	R	An external locus of control is a hindrance to coping with challenges and is associated with negative feelings.
2. Diamond & Shapiro (1973)	R	Deliberate attempts were made to alter locus of control; reported a shift toward internality.
3. Foulds et al. (1974)	L	
4. McCallister et al. (1978)	L	

continued

EXHIBIT 9.2 *concluded*

Topic: Interpersonal Perception & Behavior		
Author (Date)	**Construct Utilized**	**Findings**
1. Ubbink & Sadova (1974)	R&L	Helpers tended to be internals.
2. Levenson (1975)	L	The more individuals felt they were controlled by powerful others, the more they perceived others as untrustworthy.
3. Mahler (1975)	L	Machiavellian individuals were internals.

cations for the training and development of entrepreneurs and the expansion of entrepreneurial activity.

Locus of Control Studies in Organizational and Managerial Settings

Exhibit 9.3 contains a selected review of the research that has employed locus of control in studies focusing on organizational and managerial issues. Clearly, many of these topics and findings are pertinent for entrepreneurial research.

At least two summary comments are relevant. First, internals outperformed externals in most organizational or managerial settings. Internals reacted better under stress, exhibited task-oriented behaviors, were less risk-averse, made more reliable decisions, and tended to be more innovative. Second, all of the studies reviewed used Rotter's unidimensional construct. Spector (1982) called for the use of a multidimensional construct to examine the effects of locus of control in organizations, as well as improved statistical analysis and better assessment techniques.

Locus of Control in Entrepreneurial Research

Exhibit 9.4 presents a summary of research that has explicitly examined locus of control among entrepreneurs. Once again, all studies included in this table used Rotter's I-E construct.

Hornaday (1971) examined the characteristics of successful entrepreneurs and reported that they had a "high" internal locus of control. Brockhaus (1975) and Rupkey (1978) found that individuals with entrepreneurial intentions tended to have an internal locus of control. Borland (1975) and Pandey and Tewary (1979) investigated the relationship between need for achievement, locus of control, and entrepreneurial activities. Both studies revealed that entrepreneurs had a high need for achievement and an internal locus of control. Borland further examined the characteristics of management students who intended to become

EXHIBIT 9.3 Locus of Control Research Within an Organizational Setting*

Topic	Author (Date)	Findings
Leadership	1. Watson & Baumal (1967)	Locus of control may help to explain differences in individual task performance in stressful situations; internals tended to perform better.
	2. Anderson, Hellriegel, & Slocum (1977)	Confirmed Watson & Baumal's hypothesis; internal managers were more likely to express a task orientation and to out-perform externals in a stress situation.
	3. Goodstadt (1973) 4. Mitchell, Smyser, & Weed (1975)	Externals were more likely to utilize a coercive power base, while internal managers were more likely to rely on persuasive forms of power. Internals had more job satisfaction and were more likely to be in managerial positions.
	5. Runyon (1973)	Internals were more satisfied with a participative management style.
	6. Durant & Nord (1976)	Externals had more job satisfaction and were more likely to be in managerial positions.
	7. Anderson & Schneier (1978)	Group leaders of college students tended to be internals; internals were superior performers both on a group basis and individually; externals exhibited behaviors pointing to a social emotional style while internals exhibited behaviors of an instrumental, task-oriented style.
	8. Runyon (1973) 9. Goodstadt & Hjelle (1973) 10. Abed-Halim (1981)	External supervisors tended to be directive while internal supervisors tended to be participative. Internal subordinates tended to prefer supervisors who used a participative style while externals tended to prefer supervisors who used a directive style.
Decision making	1. Kets de Vries (1977) 2. Rice (1978) 3. Bonoma & Johnston (1979)	Internals generated more reliable decisional solutions by using previously provided information and sought out available choice information more fully before making decisions. Internals tended also to be less affected by risk aversion in choice.
Strategy formulation	1. Miller et al. (1982)	The more internal the top executive, the more innovative the firm. The action orientation of internals in a managerial situation appeared to have broad repercussions (risk taking, proactiveness, futurity) on the strategy of the firm.
Organizational behavior	1. Organ & Greene (1974)	Internals reported a greater satisfaction with work than externals.
	2. Evans (1974)	Internals reported higher motivation than externals; internals perceived and responded to environmental contingencies more consistently than externals.
	3. Spector (1982)	Reviewed locus of control studies in organizational settings; supported general theory with some limitations.

* All studies included in Exhibit 9.3 used the Rotter scale.

entrepreneurs. She reported: (1) students with a high need for achievement and an internal locus of control had a higher expectancy of starting a company, (2) locus of control may moderate the influence of achievement since only those students with an internal locus of control expressed a high achievement oriented behavior, and (3) whether or not the student's father had ever started a company proved to be the most important variable predicting the intention to start a business. Andrisani and Nestel (1976) conducted a longitudinal study of male career mobility among entrepreneurs and determined that individuals who reported greater career success were internals. Initial differences in locus of control were not investigated. Scanlan (1979) studied two types of entrepreneurs—those interested in growth and organization building and those who were small business owners. Both types scored relatively the same as internals.

Anderson (1977) conducted a longitudinal field study of entrepreneurs whose businesses had been extensively damaged by a major flood. The Rotter scale was administered to participants eight months after the flood, and then again after 36 months. Locus of control was related to business performance under these stressful conditions. The results showed a shift toward greater internality for internals whose performance improved and a shift toward greater externality for externals whose performance declined. The improved externals did not shift toward internality and the poorer internals did not become external. Finally, Krolick (1979) studied entrepreneurs and others in stressful situations. He found a shift for internals in an external direction.

EXHIBIT   9.4   Locus of Control Research with Entrepreneurs*

Author (Date)	Findings
1. Hornaday (1971)	Successful entrepreneurs had a high internal locus of control.
2. Brockhaus (1975) 3. Rupkey (1978)	Individuals with entrepreneurial intentions had an internal locus of control.
4. Borland (1975) 5. Pandey & Tewary (1979)	Entrepreneurs tended to have a high need for achievement and an internal locus of control.
6. Andrisani & Nestel (1976)	Longitudinal study of career mobility of entrepreneurs. Internals reported greater career success.
7. Scanlan (1979)	Studied two types of entrepreneurs; both groups were internals.
8. Anderson (1977)	Longitudinal study of entrepreneurs in a stressful situation. Reported a shift toward greater internality for internals whose performance improved and a shift toward greater externality for externals whose performance declined.
9. Krolick (1979)	Entrepreneurs in stressful situations. Reported a shift only for internals in an external direction.

* All studies included in Exhibit 9.4 used the Rotter scale.

Research Implications and Discussion

Despite extensive use of the locus of control construct and its support in empirical studies, there are many unanswered questions, particularly with respect to locus of control and entrepreneurial research.

First, increased attention should be devoted to the formulation of the locus of control construct for studying entrepreneurs. Clearly, there is considerable disagreement concerning the relative merits of a unidimensional versus a multidimensional construct. Since existing studies in this field have employed Rotter's approach exclusively, it is time to develop a more sophisticated, multidimensional approach similar to other disciplines. A scale designed specifically for entrepreneurs may be appropriate. This would allow for the replication and refinement of previous entrepreneurial–locus of control research, and contribute perhaps to better understanding of the general construct. Earlier research suggests that factors such as success expectancy, need for achievement, tolerance for ambiguity, and anxiety are potential candidates for inclusion in a multidimensional construct. Consistent with the criticisms of Spector (1982), greater care should be exercised with respect to instrument development and assessment techniques. These measurement and methodological improvements alone should greatly enhance the understanding of entrepreneurs.

Second, previous research has inadvertently given internals and externals a connotation of good and bad. Internals are viewed typically as successful, intelligent, and decisive, while externals are perceived as inadequate, dull, and failure ridden. Such value judgments are very dangerous. There has been little research that has examined the long-term implications of locus of control, or the relationship between locus of control and other factors (both internal and external) critical to entrepreneurial success. Depending on these factors, certain locus of control "types" may be more or less suited to be entrepreneurs. Research in this area may find that certain locus of control behaviors are appropriate on a situational basis. Once again, a multidimensional construct may contribute to this approach.

Third, research consideration should be given to the relationship between various locus of control types within entrepreneurial organizations. For example, assuming that successful entrepreneurs tend to be internals, what managerial practices will facilitate the operation of their organizations and their dealing with externals and other internals? Stated alternatively, do externals have a significant role in entrepreneurial firms, and, if so, what should that role be? An important function of management is the delicate art of balancing external demands and constraints, vision, entrepreneurship, and internal politics (Quinn, 1977; Yavitz, 1982). Locus of control may have an influence on the effective alignment of these factors.

Fourth, research that examines the use of the locus of control construct for high potential entrepreneur identification and training would be an important contribution. Quality entrepreneur identification programs employing valid and reliable locus of control measures would be an asset to career guidance efforts and to individuals and organizations interested in selecting high potential entrepreneurs. In addition, research (see Exhibit 9.2) indicates that locus of control may be influenced through systematic training programs. These training efforts may benefit existing entrepreneurs, individuals embarking on entrepreneurial endeavors, and those with a long-term interest in entrepreneurial involvement.

Conclusion

The objective of this article was to provide a comprehensive background for researchers interested in using the locus of control construct. While the research issues outlined in the previous section do not represent an exhaustive list of potential topics, they are intended to stimulate entrepreneurial research within the area. Locus of control appears to hold considerable promise for further research development.

Source: This article excerpted from D. Jennings and C. Zeithaml, "Locus of Control: A Review and Directions for Entrepreneurial Research," *National Academy of Management Proceedings* (1983), 42–46.

ENDNOTES

1. For a review of these studies see R. D. Hisrich and M. P. Peters, *Entrepreneurship: Starting, Developing, and Managing a New Enterprise* (Homewood, Ill.: BPI-Irwin, 1989), 49–64; B. J. Bird, *Entrepreneurial Behavior* (Glenview, Ill.: Scott, Foresman, 1989), 77–127.
2. This rationale has been suggested by W. D. Guth, "Research in Entrepreneurship," *The Entrepreneurship Forum* (New York: Center for Entrepreneurial Studies, New York University, 1991).
3. Ibid. This stream of research has established, however, that successful entrepreneurs more frequently than nonentrepreneurs take a high degree of personal responsibility for their decisions, actions, and outcomes and have a high level of tolerance for ambiguity in comparision to nonentrepreneurs.
4. D. C. McClelland, *The Achieving Society* (Princeton, N. J.: Van Nostrand, 1961).
5. J. A. Hornaday and J. Aboud, "Characteristics of Successful Entrepreneurs," *Personnel Psychology* 24 (1971): 141–53.
6. T. M. Begley and D. P. Boyd, "Psychological Characteristics Associated with Performance in Entrepreneurial Firms and Smaller Businesses," *Journal of Business Venturing* 2 (1987): 79–93.
7. See Chapter 8 for a discussion of the entrepreneur as an uncertainty bearer. For the notion of uncertainty bearer in economic thought, the entrepreneur is the bearer of uncertainty. Without the entrepreneur, production could not take place in an uncertain environment.
8. J. L. Schere, "Tolerance of Ambiguity as a Discriminating Variable Between Entrepreneurs and Managers," *Academy of Management Proceedings* (1982): 404–8.
9. P. Liles, "Who Are the Entrepreneurs?" *Business Topics* 22 (1974): 5–14.
10. W. Long and W. E. McMullen, "Mapping the New Venture Opportunity Identification Process," *Frontiers of Entrepreneurship Research* 4 (1984): 56–68.
11. N. R. Smith and J. B. Miner, "Type of Entrepreneur, Type of Firm, and Managerial Motivation: Implications for Organizational Life Cycle Theory," *Strategic Management Journal* 4 (1983): 325–40.
12. P. Liles, *New Business Ventures and the Entrepreneur* (Homewood, Ill.: Richard D. Irwin, 1974).
13. M. E. R. Kets de Vries, "The Dark Side of Entrepreneurship," *Harvard Business Review* 63 (1985): 160–67.
14. Ibid.

CHAPTER 10

Are Entrepreneurs Really Different from Nonentrepreneurs?

A ttempts to differentiate individuals who have chosen to start their own businesses from those who have selected other career paths have been a recurring theme in entrepreneurship research. A critical assumption in this literature is that an entrepreneur is somehow different in terms of personality and that this *individual difference* can be used to predict the selection of an entrepreneurial career. Yet these studies have been criticized for their failure to address why some individuals are more likely than others to pursue an entrepreneurial career.[1]

This lack of research support for the argument that individual differences exist between entrepreneurs and nonentrepreneurs leads to an important question: are entrepreneurs really different from nonentrepreneurs? The first section of this chapter describes the nature of individual differences, while the second section reviews two research studies regarding the individual differences between entrepreneurs and nonentrepreneurs. The third section reviews Nobel laureate Theodore Schultz's argument that "the notion that entrepreneurs are only entrepreneurs is pure fiction."[2] The chapter concludes with a discussion of the three factors of personality.

NATURE OF INDIVIDUAL DIFFERENCES

Each person is similar to everyone else in many ways. For example, our basic appearances as well as our biological systems are much the same. However, each person is also very different from everyone else. The manner in which individuals interpret and respond to the environment and the way they think are unique. This uniqueness is called *individual differences* and consists of both physical and psychological differences.[3] Exhibit 10.1 illustrates the more common attributes that differentiate people from one another.

Two important individual differences are personality and a person's attitude. Personality has been described as consisting of determinants, stages, and traits,[4] as presented in the last section of this chapter. Attitudes have been viewed as either dispositional or situational. The dispositional view suggests that stable dis-

EXHIBIT 10.1 The Uniqueness of People

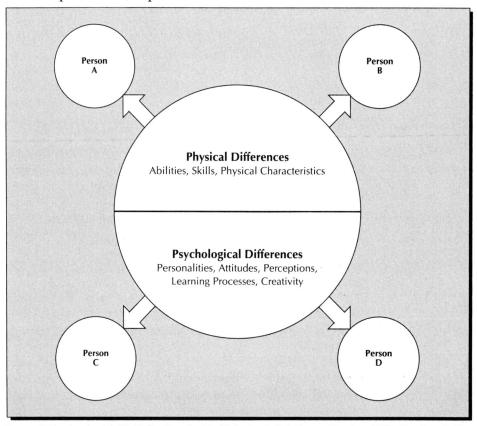

Source: G. Moorhead and R. W. Griffin, *Organizational Behavior,* 2nd ed. (Boston: Houghton Mifflin Company, 1989). Used by permission.

positions occur and lead to behavior toward objects in a certain way as a result of experience.[5] For example, if an individual did not like a certain restaurant (a disposition), then that individual would be expected to express consistently negative opinions of the restaurant and to maintain the consistent and predictable intention of not patronizing the restaurant.[6]

The situational view of attitudes challenges the dispositional view by arguing that attitudes are not stable dispositions composed of precise components that are consistently reflected in individual responses. Instead the situationalists argue that attitudes evolve from socially constructed realities.[7] Exhibit 10.2 describes the situational perspective.

In summary, most of the research focusing on behavioral aspects of entrepreneurs have tended to utilize the individual-difference dimensions of personality and have excluded the notion of attitudes. The situational perspective of attitudes illustrated in Exhibit 10.2 may provide new research directions for entrepreneurship.

We now turn our attention to two empirical studies that have investigated the individual differences between entrepreneurs and nonentrepreneurs.

RESEARCH STUDIES INVOLVING INDIVIDUAL DIFFERENCES BETWEEN ENTREPRENEURS AND NONENTREPRENEURS

Nancy Robbins conducted a study involving 78 entrepreneurs from the Minneapolis area and 84 middle and upper-level managers from a single Minneapolis corporation.[8] Specifics of the study are described in Exhibit 10.3. Using a variety of personality variables depicted in Exhibit 10.4, Robbins reported that no statistically significant differences existed between the entrepreneurs and the managers in her study with respect to the personality variables she used. Robbins noted that all the entrepreneurs were from one geographical locale and that all the managers were from one organization, which affects the generalizability of her study. Robbins commented that (1) the organization from

EXHIBIT   10.2   The Situational Perspective of Attitudes

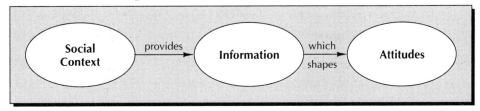

The situational perspective of attitudes argues that the social context delivers information that shapes the individual's attitudes. Through cues and guides, social information provides a specific prescription for socially acceptable attitudes and behaviors.

10.3 Specifics of Robbins's Study Involving Individual Differences Between Entrepreneurs and Managers

In this study, entrepreneurs were defined as individuals who had started a business where none existed before. Managers were individuals who held middle-·and upper-level management positions.

	Entrepreneurs	Managers
Number invited to participate	264	122
Study participants	78	84
Response rate	30%	69%
Number of males responding	50	84
Number of females responding	28	0
Average age of participants	42	48
Age range of participants	25 to 62	37 to 63

Entrepreneur Participants

Type of Business

Service-oriented	65%
Manufacturing	23%
Retail sales	12%
	100%

Number of Employees

More than 100	7%
51 to 100	4%
Fewer than 50	89%
	100%

Length of Time Spent in Current Business

More than five years	21%
Three to five years	29%
Two years or less	50%
	100%

Management Participants

Job Level

Upper level	36%
Middle level	64%
	100%

Source: Data developed from N. E. G. Robbins, "Entrepreneurial Assessment: Characteristics Which Differentiate Entrepreneurs, Intrapreneurs, and Managers" (Ph. D. diss., University of Minnesota, 1986).

which the management sample was obtained tended to have an "entrepreneurial bent to it—entrepreneurship and entrepreneurial behavior were highly valued by top management" and (2) this organizational entrepreneurial tendency may have created a bias in that managers in the focal organization may have been more entrepreneurial than managers in other organizations.[9]

In another study Peter Robinson developed an Entrepreneurial Attitude Orientation Scale, which consists of the four characteristics of achievement, innovation, locus of control, and self-esteem.[10] Robinson's survey instrument was designed to measure these four characteristics as well as the affective, cognitive, and conative aspects of entrepreneurs.[11] Robinson used four groups of subjects in his study—two control groups and two experimental groups. College students made up one set of subjects, including a control group and an experimental group. The other set of subjects also included both a control group and an experimental group and were nonstudents.

EXHIBIT   10.4   Personality Variables Used in Robbins's Study

Variables from Jackson Personality Research Form (PRF)
   Abasement
   Achievement
   Affiliation
   Aggression
   Autonomy
   Change
   Cognitive structure
   Dominance
   Endurance
   Nurturance
   Social recognition
   Succorance
Variables from Jackson Personality Inventory (JPI) Scales
   Anxiety
   Complexity
   Conformity
   Energy level
   Innovation
   Interpersonal affect
   Risk taking
   Self-esteem
   Social participation
Locus of control measured by Rotter's Instrument
California Psychological Inventory (short form)

Source: Data developed from N. E. G. Robbins, "Entrepreneurial Assessment: Characteristics Which Differentiate Entrepreneurs, Intrapreneurs, and Managers" (Ph. D. diss., University of Minnesota, 1986).

The student experimental group consisted of 24 student entrepreneurs who (1) owned their own business at the time of the study, (2) had previously owned a business, or (3) were working on a business project without the formal organization yet being in place. Student entrepreneurs were located at three universities and were juniors, seniors, or first-year M.B.A. students. The student control group involved 63 freshmen or sophomores from an introductory psychology course who had no prior business experience.

The nonstudent experimental group contained 54 businesspersons who (1) had started a business within the last five years and (2) had a history of more than one business startup. The nonstudent control group numbered 57 nonentrepreneurial individuals who were career, white collar, nonmanagement employees. These nonentrepreneurs were screened to avoid selecting "closet entrepreneurs" (individuals with a full-time job who also owned a small business).[12]

Robinson noted that while his study identified a "constellation of attitudes" relating to entrepreneurship, his Entrepreneurial Attitude Orientation Scale needs to be "readministered to other groups of subjects to check its reliability and validity as an independent scale."[13]

THEODORE SCHULTZ'S ARGUMENT

Professor Theodore Schultz makes the argument[14] that there is a distinction between the "abilities" and "capacities" of individuals and suggests that it is better to think that people have abilities and that nonhuman factors have capacities. For example, the capacity of farmland can be increased by irrigation and the application of fertilizers and lime. The capacity of machines and equipment can be increased by changes in design. Individuals, however, have abilities that are both innate and acquired. According to Schultz, the differences in acquired abilities may explain entrepreneurial behavior, because the distribution of genetic abilities in large populations is about equal, but there are differences in acquired abilities. These acquired abilities are influenced by investments in human capital: experience, education, and health.[15] However, Schultz also argues that entrepreneurial abilities are not limited to a certain group of individuals. For example, Schultz states that "in analyzing entrepreneurship, no able-bodied adult has only entrepreneurial abilities. The notion that entrepreneurs are only entrepreneurs is pure fiction."[16] Referring to the scenario in Exhibit 10.5, Schultz describes a situation in which specialists have abilities that are not specific to their specialized work.

Schultz also notes that entrepreneurial ability is not transferable. According to Schultz:

A human being's stock of entrepreneurial ability cannot be separated from the person who has it. The implications are it cannot be sold to someone else and it cannot be transferred to heirs. The heirs of fathers who are successful entrepreneurs are, as a rule, not up to that of their father's achievements, genetic endowment notwithstanding. A person's stock of entrepreneurial ability cannot be appropriated by governments. Jews and other ethnic groups facing the danger of being expelled have known this fact for ages. Since their property has often been confiscated, one of their responses has been to invest more in their human capital, including entrepreneurial ability, than they otherwise would have, as have the Chinese in countries in parts of Asia, Indians in Africa, Parsees in Bombay, Lebanese in the Middle East, Jews in Europe, and Huguenots in France.[17]

In essence Schultz argues that *every* individual can acquire the abilities to become an entrepreneur. These acquired abilities include learning from experience and investments in education and health.

THREE FACTORS OF PERSONALITY: DETERMINANTS, STAGES, AND TRAITS

Determinants

Three components have been identified as determinants of personality: heredity or biological components, social or situational components, and cultural or environmental components.

Heredity or Biological Components

Heredity or biological components are those factors that one inherits from one's parents. For example, physical stature, facial attractiveness, sex, muscle composition, and reflexes are characteristics that are either completely or substantially influenced by one's parents. In essence this perspective argues that personality characteristics such as temperament and sociability are determined in much the same way as facial features or body build. These characteristics affect how an individual feels about himself or herself. As an example, facial attractiveness may cause a man to "feel good" about his physical appearance. While earlier arguments suggested that heredity or biological factors completely dictate personality, organizational-science researchers have rejected that notion as an inadequate explanation of personality.[18]

EXHIBIT   10.5   Specialists with Abilities Not Specific to Their Specialized Work Who Become Entrepreneurs

> Every individual who is an economic agent, however specialized his or her work may be, has a variety of abilities that are not specific to his or her specialized work. For example, a druggist, who is qualified in pharmacology, has the expertise and the credentials to operate a drugstore. This druggist may earn a satisfactory return on his or her investment in specialized abilities and on his or her physical capital invested in the drugstore. However, Schultz argues, when the economic environment of the druggist changes, the druggist's response is that of an entrepreneur.

Source: Adapted from T. W. Schultz, "Demand and Supply," *Restoring Economic Equilibrium: Human Capital in the Modernizing Economy* (London: Basil Blackwell, 1990).

Social or Situational Components

An individual's personality, while generally stable and consistent, does change in different situations. For example, the kind of people that individuals interact with may influence their own behavior. An increasing body of literature on socialization suggests that social forces in the workplace affect an individual's personality and behavior.[19]

Cultural or Environmental Components

The environment that individuals are exposed to plays a role in shaping their personality. For example, research on the relationship of birth order to personality has revealed some interesting findings. First-born children tend to be more ambitious, more cooperative, and more concerned with being socially accepted than are later-born children.[20]

Culture establishes the norms, attitudes, and values that are passed along from one generation to the next and creates consistency over time. In addition an ideology that is important in one culture may have only moderate influence in others.[21] For example, a strong sense of competitiveness may prevail in one culture, while individuals from another culture may be more comfortable with cooperation. Research into the cultural determinants of personality is still in its infancy.[22]

Stages

A number of psychologists have argued that as time passes individuals change. These changes are somewhat predictable rather than being purely random and unstable and are considered to be both healthy and desirable for both the individual and the social system. For example, Freud argued that personality is shaped by unconscious motives, which are developed in a variety of stages. These motives were considered as occurring in the following four stages: dependent, compulsive, oedipal, and mature.[23] Freud's precise stages generally are not accepted by contemporary theorists.[24]

Erik Erikson, however, noted that Freud's stages were heavily slanted toward biological and sexual factors and conceptualized eight stages based on the social adaptations people have to make as they grow older.[25] Certain researchers have suggested that Erikson's stages may appear in the form of the crises individuals face as they move from being a newcomer to being a mature member and then a senior member of an organization.[26]

Jean Piaget, whose work is supported by empirical research,[27] also suggested that individuals pass through precise stages of personality development.[28] Piaget's stages are not specifically relevant to organizational settings.[29]

Traits

The trait approach for studying personality formation attempts to identify a configuration of traits that best reflect personality. Allport suggested that all individuals have a set of common personality traits and also a set of unique traits, which he called personal dispositions.[30] Cattell argued that an individual's personality can be characterized along two dimensions: surface traits and source traits. According to Cattell, surface traits reflect the observable and consistent behaviors of individuals, while source traits are more difficult to discern because they often are kept hidden.[31]

Efforts to isolate traits have been hindered because there are so many of them. For example, one study identified 17,953 traits.[32] While several traits have been identified as having direct relevance for the workplace,[33] the traits of the majority of individuals are not predictable and must be considered in their situational context.[34]

ENDNOTES

1. For a review of the criticism directed toward studies focusing on individual differences between entrepreneurs and nonentrepreneurs, see R. F. Scherer et al., "Role Model Performance Effects on Development of Entrepreneurial Career Preference," *Entrepreneurship Theory and Practice* 13 (1989): 53–71.
2. T. W. Schultz, *Restoring Economic Equilibrium: Human Capital in the Modernizing Economy* (London: Basil Blackwell, 1990), 96.
3. G. Moorhead and R. W. Griffin, "Individual Differences," *Organizational Behavior,* 3rd ed. (Boston: Houghton Mifflin, 1992), 72–101.
4. For an earlier review of personality, see W. Mischel, *Introduction to Personality* (New York: Holt, 1971). Recent reviews are described in L. Pervin, "Personality," in *Annual Review of Psychology,* vol. 36, ed. M. Rosenzweig and L. Porter (Palo Alto, Calif.: Annual Reviews, 1985), 83–114.
5. G. W. Allport, "Attitudes," in *Handbook of Social Psychology,* ed. C. Murchison (Worcester, Mass.: Clark University Press, 1935), 798–844; B. Gerhart, "How Important Are Dispositional Factors as Determinants of Job Satisfaction? Implications for Job Design and Other Personnel Programs," *Journal of Applied Psychology* 72 (1987): 366–73.
6. This example was developed from Moorhead and Griffin, "Individual Differences."
7. G. Salancik and J. Pfeffer, "A Social Information Processing Approach to Job Attitudes and Task Design," *Administrative Science Quarterly* 23 (1978): 224–53; J. Thomas and R. W. Griffin, "The Social Information Processing Model of Task Design: A Review of the Literature," *Academy of Management Review* 8 (1983): 672–82.
8. N. E. G. Robbins, "Entrepreneurial Assessment: Characteristics Which Differentiate Entrepreneurs, Intrapreneurs and Managers" (Ph. D. diss., University of Minnesota, 1986.)
9. Ibid., 132–33.
10. P. B. Robinson, "Prediction of Entrepreneurship Based on an Attitude Consistency Model" (Ph. D. diss., Brigham Young University, 1987). Robinson has suggested that attitude theory can be used as an alternative to trait and demographic approaches used to study entrepreneurs. For a detailed discussion of this approach, see P. B. Robinson et al., "An Attitude Approach to the Prediction of Entrepreneurship," *Entrepreneurship Theory and Practice* 15 (1991): 13–32.
11. Ibid., 76–77.
12. Ibid., 78.
13. Ibid., 80.
14. See Chapter 7 of this text for Schultz's article on entrepreneurship and human capital.

15. Schultz, *Restoring Economic Equilibrium*, 219–21.

16. Ibid., 96.

17. Ibid., 96.

18. S. P. Robbins, *Organizational Behavior*, 5th ed. (Englewood Cliffs, N. J.: Prentice-Hall, 1992), 52.

19. J. P. Wanous, A. E. Reichers, and S. D. Malik, "Organizational Socialization and Group Development: Toward An Integrative Perspective," *Academy of Management Review* 9 (1984): 670–83.

20. J. R. Warren, "Birth Order and Social Behavior," *Psychological Bulletin* 65 (1966): 38–49.

21. N. J. Adler, *International Dimensions of Organizational Behavior*, 2nd ed. (Boston: PWS Kent, 1989).

22. Moorhead and Griffin, "Individual Differences," 79.

23. S. Freud, "Lecture XXXIII," *New Introductory Lectures on Psychoanalysis* (New York: Norton, 1933), 153–86.

24. R. Cattell, *The Scientific Analysis of Personality* (Chicago: Aldine, 1965).

25. E. Erikson, *Childhood and Society*, 2nd ed. (New York: Norton, 1933).

26. Moorhead and Griffin, "Individual Differences," 79.

27. Mischel, *Introduction to Personality*.

28. J. Piaget, "The General Problems of the Psychological Development of the Child," in *Discussions on Child Development*, ed. J. M. Tanner and B. Inhelder (New York: International Universities Press, 1960), 3–27.

29. Moorhead and Griffin, "Individual Differences," 80–81.

30. G. W. Allport, *Pattern and Growth in Personality* (New York: Holt, 1961).

31. Cattell, *The Scientific Analysis of Personality*.

32. G. W. Allport and H. S. Odbert, "Trait Names: A Psycholexical Study," *Psychological Monographs* 47 (1936): 5–29.

33. Most organizational behavior textbooks identify the following six traits: locus of control, authoritarianism, Machiavellianism, risk taking, achievement orientation, and self-esteem.

34. Robbins, *Organizational Behavior*, 55–56.

Corporate Entrepreneurship

Overview of Corporate Entrepreneurship

C hapters 11, 12, 13, and 14 describe the corporate entrepreneurship school of thought. This chapter defines the concept of corporate entrepreneurship and gives an overview of three distinct research activities involving different aspects of corporate entrepreneurship. Because there is some discussion concerning the relationship between organizational innovation and corporate entrepreneurship, a section in Chapter 11 describes organizational innovation. Chapter 11 concludes with a discussion regarding how organizational size affects corporate entrepreneurship. Chapter 12 focuses on research studies of organizational factors that foster or hinder corporate entrepreneurship at an organizational level of analysis. Chapter 13 examines conceptual studies that explore the notion of corporate venturing. Articles presented in Chapter 14 describe the process of intrapreneurship and compare this concept with corporate entrepreneurship.

We are now ready to begin Chapter 11 and to consider the concept of corporate entrepreneurship.

CONCEPT OF CORPORATE ENTREPRENEURSHIP

There has been a tendency to identify entrepreneurship with dominant, independent-minded owner-managers who make the strategic decisions for their firms.[1] Recently, however, researchers have shifted their interests to the entrepreneurial activities of the firm, thus creating the notion of corporate entrepreneurship.[2] These researchers consider corporate entrepreneurship to be a multidimensional concept that incorporates a firm's activities directed at product and technological innovation, risk taking, and proactiveness. There is some debate, however, regarding the role of innovation in defining entrepreneurship. As stated in Chapter 1, Schumpeter argued that an individual is an entrepreneur only when he or she is engaged in innovative behavior, while other researchers consider entrepreneurship to include the administrative activities involved in managing an enterprise.[3] In Module 1, which described entrepreneurship as an economic function, we learned that a number of economists agree with Schumpeter's view regarding entrepreneurship and innovative behavior.

The following section provides an overview of organizational innovation.

Organizational Innovation

Organizational-science researchers have identified three types of innovation: technological, administrative, and ancillary. Technological innovations are those that bring change to organizations by introducing changes in technology. Administrative innovations are those that change an organization's structure or its administrative processes. Ancillary innovations are programs developed between a focal organization and groups outside the boundary of the focal organization. Examples of ancillary innovations include library community service activities, career development projects, and continuing education programs.[4]

Both technological and administrative innovations occur within an organization and are under the control of the focal organization's management. Ancillary innovations occur at an organization's interface with sectors of its external environment and are outside the focal organization. This type of innovation is not fully controlled by the focal organization's management.[5]

Organizational science researchers have identified three groups of factors that influence the adoption of a particular type of innovation. These include individual, organizational, and environmental variables. For example, individual variables are the values, roles, and personalities of an organization's leaders. Organizational variables include specialization, functional differentiation, professionalism, size, slack, and administrative intensity. Environmental variables are described along six dimensions, including whether the environment is stable or unstable, homogeneous or heterogeneous, concentrated or dispersed, simple or complex; the extent of turbulence; and the amount of resources available to support the organization.[6]

There is continuing debate regarding which group of these factors has the greatest influence on an organization's adoption of an innovation. Several researchers have reported that organizational variables are the most important in the adoption process.[7]

A number of researchers have linked various aspects of entrepreneurship with types of innovation at both individual and organizational levels of analysis.[8] For example, Miller and Friesen used the notion of organizational configurations to study product innovation. These two researchers developed a continuum ranging from "entrepreneurial" to "conservative" firms. An entrepreneurial organization was viewed as engaging in innovative activities to develop a distinctive competence, while a conservative organization viewed innovation as something done in response to challenges, occurring only when necessary. Miller and Friesen found significant differences between their entrepreneurial and conservative organizations with respect to environmental, information-processing, structural, and decision-making variables.[9] These variables are described in Exhibit 11.1.

EXHIBIT   11.1   Relationships Among Environmental, Information-Processing, Structural, and Decision-Making Variables and Entrepreneurial Activities

Environmental Variables

- The more competitive the environment, the greater the need for innovation and the more likely it is that firms will be innovative.
- Firms with a diversity in personnel, operating procedures, technologies, and administrative practices that operate in many different markets tend to be innovative because ideas are borrowed from one market and applied in another.

Information-Processing Variables

- The technique of gathering and processing information concerning a firm's environment is known as *environmental scanning.*
- A limitation on a firm's ability to innovate is its ability to recognize the needs and demands of its external environment. Perceived market needs account for ideas for innovation. Entrepreneurial firms scan their environments searching for opportunities.
- Financial controls may identify areas of weakness and encourage remedial innovations. Nonentrepreneurial firms scan their environments in search for threats.

Structural Variables

- A powerful leader is able to overcome resistance to change and make bold innovations.
- Professional employees possess the knowledge and training to recognize the need for change. Structures that have a high percentage of influential professionals tend to be the most innovative.
- The extent to which a firm's products require different marketing and production methods and procedures provides more varied sources of information for developing new programs.
- Most major innovations are too costly to be undertaken by firms that are short of organizational resources such as laboratories, scientists, and financial capital.

Decision-Making Variables

- The more analysis is performed by key decision makers—the more they search deeply for the roots of problems and try to generate the best solutions—the more likely it is that opportunities for innovation will be discovered and pursued.
- Managers who make seat-of-the-pants decisions are unlikely to spend the time and effort required to recognize the need for innovations.

Source: Adapted from D. Miller and P. H. Friesen, "Innovation in Conservative and Entrepreneurial Firms: Two Models of Strategic Momentum," *Strategic Management Journal* 3 (1982): 1–25.

Chapter 3 described how economists have studied innovation. The following section details organizational factors that can foster or hinder entrepreneurship.

Organizational Factors That Foster or Hinder Entrepreneurship

From the organizational factors viewpoint, earlier researchers have investigated how changes in the task of work affect performance and innovation. For example, Tisk and Bamforth reported that changes in the task can inadvertently disrupt the social system of the organization, causing serious difficulties.[10] Kanter, Stevenson, and Sathe have written that large corporations use rules and policies to properly administer the routine tasks of the organization. These regulations often stifle innovative, entrepreneurial activities.[11]

Other researchers have investigated the relationship between entrepreneurship and organizational factors by examining to what extent different organizational structures are utilized to deal with changing environmental conditions. Burns and Stalker[12] were the first researchers to determine empirically that organizational structure varies with a changing environment. Burns and Stalker examined twenty manufacturing firms in Scotland and England and reported that a number of these organizations facing a stable environment used a structure similar to Weber's bureaucratic concept.[13] Burns and Stalker described this structure as mechanistic because the organizations that were studied had defined the decision-authority relationships and rules almost to the point of mechanizing them. Burns and Stalker identified another organizational context, with opposite characteristics to the mechanistic structure, that they called the organic structure. Later researchers have characterized the image of an innovative or entrepreneurial organization as having features similar to Burns and Stalker's organic organization. These similar characteristics include decentralization, flexibility, and the absence of rules and regulations.[14]

Continuing with research regarding organizational structure and entrepreneurship, Wilson argued that the structure of an organization that generates innovative ideas conflicts with the structure that eventually implements the idea.[15] Duncan suggested that organizations must be "ambidextrous" to accomplish innovative or entrepreneurial activities. For example, structures must exist that are appropriate for the initiation and implementation of new ideas. According to Duncan, the organization should be "organic" when new ideas are being initiated and "mechanistic" during the implementation phase.[16]

Corporate Venturing

The second perspective of corporate entrepreneurship is the notion of internal corporate venturing and deals with how corporations engage in internal ventures to take advantage of various opportunities.[17] A process model of internal corporate venturing has been developed by exploring how corporations transform their research and development activities at the "frontier of corporate technology" into new businesses that are not in the "mainstream" of existing corporate operations. This model suggests that the success of the process of internal corporate venturing depends on the availability of autonomous entrepreneurial activity on the part of operational-level participants, on the ability of middle-level managers to conceptualize the strategic implications of these initiatives in more general terms, and on the capacity of top management to allow viable entrepreneurial initiatives to change the corporate strategy.[18]

In a review of the corporate venturing literature, MacMillan reported that most of the research on corporate venturing in established firms has focused on the venturing process itself.[19] Other studies have investigated the relationship of certain variables to the corporate venture. These studies include *Corporate Culture and Support*,[20] *Mission Statement Definition*,[21] *Venture Strategy*,[22] *Structure of the Venture Activity*,[23] *Staffing the Venture Activity*,[24] and *Reward Systems for Venture Management*.[25]

Despite this interest in corporate venturing, MacMillan has suggested that several definitional problems still exist. For example, while researchers have used a variety of ways to define a corporate venture, there has been little agreement about where the venturing process begins. Some researchers have suggested that venturing begins as something new is created (invention); others believe that venturing begins when an idea has been converted into a commercial application (innovation); and still others tend to define venturing as the marketing of a new creation (diffusion).[26]

Definitional problems aside, other questions remain. Are there, for example, certain organizational variables that can foster or impede corporate venturing in established firms? Certain researchers suggest that corporate venturing may be related to industry structure. In the same way that Porter[27] talks about industry structure constraining a firm's strategy, these researchers have posited that industry structure constrains a firm's ability to form corporate ventures.[28] Another important research question concerning how established firms respond to new business opportunities is the relationship between organizational structure and strategy and a firm's response to new business ventures.

One research study investigated how established financial firms respond to new business opportunities following an industry deregulation and then compared those activities to accepted, well-known strategy typologies and structural arrangements. This study reported that firms with high levels of venturing activities tend to have a prospector strategy and organic structure. Firms with a low level of venturing activity tend to have a defender strategy and mechanistic structure.[29] Integrating these well-known and defined strategy and structure classifications with other variables provides fertile ground for further corporate venturing research.

Another aspect of the venturing process involves obtaining venture capital as a source of financing. While many entrepreneurial firms utilize venture capital as a major source of financing for the first stage or initiation of the venture, a number of firms utilize venture capital for second- and third-stage financing.[30]

A review of the "academic" literature regarding venture capital research from 1981 to 1986 indicates that (1) venture capital research is embryonic and fragmented and (2) attempts to apply financial theory to venture capital research have been unsuccessful.[31] This review indicated that certain fundamental problems plague venture capital research, including the following: (1) the level of uncertainty in a venture is extremely high; (2) venture capitalists are not totally rational decision makers; and (3) contributions of the venture capitalists to the entrepreneurial firm are more than financial.[32]

The following is a descriptive model developed for the venture capital process:

> The process can be broken into three levels. At the extremes are the investor and the investee, an entrepreneurial firm. The investor has both funds to invest and a desire to invest in entrepreneurial firms. The investee has developed to an extent that it is in need of outside capital and has chosen venture capital as its source. In the middle lies the venture capitalist who serves as intermediary between the investor and the entrepreneurial firm. Venture capital research is primarily concerned with three areas: 1. the relationship between investor and venture capital firm, 2. the relationship between the venture capital firm and the investee and 3. the operation of the venture capital firm.[33]

In another approach toward studying the venture capital process, concepts from organizational economics have been utilized to develop a theory that explains the level of monitoring and control built into the relationship between venture capital firms and new ventures. This approach indicates that the level of monitoring and control depends on the level of business and agency risk associated with investing in a new firm.[34] Exhibit 11.2 describes how a previously successful venture capital firm failed to implement a high-tech venture.

EXHIBIT   11.2   A Venture Capital Star Flops

Kleiner Perkins Caulfield & Byers—a prestigious high-tech venture capital group that has helped launch a number of high-tech companies, including Genentech, Tandem, Lotus, Compaq, and Sun—is suffering from a host of errors after attempting to develop a laptop computer. Unlike most venture capital firms that finance ideas brought to them, Kleiner Perkins finances the ideas of its own partners and then lets them staff the new companies.

In early 1987 a Kleiner Perkins partner, Vinod Khosla, was approached by a San Jose, California, technology firm offering a new technology in manufacturing laptop computers. The owner of the San Jose company, Todd Morgenthaler, indicated that he had developed a method to produce the main circuitry of IBM's PC AT on a single piece of silicone. Even today such a design is difficult, but the benefits are enormous: lower manufacturing costs and lower power consumption, which are big pluses for a new laptop.

continued

EXHIBIT   11.2   *concluded*

Khosla and another Kleiner Perkins partner, John Doerr, agreed to use Morgenthaler's design and approached their firm for funding. Both Khosla and Doerr had previously developed several high-tech companies for Kleiner Perkins. In late 1987 Kleiner Perkins agreed to finance the venture, and Dynabook Technologies Corporation was founded to produce laptop computers.

Over the next three years, Khosla and Doerr raised $37 million, including $3 million of their own money and $8 million from Kleiner Perkins, making Dynabook one of the best-ever financed computer startups.

Despite this endowment, Dynabook failed miserably. Instead of hiring a full-time engineering chief, Dynabook relied on consultants, outside contractors, and part-time engineers to design both the product and the manufacturing process. A key manufacturing manager was fired and not replaced. Morgenthaler, who fell behind in developing his design because of the distraction of a brother dying with cancer, reported that he was treated like a "hired hand" by Khosla and Doerr rather than as a valued associate. Morgenthaler was also fired by Khosla and Doerr. Consequently manufacturing was botched.

One former employee commented that Khosla and Doerr spent their time raising money and hired consultants to solve manufacturing problems. This same employee noted that Dynabook developed a "rent-a-company" image. Management became confused and fragmented. By early 1990, after failing to meet delivery dates and experiencing defects in the laptop's screen, Khosla and Doerr decided to stop production of the laptop and concentrated on designing future machines from scratch. In late 1990 Dynabook downsized from a staff of 140 to 28 and placed its assets on the selling block. Unisys announced an offer to purchase Dynabook's assets for only $5 million.

Why did such a successful venture capital firm as Kleiner Perkins make a host of errors in trying to operate Dynabook?

Kleiner Perkins' mishandling of Dynabook provides ammunition to critics of its practice—avoided by many venture capital firms—of providing funding for ventures dreamed up by its partners.

According to Pascal Zachary, who has studied Kleiner Perkins' mistakes, Dynabook's failure suggests "with high tech being increasingly dominated by global companies, venture capitalists will have a difficult time in reaping the bonanzas common a decade ago. This failure also makes it clear that entrepreneurs, not venture capitalists, are critical in forging new companies." Kleiner Perkins' president states that "Dynabook got into trouble because it didn't have that entrepreneur. It relied on a professional team that came in to execute someone else's ideas. It is hard to tell when hired managers have the requisite passion for a venture because if you make the venture tempting enough, everyone becomes an entrepreneur."

Source: Adapted from P. Zachary, "Computer Glitch: Venture-Capital Star, Kleiner-Perkins, Flops as a Maker of Laptops," *Wall Street Journal,* 26 July 1990, A1.

Intrapreneurship

The third perspective of corporate entrepreneurship focuses on *intrapreneurship,* or how entrepreneurs function within large organizations. One writer reported that entrepreneurs get fired from large organizations because "asking for a large company to engage in entrepreneurship is like trying to get an elephant to ice skate."[35] Kanter, however, has noted that many large firms are now aware that internal entrepreneurs are necessary to achieve growth. The internal entrepreneur, like the external entrepreneur, enacts new opportunities and drives the development of new resource combinations or recombinations. Kanter has indicated that large firms are utilizing new organizational forms and arrangements to facilitate internal entrepreneurship.[36] Exhibit 11.3 describes how a large company failed to successfully implement a program of internal entrepreneurship.

Internal entrepreneurs do have problems functioning in certain large organizations. One study concluded that individual entrepreneurship and the large corporation should be viewed as existing on opposite ends of an organization scale.[37] One prominent executive noted that the corporate culture of large companies leaves little room for in-house entrepreneurs.[38]

EXHIBIT 11.3   Eastman Kodak Fails at Internal Entrepreneurship

Eastman Kodak Company, incorporated in 1901, obtained a superior position in the world photography industry and became one of the most profitable American corporations by using the following four principles: (1) mass production to lower production costs, (2) maintaining a lead in technological development, (3) extensive product advertising, and (4) developing a multinational business to exploit the world market. However, during the 1980s the environment of the photographic industry surrounding Kodak changed dramatically. For example, Fuji of Japan became the cost and quality leader in photographic film. A federal judge ordered Kodak out of the instant photography business for violating seven of Polaroid's patents in Kodak's rush to produce an instant camera. The emergence of new industries that provided alternative means for producing and recording images such as VCRs destroyed Kodak's profitable film-based home-movie business. These changes in the competitive environment caused enormous difficulties for Kodak. For example, between 1972 and 1986 profit margins from sales declined from nearly 16 percent to 3 percent. Kodak stock, once outstanding, was the worst performer among the thirty blue-chip issues in the Dow Jones industrial average. Kodak's deteriorating position was apparent when net earnings plummeted by 68 percent, from $1.2 billion in 1982 to $374 million in 1986.

Colby Chandler, who became chief executive officer in July 1983, attempted to improve Kodak's profitability by implementing a twofold strategy: (1) increase control of existing businesses by introducing new products made by Kodak or bought from Japanese manufacturers and sold under its name and (2) diversify into new businesses. To instill an entrepreneurial zeal, Kodak created fourteen internal ventures to commercialize technologies that did not have a home in its core business groups of photography, information systems, and pharmaceuticals. The idea was that Kodak, the parent company, would provide seed money to employees, who would gain the satisfaction of running their own shop while producing products that benefited their corporate sponsor.

continued

EXHIBIT 11.3 *concluded*

> While Kodak's efforts at creating internal ventures were praised in the management book *When Giants Learn to Dance,* the program was always an awkward minuet. By 1990 the dance was clearly over. Of the fourteen ventures Kodak created, six have been shut down, three have been sold, four have been merged into the company, and only one is operating independently. Furthermore, Kodak said it would no longer seek new ventures and instead would focus on its core businesses.
>
> What went wrong at Kodak? James Hirsch, a reporter for the *Wall Street Journal,* states that the practices that make corporations successful—training procedures, personnel policies, hierarchical management structures—are anathema to risk-taking, free-wheeling entrepreneurs. In addition, employees-turned-entrepreneurs are often ill-prepared for their new roles. Researchers, for example, who have spent their careers in the lab are unfamiliar with the rigors of the marketplace. According to interviews obtained by Hirsch, many of the venture managers were terminated when Kodak became dissatisfied with their performance. These terminated managers reported that Kodak established unrealistic sales goals and did not give them the autonomy they needed. One former manager indicated that Kodak "killed his entrepreneurial spirit" as a result of bureaucratic controls.

Source: Adapted from T. Moore, "Embattled Kodak Enters the Electronic Age," *Fortune,* 22 August 1983, 120–28; C. Chandler, "Eastman Kodak Opens Windows of Opportunity," *Journal of Business Strategy* 7 (1986): 5–9; A. Taylor, "Kodak Scrambles to Refocus," *Fortune* 3 (1986): 34–38; J. Hirsch, "Kodak Effort at 'Intrapreneurship' Fails," *Wall Street Journal,* 17 August 1990, B1 and B8.

While Pinchot has been given credit for developing the term *intrapreneur* to describe individuals in large companies who are entrepreneurs,[39] other researchers have reported a difference between intrapreneurship and corporate venturing.[40] (Chapter 14 contains an article that describes this difference.)

Pinchot stated that intrapreneurs are concerned with both designing products or projects and then being personally involved in the implementation process. Autonomy is valued more than the traditional corporate rewards. But, asked Pinchot, what happens when autonomy or freedom to act is removed? Intrapreneurs should "come to work each day willing to be fired, to circumvent any order aimed at stopping your dream."[41]

Innovative firms with a "passion for excellence" have been described as having the attributes of discipline, purpose, and concern for the future.[42] Innovative firms are described as practicing entrepreneurship by converting "bright ideas" into organized activities through a "systematic management approach and focused strategy."[43]

Sathe used the notion of corporate culture to present some insights on how entrepreneurs will function in future organizational settings. According to Sathe, innovation can be achieved by avoiding the friction between new ideas and established norms when the organization's culture involves a socialization process that fosters cooperation, integrity, and communication.[44]

The essence of intrapreneurship was stated by Peterson and Berger, who used Schumpeter's 1934 description of entrepreneurship. As described by

Schumpeter, "new combinations" most often are made by employees of large firms rather than by self-employed business men or women. According to Schumpeter, entrepreneurship emerges only when the objective possibilities for new combinations are present, and that entrepreneurship does not emerge automatically. The exercise of entrepreneurship in large firms requires the freedom to work outside normal channels; thus, there is a tension between the intermittent organizational need for entrepreneurship and the entrepreneur's empire-building way of working, so that the intrapreneur is likely to find the organization stultifying, while the organization may often find the intrapreneur disruptive.[45]

Organizational Size and Corporate Entrepreneurship

What is the relationship between organizational size and corporate entrepreneurship? Conventional wisdom suggests that entrepreneurship may bloom and grow better in smaller, flexible organizations than in larger, bureaucratic forms. Organizational size alone may not be the determining factor. Other organizational variables exist, as described earlier in this chapter, that can foster or hinder entrepreneurship within an organizational setting.

There are also glimpses from researchers that indicate mixed theories regarding organizational size as a single variable and entrepreneurship. For example, Macrae predicted that small-size entrepreneurial organizations will grow in number and will eventually replace the multinational corporation by the year 2010.[46] Yet Schumpeter suggested that, in some cases, large oligopolistic firms may outperform small, perfectly competitive firms in dynamic terms.[47]

Libecap made the following observation regarding organization size and entrepreneurship:

> Differences between large and small firms with respect to entrepreneurship is a matter of degree and not absolutes. In large, well-run organizations, executives seek to achieve objectives in terms of established priorities. If entrepreneurs are frustrated because management won't pursue new product development, for example, it may be that management does not view the idea as feasible within the order of priorities, rather than an inflexibility toward change. In the long run, management may be contributing just as much or maybe more, if they pursue their objectives for product development and other improvements. If the priorities are set, a good management team cannot listen to every new idea because they won't be successful in achieving their plans and goals. Whether or not management has selected the correct priorities, however, is another issue. But it should not be argued that large organizations are a poor environment for entrepreneurs.[48]

From a research methodology perspective, several researchers have argued that small-size firms may exhibit different organizational characteristics than their large-size counterparts and suggest that this factor be considered in data analysis.[49] In the article by Jennings and Lumpkin presented at the end of Chapter 12, a statistical technique is used to successfully control for organizational size.[50]

Another interesting question regarding organizational size and entrepreneurship is related to firm growth. As an organization grows and is successful, is it possible to sustain an entrepreneurial environment? Does the success of a venture inevitably lead to a more structured and less innovative environment? For example, Kanter reported that segmentation and bureaucratic procedures occur when organizational size and complexity increase, which often constrains internal entrepreneurship and innovation unless special systems are put into place to motivate and enable entrepreneurial and innovative behavior. Kanter suggested that key motivating factors should include a balance of intrinsic and extrinsic rewards for entrepreneurial and innovative behavior. According to Kanter, pay, in itself, is a relatively weak motivation for innovation and often serves only as a proxy for recognition.[51]

Researchers have argued that motivating factors by themselves will not stimulate innovative behavior. Instead the organization must develop a context that "enables" innovation to occur. These "enabling conditions" are described as the following:

- resources for innovation
- frequent communications across departmental lines and among people with dissimilar viewpoints
- moderate environmental uncertainty and mechanisms for focusing attention on changing conditions
- cohesive work groups with open conflict resolution mechanisms that integrate creative personalities into the mainstream
- structures that provide access to innovation role models and mentors
- moderate personnel turnover
- psychological contracts that legitimate and solicit spontaneous innovative behavior[52]

Several researchers have indicated that a major factor in determining a firm's success in innovation, regardless of its size, is the role played by its top manager.[53] Van de Ven suggested that top managers should enact at least the following four roles:[54] sponsor, mentor, critic, and institutional leader. These roles are described in greater detail in Exhibit 11.4.

EXHIBIT 11.4 Managerial Roles That Promote the Development of Innovation

Sponsor

The sponsor's role is performed by a high-level manager with the power and the resources to push an innovation into a finished product. The sponsor may or may not be the individual who first thought of the innovation idea but is clearly the person who "carries the ball" as an advocate for the innovation in corporate and investor circles where resources are allocated. The sponsor, also described as the "champion" by other researchers, runs interference in the firm for the innovation. The sponsor's role may be performed by more than one individual.

continued

EXHIBIT 11.4 *concluded*

Mentor

The mentor is usually an experienced and successful innovator who is assigned the managerial responsibility of coaching the innovation team leader. The mentor serves as a role model and, together with the sponsor, provides encouragement, guidance, and other types of support to the innovation team leader.

Critic

The critic acts as a devil's advocate who counterbalances the innovation idea. The critic applies dispassionate, hard-nosed business criteria to the innovation idea and its development. The critic's role generally is shared by several persons.

Institutional Leader

The institutional leader is removed from the battlefield and is not subject to any partisan myopia that may affect those closer to the innovation. The institutional leader's function is to maintain a balance of power between the pro-innovation influences of the sponsor-mentor coalition and the reality-testing influences of the critic in such a manner that conflicts can be resolved on their particular merits rather than on power alone.

Source: Adapted from A. H. Van de Ven, "Central Problems in the Management of Innovation," *Management Science* 32 (1986), 590–607.

ENDNOTES

1. This view of entrepreneurship has been described by O. F. Collins and D. G. Moore, *The Organization Makers: A Behavioral Study of Independent Entrepreneurs* (New York: Meredith Press, 1970); A. Shapero, "The Displaced, Uncomfortable Entrepreneur," *Psychology Today* (1975) 83–89; F. A. Webster, "Entrepreneurs and Ventures: An Attempt of Classification and Clarification," *Academy of Management Review* 2 (1977), 54–61.
2. The notion of corporate entrepreneurship has been presented by D. Miller and P. H. Friesen, "Innovation in Conservative and Entrepreneurial Firms: Two Models of Strategic Momentum," *Strategic Management Journal* 3 (1982) 1-25; R. A. Burgelman, "A Process Model of Internal Corporate Venturing in the Major Diversified Firm," *Administrative Science Quarterly* 28 (1983), 223–44; R. M. Kanter, *The Change Masters* (New York: Simon and Schuster, 1983).
3. Participants in this debate include J. Schumpeter, *The Theory of Economic Development* (Cambridge: Harvard University Press, 1934); A. Cole, "Entrepreneurship as an Area of Research," *Journal of Economic History* 2 (1942), 118–26; D. G. Moore, *The Organization Makers* (New York: Appleton-Century-Crofts, 1970); Shapero, "The Displaced, Uncomfortable Entrepreneur"; Webster, "Entrepreneurs and Ventures."
4. F. Damanpour, "The Adoption of Technological, Administrative, and Ancillary Innovations: Impact of Organizational Factors," *Journal of Management* 13 (1987), 675–88.

5. Ibid.

6. J. V. Baldridge and R. Burnham, "Organizational Innovation: Industrial, Organizational, and Environmental Impact," *Administrative Science Quarterly* 20 (1975), 165–76; R. L. Daft, "A Dual-Core Model of Organizational Innovation," *Academy of Management Journal* 21 (1978), 193–210; J. R. Kimberly and M. Evanisko, "Organizational Innovation: The Influence of Individual, Organizational, and Contextual Factors on Hospital Adoption of Technological and Administrative Innovations," *Academy of Management Journal* 24 (1981), 689–713.

7. L. Kim, "Organizational Innovation and Structure," *Journal of Business Research* 8 (1980), 225–45; Kimberly and Evanisko, "Organizational Innovation."

8. D. A. Tansik and G. Wolf, "Entrepreneurial Roles in the Process of Technological Innovation," in *Advances in the Study of Entrepreneurship, Innovation, and Economic Growth*, ed. G. D. Libecap (Greenwich, Conn.: JAI Press, 1986), 115–27.

9. Miller and Friesen, "Innovation in Conservative And Entrepreneurial Firms."

10. E. Tisk and K. W. Bamforth, "Some Social and Psychological Consequences of the Long Wall Method of Goal Setting," *Human Relations* 4 (1951), 3–38.

11. Kanter, "The Change Masters"; H. H. Stevenson, "Entrepreneurship: A Process of Creating Value" (Cambridge: Division of Research, Harvard Business School, 1983); V. Sathe, "Intrapreneurship: A New Form of Corporate Entrepreneurship," (Cambridge: Division of Research, Harvard Business School, 1983).

12. T. Burns and G. M. Stalker, *The Management of Innovation* (London: Tavistock Publications, 1961).

13. M. Weber, *The Theory of Social and Economic Organization,* trans. A. M. Henderson and T. Parsons (New York: Free Press, 1947).

14. M. Aiken and J. Hage, "The Organic Organization and Innovation," *Sociology* 5 (1971), 63–82; R. L. Daft and S. Becker, *Innovation in Organizations* (New York: Elsevier, 1978); H. Mintzberg, *The Structure of Organizations* (Englewood Cliffs, N. J.: Prentice-Hall, 1979).

15. J. Q. Wilson, "Innovation in Organizations: Notes Toward a Theory" in *Approaches to Organizational Design,* ed. J. D. Thompson (Pittsburgh: University of Pittsburgh Press, 1966).

16. R. B. Duncan, "The Ambidextrous Organization: Designing Dual Structures for Innovation," in *The Management Of Organizations,* ed. R. H. Killman et al. (New York: North-Hollard, 1976).

17. M. S. Salter and W. A. Weinhold, *Diversification through Acquisition* (New York: Free Press, 1979).

18. Burgelman, "A Process Model of Internal Corporate Venturing."

19. I. C. MacMillan, "Progress in Research on Corporate Venturing," in *The Art and Science of Entrepreneurship,* ed. D. Sexton and R. Smilor (Cambridge, Mass.: Ballinger, 1986).

20. D. A. Schon, "The Fear of Innovation," *International Science and Technology* 12 (1966), 70–78; J. D. Hlavacek and V. A. Thompson, "Bureaucracy and Venture Failure," *Academy of Management Review* 3 (1978), 242–48; M. A. Maidique, "Entrepreneurs, Champions, and Technological Innovation," *Sloan Management Review* 20 (1980), 59–76; Kanter, "The Change Masters"; N. D. Fast and S. E. Pratt, "Individual Entrepreneurship and the Large Corporation," in *Frontiers of Entrepreneurial Research* (Wellesley, Mass.: Babson College, 1981).

21. I. C. MacMillan, Z. Block, and P. N. Subba Narasimha, "Corporate Venturing: Alternatives, Obstacles Encountered and Experience Effects," *Journal of Business Venturing* 1 (1986), 177–92.

22. R. Biggadike, "The Risky Business of Diversification," *Harvard Business Review* (May-June 1979), 103–11; K. G. Cooper, "The Dimensions of Industrial New Product Success and Failure," *Journal of Marketing* 43 (1979), 93–103; E. B. Roberts, "New Ventures for Corporate Growth," *Harvard Business Review* (July-August 1980), 132–42; N. D. Fast, "Pitfalls of Corporate Venturing," *Research Management* (1981), 21–24; M. A. Maidique and B. J. Zirger, "The Stanford Innovation Project, Phase I: A Study of Success and Failure in High Technology Innovation," *IEEE Transactions on Engineering Management* (1984), 192–203; E. L. Hobson and R. M. Morrison, "How Do Corporate Start-up Ventures Fare?," J. Hornaday, J. Timmons, and K. Vesper (eds.), *Frontiers of Entrepreneurship Research* (Wellesley, Mass.: Babson College, 1983), 390–440; I. C. MacMillan and D. L. Day, "Corporate Ventures into Industrial Markets: Dynamics of Aggressive Entry," *Journal of Business Venturing* 2 (1987), 29–39.

23. Burgelman, "A Process Model of Internal Corporate Venturing"; D. F. Jennings and S. L. Seaman, "Aggressiveness of Response to New Business Opportunities Following Deregulation: An Empirical Study of Established Financial Firms," *Journal of Business Venturing* 5 (1990), 177–89.

24. R. M. Hill and J. D. Hlavacek, "The Venture Team: A New Concept in Marketing Organizations," *Journal of Marketing* 36 (1972), 44–50; M. L. Tushman, "Special Boundary Roles in the Innovation Process," *Administrative Science Quarterly* 22 (1977), 587–605; E. Von Hippel, "Successful Industrial Products from Customer Ideas," *Journal of Marketing* (1978), 39–49; T. Kidder, *The Soul of a New Machine* (Boston: Little, Brown, 1981); R. M. Kanter, "The Middle Manager as Innovator," *Harvard Business Review* (September-October 1982), 26–37; M. A. Maidique and R. H. Hayes, "The Art of High-Technology Management," *Sloan Management Review* 24 (1984), 17–31; R. A. Burgelman, "Managing the Internal Corporate Venturing Process," *Sloan Management Review* 24 (1984), 33–48.

25. K. H. Vesper and T. G. Holmdahl, "How Venture Management Fares in Innovative Companies," *Research Management* (1973), 30–32; Z. Block, "Can Corporate Venturing Succeed?" *Journal of Business Strategy* 3 (1982), 21–33; Z. Block and O. A. Ornati, "Compensating Corporate Venture Managers," *Journal of Business Venturing* 2 (1987), 41–51.

26. MacMillan, "Progress in Research on Corporate Venturing."

27. W. R. Sandberg and C. W. Hofer, "Improving New Venture Performance: The Role of Strategy, Industry Structure, and the Entrepreneur," *Journal of Business Venturing* 2 (1987), 5–28.

28. M. E. Porter, *Competitive Strategy* (New York: Free Press, 1980).

29. Jennings and Seaman, "Aggressiveness of Response."

30. T. T. Tyebjee and A. V. Bruno, "A Model of Venture Capitalist Investment Activity," *Management Science* 30 (1984), 1051–66.

31. V. H. Fried and R. D. Hisrich, "Venture Capital Research: Past, Present and Future," *Entrepreneurship Theory and Practice* 13 (1988), 15–28.

32. Ibid.

33. Ibid.

34. J. B. Barney et al., "The Structure of Venture Capital Governance: An Organizational Economic Analysis of Relations between Venture Capital Firms and New Ventures" (Proceedings, National Academy of Management, 1989).

35. I. Barmash, *Welcome to Our Conglomerate—You're Fired* (New York: Delacorte, 1971).

36. R. M. Kanter, *When Giants Learn to Dance* (New York: Simon and Schuster, 1989).

37. Fast and Pratt, "Individual Entrepreneurship and the Large Corporation."

38. H. Geneen, *Managing* (New York: Doubleday, 1984).

39. N. Macrae, "The Coming Entrepreneurial Revolution: A Survey," *The Economist* 11 (1976), 41–44, 53–65; G. Pinchot, *Intrapreneuring, Or Why You Don't Have to Leave the Corporation to Become an Entrepreneur* (New York: Harper and Row, 1985).

40. R. P. Nielsen, M. P. Peters, and R. D. Hisrich, "Intrapreneurship Strategy for Internal Markets—Corporate, Non-Profit and Government Institution Cases," *Strategic Management Journal* 6 (1985), 181–89.

41. Pinchot, *Intrapreneuring.*

42. T. J. Peters and N. Austin, *A Passion for Excellence* (New York: Random House, 1985).

43. P. Drucker, *Innovation and Entrepreneurship* (New York: Harper and Row, 1985).

44. V. J. Sathe, *Culture and Related Corporate Realities* (Homewood, Ill.: Richard Irwin, 1985).

45. R. A. Peterson and D. G. Berger, "Entrepreneurship in Organizations: Evidence from the Popular Music Industry," *Administrative Science Quarterly* 16 (1971), 97–107.

46. Macrae, "The Coming Entrepreneurial Revolution."

47. Schumpeter, *The Theory of Economic Development.*

48. G. D. Libecap, "Do Large Corporations Provide an Environment for Entrepreneurs?" in *Advances in the Study of Entrepreneurship, Innovation, and Economic Growth,* ed. G. D. Libecap (Greenwich, Conn.: JAI Press, 1986).

49. W. M. Lindsay and L. W. Rue, "Impact of the Organization Environment on the Long-Range Planning Process: A Contingency View," *Academy of Management Journal* 23 (1980), 385–404; R. B. Robinson, Jr., "The Importance of 'Outsiders' in Small Firm Strategic Planning," *Academy of Management Journal* 25 (1982), 80–93.

50. The article by Jennings and Lumpkin that appears at the end of Chapter 12 employs a multivariate analysis of covariance (MANOCOVA) to control for organizational size. A description of this statistical technique is beyond the scope of this text. However, most good statistical textbooks offer detailed explanations. See, for example, W. W. Cooley and P. R. Lohnes, *Multivariate Data Analysis* (New York: Wiley, 1971).

51. Kanter, *The Change Masters.*

52. H. L. Angle and A. H. Van de Ven, "Suggestions for Managing the Innovation Journey," in *Research on the Management of Innovation,* ed. A. H. Van de Ven et al. (New York: Harper and Row, 1989).

53. Ibid.

54. A. H. Van de Ven, "Central Problems in the Management of Innovation," *Management Science* 32 (1986), 590–607.

Organizational Factors That Affect Corporate Entrepreneurship

T he popular press has stressed that organizations should utilize the notion of entrepreneurship as a means of adapting to a complex, turbulent environment. Companies are searching for executives who not only can develop long-term product marketing strategies but also can instill an entrepreneurial spirit.[1]

The organizational-science research literature contains many instances where the word *entrepreneurial* is used to describe certain firms. Whether there are industry settings where entrepreneurship does not exist makes an interesting argument. For instance, Miller and Friesen stated that entrepreneurship is not a "natural state of affairs" in some instances. According to Miller and Friesen, "conservative" managers are reluctant to engage in entrepreneurial activities unless they are encouraged by challenges and threats.[2] Examples of these firms are provided by Miller and Friesen and include Miles and Snow's "reactors,"[3] Mintzberg's "adapters"[4] and Miller and Friesen's "stagnant bureaucracy" and "headless giant."[5] These strategy types are described in Exhibit 12.1.

Dolan and Lindsey, however, asserted that under favorable conditions firms of all sizes, in all markets, and with all degrees of concentration can engage in entrepreneurial activities.[6]

Very little is known about the actual processes of corporate entrepreneurship at an organizational level of analysis, because of existing definitional disagreements. Despite these problems, a number of researchers have conceptualized the

EXHIBIT 12.1 Strategic Types: Reactors, Adapters, Stagnant Bureaucracies, and Headless Giants

Reactors

According to Miles and Snow, a "reactor" is a form of strategic failure that lacks any type of response mechanism that it can consistently utilize when faced with a changing environment. Reactors usually respond inappropriately to environmental change, performing poorly as a result, and then being reluctant to act aggressively in the future.

Adapters

"Adapters," as described by Mintzberg, have the following four major characteristics:

- Clear goals do not exist. The adaptive organization is caught in a complex web of political forces. Unions, managers, owners, lobby groups, governmental agencies—each with their own needs—seek to influence decisions. There is no one central source of power, no one simple goal.

- Strategy-making is characterized by the reactive solution to existing problems rather than a proactive search for new opportunities. Adapters seek to reduce existing uncertainties by establishing cartels to ensure markets and negotiating long-term purchasing arrangements to stabilize sources of supply.

- Decisions are made in incremental steps. Adapters cannot make large decisions for fear of venturing too far into the unknown. The strategy maker focuses first on what is familiar, considering convenient alternatives and ones that differ only slightly from the status quo.

- Decisions are disjointed. The demands on the organization are diverse, and no manager has the mental capacity to reconcile all of them. Sometimes it simply is easier and less expensive to make decisions in disjointed fashion, so that each problem is treated independently and little attention is paid to coordination. Strategy making is fragmented, but the strategy maker remains flexible to adapt to the needs of the moment.

Stagnant Bureaucracies

A "stagnant bureaucracy" is a firm whose top managers fail to allow it to live in the present or adapt to the current conditions of the marketplace. Traditional strategies are clung to, as are the structural and interpersonal orientations that were appropriate to much simpler and stabler firms. Since lower and middle echelons are powerless to redirect the firm, human disillusionment and corporate demise result.

Stagnant bureaucracies are highly bureaucratic organizations that have become bound up with past traditions and outdated product lines. A previously placid and simple environment has lulled the firm to sleep. Top management is emotionally committed to the old strategies, and the firm's information systems are too feeble to provide it with evidence of the need to change. Lower-level managers who are convinced of this need are ignored and alienated.

Eastern Air Lines during the 1950s is a good example of a stagnant bureaucracy. As described in a *Fortune* (July 1964) article, the top manager of Eastern was Eddie Rickenbacker, an autocratic and flamboyant World War I flying ace. While Rickenbacker was a charismatic personality, his financial conservatism was legendary.

continued

EXHIBIT 12.1 *continued*

During the early years of Eastern's existence, Rickenbacker's management style did little damage because the firm held a monopoly on a number of highly profitable routes. In the 1950s, however, Eastern's environment was changing. For example, the Civil Aeronautics Board opened some of Eastern's routes to other competitors, and the age of the jet was dawning. Eastern was not prepared to meet those challenges—it was not used to competing because of its former monopoly. Rickenbacker's earlier successes made him reluctant to change old policies. As a result, Eastern continued to provide substandard service, had a lackluster marketing effort, flew shorter, less profitable routes, and purchased airplanes that were quickly becoming obsolete. Rickenbacker's penny pinching ultimately cost Eastern a great deal of money.

Headless Giants

"Headless giants" are leaderless firms in which no one has taken charge. These firms are large, internally differentiated, and often geographically dispersed. They no longer are managed by the individuals who built them or even those who presided over any important projects or transitional periods. Headless giants are firms between true leaders and are in a state of limbo, in which they drift aimlessly. Little innovation or change takes place and the firms muddle through.

Most of the administrative activity in headless giants takes place at the divisional or departmental levels. Managers at this level are highly independent—so much so that subunits often operate at cross-purposes without any interference from higher-level administrators. For example, divisions will introduce new products that compete with those of other divisions, duplicating costly developmental expenditures and narrowing the potential breadth of target markets. In headless giants that do have a functional organizational structure, there is a great deal of difficulty in getting managers to cooperate with one another. Department heads are about equally powerful, and each may have ambitions of filling the leadership vacuum at the top. This competitive spirit, coupled with the absence of any authority to thwart it, channel it, or arbitrate in disputes, stymies interdepartmental collaboration. As a result, complex projects founder or are avoided. The firm is restricted to intrafunctional changes that are minor and inconsequential. Headless giants drift, utilizing existing methods, markets, and products. Nothing much changes except the external environment.

Société Générale de Belgique, a Belgian conglomerate that operated in banking, mining, steel, chemical, petroleum, and electrical industries, was one of the world's largest headless giants. Société Générale operated as a monopoly in both Europe and Africa and was isolated from stockholder criticism because of its financial structure. The conglomerate was managed by a governor and nine directors. Each director was the president of one or more groups of companies and focused attention primarily on his own industry. While the governor developed overall policies and strategies for the conglomerate, he lacked the power of implementation. The governor was elected by the directors and received funding from them for both his salary and those of his staff. As a result, there was no effective communication or guidance from the top. The member firms went their own way. It was impossible to take money from the poorly performing firms to invest in more promising areas, because the powerful directors losing funds would protest. Serious problems developed when foreign companies

continued

EXHIBIT 12.1 *concluded*

entered markets neglected by Société Générale. Certain African properties were nationalized, and competition from within the European Common Market was severe. Societe Generale became stuck with a group of businesses so archaic that its overall rate of return on invested capital was lower than the yield on government bonds.

Allis Chalmers went through a period as a headless giant during the 1960s. It drifted along conservatively, in all directions, as its myriad divisions independently pursued their own, often conflicting, ends.

Source: Descriptions of these strategic types were developed from the following sources: "reactors" from R. Miles et al., "Organizational Strategy, Structure, and Process," *Academy of Management Review* 3 (1978), 546–62; "adapters" from H. Mintzberg, "Strategy Making in Three Modes," *California Management Review* 16 (1973), 44-58; "stagnant bureaucracies" and "headless giants" from D. Miller and P. Friesen, *Organizations: A Quantum View* (Englewood Cliffs, N. J.: Prentice-Hall, 1984).

organizational structure of an entrepreneurial organization. One viewpoint is that an entrepreneurial organization would have the framework of a "simple structure," using Mintzberg's typology of organizational structure.[7] Khandwalla found evidences of firms with simple structures in research on Canadian companies. These firms had rudimentary financial controls, no staff training, and little research and development and marketing research activities. Communication flowed informally, most of it between the chief executive and everyone else.[8]

Another viewpoint used by researchers focuses on how large organizations adapt to the requirements of entrepreneurship that occurs when the organization cannot reduce the turbulence of at least one important segment of its environment. As an example, certain researchers have argued that the top managers of entrepreneurial organizations promote entrepreneurship at every organizational level.[9] A typical entrepreneurial organization has been described as "loathing bureaucratic procedures as impositions on their flexibility."[10] Mintzberg stated that it is an unpredictable maneuvering that keeps the structure of an entrepreneurial organization "lean, flexible, and organic."[11]

From these descriptions it is not surprising that the meaning of entrepreneurship never has been conceptualized. It is extremely difficult to concretely identify a lean, informal organization. Structural characteristics may not adequately describe an organization's entrepreneurial ability.

Both academic researchers and practicing managers, however, have described problems that result when top managers attempt to utilize entrepreneurial concepts. For example, Eugene Jennings has said that corporate executives who stress the need for entrepreneurial activities also create an atmosphere that cannot accommodate entrepreneurship.[12] Other researchers have argued that corporations use rules and policies to properly administer the routine tasks of the organization. Entrepreneurs working in these organizational climates can present serious problems to the established "bureaucracy."[13]

Given this apparent conflict between organizational procedures and entrepreneurship, an interesting question arises. How can an organization use the notion of entrepreneurship to cope with changing environmental conditions? A more fundamental set of questions is: Do entrepreneurial organizations exist and can they be distinguished from other organizations? What are the differences between an entrepreneurial and a nonentrepreneurial organization? These fundamental questions raise a major issue regarding the notion of entrepreneurship. Can the concept of entrepreneurship be functionally modeled in such a way as to suggest testable hypotheses?

To describe the differences between entrepreneurial and nonentrepreneurial organizations with respect to certain organizational variables, the rest of this chapter presents a summary of Miller and Friesen's research on entrepreneurial and conservative organizations and excerpts from an article by Jennings and Lumpkin that functionally models corporate entrepreneurship using an objective definition and empirically tests certain hypotheses.

MILLER AND FRIESEN'S STUDY

Miller and Friesen argued that both entrepreneurial and nonentrepreneurial organizations exist and that each uses different strategies.[14] For example, an entrepreneurial organization is viewed as engaging in innovative activities to develop a distinctive competence, while a nonentrepreneurial organization views innovation as something that is done in response to challenges, occurring only when necessary. Miller and Friesen described nonentrepreneurial organizations as "conservative" and used the self-report measures of chief executive officers to classify fifty-two Canadian firms as being either entrepreneurial or conservative. The self-report measures contained questions focusing on risk taking and innovative activities.

ARTICLE 12.1   FUNCTIONALLY MODELING CORPORATE ENTREPRENEURSHIP: AN EMPIRICAL INTEGRATIVE ANALYSIS
by Daniel F. Jennings and James D. Lumpkin

Miller and Friesen's (1982) research where corporate entrepreneurship (CE) was defined using subjective measures could be extended by developing an objective definition of CE. This objective measure could be used, then, to classify organizations as being entrepreneurial or conservative (non-entrepreneurial). By having a method of objective classification, various hypotheses could be developed and tested with respect to CE.

Developing an Objective Definition of CE

Previous research suggests that various definitions can be linked together to develop an objective definition of CE. For example, Schumpeter (1947) argued that a manager becomes an entrepreneur only when he or she is innovative with respect to market forces. Ansoff's (1979) definition where entrepreneurship is viewed as replacing obsolete product market combinations with newer ones of greater profit potential is an extension of Schumpeter's work. Hambrick (1983) used Ansoff's definition and measured entrepreneurship by the extent of product market additions.

In the present research, CE is defined as the extent to which new products and/or new markets are developed. An organization is entrepreneurial if it develops a higher than average number of new products and/or new markets.

This definition can be utilized to study entrepreneurial behavior in both large and small firms. For example, entrepreneurship has been equated with small business ownership and management (Carland et al., 1984) while intrapreneurship (Pinchot, 1984) has been associated with large firms. Nielsen, Peters, and Hisrich (1985, page 181) state that:

> intrapreneurship is the development within a large organization of internal markets and relatively small and independent units designed to create, internally test-market, and expand improved and/or innovative staff services, technologies or methods within the organization. This is different from the large organization entrepreneurship/ venture management strategy that tries to develop internal entrepreneurial/venture units whose purpose is to develop profitable positions in external markets.

In essence, Nielsen, Peters, and Hisrich (1985) are saying that intrapreneurship is the practice of entrepreneurship *within* a large organization while there is another type of entrepreneurship practiced in developing *external* markets. This "other type of entrepreneurship" is a form of CE. The authors of this study argue that CE occurs both in large-sized and small-sized firms.

Operationalizing the Definition of Corporate Entrepreneurship

Two requirements had to be satisfied before CE could be operationalized. First, an industry had to be selected when published information was available to satisfy the requirements of the objective definition. Secondly, the industry had to operate where there was a possibility for entrepreneurship. In addition, various researchers have argued for single industry studies (Hirsch, 1975; Porter, 1980; Chakravarthy, 1986) to minimize confounding effects. For example, Porter (1980) has noted that industry structure constrains a firm's strategy.

The Texas savings and loan (S&L) industry was chosen because recent regulatory changes have created the opportunity for increased entrepreneurship. The entire S&L industry was deregulated in 1980 and given "new powers" (Public Law 96-221 and Public Law 97-320). These new powers created over 100 new ways for S&Ls to transact business (Eisenbeiss, 1983). Before 1980, S&Ls could only finance residential mortgages and make certain equipment loans. The two new acts allowed S&Ls to offer most types of commercial loans, consumer loans, credit cards, and to make loans to state and local governments. Negotiable orders of withdrawal (NOW accounts) where customers can write checks withdrawing money from interest-bearing accounts were also allowed. Rose and Fraser (1985) and Gart (1985) suggest S&Ls of the future will be different from the traditional S&L which began more than a century ago because of these broader loan and investment powers. After 1980, the charters of many Texas S&Ls were acquired by commercial bankers, real estate developers, and other newcomers (Gart, 1985). In essence, with deregulation came new entrants (Porter, 1980) who used their newly acquired S&Ls to engage in commercial banking activities and to enter into both short-term and long-term consumer lending practices.

Previously, we defined CE as the extent to which new products and/or new markets are developed. For the purpose of this research setting, our definition was operationalized using Goudreau's (1984) conceptualization. He proposed that these liberalized powers brought about by deregulation could be grouped into six major categories that represent new products or markets. Goudreau then developed six financial ratios to measure how extensively each category was being implemented by S&Ls. Since these ratios are proxies for new products and new services, they are used as indicators of CE based on our definition. Goudreau's six ratios are defined as follows:

(1) $\dfrac{\text{consumer loans}}{\text{total assets}}$ (2) $\dfrac{\text{commercial loans}}{\text{total assets}}$

(3) $\dfrac{\text{liquid investments}}{\text{total assets}}$ (4) $\dfrac{\text{investments in service corporations}}{\text{total assets}}$

(5) $\dfrac{\text{"NOW" accounts}}{\text{total liabilities}}$ (6) $\dfrac{\text{"NINOW" accounts}}{\text{total liabilities}}$

The six ratios were calculated individually for each S&L involved in the sample. Using a product/market addition classification scheme, S&Ls were classified as entrepreneurial or non-entrepreneurial (conservative).

Organizational Differences

This research investigated the organizational differences between entrepreneurial and non-entrepreneurial organizations. The following variables were considered to be related to CE: (1) three elements of management structure—centralization of decision making (Burns & Stalker, 1961); specialization (Pugh, Hickson, Hinnings, & Turner, 1988); integration processes (Lawrence & Lorsch, 1967); (2) performance objectives (Hrebiniak & Joyce, 1984); and (3) rewards and sanctions (Salter, 1973).

Centralization of Decision Making

Centralization of decision making is viewed as the concentration of authority for decision making. Both Thompson (1969) and Hage and Aiken (1970) argued that dispersed power makes possible a large number and variety of subcoalitions which tend to support innovative activities. Normann (1971) posited, however, that only "powerful leaders" are able to accomplish major innovations. Miller and Friesen (1982) viewed centralization as the extent to which decision making remains with the top manager of the organization and hypothesized that centralization would be positively correlated with the entrepreneurial organization. Their findings, however, did not support the hypothesis. Miller and Friesen also used a self report or subjective measure to define their entrepreneurial and conservative organizations. Would different results have been obtained by using an objective measure of entrepreneurial and conservative organizations? Based on Thompson (1969) and Hage and Aiken (1970), the following hypothesis was formulated:

> H1: Decision making in entrepreneurial organizations (EO) will tend to be more participative (decentralized) than in conservative organizations (CO).

Specialization

Specialization is viewed as the extent to which professionals who possess specific knowledge and training are employed within an organization. Wilson (1966) reported that diverse groups of managers and specialists will tend to promote innovation because of the differences in their expertise and perspectives. Hage and Aiken (1970) argued that professional employees tend to recognize the need for change and that firms with a high percentage of specialists will tend to be more innovative. Miller and Friesen (1982) found a positive relationship between specialization and entrepreneurial organizations. Accordingly, the following hypothesis was formulated:

> H2: Decision making in EO will tend to rely more on personnel with specialized training than in CO.

Integration Processes

Integration processes refers to the liaison devices used to encourage adjustment both within and among units of the organization. Lawrence and Lorsch (1967) viewed integration as promoting innovation while Galbraith (1973) argued that integration restrains innovation because the integrative mechanisms tend to warn managers of potential problems resulting from excessive innovation. Miller and Friesen (1982) found a positive relationship between integration and conservative organizations. Based on this evidence, the following hypothesis was formulated:

> H3: EO will tend to use less integrating devices in decision making than CO.

Developing Performance Objectives

Hrebiniak and Joyce (1984) suggest procedures used in establishing objectives can affect behavior within the organization. They noted that when objectives are developed unilaterally by top management with an emphasis on formal accountability and a strict enforcement of rules; there is a tendency for organization members to be concerned with a "defensibility of action, the breeding of conservatism, and a rigidity of behavior." Organizational members tend to be more innovative when performance objectives are developed from a shared participation. Based on this evidence, the following hypothesis was formulated:

> H4: Performance objectives in EO will tend to be developed from a shared participation while CO performance objectives will tend to be developed unilaterally by top management.

Rewards and Sanctions

The measures of rewards and sanctions deal with how organizations sanction failure. Pascale and Athos (1981) reported that innovative firms have a management that encourages risk taking and developing skills that translate ideas into action. Conservative organizations tend to emphasize risk aversion, stability, and efficiency. Managers in these organizations who undertake "risky" projects and fail are fired or suffer damage to their careers (Fast, 1979). Based on this evidence, the following hypothesis was formulated:

> H5: Managers in EO will tend not to be penalized if risky projects fail while managers in CO will tend to suffer career damage by undertaking risky projects that fail.

Research Methods

Archival Data Analysis

The product/market addition number discussed in Exhibit 12.2 was applied to the total population (270) of Texas S&Ls. Of these S&Ls, 44 were classified as entrepreneurial and 71 were classified as conservative. The remaining 155 S&Ls were considered to be neither entrepreneurial nor conservative based on the measure of CE used in this research. An important methodological issue in this study is the possible restriction of range. We wanted to capture polar behaviors—entrepreneurial on one extreme and conservative on the other. This classification system allowed us to study extremes. One group of S&Ls (44) was considered as one extreme—entrepreneurial—while another group (71) was considered as another extreme—conservative.

Sample Size

Twenty-eight S&Ls were randomly chosen for study from each of two groups (entrepreneurial and conservative) for a total sample size of 56. Total assets of the sample S&Ls ranged from 4.1 billion dollars to 10.2 million dollars.

EXHIBIT 12.2 Classification of S&Ls

Goudreau's six ratios were calculated individually for each S&L involved in the sample. For each ratio, a value of plus one was assigned to the S&L if it was in the top third of all S&Ls on that ratio, a value of minus one was assigned if the S&L was in the bottom third, and a value of zero if the S&L was in the middle third. Each S&L was assigned a product/market addition number that was the arithmetic sum of these values. S&Ls with a product/market addition number ranging from plus two to plus six were classified as entrepreneurial, and S&Ls with a product/market addition number ranging from minus two to minus six were classified as conservative. The following graph illustrates the results of this classification scheme.

Product/market addition number

		+6
Number of entrepreneurial S&Ls	44	
		+2
Neither entrepreneurial nor conservative	155	
		−2
Number of conservative S&Ls	71	
		−6

Data Collection

A pilot-tested list of questions together with a cover letter requesting a telephone interview was sent to the CEO of each S&L in the sample. These CEOs were contacted by telephone to determine if they would participate and a telephone interview was arranged. During the telephone interview, these CEOs were asked to respond to the previously mailed questions and the researcher marked telephone responses to identical questions on a questionnaire. Lenz (1980) tested the combination questionnaire/telephone interview and reported it was superior to premailed questions because the respondent could ask questions or clarify responses. Telephone interviews were obtained from 49 of the 56 CEOs who received questionnaires—an 87.5 percent response. CEOs from 24 entrepreneurial S&Ls and 25 conservative S&Ls responded.

While only interviewing one executive from each organization can be considered a limitation of this study, Miller and Friesen (1982) sampled only CEOs. In essence, this research replicates their data collection procedures with respect to sampling one individual from each organization.

Measurements

The five organizational variables were measured by multi-item, 5-point or 4-point, appropriately anchored Likert scales (Exhibits 12.4 and 12.5 describe the scale values). Each construct included items developed by Miller and Friesen (1982) and Lawrence and Lorsch (1967). These items were rewritten in such a manner that they conformed to the savings and loan industry. This revision was necessary because both Miller and Friesen and Lawrence and Lorsch studied manufacturing firms. A reliability analysis was used to verify four of the five scales using inter-item correlations and Cronbach's alpha (Cronbach, 1951). The centralization of decision making scale was designed in such a manner that a reliability analysis was inappropriate.

Three of the four scales—integration processes, rewards and sanctions, developing performance objectives—had reliabilities above the .70 level suggested by Nunnally (1978) and Van De Ven and Ferry (1980) as satisfactory. The specialization scale failed to exhibit a high reliability (r = .46). Exhibit 12.3 reports inter-item correlations and reliabilities for the four organizational differences constructs. The six decision processes used for the centralization of decision making construct are shown in Exhibit 12.5.

Data Analysis

Multivariate analysis of covariance (MANOCOVA) was employed to determine whether or not the entrepreneurial and conservative S&Ls exhibited significant statistical differences on four of the five organizational variables. Because researchers (Lindsay & Rue, 1980; Robinson, 1982) have argued that in studies involving various organizational sizes, small-sized firms may exhibit different characteristics and should be considered as a separate class, the covariance analysis was used to control for organizational size.

If the MANOCOVA indicates that overall differences exist, further analysis to determine the source of these differences is appropriate (Timm, 1975). Univariate analysis of variance of each criterion variable is the traditional form of the test (Cooley & Lohnes, 1971). Exhibit 12.4 describes the MANOCOVA analysis together with the means and standard deviations for the four organizational variables of (1) rewards and sanctions, (2) specialization, (3) developing performance objectives, and (4) integration processes. Chi-square was used to test for differences in the six decision processes associated with centralization. The results are shown in Exhibit 12.5.

Results and Discussion

Overall Results

The MANOCOVA test indicated a significant difference in three of the four organizational variables between entrepreneurial and conservative S&Ls: rewarding risk taking, specialized personnel, and participating in objective setting. No significant difference was found in integration processes. The six decision-making

EXHIBIT   12.3   Inter-Item Correlations and Reliabilities for Organizational
Differences Scales*

	Inter-item Correlation	Alpha Coefficients
Integration Processes		.72
Temporary task force	.21	
Standardized rules and regulations	.36	
Memos sent to advise of decisions	.16	
Specialization		.46
Rely on long-term managers (negatively scored)	.32	
Managers with specialized training and formal education	.29	
Staff specialists to investigate and write reports	.29	
Hire managers with technical expertise	.16	
Rewards and Sanctions		.79
Performance based on avoiding risks (negatively scored)	.50	
Fired or damage career if fail on risky project (negatively scored)	.53	
Performance based on risk taking and creativity	.76	
Managing risky projects is a valuable learning experience	.60	
Developing Performance Objectives		.72
Develop objective in consultation with the managers	.57	
Top management develops objectives unilaterally (negatively scored)	.57	

* All values are based on data from 49 firms used in the sample.

EXHIBIT   12.4   MANOCOVA[a] of Differences in Organizational Differences Variables Between Entrepreneurial and Conservative Organizations

Dimensions	F-Ratio	Significance Level	Entrepreneurial (N = 24) Means[b]	S.D.	Conservative (N = 25) Means	S.D.
Multivariate Statistics	15.396	.000				
Univariate Statistics						
Rewards and Sanctions	53.296	.000	3.425	.676	2.160	.564
Specialized Personnel	4.200	.046	3.833	3.020	2.584	.348
Participating in Objective Setting	17.575	.000	4.166	.637	3.080	1.115
Integrating Processes	1.960	.168	2.495	.520	2.708	.554

[a] Size of organization controlled for by covariance analysis.

[b] Based on 5-point scale from Never (1) to Always (5).

EXHIBIT   12.5   Chi-Square Test and Percentage Distribution of Centralization of Decision-Making Processes Between Entrepreneurial and Conservative Organizations

Decision-Making Process		All Managers	Most Managers	Some Subordinates	CEO Only	Total Percent	Chi-Square Significance Level
Hiring/Firing Managerial Personnel	E[a]	45.8[b]	29.2	20.8	4.2	100	.000
	C	4.0	8.0	36.0	52.0	100	
New Products/Services	E	4.2	75.0	20.8	—	100	.000
	C	8.0	8.0	48.0	36.0	100	
Interest Rates/Points for Mortgage Loans	E	—	75.0	20.8	4.2	100	.000
	C	—	8.0	44.0	48.0	100	
Opening Branch Offices	E	—	16.7	66.6	16.7	100	.001
	C	—	—	36.0	64.0	100	
Acquiring Another Association	E	—	—	58.3	41.7	100	.002
	C	—	—	16.0	84.0	100	
Sources and Uses of Funds	E	—	50.0	50.0	—	100	.000
	C	—	4.0	68.0	28.0	100	

Percent Participation in the Process

[a] E = Entrepreneurial; C = Conservative. N = 49 (24 entrepreneurial + 25 conservative).

[b] Read—45.8 percent of reporting entrepreneurial organizations say that "all managers" participate in hiring/firing managerial personnel. Similarly, in only 4.2 percent of the entrepreneurial organizations the CEO, only, does the hiring/firing.

processes were also significantly different between entrepreneurial and conservative S&Ls (Exhibit 12.5). Four of the five hypotheses were supported as follows:

Hypotheses	Summary Indication of Support	P Value
1. Decision making to be more participative in EO than in CO.	Supported	.000
2. Decision making in EO will rely more on specialized trained personnel than CO.	Supported	.046
3. EO will tend to use less integration processes in decision making than CO.	Not Supported	.168
4. Performance objectives in EO will tend to be developed from a shared participation while performance objectives in CO will tend to be developed unilaterally by top management.	Supported	.000
5. Managers in EO will tend not to be penalized if risky projects fail while managers in CO will tend to suffer career damage by undertaking risky projects that fail.	Supported	.000

Decision Making

Support was found for the hypothesis that decision making in entrepreneurial organizations is participative. Many levels of managers are involved in the decision-making process. In contrast, decision making in conservative organizations tends to be unilateral. The top manager makes the decision with relatively little involvement from subordinates. Thompson (1969) and Hage and Aitken (1970) argued that dispersed power makes possible a large number and variety of subcoalitions which tend to support innovative activities. The findings of this research agree with Burns and Stalker's (1961) locus of authority concept within an organic organizational structure and supports the argument of Pearce and David (1983) that organic, innovative organizations are characterized by a participative management style.

Specialization

Support was found for other research suggesting entrepreneurial organizations tend to rely more on specialized personnel in their decision-making activities than conservative organizations (Wilson, 1966; Bigoness & Perreault, 1981; Miller & Friesen, 1982). This finding discounts the notion that CE managers tend to act without having specialized analysis of the particular situation. Knight (1921, pp. 277–82) stated that:

the essential factors of entrepreneurship include foresight and executive capacity, the knowledge of their own powers and a disposition to trust them in action, and a knowledge of other men's powers and judgment.

Perhaps the greater use of specialists provides this knowledge that Knight described.

Integration Processes

Although the direction of our findings indicates that entrepreneurial organizations tend to use less integrating devices in decision making than conservative organizations (Exhibit 12.4; EO mean for integrating processes = 2.495, CO mean = 2.708), no significant statistical support was found for our hypothesis that entrepreneurial organizations will tend to rely less on integration processes than conservative organizations. This differs from past research. Lawrence and Lorsch (1967) argued that integrative mechanisms can foster innovation because they "bring important facts" to bear upon the decision. These integrative mechanisms also ensure an effective collaboration that is necessary in achieving complex new-product innovations (Miller & Friesen, 1982).

In addition, Galbraith (1973) argued that integration restrains innovation because the integrative mechanisms will warn managers of potential problems resulting from excessive innovation. Galbraith appeared to have viewed integration as behavior as an information-processing device; serving to warn managers of the costs or dangers of too much information.

Developing Performance Objectives

Support was found for Hrebiniak and Joyce's (1984) argument that organizational members tend to be more innovative when performance objectives are developed from a shared participation. Support is also indicated for Hrebiniak and Joyce's (1984) assertion that there is a tendency for organizations to become conservative when objectives are developed unilaterally by top management with an emphasis on formal accountability and strict enforcement of rules.

Rewards and Sanctions

The conclusions of Pascale and Athos (1981) that innovative firms have a management that encourages risk taking and developing skills that translate ideas into action was supported. Entrepreneurial S&L managers are allowed more product or service failures before their long-term career prospects are affected than conservative S&L managers.

Discussion

The purpose of this study was to develop an operational measure for CE, classify firms from one industry as being either entrepreneurial or conservative and to investigate how these firms differ with respect to a variety of organizational variables.

The results indicate that using an objective measure of CE developed from the literature can be an effective approach in studying entrepreneurship. This is significant when one considers that a major criticism of entrepreneurial research is its lack of an integrative nature with respect to other research studies.

The findings of this study support a variety of theoretical research and empirical studies where CE was measured by self-report techniques regarding certain organizational variables. For example, decision making is more participative, more specialized personnel are employed, performance objectives are developed from a shared objective, and managers are not penalized if risky projects fail, respectively, for entrepreneurial firms compared to conservative firms. No support was found that entrepreneurial organizations use less integration processes in decision making than conservative organizations.

Another important feature of this research is its methodological rigor. For example, Harrigan (1983, p. 85) in describing "medium-grained" methodology states:

> few studies have exploited opportunities to impose greater rigor on their analyses by incorporating testable hypotheses in their sample designs. If samples could be gathered using a design that categorizes target firms according to important explanatory variables, greater control in isolating the effects of these key variables could be imposed.

By using archival data to classify firms as either entrepreneurial or conservative, a procedure has been developed that will allow target firms to be categorized according to important explanatory variables. By using a combination questionnaire/interview technique to test the research hypotheses, "greater rigor" has been imposed.

Using an objective measure to model CE provides fertile ground for future research in this area.

Source: This article excerpted from D. F. Jennings and J. R. Lumpkin, "Functionally Modeling Corporate Entrepreneurship: An Empirical Integrative Analysis," *Journal of Management* 15 (1989), 485–502. Used by permission of the *Journal of Management* and the authors.

ENDNOTES

1. "Entrepreneurship and Mass Marketing," *Business Week* (21 November 1983), 80–94.
2. D. Miller and P. H. Friesen, "Innovation in Conservative and Entrepreneurial Firms: Two Models of Strategic Momentum," *Strategic Management Journal* 3 (1982), 1–25.
3. R. Miles and C. Snow, *Organizational Strategy, Structure, and Process* (New York: McGraw-Hill, 1978).
4. H. Mintzberg, "Strategy Making in Three Modes," *California Management Review* 16 (1973), 44–58.

5. D. Miller and P. H. Friesen, "Archetypes of Organizational Transition," *Administrative Science Quarterly* 25 (1980), 268–99.

6. E. G. Dolan and D. E. Lindsey, *Economics,* 5th ed. (New York: Dryden Press, 1988).

7. H. Mintzberg, *The Structuring of Organizations* (Englewood Cliffs, N. J.: Prentice-Hall, 1979).

8. P. N. Khandwalla, "Viable and Effective Organizational Designs," *Academy of Management Journal* 16 (1973), 481–95.

9. R. A. Peterson and D. G. Berger, "Entrepreneurship in Organizations: Evidence from the Popular Music Industry," *Administrative Science Quarterly* 16 (1971), 97–106.

10. A. Toffler, *Future Shock* (New York: Bantam Books, 1970).

11. Mintzberg, *The Structuring of Organizations.*

12. E. Jennings, personal correspondence.

13. V. Sathe, "Intrapreneurship: A New Form of Corporate Entrepreneurship" (Cambridge: Division of Research, Harvard Business School, 1983).

14. Miller and Friesen, "Innovation in Conservative and Entrepreneurial Firms."

CHAPTER 13

Corporate
Venturing

C orporate ventures provide a means for firms to grow and diversify and offer the promise of facilitating entry into new business areas with innovative, usually technology-based products. In some situations a corporate venture may be undertaken to satisfy customer needs by entering new markets or by selling dramatically different products in existing markets. For large firms with many layers of management and detailed control systems, corporate ventures offer a special promise of creating entrepreneurial activity. For example, large firms attempt to emulate the actions of small entrepreneurial companies in their venturing activity. These large firms try to scale down their manner of operating when they want to enter new business areas. They have rediscovered the special virtues of building an entrepreneurial organization and "harnessing entrepreneurial energy."[1]

Selecting readings for this chapter was difficult because of the diverse nature of many published research articles. As stated earlier, MacMillan has reported that it is difficult to compare research results because of a lack of agreement on fundamental definitions.[2] Rather than attempting to develop a particular classification scheme to compare research results on corporate venturing, we have selected three theoretical articles. The first article, by Robert Burgelman, reports the findings of a field study of the internal corporate venturing (ICV) activities of a diversified major firm. Burgelman develops a process model of internal corporate venturing and describes the factors involved in successful internal corporate ventures. The second article, by Daniel F. Jennings, suggests that contextual factors affect venturing activities. Jennings uses a technological process model to develop a framework for studying venturing through an analysis of contextual factors. The third article, also by Robert Burgelman, describes how internal corporate ventures can be better managed.[3]

Because of the theoretical nature of these three selected readings, summaries are provided for each article. The summaries are placed together, preceding the first article. The rationale for including summaries is that we believe our readers will benefit from knowing basically what is in each article before reading it.

SUMMARY OF BURGELMAN'S INTERNAL CORPORATE VENTURING ARTICLE

An internal corporate venture is a situation in which a company sets up a separate division or group within itself for the purpose of entering different markets or developing radically different products. A typical discussion of an internal corporate venture uses a "stage model"[4] to describe the problems associated with the step-by-step development of the new venture. Most stage models of internal corporate ventures emphasize different requirements for each stage of the model in terms of tasks, personnel, organization structure, and leadership styles. While these requirements are important in growing a business, another set of problems arises when a new business is developed in the context of a large established firm. For example, strategic activities related to both the large firm and the internal venture occur simultaneously at different management levels.

Burgelman developed a process model that describes the activities of the venturing process together with other strategic activities occurring in the firm that affect the venture. As depicted in Exhibit 13.1, Burgelman describes the activities of the venture itself as a *core process* and the strategic context of the firm as an *overlaying process*.

The core processes describe how a new business venture is created and developed within the firm. Burgelman defines these activities as *definition* and *impetus*. The overlaying processes describe how the strategic and structural contexts of the firm are determined. Burgelman's structural context refers to the various organizational and administrative mechanisms put in place by corporate management to implement the current corporate strategy. Burgelman refers to strategic context as the process through which the current corporate strategy is extended to accommodate the new business that results from the venturing activity. Both the core and the overlaying processes involve key activities (the shaded area of Exhibit 13.1) and more peripheral activities (the nonshaded area of Exhibit 13.1), situated at different levels of the organization.

SUMMARY OF JENNINGS'S ARTICLE ON CONTEXTUAL FACTORS OF VENTURING ACTIVITIES

Jennings's article suggests that while process models (the way in which the venture is implemented) have been used to study venturing activities, another

EXHIBIT 13.1 Key and Peripheral Activities in a Process Model of an ICV

		Core Processes		Overlaying Processes	
☐ = Key activities		Definition	Impetus	Strategic Context	Structural Context
Levels	Corporate management	Monitoring	Authorizing	Rationalizing	Structuring
				Selecting	
	New venture division management	Coaching Stewardship	Strategic building	Organizational championing Delineating	Negotiating
	Group leader/ venture manager	Technical and need linking	*Product championing* Strategic forcing	Gatekeeping Idea generating Bootlegging	Questioning

Source: R. A. Burgelman, "A Process Model of Internal Corporate Venturing in the Diversified Major Firm," *Administrative Science Quarterly* 28 (1983), 223–44. Used by permission of *Administrative Science Quarterly* and the author.

dimension of venturing exists, which is referred to as the "context" of the venture. Context deals with the environment and the organizational elements in which the venture is situated. The environment of the venture activity is considered as occurring within the technological progress model. After describing this environment and model, the article suggests that five factors affect the positioning of the venture activity, as well as the venture implementation.

SUMMARY OF BURGELMAN'S MANAGING THE INTERNAL VENTURING PROCESS ARTICLE

In this article Burgelman extends his internal corporate venturing process article by identifying problem areas that involve managerial levels in the firm with respect to both the core processes and the overlaying processes. A description of major managerial problems in the ICV process are illustrated in Exhibit 13.2. The "NVD management" level depicted in Exhibit 13.2 is the new venture division (NVD) of the large, diversified firm that Burgelman studied. These problems occur because ICV is an "uncomfortable process" for large, complex firms, because carefully evolved routines and planning mechanisms are threatened by the venture. Various recommendations are presented in Exhibit 13.3 to improve the entrepreneurial resources of large, complex firms.

EXHIBIT 13.2   Major Problems in the ICV Process

| Level | Core Processes | | Overlaying Processes | |
	Definition	Impetus	Strategic Context	Structural Context
Corporate management	Top management lacks capacity to assess merits of specific new-venture proposals for corporate development.	Top management relies on purely quantitative growth results to continue support for new venture.	Top management considers ICV as insurance against mainstream business going badly. ICV objectives are ambiguous and shift erratically.	Top management relies on reactive structural changes to deal with problems related to ICV.
NVD management	Middle-level managers in corporate R&D are not capable of coaching ICV project initiators.	Middle-level managers in new business development find it difficult to balance strategic building efforts with efforts to coach venture managers.	Middle-level managers struggle to delineate boundaries of new business field. They spend significant amounts of time on political activities to maintain corporate support.	Middle-level managers struggle with unanticipated structural impediments to new-venture activities. There is little incentive for star performers to engage in ICV activities.
Group leader/ venture leader	Project initiators cannot convincingly demonstrate in advance that resources will be used effectively. They need to engage in scavenging to get resources.	Venture managers find it difficult to balance strategic forcing efforts with efforts to develop administrative framework of emerging ventures	Project initiators do not have clear idea of which kind of ICV projects will be viable in corporate context. Bootlegging is necessary to get new idea tested.	Venture managers do not have clear idea of what type of performance will be rewarded, except fast growth.

Source: R. A. Burgelman, "Managing the Internal Corporate Venturing Process," *Sloan Management Review* 25 (1985), 33–48. Used by permission of *Sloan Management Review* and the author.

ARTICLE 13.1   **INTERNAL CORPORATE VENTURING IN THE DIVERSIFIED MAJOR FIRM**
by Robert A. Burgelman

Despite a number of studies on the relationships between strategy, structure, degree of diversification, and economic performance in the divisionalized firm, the actual processes of corporate entrepreneurship and strategic change remain less well understood. This is probably because these processes in such firms are complex and are difficult and costly to research.

This research investigates the process through which a diversified major firm transforms R&D activities at the frontier of corporate technology into new businesses through internal corporate venturing (ICV). These new businesses enable the firm to diversify into new areas that involve competencies not readily avail-

EXHIBIT 13.3 Recommendations for Making ICV Strategy Work Better

Level	Core Processes		Overlaying Processes	
	Definition	**Impetus**	**Strategic Context**	**Structural Context**
Corporate management	ICV proposals are evaluated in light of corporate development strategy. Conscious efforts are made to avoid subjecting them to conventional corporate wisdom.	New-venture progress is evaluated in substantive terms by top managers who have experience in organizational championing.	A process is in place for developing long-term corporate development strategy. This strategy takes shape as result of ongoing interactive learning process involving top and middle levels of management.	Mangers with successful ICV experience are appointed to top management. Top management is rewarded financially and symbolically for long-term corporate development success.
NVD management	Middle-level managers in corporate R&D are selected who have both technical depth and business knowledge necessary to determine minimum amount of resources for project and who can coach star players.	Middle-level managers are responsible for use and development of venture managers as scarce resources of corporation, and they facilitate intrafirm project transfers if new business strategy warrants it.	Substantive interaction between corporate and middle-level management leads to clarifying merits of new business field in light of corporate development strategy.	Star performers at middle level are attracted to ICV activities. Collaboration of mainstream middle level with ICV activities is rewarded. Integrating mechanisms can easily be mobilized.
Group leader/ venture leader	Project initiators are encouraged to integrate technical and business perspectives. They are provided access to resources. Project initiators can be rewarded by means other than promotion to venture manager.	Venture managers are responsible for developing functional capabilities of emerging venture organizations and for codification of what has been learned in terms of required functional capabilities while pursuing new business opportunity.	Slack resources determine level of emergence of mutant ideas. Existence of substantive corporate development strategy provides preliminary self-selection of mutant ideas.	A wide array of venture structures and supporting measurement and reward systems clarifies expected performance for ICV personnel.

Source: R. A. Burgelman, "Managing the Internal Corporate Venturing Process," *Sloan Management Review* 25 (1985), 33–48. Used by permission of *Sloan Management Review* and the author.

able in the operating system of the mainstream businesses of the corporation. Previous systematic research of ICV has not clearly distinguished between new product and new business development and has investigated the ICV development process only up to the "first commercialization" phase (von Hippel, 1977). The present study specifically examines the relationship between project development and business development, showing how new organizational units developed around new businesses become integrated into the operating system of the corporation either as new freestanding divisions or as new departments in existing divisions. The rationale for studying projects utilizing new technologies is that the strategic management problems involved in corporate entrepreneurship are likely to be most accentuated and most identifiable in projects in which innovative efforts are radical (Zaltman, Duncan, and Holbek, 1973).

Methodology and Research Design

A qualitative method was chosen as the best way to arrive at an encompassing view of ICV. Concerns of external validity were traded off against opportunities to gain insight into as yet incompletely documented phenomena. The caveats pertaining to field methods described by Kimberly (1979) are in order. ICV project development has a ten- to twelve-year time horizon (Biggadike, 1979), and a truly longitudinal study was thus beyond the available resources. Instead, a longitudinal-processual approach (Pettigrew, 1979) was adopted. The ICV process was studied exhaustively in one setting. Data were collected on six ongoing ICV projects that were in various stages of development. The historical development of each case was traced and the progress of each case during a fifteen-month research period was observed and recorded. These materials formed the basis for a comparative analysis of the six projects. This approach should not be confused with the so-called "comparative method" of early sociology, which used, often selectively, cross-sectional data to support a priori theories—most aptly called metaphors—of stages of development (Nisbet, 1969). No such theory guided the present research, nor is one proposed as a result of it.

In fact, because of the exploratory nature of the study and the objective of generating a descriptive model of as yet incompletely documented phenomena, Glaser and Strauss's (1967) strategy for the discovery of "grounded theory" was adopted. This strategy requires the researcher " . . . at first, literally to ignore the literature of theory and fact on the area under study, in order to assure that the emergence of categories will not be contaminated by concepts more suited to different areas" (Glaser and Strauss, 1967, p. 37). It also requires joint collection, coding, and analysis of the data. Data must be collected until patterns have clearly emerged and additional data no longer add to the refinement of the concepts.

The lack of previous research at the ICV project level of analysis made it fairly easy to follow these guidelines. By the same token, great uncertainty existed as to what conceptual framework would emerge from the data. Throughout the research period, idea booklets were used to write down new insights and interpretations of data already collected. These ongoing, iterative conceptualization efforts resulted in the creation of a new set of terms for the key activities in ICV and provided the bits and pieces out of which the conceptual framework finally emerged.

Research Setting

This research was carried out in one large, U.S.-based, high-technology firm of the diversified major type which I shall refer to as GAMMA. GAMMA had traditionally produced and sold various commodities in large volume, but it had also tried to diversify through the internal development of new products, processes, and systems so as to get closer to the final user or consumer and to catch a greater portion of the total value added in the chain from raw materials to end products. During the sixties, diversification efforts were carried out within existing corporate divisions, but in the early seventies, the company established a separate new venture division (NVD). Exhibit 13.4 illustrates the structure of GAMMA at the time of the study.

Data were obtained on the functioning of the NVD. The chapters of its various departments, the job descriptions of the major positions in the division, the reporting relationships and mechanisms of coordination, and the reward system were studied. Data were also obtained on the relationships of the NVD with the rest of the corporation. In particular, the collaboration between the corporate R&D department and divisional R&D groups was studied. Finally, data were also obtained on the role of the NVD in the implementation of the corporate strategy of unrelated diversification to help explain why it had been created, how its activities fit in the corporation's Strategic Business Unit system, and how it articulated with corporate management. These data describe the historical evolution of the structural context of ICV development at GAMMA before and during the research period. The bulk of the data was collected in studying the six major ICV projects in progress at GAMMA at the time of the research.

Fermentation Products was in the earliest stage of development. The new business opportunity was still being defined and no project had been formally started. Five people from this project were interviewed, some several times, between November 1976 and August 1977.

Fibre Components was a project for which a team of R&D and business people were investigating business opportunities and their technical implications. Five people in this group were interviewed between January 1977 and May 1977.

Improved Plastics had reached a point where a decision was imminent as to whether the project would receive venture status and be transferred from the corporate R&D department to the venture development department of the NVD. Seven people from this project were interviewed, some several times, between February 1977 and April 1977.

Farming Systems had achieved venture status, but development had been limited to the one product around which it had been initially developed. Efforts were being made to articulate a broader strategy for further development of the venture. This was achieved during the research period and an additional project was started. Seven people were interviewed, some several times, between November 1976 and August 1977.

Environmental Systems had also achieved venture status, but was struggling to deal with the technical flaws of the product around which its initial

EXHIBIT 13.4 The Structure of GAMMA Corporation

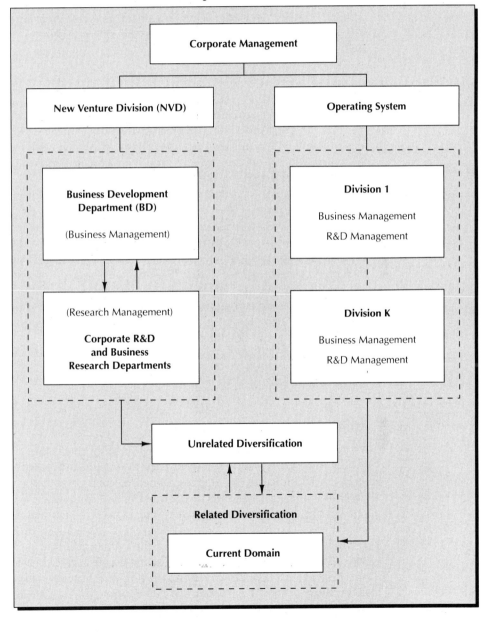

development had taken place. It also was trying to develop a broader strategy for further development. It failed to do so, however, and the venture was halted during the research period. Six people from the project were interviewed between March 1977 and June 1977.

Medical Equipment was rapidly becoming a mature new business. It had grown quickly around one major new product, but had then developed a broader strategy that allowed it to agglomerate medically related projects from other parts of the corporation and to make a number of external acquisitions. After the research period, this venture became a new freestanding division of the corporation. Eleven people were interviewed, some several times, between June 1976 and September 1977.

Data Collection

In addition to the participants in the six ICV projects, I interviewed NVD administrators, people from several operating divisions, and one person from corporate management. All in all, sixty-one people were interviewed. Exhibit 13.5 indicates the distribution of persons interviewed over job categories.

The research also involved the study of documents. As could be expected, the ICV project participants relied little on written procedures in their day-to-day working relationships with other participants. One key set of documents, however, was the set of written corporate long-range plans concerning the NVD and each of the ICV projects. After repeated requests, I received permission to read the plans on site and to make notes. These official descriptions of the evolution of each project between 1973 and 1977 were compared with the interview data.

Finally, occasional behavioral observations were made, for example when other people would call or stop by during an interview or in informal discussions during lunch at the research site. These observations, though not systematic, led to the formulation of new questions for further interviews.

A Process Model of ICV

A Stage Model

As the research progressed, four stages of ICV development were identified—a conceptual, a pre-venture, an entrepreneurial, and an organizational stage. Exhibit 13.6 indicates the stages reached in each project, the number of projects observed for each stage, and the number of real time observations of each stage.

This research design thus resulted in seven case histories. At the project level, the comparative analysis of the six ICV cases allowed the construction of a grounded stage model that described the sequence of stages and their key activities. At the level of the corporation, the research constituted a case study of how one diversified major firm went about ICV and how the corporate context influenced the activities in each stage of development of an ICV project.

A stage model describes the chronological development of a project. It provides a description of the development activities and problems in a series of stages, which is convenient for narrative purposes. Such a model, however, is somewhat deceptive because it does not capture the fact that strategic activities take place at different levels in the organization simultaneously as well as sequentially and, sometimes, in a different order than would be expected.

ICV Process

The process-model approach proposed by Bower (1970) for strategic capital investment projects permits one to connect the project and corporate level of

EXHIBIT 13.5 Distribution of Persons Interviewed, by Job Title

	Number
Top management of the New Venture Division (NVD)	
Director of NVD	2
Director of corporate R&D Department	1
Director of Business Research Department	1
Director of Business Development Department	2
Participants from corporate R&D Department	
R&D managers	4
Group leaders	10
Bench scientists	6
Participants from Business Research Department	
Business managers	2
Business researchers	4
Participants from Business Development Department	
Venture managers	5
Business managers	1
Technology managers	3
Group leaders in venture R&D group	3
Marketing managers	4
Marketing researchers	2
Operations managers	4
Project managers	1
Administration of NVD	
Personnel managers	1
Operations managers	1
Participants from other operating divisions	
R&D managers	1
Group leaders	2
Corporate management	
Executive staff	1
Total	61

analysis and to depict simultaneous as well as sequential strategic activities. Subsequent research has established the usefulness and generalizability of the process-model approach for conceptualizing strategic decision making in and around projects other than capital investment in large, complex firms (Hofer, 1976; Bower & Doz, 1979).

The inductively derived process model for ICV at GAMMA presented below shows how managers from different generic levels in the organization got involved in the development of ICV projects. The first step was to map the stages of ICV development onto the *definition* and *impetus* processes of the model. The definition process encompassed the activities involved in articulating the technical-economic aspects of an ICV project. Through the impetus process, it gained and maintained support in the organization. Definition and impetus were identified as the *core* processes of ICV.

The second step was to map the corporate-level findings onto the *strategic context* and *structural context* determination processes, which make up the corporate context in which ICV development takes shape. Structural context refers to the various organizational and administrative mechanisms put in place by corporate management to implement the current corporate strategy. It operated as a selection mechanism on the strategic behavior of operational and middle-level managers. Strategic context determination refers to the process through which the current corporate strategy was extended to accommodate the new business activities resulting from ICV that fell outside the scope of the current corporate strategy. Strategic and structural context determination were identified as the *overlaying* processes of ICV.

The third step was the documentation of the managerial activities that constitute these different processes.

EXHIBIT 13.6 Stages of Development Reached by Six ICV Projects

Project	Stages			
	Conceptual	Pre-venture	Entrepreneurial	Organizational
Medical Equipment	*	*	*	*
Environmental Systems	*	*	*	
Farming Systems	*	*	*	
Improved Plastics	*	*		
Fibre Components	*	*		
Fermentation Products	*			
Projects observed	6	5	3	1
Real time observations	1	2	2	1

Note: An asterisk indicates that the project reached this stage prior to the conclusion of the study.

Exhibit 13.7 maps the activities involved in ICV onto the process model. It shows how the strategic process in and around ICV is constituted by a set of key activities (the shaded area) and by a set of more peripheral activities (the non-shaded area). These activities are situated at the corporate, NVD, and operational levels of management.

Exhibit 13.8, which can be superimposed on Exhibit 13.7, shows how these different activities interlock with each other, forming a pattern of connections. The relative importance of activities is indicated by the different types of line segments. The data also suggested a sequential flow of activities in this pattern, as indicated by the numbers in Exhibit 13.8.

Exhibit 13.8 shows that ICV is primarily a bottom-up process and depicts the key role performed by middle management. Looking at Exhibit 13.8, entrepreneurial activities at the operational and middle levels (1, 2, 3) can be seen to interact with the selective mechanisms of the structural context (5). These selective mechanisms can be circumvented by activating, through organizational championing (6), the strategic context, which allows successful ICV projects to become retroactively rationalized by corporate management in fields of new business delineated by the middle level (7, 8). These parts of the pattern, represented by the full line segments in Exhibit 13.8, constitute the major forces generated and encountered by ICV projects.

The finely dotted lines in Exhibit 13.8 (4, 9) represent the connection between the more peripheral activities in the ICV process and their linkages with the key activities. Corporate management was found to monitor the resource allocation to ICV projects. Middle-level managers managed these resources and facilitated collaboration between R&D and business people in the definition of new business opportunities; however, these activities seemed to support, rather than drive the definition process. In the same fashion, authorizing further development was clearly the prerogative of corporate management, but this was a result, not a determinant of the impetus process. In the strategic context determination, operational level participants were all found to be important in developing a basis for further definition processes but seemed to be more a result of the process than a determinant of it. In the process of structural context determination, questioning of the structural context by operational level participants and efforts by middle managers to negotiate changes in it seemed to be reactive rather than primary.

The broken line segments in Exhibit 13.8 (10, 11) indicate two important delayed effects in the ICV process. First, the successful activation of the process of strategic context determination encouraged further entrepreneurial activities at the operational level, thus creating a feedforward loop to the definition process (10). Second, corporate management attempted to influence the ICV process primarily through its manipulations of the structural context. These manipulations appeared to be in reaction to the results of the previously authorized ICV projects. This created a feedback loop (11) between the core and overlaying processes.

Exhibits 13.7 and 13.8 and the preceding overview of the process model can now serve as a road map for detailed examination of the interlocking key activi-

EXHIBIT   13.7   Key and Peripheral Activities in a Process Model of ICV

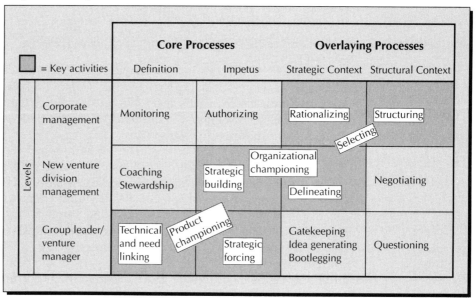

EXHIBIT   13.8   Flow of Activities in a Process Model of ICV

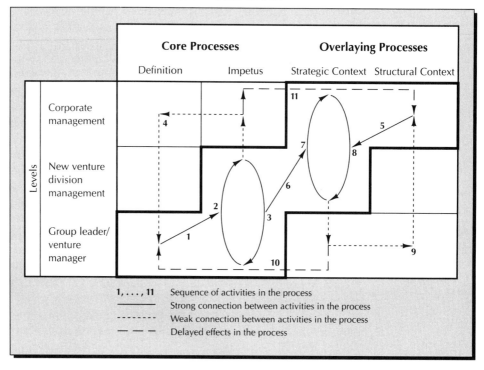

ties that constitute the major driving forces in the four processes—definition, impetus, strategic context determination, and structural context determination—that together constitute ICV.

Defining New Business Opportunities

The case data of the present study suggest that the definition process of an ICV project encompasses the conceptualization and pre-venture stages of the development process. As the definition process takes shape, an idea for a new business opportunity evolves into a concrete new product, process, or system around which a pre-venture team of R&D and business people is formed. As a result of the successful technical and market development efforts of this pre-venture team, a project grows into an embryonic business organization. These stages take place in the context of the corporate R&D department. Critical for the definition of new business opportunities are *linking processes* and *product-championing* activities.

Linking Processes

In all of the cases studied, the initiation of the definition process involved a double linking process. Technical linking activities led to the assembling of external and/or internal pieces of technological knowledge to create solutions for new, or known but unsolved, technical problems. Need linking activities involved the matching of new technical solutions to new, or poorly served, market needs.

In five out of six cases, the definition of the new business opportunity had its origin in technical linking activities in the context of ongoing research activities in the corporate R&D department. In the Fibre Components case, the idea came from a business-oriented manager, but once the idea was to be made concrete, technical linking activities began to dominate the definition process there, too. This suggests "technology first" (Schon, 1967) as the dominant mode of conceiving of a new venture. However, the case data also suggest that the continued viability of a project depended to a very great extent on the integration of technical and marketing considerations in the definition process.[a]

---

[a] This is how the originator of the medical-equipment venture recounted a story that illustrated the importance of integrating technical and marketing considerations in the definition process:

> In 1988, we had a think tank session in Connecticut. A scientist from our government-sponsored lab, I found out, was working on a new way to handle and transfer blood samples, an entirely new concept . . . but the scientist had very fixed ideas about how the product should look as a commercial product . . . .

> An outside group also had discovered the existence of the scientist's idea and followed closely his recommendations. It was a small company, with a sales volume of some eight million dollars. I decided not to make "Chinese copies" of their approach. I insisted on doing market research, and actually spent two months full-time doing this. We ended up with a radical departure from the scientist's approach; we used only the nucleus of his physical concepts. We had found out some advisable product characteristics from our market research, which led, for instance, to a broader-sized "reader." We also combined the analyzer with a computer.

A further discussion of how this integration is achieved and of the issues related to the collaboration between R&D and business people in the definition process is provided in Burgelman (1980).

An important characteristic of ICV project definition was its autonomy from current corporate strategy. ICV project initiators perceived their initiatives to fall outside the current strategy but felt that there was a good chance for them to be included in future strategic development if they proved to be successful. For instance, in the Improved Plastics project, SURF was a process through which cheap plastics—a major business of GAMMA—could be given certain properties of expensive plastics. However, since knowledgeable and influential people at GAMMA were convinced that SURF could not work because it was too violent a process, it was very difficult to obtain formal support for work in this area.[b] The leader of the efforts in SURF persisted, however, and was capable of developing an application of the process with plastic aerosol bottles. Later on, it turned out that they had focused their efforts on the wrong size bottles for commercial application, but in the meantime a basis for corporate support had been demonstrated.

The key position in the definition process turned out to be that of group leader, a first-line supervisory position, in the corporate R&D department. This person had sufficient direct involvement in the research activities to perform technical linking activities, sufficient contact with the business side to be aware of market needs and start the need linking activities, and sufficient experience of the corporate tradition to know what might be included in corporate strategy.[c] Fermentation Products, Improved Plastics, Farming Systems, and Medical Equipment all clearly illustrated the importance of the group leader in the definition process. Fibre Components and Environmental Systems involved higher levels of management in a very superficial way in the initiating phase, but it was the group leader who was able to perform the concrete linking activities, and the higher level involvement soon became very remote even in these two cases.

Product Championing: Linking Definition and Impetus

Because group leaders were most deeply involved in the definition process, they tended to take on the product-championing activities (Schon, 1967) that formed the connection between the definition and impetus processes. Product championing was required to turn a new idea into a concrete new product in which technical and marketing development could begin to take shape. These activities required the ability to mobilize the resources necessary to demonstrate that what

---

[b] In the words of the group leader:

> As with most new ideas, people would give little time to it. People "knew" that SURF was "unpractical," so the divisions did not really get involved, except in an informal way.

[c] Argyris and Schon (1978: 214) noted a similar phenomenon in their Mercury case, in which key participants were those who could recognize "a Mercury problem." In the present study, however, initiators were more concerned with avoiding the work on projects that would be perceived by top management as *not* a GAMMA problem. Projects were avoided in those areas in which there had been failures in the past, in those where there might be risk to the corporation's image, or in areas having special legal liabilities.

conventional corporate wisdom had classified as impossible was, in fact, possible. To overcome difficulties in resource procurement resulting from this conventional wisdom, product champions acted as scavengers, reaching for hidden or forgotten resources to demonstrate feasibility. SURF, for instance, demonstrated the validity of its need for pumps by using modified pumps from the corporate reserve list.[d]

Product championing also set the stage for the impetus process by creating market interest in the new product, process, or system while, from the corporate point of view, it was still in the definition process. To do so, the product champion sometimes cut corners in corporate procedures, as in a case where unauthorized selling efforts were started from the R&D site before the project had become an official venture.[e] ICV projects of the nature investigated in this study thus had to be fought for by their originators. Hiding their efforts until they could show positive results clearly had survival value for product champions. Once such positive results were available, however, pressure began to build to give a project venture status and to transfer it to the business development department, where the impetus process took further shape.

The importance of product championing was especially clear in the cases where it was lacking. In the Fibre Components case, a product champion had not yet emerged, and this hampered the momentum of the project. The more careful balance between the technical and business considerations fostered in this case seemed to make the emergence of a champion more difficult. In Improved Plastics, the original product champion returned to more basic research, and the subsequent reorganization of the pre-venture team with greater balance between R&D and business people made the emergence of a new product champion more difficult. In the Farming Systems, Environmental Systems, and Medical Equipment cases, however, a product champion was able to develop a single product or system around which an embryonic business organization could be formed.

Impetus

The impetus process of an ICV project encompasses the entrepreneurial and organizational stages of development. Major impetus was received when a project was transferred with venture status to the business development department. At this

---

[d] Said the group leader:

> But these pumps are costly, and people at the management level are afraid to commit themselves to such outlays. At that time, however, an engineer came on the project. He knew of the corporate surplus lists and got some old pumps. We rebuilt them and showed that we could pump 35 percent to 49 percent solutions. Having showed that, we could now get the pumps we needed.

[e] As the product champion in this case explained:

> When we proposed to sell the ANA product by our own selling force, there was a lot of resistance, out of ignorance. Management did numerous studies, had outside consultants on which they spent tens of thousands of dollars; they looked at XYZ Company for a possible partnership. Management was just very unsure about its marketing capability. I proposed to have a test marketing phase with 20 to 25 installations in the field. We built our own service group; we pulled ourselves up by the "bootstrap." I guess we had more guts than sense.

time it acquired its own organization, general manager, and operating budget, thus becoming an embryonic new business organization in the department. In the course of the impetus process, the embryonic business grew into a viable one-product business and then, possibly, into a more complex new business with several products. The impetus process reached its conclusion in the decision to integrate this new unit into the operating system of the corporation as a freestanding new division or as a major new department of an existing division. The data indicate that there were no clear general criteria that guided the decisions to transfer projects to the business development department. Although formal screening models existed and the participants in all cases were very able in quantitative analysis, there was little reliance on formal analytical techniques in the ICV process. This is understandable, since each project was unique and could not easily be judged by prior experience. Not surprisingly, the transfer decision thus tended to be greatly influenced by the success of the product-championing activities. The latter allowed a project to reach a threshold level of commercial activity which, in turn, created pressure for it to be given venture status. Farming Systems, Environmental Systems, and Medical Equipment all manifested this pattern. The data on these cases also indicate that after a project was transferred, its further development was highly dependent on the combination of *strategic forcing* and *strategic building* activities and their corollary forms of *strategic neglect*. These activities together give shape to the impetus process.

Strategic Forcing

In the first phase of the impetus process, product-championing activities were transformed into strategic forcing by the entrepreneurial venture manager. This transformation happened naturally, because, in the cases studied, the product champion had become the venture manager. Even though normative theory might question this practice, there were very strong pressures to let the technically oriented product champion become the venture manager. These pressures were in part motivational, because product champions were attracted by the opportunity to become general managers, but they also resulted because there was nobody else around who could take over and maintain momentum. Strategic forcing required that the venture manager concentrate his efforts on the commercialization of the new product, process, or system. In particular, it required a narrow and short-term focus on market penetration.

The Medical Equipment case illustrates successful strategic forcing. Under the impulse of a product champion/venture manager, this ICV project doubled its sales volume each year for five consecutive years. This created the beachhead for further development into a new, mature business.[f] Such successful strategic

---

[f] In the words of the venture manager:

> We were convinced that we could develop simultaneously domestically and internationally. We were fearless, and, management being ignorant, we just started to do it. What we did was, in fact, a parallel international new development. That made our sales 55 percent larger profit fraction. If we had not done this, we might have lost the business.

forcing created a success-breeds-success pattern that allowed the new venture to maintain support from top management and facilitated collaboration from people in other parts of the corporation who liked to be part of the action of a winner. In addition, the success of strategic forcing allowed the emerging venture organization to acquire substantial assets that could not easily be disposed of, thus committing the corporation.[g]

The Environmental Systems case, on the other hand, illustrates unsuccessful strategic forcing. In this case, premature commercialization caused strategic forcing to degenerate into mere selling, and technical people were forced to spend their time correcting the technical flaws of systems already sold. The resulting failure-breeds-failure pattern led first to a reduction of the control of the product champion/venture manager, then to management-by-committee, then to the termination of the venture.

The corollary of successful strategic forcing, however, was strategic neglect of the development of the administrative framework of the new venture. Strategic neglect refers to the more or less deliberate tendency of venture managers to attend only to performance criteria on which the venture's survival is critically dependent; that is, those related to fast growth. To carry out the strategic forcing efforts, the entrepreneurial venture manager attracted or was assigned generalist helpers who usually took care of more than one of the emerging functional areas of the venture organization. This was inexpensive and worked sufficiently well until the volume of activity grew so large that operating efficiency became an important issue. Also, as the new product, process, or system reached a stage of maturity in its life cycle, the need for additional new product development was increasingly felt. To deal with the operating problems and to maintain product development, some of the generalists were replaced with functional specialists who put pressure on the entrepreneurial venture manager to pay more attention to administrative development. In the cases studied, this led to severe friction between the venture manager, who continued to be pressured by forces in the corporate context to maintain a high growth rate, and the functional specialists.[h]

In the successful Medical Equipment venture, the venture manager neglected the administrative development of the venture and experienced increasingly strong conflicts with the professional functional managers brought in to replace the generalists. This became a problem especially in manufacturing. The venture

---

[g] In the words of one of the key participants in a venture:

> The mechanism is to double each year your size. The next step is then to acquire assets that are not easily disposed of. Then management cannot get rid of you that easily, and you can relax if you have a bad year.

[h] Arrow (1974) uses "salutary neglect" to denote the situation in which problems for which there are no satisfactory solutions are not placed on the agenda of the organization. Strategic neglect, independently observed in the present study, has a similar meaning. Arrow points out that neglect is never productive. In the long run, and from the perspective of the larger system, this may be true, and of course the larger system will, in time, correct for neglect. From the perspective of the entrepreneurial actor, however, strategic neglect of administrative issues was the necessary cost of forcing growth.

manager also neglected to maintain close relationships with the corporate R&D group and focused everything on development efforts related to the original product. The venture R&D group, seeking its own identity, sealed itself off from corporate R&D.[i] One of the problematic results of this was that the flow of new product development never got under control. Eventually, the organizational problems and the difficulties in new product development required the replacement of the venture manager.

This study of ICV thus reveals an important dilemma in the process of radical corporate innovation. Successful strategic forcing is required if a project is to gain and maintain impetus in the corporate context. Yet, the very success of strategic forcing seems to imply strategic neglect of the administrative development of the venture. This, in turn, leads to the ironic result that the new product development may become a major problem, and to the tragic result that the entrepreneur may become a casualty in the process of gaining a beachhead for the venture.

Strategic Building

Successful strategic forcing was a necessary, but not sufficient, condition for the continuation of the impetus process. Strategic forcing had to be supplemented by strategic building activities if the project was to overcome the limitations of a one-product venture and maintain the growth rate required for continued support from corporate management. Strategic building took place at the level of the business development (BD) department manager (the venture manager's manager). Thus, consistent with Kusiatin's (1976) and von Hippel's (1977) findings, the present study identifies the venture manager's manager as a key position in the ICV process.

Strategic building involved the articulation of a master strategy for the broader field of new business development opened up by the product champion/venture manager and the implementation of this strategy through the agglomeration of additional new businesses with the original venture. This involved negotiating the transfer of related projects from other parts of the corporation and/or acquisition of small companies with complementary technologies from the outside.

The Medical Equipment case illustrates successful strategic building. From year to year, the written long-range plans showed an increase in depth of understanding of what the real opportunity was. Strategic plans grew more specific, and there was a progression in identifying problems and solving them. Based on this articulation of the principles underlying success, the BD manager negotiated the transfer of one major medically related project from one of the divisions and

---

[i] In the words of one person who was transferred from corporate R&D to the venture:

> We were, at the time, basically separated from the group in the venture. The group there wanted to identify itself. They did it to such an extent that they put a wall between themselves and us . . . . In a way, it was ironic. We were funded by the venture, and the technology that we developed was not accepted by them!

was able to identify suitable acquisition candidates and convince top management to provide the resources to get them.

Strategic building was iterative in nature. The evolving master strategy reflected the learning-by-doing that resulted from the assessment of the success of the strategic forcing efforts of the venture manager. The BD manager learned to understand the reasons for the success of these efforts and used this insight to further articulate the strategy. This, in turn, increased his credibility and provided a basis on which to claim further support of the venture.j

The Environmental Systems case illustrates how failure to understand the nature of the opportunity prevented further progress. Over a five-year period, the long-range plans remained vague about what the opportunity was. There was no progress in terms of identifying and then solving problems. An acquisition was actually made, but it turned out to be as much technically flawed as the original system around which the venture was formed.

The Farming Systems case illustrates how the impetus received from fairly successful strategic forcing can slow down, and even halt, when strategic building is lacking. Only after a new BD manager took over and an analysis was made of the underlying principles of the business opportunity did the impetus process pick up again. The new BD manager discarded the original product, which had been the vehicle for strategic forcing, and articulated a new master strategy that led first to the redirection of the R&D efforts and then to the acquisition of two small companies with complementary technology.

Strategic building, like strategic forcing, was accompanied by strategic neglect in the Medical Equipment case. Because forces in the corporate context emphasized fast growth, the BD manager got absorbed in the search and evaluation of companies that could be acquired, in negotiations with divisions to transfer related projects, and in courting top management. The coaching of the venture manager was, again more or less deliberately, neglected, which seemed to suit the venture manager. As a result, the emerging administrative problems in the venture organization deteriorated from petty and trivial to severe and disruptive, and some high-quality people left the venture.

The personal orientations of the venture managers further reinforced this tendency in the cases in my study. The venture manager of Medical Equipment complained about a lack of guidance from the BD manager, but he also pointed out that the situation gave him leeway for his mistakes. Furthermore, he pointed out that because the venture was growing very fast, there was little time for

---

j Explaining his approach, one BD manager said:

First, I look for demonstrated performance on an arbitrarily chosen—sometimes not even the right one—tactic. For instance, developing a new analyzer may not be the right move, but it can be done and one can gain credibility by doing it. So, what I am really looking for is the ability to predict and plan adequately. I want to verify your claim that you know how to predict and plan, so you need a "demonstration project" even if it is only an experiment. The second thing that I look for is the strategy of the business. That is the most important milestone. The strategy should be attractive and workable. It should answer the questions where you want to be in the future and how you are going to get there . . . .And that, in turn, allows you to go to the corporation and stick your neck out.

coaching. He also admitted that his style was probably considered a bit "adversarial" by the BD manager, and that this did not facilitate the coaching process.

The venture manager of Environmental Systems also complained about a lack of guidance.[k] This manager, however, admitted that he had been eager to get the venture manager's job in spite of his lack of experience. Others in the venture organization pointed to this manager's stubbornness and lack of responsiveness to others' inputs.

The present study thus suggests a second important dilemma in the strategic management process. The BD manager can spend more time trying to guide the impetuous venture manager, but this may both interfere with the strategic forcing efforts of the venture manager and limit the time available to the BD manager for strategic building activities. Or, he can leave the venture manager alone and let him run his course until the problems in the growing venture organization require his replacement, but by that time the venture itself should have reached a viable position in terms of commercial activity. The data suggest that the forces exerted by the corporate context—the emphasis on fast growth—seem to favor the second of these possibilities.

Successful strategic forcing and strategic building created a new business organization with several products and a sales volume of about 35 million dollars in the case of Medical Equipment, but important managerial problems remained to be solved. First, the effects of the strategic neglect of the administrative framework of the venture became particularly pronounced. This administrative instability was exacerbated by the fact that there was not yet a strong common orientation, and there was still a lot of opportunistic behavior on the part of some key participants in the venture organization, who seemed to work more to improve their resumes to get a better position elsewhere than for the overall success of the venture. Also, the delayed effects of the strategic neglect of new product development in the original area of business manifested themselves. Furthermore, strategic building efforts had led to the creation of a complex new business organization, where growth could no longer be maintained solely by the hard work of the venture manager. New strategies for the different business thrusts had to be generated by the organization, but this required that people work in a strategic planning framework in which the concerns of the different new business thrusts could be traded off and reconciled, and the participants were still learning to do this.

In addition to these internal managerial problems, this new venture also had to cope with the problem of securing its position in the corporation. The venture's size made it visible in the external and internal environments, and corporate management became increasingly aware of the differences in modus

---

[k] Right after his replacement, this manager observed:

> I should have gotten help from my management—counseling and education. Most venture managers tend to come from the technology side because these ventures require a lot of high technology input. But in the technology area there is relatively little need for broad general management skill development. I was lacking that kind of judgment.

operandi between the new business and the rest of the corporation and of the effects of these differences on the corporate image. NVD management thus was faced with the problem of convincing corporate management that the new venture was compatible with the rest of the corporation and was moving toward institutionalization.

Strategic Context

For institutionalization to take place, an area of new venturing must become integrated into the corporation's concept of strategy. Adaptation of corporate strategy at GAMMA involved complex interactions between managers of the NVD and corporate management in the process of *strategic context* determination.

Strategic context determination refers to the political process through which middle-level managers attempt to convince top management that the current concept of strategy needs to be changed so as to accommodate successful new ventures. Strategic context determination constitutes an internal selection mechanism that operates on the stream of autonomous strategic behavior in the firm. The key to understanding the activation of this process is that corporate management knows when the current strategy is no longer entirely adequate but does not know how it should be changed until, through the selection of autonomous strategic initiatives from below, it is apparent which new businesses can become part of the business portfolio.[1]

Critical activities in this process involve *delineating* new fields of business development and *retroactive rationalizing* of successful new venture activities. The link between the process of strategic context determination and the impetus process of a particular new venture is constituted by *organizational championing* activities.

Organizational Championing: Linking Impetus and Strategic Context Determination

The case data indicate that during the impetus process, organizational championing activities became the crucial link between the emerging new business organization and the corporate context. Organizational championing involved the establishment of contact with top management to keep them informed and enthusiastic about a particular area of development. This, in turn, involved the ability to articulate a convincing master strategy for the new field, so as to be able to communicate where the development was leading and to explain why support

---

[1] The identification of the process of strategic context determination leads to a major extension of the process model. It suggests that the corporate context is more complex than was revealed by Bower's (1970) study of strategic capital investment projects. These projects were situated in the operating system of the corporation. Even though they were clearly strategic because of the large amounts of resources involved, they did not require a change in the business portfolio of the corporation. These projects fell within the scope of and were induced by the current concept of strategy of the corporation.

was needed for major moves. These activities were also performed at the level of the business development manager.

Organizational championing was, to a large extent, a political activity. The BD manager committed his judgment and put his reputation on the line. Astute organizational champions learned what the dispositions of top management were and made sure that the projects they championed were consistent with the current corporate strategy. More brilliant organizational champions were able to influence the dispositions of top management and make corporate management see the strategic importance of a particular new business field for corporate development.

Organizational championing required more than mere political savvy, however. It required the rare capacity to evaluate the merit of the proposals and activities of different product champions in strategic rather than in technical terms. Thus, in the Medical Equipment venture, a sound master strategy for the new venture and corresponding strategic building moves allowed the organizational champion to convince top management that the medical field was an attractive and viable one for the corporation. In the Environmental Systems venture, on the other hand, the failure to come up with a master strategy prevented the organizational champion from obtaining the resources needed to straighten out the technological problems of the new venture and prevented him from engaging in strategic building. His organizational championing was limited to gaining more time, but eventually top management concluded that the opportunity just wasn't there. Finally, in the Farming Systems venture, new impetus was developed as a result of the involvement of the same person who was the organizational champion in Medical Equipment.

Delineating

Through organizational championing based on strategic building, middle-level managers were capable of delineating in concrete terms the content of new fields of business development for the corporation. It is a critical finding of this study that these new fields became defined out of the agglomeration of specific commercial activities related to single new products, processes, or systems, developed at the level of venture projects rather than the other way around. Delineating activities were thus iterative and aggregative in nature. This was clearly reflected in the written long-range plans of the NVD in 1975, which stated: "Instead of dealing with an ever-growing number of separate arenas, the NVD should henceforth focus its attention on a critical few major fields, within each of which arenas may be expanded, grouped together, or added."

Retroactive Rationalizing

To be sure, corporate management, too, got involved in the process of strategic context determination. Top management gave indications of interest in venture activity in certain general fields and expressed concern about the fit of ongoing ICV activities with corporate resources and strategy. In the final analysis, however, corporate management's role was limited to rejecting or rationalizing, retroactively, the ICV initiatives of lower-level participants in fields delineated by middle-level management.

These findings corroborate and extend the findings of previous research. They confirm the critical role of middle-level managers in shaping the strategy of internal development in the diversified major firm (Kusiatin, 1976). More generally, these findings also extend Kimberly's (1979) observation of the paradox that the success of a new, nonconformist unit creates pressures in the larger organizational context toward conformity, thereby affecting the very basis of success. Entrepreneurial and institutional existence seem to be inherently discrete states, and middle-level management needs to bridge the discontinuity.

Structural Context

Given the limited substantive involvement of corporate management in the process of strategic context determination, how do they try to exert control over the ICV process? The present study suggests that they did so by *structuring* an internal selection environment.

Structuring

As in the situation studied by Bower (1970), corporate management relied on the determination of the structural context in its attempts to influence the strategic process concerning ICV. The structural context includes the diverse organizational and administrative elements whose manipulation is likely to affect the perception of the strategic actors concerning what needs to be done to gain corporate support for particular initiatives. The creation of the NVD as a separate organizational unit, the definition of positions and responsibilities in the departments of the NVD, the establishment of criteria for measuring and evaluating venture and venture-manager performance, and the assignment of either entrepreneurially or administratively inclined managers to key positions in the NVD all seemed intended to affect the course of ICV activity.

The corporate level seemed dominant in the determination of structural context. Corporate management's manipulations of the structural context seemed to be guided primarily by strategic concerns at their level, reflecting emphasis on either expansion of mainstream businesses or diversification, depending on perceptions at different times of the prospects of current mainstream businesses.

These changes in structural context did not reflect a well-conceived strategy for diversification, however, and seemed to be aimed at consolidating ICV efforts at different levels of activity rather than at guiding and directing these efforts. The NVD was created in the early seventies because people in the divisions had been engaging in what some managers called a "wild spree" of diversification efforts. Corporate management wanted to consolidate these efforts, although at a relatively high level of activity. Key managers involved in those earlier decisions pointed out that the direction of these consolidated efforts was based on preceding lower-level initiatives that had created resource commitments, rather than on a clear corporate strategy of diversification.

The lack of a clear strategy for directing diversification was also evident in 1977, when significant changes in the functioning of the NVD took place. The newly appointed NVD manager pointed out that corporate management had not expressed clear guiding principles for further diversification beyond the emphasis on consolidation and the need to reduce the number of fields in which ICV activity was taking place.

Selecting

Structural context determination thus remained a rather crude tool for influencing ICV efforts. It resulted in an internal selection environment in which the autonomous strategic incentives emerging from below competed for survival. In all the ICV cases, strong signals of fast growth and large size as criteria for survival were read into the structural context by the participants. This affected the process, if not so much the specific content, of their behavior. The importance of product championing, strategic forcing, strategic building, and the corresponding forms of strategic neglect would seem to indicate this. The inherent crudeness of the structural context as a tool for influencing the ICV process provided, of course, the rationale as well as the opportunity for the activation of the strategic context determination process discussed earlier.

Conclusions and Implications

The preceding discussion of a process model of ICV does not, to be sure, treat the entire range of phenomena associated with new ventures (Roberts, 1980) and corporate entrepreneurship (Peterson, 1981). Reasons of focus as well as space constraints prevent discussion of issues such as management of the interfaces between business and R&D people and structural and managerial innovation associated with the separate new venture division.

The purpose here has been to construct a grounded model and to use this model as a framework for insights into the generative mechanisms of one form of corporate entrepreneurship in one type of large business organization. Verification is necessary to identify the generalizable relationships embedded in the process model generated in this paper and to identify the contingency factors that might explain variance across organizations in these relationships. The major insights gained from this exploratory study of the ICV process are recapitulated below and some major implications are briefly discussed.

First, the findings suggest strongly that the motor of corporate entrepreneurship resides in the autonomous strategic initiatives of individuals at the operational levels in the organization. High-technology ventures are initiated because entrepreneurially inclined technologists, usually at the group-leader level, engage in strategic initiatives that fall outside the current concept of corporate strategy. They risk their reputations and, in some cases, their careers, because they are attracted by the perceived opportunity to become the general manager of an important new business in the corporation. This stream of autonomous strategic initiatives may be one of the most important resources for maintaining the corporate capability for renewal through internal development. It constitutes one major source of variation out of which the corporation can select new products and markets for incorporation into a new strategy.

Second, because of their very nature, autonomous initiatives are likely to encounter serious difficulties in the diversified major firm. Their proponents often have to cope with problems of resource procurement, because they attempt to achieve objectives that have been categorized by the corporation as impossible. Because such initiatives require unusual, even unorthodox, approaches, they create managerial dilemmas that are temporarily resolved through the more or less deliberate neglect of administrative issues during the entrepreneurial stage. The success of the entrepreneurial stage thus depends on behaviors that, paradoxically, have a high probability of eliminating the key actors from participation in the organizational stage. There seems to be an inherent discontinuity in the transition from entrepreneurial to institutionalized existence, as well as a possible asymmetry in the distribution of costs and benefits for the actors that may underlie the myth of the entrepreneur as tragic hero in the large corporation.

Third, the study of ICV elucidates the key role of middle-level managers in the strategy-making process in the diversified major firm. The venture manager's manager performs the crucial role of linking successful autonomous strategic behavior at the operational level with the corporate concept of strategy. Both the continuation of the impetus process of a particular ICV project and the change of the corporate strategy through the activation of the process of strategic context determination depend on the conceptual and political capabilities of managers at this level. The importance of this role seems to confirm the above-mentioned discontinuity between entrepreneurial activity and the mainstream of corporate activity.

Fourth, corporate management's role in the ICV process seems to be limited to the retroactive rationalization of autonomous strategic initiatives that have been selected by both the external environment at the market level and the internal corporate environment. Top management's direct influence in the ICV process is through the manipulation of structural context. These manipulations, however, seem to be predicated less on a clearly formulated corporate strategy for unrelated diversification than on concerns of consolidation. Ironically, from this perspective, the establishment of a separate, new venture division may be more a manifestation of corporate management's uneasiness with autonomous strategic behavior in the operating system than the adaptation of the structure to implement a clearly formulated strategy. The present study thus suggests that the observed oscillations in ICV activity at GAMMA may have been due to the lack of articulation between these manipulations of the structural context and a corporate strategy for unrelated diversification. It also provides further corroboration for the similar findings of Fast (1979) on the unstable position of NVDs in many corporations and for Peterson and Berger's (1971) suggestion that top management may view corporate entrepreneurship more as insurance for coping with perceived environmental turbulence than as an end in itself.

Implications for Organization Theory and Strategic Management

The research findings presented in this paper can be related to the current discussions in organization theory of the validity of rational versus natural selection models to explain organizational growth and development (Pfeffer & Salancik, 1978; Aldrich, 1979; Weick, 1979). Relatively successful, large diversified major firms like GAMMA would seem to be representative of the class of organizations that have sufficient control over their required resources to escape, to a great extent, the tight control of external selection and to engage in strategic choice (Child, 1972; Aldrich, 1979). The detailed, multilayered picture of the strategic management process presented in this paper suggests, however, that these strategic choice processes, when exercised in radical innovation, take on the form of experimentation and selection, rather than strategic planning. This is fundamentally different from the view that administrative systems "program" their own radical change (Jelinek, 1979).

Further research is needed to establish the conditions under which different systems for innovation in organizations can be adequate. The limited evidence of the present study, however, suggests that the tight coupling implied in the institutionalized approach may be inadequate for organizations with multiple, mostly mature technologies in their operating system. In an organization like GAMMA, there seems to be relatively little opportunity for generating radical innovation from within the operating system through the imposition of a strategic planning approach.

Large, complex business organizations have separate variation and selection mechanisms. Previously unplanned, radically new projects at the product/market level are generated from the relatively unique combination of productive resources of such firms. Not all of these projects are adopted, not so much because the market may turn out to be unreceptive but because they must overcome the selection mechanisms in the internal administrative environment of the firm, which reflect, normally, the current strategy of the corporation, i.e., the retained wisdom of previously selected strategic behavior. Thus, the experimentation and selection model draws attention to the possibility that firms may adopt externally unviable projects or may fail to adopt externally viable ones and provides a clue to why firms occasionally produce strange innovations.[m] This analysis posits a conceptual continuity between internal and external selection processes, analogous to Williamson's (1975) analysis of external and internal capital markets, to explain the existence of the conglomerate form of the divisionalized firm. Because corporate entrepreneurship, as exemplified by the ICV activities in this paper, seems to differ from traditional individual entrepreneurship, as well as from traditional organizational economic activity, it may be necessary to devise different arrangements between the corporate resource

---

[m] In the course of the present study, anecdotal evidence for the emergence of very unusual projects was amply available. In one case, a scientist pulled out a file with a whole series of such abortive projects, e.g., the mining of gold from sea water.

providers and their entrepreneurial agents. Further research, both theoretical and empirical, would seem useful here.

The insights generated by the present study also have some implications for further research on the management of the strategy-making process in general. Comparative research studies of a longitudinal-processual nature, carried out at multiple levels of analysis, are necessary to document and conceptualize the multilayered, more or less loosely coupled network of interlocking, simultaneous, and sequential key activities that constitute the strategy-making process. Following Bower (1970), the present study has found it useful to focus the research on a particular strategic project rather than on the strategy-making process in general. This is consistent with Quinn's (1980, p. 52) observation that top managers "deal with the logic of each subsystem of strategy formulation largely on its own merits and usually with a different subset of people." A concrete focus, it would seem, is more likely to produce data on the vicious circles, dilemmas, paradoxes, and creative tensions that are embedded in the strategy-making process.

Comparative analysis of process models of various strategic projects could produce grounded concepts and categories that would initially be somewhat rudimentary and evocative. Hopefully, these would stimulate the imagination of other scholars and provide the base for more formal and precise concepts of managerial activity in the strategy-making process. Eventually, this could lead to a general theory of the management of strategic behavior in complex organizations and to the conceptual integration of content and process, formulation and implementation.

The present study may then be viewed as an attempt to augment the substratum of rudimentary and evocative concepts and categories. One result of this attempt is the identification of the new concepts of autonomous strategic behavior and strategic context determination and categories of key strategic activities. Further research along these lines may be able to provide a clearer understanding of the interactions between strategy, structure, and managerial activities and skills.

Source: Article 13.1 excerpted from R. A. Burgelman, "A Process Model of Internal Corporate Venturing in the Diversified Major Firm," *Administrative Science Quarterly* 28 (1983), 223–44. Used by permission of *Administrative Science Quarterly* and the author.

ARTICLE 13.2   TECHNOLOGICAL PROGRESS AND VENTURE ACTIVITIES: CONSIDERING THE IMPLICATIONS OF CONTEXTUAL FACTORS
by Daniel F. Jennings

A review of the literature on venturing activities indicates that most of the focus regarding venture activities is on process factors. Process refers to the way in which the venture, itself, is implemented. However, another dimension of venturing exists which can be referred to as the context of the venture. Context deals with the environment and organizational elements in which the venture is situated. Timmons and Bygrave stated that within the United States there are "conspicuous oases" of highly innovative technological ventures where "entrepreneurs, technologists, and venture capitalists have agglomerated." An important question is why have these "conspicuous oases" developed in certain locations and not in others.

The primary purpose of this article is to stimulate thinking and interest on the concept and conditions regarding the context of venturing and implications for future research. The venturing activities, in this article, are considered as occurring within the stages of technological progress. The first part of this article describes a model of technological progress, the second part introduces venturing activities into the technological progress model, and the third part posits contextual factors that affect venturing activities. Finally, implications for future research are discussed.

Technological Progress Model

Building on the work of Fraas and Greer, technological advances can be viewed as a three-stage phenomenon as depicted in Exhibit 13.9.

Invention has been described as the "first confidence that something should work and the first rough test that it will, in fact, work." This suggests that there must be an initial concept and some proof that the idea will work. Kamien and Schwartz argue that invention must possess utility and is the "seed" of technical progress.

Innovation is the first commercial application of an invention. This is a costly process. Publications developed by the U.S. Department of Commerce indicate that 5–15% of a successful new product's cost is incurred from engineering and design, 40–60% is spent on setting up the manufacturing process, 5–15% into startup expenses, and 10–25% covers initial marketing expenses. The National Science Foundation reports that 3% of total research expenditures, both private and public, is for basic research and can be viewed as the advancement of scientific knowledge; 17% is spent for applied research, which can be called inventions; and 80% is spent on development, which can be considered as innovative activities—translating research findings into commercial products. To the venture capitalists, funding at this stage is referred to as "seed money."

EXHIBIT 13.9   A Model of Technological Progress

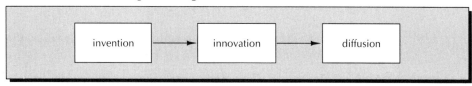

Enos writes that innovation consumes a tremendous amount of time and effort as the basic idea is tested, refined, debugged, produced, and marketed, and further asserts that "in the majority of cases there is not a clear boundary between invention and innovation." From an organizational perspective, innovation studies yield mixed results. While Downs and Mohr, Kets de Vries, and Arrow have reported that factors found to be important for innovation in one study are found to be less important in another, Miller and Friesen argue that these conflicts occur because researchers have failed to consider the strategy or philosophy behind innovation.

Diffusion is the third stage of the model. This aspect, or stage, deals with the spread of the commercial application of the invention. Buyers and investors assume some risks during this period with regard to whether or not the product or service will perform. This is the area of the majority of venture capital activity.

Each part of the three-stage model of technological progress requires different talents and resources. Although not considered in this article, progress is also affected by economic conditions and other factors. A great deal of study has been devoted toward attempting to discern the relationship among firm size, market structure, organizational factors, and technological progress. These reviews are presented in the appendix to this article on page 247.

Venturing Activities and the Technological Process Model

As depicted in Exhibit 13.10, venturing activities (VA) can occur between the invention and innovation stages and between the innovation and diffusion stages.

We suggest that five factors determine whether or not the venturing activity occurs between the invention and innovation stages or between the innovation and diffusion stages and also affect venture implementation. These factors include: (1) market structures, (2) basic government policies concerning markets, (3) availability of tax incentives, (4) technological opportunity, and (5) organizational structure and congruence. Following is a brief description of each of these five factors.

EXHIBIT 13.10 The Relationship Between Venturing Activities and Technological Progress Stages

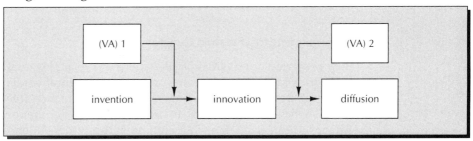

Market Structures

Market structure refers to such conditions as the size, distribution, and number of buyers and sellers, the conditions of entry, and product differentiation.

Basic Government Policies Concerning Markets

Greer writes that governmental policies can be classified in terms of how the policy relates to competition and offers three classifications. These classifications are (1) the maintenance of competition, (2) setting the plans of competition, and (3) reliance on a particular type of regulation instead of competition.

The first classification, maintenance of competition, deals with monopoly and merger laws, price fixing, exclusive dealing, tying, and price discrimination. The second classification, setting the plans of competition, focuses on information disclosure, trademark and copyright protection, false advertising, deceptive practices, health and safety disclosures, and pollution limitations. The third classification, reliance on a particular type of regulation instead of competition, concerns the availability of credit, price regulation, service abandonment, profit regulation, service requirements, safety, and innovation regulation.

Availability of Tax Incentives

While Adam Smith wrote that taxes should have the virtue of neutrality—"The private production and consumption decisions are not affected, and that the allocation of resources in the private sector remains undisturbed"—both Federal and state governments have devised various tax incentives to encourage investment. These incentives are a departure from neutrality because they are designed to get businessmen to change their decisions and to undertake more investment than their ordinary judgment dictates. Tax incentives are devised in such a manner that the government pays a subsidy on investments by giving back to the investor some amount of the investment cost through a special tax credit.

Technological Opportunity

Comanor writes that "technological opportunity" can be associated with the ease of product differentiation. Hambrick and MacMillan argue that technological opportunity requires a market reference. Opportunity is a function to which the market seeks or accepts product changes.

Organizational Structure and Congruence

Miller and Friesen write that organizations are "complex entities whose elements of structure, strategy, and environment have a natural tendency to coalesce into quantum states or configurations which tend to influence each other."

This article postulates that an organization's configuration develops from the activities of differentiation, integration, and interdependence, and that the factors, together with a degree of congruence, are important contextual factors affecting venturing activities.

Implications for Future Research

The article began with a discussion of the need to study the context of venturing. A framework describing the relationship between venturing activities and stages of technological progress is presented. Contextual factors affecting the implementation of the venture as well as which stage in the technological process model the venture will occur are suggested. While specific hypotheses are not developed, the following implications exist for future research.

- How do the contextual factors affect the venturing activity within different stages of the technological progress model?
- Two situations of venture capital activity are noted: one occurring between the invention and innovation stages and the other between the innovation and diffusion stages. To what extent are these situations different? Do more than two situations occur?
- To what extent do the contextual factors affect the internal venture developed by a corporation as opposed to the independent venture activities?
- To what extent do the contextual factors affect the venture as opposed to the activities of a venture capital firm?
- What hypotheses can be developed to test the contextual factors?

The article ends with more questions than answers. Certainly, sophisticated techniques will provide additional insight. The purpose is to stimulate critical thinking toward developing a better understanding of the "conspicuous oases" where venturing occurs.

APPENDIX TO ARTICLE 3.2

Relationships Among Firm Size, Market Structure, Organizational Elements and Technological Progress

Firm Size and Technological Progress

Despite Galbraith's comment that "a benign providence has made the modern industry of a few large firms an excellent instrument for inducing technical progress," the emphasis on bigness may be misplaced. Mansfield, et al., investigated firm size and invention using the measures of inputs (R&D money and personnel) and outputs (number of patents) and summarized as follows:

> Early theorizing on the relation between technological advancement and firm size stressed the virtues of bigness. But two decades of subsequent study have shown that the hypotheses of firm size and advancement tend to be misplaced. In the aggregate, R&D effort is concentrated in the hands of the top 600 firms, but inventive output is

not commensurate with the input of these firms. Within specific industries there is no evidence indicating that R&D intensity, relative to firm size, increases beyond medium-sized firms. Indeed, the largest firms are much less spirited than medium-sized firms in many industries. Moreover, within most industries, inventive output does not match measured input, apparently because diseconomies of scale occur beyond moderate size levels.

Greer and Rhoades wrote that with the exception of the chemical industry, large firms account for a "disproportionate" share of innovations. Romeo empirically tested the rate of diffusion of a single innovation, numerically controlled machine tools, by gathering adoption data from 140 firms in ten manufacturing industries. Romeo learned that the less concentrated industries adopted the innovation "more quickly" than industries that were more highly concentrated. Scherer provides an overview of firm size as follows: "a little bit of bigness is good; too much often seems bad. The most favorable industrial environment for rapid technological progress would appear to be a firm size distribution which includes a preponderance of companies with sales below $200 million, pressed on one side by a horde of small technology-oriented enterprises bubbling over with bright new ideas and on the other by a few larger corporations with the capacity to undertake exceptionally ambitious developments."

Thus, we see that a range of sizes may be best for a particular industry. The stages of invention, innovation, and diffusion include projects that vary widely in size and scope demanding different talents and resources. Consequently, size alone cannot be considered as a determinant factor in the model.

Market Structure and Technological Progress

Once the departure is made from the world of perfect competition, the key issue relating to market structure becomes market power. Rothschild defined market power as "the ability to influence market price perceptibly."

Early researchers tended to consider the notion of rivalry in developing theories of the relationship between market structure and progress. Galbraith argued that high barriers to entry and high concentration tended to promote progress. A lack of rivalry was viewed as increasing profits which would provide more funds for risky R&D projects. Innovators would be protected from those that might "steal" their ideas. Williamson argued, however, that the relative performance of leading firms is greater where competition exists and concentration is lower. He stated: "The relative innovative performance of the largest firms may decline as monopoly power increases. Hence, the incentives to innovate are held to be particularly keen where competitive conditions prevail."

Greer summarized the research on the relationship of market structure and progress as follows:

> The influence of market structure is still somewhat uncertain because test results conflict. Nevertheless, several faint outlines seem discernable. First, it is perhaps most

plausible to suppose that neither monopoly nor pure competition are very good for vigorous advance. Incentive and ability blend in the middle ranges of structure, as evidence on R&D effort seems to bear out. Second, the facts concerning innovation indicate that the relative performance of leading firms diminishes as concentration increases. Data on productivity changes are mixed, but if concentration does make some positive contribution it is a small one. Finally, several studies of diffusion testify to the benefits of competitive structures. Other things being equal, high concentration and lofty entry barriers hinder the spread of technological breakthroughs.

Organizational Elements and Technological Progress

The role of organizational elements such as structure, culture, and congruence has been stressed by numerous researchers as having an impact on technological progress. Following is a review of each of these organizational elements.

Structure. Burns and Stalker conceptualized that adaptive firms operating in a dynamic environment with heterogeneous markets would adopt an organic structure.

Lawrence and Lorsch reported that the dimensions of differentiation and integration have a strong interrelationship on the design of an organization. Differentiation is defined as segmenting parts of the organization into subsystems. Each of these subsystems faces a different task environment and these differences account for the organization's differentiation. As an example, the marketing department is concerned with customer desires while the research and development department is concerned with technological advances. Integration is defined as the process of unifying the various subsystems. Thompson argued that differentiation among subsystems creates conflicts unless integrative devices are used to insure collaboration. Thompson's notion of achieving integration was through interdependence based on the extent to which the various organizational subsystems depend on each other's tasks. Mintzberg built upon Thompson's interdependencies and viewed them as devices dealing with the organization's work flow, classifying the work flow interdependencies as process, scale, and social. Process deals with relationships among specialists. Scale relates to efficiency, and social interdependence takes into account the psychological and social needs of individual workers.

Frequently, organizations are differentiated by function or by markets served. The advantages of functional differentiation are the achievement of economies of scale and specialization of labor. A disadvantage is that the subsystems may work toward achieving their own objectives rather than the overall goals of the organization.

An advantage of differentiation by markets is that less formalization is required, an "esprit de corps" among members is achieved, and there is a concern for the "end" rather than the "means." Some disadvantages of market differentiation are inefficiency in utilizing personnel and equipment, and problems in dealing with organizational specialists who are within the subsystem.

Wilson advises that a diverse group of managers and specialists will tend to promote innovation. Galbraith argues (1) that differentiation has a negative effect on innovation because collaboration is hindered, and (2) that integration will restrain innovation because integrative mechanisms will warn managers of the excessive costs of innovation. Miller and Friesen reported empirical support for Galbraith's arguments.

Culture. Sathe stated that culture is the set of values, guiding beliefs, and understandings that are shared by members of an organization. It defines basic organizational values, and communicates to new members the correct way to think and act, and how things ought to be done.

Deal and Kennedy noted that a strong culture can be a positive force when used to reinforce and support the strategy of a firm. For this reason, senior executives often try to influence culture to be consistent with corporate strategy.

Trice and Beyer argued that organizational leaders can plan an active role in shaping corporate culture and proposed four types of cultural leadership in organizations. Trice and Beyer suggested that leaders can create, embody, change, or integrate the cultures of their organizations.

Congruence. If the components of an organization "fit well," then the organization functions effectively—if they "fit poorly," it will not. The term "fit" in this article refers to congruence effects. Conceptualizations of congruence are found early in the strategic management literature. For example, Chandler found that new strategies necessitate changes in the firm's structure. Galbraith and Nathanson noted that the organization also must match its employees to tasks, the organization's structure, reward system, and information technology. Thompson felt that one of the chief administrative functions of top management was to coalign the organization's technology and task environment with a viable domain, and to adopt an organization design appropriate to that domain. Thompson suggested that in both cases, "matches" could be made that would maximize the effectiveness of the organization.

While a number of researchers (Egelhoff, Nadler & Tushman; Nightingdale & Toulouse; Venkatraman & Camillus; Fry & Smith) have made contributions toward developing contingency models explaining congruence, our approach is to suggest that from a venturing perspective, the work of Galbraith and Nathanson is more appropriate.

ARTICLE 13.3   MANAGING THE INTERNAL CORPORATE VENTURING PROCESS
by Robert A. Burgelman

Many large established firms currently seem to be trying hard to improve their capacity for managing internal entrepreneurship and new ventures. Companies like DuPont and General Electric have appointed CEOs with a deep understanding of the innovation process.[a] IBM has generated much interest with its concept of "independent business units."[b] To head its new ventures division, Allied Corporation has attracted the person who ran 3M's new ventures group for many years.[c] These are only some of the better publicized cases.

Most managers in large established firms will probably agree that internal corporate venturing (ICV) is an important avenue for corporate growth and diversification. However, they will also probably observe that it is a hazardous one, and will be ready to give examples of new ventures (and managerial careers) gone for naught.

Systematic research suggests that such apprehension is not unfounded. In a large sample study of firms attempting to diversify through internal development, Ralph Biggadike found that it takes on the average about eight years for a venture to reach profitability, and about ten to twelve years before its ROI equals that of mainstream business activities.[d] He concludes his study with the caveat that new business development is "not an activity for the impatient or for the fainthearted." Norman Fast did a study of firms that had created a separate new venture division to facilitate internally developed ventures.[e] He found that the position of such new venture divisions was precarious. Many of these were short-lived, and most others suffered rather dramatic changes as a result of often erratic changes in the corporate strategy and/or in their political position. An overview of earlier studies on new ventures is provided by Eric von Hippel, who observed a great diversity of new venture practices.[f] He also identified some key factors associated with the success and failure of new ventures, but did not document how the ICV *process* takes shape.

The purpose of this article is to shed additional light on some of the more deep-rooted problems inherent in the ICV *process* and to suggest recommendations for making a firm's ICV strategy more effective. This article presents a new model capable of capturing the intricacies of managerial activities involved in the ICV process. This model provides a fairly complete picture of the organizational dynamics of the ICV process. By using this new tool, we can identify and discuss

---

[a] See "DuPont: Seeking a Future in Biosciences," *Business Week* 24 (November 1980), 86–98; "General Electric: The Financial Wizards Switch Back to Technology," *Business Week,* 16 March 1981, 110–14.

[b] See "Meet the New Lean, Mean IBM," *Fortune,* 13 June 1983, 68–82.

[c] "Allied after Bendix: R&D Is the Key," *Business Week,* 12 December 1983, 76–86.

[d] See R. Biggadike, "The Risky Business of Diversification," *Harvard Business Review,* May-June 1979, 111.

[e] See N. D. Fast, "The Future of Industrial New Venture Departments," *Industrial Marketing Management* (1979): 264–73.

[f] See E. von Hippel, "Successful and Failing Internal Corporate Ventures: An Empirical Analysis," *Industrial Marketing Management* (1977): 163–74. Some of the diversity found by von Hippel, however, may be due to a somewhat unclear distinction between new product development and new business development.

key problems and their interrelationships and then suggest some ideas for alleviating, if not eliminating, these deep-rooted problems.

A New Model of the ICV Process

The hazards facing internal corporate ventures are similar in many ways to those confronting new businesses developed by external entrepreneurs. Not surprisingly, the ICV process has typically been conceptualized in terms of a "stages model" which describes the evolution and organization development of a venture as a *separate* new business. Such a model emphasizes the *sequential* aspects of the development process, and focuses on problems within the various stages and on issues pertaining to the transitions between stages. For example, Jay Galbraith has recently proposed a model of new venture development that encompasses five generic stages: (1) proof of principle, prototype; (2) model shop; (3) start-up volume production; (4) natural growth; (5) strategic maneuvering.ᵍ He discusses the different requirements of these five stages in terms of tasks, people, rewards, processes, structures, and leadership.

Such a stages model is useful for helping managers to organize their experiences and to anticipate problems of fledgling businesses. However, it does not really address the problems of growing a new business *in a corporate context*. Many difficult problems generated and encountered by ICV result from the fact that related strategic activities take place at multiple levels of corporate management. These must be considered *simultaneously* as well as sequentially in order to understand the special problems associated with ICV.

A Process Model of ICV

The work of Joseph Bower and his associates has laid the foundation for a "process model" approach which depicts the simultaneous as well as sequential managerial activities involved in strategic decision making in large complex firms.ʰ Recently, I have proposed an extension of this approach that has generated a new model of the ICV process.ⁱ This new model is based on the findings of an in-depth study of the complete development process of six ICV projects in the context of the new venture division of one large diversified firm. These ICV projects purported to develop new businesses based on new technologies, and constituted radical innovation efforts from the corporation's viewpoint.

ᵍ See J. R. Galbraith, "The Stages of Growth," *Journal of Business Strategy* 4 (1983) 70–79.

ʰ See J. L. Bower, *Managing the Resource Allocation Process* (Boston: Graduate School of Business Administration, Harvard University, 1970).

ⁱ See R. A. Burgelman, "Managing Innovating Systems: A Study of the Process of Internal Corporate Venturing" (Ph. D. diss., Columbia University, 1980); R. A. Burgelman, "A Process Model of Internal Corporate Venturing in the Diversified Major Firm," *Administrative Science Quarterly*, June 1983, 223–44.

Exhibit 13.11 shows the *core* processes of an ICV project and the *overlaying* processes (the corporate context) in which the core processes take shape. The core processes of ICV comprise the activities through which a new business becomes defined (definition process) and its development gains momentum in the corporation (impetus process). The overlaying processes comprise the activities through which the current corporate strategy is extended to accommodate the new business thrusts resulting from ICV (strategic context determination), and the activities involved in establishing the administrative mechanisms to implement corporate strategy (structural context determination).

The model shows how each of the processes is constituted by activities of managers at different levels in the organization. Some of these activities were found to be more important for the ICV process than others. These key activities are indicated by the shaded areas. They represent new concepts which are useful to provide a more complete description of the complexities of the ICV process. Because they allow us to refer to these complexities in a concise way, they also serve to keep the discussion manageable. The process model shown in Exhibit 13.11 is *descriptive*. It does *not* suggest that the pattern of activities is optimal from a managerial viewpoint. In fact, many of the problems discussed below result from this particular pattern that the ICV process seems to take on naturally.

EXHIBIT 13.11 Key and Peripheral Activities in a Process Model of ICV

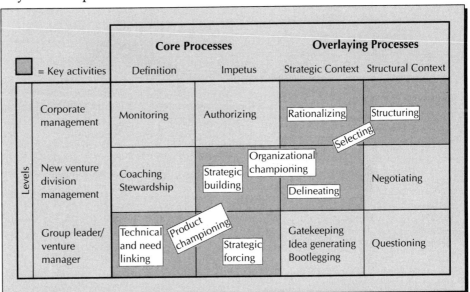

Source: Reprinted from "A Process Model of Internal Corporate Venturing in the Diversified Major Firm" by R. A. Burgelman, published in the *Administrative Science Quarterly*, vol. 28, no. 2, June 1983 by permission of the *Administrative Science Quarterly*. Copyright 1983 Cornell University.

Major Problems in the ICV Process

The process model provides a framework for elucidating four important problem areas observed in my study:

- Vicious circles in the definition process,
- Managerial dilemmas in the impetus process,
- Indeterminateness of the strategic context of ICV development, and
- Perverse selective pressures exerted by the structural context on ICV development.

Exhibit 13.12 serves as a road map for discussing each of these problem areas.

EXHIBIT 13.12 Major Problems in the ICV Process

| Level | Core Processes | | Overlaying Processes | |
	Definition	Impetus	Strategic Context	Structural Context
Corporate management	Top management lacks capacity to assess merits of specific new-venture proposals for corporate development.	Top management relies on purely quantitative growth results to continue support for new venture.	Top management considers ICV as insurance against mainstream business going badly. ICV objectives are ambiguous and shift erratically.	Top management relies on reactive structural changes to deal with problems related to ICV.
NVD management	Middle-level managers in corporate R&D are not capable of coaching ICV project initiators.	Middle-level managers in new business development find it difficult to balance strategic building efforts with efforts to coach venture managers.	Middle-level managers struggle to delineate boundaries of new business field. They spend significant amounts of time on political activities to maintain corporate support.	Middle-level managers struggle with unanticipated structural impediments to new-venture activities. There is little incentive for star performers to engage in ICV activities.
Group leader/ venture leader	Project initiators cannot convincingly demonstrate in advance that resources will be used effectively. They need to engage in scavenging to get resources.	Venture managers find it difficult to balance strategic forcing efforts with efforts to develop administrative framework of emerging ventures.	Project initiators do not have clear idea of which kind of ICV projects will be viable in corporate context. Bootlegging is necessary to get new idea tested.	Venture managers do not have clear idea of what type of performance will be rewarded, except fast growth.

Vicious Circles in the Definition Process

The ICV projects in my study typically started with opportunistic search activities at the group level (first-level supervisor) in the firm's research function. Technical linking activities led to the assembling of external and/or internal pieces of technological knowledge to create solutions for new or known, but unsolved, technical problems. Need linking activities involved the matching of new technical solutions to new or poorly served market needs. Both types of linking activities took place in an iterative fashion. Initiators of ICV projects perceived their initiatives to fall outside of the current strategy of the firm, but felt that there was a good chance they would be included in future strategic development if they proved to be successful.

At the outset, however, project initiators typically encountered resistance and found it difficult to obtain resources from their managers to demonstrate the feasibility of their project. Hence, the emergence of *vicious circles:* resources could be obtained if technical feasibility was demonstrated, but such a demonstration required resources. Similar problems arose with efforts to demonstrate commercial feasibility. Even when a technically demonstrated product, process, or system existed, corporate management was often reluctant to start commercialization efforts, because they were unsure about the firm's capabilities to do this effectively.

Product championing activities, which have been well documented in the literature, served to break through these vicious circles.[j] Using bootlegging and scavenging tactics, the successful product champion was able to provide positive information which reassured middle-level management and provided them with a basis for claiming support for ICV projects in their formal plans. As the product initiator of a medical equipment venture explained:

> When we proposed to sell the ANA product by our own selling force, there was a lot of resistance, out of ignorance. Management did numerous studies, had outside consultants on which they spent tens of thousands of dollars; they looked at ZYZ Company for a possible partnership. Management was just very unsure about its marketing capability. I proposed to have a test marketing phase with twenty to twenty-five installations in the field. We built our own service group; we pulled ourselves up by the "bootstrap." I guess we had more guts than sense.

Why Does the Problem of Vicious Circles Exist? The process model provides some insight about this by showing the connection between the activities of the different levels of management involved in the definition process (see Exhibit

---

j See D. A. Schon, "Champions for Radical New Inventions," *Harvard Business Review*, March–April 1963, 77–86; E. B. Roberts, "Generating Effective Corporate Innovation," *Technology Review*, October–November 1977, 27–33.

13.12). Operational-level managers typically struggled to conceptualize their somewhat nebulous (at least to outsiders) business ideas, which made communication with management difficult. Their proposals often went against conventional corporate wisdom. They could not clearly specify the development path of their projects, and they could not demonstrate in advance that the resources needed would be used effectively in uncharted domains.

Middle-level managers in corporate R&D (where new ventures usually originated) were most concerned about maintaining the integrity of the R&D work environment, which is quite different from a business-oriented work environment. They were comfortable with managing relatively slow-moving exploratory research projects and well-defined development projects. However, they were reluctant to commit significant amounts of resources (especially people) to suddenly fast-moving areas of new development activity that fell outside of the scope of their current plans and that did not yet have demonstrated technical and commercial feasibility. In fact, the middle-level manager often seemed to encourage, not just tolerate, the sub-rosa activities of a project's champion. As one such manager said, "I encourage them to do 'bootleg' research; tell them to come back [for support] when they have results."

At the corporate level, managers seemed to have a highly reliable frame of reference to evaluate business strategies and resource allocation proposals pertaining to the main lines of the corporation's business. However, their capacity to deal with substantive issues of new business opportunities was limited, and their expectations concerning what could be accomplished in a short time frame were often somewhat unrealistic. Also, ICV proposals competed for scarce top management time. Their relatively small size combined with the relative difficulty in assessing their merit made it at the outset seem uneconomical for top management to allocate much time to them.

The process model shows the lack of articulation between the activities of different levels of management; this may, to a large extent, account for the vicious circles encountered in the definition process.

Managerial Dilemmas in the Impetus Process

Successful efforts at product championing demonstrated that the technical and commercial potential of a new product, process, or system was sufficient to result in a sizeable new business. This, in turn, allowed an ICV project to receive "venture" status: to become a quasi-independent, embryonic new business organization with its own budget and general manager. From then on, continued impetus for its development seemed entirely dependent on achieving fast growth in order to convince top management that it could grow to a $50 to $100 million business within a five- to ten-year period.

My findings suggest that this created a *dilemmatic* situation for the venture manager: maximizing growth with the one product, process, or system available versus building the functional capabilities of the embryonic business organization. Similarly, the middle-level manager was confronted with a *dilemmatic* situation: focusing on expanding the scope of the new business versus spending time coaching the (often recalcitrant) venture manager.

Ironically, my study indicates that new product development was likely to be a major problem of new ventures.[k] Lacking the carefully evolved relationships between R&D, engineering, marketing, and manufacturing typical for the mainstream operations of the firm, the venture's new product development schedules tended to be delayed and completed products often showed serious flaws. This was exacerbated by the tendency of the venture's emerging R&D group to isolate itself from the corporate R&D department, partly in order to establish its own "identity." A related, and somewhat disturbing, finding was that new venture managers seemed to become the victims of their own success at maintaining impetus for the venture's development. Here are some examples from my study:

- In an environmental systems venture, the perceived need to grow very fast led to premature emphasis on commercialization. Instead of working on the technical improvement of the new system, the venture's resources were wasted on (very costly) remedial work on systems already sold. After a quick rise, stagnation set in and the venture collapsed.

- In a medical equipment venture, growth with one new system was very fast and could be sustained. However, after about five years, the new products needed for sustaining the growth rate turned out to be flawed. As one manager in the venture commented: "Every ounce of effort with Dr. S. [the venture manager] was spent on the short run. There was no strategizing. New product development was delayed, was put to corporate R&D. Every year we had doubled in size, but things never got any simpler."

In both cases the venture manager was eventually removed.

How Do These Dilemmas Arise?   The process model shows how the strategic situation at each level of management in the impetus process is different, with fast growth being the only shared interest (see Exhibit 13.12).

At the venture manager level, continued impetus depended on strategic forcing efforts: attaining a significant sales volume and market share position centered on the original product, process, or system within a limited time horizon.[l] To implement a strategy of fast growth, the venture manager attracted generalists who could cover a number of different functional areas reasonably well.

---

[k] One of the key problems encountered by Exxon Enterprises was precisely the existence of these new product development problems in the entrepreneurial ventures (Qyx, Qwip, and Vydec) it had acquired and was trying to integrate. See "What's Wrong at Exxon Enterprises," *Business Week*, 24 August 1981, 87.

[l] The need for strategic forcing is consistent with findings suggesting that attaining large market share fast at the cost of early profitability is critical for venture survival. See Biggadike (May–June 1979).

Efficiency considerations became increasingly important with the growth of the venture organization and with competitive pressures due to product maturation. New functional managers were brought in to replace the generalists. They emphasized the development of routines, standard operating procedures, and the establishment of an administrative framework for the venture. This, however, was time-consuming and detracted from the all-out efforts to grow fast. Growth concerns tended to win out, and organization building was more or less purposefully neglected.

While the venture manager created a "beachhead" for the new business, the middle-level manager engaged in strategic building efforts to sustain the impetus process. Such efforts involved the conceptualization of a master strategy for the broader new field within which the venture could fit. They also involved the integration of projects existing elsewhere in the corporation, and/or of small firms that could be acquired with the burgeoning venture. These efforts became increasingly important as the strategic forcing activities of the venture manager reached their limit, and major discontinuities in new product development put more stress on the middle-level manager to find supplementary products elsewhere to help maintain the growth rate. At the same time, the administrative problems created by the strategic forcing efforts increasingly required the attention of the venture manager's manager. Given the overwhelming importance of growth, however, the coaching activities and organization building were more or less purposefully neglected.

The decision by corporate-level management to authorize further resource allocations to a new venture was, to a large extent, dependent on the credibility of the managers involved. Credibility, in turn, depended primarily on the quantitative results produced. Corporate management seemed to have somewhat unrealistic expectations about new ventures. They sent strong signals concerning the importance of making an impact on the overall corporate position soon. This, not surprisingly, reinforced the emphasis to achieve growth on the part of the middle and operational levels of management. One manager in a very successful venture said, "Even in the face of the extraordinary growth rate of the ME venture, the questions corporate management raised when they came here concerned our impact on the overall position of GAMMA, rather than the performance of the venture per se."

Indeterminateness of the Strategic Context of ICV

The problems encountered in the core process of ICV are more readily understood when examining the nature of the overlaying processes (the corporate context) within which ICV projects took shape. My findings indicated a high level of indeterminateness in the strategic context of ICV. Strategic guidance on the part of top management was limited to declaring corporate interest in broadly defined fields like "health" or "energy." Also, there seemed to be a tendency for severe oscillations in top management's interest in ICV—a "now we do it, now we don't" approach. It looked very much as if new ventures were viewed by top management as insurance against mainstream business going badly, rather than as a corporate objective per se.[m] As one experienced middle-level manager said:

> They are going into new areas because they are not sure that we will be able to stay in the current mainstream businesses. That is also the reason why the time of maturity of a new venture is never right. If current business goes OK, then it is always too early, but when current business is not going too well, then we will just jump into anything!

In other words, corporate management's interest in new ventures seemed to be activated primarily by the expectation of a relatively poor performance record with mainstream business activities—a legacy most managers want to avoid. Treating ICV as "insurance" against such an undesirable situation, however, implies the unrealistic assumption that new ventures can be developed at will within a relatively short time frame, and plays down the importance of crafting a corporate development strategy in substantive terms. Lacking an understanding of substantive issues and problems in particular new venture developments, top management is likely to become disenchanted when progress is slower than desired. Perhaps not surprisingly, venture managers in my study seemed to prefer less rather than more top management attention until the strategic context of their activities was more clearly defined.

Why This Indeterminateness? In determining the strategic context (even more than the impetus process), the strategies of the various levels of management showed a lack of articulation with each other. The process model in Exhibit 13.12 allows us to depict this.

Corporate management's objectives concerning ICV seemed to be ambiguous. Top management did not really know which specific new businesses they wanted until those businesses had taken some concrete form and size, and decisions had to be made about whether to integrate them into the corporate portfolio through a process of retroactive rationalizing. Top management's actual (as opposed to declared) time horizon was typically limited to three to five years, even though new ventures take between eight and twelve years on the average to become mature and profitable.

Middle managers were aware that they had to take advantage of the short-term windows for corporate acceptance. They struggled with delineating the boundaries of a new business field. They were aware that it was only through their strategic building efforts and the concomitant articulation of a master strat-

---

[m] Entrepreneurial activity used as insurance against environmental turbulence was first documented by R. A. Peterson and D. G. Berger, "Entrepreneurship in Organizations: Evidence from the Popular Music Industry," *Administrative Science Quarterly* 16 (1971): 97–106; R. A. Burgelman, "Corporate Entrepreneurship and Strategic Management: Insights from a Process Study," *Management Science* 29 (1983): 1649–64.

egy for the ongoing venture initiatives that the new business fields could be concretely delineated and possible new strategic directions determined. This indeterminateness of the strategic context of ICV required middle-level managers to engage in organizational championing activities.[n] Such activities were of a political nature and time-consuming. As one venture manager explained, these activities required an "upward" orientation which is very different from the venture manager's substantive and downward (hands-on) orientation. One person who had been general manager of the new venture division said: "It is always difficult to get endorsement from the management committee for ventures which require significant amounts of resources but where they cannot clearly see what is going to be done with these resources. It is a matter of proportion on the one hand, but it is also a matter of educating the management committee which is very difficult to do."

The middle-level manager also had to spend time working out frictions with the operating system that were created when the strategies of the venture and mainstream businesses interfered with each other. The need for these activities further reduced the amount of time and effort the middle-level manager spent coaching the venture manager.

At the operational level, managers engaged in opportunistic search activities which led to the definition of ICV projects in new areas. These activities were basically independent of the current strategy of the firm. The rate at which mutant ideas were pursued seemed to depend on the amount of slack resources available at the operational level. Many of these autonomous efforts were started as "bootlegged" projects.

Perverse Selective Pressures of the Structural Context

Previous research indicates that reaching high market share fast has survival value for new ventures.[o] Hence, the efforts to grow fast which I found pervading the core processes correspond to the managers' correct assessment of the external strategic situation.

My study, however, suggests that the firm's structural context exerted *perverse selective pressures* to grow fast which exacerbated the external ones. This seemed in part due to the incompleteness of the structural context in relation to the special nature of the ICV process. Establishing a separate new venture division was useful for nurturing and developing new businesses that fell outside of

---

[n] The importance of the middle-level manager in ICV was already recognized by E. von Hippel (1977). The role of a "manager champion" or "executive champion" has also been discussed by I. Kusiatin, "The Process and Capacity for Diversification through Internal Development" (Ph. D. diss., Harvard University, 1976); M. A. Maidique, "Entrepreneurs, Champions, and Technological Innovation," *Sloan Management Review*, Winter 1980, 59–76.

[o] See Biggadike (May–June 1979).

the current corporate strategy. (It was also convenient to have a separate "address" for projects that were "misfits" or "orphans" in the operating divisions.) However, because the managerial work involved in these was very different from that of the mainstream business, the corporate measurement and reward systems were not adequate, and yet they remained in effect, mostly, in the new venture division (NVD).

Another part of the structural context problems resulted from the widely shared perception that the position of the NVD was precarious.[P] This, in turn, created an "it's now or never" attitude on the part of the participants in the NVD, adding to the pressures to grow fast.

How Do These Selective Pressures Arise? Exhibit 13.12 shows the situation at each of the management levels. Corporate management did not seem to have a clear purpose or strong commitment to new ventures. It seemed that when ICV activities expanded beyond a level that corporate management found opportune to support in light of their assessment of the prospects of mainstream business activities, changes were effected in the structural context to "consolidate" ICV activities. These changes seemed reactive and indicative of the lack of a clear strategy for diversification in the firm. One high-level manager charged with making a number of changes in which the NVD would operate in the future said:

> To be frank, I don't feel corporate management has a clear idea. Recently, we had a meeting with the management committee, and there are now new directives. Basically, it de-emphasizes diversification for the moment. The emphasis is on consolidation, with the recognition that diversification will be important in the future. . . . The point is that we will not continue in four or five different areas anymore.

At the middle level, the incompleteness of the structural context also manifested itself in the lack of integration between the ICV activities and the mainstream businesses. Middle-level managers of the new venture division experienced resistance from managers in the operating divisions when their activities had the potential to overlap. Ad hoc negotiations and reliance on political savvy substituted for long-term, joint optimization arrangements.[q] This also created the perception that there was not much to gain for middle-level star performers by participating directly in the ICV activities. In addition, the lack of adequate reward systems also made middle-level managers reluctant to remove venture managers in trouble. One middle-level manager talked about the case of a venture manager in trouble who had grown a project from zero to about $30 million in a few years:

[P] See Fast (1979).

[q] These frictions are discussed in more detail in R. A. Burgelman, "Managing the New Venture Division: Research Findings and Implications for Strategic Management," *Strategic Management Journal* 7 (1986): 21–49.

When the business reached, say, $10 million, they should have talked to him; have given him a free trip around the world, $50 thousand, and six months off; and then have persuaded him to take on a new assignment. But that's not the way it happened. For almost two years, we knew that there were problems, but no one would touch the problem until it was too late and he had put himself in a real bind. We lost some good people during this period, and we lost an entrepreneur.

At the operational level, managers felt that the only reward available was to become general manager of a sizeable new business in the corporate structure. This "lure of the big office" affected the way in which they searched for new opportunities. One high-level manager observed, "People are looking around to find a program to latch onto, and that could be developed into a demonstration plan. Business research always stops after one week, so to speak."

Making the ICV Strategy Work Better

Having identified major problem areas with the help of the process model, we can now propose recommendations for improving the strategic management of ICV. They serve to alleviate, if not eliminate, the problems by making the corporate context more hospitable to ICV. This could allow management to focus more effectively on the problems inherent in the core processes.

There are four "themes" for the recommendations which correspond to the four major problem areas already discussed:

- Facilitating the definition process,
- Moderating the impetus process,
- Elaborating the strategic context of ICV, and
- Refining the structural context of ICV.

Each of these themes encompasses more specific action items for management. Exhibit 13.13 summarizes the various recommendations and their expected effects on the ICV process.

Facilitating the Definition Process

Timely assessment of the true potential of an ICV project remains a difficult problem. This follows from the very nature of such projects: the many uncertainties around the technical and marketing aspects of the new business, and the fact that each case is significantly different from all others. These factors make it difficult to develop standardized evaluation procedures and development programs, without screening to death truly innovative projects.

Managing the definition process effectively poses serious challenges for middle-level managers in the corporate R&D department. They must facilitate the integration of technical and business perspectives, and they must maintain a life line to the technology developed in corporate R&D as the project takes off.

As stated earlier, the need for product championing efforts, if excessive, may cut that life line early on and lead to severe discontinuities in new product development after the project has reached the venture stage. The middle-level manager's efforts must facilitate both the product championing efforts and the

13.13   Recommendations for Making ICV Strategy Work Better

| Level | Core Processes | | Overlaying Processes | |
	Definition	Impetus	Strategic Context	Structural Context
Corporate management	ICV proposals are evaluated in light of corporate development strategy. Conscious efforts are made to avoid subjecting them to conventional corporate wisdom.	New-venture progress is evaluated in substantive terms by top managers who have experience in organizational championing.	A process is in place for developing long-term corporate development strategy. This strategy takes shape as result of ongoing interactive learning process involving top and middle levels of management.	Mangers with successful ICV experience are appointed to top management. Top management is rewarded financially and symbolically for long-term corporate development success.
NVD management	Middle-level managers in corporate R&D are selected who have both technical depth and business knowledge necessary to determine minimum amount of resources for project and who can coach star players.	Middle-level managers are responsible for use and development of venture managers as scarce resources of corporation, and they facilitate intrafirm project transfers if new business strategy warrants it.	Substantive interaction between corporate and middle-level management leads to clarifying merits of new business field in light of corporate development strategy.	Star performers at middle level are attracted to ICV activities. Collaboration of mainstream middle level with ICV activities is rewarded. Integrating mechanisms can easily be mobilized.
Group leader/ venture leader	Project initiators are encouraged to integrate technical and business perspectives. They are provided access to resources. Project initiators can be rewarded by means other than promotion to venture manager.	Venture managers are responsible for developing functional capabilities of emerging venture organizations and for codification of what has been learned in terms of required functional capabilities while pursuing new business opportunity.	Slack resources determine level of emergence of mutant ideas. Existence of substantive corporate development strategy provides preliminary self-selection of mutant ideas.	A wide array of venture structures and supporting measurement and reward systems clarifies expected performance for ICV personnel.

continued development of the technology base by putting the former in perspective and by making sure that the interface between R&D and businesspeople works smoothly.

Facilitating the Integration of R&D-Business Perspectives

To facilitate the integration of technical and business perspectives, the middle manager must understand the operating logic of both groups, and must avoid getting bogged down in technical details yet have sufficient technical depth to be respected by the R&D people. Such managers must be able to motivate the R&D people to collaborate with the businesspeople toward the formulation of business objectives against which progress can be measured. Formulating adequate business objectives is especially important if corporate management becomes more actively involved in ICV and develops a greater capacity to evaluate the fit of new projects with the corporate development strategy.

Middle-level managers in R&D must be capable of facilitating give-and-take between the two groups in a process of mutual adjustment toward the common goal of advancing the progress of the new business project. It is crucial to create mutual respect between technical and businesspeople. If the R&D manager shows respect for the contribution of the businesspeople, this is likely to affect the attitudes of the other R&D people. Efforts will probably be better integrated if regular meetings are held with both groups to evaluate, as peers, the contribution of different team members.

The Middle Manager as Coach. Such meetings also provide a vehicle to better coach the product champion, who is really the motor of the ICV project in this state of development. There are some similarities between this role and that of the star player on a sports team. Product champions are often viewed in either/or terms: either they can do their thing and chances are the project will succeed (although there may be discontinuities and not fully exploited ancillary opportunities), or we harness them but they will not play.

A more balanced approach is for the middle-level manager to use a process that recognizes the product champion as the star player, but that, at times, challenges him or her to maintain breadth by having to respond to queries:

- How is the team benefiting more from this particular action than from others that the team may think to be important?
- How will the continuity of the team's efforts be preserved?
- What will the next step be?

To support this approach, the middle manager should be able to reward team members differently. This, of course, refers back to the determination of the structural context, and reemphasizes the importance of recognizing at the corporate level, that different reward systems are necessary for different business activities.

Moderating the Impetus Process

The recommendations for improving the corporate context (the overlaying processes of ICV) have implications for the way in which the impetus process is allowed to take shape. Corporate management should expect the middle-level managers to think and act as corporate strategists and the operational-level managers to view themselves as organization builders.

The Middle-Level Managers as Corporate Strategists. Strategy making in new ventures depends, to a very great extent, on the middle-level managers. Because new ventures often intersect with multiple parts of mainstream businesses, middle managers learn what the corporate capabilities and skills—and shortcomings—are, and they learn to articulate new strategies and build new businesses based on new combinations of these capabilities and skills. This, in turn, also creates possibilities to enhance the realization of new operational synergies existing in the firm. Middle-level managers can thus serve as crucial integrating and technology transfer mechanisms in the corporation, and corporate management should expect them to perform this role as they develop a strategy for a new venture.

The Venture Managers as Organization Builders. Pursuing fast growth and the administrative development of the venture simultaneously is a major challenge during the impetus process. This challenge, which exists for any start-up business, is especially treacherous for one in the context of an established firm. This is because managers in ICV typically have less control over the selection of key venture personnel, yet, at the same time, have access to a variety of corporate resources. These seems to be less pressure on the venture manager and the middle-level manager to show progress in building the organization than there is to show growth.

The recommendations concerning measurement and reward systems should encourage the venture manager to balance the two concerns better. The venture manager should have leeway in hiring and firing decisions, but should also be held responsible for the development of new functional capabilities and the administrative framework of the venture. This would reduce the probability of major discontinuities in new product development mentioned earlier. In addition, it would provide the corporation with codified know-how and information which can be transferred to other parts of the firm or to other new ventures, even if the one from which it is derived ultimately fails as a business. Know-how and information, as well as sales and profit, become important outputs of the ICV process.

Often the product champion or venture manager will not have the required capabilities to achieve these additional objectives. The availability of compensatory rewards and of avenues for recycling the product champion or venture manager would make it possible for middle management to better tackle deteriorating managerial conditions in the new business organization. Furthermore, the availability of a competent replacement (after systematic corporate search) may induce the product champion or venture manager to relinquish his or her position, rather than see the venture go under.

Elaborating the Strategic Context of ICV

Determining the strategic context of ICV is a subtle and somewhat elusive process involving corporate and middle-level managers. More effort should be spent on developing a long-term corporate development strategy explicitly encompassing ICV. At the same time measures should be taken to increase corporate management's capacity to assess venture strategies in substantive terms as well as in terms of projected quantitative results.

The Need for a Corporate Development Strategy. Top management should recognize that ICV is an important source of strategic renewal for the firm and that it is unlikely to work well if treated as insurance against poor mainstream business prospects. ICV should, therefore, be considered an integral and continuous part of the strategy-making process. To dampen the oscillations in corporate support for ICV, top management should create a process for developing an explicit long-term (ten to twelve years) strategy for corporate development, supported by a resource generation and allocation strategy. Both should be based on ongoing efforts to determine the remaining growth opportunities in the current mainstream businesses and the resource levels necessary to exploit them. Given the corporate objectives of growth and profitability, a resource pool should be reserved for activities outside the mainstream business. This pool should not be affected by short-term fluctuations in current mainstream activities. The existence of this pool of "slack" (or perhaps better, "uncommitted") resources would allow top management to affect the rate at which new venture initiatives will emerge (if not their particular content). This approach reflects a broader concept of strategy making than maintaining corporate R&D at a certain percentage of sales.

Substantive Assessment of Venture Strategies

To more effectively determine the strategic context of ICV and to reduce the political emphasis in organizational championing activities, top management should increase their capacity to make substantive assessments of the merits of new ventures for corporate development. Top management should learn to assess better the strategic importance of ICV projects to corporate development and their degree of relatedness to core corporate capabilities. One way to achieve this capacity is to include in top management people with significant experience in new business development. In addition, top management should require middle-level organizational champions to explain how a new field of business would further the corporate development objectives in substantive rather than purely numerical terms and how they expect to create value from the corporate viewpoint with a new business field. Operational-level managers would then be able to assess better which of the possible directions their envisaged projects could take and would be more likely to receive corporate support.

Refining the Structural Context of ICV

Refining the structural context requires corporate management to use the new venture division design in a more deliberate fashion, and to complement the organization design effort with supporting measurement and reward systems.

More Deliberate Use of the New Venture Division Design. Corporate management should develop greater flexibility in structuring the relationship between new venture projects and the corporation. In some instances, greater efforts would seem to be in order to integrate new venture projects directly into the mainstream businesses, rather than transferring them to the NVD because of lack of support in the operating division where they originated. In other cases, projects should be developed using external venture arrangements. Where and how a new venture project is developed should depend on top management's assessment of its strategic importance for the firm, and of the degree to which the required capabilities are related to the firm's core capabilities. Such assessments should be easier to implement by having a wide range of available structures for venture-corporation relationships.[r]

Also, the NVD is a mechanism for decoupling the activities of new ventures and those of mainstream businesses. However, because this decoupling usually cannot be perfect, integrative mechanisms should be established to deal constructively with conflicts that will unavoidably and unpredictably arise. One such mechanism is a "steering committee" involving managers from operating divisions and the NVD.

Finally, top management should facilitate greater acceptance of differences between the management processes of the NVD and the mainstream businesses. This may lead to more careful personnel assignment policies and to greater flexibility in hiring and firing policies in the NVD to reflect the special needs of emerging businesses.

Measurement and Reward Systems in Support of ICV

Perhaps the most difficult aspect concerns how to provide incentives for top management to seriously and continuously support ICV as part of corporate

---

[r] An overview of different forms of corporate venturing is provided in E. B. Roberts, "New Ventures for Corporate Growth," *Harvard Business Review,* July–August 1980, 132–42. A design framework is suggested in R. A . Burgelman, "Designs for Corporate Entrepreneurship in Established Firms," *California Management Review,* in press.

strategy making. Corporate history writing might be an effective mechanism to achieve this. This would involve the careful tracing and periodical publication (e.g., a special section in annual reports) of decisions whose positive or negative results may become clear only after ten or more years. Corporate leaders (like political ones) would, presumably, make efforts to preserve their position in corporate history.[s] Another mechanism is to attract "top performers" from the mainstream businesses of the corporation to ICV activities. To do this, at least a few spots on the top management team should always be filled with managers who have had significant experience in new business development. This will also eliminate the perception that NVD participants are not part of the real world and, therefore, have little chance to advance in the corporation as a result of ICV experience.

The measurement and reward systems should be used to alleviate some of the more destructive consequences of the necessary emphasis on fast growth in venture development. This would mean, for instance, rewarding accomplishments in the areas of problem finding, problem solving, and know-how development. Success in developing the administrative aspects of the emerging venture organization should also be included, as well as effectiveness in managing the interfaces with the operating division.

At the operational level where some managerial failures are virtually unavoidable, top management should create a reasonably foolproof safety net. Product champions at this level should not have to feel that running the business is the only possible reward for getting it started. Systematic search for and screening of potential venture managers should make it easier to provide a successor for the product champion *in time*. Avenues for recycling product champions and venture managers should be developed and/or their reentry into the mainstream businesses facilitated.

Finally, more flexible systems for measuring and rewarding performance should accompany the greater flexibility in structuring the venture-corporate relations mentioned earlier. This would mean greater reliance on negotiation processes between the firm and its entrepreneurial actors. In general, the higher the degree of relatedness (the more dependent the new venture is on the firm's resources) and the lower the expected strategic importance for corporate development, the lower the rewards the internal entrepreneurs would be able to negotiate. As the venture evolves, milestone points could be agreed upon to revise the negotiations. To make such processes symmetrical (and more acceptable to

---

[s] Some firms seem to have developed the position of corporate historian. See "Historians Discover the Pitfalls of Doing the Story of a Firm," *Wall Street Journal*, 27 December 1983. Without underestimating the difficulties such a position is likely to hold, one can imagine the possibility of structuring it in such a way that the relevant data would be recorded. Another instance, possibly a board-appointed committee, could periodically interpret these data along the lines suggested.

the nonentrepreneurial participants in the organization), the internal entrepreneurs should be required to substitute negotiated for regular membership awards and benefits.[t]

Conclusion: No Panaceas

This article proposes that managers can make ICV strategy work better if they increase their capacity to conceptualize the managerial activities involved in ICV in process model terms. This is because the process model approach allows the managers involved to think through how their strategic situation relates to the strategic situation of managers at different levels who are simultaneously involved in the process. Understanding the interplay of these different strategic situations allows managers to see the relationships between problems which otherwise remain unanticipated and seemingly disparate. This may help them perform better as *individual* strategists while also enhancing the *corporate* strategy-making process.

Of course, by focusing on the embedded, nested problems and internal organizational dynamics of ICV strategy making, this article has not addressed other important problems. I believe, however, that the vicious circles, managerial dilemmas, indeterminateness of the strategic context, and perverse selective pressures of the structural context are problem areas that have received the least systematic attention.

The recommendations (based on this viewpoint) should result in a somewhat better use of the individual entrepreneurial resources of the corporation and, therefore, in an improvement of the corporate entrepreneurial capability. Yet, the implication is not that this process can or should become a planned one, or that the discontinuities associated with entrepreneurial activity can be avoided. ICV is likely to remain an uncomfortable process for the large complex organization. This is because ICV upsets carefully evolved routines and planning mechanisms, threatens the internal equilibrium of interests, and requires revising a firm's self-image. The success of radical innovations, however, is ultimately dependent on whether they can become institutionalized. This may pose the most important challenge for managers of large established firms in the eighties.

Source: Article 13.3 excerpted from R. A. Burgelman, "Managing the Internal Venturing Process," *Sloan Management Review* 25 (1985), 33–48. Used by permission of *Sloan Management Review* and the author.

---

[t] Some companies have developed innovative types of arrangements to structure their relationships with internal entrepreneurs. Other companies have established procedures to help would-be entrepreneurs with their decision to stay with the company or to spin off. Control Data Corporation, for example, has established an "Employee Entrepreneurial Advisory Office."

ENDNOTES

1. E. B. Roberts, "New Ventures for Corporate Growth," *Harvard Business Review* 58 (July-August 1980), 134–42.
2. I. C. MacMillan, "Progress in Research on Corporate Venturing," in *The Art and Science of Entrepreneurship,* ed. D. L. Sexton and R. W. Smilor (Cambridge, Mass.: Ballinger, 1986).
3. R. A. Burgelman, "Managing the Internal Corporate Venturing Process," *Sloan Management Review* 25 (1985), 33–48.
4. See J. R. Galbraith, "The Stages of Growth," *Journal of Business Strategy* 9 (1983), 21–29.

14

Intrapreneurship

Earlier in this text intrapreneurs were described as those individuals who operate entrepreneurially in a larger organization. While Wortman has reported that most of the research regarding intrapreneurship is anecdotal,[1] MacMillan has suggested that there are certain differences between entrepreneurs and intrapreneurs.[2] For example, Bird has described these differences as follows:

> Intrapreneurs operate under some form of corporate accounting system, with reporting relationships to hierarchical superiors; entrepreneurs stand alone. Intrapreneurs do not personally face the financial risks that entrepreneurs do, nor do they foresee the same rewards. As a result, their experiences and behaviors differ somewhat from those of the entrepreneurial sole proprietor or partner. Differences in perceptions of risk, resource availability, and autonomy might be expected to influence decision making, relationships, commitment, and other behavior. Likewise, the individuals who choose the career of corporate entrepreneur over that of an independent entrepreneur might need different competencies to success such as being skilled at corporate politics. Most independent entrepreneurs find corporate politics reprehensible which motivates them to resist working for anyone but themselves.[3]

Three articles are included in this chapter. The first article, by Nielsen, Peters, and Hisrich, explains the conceptual foundations for an intrapreneurship strategy, why an organization might consider adopting such a strategy, and the limitations to that strategy. These researchers also draw a distinction between corporate entrepreneurship and intrapreneurship.

The second article, by Erik Rule and Donald Irwin, describes how top managers can encourage and foster intrapreneurship in an organizational setting. The third article, by Marsha Sinetar, describes two types of entrepreneurs that exist in organizations and how creative personalities and creative thinking can cause "chaos" in a "well-oiled" organizational process. Sinetar demonstrates how management can identify and cultivate creative talent while still maintaining the orderly functions of the company.

ARTICLE 14.1   INTRAPRENEURSHIP VERSUS INTERNAL ENTREPRENEURSHIP
by Richard Nielsen, Michael Peters, and Robert Hisrich

It is often important that an organization maintains both its line and staff units' integration with the organization's central mission while flexibly and innovatively responding to evolving and changing external markets and environments. A dilemma facing top managers, however, is that internal flexibility/innovation and integration needs often conflict.

One strategy that can help organizations to resolve internal conflicts between integration and flexibility/innovation needs is intrapreneurship. Intrapreneurship, a term perhaps first used by Gifford Pinchot (Macrae, 1982), is the development within a large organization of internal markets and relatively small and independent units designed to create, internally test-market and expand improved and/or innovative staff services, technologies or methods within the organization. This is different from the large organization entrepreneurship/venture management strategy that tries to develop internal entrepreneurial/venture units whose purpose is to develop profitable positions in external markets.

By using three cases: a corporation, Texas Instruments; a non-profit institution, Harvard University and its Harvard Student Agencies, Inc.; and a government agency, the U.S. Department of Energy and its Solar Energy Research Institute—conceptual foundations are developed for the intrapreneurship strategy, the reasons why an organization might consider adopting the strategy and some important limits to the strategy.

Conceptual Foundations for Intrapreneurship

The work of economic historians such as Chandler (1962, 1977, 1980) and industrial organization economists such as Williamson (1975) and Baumol (1982) is challenging central principles of classical and neoclassical market economics as well as much of U.S. antitrust law. What these researchers have found is that internal administrative coordination within large organizations is often more efficient than co-ordination through market mechanisms. As Chandler (1977: 6) concludes:

> Modern multiunit business enterprise replaced small traditional enterprise when administrative coordination permitted greater productivity, lower costs, and higher profits than coordination by market mechanisms.

Williamson (1975: 248, 253) comes to a similar conclusion:

> The shift of transactions from autonomous market contracting to hierarchy is principally explained by the transactional economies that attend such assignments. . . . A comparative institutional attitude is maintained: markets and hierarchies are regarded as alternative contracting modes.

However, the classical organization theorists such as Fayol (1925), the bureaucratic sociologists such as Goulder (1954) and the many management scholars and practitioners such as Greiner (1972), Sloan (1963) and Lorsch and Allen (1973) have found that large scale internal integration is, nonetheless, very difficult to manage. One of the main sources of difficulty is managing a good balance among centralization vs. decentralization, interdependence vs. diversity and integration vs. flexibility/innovation needs.

One generalized solution that many large organizations have found useful is multidivisionalization. Multidivisionalization helped solve the problem of lack of autonomy (Chandler, 1977). However, after divisionalization, many organizations experienced a co-ordination problem. Matrix organization helped alleviate this problem by increasing integration between product lines and pooled functional resources (Sayles, 1976). In addition, strategic planning helped solve the co-ordination problem. However, both matrix organization and strategic planning frequently contributed to problems of excessive, top-down administrative co-ordination and red tape (Davis & Lawrence, 1978). In partial response to this problem, several organizations have further evolved into strategic planning with more bottom-up consensus building models (Galbraith & Nathanson, 1978; Quinn, 1980; Nielsen, 1981, 1983d).

Reasons Motivating Use of Intrapreneurship

Problems that can sometimes accompany both formal and informal strategic planning consensus building and collaboration models are: integration of secondary activities not directly related to an institution's central mission can be ignored; flexibility/innovation needs of secondary activities can also be ignored; integration planning and implementation for secondary activities can take too long; and the tendency to compromise rather than adopt best solutions in areas considered non-central.

1. Intrapreneurship can help integrate secondary activities not directly related to an organization's central mission. Texas Instruments has developed an elaborate strategic planning and consensus building system built on the units of product divisions and the hundreds of product-customer centres within the divisions. In order to co-ordinate the activities of the several product divisions and hundreds of product-customer centres (PCCs) an elaborate strategic planning consensus building system was built, the OST System. Jelinek describes the system as follows:

The OST System then was a hierarchy of goals linking long-term activities to current funding and programs intended to achieve those goals. The OST operated as a three-level allocation and management system. Goals and Strategies were initiated by Strategy and Objectives Managers, generally people with line operating responsibilities and consequent close contact with the operating realities and technical details of the businesses and technologies upon which planning must be based. Proposed goals and directions were reviewed and approved—perhaps after several iterations of the negotiation process, allowing for top-level input—by the Corporate Development Committee. Finally, the Objectives and Policies Committee of the Board of Directors examined a summary of proposals earmarked for approval, for comparison with Corporate goals (1979: 90).

Managers from the product divisions and PCCs were involved throughout the process. The OST planning cycle represents one of the most massive planning, communication and consensus building systems at all levels and across the various divisions and profit centres of any large corporation. Despite such a very elaborate system, not all corporate activities are included in the system. For example, managers of the engineering service units and marketing service units were not included. They were not included because their function was viewed more as a service than as a strategic profit centre. Although important, the function of the service units was considered secondary to that of the profit centres. Since the OST System was already so elaborate it was considered desirable not to overburden the system with units not considered key to strategic planning.

Nevertheless, it was considered important to integrate the service activity units with the strategic directions of the product divisions and PCCs. An intrapreneurship system was developed. In the Texas Instruments intrapreneurship system internal markets were created with the PCCs serving as potential customers for the service units. For example, the PCCs could choose to perform as marketing and engineering services units, or buy the services from outside organizations. As a consequence, the marketing services and engineering services units had to compete for, and respond adequately to, the needs of the PCCs or they would not get the resources they needed to survive and/or expand. This system integrated the activities and attentions of the services units into the strategic needs of the PCCs without involving them in the OST System.

At Harvard University, at one time, all support services such as publishing, copying, catering, travel services, custodial services, etc. were centrally organized. However, as the various schools, institutes, hospitals, etc. evolved in their different field-specific strategic directions, it was found that their service needs were quite different. Partly in order better to integrate services with the various line units' strategic directions, the line units were given budget flexibility so that they could choose to produce the services themselves, buy the services from outside organizations, buy the services from the central administration, or buy the services from the HSA. In order to compete successfully for business from the line units both the central administration service units and the HSA had to direct their attention and respond to the strategic needs of the line units. This intrapreneurship system integrated the performance of the services units into the strategic directions of the line units (Riley & Donovan, 1982; Nielsen, 1983c).

In the case of the Solar Energy Research Institute of the Department of Energy, the DOE requires SERI to justify its usefulness in part by selling its research services to other federal government agencies. The various units of the DOE and other U.S. government units have the option of buying energy research services from SERI or from outside organizations, or performing such research services themselves. The various government units act as potential customers for SERI within an internal U.S. government market. The idea behind this system is that for research activities to be useful, they must satisfy some strategic needs. A test developed to determine whether the solar research activities are integrated into the strategic needs of the various U.S. government units is whether SERI can sell its services to these units (Ashworth, 1981).

2. Intrapreneurship can help realize the flexibility/innovation needs of secondary activity units not directly related to an organization's central mission. At Texas Instruments even though the marketing services and engineering services units are not considered strategic business units, they still have flexibility/innovation needs. In order for service activities to adequately service the PCCs, they must keep up to date in their own fields as well as be flexible and responsive to the evolving needs of the PCCs. When the service activity units have to compete against outside service organizations as well as the PCCs performing the services themselves, they are forced to remain both state of the art and responsive to the PCCs' needs. In order to remain state of the art and competitive the service units act much like outside smaller entrepreneurs in trying to come up with constantly better ways to service their clients, the PCCs. If they fail to be flexible and innovate, then the PCCs can buy the services from organizations that are more flexible and innovative.

At Harvard University, one of the primary reasons for starting the HSA was because the line schools, departments, hospitals, etc. had become dissatisfied with the flexibility and innovativeness of the centrally based services. Many of the line units were finding that they could find both more innovative and less expensive services from outside organizations. In addition, many of the centrally planned and administered services were finding it very difficult to respond flexibly to the many different types of needs of the many different types of line units within Harvard University. They were becoming dissatisfied with their need and ability to satisfy all their internal clients well. The creation of the HSA released some of the pressure on the central services while allowing both the central services and the HSA to be more innovative and flexible in which types of services they tried to provide. The creation of the HSA released some of the pressure from the central services because the line units had an internal alternative they could go to for very specialized needs. At the same time, the existence of the HSA gave the central services more room to plan and prioritize how they might try to target innovation areas.

One of the major frustrations of the Solar Energy Research Institute of the Department of Energy was that they considered their primary mission as one of innovative research. Yet they had to justify their mission, objectives and projects within a very large scale planning and programming budget that demanded that SERI justify how its activities were fitting into a large scale master plan. SERI found it difficult both to seek innovative directions and fit into a central energy plan. The problem was also compounded by the fact that the top management did not consider solar energy a likely viable energy alternative. The DOE decided that for funds received from DOE, SERI would have to justify its activities with the central energy master plan, but could seek research funds from other government agencies for different types of solar energy research projects. This increased the flexibility and innovative potential of SERI because it greatly increased the number of potential funders and supporters of its research projects. Although SERI preferred to have, in effect, minimally constrained research funds from DOE, the intrapreneurship alternative was preferable to having to justify all its research activities within a central energy master plan.

3. Intrapreneurship can shorten response time. Both comprehensive planning and strategic planning can take a long time. By their nature as secondary activities, the time priority they receive in the planning process is typically secondary. That is, the people working on an organization's plan tend not to direct their attention to activities considered secondary until primary issues have been addressed. This can result in secondary activities being put on hold for so long that they lose initiative and capacity to respond to needs that are currently developing (Simon, 1947; Cyert & March, 1963; Simon, 1983).

Intrapreneurship shortening response time has been the situation in all the cases considered here. For example, it was an important reason for Texas Instruments' decision not to include the marketing and engineering service units in its elaborate strategic planning system. Similarly, SERI was able to provide services much more quickly when it was acting more independently of the central planning of the DOE. Response time is shortened through bilateral transactions. The bilateral transactions have shorter response times because they are not part of a planning process that involves more items and more complex multi-party transactions.

4. Intrapreneurship can help avoid the tendency to compromise rather than adopt "best" solutions in areas considered non-central. Planning systems are also political systems. If the individuals involved in debating and disputing issues considered primary are sufficiently involved with and exhausted by the politics revolving around the primary issues, then they may not be eager to extend similar energy and commitment to issues considered secondary (Nielsen, 1984a). Instead of different individuals and groups actively trying to advance positions that they think are best for the organization, in order to reduce further conflict and energy expenditures, they may prefer to compromise on secondary issues rather than go through the difficult process of debating and advocating what they consider "best" positions. This particularly may be the case after difficult debates concerning primary issues when the various participants are more interested in demonstrating reasonableness and settling issues simply than hashing out "best" solutions. Compromise can be easier to arrive at than searches for "best" solutions (Fisher & Ury, 1981; Raiffa, 1982). Intrapreneurship can largely remove secondary issues from the politics of the planning process and allow "best" solutions to be found through internal market operations. For example, at Texas Instruments, managers from different divisions do not have to compromise on what types of marketing or engineering services are best for Texas Instruments. Each division manager and PCC manager can buy the types of services that are best for them. Similarly, different schools within Harvard University do not have to compromise on, for example, the same types of food for catered occasions; they can buy the type of catering that is best for them. In the SERI situation, the various government departments do not have to compromise on the one type of solar energy research program that is best for all. They can buy the type of research that is best for their individual needs and concerns.

Limits of Intrapreneurship

Although the above discussion indicated that there are many reasons and circumstances where intrapreneurship should probably be seriously considered, there are also some important limits to the principle. Intrapreneurship is not applicable or desirable in all circumstances.

1. Intrapreneurship applies more to large than small organizations. Just as in external markets there are minimum market sizes required to justify the existence of multiple competitors (Williamson, 1975; Baumol, 1982), so also it is probably the case with respect to internal markets. If an organization is not large enough, it may not be possible to justify more than one group performing any particular function. Therefore, the larger the organization, the more likely will there be sufficient volume to justify multiple consumer units and multiple supplier units within an organization.

2. Intrapreneurship applies primarily to secondary rather than primary strategic activities. It is the purpose of strategic planning to include strategic activities in the strategic planning process. Therefore, it would normally not make very much sense to leave these activities to just internal markets. However, for secondary activities which are not of primary interest to the strategic planning process, intrapreneurship is applicable.

3. Intrapreneurship applies more to secondary activities that need to be at least partially performed in-house rather than secondary activities that can be performed solely by outside specialists. The question can be asked, why bother with intrapreneurship instead of relying on the flexibility and innovation of external suppliers? One reason would be if the external suppliers were not as flexible and innovative as internal intrapreneurial units. However, a more important reason within the context of this article is that an organization may need to perform at least part of the service activities within house. For example, even if an outside research and development organization could adequately perform research services, it might be necessary to retain some internal research services so that there is an internal capability of generating and evaluating research processes and outputs related to the organization's central mission. An intrapreneurial research unit combines the advantages of maintaining an internal capability that needs to respond to internal needs with the non-exclusive reliance on internal units and the participation of external suppliers.

4. Intrapreneurship applies more in rapidly than slowly evolving environments. One of the main advantages of intrapreneurship as discussed above is that the intrapreneurial units can respond flexibly and innovatively to changing environments. Intrapreneurship can help overcome the sluggishness of large scale planning systems with respect to the flexibility/innovation needs of secondary activities. However, if the environments within which the secondary activities exist are very stable and unchanging, then they may not have very urgent needs to react quickly and could conceivably be planned much more than secondary activities that operate in rapidly evolving environments (Drucker, 1980; Simon, 1983).

5. Overduplication limits. As referred to above, intrapreneurship applies more to large organizations than small. However, even in large organizations where the scale of activities is large enough to justify multiple consumer and producer units, there is also probably a limit to how many intrapreneurial units can effectively compete against each other or outside organizations for the business of internal consuming units. At some point, the advantages of flexibility and innovation will be outweighed by the disadvantages and costs of overduplication of efforts. Too many units doing similar things can cause waste of resources.

6. Legal constraints. There can also be legal factors that can limit the scope of the intrapreneurial strategy. For example, there are limits to the types of revenue-producing activities that non-profit organizations can engage in while maintaining their non-profit status (Nielsen, 1982, 1984b). In the HSA case the intrapreneurial units sell services not only to other Harvard University units, but also to outside organizations. Harvard University and HSA are currently considering whether to make HSA or part of HSA profit seeking subsidiaries of Harvard University.

Also, union contracts that contain work jurisdiction clauses may constrain a strategic business unit from having the option of using external organizations instead of internal units. If the internal consuming units do not have the option of using outside organizations, this can create something of a monopoly situation for the internal units where the consuming units are in effect captive customers. Internal monopoly situations can have many of the same negative consequences as external monopoly situations (Nielsen, 1979).

Conclusion

This article has considered the conceptual foundations for the intrapreneurship strategy. Reasons motivating use of the intrapreneurship strategy were also explored. The motivating reasons were explored within the context of three different types of case studies. In addition, the limits of the intrapreneurship strategy were recognized and discussed. Even though there are several important limits to the intrapreneurship strategy, since there are also some very important potential benefits that can be realized from intrapreneurship, then it would appear reasonable that many organizations should seriously consider adopting at least a limited intrapreneurship strategy. For many organizations and environments, intrapreneurship may provide at least a very useful supplemental solution strategy for the continuing and evolving conflicts among centralization vs decentralization, interdependence vs diversity and integration vs flexibility/innovation needs. On a larger level, as our cases revealed, intrapreneurship may provide some basis for a synthesis of planning vs market systems benefits and needs in situations so diverse as large corporations, non-profit institutions, government institutions and perhaps even national political economic systems (Nielsen, 1983a, 1983b).

In addition, from a more theoretical perspective, intrapreneurship for internal markets may add something to the continuing evolution of economic theory represented by the work of Chandler (1962, 1977), Chandler and Daems (1980), Williamson (1975) and Baumol (1982) concerning the circumstances under which planning systems and internal markets within large organizations can be more efficient and effective than reliance on the assumptions of ideal classical and neoclassical external market systems. Furthermore, what might be the next higher level of economic aggregation and unit of competition beyond the large corporation? If planning systems and internal markets can be more efficient within large organizations than reliance on external market mechanisms, could there also be circumstances where the same would be true for a situation where the country was more the unit of competition in world markets than the corporation, i.e. where the unit of competition is more the U.S. competing against Japan in world markets than it is IBM competing against Hitachi (Nielsen, 1983a, 1983b)?

Source: Article 14.1 excerpted from R. P. Nielsen, M. P. Peters, and R. D. Hisrich, "Intrapreneurship Strategy for Internal Markets—Corporate Non-Profit and Government Institution Cases," *Strategic Management Journal* 6 (1985), 181–89. Reproduced by permission of John Wiley and Sons Limited and the authors.

ARTICLE 14.2 FOSTERING INTRAPRENEURSHIP
by Erik G. Rule and Donald W. Irwin

To gain insight into intrapreneurship, The Coopers & Lybrand Consulting Group recently carried out a survey of senior managers in 104 Canadian organizations. Respondents were asked to judge the extent to which their company practices intrapreneurship relative to other companies in their industry. Over 85 percent of the senior managers responded that their companies are either more than or equally as intrapreneurially oriented as other companies. Only 15 percent judged their companies' intrapreneurial abilities to be less than that of their competitors.

Surprisingly, however, when senior managers were asked to indicate their level of satisfaction with their current intrapreneurial ability, almost 50 percent indicated that they were dissatisfied to very dissatisfied.

This finding implies that most top-level managers believe that they must substantially improve their companies' intrapreneurial abilities to remain competitive. It is significant that almost 70 percent of the respondents indicated that they plan to increase efforts to encourage intrapreneurship over the next ten years. Clearly, cultivating an innovative corporate environment is a strategic priority for many companies.

There is, of course, no single, simple way for a company to become intrapreneurial. While respondents identified a large variety of approaches described in Exhibit 14.1, they isolated the following five methods as being the most effective at contributing to intrapreneurship within their organizations:

(1) Innovation teams and task forces;

(2) Recruitment of new staff to transfer new ideas to the organization;

(3) Application of strategic planning focused on achieving innovation;

(4) Customer focus groups organized to identify new innovations; and

(5) In-house research and development.

Although these methods were judged to be highly effective, the responding companies did not report using them as frequently as might be expected. This implies that most companies have not yet found the right combination of culture and management systems necessary to support innovation.

Six Keys to Successful Intrapreneurship

How can an organization develop a more intrapreneurial culture? When establishing an intrapreneurship program, senior management must focus on the following.

1. Generate New Ideas. There is no shortage of innovative ideas in most organizations. To uncover these innovations, senior executives must communicate the importance of innovation to all levels of the organization through a variety of channels. They should invite ideas, establish a conduit for submissions, and ensure that the whole organization is empowered to submit suggestions.

For example, Connaught Laboratories, a world leader in the production of human vaccines, annually holds "strategy circles" with small groups of employees representing a cross section of the organization. These sessions are designed to identify innovative ideas to improve productivity, to develop new products,

EXHIBIT 14.1 Thirty-Three Ways to Encourage Intrapreneurship

1. In-house market research
2. In-house research and development
3. Competitor tracking and assessment
4. Market research using consultants
5. Collaborative ventures with others
6. Monitoring trade shows
7. New product screening systems
8. Customer focus groups
9. Suggestion box systems
10. Objective setting and performance standards for innovation
11. Innovation teams/task forces
12. Dedicated new venture group
13. Recruiting new staff to bring in innovative ideas
14. Scenario planning
15. Licensing-in of new technology
16. Monitoring federal R&D activities
17. Staff rotation program
18. Liaison with university labs
19. Strategic planning focused on innovation
20. Technology forecasting
21. Publication of innovations in company house organ
22. Contracting for external R&D
23. Training in creative thinking
24. Acquisition of entrepreneurial company
25. Creativity/innovation workshops
26. Bonus system linked to innovation
27. Accessing external venture capital
28. Training in entrepreneurship
29. Senior management innovation screening committee
30. Internal venture capital fund
31. Sabbatical programs
32. In-house innovation fairs
33. External inventor relations programs

and to achieve a differentiated position through marketing and service. A valuable means of introducing change into the organization, Connaught's "strategy circles" have contributed to the company's healthy annual growth rate of over 15 percent since 1980.

2. Screen New Ideas to Allocate Resources. It has been said that corporate entrepreneurs are often the authors not of the grand gesture but of the quiet innovation. How does a company decide whether to explore small, uncertain, unprofitable, ambiguous ideas concerning new products or services? The challenge is to screen out projects with poor prospects while accepting projects with substantial merit.

Experience has shown that large, complex organizations need some structured approach to screen new opportunities.

Screening ensures that the best ideas are allocated sufficient resources and given a high enough priority to be successfully developed and implemented.

Honeywell, for instance, has established a permanent senior management steering committee focused on the management of innovation and change. Connaught Laboratories uses cross-functional teams to screen new ideas generated in the strategy circles discussed above.

Because of the nature of the innovation process, certain screening criteria are inappropriate. Using cost-benefit calculations and rate of return estimates, for example, often results in the dismissal of promising new ideas. The following criteria may be useful in the screening process:

The personal commitment and passion of the proponent. As venture capital investors know, the energy, commitment, and drive of entrepreneurs are often the key to success. Within a corporation, the entrepreneur's role is filled by a proponent or champion of the new idea or opportunity, an individual who Peters and Waterman describe in *In Search of Excellence* as having "the energy required to cope with the indifference and resistance that major change provides."

Support among middle managers. If there is some support among managers, this provides evidence that there may be substance to a new idea. It is middle managers who run organizations—they are the ones who have to live with the results of innovation. Their judgments regarding new ideas are critically important.

Support and commitment of a sponsor or mentor. Unless someone in senior management is willing to provide support and give legitimacy to the exploration of a new idea, innovation will not be successful.

A good fit with the corporate mission. Unless the organization is seeking unrelated diversification, new business opportunities should be fundamentally consistent with the mission of the corporation—that is, compatible with the markets served and the range of products and services offered, and supportive of corporate values.

3. Support Idea Development. The generation and screening processes should be supported by real commitments of resources, time, and money for idea exploration and development. New opportunities will be strongly encouraged if the firm makes an investment in exploring an innovative idea. New ideas will also be encouraged if the firm celebrates and rewards achievement.

It is particularly important for management to recognize small accomplishments. All ideas start small, and management cannot tell initially which small ideas will become the key to future profits. Development of 3M's masking tape began with a salesman who recognized a customer need. The company's highly successful Post-it pads began when an employee needed a removable adhesive hymnal marker.

It is important to let the innovator and sponsor decide what human resources are needed to explore an idea—these individuals know their strengths and weaknesses and are therefore in the best position to identify the needed resources. After all, management should ensure that membership on the innovation development team is voluntary. Unless the intrapreneur and the sponsor can convince staff that the idea warrants attention, the team will lack the commitment from its members needed to follow through.

4. Encourage Flexibility. Management should let the innovation team define its resource requirements and time schedule while maintaining control over the total budget and the overall time schedule. This flexible approach provides for overall project control while giving the innovation team the freedom to make expenditures as required. The team should also be responsible for evaluating the financial viability of the idea.

It is important for management to protect the innovation team from the central work activities of the organization. Without nurturing and protection, small, unprofitable, and ambiguous projects will always lose out to the demands of a firm's core business in the competition for scarce management time. The idea of encouraging a separate "skunk works" is one mechanism that can be used to protect innovators from the demands of other work. IBM, for example, used an autonomous work group to develop the personal computer. Pontiac adopted this approach in developing the Fiero.

5. Reward the Contributors. A wide range of techniques is available to reward intrapreneurs. Perhaps the most important reward is not monetary—it is the freedom given to intrapreneurs to solve problems or to follow up on pet projects. Some firms have created "intracapital" to reward and fund innovation. This is a system that provides intrapreneurs with a timeless discretionary budget to be used to fund the creation of new enterprises and innovations.

More traditional financial rewards such as bonuses, salary increases, and participation in the profits generated from new products or services are also valuable motivators. Magna International, a Canadian manufacturer of auto parts with sales of over $1 billion and an average growth rate of 30 percent since 1979, is one company that has effectively used financial rewards to motivate intrapreneurship. The firm guarantees employees 10 percent of pretax profits. In 1985, incentive systems paid $8.3 million to employees.

6. Provide Leadership. Finally, senior management must make a personal commitment to support innovation. It is not so much what leaders say but what they do to support innovation and encourage intrapreneurship that counts. More than any other group, senior managers must understand and communicate that new solutions are required, and that companies are operating in a new environment where change is the key to success.

Leaders must be willing and confident enough to share power because, in the long run, the future success of the firm rests upon the new products and new services not yet developed. Soichiro Honda, the legendary founder and leader of the motorcycle and automotive giant Honda, is an excellent example of this forward-looking attitude; even as chairman, he regularly worked alongside his associates in the engineering department to provide hands-on assistance in the development of new engineering innovations.

In large part, intrapreneurship is a process of problem solving and team work in organizations. An environment that encourages integrative team building and collaborative problem-solving approaches is one where valuable skills are learned, which can then be applied to intrapreneurial projects.

Conclusion

Many business leaders today are dissatisfied with their ability to innovate. They value the need for intrapreneurial activities within their firms and expect such activities to become more strategically important in the next decade.

Achieving a consistent record of intrapreneurship requires that management focus on generating new ideas, establishing a structured screening system, giving innovators freedom, rewarding the contributors, and providing strong leadership. By cultivating these intrapreneurial skills, corporations can build the competitive advantage that will be needed to thrive in increasingly global markets in the years ahead.

Source: Article 14.2 excerpted from E. G. Rule and D. W. Irwin, "Fostering Intrapreneurship: The New Competitive Edge," *Journal of Business Strategy* (May-June 1988), 44–47. Reprinted with permission from the *Journal of Business Strategy,* copyright 1988, Warren Gorham & Lamont Inc., 210 South Street, Boston, MA 02111. All rights reserved.

ARTICLE 14.3   ENTREPRENEURS, CHAOS, AND CREATIVITY: CAN CREATIVE PEOPLE REALLY SURVIVE LARGE COMPANY STRUCTURE?
by Marsha Sinetar

> "I love Chaos: it is the mysterious, unknown road. It is the ever-unexpected, the way out: it is freedom, it is man's only hope. It is the poetic element in a dull and orderly world."
>
> American artist, Ben Shahn, 1966

Suddenly, big business is in love with creativity. With the same fervor with which it courted MBAs in the 1970s, American industry is now trying to lure entrepreneurs into managerial positions. It has discovered that survival in today's volatile, global marketplace means finding, developing, and sustaining the very mavericks it rejected only a few years ago.

Why this dramatic shift in focus? One of the reasons is apparent as soon as we examine the entrepreneur's instinctive intelligence: entrepreneurs are better able to spot options and create new directions for an industry. Typically, they deal well with ambiguity and change, and that is a prerequisite for success in today's fast-paced business world. They can distinguish real from imaginary pitfalls, and the brightest among them can turn error into opportunity. Small wonder then that industry is scurrying to acquire creative thinkers.

Even current buzzwords point to the important place creativity holds in business. Intrapreneurial describes entrepreneurial characteristics when these turn inward, for organizational benefit. Entrepreneurialize is jargon used to describe any business activity that allows large, calcified organizations to internalize the advantages of smaller, more nimble companies. But, whatever the terminology, progressive corporations are hiring entrepreneurs, sending managers to creativity seminars, and bringing in creativity specialists to teach executives how to think in original ways.

However, just because big business wants entrepreneurs doesn't mean it is prepared to accept or appreciate their way of working. There is much evidence suggesting that most large organizations are insensitive to the nuances and idiosyncratic work style of the creative personality. In reality, a substantial number of creatives are strangled within the orderly, systematic cultures of large companies: they can't work in these structured environments. Sometimes they leave, and sometimes their ideas just die, unused and unnoticed. But because business needs creative people, it must learn to understand—and support—this inventive breed of worker.

Who and What Is a Creative Entrepreneur?

It is possible to distinguish two types of creative entrepreneurs: the activist and the creative thinker. Actually these two categories are not at all clear-cut, since all entrepreneurs if successful possess healthy doses of business acumen and original/

resourceful thinking skills. What distinguishes one type from another is a subtle, almost elusive difference in thinking mode and in the manner of getting a job done. The activist is a doer. He has an innate understanding of what it takes to run, expand, reconceptualize, or create a business. This person's thought processes—the steady, incremental way of thinking, doing, communicating—fit into and naturally complement the core of organizational life. The activist is a natural dance partner to business, and activists have an intuitive, sixth sense when it comes to motivating personnel, marketing new products, and dealing with financial issues. They know, without having to learn through academic institutions or books, how to put business principles to use within organizations so that both principle and organization succeed.

Victor Kiam, president of Remington Products, Inc., serves as an excellent and well-known media model of the activist entrepreneur. With effectiveness and energy he participates in all facets of his company's operations. He markets and even sells the product: his ad campaign, "I liked this shaver so much I bought the company," is now nationally familiar. He meets regularly with employees to motivate and inspire them. Kiam has built an impressive, clear corporate identity. In fact, if media reports are accurate, this activist entrepreneur is doing so well he is currently moving his products into the Japanese marketplace, thus reversing a global trend of Japanese products encroaching on U.S. markets. An impressive achievement.

The creative thinker, on the other hand, is more like an artist or inventor. Primarily a thinker, he derives his greatest pleasure from the act of thinking itself, from the creative process in action. Achievement for him comes when mental abstractions are transformed into concrete forms—when idea becomes reality. Indeed, the creative thinker loves the conceptional work of his technical specialty so much that sometimes practical business needs get overshadowed by the images of his professional frame of reference (e.g., engineering, computer technology, genetics, mathematics, etc.). This person is totally absorbed in experimentation, investigation, and innovation. Money, status, the outcomes of business are secondary to the act of creation. It is thinking itself which provides deep, visceral satisfaction: a fact industry must not overlook or misinterpret.

For the creative thinker, problems are sorted out in a stylized, unpredictable, and often disorganized manner; herein lies the greatest conflict that creatives have within organized, corporate structures. Often, creative thinkers are hard to get to know. As managers they frustrate and surprise people in their departments; as employees they don't conform. In any role their habits contradict organizational expectations and mores.

One such manager, a nationally respected visionary known best for his grasp and application of computer technology, arrives at work early each morning and makes coffee for everyone. Accustomed to working late into the night, he then cleans up the coffee room before the custodians can get to it. He is oblivious to his company's unwritten social law that says senior executives must not engage in such activities. Thus he unknowingly thwarts lower level employees' ego needs to do a job they feel is rightly theirs.

Another creative thinker, a corporate vice president, upsets subordinates and superiors alike by refusing all clerical help, including a secretary to answer his phone and type his letters. Instead, he scrawls all memos on yellow legal pads, unaware that his colleagues get irritated because of this and because they can't get in touch with him when he's away from his office.

For all that, the creative thinker is not a wild-eyed nonconformist. With respect to most of the small customs of life, innovators may be very ordinary, even boring, people. But these personalities thrive on freedom in three important areas of life:

- Freedom in the general area of their work and the way in which the work gets done.
- Freedom to ask novel or disturbing questions.
- Freedom to come up with unusual solutions to the things they're thinking about (sometimes in the form of what seems, to others, to be impractical ideas).

In other words, these types must have lots of room for experimentation and "play." Such license is like air for breathing to the bright, inventive mind, yet it is only the rare organization that can provide this.

Creativity Means Disturbing the Status Quo

Creativity means bringing into existence something that has never existed before. For the person who creates, thinking is play, and this becomes both his motive ("I desire to think") *and* his goal ("so that I can think some more"). Part of his recreation is experimentation: this is unsettling to others, and disruptive to organizational life. Courting error, taking a "let's see what happens" stance is natural to the creative thinker, but anathema to large organizations.

Because of size and structure, big companies are risk-averse, even though they may give lip service to being otherwise. Errors, mistakes, failures: these must be avoided because they destroy careers, departmental efficiency, record keeping, and the like. *Organizations are designed to administer, maintain, and protect what already exists; creative thinkers are designed to bring into existence that which has never been before.* The creative's need to think and invent disturbs the well-oiled machinery of organizational process; thus, creativity is experienced as chaotic in most business environments. Some examples will help illustrate this fact.

The head of a technical unit of a prosperous, multinational corporation thinks nothing of spending vast sums of money to experiment with state-of-the-art systems equipment. Colleagues who are responsible for the corporate bottom line wonder if he is sane. "Just buy something reputable and stop playing games," they plead in an effort to keep expenditures down, but he continues to load his offices and theirs with a variety of experimental equipment and spends freely. While his associates think he's irresponsible, he thinks about the future, and electronics, and how to bring his company into the forefront of technology.

Because he cannot (or will not) communicate in terms familiar to others, a knowledge and goals gap grows between himself and those important to his success.

Another entrepreneur, hired to help a corporation reconceptualize itself into new markets, spent the majority of his first year wandering about the halls, asking people vague, unanswerable questions. His incomprehensible approach alarmed fellow executives; more action-oriented business colleagues considered his constant probing a waste of time. Months passed without formal meetings or the development of a strategic game plan. This creative thinker appeared to lack the logic and discipline of a businessman.

In time, the man successfully accomplished what he'd been hired to do. His style of handling the project, however, put him on thin ice even with those who'd hired him in the first place, again underscoring the difficulty that creatives have in a structured setting and the difficulty structured organizations have with the creative process.

What Do Creative Entrepreneurs Have in Common?

Every truly creative individual is a minority of one. There is no one else like him or her. It is difficult to group such persons into neat descriptive categories, except to say, as we have, that they don't fit the stereotypical way of doing business. However, the broadest area of their thinking skills and style of pursuing goals can be codified:

- They are easily bored, and would rather move into untried areas.
- They are comfortable with ambiguity, at least when it comes to work.
- They are neither risk-averse nor troubled by ambiguity.
- They may be uninterested in social matters, and thus may not be socially "well-rounded."
- They need to use their minds to solve difficult, personally fulfilling problems.
- The healthier their personalities, the more likely it is that they experience their work as a calling or dedicated vocation.

When working in unexplored problem areas, creative entrepreneurs are able to cope without support or approval from others. According to research done by Paul Torrance, creativity researcher at the University of Georgia, Athens, creative people are happy with solitude, and they are less in need of discipline or order. Their dominant need may be to use their brains on complex problems; this often overshadows their dependency on the approval or opinions of others.

One such individual expressed his need to use his mind this way: "I love to use my brain . . . it actually feels good in a physical sense. The best times for me are when I'm working, uninterrupted, on something that needs a solution. My ideal job would be if I could sit in a room with the door shut with no one to bother me, and the company would just slide problems it needed solved under the door."

Such attitudes are disruptive to, if not disrespectful of, others. An all too familiar example is the creative entrepreneur who walks away from a successful business to work on a new project. His actions confuse family and colleagues alike. The energy, money, and time he must put into the new venture could so easily go into expanding the existing, profitable business. But, for a creative mind, moving on to a new challenge is natural, perhaps necessary. As a creative friend once told me, "Show me something easy, and I'll show you something dull."

How Can Organizations Sustain Creative Talent?

After all has been said about creative entrepreneurs, it must be clear that there are no instant answers, no quick-fix formulas that large organizations can use to harness the potential of creative people. There are, however, a few basic principles that can help businesses utilize the ideas and energy of entrepreneurs with more probability of success. (See Exhibit 14.2 for analysis of the creative entrepreneur as subordinate, team member, manager, and founder of company.)

First of all, management must be able to identify creative talent, then it must know how to use it. To accomplish the task, it should ask itself the following questions:

1. Who are our creative people, and how do we know they are creative? (This implies setting criteria for identifying innovators.)
2. What opportunities exist for creative people within this organization?
3. What barriers have key managers placed in the way of creative thinkers?

Once the organization knows who its creative people are, it must become introspective and ask itself:

1. In what ways do we reward creativity?
2. Do we punish, that is, do we negatively reinforce, reject, or embarrass those in the organization who look different or experiment freely?
3. In what specific ways do we encourage or promote experimentation and independent thinking?

Finally, in order to cultivate more independent, inventive thinking practices, organizations should audit thinking time. An expert isn't needed at this juncture, but opportunities to think are. An organization can ask itself:

1. What problem-solving opportunities exist for nonmanagers?
2. Do managers usually make all important decisions? What types of decisions are nonmanagers encouraged to make?
3. Are staff meetings, round table discussions or small group meetings agenda bound, tightly structured, or time restricted? Or are these used, on occasion, as brainstorming sessions?

EXHIBIT   14.2   Common Challenges Facing the Creative Entrepreneur

Creative Entrepreneur as Subordinate:

- Style, thinking, expectancies can clash when reporting to logical, linear thinker.
- Can suffocate in rigid cultures.
- Can suffer (or cause distress) when not managed (i.e., guided) into corporate culture.
- Can experience management and/or the company as punitive to creative efforts.
- Can be impatient to utilize brain, resulting in premature termination.
- Can irritate and/or threaten own manager.

Creative Entrepreneur as Team Member:

- Can alienate others by intensive drive, focus on pet projects, idiosyncrasies.
- Can be isolated, misunderstood, a loner.
- Can be perceived as self-serving, disruptive to team effort, a rule/protocol breaker.
- Can suffer from feelings of loneliness, isolation, being different.

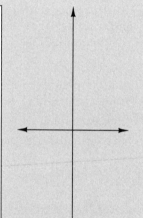

Creative Entrepreneur as Founder and Chief of Company:

- Can grow to rely on unreliable "sidekicks."
- Often unwilling/unable to delegate.
- Impatient with day-to-day operating details.
- Impulsive, can be perceived as erratic.
- Can be perceived as condescending, scattered, feeling superior to others.
- Can be highly dictatorial.

Creative Entrepreneur as Manager:

- Can see management activities as uninteresting, irritating.
- Can be perceived as "ivory tower," impractical; lacking in short-range follow-through.
- Can develop interpersonal communication barriers with subordinates (e.g., by avoiding coaching, corrective, appraisal-type conversations).
- Can be perceived as withdrawing and/or avoiding selected aspects of the job.

The Challenge to Business

One of the greatest challenges facing business today is encouraging creative people to express themselves innovatively while still maintaining the orderly functions of the company. If this is not done, creative entrepreneurs will leave generous salaries, incentives, and fringe benefits for more exciting, personally meaningful ventures.

In the words of one executive who left a large corporation to start his own company, "I needed the basic kick of using my brain on things that really mattered. I was bored in my other job, even though I was handsomely paid. There was no way of really thinking through the tough issues, no accountability or feedback in any immediate way. What I needed was the chance to use my mind. The company was too generous, but they didn't give me what I needed most—a real challenge."

Source: Article 14.3 excerpted from M. Sinetar, "Entrepreneurs, Chaos, and Creativity: Can Creative People Really Survive Large Company Structure?" *Sloan Management Review* 25 (1985), 57–62. Used by permission of *Sloan Management Review* and the author. Copyright 1985 by the Sloan Management Review Association. All rights reserved.

ENDNOTES

1. M. S. Wortman, Jr., "Entrepreneurship: An Integrating Typology and Evaluation of the Empirical Research in the Field," *Journal of Management* 13 (1987), 259–79.
2. I. C. MacMillan, "The Politics of New Venture Management," *Harvard Business Review* (November-December, 1983), 8–16.
3. B. J. Bird, *Entrepreneurial Behavior* (Glenview, Ill.: Scott, Foresman, 1989).

Entrepreneurship
in the Future

Perhaps the greatest challenge facing modern American business organizations of all sizes is the need to nurture and maintain entrepreneurship. The imperatives of global competition demand that organizations develop new products, services, processes, and organizational forms to improve performance and ensure survival. In this chapter we consider the future of entrepreneurship from several vantage points. The first section describes how entrepreneurship is related to underdeveloped countries. The second section considers entrepreneurship from a global perspective. The third section discusses how entrepreneurship can flourish in large organizations, while the fourth section identifies trends for the creation of small, entrepreneurial businesses. In the fifth section implications regarding future research activities for entrepreneurship are presented. Finally, the chapter concludes with a review of Robert Reich's discussion of the "new entrepreneurs."

UNDERDEVELOPED COUNTRIES AND THE FUTURE OF ENTREPRENEURSHIP

Is there a demand for entrepreneurship in underdeveloped countries? A number of studies have shown that while people in underdeveloped countries are often viewed as strangers to the idea of economic growth and market gains, there is evidence that the supply of effort is responsive to incentives for improvement and that wants are elastic through time in large parts of the underdeveloped world.[1] Given that there is a demand for entrepreneurship in underdeveloped countries, what about the supply of entrepreneurially talented people? How is this supply developed? In discussing how entrepreneurship can be developed, certain economists have argued that economic growth cannot be wholly explained in terms of an economy's stock of physical capital and the number of workers. The *residual*, which is the name given to the portion of growth that is not accounted for by increases in the stock of physical capital and increases in the labor force, has been attributed in part to improvements in human capital.[2] These same economists argue that investments in human capital play a major role in creating a supply of entrepreneurs. Chapter 7 discussed Theodore Schultz's theory of entrepreneurship based on his concept of human capital in which education is a vital ingredient.[3] Furthermore, Milton Friedman states that an important factor in the economic growth of an undeveloped country is the "release of the energies of millions of able, active, and vigorous people in an atmosphere of freedom, and a maximum opportunity to experiment in new ways of doing things." According to Friedman, this type of atmosphere can be accomplished by providing education, information, and an environment for economic agents to be mobile and flexible. Friedman argues that creating this kind of environment will require a minimal administrative apparatus and very little policing other than the provision of a legal system for the enforcement of contracts.[4]

In summary, economic studies indicate that the demand for entrepreneurship exists in underdeveloped countries and that a supply of entrepreneurship can be created by investments in education together with an environment that does not militate against economic development and contributes in a positive way to its realization. Certainly recent events in China, Mexico, the former Soviet Union, and Eastern Europe support the notion that a demand for entrepreneurship exists in many areas of our world. Whether the supply of entrepreneurship is developed, however, remains an interesting question.

ENTREPRENEURSHIP: A GLOBAL PERSPECTIVE

During the late 1950s and early 1960s, U.S.-based companies originated sixty percent of the world's significant innovations.[5] Certainly these efforts contributed to the technological leadership capabilities of many U.S. firms. In more recent times, however, U.S. companies have lost their leadership positions in automobile design and quality, steel making, consumer electronic goods, shipbuilding, textile machinery, numerically controlled machine tools, ceramics, nuclear-power reactors, and many others.[6] Other changes are also occurring. For example, the Berlin Wall came tumbling down, with East and West Germany being united. The Soviet Union split asunder and communism ended in Europe. What are the implications for the future of entrepreneurship regarding these changes? Scherer argues that successful global competition is linked to technological innovation and economies of scale.[7] The role of entrepreneurship in these areas is not clear. A quick response would be to argue for an increase in the research and development efforts of U.S. firms. "Let's be more innovative and create more new products" is an interesting response. However, the development of new products and production processes often takes considerable time and large amounts of resources that once invested, become sunk costs. Also when several rivals struggle for comparative advantage of a new technology, duplicate investments may occur before a winner emerges.[8] Certainly the consequences of expanding global high-technology competition need further study.

What is the future of entrepreneurship in foreign economies? Some economies are more successful in promoting entrepreneurship than others. For example, Japan has been very innovative, while the economies of the former Soviet Union and Eastern Europe during the 1970s and 1980s experienced very low rates of innovation. In fact Eastern European countries have lacked the ability to create new value through entrepreneurship.[9] In part the poor entrepreneurial performance of the former Soviet Union stems from a lack of incentives in a system that involved central planning. This central planning system contained powerful disincentives for innovation and entrepreneurship. Most entrepreneurial activity tends to disrupt existing ways of doing things during its implementation. Soviet managers avoided those interruptions, because they focused on meeting quarterly targets. The central planning system also took away any gains resulting from innovation and entrepreneurship.[10] Currently, countries of the former Soviet Union are attempting to move from central planning to a market economy. However, much needs to be done in developing the prerequisites for a market economy—flexible prices, financial markets, and private property.[11] Remembering Professor Schultz's arguments for investments in human capital (health and education), we realize that these investments will work in Eastern Europe. All the money that governments spend on education and science may be wasted, however, if entrepreneurs are forced to deal with government regulations, red tape, and bureaucracy to bring their ideas to fruition. Governments must be willing to allow market incentives to work.

HOW ENTREPRENEURSHIP CAN FLOURISH IN LARGE ORGANIZATIONS

A number of organization-science researchers have indicated that organizations do not generally search for innovations but instead respond to perceived performance gaps. Other organization science researchers have identified large firms that are highly innovative and proactive in their search for innovation.[12] How can entrepreneurship flourish in large companies? Is it a reactive or a proactive process? Joseph Bower conducted an in-depth study of one large company and demonstrated that the structural context (corporate structure, measurement and control system, and reward system) had a powerful influence on the thinking and entrepreneurial actions of the company's managers.[13] Later Burgelman extended Bower's model in a detailed study of internal corporate venturing in one large organization. Burgelman reported that successful venturing requires entrepreneurial initiatives by individuals at the operational levels, the ability of middle managers to conceptualize the strategic implications of these initiatives, and the capacity of top management to allow viable entrepreneurial initiatives to change the organization's strategy.[14]

Peter Drucker, drawing on his many years of studying large entrepreneurial companies, suggested that success in creating an entrepreneurial environment comes from the careful implementation of an unspectacular but systematic management discipline. A key aspect of this discipline, according to Drucker, lies in the knowledge of where to look for entrepreneurial opportunities and how to identify them.[15]

James Brian Quinn studied several large innovative firms in Europe, Japan, and the United States and concluded that large firms stay innovative by behaving like small entrepreneurial ventures. Quinn noted that few, if any, major innovations result from a highly structured planning system. Instead, major innovations are best managed as incremental, goal-oriented, interactive learning processes.[16]

Vijay Sathe studied eight large corporations (four American and four European), each with annual sales exceeding one billion dollars and each having a long track record of successful entrepreneurship. Exhibit 15.1 describes a set of recommendations developed by Sathe for top executives who are committed to promoting entrepreneurship in their firms.[17]

Not all attempts at fostering entrepreneurship are successful. For example, Exxon Enterprises created nineteen new ventures and *all* failed to produce a business with significant profits.[18]

EXHIBIT   15.1   A Process for Promoting Entrepreneurship in Large Firms

1. *Consider "knowledge of territory" and "benefit of contrast" when moving managers around.* Managers should have a sufficiently deep knowledge of their "territory" (products, markets, and technologies) to be able to identify really promising entrepreneurial opportunities.

2. *Selectively hire new managers from the outside who know a product, market, or technological territory of interest.* These managers have the benefit of previous experience, which they can use to set up a contrast with the current environment.

3. *Play up and promote the company's own success stories and champions.* Even in the absence of an entrepreneurial culture, virtually every company has experienced some entrepreneurial success. It pays to play up these accomplishments and encourage more of them with mild financial incentives and strong company recognition.

4. *Don't penalize for failure.* Failure should be regarded as normal and as an invitation to learning. Failure should not be treated as an occasion for finding fault or apportioning blame.

5. *Heighten visibility of results and keep top management well informed.* Top management needs to trust its entrepreneurs. Trust is built and maintained with openness, not secrecy.

continued

EXHIBIT 15.1 *concluded*

6. *Bet on people who know their territory, rather than on formal analysis or your own judgment of the attractiveness of the opportunity.* Entrepreneurial activity by its very nature involves great uncertainty. Knowledgeable people may differ on such basic differences as the attractiveness of an opportunity, how much to invest in it, and how long to pursue it.

7. *Use supportive challenge to test the entrepreneur's conviction and to help uncover his or her blind spots.* Top management's aim should be to provide a second opinion, not to second-guess the entrepreneur. This is best accomplished by questioning the entrepreneur's assumptions, reasoning with empathy and understanding, and not dictating what the entrepreneur should do about specific ventures.

8. *Use betting rules to contain entrepreneurial risk.* Entrepreneurial activity is inherently risky. Successful entrepreneurial companies allow the entrepreneur the discretion to pursue his or her own convictions about a particular venture. At the same time these firms contain the overall risk to the company by placing limits on the total venture portfolio of each entrepreneur. Such limits may be specified in the form of betting rules that allow the entrepreneur to call the shots on his or her specific ventures but that limit the company's total exposure.

9. *Ask for additional contributions and budget cuts without calling the shots on specific ventures.* Selected business units are asked for profit contributions over and above the budgeted amount. This is done to compensate for anticipated shortfalls in the budgeted contributions of other units.

Source: Adapted from V. Sathe, "Fostering Entrepreneurship in the Large, Diversified Firm," *Organizational Dynamics* (Summer 1989), 20–32. Used by permission of the American Management Association.

Exhibit 15.2 describes how one large American firm, General Electric, is changing its organization to promote entrepreneurship.

EXHIBIT 15.2 Changing Organizational Factors to Promote Entrepreneurship

General Electric (GE) is turning around the equation of U.S. business. Instead of pushing marketers to come up with ideas and then asking scientists to make them work, GE increasingly gives researchers a wide berth to imagine and invent—and then shop the invention around GE's divisions. The result is that GE's scientists and salespeople regularly manage to transfer technology from the laboratory to the marketplace, a transition that frequently baffles American business. U.S. companies lead the world in inventing and innovating but drop the ball after that. GE's record is hardly flawless. For example, the company developed a new compressor for its refrigerators and then lost $450 million when it turned out to be unreliable. However, an internal study conducted by a major consulting firm indicated that during a recent four-year period, GE

continued

EXHIBIT 15.2 *concluded*

produced 150 successful products from 250 technology projects—a success rate of 60 percent. The average for all U.S. firms during this time period was 10 percent, according to a GE spokesperson.

At GE, because researchers are supposed to sell their ideas around the whole company, they sometimes find applications far afield from the original intentions. Something invented to protect coal spraying nozzles in an experimental locomotive ended up creating a new generation of energy-saving light bulbs. A medical diagnostic technology used for imaging the human body became a cost-saving device for inspecting jet engines. Sophisticated coating and machining techniques developed for aircraft engines got transferred to GE's power-generation business.

How did GE accomplish their successes in moving ideas from the laboratory to the market place? By changing the culture and organizational structure of R&D. A GE executive stated, "We have the finest laboratories and equipment in the world, but company rules and regulations were hampering our entrepreneurial abilities." GE changed the culture of its R&D operation by providing an informal atmosphere where free beer, pretzels, and pizza are served on Friday afternoons. Scientists and engineers frequently meet and exchange ideas. Interdisciplinary work projects develop during these meetings. Researchers are regularly treated to art exhibits and classical music concerts to emphasize creativity. In the past, it was not only difficult for researchers to transfer from their labs to manufacturing operations, but they were assigned to a specific business unit. Researchers can now transfer annually to various manufacturing operations and across business units. For example, an electrical engineer moved from appliances to power generation, to electrical distribution, to aerospace—cross-pollinating technology all the while.

Source: Adapted from A. Naj, "GE's Latest Invention: A Way to Move Ideas from Lab to Market," *Wall Street Journal* (14 June 1990), A1.

CREATING SMALL ENTREPRENEURIAL BUSINESSES

Defining a small business is detailed and complex. For example, the Small Business Administration (SBA) uses 37 pages of regulations to define small businesses by industry. Generally a business is considered small if it has fewer than 500 employees. This general definition works fine, but the SBA has added additional qualifications based on type of industry.[19]

The future of small, entrepreneurial companies appears to be high because changes in the U.S. economy provides many opportunities for new businesses. For example, the demand for services is booming, and most service firms are small, with fewer than 100 employees. The government's deregulation of the trucking and airline industries removed restrictions that inhibited small-business formation. More than 13,000 trucking companies have been started since 1980.[20]

The impact of small, entrepreneurial companies in the U.S. economy is underscored by the following figures:[21] approximately 700,000 businesses are incorporated in the U.S. each year, along with another 600,000 unincorporated start-ups, for a total of about 1.3 million new businesses. (Only 90,000 new incorporations occurred in 1950.) Furthermore data indicate that most new businesses survive at least three to five years.

Several trends, which are described in Exhibit 15.3, have been identified that indicate an increased interest in entrepreneurship.

Recent occurrences of corporate downsizing (the process by which firms reduce their total number of employees) are spurring an exodus of managers, professionals, and workers into the ranks of self-employment. A growing army of people is leaving corporate America to strike out on their own, enticed by early retirement incentives and buyouts. In some cases, they are pushed out. Others leave before the ax falls—or they simply make the decision that there is a better way to earn a living. One measure of growth for this new sector is the increase in the number of people counted by the U.S. Census Bureau as self-employed. From 1980 to 1990 the number of self-employed people grew by 29.3 percent, while overall employment grew by 19.9 percent. These "defensive entrepreneurs" are described in Exhibit 15.4.

Certainly the phenomenon of small entrepreneurial companies is a miracle for job creation, innovation, and opportunities for women and minorities. For example, small entrepreneurial companies are responsible for the creation each year of from 40 to 80 percent of all new jobs in the United States. Over 65 percent of all initial jobs for Americans are in a small business.[22] As discussed in Chapter 3, small entrepreneurial firms create a disproportionate number of new products and services.[23] Women and minorities also are discovering the promise of entrepreneurship as they find themselves blocked in established firms.[24] Nearly four million women own businesses in the United States, and the growth of women-owned firms is spectacular. One projection is that by the year 2000 half of all business owners will be women. [25]

EXHIBIT 15.3 Trends in Entrepreneurship

- Large firms are striving to utilize entrepreneurship in their operations.
- Managers, professionals, and workers are leaving large firms to start their own businesses.
- The number of female entrepreneurs has increased significantly.
- All over the world entrepreneurship is gaining popularity.
- In the past the sons and daughters of entrepreneurs did not choose to work in the family business. Recent data suggest that this trend may be changing.
- An increasing number of college students are starting their own businesses. These range from printing calendars and writing software to opening pizza parlors.

EXHIBIT 15.4 The Defensive Entrepreneurs

A growing number of individuals are being called defensive entrepreneurs: people who, while continuing in their regular jobs, are developing new careers—for psychic as well as financial reasons. They are sacrificing weekends and vacations to moonlight as small scale landlords, innkeepers, studio photographers, mechanics, and owners of hardware stores and hair salons. Certainly, people have always had hobbies, and moonlighting is not new. But the tremendous restructuring that has hit Corporate America brought a new sense of insecurity to many employees. Hundreds of thousands faced unexpected layoff. Now, most people do not trust their company anymore.

Individuals who began their careers 20 or more years ago at paternalistic companies tended to feel they had an implicit contract guaranteeing them employment as long as they did their job well. Now, that contract does not exist. Defensive entrepreneuring is not easy. Nurturing side ventures demands time and resources. There are no guarantees these businesses will succeed, to say nothing of growing enough to provide support if a job is lost. If the business founders, invested money will vanish with it. Following is a description of a defensive entrepreneur.

Greg Cesario spent eight of his last 19 years with IBM as a middle manager. "I had visions of being in one of the top corporate echelons but instead I dodged five departmental mergers. It became corporate musical chairs. When the music stopped, there were fewer chairs than there were people."

Concerned about his future, Cesario began buying modestly priced resort property to manage. In early 1988 he began planning to purchase his first restaurant. In December 1988, during another restructuring, IBM offered Cesario two years' salary plus $25,000 if he would take early retirement. Mr. Cesario, now part-owner of three restaurants, had traded managing an IBM department for dish washing, table clearing, and cleaning bathrooms. His real estate holdings have expanded to include condos and single-family residences, which he may rent out or fix up and resell. Mr. Cesario states that while his businesses are growing, it was not easy giving up a $90,000-a-year salary, bonuses, and frequent expense-account trips. The restaurant and real estate operations generate only about a third of what IBM paid him. Cesario indicates that he has not played golf in a year (which he used to play twice a week) and his personal relationships are in jeopardy because of the time he spends with his businesses.

Richard Morgan was a senior vice president of marketing for a $100 million dollar tire company until it was purchased by Goodyear. Afraid that he would not be retained, Morgan started a marketing research company working nights and on weekends. After being offered a severance package, Morgan began working full-time in his consulting company. "I am having so much fun it is hard to imagine going to work for another firm," states Morgan.

Connie Shortes, a CPA working part-time for a large accounting firm, is building an entirely new career as a college professor. She wants to eventually get a Ph.D. with a focus on women's studies, write and teach. Meanwhile, her part-time work pays the tuition bills.

Source: Adapted from J. Mitchell, "Fear of Layoff Spurs Employees to Launch Part-Time Businesses," *Wall Street Journal* (25 May 1990), A1; D. Kunde, "Striking Out on Their Own," *Dallas Morning News* (19 February 1991), D1.

FUTURE RESEARCH ACTIVITIES FOR ENTREPRENEURSHIP

As discussed in Chapters 8 and 9, a considerable amount of earlier research on entrepreneurship focused on determining the psychological and personality factors of successful entrepreneurs. Unfortunately the objective of this research has not been achieved. There appears to be no discoverable pattern of traits that distinguishes successful entrepreneurs from nonentrepreneurs.[26] Researchers are now focusing on contextual factors that moderate the relationship between corporate entrepreneurship and firm performance by investigating the influence of environmental, organizational, and strategic variables on the level of performance achieved by entrepreneurial firms. Three streams of research are involved with this perspective, based on paradigms from strategic management, organizational ecology, and organization theory.[27]

Research involving new-venture performance from the strategic management paradigm has already demonstrated that industry structures and strategies of the new ventures have a significant influence on new-venture performance. Although this stream of research is in an early stage of development, the importance of these variables in explaining performance variation has already been clearly demonstrated, with the suspicion that they may significantly overshadow characteristics of entrepreneurs as explanatory variables. Should this stream of research continue to produce interesting findings, much of value will be discovered about what to teach and how to learn about successful new-venture creation.

Research focusing on new-venture creation from the organization ecology paradigm highlights the need to document and understand intrapopulation processes, interpopulation processes, and institutional factors that shape the context in which new ventures are founded. Adding the historical, substantive context to their investigations makes it possible for organization-ecology researchers to develop more comprehensive understanding of why entrepreneurs behave as they do. In addition knowing how appropriate organizational forms vary over a population's life cycle and how these forms are linked, for example, to population density can be of value to entrepreneurs in making decisions about how to structure new and growing business ventures.

Research that investigates research and development expenditures and new-venture start-ups from an organization theory paradigm highlights the impact of organizational variables on the frequency and success rate of innovative and entrepreneurial activities within ongoing organizations. Such studies increasingly document the significant role of organizational strategy, structure, management processes, and culture on patterns of R&D expenditures and new-venture creation. The findings of many of these studies point corporate managers interested in increasing innovative and entrepreneurial behavior in their firms to a number of significant variables that can be managed toward that end.[28]

This chapter concludes with a review of Robert Reich's views concerning the "new entrepreneurs"[29] which is presented in Exhibit 15.5.

EXHIBIT 15.5 Robert Reich's New Entrepreneurs

Reich argues that many economic truths of the past are no longer relevant and that clinging to old realities (for one, that a nation's economy depends on the health of a few core firms such as GM and IBM) can be fatal. Reich explains that as money, technology, ideas, and jobs flow freely across borders, corporations are losing their national identity altogether. All that remains within a nation is its people, the skills of which are a country's single most important national resource. What matters, Reich argues, is not what a nation or its companies own, but the knowledge its people possess and the work their knowledge enables them to do. The wealth of nations is the human capital of the people who live in them. As a result, we are not rich or poor because we are citizens of rich or poor nations. Instead, we are either rich or poor based on the value the global marketplace places on the work we do as individuals. Because of this, the fortunes of Americans no longer tend to rise and fall together. From an economic perspective, we are no longer in the same boat. Instead, most Americans are dispersed among three different boats according to the function they perform in the world market. Two of these boats are sinking, one is rising.

The rising boat holds "symbolic analysts"—professionals, managers, and creative types who "solve, identify, and broker problems." Also included in this group are the "new entrepreneurs," individuals who create value from a recombination of existing factors. The people in Reich's rising boat make up about a fifth of the U.S. population, and amid booming worldwide demand for their services, spurred by the digital communications revolution, their incomes have been rising smartly.

Suffering the opposite fate are the "routine producers," that is, the factory workers and low- and middle-level managers supervising them, who constitute a quarter of the American work force. Once beneficiaries of unions' clout and oligopolies' largess, they have been increasingly competing with lower-paid, often more productive workers around the globe, and over the years have taken a terrible beating. Routine producers' wages are way down, their jobs are disappearing, and their boat is capsizing.

Stuffed into the third boat are the "in-person service" workers—the biggest, fastest-growing part of the work force. Some three million new in-person service jobs were created in bars, restaurants, and fast-food outlets alone in the 1980s—more than the total number of routine production jobs in U.S. auto, steel, and textile companies at decade's end. Wages in this sector, never high, have been drifting down unevenly under pressure from forces such as automation and immigration. With exceptions, Reich expects this boat to continue sinking.

If Reich is right, then America is in for a bumpy ride, and we should all be doing some serious worrying and thinking about our future together.

Source: This material is excerpted from a book review written by Paul H. Weaver for *Fortune* magazine of the book *The Work of Nations*, by Robert Reich. The review is copyrighted 1991 *The Time Inc. Magazine Company*. All rights reserved.

ENDNOTES

1. P. T. Bauer and B. S. Yancey, *The Economics of Underdeveloped Countries* (Chicago: University of Chicago Press, 1957); I. H. Rima, *Development of Economic Analysis*, 4th ed. (Homewood, Ill.: Irwin, 1986).

2. F. H. Harbison and C. A. Myers, *Education, Manpower and Economic Growth* (New York: McGraw-Hill, 1987).

3. T. W. Schultz, "The Value of the Ability to Deal with Disequilibria," *Journal of Economic Literature* 13 (1975), 827–46.

4. M. Friedman, *Capitalism and Freedom* (Chicago: University of Chicago Press, 1962).

5. Organization for Economic Cooperation and Development, "General Report: Gaps in Technology" (Washington, D. C.: 1991).

6. F. M. Scherer, "Competing for Comparative Advantage through Technological Innovation," *Business and Contemporary World* 4 (1992), 30–39.

7. Ibid.

8. A. Meron and R. Graves, "Rivalry among Firms in Research and Development Outlays" (Working paper, Harvard University, 1990).

9. E. G. Dolan and D. E. Lindsey, *Economics,* 6th ed. (Chicago: Dryden Press, 1991), 795–99.

10. Ibid., 981–86.

11. Ibid.

12. A. H. Van de Ven, H. L. Angle, and M. S. Poole, *Research on the Management of Innovation* (New York: Harper and Row, 1989); J. B. Quinn, "Managing Innovation: Controlled Chaos," *Harvard Business Review* (May-June, 1985), 73–84.

13. J. L. Bower, *Managing the Resource Allocation* (Cambridge: Harvard Business School, 1970).

14. R. A. Burgelman, "A Process Model of Internal Corporate Venturing in the Diversified Major Firm," *Administrative Science Quarterly* 28 (1983), 223–44.

15. P. Drucker, *Innovation and Entrepreneurship* (New York: Harper and Row, 1985).

16. J. B. Quinn, "Managing Innovation."

17. V. Sathe, "Fostering Entrepreneurship in the Large, Diversified Firm," *Organizational Dynamics* (Summer 1989), 20–32.

18. G. G. Dess and A. Miller, *Strategic Management* (New York: McGraw-Hill, 1993), 195.

19. For an expanded definition of small business, see C. R. Kuehl and P. A. Lambing, *Small Business: Planning and Management* (Chicago: Dryden Press, 1990), and "The State of Small Business: A Report to the President." (Washington, D. C.: GPO, 1990).

20. D. L. Birch, "The Truth about Start-Ups," *Inc.* (January 1988), 14–18.

21. Kuehl and Lambing, *Small Business: Planning and Management.*

22. *Entrepreneurship and National Policy* (Chicago: Heller Institute, 1988).

23. F. M. Scherer, *Industrial Market Structure and Economic Performance,* 2nd ed. (Chicago: Rand McNally, 1972).

24. R. L. Daft, "Entrepreneurship and Small Business Management," in *Management,* 2nd ed. (Chicago: Dryden Press, 1991), 633–35.

25. "What Do Women Want? A Company They Can Call Their Own," *Business Week* (22 December 1986), 58-61.

26. W. D. Guth, "Research in Entrepreneurship," *The Entrepreneurial Forum* (New York: Center for Entrepreneurial Studies, New York University, 1991).

27. This approach was discussed at a symposium, "Corporate Entrepreneurship and Innovation," presented at the Southern Management Association in Atlanta, Ga., 1991, by S. A. Zahra, J. A. Pearce II, D. F. Jennings, J. G. Covin, and S. Brown.

28. Ibid.

29. R. B. Reich, *The Work of Nations* (New York: Knopf, 1991).

C A S E

1

A Note on Starting an Entrepreneurial Business through Venture Capital

Jeffrey S. Bracker
University of Louisville

Throughout America more and more entrepreneurs are building successful businesses, which range from high technology to food franchising, from manufacturing products to providing services. Venture capital investments are spurring a good deal of the entrepreneurial momentum. In recent years investment bankers and venture capital firms have channeled funds into a variety of companies that demonstrated solid potential for profitable growth.[1]

Owning and managing a small firm is a risky undertaking, however. About 400,000 small businesses fail each year.[2] In fact, by their tenth year of existence, almost 90 percent of all small firms fail (Exhibit C1.1a). Exhibits 1.1b and 1.1c present the overall new business failure rates and survival rates for one year and four years based on firm size.

The key to starting a successful firm is a good idea. Let us assume for this case study that the idea is a new one and that it is patentable.

EXHIBIT C1.1a
Overall New Business Failure Rates

By the End of:	Percentage of New Businesses That Fail
First year	40
Second year	60
Tenth year	90

Sources: U. S. Department of Commerce, Small Business Administration; Dun & Bradstreet

EXHIBIT C1.1b
One-Year Survival Rates by Firm Size

Firm Size (Employees)	Survival Rate (Percent)
0–9	77.8
10–19	85.5
20–99	95.3
100–249	95.2
250+	100.0

Source: M. B. Teitz et al., "Small Business and Employment Growth in California," Working Paper No. 348 (Berkeley, Calif.: University of California, March 1981), 42.

EXHIBIT C1.1c
Four-Year Survival Rates by Firm Size

Firm Size (Employees)	Four-Year Survival Rate (Percentage)	
	D&B Study (1969–1976)	California Study (1976–1980)
0–19	37.4	49.9
20–49	53.6	66.9
50–99	55.7	66.9
100–499	67.7	70.0

Sources: D. L. Birch, *MIT Studies, 1979–80;* M. B. Teitz et al., "Small Business and Employment Growth in California," Working Paper No. 348 (Berkeley, Calif.: University of California, March 1981), 22.

This case is intended for classroom discussion only, not to depict effective or ineffective handling of administrative situations. All rights reserved to the author.

Let us further assume that the entrepreneur has completed the necessary market research and has found the potential for this product, process, or service to be outstanding. What he or she lacks is funding.

WHAT VENTURE CAPITALISTS LOOK FOR

Studies of successful and unsuccessful firms have indicated that firms with properly developed, implemented, and controlled plans are more likely to be successful in obtaining venture capital. A study that considered only the structure of the plan, not the content, distinguished funded from unfunded business plans evaluated by venture capitalists[3] (see Exhibits C1.2 and C1.3). The data revealed that plans that exhibit wide values from the norm go unfunded. It seems clear from the data that financial projections should conform to financial ratios for firms in similar competitive situations. Venture capitalists most often compare forecast figures and typical industry statistics in their early screening. Any differences from the industry should be explained in the plan. Failure to do this usually results in a rejection letter.

Many investment companies publish their investment criteria (Exhibit C1.4), yet it is still very difficult to obtain venture funding. In fact, only an estimated one in a hundred firms is funded through traditional venture capitalists. Exhibit C1.5 shows the sources of capital for entrepreneurs starting businesses that were previously nonexistent.

EXHIBIT   C1.2   Standard Deviations, *F*-Values: Projected Financial Ratios

	No. Samples Funded	No. Samples Unfunded	Std. Dev. Funded	Std. Dev. Unfunded	*F*-Values
Asset Management					
Sales/fixed assets	15	20	61.83	131.10	4.61[a]
Sales/current assets	16	21	0.92	1.36	2.18[a]
Working capital/total assets	17	22	0.51	0.63	1.53
Working capital/sales	16	20	0.32	0.61	3.52[b]
Profitability					
EBIT/sales	24	37	0.41	0.29	1.99
EBIT/total assets	17	22	0.61	0.54	1.40
EBIT/equity	13	20	0.68	0.56	1.47
Expense Management					
Fixed costs/sales	15	26	0.35	0.46	1.73
Gross margin	20	29	0.53	0.63	1.41
Capital Structure					
LT debt/equity	14	21	0.17	1.93	128.89[b]

[a] $p = 0.01$; [b] $p = 0.05$

Due to lack of data in some plans it was impossible to calculate all ratios, so sample sizes vary.

Source: I. C. MacMillan and P. N. Subba Narasimha, "Characteristics Distinguishing Funded from Unfunded Business Plans Evaluated by Venture Capitalists," *Strategic Management Journal* 8 (issue 6, 1987), 583.

C1.3   Standard Deviations, *F*-Values for Plan Structure

	No. Samples Funded	No. Samples Unfunded	Std. Dev. Funded	Std. Dev. Unfunded	*F*-Value
Marketing percentage of plan	27	55	0.12	0.31	6.67[a]
Financial percentage of plan	27	55	0.13	0.34	6.81[a]
Production percentage of plan	27	55	0.12	0.31	6.67[a]
Management percentage of plan	27	55	0.09	0.18	6.00[a]
Smallest expense item/ largest expense item	16	34	0.12	0.30	6.25[a]

[a] $p < 0.01$.

Due to lack of data in some plans it was impossible to calculate all ratios, so sample sizes vary.

Source: I. C. MacMillan and P. N. Subba Narsimha, "Characteristics Distinguishing Funded from Unfunded Business Plans Evaluated by Venture Capitalists," *Strategic Management Journal* 8 (issue 6, 1987), 582.

C1.4   Investment Criteria of a Typical Investment Company

Industry
- Stable industries not subject to rapid technological change or wide cyclical swings in volume and profit
- Presence of barriers to market entry

Size
- Revenues of at least $20 million
- Net income after tax of at least $1.5 million in the latest fiscal year or the average of the last three years

Profitability
- Proven record of profitability for a minimum of three years

Balance Sheet
- Relatively low debt/equity ratio

Price
- Purchase price that represents a realistic relationship to demonstrated profit performance

Location
- Anywhere in the United States

Equity Features
- Always required
- Percentage negotiable, never control

Preferred Size of Investment
- $1.0 million to $10.0 million

Purpose of Investments
- Leveraged buyouts
- Divestitures of subsidiaries and divisions
- Leveraged ESOP
- Growing companies

Types of Securities
- Private placements of
  - Subordinated debentures with common stock
  - Subordinated debentures with warrants
  - Preferred stock with common stock
  - Preferred stock with warrants

Types of Financing
- Sole investor/leader
- Lead with participants
- Participant, with another investor leading

continued

C1.4 *concluded*

Amortization/Redemption Schedules	• Breaking even or unprofitable operations
• 5–10 years	• Real estate
Board of Directors Participation	• Commodity businesses with little or no control over pricing
• Attend board meeting as observer and/or have the right to sit on the board	• Highly capital-intensive businesses that must reinvest most of their cash flow in plant and equipment or working capital to remain competitive
Businesses Not Favored	
• Start-ups	
• Turnarounds	

Source: Venture Capital Group, Bankers Trust Company, New York, N. Y.

Most venture capitalists look for established industry niches to fund. Because they expect to see sound management practices, it is rare to see a venture funded that has limited management expertise. Mergers and acquisitions expert Robert Ouriel believes that venture capitalists look at three things: management, management, and management.

A summary of characteristics of entrepreneurs, as proposed by various authors since the mid-1800s, is given in Exhibit C1.6. Miner has developed a comprehensive theory of entrepreneurial achievement having at its root McClelland's[4] psychological theory of nAch. Miner's theory specifies five role characteristics and their related motivational patterns.[5] These relationships are summarized as follows:

- Achievement orientation: a desire to achieve through one's own efforts
- Personal risk: a desire to take moderate risks
- Feedback: a desire for some clear index of the level of performance
- Personal innovation: a desire to introduce novel, creative, or innovative solutions
- Planning: a desire to think about the future and anticipate future possibilities

A study of technologically innovative entrepreneurs found that these characteristics or motives were relatively strong among more successful entrepreneurs.[6] Entrepreneurs who owned and managed small high-growth electronic firms were found to possess these characteristics as well as sophisticated business plans.[7]

These studies and others lead us to believe that many entrepreneurs are doomed because of

EXHIBIT C1.5
Sources of Capital for Entrepreneurs
Starting Businesses Previously Nonexistent

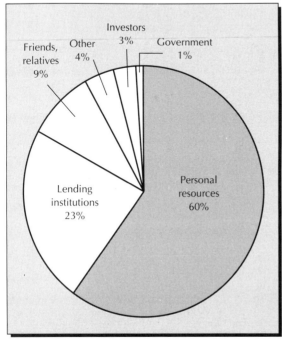

Source: National Federation of Independent Business.

EXHIBIT   C1.6   Characteristics of Entrepreneurs

Date	Author(s)	Characteristic(s)	Normative	Empirical
1848	Mill	Riskbearing	x	
1917	Weber	Source of formal authority	x	
1934	Schumpeter	Innovation, initiative	x	
1954	Sutton	Desire for responsibility	x	
1959	Hartman	Source of formal authority	x	
1961	McClelland	Risk taking, need for achievement		x
1963	Davids	Ambition, desire for independence, responsibility, self-confidence		x
1964	Pickle	Drive/mental; human relations; communication ability; technical knowledge		x
1971	Palmer	Risk measurement		x
1971	Hornaday & Aboud	Need for achievement, autonomy, aggression, power, recognition; innovative/independent		x
1973	Winter	Need for power	x	
1974	Borland	Internal locus of control		x
1974	Liles	Need for achievement		x
1977	Gasse	Personal value orientation		x
1978	Timmons	Drive/self-confidence, goal oriented, moderate risk taker, internal locus of control, creativity/innovation	x	x
1980	Sexton	Energetic/ambitious, positive setbacks		x
1981	Welsh & White	Need to control, responsibility seeker, self-confidence/drive, challenge taker, moderate risk taker		x
1982	Dunkelberg & Cooper	Growth oriented, independence oriented, craftsman oriented		x

Source: J. W. Carland, et al., "Differentiating Entrepreneurs from Small Buess Owners: A Conceptualization," *Academy of Management Review* 9 (no. 2, 1984), 356.

a lack of drive and achievement. Barbato and Bracker (1988) studied dislocated (laid off) workers who desired to start their own businesses.[8] Even though they had been in sophisticated positions in large firms, they failed to produce sophisticated business plans for their potential companies after a twelve-week training program. Further investigation also found them lacking in many of the motivational areas described by Miner. Therefore, there is a distinct difference between small business owners and

entrepreneurs. Entrepreneurship reflects a constellation of characteristics and behaviors, and these vary among all individuals, including small business owners.

Smith identified two types of entrepreneur: opportunist and craftsman.[9] According to his typology, the opportunist reflects an individual who reacts to a broad range of culture, exhibits breadth in education and training, and possesses a high level of social awareness, involvement, flexibility, confidence, and awareness of and orientation toward the future. The craftsman reflects the opposite on each dimension.

Smith's types are consistent with the literature.[10] In general these typologies suggest that individuals who tend toward the craftsman orientation are motivated to do what they want to do, meet their personal and family needs, and avoid working for others. The opportunistic or managerial types are motivated by a desire to achieve economic gain and build an organization. This motivation is consistent with the goals of venture capital firms with regard to funding and represents the ability to build an organization that will return a significantly higher rate of return than a typical security investment.

Based on our knowledge of venture capital firm funding, it seems clear that the business plan developed by the true entrepreneur plays a critical role not only in the success of the firm but in the acquisition of funds to start the firm. Numerous papers and books detail the structure of the plan. At a minimum the plan should contain fundamental objectives, description of the company, the products, processes or services, the market, the competition, production and distribution, management, key business advisors, organizational chart, and projected financial information. Central to the plan is a section on how investors will see a return on their investment. The following is taken from a typical business plan:

> The company intends to go public in three to five years. If the company does not go public within that time, investors may realize a return on their investment from either a purchase of the company by a larger health care company, or the exchange of ownership through a pay-out schedule.[11]

The key to investment besides strong management is the construction and presentation of sound financial figures. The accounting firm of Deloitte, Haskins, and Sells has put together an outline of what the figures should look like. They are contained in three important sections: cash-flow forecast, income statement, and pro forma balance sheet (Exhibits C1.7, C1.8, and C1.9).

A METHOD FOR APPROACHING VENTURE CAPITALISTS

Critical to making the venture capital deal is the method of approaching the venture capitalist. Many firms take a shotgun approach and send business plans to every venture capital firm

EXHIBIT   C1.7
Cash Flow Forecast

The following format can be used to prepare the cash flow forecast:

BEGINNING CASH BALANCE
CASH RECEIPTS:
    Collection of Receivables
    Interest Income
      Total
CASH DISBURSEMENTS:
    Accounts Payable
    Payments of Other Expenses
    Income Tax Payments
      Total
NET CASH FROM (USED FOR) OPERATIONS
SALE OF STOCK
PURCHASE OF EQUIPMENT
DECREASE (INCREASE) IN FUNDS INVESTED
SHORT-TERM BORROWINGS (REPAYMENTS)
LONG-TERM BORROWINGS (REPAYMENTS)
ENDING CASH BALANCE

This format shows cash receipts and disbursements from operations separate from financing activities and capital acquisitions. It clearly shows the monthly changes in cash flow from operations and will indicate when operations will begin to generate a positive cash flow.

The financing activities are segregated. In using this format, estimate a minimum cash balance to be maintained at the end of every month and project enough borrowings to give you that minimum cash balance. Any excess cash generated during a month is used to repay debt or is invested in money market funds; any shortage of cash is made up by drawdowns of funds previously invested or by additional borrowings.

Source: Deloitte, Haskins, and Sells, *Raising Venture Capital: An Entrepreneur's Guidebook,* 1985.

mentioned in magazines such as *Inc.* or *Venture.* This approach usually brings multiple rejection letters, because the typical large firm might receive nearly a hundred plans a day to evaluate.

Venture capitalists like to have input into the firm by way of board seats. It would be quite difficult for partners of a California firm to sit on the board of a firm in Maine. Thus, logistics of travel and time prompt the new firm to look for funding in its own region.

Most cities have venture capital clubs or associations. Often a contact through the entrepreneur's legal or accounting representation will result in a presentation to these groups. Many times press releases that result in newspaper articles alert venture capitalists to a firm's needs. An example is BioSurge, Inc., in Rochester, New York. A short article about its product in The Wall Street Journal resulted in eight calls from local and regional venture capital firms.

EXHIBIT   C1.8
Income Statement

The following format can be used in preparing the income statement:

SALES
COST OF SALES:
    Material
    Labor
    Overhead
        Total
GROSS MARGIN
OPERATING EXPENSES:
    Marketing
    Research and Development
    General and Administrative
        Total
INCOME (LOSS) FROM OPERATIONS
INTEREST INCOME (EXPENSE)
INCOME (LOSS) BEFORE TAXES
TAXES ON INCOME
NET INCOME (LOSS)

To assist the potential investor in evaluating your company, include some operating statistics on the income statement. Calculate your gross margin and each major expense category as a percentage of sales. If any of these statistics are significantly different from industry averages, you should explain why.

Source: Deloitte, Haskins, and Sells, *Raising Venture Capital: An Entrepreneur's Guidebook*, 1985.

EXHIBIT   C1.9
Pro Forma Balance Sheet

The following format can be used for a pro forma balance sheet:
ASSETS:
Current Assets:
    Cash
    Investments
    Accounts Receivable
    Inventory
        Total
Property, Plant and Equipment–net
    TOTAL ASSETS
LIABILITIES AND STOCKHOLDERS' EQUITY:
Current Liabilities:
    Short-Term Debt
    Accounts Payable
    Income Taxes Payable
    Accrued Liabilities
        Total
Long-Term Debt
Stockholders' Equity:
    Preferred Stock
    Common Stock
    Retained Earnings (Deficit)
        Total
    TOTAL LIABILITIES AND STOCKHOLDERS' EQUITY

The pro forma balance sheets will help investors to evaluate your understanding of asset management.

Investors use a variety of financial statistics to assist them in evaluating companies. You should calculate these statistics and include them in your forecast. This will make the investors' evaluations easier and show them that you considered these ratios in formulating your plan.

Source: Deloitte, Haskins, and Sells, *Raising Venture Capital: An Entrepreneur's Guidebook*, 1985.

The key, though, to contacting venture capitalists is personal contacts. Rarely do cold calls or unsolicited letters produce results.

Once the venture capitalist has become interested, the firm must prepare for initial meetings at both its own office and that of the venture firm. Usually the CEO or top financial officer meets initially with the venture capitalist. This meeting is usually a check on figures, a discussion of possible forms of financial participation, and an expressed desire to examine additional information. Often this information is referred to as due diligence. Exhibit C1.10 is taken from BioSurge's due diligence package. This presents further knowledge of the company and allows the venture capitalist's staff to examine specific technical details. In the example of BioSurge, these would be its FDA documentation and the strength of its patent applications.

Up to this point the entrepreneur has not revealed any significant technical or marketing information that would have been considered confidential. The presentation of filed patents and, in the case of BioSurge, FDA documentation are crucial business secrets that must be closely controlled. The entrepreneur must make sure that the venture capitalist does not represent a competitor or potential competitor. A signed confidentiality agreement is crucial at this stage. Exhibit C1.11 provides an example of such an agreement.

What remains now are the negotiations with the venture capital firm. If this is the entrepreneur's first deal, it is important to be accompanied by legal counsel at all times. Most venture capitalists do not like to negotiate initially with attorneys, but having them present is in the best interest of the entrepreneur. However, a consulting firm can easily assist in lieu of an attorney in the early stages. One such firm is Alimansky Venture Group in New York. Exhibit C1.12 lists many of the items about which the entrepreneur needs to be knowledgeable when negotiating the deal.

EXHIBIT   C1.10
Contents Page from a Due Diligence Package

> TABLE OF CONTENTS
> Introduction to Officers/Directors
> Listing of Business Advisors
> Organizational Structure
> Corporate Resolutions/Agreements
> FDA Documentation
> Patent Applications

The final decision for the entrepreneur is the percentage of the company to give up. This is a function of economic position, experience, stage of business development, risk involved, and many additional factors. Two of the most common methods today are the sale of preferred stock or private placements. Exhibits C1.13 and C1.14 present some of the advantages and disadvantages of each method.

Ultimately the entrepreneur will determine whether the firm is successful. No amount of advisors or money can make a poor idea work. Careful attention to detail and a willingness to work long hard hours and plow revenues back into the firm are musts.

ENDNOTES

1. *Raising Venture Capital: An Entrepreneur's Guidebook* (Chicago: Deloitte, Haskins, and Sells, 1985), 72.
2. Small Business Administration, *The State of Small Business,* 1986.
3. I. C. MacMillan and P. N. Subba Narasimha, "Characteristics Distinguishing Funded from Unfunded Business Plans Evaluated by Venture Capitalists," *Strategic Management Journal* 8 (issue 6, 1987), 582–83.
4. J. B. Miner, "Limited Domain Theories of Organization Energy," in *Middle Range Theory and Study of Organizations,* ed. C. C. Tinder and L. F. Moore (Boston: Martinus Nijhoff, 1980), 279–80.

EXHIBIT   C1.11   Sample Confidentiality Agreement to Business Secrets

CONFIDENTIALITY AGREEMENT

This Agreement is made this _____ day of _____, 1988, by and between BioSurge, Inc., a Delaware corporation with a place of business of 919 Westfall Road, Rochester, New York 14618 (hereinafter referred to as "BioSurge") and _____, a _____ organized and existing under the laws of _____ and having a place of business at _____ _____ (hereinafter referred to as "Company").

WHEREAS, the parties hereto desire to discuss areas of mutual interest and benefit, including but not limited to Company investing in BioSurge; and

WHEREAS, in the course of such discussions Company desires to review and evaluate certain Confidential Information (as hereinafter defined) of BioSurge; and

WHEREAS, BioSurge is willing to disclose the Confidential Information to Company only pursuant to the terms of this Agreement;

NOW THEREFORE, in consideration of these premises and mutual covenants herein contained, the parties mutually agree as follows:

1. CONFIDENTIAL INFORMATION. The term "Confidential Information" shall include all information disclosed by BioSurge to Company, or known to Company as a consequence of the relationship between BioSurge and Company, whether in oral, written, graphic or machine-readable form including but not limited to products, plans, procedures, prototypes, clients, trade secrets, patents, copyrights, business information, financial information, ideas and data, including information relating to research, development, manufacturing, purchasing, pricing, selling and marketing. Confidential Information shall not include any information that was known to Company and documented in its files or was in the public domain, publicly known or readily available to the trade or public prior to the date of disclosure by BioSurge, and which is made known by Company to BioSurge with ten (10) days of such disclosure.

2. NON-DISCLOSURE COVENANT. Company agrees that the Confidential Information shall at all times remain property of BioSurge, and that it shall not use the Confidential Information for its own benefit or the benefit of any third party or disclose the Confidential Information to any third party without prior written consent by BioSurge.

3. PROTECTION OF CONFIDENTIAL INFORMATION. Company agrees to use all reasonable means, not less than those employed by Company to preserve and safeguard its own confidential information to maintain the Confidential Information secret and confidential. The Confidential Information shall not be disclosed or revealed to anyone except employees of Company who have a need to know the information and who have entered into a secrecy agreement with Company under which such employees are required to keep confidential the proprietary information of Company, and such employees shall be advised by Company of the confidential nature of the information and that the information shall be treated accordingly. Company shall be responsible for any use or disclosure of the Confidential Information by any of its employees or agents.

4. RETURN OF CONFIDENTIAL INFORMATION. Upon termination of discussions between the parties, or upon request of BioSurge, Company shall immediately return to BioSurge (or at BioSurge's request, destroy) all Confidential Information, including any copies thereof.

5. REPRESENTATION. Company warrants and represents that it is not currently an affiliate of or a substantial investor (with 5% or more equity or voting interest) in an entity whose products are substantially similar to or competitive with BioSurge's proposed products and will immediately inform BioSurge of any such affiliation or interest.

continued

6. EQUITABLE RELIEF. The parties hereto agree that monetary damages shall be insufficient to fully compensate BioSurge for its losses in the event Company violates the provisions of this Agreement. In addition to seeking monetary damages, BioSurge therefore shall be entitled to enjoin Company from violating or continuing to violate the provisions of this Agreement, and Company shall not raise as a defense to any action or proceeding for any injunction the claim that BioSurge would be adequately compensated by monetary damages.

7. TERM. This agreement shall remain in full force and effect both during discussions between the parties and thereafter, whether or not Company actually invests in BioSurge.

8. MISCELLANEOUS.

8.1 *Severability.* If any part, term or provision of this Agreement shall be held unenforceable, the validity of the remaining portions or provisions shall not be affected thereby.

8.2 *Modification.* This Agreement shall not be modified or terminated except in writing signed by both parties.

8.3 *Governing Law.* This Agreement shall be governed by and construed in accordance with the laws of the State of New York.

IN WITNESS WHEREOF, the parties hereto have executed this Agreement as of the day and year first above written.

> BIOSURGE, INC.
>
> By: _____
>
> Name: _____
>
> Title: _____
>
> COMPANY
>
> By: _____
>
> Name _____
>
> Title: _____

Endnotes Concluded:

5. Miner, "Limited Domain Theories," 334–36.

6. N. R. Smith, J. S. Bracker, and J. B. Miner, "Correlates of Firm and Entrepreneur Success in Technologically Innovative Companies," *Frontiers of Entrepreneurship Research* 7, 337–53.

7. J. S. Bracker, et al., "Task Motivation, Planning Orientation, and Firm Performance" (Paper presented at the National Academy of Management Meeting, Anaheim, Calif., 1988).

8. R. Barbato and J. S. Bracker, "Dislocation and Potential Entrepreneurship," in *Proceedings,* Santa Barbara Institute Directors Association National Meeting (San Francisco: 1988).

9. N. R. Smith, "The Entrepreneur and His Firm: The Relationship between Type of Man and Type of Company," Michigan State University, East Lansing, Mich., 1967.

10. See J. W. Carland, et al., "Differentiating Entrepreneurs from Small Business Owners: A Conceptualization," *Academy of Management Review* 9 (no. 1, 1984), 356; M. C. Casson, *The Entrepreneur* (Oxford, England: Martin Robertson, 1982); and A. C. Filley and R. J. Aldag, "Characteristics and Measurement of an Organizational Typology," *Academy of Management Journal* 21 (1978), 578–91.

11. Biosurge, Inc., business plan, 1987.

EXHIBIT   C1.12   Venture Capital Negotiation Checklist

1. Amount of financing
2. Type of security (e.g., convertible preferred)
3. Price (possibly including performance-based securities)
4. Prefinancing valuation
5. Purchasers
6. Exchange of debt securities
7. Dividend provisions (e.g., preference)
8. Liquidation preference
9. Rights upon merger or consolidation
10. Conversion rights (if applicable)
11. Rights upon a public offering (e.g., automatic conversion, payment of accrued dividends)
12. Antidilution provisions (e.g., stock splits, stock dividends, new stock issued at a purchase price less than the conversion price for this round)
13. Option to require the company to repurchase all or part of the securities issued
14. Voting rights (e.g., preferred stock)
15. Protective provisions (e.g., consent of 50 percent of holders of new securities required for change in rights)
16. Information rights (e.g., monthly financial statements, annual operating plan, board seat, etc.)
17. Registration rights (e.g., demand registration, "piggyback" registration, S-3 rights, registration expenses, transfer of rights, standoff provisions within 90 days, etc.)
18. Right of first refusal to purchase pro rata any new shares
19. Key man insurance
20. Market standoff agreement (e.g., for 90 days)
21. Employee matters:
    A. Vesting of stock granted to new employees
    B. Proprietary information
    C. Reserved employee shares
    D. Employment contracts
22. Amendments to rights of existing stockholders
23. Conditions to financing (e.g., legal documentation, due diligence, etc.)
24. Investment banking agreement with [our company]
25. Legal fees and expenses to investor's attorney
26. Approval of accounting firm
27. Shareholders agreement
28. Representations and warranties

Source: Alimansky Venture Group Inc., New York, N.Y., 1988.

E X H I B I T   C1.13   Obtaining Capital through the Sale of Preferred Stock

Advantages

1. Failure to meet offering terms will not result in bankruptcy.
2. The cost of raising capital is about 30 percent less when preferred is issued instead of secondary common stock.
3. Borrowing reserve and financial insurance are preserved.
4. Preferred carries no maturity unless investors require a sinking fund to guarantee the annual buy-back of a certain number of outstanding shares.
5. If the financial condition of the company is strong, the quality of the common shares is undiminished, and debt ratios are not altered by a preferred offering.

Disadvantages

1. In order to guarantee buy-back of a certain number of shares outstanding every year, the company may have to either establish a sinking fund from available cash or reissue new shares of preferred to finance the buy-back.
2. If the offering terms are too restrictive in order to satisfy investors, the offering may limit future unsecured borrowing or other long-term debt financing.
3. The quality of common shares may diminish during bad economic times if too much preferred is issued.
4. Management must pay ongoing costs to keep the preferred offering in registration.

Source: J. Lindsay, *The Entrepreneur's Guide to Capital: The Techniques for Capitalizing and Refinancing New and Growing Businesses* (Chicago: Probus Publishing, 1986), 45.

E X H I B I T   C1.14   Obtaining Capital from Private Investors

Advantages

1. Management can avoid some or all of the time-consuming SEC registration/disclosure requirements of public ownership.
2. Management can raise capital in less time and at slightly less cost by not going public.
3. Friends, employees, and associates can acquire private company stock at a more beneficial price with a private offering.
4. More control is retained by company founders/owners/management by remaining private with an exempt offering.

Disadvantages

1. Regulation D limits the number and qualification of private investors, as well as the amount raised, in some offerings.
2. Resale of private shares is restricted, and lack of a public market creates other obvious resale constraints.
3. Private companies do not receive as much media and analyst attention as public entities do.
4. Share price may be lower because of limitations on the number of purchasers and on resale of shares.
5. Private companies cannot apply for NASDAQ or stock exchange listing.

Source: J. Lindsay, *The Entrepreneur's Guide to Capital: The Techniques for Capitalizing and Refinancing New and Growing Businesses* (Chicago: Probus Publishing, 1986), 54–55.

Applied CAD Knowledge, Inc.: The "Boom/Splat" Syndrome

John A. Seeger
Bentley College

Raymond M. Kinnunen
Northeastern University

Something is seriously wrong with this planet. Look at us. I'm working a hundred and twenty hours a week or more and not catching up. I've got these two friends—both recently divorced, like me—who aren't working at all: they're living off their girl friends, and loving it. One of them is basking in Hawaii. But here I am, busting my ass and giving my customers problems anyhow.

Some guys go on television and say, "Send money now," and people *do*. I ask my best customer to send $30,000, and he goes bankrupt instead. What's wrong with this picture?

Jeff Stevens, president and 90-percent owner of Applied CAD Knowledge, Inc., was reporting on current sales and production levels to the two business school professors who made up his board of directors. It was late August of 1987, and the three men sat in a booth at Bogie's restaurant. The waitress, Patty, was accustomed

to these monthly meetings; she offered another round of Lite beer. "Make mine cyanide," said Stevens. "On the rocks, please."

Applied CAD, a small service bureau that designed electronic circuit boards, was experiencing the highest sales levels in its three-year history. June sales had reached $50,000—leaving a backlog of $90,000; July shipments had set a record at $58,000; August would be nearly as high. The problem facing Stevens through the summer of 1987 was a shortage of good designers to work as part-time freelancers. The surge in business saw Stevens sitting at the computer consoles himself, doing design work on second and third shifts, six or seven days a week. After eight weeks of this schedule, the strain was showing. One director asked about the longer-range sales picture, and Stevens summed it up:

> There's nothing on the books at all for late Fall, and not much likely. Every major customer we have is in "busy phase" right now. When these designs are finished, it will be another four to six months before their next generation of product revisions. In the meantime, everybody is burned out. All I'm hoping for right now is a front porch, a rocking chair, a lobotomy, and a drool cup.

THE ELECTRONICS INDUSTRY AND CIRCUIT BOARD DESIGN

The United States electronics industry in 1987 was a sprawling giant, some of whose sectors were growing while others remained in a protracted slump. In 1986 total industry size was variously estimated as $100 billion to $182 billion.

A basic part of nearly every electronic product was the printed circuit board (PCB), to which a variety of electronic components were attached. These components ranged from old-fashioned resistors and capacitors to transistors and the most modern integrated circuit chips. All components needed some sort of platform to sit on and some way to make connection with other components.

In the 1930s and '40s, circuit boards were made from thin, nonconducting fiberboard with metal pins and sockets attached. Assembly operators wound the wire leads of the circuit's resistors, capacitors, etc., around the proper pins and soldered them in place. By the 1960s this technology had become highly automated. Numerically controlled machines positioned the components and connected the pins to one another with wires. By the 1980s both the pins and the wires had disappeared, replaced by electrically conductive lines that are "printed," or plated, onto (or under) the surface of the board itself. Wire leads from electrical components are inserted through small holes in the board and soldered on the underside.

The increasing complexity of electronic circuits presented a problem for PCB technology. When connections were made with wires, assemblers simply attached one end, routed the wire over the top of everything between the two pins involved, and attached the other end where it belonged. With printed circuits, however, designers are constrained to two dimensions on a flat board; they must route the line between two pins without touching any other lines. Furthermore, efficient design calls for the components to be tightly packed together, grouped by function. Designers frequently find situations where they cannot lay out a trace from one point to another without interfering with other traces.

"Multilayer" PCBs ease this problem by providing "upstairs" layers on the board, allowing the designer to "go over the top." Multilayer boards contain at least three layers of traces, and sometimes more than twenty layers. Skilled designers seek to minimize the number of layers required for a given circuit, in order to reduce manufacturing costs: multilayer PCBs are far more expensive to manufacture.

Board design was made more complicated by increasing density of components, by sensitivity of components to heat (some threw off large amounts of heat, while others would go haywire if their operating temperature was disturbed), and by radio-frequency interference (some components generated static, while others might "hear" the noise and try to process it). The layout of components on the board had tremendous impact on how well the finished product worked, as well as on its manufacturing cost.

In 1983, according to *Electronic Business* magazine, multilayer boards had sales of $900 million, or 25 percent of the PCB market. By 1993 multilayer boards were forecast to reach sales of $5.6 billion, or 41 percent market share. Exhibit C2.1 shows PCB sales and projections by type of board.

Frost and Sullivan, Inc., a New York market research firm, estimated in 1986 that the total U.S. PCB market reached $3.7 billion in sales in 1985, a decrease of 12 percent from 1984's production. PCBs were projected to grow to a likely $6.5 billion by 1990 and to $10.8 billion in 1995. Multilayer PCBs were expected to be the fastest-growing type, averaging 15.7 percent per year annual growth. A little over half the market was served in 1985 by independent PCB fabricators, as opposed to captive suppliers, Frost & Sullivan said.[1]

TRENDS IN CIRCUIT BOARD DESIGN EQUIPMENT

Originally (and still, for simple circuits) an engineer or technician worked from a "schematic" drawing of the circuit, which showed how the various components were connected. On a large layout table the PCB designer manually drew in the components and linked them with black tape (or ink) to produce a "photo master" film, which was in turn used to manufacture the circuit board. As circuits became more complex, the manual process bogged down.

By the mid 1970s computer-aided design (CAD) vendors began to offer computer systems specifically for PCB designing. Racal-Redac, Inc., a British firm, was the first to offer a system that permitted PCB designers to interact with the computer, trying various routings of traces to see how they looked on the graphic display. This approach, based on the moderate-price DEC PDP-11, competed well against established CAD systems such as those made by Gerber Scientific or Computervision, whose equipment was priced in the $500,000 class and still lacked interactive design capability.

By 1982 prices for PCB design systems had fallen below $100,000. New CAD equipment makers entered the field with automated routing or documentation features that carried substantial advantages over the established Redac software. Calay and Cadnetix, as examples, introduced strong entries—neither being compatible with the Redac, Sci-Cards, or Telesis equipment already in the field. Racal-Redac Ltd. had perhaps taken the greatest strides to tailor its software to run on a variety of computers. Said Ian Orrock, chief executive of Redac's CAD division in England, "We're all going to end up being software houses."

Another important feature of the new CAD equipment was ease of use; the older systems might require months of learning time before a designer became proficient.

SERVICE BUREAU OPERATIONS

In the late 1970s, with high equipment costs and low availability of trained designers, only the largest electronics firms designed and produced their own PCBs. Service bureaus took advantage of the market opportunity, acting as the primary design resource for smaller clients and as peak load designers for firms with in-house capacity. These small service firms specialized in design, working for electronics companies in the same way an architect works for real estate developers. (Exhibit C2.2 shows the relationship between firms in the PCB production process.)

When the design phase of a job was finished, the computer tape or disk containing the final output would be carried to a photoplotting service bureau for creation of the precision film needed for manufacturing. The equipment for photoplotting was far more complex and expensive than the computer systems needed for design. Only a few design shops in the New England area had their own photoplotting capability; they performed this work for other service bureaus and for electronics firms' in-house design departments as well as for their own design clients.

The actual production of PCBs might be done by the electronics company itself or by a fabrication shop that specialized in the work. The New England area was home to some

EXHIBIT C2.1   Sales and Projections for PCBs by Type of Board

PCB Type	1983		Annual Growth Rate, Percent	1993	
	Sales, in $ Millions	Market Share, Percent		Sales, in $ Millions	Market Share, Percent
Multilayer	900	25	20	5,600	41
Double-sided	2,000	56	13	6,700	49
Flexible	353	10	10	916	7
Single-sided	307	9	4	454	3
	3,560	100		13,670	100

Source: *Electronic Business* (Feb. 1, 1985), 87.

eighty to one hundred fab shops, many of which offered design as well as manufacturing services. A few large firms (Hadco, at $125 million in sales) were equipped to service very large orders—100,000 or more boards of a design—but most fab shops fell in the $1 million to $2 million size range, with an average order size of 25 to 30 relatively small boards. One such fabricator estimated its average low-tech PCB was priced at $22 each, with a setup charge of $150. For the most difficult boards, in small quantities with rigid testing requirements, Applied CAD's customers might pay as much as $1,000 each for fabrication.

As electronics firms purchased and began to use the newer CAD systems, they wanted service bureaus to be equipped with similar or compatible machines. A firm with its own Telesis equipment, for example, would favor Telesis-equipped service bureaus for its overload work. Service bureaus felt the pressure to acquire the most up-to-date hardware and software available, in order to qualify as bidders.

When a service bureau invested in CAD equipment, the sheer size of the investment cre-ated pressure to use the equipment intensively. Multishift operations were common, but the supply of designers to staff them was severely limited. Typically a service bureau did not hire permanent staff for all three shifts: the work load was too unpredictable. Service bureaus generally hired moonlighting designers from established electronics firms to staff their second and third shifts.

Printed circuit board design requires a pecu-liar combination of human skills, primarily in spatial geometry, circuit insight, memory, and persistence. A talented designer—perhaps capa-ble of completing a complex design in three weeks of console time—might be several times more productive than a "journeyman." In the early 1980s talented designers willing to work odd shifts were earning over $100,000 per year; few of them had college educations.

Most customers requested separate quo-tations for each board; often customers asked for bids from several service bureaus. Design clients always ran on tight schedules, Jeff Stevens observed, wanting their work to be delivered "yesterday":

EXHIBIT   C2.2   Work Flow Between Firms in Production of Printed Circuit Boards

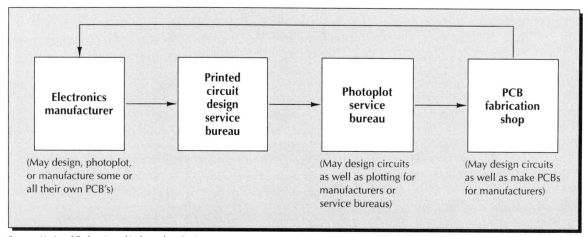

Source: National Federation of Independent Business.

Circuit board design is usually one of the last steps before a new product goes into production. Our design time may be the customer's time-to-market. It's natural for them to be in a hurry.

For the design of a large, complex, four-layered PCB a client might pay between $10,000 and $15,000. Such a project might require five to six man weeks of labor input (two-thirds of which might be designer's time); it might involve extensive communication between Applied CAD and a wide variety of the client's technical personnel, and it would often require the designer to work through the night at various project stages to make deadlines. Much of the time would be spent sorting out and coordinating conflicting information and directions from different technical people in the client company. Stevens noted,

> Even our clients themselves won't always know completely what they want. When we take their directions to their logical conclusions, problems often occur. Then we have to show them what developed. You spend a lot of time on the phone with clients, sometimes at 3 a.m. Often I make decisions for the client, so the work can go ahead; later I have to convince the client the decision was right.

Clients were inclined to stay with their existing service bureaus, unless they were severely burned. Good relationships between service staff and engineering personnel helped minimize communication errors, and availability of the data base from the original job allowed for revisions or modifications at much lower cost. Design reliability remained a key attribute of a service bureau's reputation, since whole product lines (or engineers' jobs) might depend on the PCB design's working properly and on its prompt delivery:

> We had one job, in the old days, where a satellite was literally sitting on the launch pad, waiting for a corrected module design. The engineers had discovered a design flaw. They flew into town

with the specs and then took turns sitting behind the designer at the scope or sitting beside their hotel room telephone, waiting to answer any questions that might come up. In this business, you have to deliver.

FUTURE TRENDS IN PCB DESIGN

By the end of 1986, a number of vendors had developed PCB design packages to run on personal computers—primarily the IBM XT or AT machines. These software systems, some including automatic routing, were priced as low as a few hundred dollars or as high as $13,000 and varied widely in their features and capabilities. In-house design capability thus became practical for most electronics firms, although many lacked the PCB expertise that still marked the better service bureaus. Freelance designers, too, could now acquire their own equipment. Exhibit C2.3 compares the features and prices of twenty-four such software packages.

In the 1980s, as the cost of entering the service bureau business dropped, many new firms appeared. Jeff Stevens observed, "When I started at Redac in 1978, there were three service bureaus in New England. By 1983 there were maybe a dozen. Now there might be seventy-five, and it could reach one hundred in another year." In 1987 several competing service bureaus in the area were owned by former employees of Racal-Redac, where Jeff himself had learned the business. Exhibit C2.4 lists the major competitors in the Northeastern United States in 1986. The small firms in this listing were design specialists like Applied CAD, Stevens noted; the larger firms all supplied finished boards to their customers.

For the longer run some industry analysts speculated that constant advances in miniaturizing electronic circuits might permit semiconductor technology to reduce certain whole PCBs (such as those developed for computer memory) into a single integrated circuit chip.

EXHIBIT   C2.3   Low-Cost PC Board Design Software Available, Spring 1987

Company	Product	Base Price	Required Hardware	Operating System	Auto-Router	Auto-Router Price
Abacus Software	PCBOARD Designer	$ 195	Atari 520ST or 1040ST	GEM	•	
Accel Technologies	TANGO-PCB	$ 495	IBM PC/XT or PC/AT	MS-DOS	•	$5000
APTOS Systems	Criterion II	$ 4000	Artist 1 Card and IBM PC/XT or PC/AT	MS-DOS	•	
Automated Images	Personal 870	$ 8000	IBM PC/XT or PC/AT	MS-DOS		
B&C Microsystems	PCB/DE	$ 395	IBM PC/XT or PC/AT	MS-DOS (and the AUTOCAD Drafting Package)		
CAD Software	PADS-PCS	$ 875	IBM PC/XT or PC/AT	MS-DOS	•	$ 750
CASE Technology	Vanguard PCB	$ 4250	IBM PC/AT, SUN-3, or DEC MICROVAX	MS-DOS, UNIX, or VMS	•	$5500
Daisy Systems	Personal Boardmaster	$ 8000	IBM PC/AT or Daisy PL306	DNIX		
DASOFT Design	Project: PCB	$ 950	IBM PC/XT or PC/AT	MS-DOS	•	
Design Computation	Draftsman-EE	$ 1147	IBM PC/XT or PC/AT	MS-DOS	•	$2450
Douglas Electronics	Douglas CAD/CAM	$ 395	Apple Macintosh	Macintosh		
Electronic Design Tools	PROCAD	$ 2495	IBM PC/XT or PC/AT and 68000 Coprocessor	MS-DOS	•	$2496
Electronic Industrial Equipment	Executive CAD	$11,000	IBM PC/XT or PC/AT	MS-DOS	•	
Futurenet	DASH-PCB	$13,000	IBM PC/AT and 32032 Coprocessor	UNIX	•	
Hewlett-Packard	EGS	$ 7000	HP 9000	HP-UX		
KONTRON	KAD-286	$10,400	IBM PC/AT	MS-DOS		
Personal CAD Systems	PCB-1	$ 6000	IBM PC/XT or PC/AT	MS-DOS	•	$6000
Racal-Redac	Redboard	$12,000	IBM PC/XT or PC/AT	MS-DOS	•	
SEETRAX (In U. S., Circuits and Systems)	Ranger	$ 5000	IBM PC/AT	MS-DOS	•	$2000
Softcircuits	PCLOPLUS	$ 1024	Commodore Amiga 1000	AmigaDOS	•	
VAMP	McCAD	$ 396	Apple Macintosh	Macintosh	•	$ 995
Visionics	EE Designer II	$ 1875	IBM PC/XT or PC/AT	MS-DOS	•	$1476
Wintek	Smartwork	$ 895	IBM PC/XT or PC/AT	MS-DOS	•	
Ziegler Instruments (in U. S., CADDY)	CADDY Electronic System	$ 2495	IBM PC/XT or PC/AT	MS-DOS	•	$2500

Company	Auto-Placement	Compatible Net Lists	Maximum Number of Colors	Maximum Number of Traces	Maximum Number of Components	Maximum Number of Layers	Packaging Technologies
Abacus Software			2	1100 lines	250	2	
Accel Technologies	•	Accel, Omation, ORCAD	16	26,000 lines	1000	9	SMD
APTOS Systems		APTOS, Futurenet, P-CAD	16	2000 nets	1000	50	SMD, ECL, Analog
Automated Images		Applicon, Futurenet, ORCAD	16			16	SMD, Hybrid
B&C Microsystems		B&C	16				
CAD Software	•	Futurenet	16	4511 nets	764	30	SMD, FINE-LINE
CASE Technology	•	CASE	16	2000 nets	1000	256	SMD
Daisy Systems		Daisy	7	14,000 lines	14,000	255	SMD
DASOFT Design		DASOFT	6			4	SMD
Design Computation	•		16	4000 nets	300	20	FINE-LINE
Douglas Electronics			2				SMD, Analog
Electronic Design Tools	•	Electronic Design Tools	16	10,000 nets	3000	56	SMD, Constant-Impedance
Electronic Industrial Equipment	•	Electronic Industrial Equipment	16			4	SMD, ECL
Futurenet		Futurenet	4			10	FINE-LINE
Hewlett-Packard		HP	15			255	Hybrid
KONTRON		Kontron	64	5300 lines	3200	255	ECL, SMD, Hybrid
Personal CAD Systems	•	P-CAD, Futurenet	16	1000 nets	300	50	SMD
Racal-Redac	•	Racal-Redac	16	1900 nets	511	16	SMD
SEETRAX (In U. S., Circuits and Systems)	•	Seetrax	16	10,000 lines	1400	16	SMD
Softcircuits			16				
VAMP	•	VAMP	2	32,000 lines	32,000	6	SMD, Metric
Visionics	•		16		999	26	SMD
Wintek		Wintek	3			6	
Ziegler Instruments (in U. S., CADDY)		Ziegler	16			128	Analog

Source: *EDN*, March 18, 1987, pp 140–41. Used by permission.

EXHIBIT   C2.4   PC Design Service Bureaus in New England,
by Annual Sales Volume

Less Than $1 Million	$1 Million–$2 Million
Abington Labs	Automated Images, Inc.
Berkshire Design	Automated Design, Inc.
CAD TEC	CAD Services, Inc.
Cadtronix, Ltd.	Antal Associates
Computer Aided Circuits, Inc.	Multiwire of New England
Dataline PCB Corp.	Teccon
Design Services	Tech Systems & Design
Energraphics	Kenex, Inc.
Graphics Technology Corp.	Alternate Circuit Design Technology
Herbertons, Inc.	Photofabrication Technology Inc.
HET Printed Circuit Design	
High Tech CAD Service Co.	**$2 Million–$5 Million**
Jette Fabrication	TEK-ART Associates
LSI Engineering	Stratco Reprographix
P C Design Company	Altek Co.
PAC-LAB, Inc.	Eastern Electronics Mfg. Corp.
Packaging for Electronics	Datacube, Inc.
PC Design Services	Owl Electronic Laboratories
Point Design, Inc.	
Power Processing, Inc.	**$5 Million–$10 Million**
Product Development Co.	Triad Engineering Co.
Qualitron Corp.	Photronic Labs, Inc.
Quality Circuit Design, Inc.	
Research Labs, Inc.	**More Than $10 Million**
Scientific Calculations, Inc.	Algorex Corp.
Tracor Electro-Assembly, Inc.	ASI Automated Systems, Inc.
Winter Design	Augat Interconnection Group
	Racal-Redac Service Bureau
	Synermation, Inc.

Source: Beacon Technology, "New England Printed Circuit Directory." Copyright © 1985. Reprinted by permission.

APPLIED CAD KNOWLEDGE, INC.: HISTORY

Jeff Stevens had learned the rudiments of circuit board design in his first job after high school graduation, as a technician in a five-person product development laboratory. Here, in 1975, one of his duties was to prepare enlarged prints of circuits, using black tape on white mylar. In another, concurrent job as a technician in an electronics manufacturing firm, he learned how the circuits themselves worked.

In 1977 Stevens left his two technician jobs for an entry-level design position with Racal-Redac in Littleton, Massachusetts. Redac operated a service bureau to complement its sales of DEC hardware and British software. As a pioneer in the field, Redac at the time boasted a near-monopoly in powerful systems dedicated to PCB design. Jeff Stevens, in a training rotation, joined Redac's service bureau as a data entry technician.

We had three computer systems—about 20 people altogether. A system then cost about

$200,000, and a lot of companies didn't have enough design work to justify buying one.

In data entry you prepare code to represent all the terminals and components on the board. I refused to code the first job they gave me and nearly got fired. Finally I convinced them that the job *shouldn't* be coded: the turkey who engineered it had the diodes in backward, and the circuit wasn't going to work. About a week later they put me in charge of data entry, supervising the guy who had wanted to fire me.

Stevens became a designer, then a lead designer, then operations manager of the service bureau. Under his leadership, the operation dramatically improved its reputation for quality and on-time delivery, as well as its financial performance:

> When I took over in October of 1981, monthly sales were $50,000 and monthly expenses were $110,000. In six months we turned it around: monthly sales were $110,000 and expenses were $50,000. There was a tremendous amount of dead wood. We had a big bonfire with it, and went from 26 people to 16. In some ways it was a brutal campaign, I guess.

In June 1983 Stevens left Racal-Redac to work as a consulting designer, helping electronics firms with their CAD decisions as well as doing freelance design work. He had developed design and management expertise and established a reputation in industry circles, which he could now broker directly to clients who were familiar with his previous work.

In December 1983 Jeff established Applied CAD while still working from his home in Pepperell, Massachusetts. By purchasing used computer equipment and installing it himself in his living room, Stevens was able to hold his initial investment to $35,000; the largest cost element was $28,000 for the software purchased from his former employer. (Financial data on Applied CAD's latest three years of operation are shown in Exhibit C2.5.)

The equipment pretty well filled up the living room, and through the summer I couldn't run it during the daytime: we didn't have enough electricity to cool it down. Winter solved that problem, though; the PDP-11 heated the house.

Jeff had sought the help of a business school professor who lived in Littleton, to negotiate the purchase of software from his former employer. That professor and another one, also from a well-known Boston area school, purchased small stock interests as Applied CAD was incorporated and became members of the board of directors. By the Fall of 1985 the board met monthly for three to four hours, usually during the first week of the month. At most meetings the board first discussed the previous month's sales and current levels of cash, accounts receivable, backlog, and payables. (Exhibit C2.6 shows the data recorded in these talks.) Other typical agenda items ranged from the purchase of new equipment and/or software, to marketing, to personnel problems and bank relationships.

In late 1984 Applied CAD leased a 1,000-square-foot office suite on the ground floor of a new building near the Merrimack River in Tyngsboro, Massachusetts. Jeff Stevens designed the interior space to hold a central computer room (with special air conditioning), a darkened "console room" for the actual design work, and a large front office. By January of 1985 the computing equipment was installed and operating. The console room was furnished with two Recaro ergonometric chairs (at $1,100 each) for the designers' use; the front office held a large receptionist's desk and a sparse collection of work tables, file cabinets, and spare hardware.

HARDWARE AND SOFTWARE

After moving into his new quarters, Jeff Stevens located another PDP-11/34 computer—this one for sale at $7,000. Adding it to his shop required the purchase of another Redac software package, but the added capacity was needed. Other, competing CAD systems were now available, but the decision to stick with Redac seemed straightforward to Jeff:

> Redac systems had several advantages. They were specifically dedicated to PCB design work, and they had software that was brutally efficient. They were familiar to most of the freelance designers in the area. Wide acceptance of Redac's software makes it easier to get overflow work from companies who demanded compatibility

with their own equipment. Not to mention that I know this gear backward and forward and could keep several machines busy at once.

The Redac software was originally developed in 1972, which made it very old by industry standards. Jeff pointed out, however, that because machines were slower in 1972 and had much less memory, their software *had* to be extremely efficient. Having used this software for a long time, he said, "I've been able to make

EXHIBIT   C2.5   Financial Statements of Applied CAD Knowledge, Inc.

BALANCE SHEET	1985	1986	1987
Assets			
Current assets:			
Cash	$128,568	$ 14,148	$ 33,074
Accounts receivable, trade	18,865	15,375	14,250
Prepaid taxes and other current assets	4,853	1,200	5,074
Total current assets	152,286	30,723	52,398
Property and equipment	174,079	190,079	203,079
Less accumulated depreciation	48,697	86,357	124,062
Total property and equipment	125,382	103,722	79,017
Total assets	$277,668	$134,445	$131,415
Liabilities and Stockholders' Equity			
Current liabilities:			
Accounts payable, trade	$127,685	$ 9,025	$ 21,823
Current maturities of long-term debt	13,300		
Income taxes payable	4,008		2,303
Other current liabilities	5,000	5,373	70
Total current liabilities	149,993	14,398	24,196
Long-term debt, less current maturities	41,121	83,247	53,663
Stockholders' equity:			
Common stock, no par value; authorized 15,000 shares, issued and outstanding 1,000 shares	25,000	25,000	25,000
Retained earnings	61,554	11,800	28,556
Total stockholders' equity	86,554	36,800	53,556
Total Liabilities and Stockholders' Equity	$277,668	$134,445	$131,415

continued

EXHIBIT   C2.5   *concluded*

STATEMENT OF INCOME AND RETAINED EARNINGS

	1985	1986	1987
Net revenues	$328,262	$232,540	$346,627
Cost of revenue:			
Salaries, wages, and outside services	134,686	116,835	209,998
Research and development	14,154	7,551	13,731
Software costs	65,131	18,864	
Total cost of revenue	$213,971	$143,250	$223,729
Gross profit	114,291	89,290	122,898
Selling, general, and administrative expenses	72,320	143,051	77,732
Operating profit	41,971	(53,761)	45,166
Bad-debt expense			(28,660)
Interest income (expense), net	2,331	3,176	(10,103)
Income before income taxes	44,302	(50,185)	6,403
Income taxes	4,508	0	0
Net income	39,794	(50,185)	6,403
Retained earnings, beginning of year	21,760	62,385	22,154
Retained earnings, end of year	$ 61,554	$ 11,800	$ 28,557

process modifications to improve its efficiency, and I know all its intricacies." Jeff had developed some proprietary software for PCB design work, which he believed kept him at the cutting edge of the competition. At times he wondered about the possibilities of licensing his proprietary software to other PCB design firms. He concluded, however, that the small market for this type of software product would probably not justify the necessary marketing and additional product development costs.

In addition to the original equipment purchased by Jeff in 1983, the company purchased a VAX Model 11/751 and a Calay Version 03 in December of 1985 at a cost of approximately $170,000. (See Exhibit C2.7 for the cash flow statements prepared for the bank to obtain a loan.) The VAX was intended to be used as a communications and networking device and for developing new software. The Calay was a dedicated hardware system that included an automatic router, which could completely design certain less complex boards without an operator. On more complex boards it could complete a major percentage of the board, leaving a designer to do the remainder. Jeff and the board felt that this automatic routing capability might open a new market for the company for less complex boards. They also felt that the manufacturer of the Calay, as well as the Calay user group, would supply new customer leads. Some of these expectations had been met.

In September of 1986 a software upgrade to the Calay was purchased for approximately $28,000. Although bank financing was available, Jeff decided to pay cash for this purchase, to avoid raising his monthly fixed expenses. The new purchases gave Applied CAD enough machine capacity to support some $2 million in annual sales.

The VAX, however, was not being fully used as originally intended—to allow hands-off automation of the firm's varied pieces of computing equipment, as well as providing batch data processing capacity. In its ultimate form the VAX might actually operate the older, more cumbersome systems. It would be able to juggle dozens of design tasks between work stations and autorouters, queuing and evaluating each job and calling for human intervention when needed. One director, visualizing robots sitting in Applied CAD's Recaro chairs, called this the "Robo-Router plan." To carry it out would require an additional investment of approximately $15,000 in hardware and another $10,000 to $20,000 in programming, along with a significant amount of Jeff's time. The investment would result in substantial cost reductions and reduced dependence on freelance designers, but it would pay for itself only under high-volume conditions.

APPLIED CAD'S ORGANIZATION

Jeff oversaw all operations in his company, did all the high-level marketing and sales contact work with clients, and did much of the technical design work as well. Another full-time designer was hired in May of 1985 but had to be terminated in September of 1986 due to persistent personal problems. Steve Jones, Jeff's data manager and former assistant at Redac, became a full-time employee in January 1986. Among other duties Steve covered the telephone, coordinated technical work done by freelance contractors in Jeff's absence, and performed various administrative duties. Steve had a B.S. in engineering and before Redac had worked for other PCB electronics companies. In April of 1987 Jeff hired John Macnamara, a former subcontract designer, on a full-time, salaried basis.

In May of 1987 Jeff also hired a part-time person to keep the books, write checks, and handle other office-related matters. For her first three months, she focused on straightening out the books and tax-related items. She was also trying to find time to set up an accounting package on the personal computer. The package had been purchased in August of 1986 (at the request of the board members), for the purpose of generating accurate monthly statements. Since the company's founding the board had been asking for accurate end-of-month data on sales, accounts receivable, cash balance, backlog, and accounts payable. They also wanted monthly financial statements, although Stevens himself saw little point in them: cash flow projections served his immediate needs. The accounting package was chosen by one of the board members, based partly on its broad capabilities. For example, it could assist in invoicing and aging receivables.

EXHIBIT   C2.6
Monthly Sales and Month-End Receivables, Backlogs, Cash Levels, $ Thousands

	A/R	Sales	Backlog	Cash
1986				
January	18	20	20	98
February	*	10	*	*
March	18	10	12	62
April	18	10	20	28
May	24	20	26	26
June	*	10	*	*
July	14	25	*	18
August	70	50	30	15
September	90	40	*	8
October	50	30	*	26
November	19	5	10	17
December	24	10	18	14
1987				
January	13	3	*	7
February	40	21	*	8
March	35	28	22	6
April	32	22	37	11
May	25	22	50	5
June	50	50	90	10
July	90	58	30	10

* Information not available.

Jeff had other capable designers on call, available for freelance project work when the company needed them. Depending on the market, there were periods when Jeff could obtain the services of several contractors to meet peak work loads. In general design contractors worked on a negotiated fixed-fee basis for completing a specific portion of a design project. In July of 1987, however (after sales in June reached approximately $50,000 and the backlog reached $90,000), Jeff found it hard to attract contract designers with free time. The backlog consisted of about fifteen boards ranging in price from $800 to $15,000. The electronics industry had turned upward, and in busy times everyone was busy. Consequently freelance designers were committed to their own customers or employers, who were also busy. Jeff attempted to fill the production gap by working as a third-shift designer.

At most of its meetings, the board of directors spent considerable time discussing the current business climate and the future sales outlook. This usually led to a discussion of hiring someone to take over the marketing and sales function. It was generally agreed that such a person could not only contribute to the company's growth in sales but also free up a considerable amount of Jeff's time that could be devoted to design and operational matters. When Applied CAD was busy, however, Jeff had very little time to devote to finding, hiring, and working with such a person. Even if one were hired, a salesperson would require Jeff's time for introductions to the present customers

EXHIBIT   C2.7   Applied CAD Knowledge, Inc.: Cash Flow Projections as of December 16, 1985 ($ Thousands)

	1985	1986												
	Dec.	Jan.	Feb.	Mar.	Apr.	May	June	July	Aug.	Sept.	Oct.	Nov.	Dec.	Total
Sales	25	30	30	30	30	30	30	30	30	30	30	30	30	360
Expenses[a]	20	24	29.5	29.5	29.5	29.5	29.5	29.5	29.5	29.5	29.5	29.5	9.5	348.5
Profit	5	6	.5	.5	.5	.5	.5	.5	.5	.5	.5	.5	.5	11.5
Opening Cash	141	148	102	102.5	88	88.5	89	89.5	90	90.5	91	91	91.5	
Receivables	37	17	30	30	30	30	30	30	30	30	30	30	30	
Disbursements[b]	30	24[c]	29.5[d]	29.5	29.5	29.5	29.5	29.5	29.5	29.5	29.5	29.5	29.5	
Taxes[e]		29[f]		15										
Closing Cash	148	102	102.5	88	88.5	89	89.5	90	90.5	91	91	91.5	92	

[a] Expenses include rent, heat, light, power, salaries, contract work, telephone, etc. This level of expenses will support sales double those projected.

[b] Figures do not include depreciation, which would only influence total profit.

[c] Includes loan payment of $4,000/month.

[d] Includes new employees at $66,000/year.

[e] Taxes based on the following assumptions: 1985 profit of $150,000; $50,000 software expense on new equipment; $20,000 depreciation on new equipment; $10,000 miscellaneous expenses; investment tax credit of $15,000.

[f] 25% of equipment costing $156,000.

and for responding to questions about new sales potentials.

When Applied CAD was *not* busy, Jeff's concern over the reliability of future cash flows made him hesitant to make the major salary commitment that a marketing professional would require. He was aware of the contrary pressures: "I can't get out of the 'boom-splat' syndrome," he said.

To Jeff the "splat" came when backlogs and cash balances fell. The winter of 1987, for example, had felt to him like hitting a wall. (See Exhibit C2.6 for monthly totals of sales, backlogs, etc., as estimated by Jeff at monthly board meetings.)

CURRENT BUSINESS OPTIONS

In August of 1987 Jeff was contemplating the current business climate, his accomplishments with Applied CAD over the past three years, and where the company was headed. His major objective—with which the board agreed—was growth. Jeff had discussed many times with his board the needs for a marketing person and a promotional brochure for the company. He hoped to attract someone with top management credentials who could work with him as a peer. On occasion he had talked with marketing people about the job, but most of these prospective employees lacked the level of skills and PCB experience Jeff knew they would need. He had also talked with commercial artists about design of a brochure. Jeff and his board felt that a "first-class" brochure would cost between $5,000 and $10,000.

Marketing in the PCB business, especially among companies with sales of under $1 million, was characterized as informal. Very few companies had full-time people devoted to the marketing task; in most cases it was the owner-president who handled marketing and sales. Most small companies had their own list of faithful customers, and new customers tended to come by word of mouth. In the under-

$1-million segment it was not uncommon for a company when extremely overloaded with work to farm out a board to a competitor. Also certain other services, such as photoplotting, were done by shops that also did design work. Consequently there was considerable communication among the competitors; the players seemed to know who got what jobs.

The marketing job at a company like Applied CAD would consist mainly of coordinating the advertising and a sales brochure, calling on current customers, and attempting to find new customers. Such a person needed a working knowledge of PCB design, which required experience in the industry. People with these qualifications normally made a base salary of $40,000 to $50,000 plus commissions; frequently their total compensation exceeded $100,000 per year. Of major concern to Jeff were Applied CAD's erratic history of sales and cash balances and the difficulty of predicting sales volume any further than two months in advance. He balked at taking on responsibility for an executive-level salary, lacking confidence in the future. "This would probably be somebody with kids to feed or send to college," Jeff said. "How could I pay them in slow times?"

Still, marketing appeared to be the function most critical to achieving the growth rates Jeff Stevens and his board hoped for. It was key, also, in meeting the major potential threat posed by the recent availability of inexpensive software that could enable personal computers (PCs) to design printed circuit boards (see Exhibit C2.3). Jeff had heard that some of that new software could perform almost as well as the more expensive equipment used by Applied CAD. He wondered how the advent of low-cost software might be turned into an opportunity, not a threat.

Four possible responses had occurred to Jeff and his board: Applied CAD could ignore the PC software, adopt it, distribute it, or sell its own software to the PC users. Ignoring the new technology might work in the short run, since the complex boards designed by Applied CAD would not be the first affected; in the long run, however, failure to keep up with technology would leave more and more jobs subject to low-cost competition.

By adopting the new software for his next equipment expansion, Applied CAD could take a proactive stance. Jeff could buy a system or two to see how good they were and hire people to work on the new systems on a freelance basis. Of course he would need a flow of jobs with which to experiment. A variation of this alternative was to sit back and wait while being ready to move quickly if he saw something developing.

A third alternative, acting as a distributor for the PC software, would give Applied CAD a product to sell to prospects who insisted on doing their own design. This could establish relationships with people who might later need overload capacity.

Fourth, Applied CAD could proceed with development of its proprietary software, creating a product to sell to PC users. Jeff estimated that his Automated Design Review System (ADRS) could save both time and grief for other designers. In some tasks it could cut the required design time in half. In all jobs the capability to check the finished design against the original input automatically and completely could improve quality. ADRS already existed in rough form; it was one of the elements that would make up the "Robo-Router" system, if that were implemented.

Many of these options seemed to require significant marketing skills—strengths—where the company was currently weak. The technical questions could be answered if Jeff had the time to work on them. But the marketing questions called for a person with extensive industry experience, broad contacts, a creative imagination, and the ability to make things happen.

Amid all the other problems facing him as the owner of a small business, Jeff was trying to figure out how to shape his business for the long-range future and how to attract the kind of person he could work with to ensure growth—and survival. He looked across the table at Bogie's restaurant, caught the eye of one director, and yawned. Tonight, after this meeting, he hoped to finish the design of a particularly complicated board. His best customer was desperate for this job.

ENDNOTE

1. Frost and Sullivan, Inc., "The Printed Circuit Board Market in the U. S.," July 1986. Quoted by permission.

Applied CAD Knowledge, Inc. (B)

Raymond M. Kinnunen
Northeastern University

John A. Seeger
Bentley College

In September of 1987, as the summer rush slowed, Jeff Stevens began to talk seriously with Jerry King, regional sales manager of Calay Systems, Inc., about the marketing problems of Applied CAD Knowledge, Inc. Stevens wanted someone to become, in effect, a co-owner and officer of the small firm. King had been a principal in his own service bureau in the very early days of automated PCB design and retained friendships and contacts with high-level personnel in many electronics firms. (Exhibit C3.1 shows King's resume.)

After a month of conversations and negotiations, including a meeting with the board of directors, the two men reached tentative agreement on employment terms that would give King a 3-percent commission on all company sales, a car allowance, and a base salary of $40,000 per year. Since the marketing person would be influential in pricing many jobs, it was important to preserve his regard for profitability; King was offered a stock interest in Applied CAD, contingent on the bottom line at the end of

1988. With a handshake of agreement, Stevens set out to reduce the terms to an employment contract letter.

The following night, Jerry King called Stevens to express his regret that he would be unable to accept the marketing vice president position afterall: he had just received an offer from AT&T, to set up Australian operations for a new venture. It was simply too good an offer to refuse, King said. A dejected Jeff Stevens reported the development at the next board meeting. "We're back to square one," he said. "And the next 'splat' is just about to arrive."

Applied CAD's monthly sales dropped to half their mid-1987 level, and the backlog dropped to near zero. On December 8, however, Jerry King called Jeff to say he had just decided against Australia and would like to apply again for the marketing VP position, if it was still open. Jeff agreed, and the next day Jerry presented to Jeff and the board a plan for reaching $1 million in sales in 1988 and for growing by $1 million per year in the following two years. (This plan is partially reproduced in Exhibit C3.2). Concerned with the timing of cash flows, one of the directors asked how long it would take to generate enough new sales to cover their added marketing expenses. King responded, "If I couldn't provide more than enough sales to cover my pay, I wouldn't take the job."

Although not officially joining Applied CAD until January 4, Jerry spent the rest of December in joint calling, with Jeff, on customers where Calay and Applied CAD shared some interests. In those first weeks, the "chemistry" Jeff Stevens had hoped for became readily apparent. The two men's skills complemented each other well: this would be a highly effective team, Stevens felt.

Jerry King

Married
Four Children
Excellent Health

EDUCATION:

FAIRLEIGH DICKINSON UNIVERSITY, Madison, New Jersey

Major: Business Administration

U.S. NAVY, Electronics "A" School, Pearl Harbor, Hawaii

CONTINUING EDUCATION, including numerous seminars and workshops in Corporate Finance, Power Base Selling, Territory Time Management, The Art of Negotiating, Computer Graphics in Electronics, Sales Management, and Marketing Techniques.

EXPERIENCE:

GENERAL BUSINESS MANAGEMENT: Establishing policies and procedures for high-volume cost-efficient business operations, planning promotions for new business development, hiring, training and supervising personnel, including management level, designing and conducting management, sales, marketing, and CAD/CAM training seminars internationally.

TECHNICAL BACKGROUND: Twenty-one years of direct Printed Circuit Design, Fabrication and Electronics CAD/CAM marketing experience. Helped to create detailed business plans for three start-up companies, including a high-volume printed circuit design service bureau, and raised five million dollars in venture capital used to purchase state-of-the-art CAD/CAM systems and other related equipment. Managed the development and marketing of a PCB Design Automation turn-key system that was sold exclusively to Calma/GE in 1977 and integrated with their GDS1 TRI-DESIGN system. Very strong market knowledge in Computer Aided Engineering (CAE), Computer Aided Design (CAD), Computer Aided Test (CAT), and Computer Aided Manufacturing (CAM).

ACCOMPLISHMENTS:

Particularly effective in areas of personnel management, motivation, and training, thereby increasing sales volume production flow, productivity and employee morale. Significant career accomplishments in customer relations, marketing and sales leadership, and management.

EMPLOYMENT HISTORY:

1986–Present   Calay Systems Incorporated, Waltham, Massachusetts

SENIOR ACCOUNT MANAGER

Responsible for a direct territory consisting of northern Massachusetts, Vermont, New Hampshire, Maine, and Quebec.

1985–1986   Automated Systems Incorporated, Nashua, New Hampshire

EASTERN REGIONAL SALES MANAGER

Responsible for regional design and fabrication service sales with a regional quota in excess of $5 million.

1981–1985   Engineering Automation Systems, Inc., San Jose, California.

WESTERN REGIONAL SALES MANAGER

Responsible for new Printed Circuit Design CAD/CAM system. Set up regional office, hired and trained sales and support staff of twelve people. Western regional sales were in excess of fifty percent of the company's business.

continued

EXHIBIT   C3.1   *concluded*

September 1984 PROMOTED TO NATIONAL SALES MANAGER.

1978–1981   Computervision Corporation, Bedford, Massachusetts

NATIONAL PRODUCT SALES MANAGER.

Responsible for all electronic CAD/CAM system sales and related products. Provided direct sales management and training to the national field sales team, conducted sales training internationally, assisted in developing competitive strategy, technical support, and new product development. Reported to the Vice President of North American Division.

March 1980 PROMOTED TO MANAGER, CORPORATE DEMONSTRATION and BENCHMARK CENTER.

Managed team of 38 people who performed all corporate level demonstrations and benchmarks. Supported field offices with technical information and people worldwide. Reported to the Vice President of Marketing Operations. **THIS WAS A KEY MANAGEMENT POSITION FOR THE COMPANY.**

1966-1978   King Systems, Inc., San Diego, California
(A Printed Circuit Design CAD/CAM and NC Drilling Service Bureau)

FOUNDER, PRESIDENT, CHAIRMAN, and MAJOR STOCKHOLDER.

Served as Chief Executive Officer in charge of all aspects of the operation. Primary activities in sales management, direct field sales, and customer relations. Responsible for financial administration, production operations, and personnel administration. Assessed future needs and created business planning for increasing market share and facilities capability and penetrating new market opportunity. Developed a new concept in contract services for blanket sales to large government and commercial prime contractors.

EXHIBIT   C3.2   Excerpts from Jerry King's Dec. 9, 1987, Presentation to Applied
CAD Knowledge, Inc.'s Board of Directors

Introduction

The plan is a detailed road map for taking Applied CAD Knowledge, Incorporated (ACK) from the current sales volume to more than three million annual sales volume over the next three years. It identifies target markets, competitive environment, and sales tactics that will be used for achieving the sales projections during the plan period from January 1, 1988 through December 31, 1990. The projections show a monthly breakdown for 1988 and a yearly number for 1989 and 1990. The monthly projections were created on Lotus and provide for projected, forecasted, and actual sales bookings for each month. As each month passes, the actual numbers are entered, and a goal status report is generated as part of the end-of-month reporting. At the end of each quarter a new quarter will be added so that there will always be four consecutive quarters of monthly projections.

The aggressive growth which is outlined will require significant expansion of facilities, personnel, and equipment in order to maintain consistent QUALITY and ON-TIME deliveries and ensure REPEAT BUSINESS from established customers. It is required that the management and the board of directors of ACK provide the necessary production controls and capital/operating budgets to support expansion commensurate with sales volume increases over the term of the plan.

The PCB design service market can be divided into three major segments. Each of these segments will include companies who design and manufacture electronic equipment for commercial, industrial, aerospace, and military vertical market areas.

continued

EXHIBIT C3.2 *concluded*

MAJOR ACCOUNTS and GOVERNMENT SUBCONTRACTORS (MA)

Major accounts are Fortune 1000 companies. They present a significant opportunity for multiple-board contracts and blanket purchase agreements. Any one company could fill ACK's capacity.

PRIMARY ACCOUNTS (PA)

Primary accounts are companies who have been doing business for more than three years (not a start-up) and typically do between 5 and 500 million in annual sales. These companies represent the most consistent level of business. The type of contracts available from this market segment are usually on the level of one to four board designs per month. Typically each board of a project has to be sold separately at the project engineering level.

VENTURE START-UP ACCOUNTS (VA)

Venture start-up companies usually are operating on stringent budgets. They typically have no internal CAD capability and therefore must rely on outside service. The business potential for this market segment is significant. This market represents a high risk and therefore is avoided by the major competitors, leaving more opportunity for the smaller operation. It is not unusual to obtain sole source product-level contracts from companies in this market.

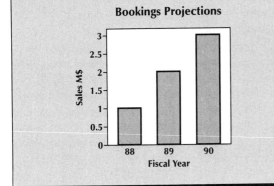

Bookings Projections

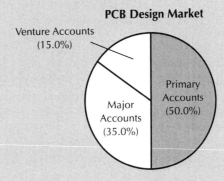

PCB Design Market

Source: Frost & Sullivan, October 1985

As 1988 began, King and Stevens continued to work closely together. Since Applied CAD's office layout did not provide the privacy needed for telephone prospecting, Jerry worked out of his home, joining Jeff several times per week on joint sales calls. At the January 8 meeting of the board of directors, the two men presented detailed sales projections for the first quarter and broader estimates for the entire year (Exhibit C3.3). One account alone—California PrinCo—held the promise of some $250,000 in sales over the next four months. An old and steady customer of Applied CAD, PrinCo was nearing a decision on a major expansion in their use of circuit boards.

January sales totalled only $6,000 but many prospects seemed close to signing for large orders. At the February 19 board meeting, Jeff and Jerry predicted sales of $100,000 per month for February and March; it appeared a 1988 sales goal of $1,000,000 might still be reachable. (Exhibit C3.4 shows monthly sales and backlogs through January 1988.)

EXHIBIT C3.3 Sales Projections Presented to the Board, January 8, 1988

Forecast Q1 1988: Sales by Customer

Account Name	Jan. 50%	Jan. 90%	Feb. 50%	Feb. 90%	Mar. 50%	Mar. 90%	Total 50%	Total 90%	Grand Total
Customer A	0.0	20.0	0.0	8.0	20.0	0.0	20.0	28.0	48.0
Prospect I	0.0	7.0	0.0	0.0	0.0	0.0	0.0	7.0	7.0
Prospect II	5.0	0.0	2.0	0.0	2.0	0.0	9.0	0.0	9.0
Customer B	0.0	0.0	12.0	0.0	0.0	0.0	12.0	0.0	12.0
Customer C	12.0	0.0	0.0	0.0	0.0	0.0	12.0	0.0	12.0
Customer D	0.0	0.0	12.0	0.0	0.0	0.0	12.0	0.0	12.0
Customer E	0.0	30.0	0.0	0.0	20.0	0.0	20.0	30.0	50.0
Prospect III	0.0	0.0	15.0	0.0	20.0	0.0	35.0	0.0	35.0
Prospect IV	0.0	0.0	15.0	0.0	20.0	0.0	35.0	0.0	35.0
Prospect V	0.0	6.5	0.0	0.8	0.0	3.8	0.0	11.1	11.1
Customer F	0.0	0.0	0.0	7.0	0.0	0.0	0.0	7.0	7.0
Total	17.0	63.5	56.0	15.8	82.0	3.8	155.0	83.1	238.1

Forecast FY 1988: Bookings by Product Type

	Service	Software	Total	Accumulated Total
January	33	15	48	48
February	48	5	53	101
March	53	15	68	169
Quarter 1	**124**	**35**	**169**	
April	60	5	65	234
May	68	15	83	317
June	75	5	80	397
Quarter 2	**203**	**25**	**228**	
July	80	15	95	492
August	85		85	577
September	88	15	103	680
Quarter 3	**253**	**30**	**283**	
October	90	8	98	778
November	95	15	110	888
December	98	15	113	1001
Quarter 4	**283**	**38**	**321**	

Q1 Forecasts

Legend: 50%, 90%, Projected

EXHIBIT   C3.4   Monthly Sales and Month-End Receivables, Backlogs, Cash Levels (in $000s)

	A/R	Sales	Backlog	Cash		A/R	Sales	Backlog	Cash
January 1986	18	20	20	98	January 1987	13	3	—	7
February	—	10	—	N/A	February	40	21	—	8
March	18	10	12	62	March	35	28	22	6
April	18	10	20	28	April	32	22	37	11
May	24	20	26	26	May	25	22	50	5
June	—	10	—	N/A	June	50	50	90	10
July	14	25	—	18	July	90	58	30	10
August	70	50	30	15	August	—	25	—	10
September	90	40	—	8	September	34	25	50	21
October	50	30	—	26	October	62	48	9	8
November	19	5	10	17	November	50	24	—	—
December	24	10	18	14	December	14	34	9	33
					January 1988	8	6	—	19

The Bates Motel and Casino

Paul R. Reed, Scott M. Bruce, and R. Dean Lewis

Sam Houston State University

The sunset was spectacular as it lit the Nevada desert. Norm Bates barely noticed the beauty as he looked out the window; he was entranced with the future of his organization. Nineteen eight-eight had been good to Norm. He married Lizzy, a nurse at the county hospital, and his corporation had netted over $137,000, despite a large amount of debt incurred from remodeling. Norm, however, was unsure of his abilities to manage the business, now that it was changing from a "mom and pop" organization into a more complex corporate structure. Furthermore, there seemed to be problems emerging that he couldn't quite put his finger on. He concluded that he would need some sage advice from one of those business consultant fellows before 1989 was history.

HISTORY

The Bates Motel and Casino was located in McLaughlin, Nevada. Founded by Norm's late mother in 1958, the Bates Motel served as a last stop for motorists before a two-hour trip across the desert. In 1964 Mother Bates's declining health seriously affected her ability to run the motel and resulted in Norm dropping out of State University in order to help out. Over the next two years Norm's responsibilities grew. In 1966 Mother Bates died, leaving the motel and a ten-acre tract of land along the highway to Norm.

Norm had a good working knowledge of plumbing and electricity and was quite capable of maintaining the motel's facilities. From time to time Norm would hire someone to watch the reception desk and clean the rooms, but for the most part he was the only employee during the sixties. In 1970 Norm was approached by Jim Curtin and Donna Showers. Jim and Donna were partners in a local cafe, and they were interested in relocating the cafe along the highway in hopes of attracting more business. Jim had considerable experience in the hotel and restaurant industry and had served as food and beverage director for a large hotel in Chicago before moving to the desert for health reasons two years earlier. Donna was a chef who grew up in McLaughlin. She was also a well-liked high school teacher who never had a problem finding good help for the restaurant. With the help of Lee Gayle, a local attorney, the Bates Motel incorporated. Jim and Donna each bought a twenty-percent share of the corporation. Lee exchanged his services for a two-percent share, and Norm held the remaining fifty-eight percent. Jim and Donna's purchase of stock allowed the corporation to build a restaurant and a swimming pool on site, and new air conditioners were put in every room.

Under the new corporation Jim managed the restaurant and motel reception desk. Donna ran the kitchen. Norm was in charge of maintenance and housekeeping. A bookkeeper,

Florence Cash, was hired to handle the day-to-day accounts, but a monthly statement was produced by a local CPA firm. During the early seventies the Bates Motel did well, and the population of the McLaughlin area had begun to grow. However, the late seventies proved to be more difficult. More cars were air conditioned, and the state had improved the highway through the desert, factors that were blamed for the sagging occupancy rates. In 1979 Norm bought six horses from a local rancher and hired Cy Kough, an ecology major at Arizona State, to give guided desert tours. These well-publicized tours became a popular attraction and seemed to increase room occupancy.

RECENT HISTORY

In 1982 an RV park was built across the highway from the Bates Motel. The park reduced the occupancy rate slightly, but the restaurant and guided desert tour business increased somewhat. Consequently the corporate income statement improved slightly. Later that year Jim and Donna were married, and Donna retired from her kitchen manager position to raise a family.

In 1984 Big Moe's Truck Stop was built next to the RV park (see the map in Exhibit C4.1). The truck stop had a restaurant, gift shop, fuel pumps, mechanic's garage, truck wash, and shower facilities. The truck stop did not affect the motel's occupancy rate but severely hurt the restaurant business and steadily eroded the appearance of the area. There always seemed to be a steady flow of trucks in and out of Big Moe's. Visible from the motel, Big Moe's had old truck tires stacked outside its garage ports, and eighteen-wheelers would park along the highway as well as the parking lot across from the motel. The truckers would usually sleep in their cabs but on occasion would check into the Bates (sometimes with one of the area's friendly ladies). Furthermore, the motel itself was in need of major remodeling. Norm, Jim, and

Donna were shocked when the contractor estimated the renovation at 1.5 million dollars.

In search of the funds to remodel, Norm met a Las Vegas developer, Louis Carminchi. Mr. Carminchi was willing to loan 2.5 million dollars and extend a line of credit for an additional 2 million. The plan was contingent on the following items: (1) Mr. Carminchi would buy 25 percent of the corporation for $500,000; (2) the motel would add a casino to its operation; and (3) the corporation would hire Al Hitchcock as its casino manager. Mr. Hitchcock was a long-time, trusted friend of Mr. Carminchi. He was also respected by the Nevada gaming authorities as one of the most honest men in the business.

On January 3, 1985, Norm called a meeting of all the shareholders as well as Flo and the local CPA. After much discussion and heated debate, the plan was accepted. Lee Gayle restructured the corporation and renamed it The Bates Motel and Casino, Inc. Norm held 43.5 percent of the common stock, Jim and Donna Curtin held 30 percent of the shares, Louis Carminchi held 25 percent of the shares, and Lee Gayle owned 1.5 percent. The remodeling was completed in May of 1985, and the grand opening of the new motel and casino was quite a success. The addition of the casino decreased the number of rooms by 25 percent, but initially total room occupancy increased significantly as did the restaurant business.

MOTEL OPERATIONS

There were seventy-five motel rooms in a two-story horseshoe shaped building. Two units were devoted to the handicapped, and two units were suites that had a jacuzzi spa and wet bar, one called the "honeymoon suite" and the other the "executive suite." There were 350 parking spaces surrounding the building, and most of the rooms opened to the parking lot. The swimming pool was in the center of the horseshoe.

EXHIBIT   C4.1   McLaughlin City Map

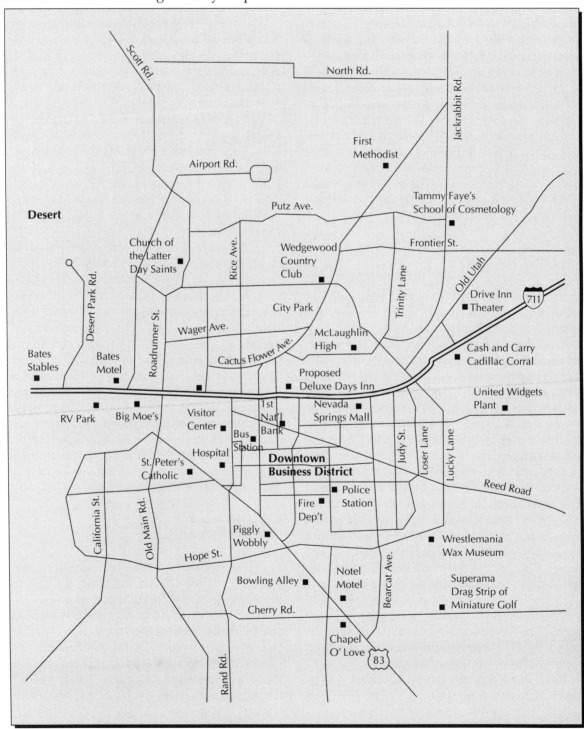

The front desk and the restaurant were on one end of the building facing the highway. The casino was on the other end and also faced the highway. The motel offices were on the second floor of the reception desk area, as were the sup-ply room and employee lounge. (Exhibit C4.2 shows a diagram of the motel complex.) Scattered around the complex were two ice machines and two snack machines for the customers' convenience.

EXHIBIT   C4.2   Diagram of Bates Motel Complex

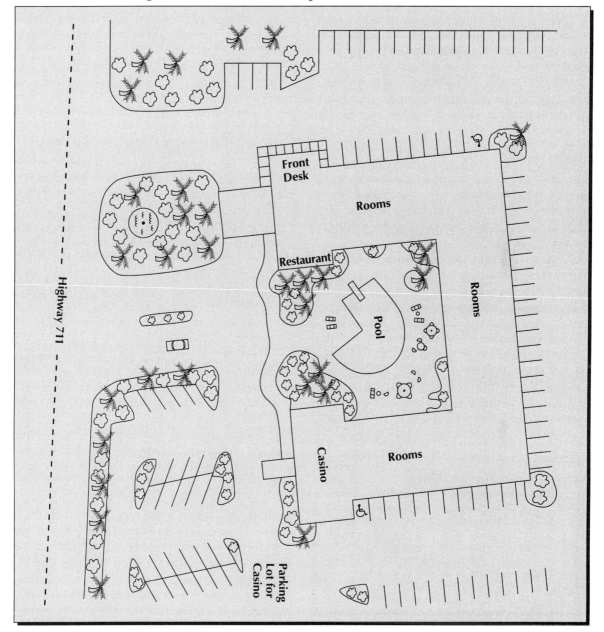

Each unit was air-conditioned and consisted of a bedroom, a bathroom, and a closet area. The rooms were equipped with a dresser, a full-length mirror, a table with four chairs, two night stands with lamps, telephones, a color television, a clock radio, and either one king-sized bed or two queen-sized beds. The bathrooms were stocked with two bars of soap, a full assortment of towels, a box of tissue, two rolls of toilet paper, an ashtray, and four plastic drinking glasses. The closet area had a clothes rod and hangers, a plastic laundry bag, and a suitcase rack.

The room rate was $36 (not including tax) per night, checkout time was noon, and there were discounts for senior citizens and certain nonprofit organizations. Local telephone calls were 50 cents, and long distance calls were billed at 75 cents per minute. International calls were billed at $2 per minute. At those rates, the new phone system just broke even if the average number of local calls was two per stay. The occupancy rates for the years 1986–1988 are shown in Exhibit C4.3.

The rooms that were occupied the night before were cleaned by Sunshine Housekeepers. Sunshine was run by Hazel Baxter. Hazel called the front desk the night before to get an occupancy count for establishing the amount of labor needed the next day. Sunshine charged a cleaning fee of $15 per room. It took one housekeeper twenty minutes to clean a room. They changed the bed sheets, pillow cases, and bath towels and placed the dirty linens in a hamper to be picked up by a linen service late in the week.

EXHIBIT   C4.3
Bates Motel Occupancy Rates

Year	Occupancy Rate	Average Room Rate
1986	63%	$33
1987	58%	$35
1988	52%	$36

Used glasses were replaced with clean ones, trash cans were emptied, and the housekeepers made inspection notes for maintenance repairs. Sunshine Housekeepers had notified Norm that their rate would go up in July to $18 per room. The linen service charged by the number of items cleaned, but the average cost per room change was three dollars. The essentials (soap, tissue, etc.) were provided by Sunshine. Hazel didn't like supplying these items and had suggested to Norm that if he would start supplying the essentials, she would not increase her price. Norm wondered if he might be better off performing these functions in-house.

FRONT-DESK AND OFFICE OPERATIONS

The front desk was staffed twenty-four hours a day. These personnel were in charge of checking guests in and out, taking reservations, answering the phone, handling guest problems, and running the computer night audit. A front-desk clerk was paid by the hour and worked in shifts. The morning shift was 5 a.m. until 1 p.m., the afternoon shift was 1 p.m. to 9 p.m., and the night shift was 9 p.m. to 5 a.m. One of the restaurant employees supervised the desk during the front clerk's break time.

Upstairs, above the front desk, were the motel offices. Norm and Jim each had his own office and shared a secretary, Peaches, who was hired last year. Peaches and Flo shared the large area outside Norm's and Jim's offices. The area also contained a Sharp copy machine, which was leased from a local dealer. The IBM 360 and dot-matrix printer were in another office just large enough to hold them.

There were five computer terminals hooked up to the IBM 360. There was one in Al's office in the casino, one in Norm's office, one in Jim's office, one on Peaches's desk, and one at the front desk. Flo had a good working knowledge of the system, but a computer representative came out when she couldn't solve the problems. The programs that the computer ran were purchased from Hotel Systems, Inc. The program was a standard hotel/motel package that had to undergo a few alterations for the Bates Motel and Casino. Flo had an AT&T personal computer on her desk, on which she ran her accounting package (Lotus 1-2-3).

RESTAURANT OPERATIONS

The restaurant was highly decorated and had a seating capacity of 182. It served a variety of short-order meals for breakfast, lunch, and dinner. The restaurant also handled room service orders. A specialty item was usually offered during the lunch hours, but the most popular items on the regular menu were hamburgers, steak sandwiches, chef's salads, fried catfish, fried chicken, and barbequed ribs. The restaurant also had a beer and wine license. It once had a full-service liquor bar but discontinued it when the casino started serving free drinks. The staff included a chef, two cooks, three waitresses (five during peak hours), and a dishwasher. The chef was responsible for ordering food and supplies as well as menu changes. The restaurant was open from 6 a.m. to 2 a.m.

CASINO OPERATIONS

The casino was run within the strict confines of the Nevada State Gaming Board. It was a 5,000-square-foot area with six blackjack tables, twenty-one slot machines, two roulette wheels, six crap tables, and a short-circuit TV viewing room that showed a variety of sporting events. There were usually four dealers, one bartender, two waitresses, a cashier, and two security guards on the floor at any given time. Al hired additional help during the holiday seasons and other peak periods. There also were several electric surveillance devices to help monitor activity on the floor. The room had a variety of lighting schemes, depending on the game areas. The waitresses wore uniforms that had a low neck-

line and that rode high on the hips with fish net hose and high heels. The dealers wore uniforms that were less revealing but more ornate. All the casino staff, except Al, were paid by the hour. The waitresses made less than minimum wage, but as Lisa, one of the waitresses put it, "The tips were great." The casino was open from 11 a.m. to 2 a.m. The waitresses and the bartenders cleaned the rooms after closing and vacuumed the floor before opening in the morning. At the end of the evening Al and a security guard were in charge of locking up the casino.

TOUR GUIDE OPERATION

The guided desert tours were not as popular since Cy resigned after his graduation. The stables were less than half a mile from the motel. The new tour guide, a geology student, was more concerned with the upkeep of the stables and horses than in promoting the tours, as Cy did. The trips were scheduled at the front desk. They were $12 per rider and lasted about two and a half hours. On weekends the horses were rented to the public for riding. Birthday parties could also be arranged, and there were usually ten or twelve a year. There were nine horses then, all of which were gentle and easy to ride. The horses were expensive to feed because there was not enough grass pasture at the stables on which they could graze. The vet bills were expensive as well, with the last check-up for the horses costing $725. Norm had been offered $19,500 for the horses by a rancher from California.

WHAT'S NEXT

The results of the past three years (Exhibits C4.4 and C4.5) were mixed for the Bates Motel and Casino. The casino increased slightly in popularity, while the restaurant and motel declined. The motel had no competition save the Notel Motel, which rented rooms by the hour on the south side of town. However, Deluxe Days Inn, a national chain of upscale hotels, proposed to build a new 300-room hotel and casino near downtown.

Norm felt something should be done, but what? He would have liked to see the occupancy rates of the motel improve but asked himself how he would be able to accomplish this when Deluxe Days Inn opened. He also was worried about the Big Moe's Truck Stop eyesore. He had complained to the city council about it, but all they did was send a letter asking Moe to keep trucks from parking on the highway shoulder. At a party honoring the Chamber of Commerce's new members, Norm overheard his banker

EXHIBIT   C4.4   Income Statement, Bates Motel and Casino, Year Ending December 31

	1988	1987	1986
Revenues			
Rooms	512,460	555,712	569,126
Casino	817,652	838,672	817,962
Restaurant	360,143	374,566	76,673
Other	59,204	54,404	72,133
Casino promotional allowances	(70,775)	(68,915)	(64,755)
Gross revenues	1,632,684	1,654,439	1,771,139
Direct Operating Expenses			
Rooms	306,230	330,661	350,016
Casino	321,722	319,452	313,732
Restaurant	219,113	223,593	270,513
Other	38,404	36,204	40,204
Depreciation and amortization	111,825	120,445	122,165
Gross profit	635,390	624,124	674,509
Indirect Operating Expenses			
Office and administration	184,292	149,082	137,016
Advertising and promotion	34,297	28,101	38,250
Interest expense	237,959	244,806	250,920
Other	8,870	5,636	6,104
Net income before taxes	169,972	196,499	242,219
Taxes	32,295	37,335	46,022
Net income	137,677	159,164	196,197

complaining to a gas station owner about Big Moe's mismanagement. Although the banker didn't say, Norm felt he might have been hinting that Big Moe's could be in financial trouble.

The sun had long set, and the stars and moon were very bright that night. Lizzy came into Norm's office and said, "Honey, why are you working so late? Is there something wrong?"

EXHIBIT   C4.5   Balance Sheet, The Bates Motel and Casino, January 1, 1989

Assets	
Current assets:	
Cash	$ 280,000
Securities	221,750
Supplies	7,620
Prepaid expenses	21,314
Other	10,560
Total current assets	$ 541,244
Land, building, and equipment	4,622,270
Accumulated depreciation and amortization	(500,391)
Total assets	$4,663,123
Liabilities	
Current liabilities:	
Accounts payable	$ 109,672
Accrued expenses	111,368
Note payable	301,867
Total current liabilities	$ 522,907
Long-term debt loan	1,919,084
Total liabilities	$2,441,991
Equity	
Common stock, $200 par value (10,000 shares outstanding)	$2,000,000
Retained earnings	221,132
Total stockholders' equity	$2,221,132
Total liabilities and equity	$4,663,123

Brooktrout Technology, Inc.

Raymond M. Kinnunen
Northeastern University

Wendy Vittori
Northeastern University

John A. Seeger
Bentley College

It's violent out there, and people in violent industries sometimes get killed. It's violent because it's changing rapidly. There are bodies all over the place in the voice mail segment. Computerm, for example, had $14 million invested and sold out for a pittance.

There are some very big companies, like AT&T, that are our potential customers, but they can also produce their own electronic messaging products. When you go to these big companies, it's like walking underneath elephants: you just hope the elephant doesn't step on you. But they don't move real fast, so you can watch out for them.

It was June of 1989, and Eric Giler, president of Brooktrout Technology, Inc., knew his company was at a crossroads. What strategy would best bring the high growth he wanted, while mini-mizing risk? Giler faced tough choices in marketing and finance as he wondered how to capitalize on his firm's technical skills.

Brooktrout designed and built electronic messaging systems, the equipment that automatically answers a business telephone and accepts a message for a specific individual. Some products were full systems in their own cabinets; others were separate electronic cards to be plugged into computers. Brooktrout sold mainly to original equipment manufacturers (OEMs) in the telecommunications industry. Its customers included some of the world's largest builders of telephone equipment.

Brooktrout Technology was founded in 1984 by Eric Giler, David Duehren, and Patrick Hynes; all had worked together previously at Teradyne, Inc. The new company lost money in each of its first five years, but Eric expected 1989 to be profitable, with sales approaching $5 million. (Exhibit C5.1 shows financial data on the company.) Eric commented:

> It's high risk but also high reward. We can build a $100 million company in this business; after all, it's a multibillion dollar industry. The expertise we have is our technology. We understand what makes it possible to do electronic messaging, and our goal in life is to sell it on an OEM basis to companies that need it. We will make a product that is cheaper or faster.

TELECOMMUNICATIONS INDUSTRY: HISTORY

On January 8, 1982, the American Telephone and Telegraph Company (AT&T) agreed to end

EXHIBIT   C5.1   Brooktrout Financial Statements

Brooktrout Technology, Inc.
Statement of Operations ($000)

	1985	1986	1987	1988	Projected 1989	1990
Revenues:						
Voice					$ 3,490	$ 6,396
Facsimile					1,231	3,444
Total revenues	$ 271	$ 510	$ 1,378	$ 2,418	$ 4,721	$ 9,840
Cost of sales:						
Voice					$ 1,920	$ 3,518
Facsimile					391	1,722
Total cost of sales	114	191	566	1,076	$ 2,311	$ 5,240
Gross profit	**$ 157**	**$ 319**	**$ 812**	**$ 1,342**	**$ 2,410**	**$ 4,600**
Operating expenses:						
Sales and marketing	$ 79	$ 134	$ 425	$ 682	$ 685	$ 1,118
Research and development	214	553	354	568	726	1,332
General and administrative	289	622	474	422	568	925
Total expenses	$ 582	$ 1,309	$ 1,253	$ 1,672	$ 1,979	$ 3,375
Net interest expense	(5)	(175)	(391)	(120)	(110)	(198)
Net income/(loss)	**$(430)**	**$(1,165)**	**$(832)**	**$(450)**	**$ 321**	**$ 1,027**

Brooktrout Technology, Inc.
Balance Sheet ($000)

	1985	1986	1987	1988
Assets				
Current assets:				
Cash	$ 96	$ 82	$ 274	$ 122
Accounts receivable	115	74	318	402
Inventory	62	44	124	236
Other current assets	0	26	5	24
Total current assets	$ 273	$ 226	$ 721	$ 784
Property and equipment (net of accumulated depreciation)	86	81	101	119
Other assets	26	16	13	8
Total assets	**$ 385**	**$ 323**	**$ 834**	**$ 912**
Liabilities and Shareholders' Equity				
Current liabilities:				
Accounts payable	$ 110	$ 126	$ 254	$ 440
Notes payable	72	160	102	90
Current portion of long-term debt	12	28	85	84
Other liabilities	70	71	86	140
Total current liabilities	$ 264	$ 385	$ 527	$ 754
Notes payable to stockholders	88	416	578	548
Other long-term debt	6	340	300	331
Total liabilities	$ 358	$1,141	$1,405	$1,633
Net stockholders' equity	28	(818)	(571)	(722)
Total liabilities and stockholder's equity	**$ 385**	**$ 323**	**$ 834**	**$ 912**

its 48-year history as a regulated monopoly. In its total lifespan of 106 years, the company had created the telecommunications system that served as a world model. AT&T provided local phone service through its wholly owned geographic subsidiaries (e.g., New England Telephone and Telegraph) to 80 percent of American homes. Through its Western Electric manufacturing arm, it made virtually all the nation's telephone equipment. Through its Bell Laboratories—renowned as the leading electronics R&D center of the world—it developed new technologies (including, for example, the first transistors). Unfettered by competition, AT&T devoted itself to providing superb quality and service. By regulation it was assured a profit based on its investment. AT&T's asset base thus grew phenomenally; by 1984, when the company was divided, its total of $150 billion in assets dwarfed the size of most nations' economies. In assets and profits, AT&T was the largest company in the world.

For most of its history, to preserve the quality of its lines, AT&T absolutely prohibited any other company's equipment from being attached to its network. The historic Carterfone decision in 1968 made it legal for non-Bell equipment to be attached to public lines; the first privately owned telephone answering machine, barred by AT&T for years, now had to be admitted to the network, and the market for terminal equipment was opened.

As a monopoly, AT&T had been restrained from competing in the open marketplace; at the same time it was often criticized for commercial practices that made market penetration difficult for makers of specialized terminal equipment. In the industry it was widely thought that AT&T saw itself as the major potential competitor to IBM in the computer industry. In the 1982 agreement, settling an antitrust suit by the government, the company officially acceded to being dismantled. Its local telephone operating companies, still working as regulated monopolies, were spun off into seven regional holding companies. The breakup—the largest financial transaction in world history—was completed in late 1983. AT&T was now free to compete. (See Exhibits C5.2 and C5.3 for comparative sizes of the units, before and after the breakup.)

TELECOMMUNICATIONS INDUSTRY: STRUCTURE

The telecommunications industry consisted of three major segments—local telephone companies, long distance carriers, and telephone equipment manufacturers—and one relatively small segment, information products and services, where Brooktrout Technology competed. (Exhibit C5.4 gives examples of leading entrants in all four segments.)

The information products and services segment resulted from the combination of computer and telecommunications technologies during the 1980s. These combined technologies made it possible for data to be processed as well as transmitted by the communications networks, thus creating "intelligent communications" (new products combining hardware innovations, computer technology, and software). By 1989 this segment of the telecommunications industry was a hotbed of competitive marketing activity, with contenders ranging from heavyweights like AT&T's own Bell Laboratories to entrepreneurial newcomers such as Brooktrout Technology, Inc.

Local Exchange Operators

Before deregulation local telephone companies were the only source for all telephone equipment and services. After deregulation many vendors began to supply the market. Businesses began to purchase and install their own private branch exchanges (PBXs), which performed all the telephone functions that were internal to a given business. PBXs were sold based on lower costs, more features, and greater control for a business over its phone usage than the telephone company's standard service could offer.

With competition increasing, local telephone companies enhanced the level of service they provided beyond simple transmission. Since pricing on local phone calls was regulated, their principal competitive weapons were additional services. The telephone companies turned to the private sector for equipment they could sell in competition with the industry newcomers. Thus, the new manufacturers of telecommunications equipment had two markets—one to businesses and another to the telephone companies, who in turn sold to businesses.

New opportunities for products and services continued to grow. In 1988 a court decision permitted local telephone companies to transmit information services. Options such as call-forwarding and call-waiting could now be offered to even single-line subscribers. In the future lay provision of services such as stock quotations and transactions and merchandise selection and purchase, all through the telephone company. A recent advance allowed multiple phone numbers to be channeled to a single line, a cost-effective solution for home businesses with only one phone line. Publishing and computer/telecommunications integration were major new business thrusts.

Long-Distance Carriers

Long-distance transmission continued to be dominated by AT&T following deregulation, with 87 percent of the long-distance customers handled by AT&T in 1988. The only major competitors to AT&T were MCI and US Sprint, each with 5–6 percent of the customer base. Both these new firms were pursuing high-growth strategies in 1989 based on the lower cost and higher quality of fiber optic, microwave, and satellite transmission technologies.

EXHIBIT C5.2 Values and Operating Results of Leading Telephone Companies

	$Millions			
	Assets	**Sales**	**Market Value**	**Net Profit**
AT&T (1983)	149,530	69,403	59,392	5,747
AT&T (1988)	35,152	35,210	30,868	–1,669
Bell Operating Companies, 1988				
Ameritech	19,163	9,903	12,888	1,237
Bell Atlantic	24,729	10,880	14,013	1,317
BellSouth	28,472	13,597	18,504	1,666
Nynex	25,378	12,661	12,997	1,315
Pacific Telesis	21,191	9,483	12,934	1,188
Southwestern Bell	20,985	8,453	12,129	1,060
U.S. West	22,416	9,221	10,548	1,132
Other Firms, 1988				
GTE	31,104	16,460	14,520	1,225
MCI Communications	5,843	5,137	5,498	356

Source: "The Forbes 500," *Forbes*, April 30, 1984, and May 1, 1989.

Low costs were vital in selling telecommunications services to business. Dedicated long-distance services, where a corporation owned its own satellite network, were also attracting a share of the total long-distance transmissions in the United States. Long-distance carriers were beginning to install these end-to-end transmission services for large customers. This connected long-distance service directly to a PBX, eliminating the need to connect via the local exchange.

Telephone Equipment Manufacturers

After deregulation the decision on what equipment to buy and where to install it was made by the customer, who could lease or purchase as much or as little equipment as desired from a vendor of its choice. Private branch exchange (PBX) equipment sales grew tremendously, breaking $3 billion per year in 1988.

Twenty years after the Carterfone decision, the market for "customer premise" equipment had grown to $8 billion per year. However, the 1988 growth rate of 8.7 percent was expected to decline to 4.89 percent in the early 1900s. Several larger firms (AT&T, Northern Telecom, Siemens) together controlled more than 50 percent of the market. However, smaller manufacturers, like TIE Communications, had made inroads by offering lower prices, enhanced features (least-cost routing, voice messaging, and

EXHIBIT   C5.3   Ranking of Leading Telephone Companies

	$Millions			
	Assets	**Sales**	**Market Value**	**Net Profit**
AT&T (1983)	1[a]	3	2	1
AT&T (1988)	36	9	4	—[b]
Bell Operating Companies, 1988				
Ameritech	85	66	28	19
Bell Atlantic	63	51	22	16
BellSouth	52	38	12	13
Nynex	60	41	26	17
Pacific Telesis	75	72	27	24
Southwestern Bell	79	83	32	30
U.S. West	69	73	38	27
Other Firms, 1988				
GTE	41	32	20	20
MCI Communications	271	154	81	142

[a] Figures give rank among the top 500 American businesses, including banks and financial services firms.

[b] Not meaningful.

Source: "The Forbes 500," *Forbes,* April 30, 1984, and May 1, 1989.

other advanced exchange and information services), quality of service, testing, and maintenance. Under this kind of competitive pressure, prices of electronic components fell by half every two to three years.

Small entrepreneurial manufacturers and software houses (like Brooktrout Technology) provided many of the innovations behind new services. These small firms might sell to the larger equipment firms, to the regional Bell operating companies, and/or to the end users themselves. Acquisition and merger activity was high (see Exhibit C5.5), as larger firms brought these high-technology skills in-house.

Information Products and Services

The compound annual growth rate for the information products and services segment was forecast to be approximately 25 percent for the next

EXHIBIT C5.4 Brooktrout Technology, Inc.—Segments of the Industry (and Examples of Active Competitors)

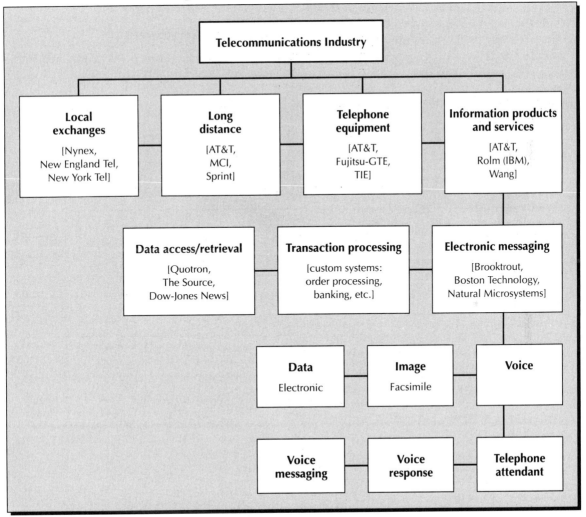

five years. Some of the major subsegments (examples are given in Exhibit C5.4) were data access and retrieval, transaction processing, and electronic messaging (the segment in which Brooktrout Technology competed).

Electronic messaging products allowed users to send and receive messages from other users, by voice, data, or image transmission. The messaging product either replaced or augmented a person-to-person phone conversation. Specific examples included electronic mail, facsimile, and voice messaging.

Principal "voice store and forward" (VSF) products were telephone attendant systems, voice messaging, and voice response systems. Telephone attendant systems replaced a switchboard operator with an automated system—a "silicon Sally" computerized voice that prompted the caller to enter codes in order to route a call to the proper extension. Voice messaging provided for recording, storing, and playing back messages, as with a simple telephone answering machine but using a much more flexible computer storage and retrieval technology. Voice response systems could carry on a dialogue with the caller in order to perform functions such as order-taking and account inquiry.[2]

Although VSF was a small subsegment in the overall telecommunications industry, in 1989 it was growing very rapidly (see Exhibit C5.6). From revenues of $200 million in 1986 and $426 million in 1988, the VSF segment was expected to reach $1 billion in the early 1990s.[3]

Voice Store and Forward

Brooktrout Technology in 1989 competed in the voice store and forward segment, with products

EXHIBIT   C5.5   Merger and Acquisition Activity in Consumer Premises Equipment Firms

	CPE Sales ($ Millions)			
CPE Manufacturer	**1986**	**1987**	**1988[a]**	**Acquired by:**
Contel/Executone	268	305	335[b]	Isotek/Vodavi
Tel Plus Comm., Inc.	255	283[b]	320	Siemens
RCA Telephone Systems	120	130	140[b]	Mitel
Universal Comm. Systems	87	106[b]	n/a	BellSouth
Jarvis Corp.	36	38[b]	40	Isotec
All American Businessphones	25	28	30[b]	TIE[c]
Gray Communications	25	22	25[b]	AIM Tel
Henkel & McCoy/Telecom	19	21[b]	25	Star Datacom
Interconnect Comm. Corp.	7	22[b]	38	Inter-Tel
Total	842	955	953	

[a] Year of acquisition.

[b] Estimated sales following acquisition.

[c] Acquisition proposed.

Source: *Telephony,* April 11, 1988.

EXHIBIT   C5.6   The Market for Telecommunications, 1988

	1988 Revenues, $ Millions	Projected Compound Annual Growth Rate, Percent*
Public Network Services		
Local services	$ 87,558	
Long-distance services	52,400	
Cellular/public data nets	2,842	
Total network services	$142,800	
Business Communications Equipment Market: Voice		
Private branch exchanges (PBXs)	$ 3,182	2.6%
Key systems	2,316	0.9
Facsimile	1,041	17.8
Voice messaging	426	23.6
Automated call distribution	284	7.1
Call accounting	281	4.4
Video teleconferencing	264	26.5
Phones	125	6.9
Integrated voice-data terminals	73	2.9
Total voice equipment market	$ 7,992	
Business Communications Equipment Market: Data		
Local area networks	$ 2,400	22.4%
Modems	1,200	−6.2
Front-end processors	625	6.7
Network management systems	457	13.8
Private packet switching	432	17.0
T-1 multiplexors	403	12.9
Statistical multiplexors	299	−5.5
Circuit/data switching units	122	12.7
Data PBXs	85	−4.7
Total data equipment market	$ 6,023	

* For the period 1988–1992.

Source: Dataquest Inc., Forecast '88

in both voice messaging and facsimile messaging. A VSF system was based on a technology known as "digital signal processing," used to capture voice signals and convert them into a string of digital "bits," which could be computer processed. Only a few VSF manufacturers, such as Brooktrout, had developed in-house expertise in this basic technology.

Traditionally voice processing applications had required the processing power of a host minicomputer, and products based on these large systems still represented the vast majority of the market in 1989 (see Exhibit C5.7). However, the new generation of more powerful personal computers was creating an increasingly strong alternative for low-end VSF host computers. In fact, the market researcher, Dataquest, had predicted:

> The low-end segment [of VSF] brings to the voice messaging market what PCs brought to the computer industry—cost-effective, flexible, powerful applications processors for small to medium-size businesses or organizations.[4]

Others had forecast that PC-based systems were not likely to achieve significant market share, because telephone answering machines and service bureaus could provide the services needed by a small user at a lower cost (almost no cost with a telephone answering machine). Service bureaus used large-scale VSF systems based on mini or mainframe computer hosts and

EXHIBIT   C5.7   VSF Equipment Market (1987)

System Size	Number of Ports*	System Size as Percent of Total Market	Percent Market Share for Segment Size	
Large systems (mainframe)	32–1500	52%	Rolm	45
			AT&T	13
Medium systems (minicomputer)	8–32	47	Centigram	17
			Opcom	17
			Rolm	14
			Wang	13
			Digital Sound	11
			Genesis	11
			AT&T	3
Small systems (personal computer)	1–8	1	Natural Microsystems	30
			Brooktrout	20
			AT&T	15

* Number of telephone lines a system is capable of accommodating simultaneously. System capacities here are estimates by Eric Giler.

Source: Frost and Sullivan, Report Number A1867, 1988. Quoted with permission.

rented voice messaging services to companies without their own on-site VSF systems. This could be a cost-effective alternative to PC-based systems for small users who needed the sophisticated capabilities of VSF. Even larger firms were contracting service bureaus for voice services. Probe Research, Inc. forecast VSF service bureau revenues to be $271 million in the early 1990s.

Local telephone companies were also looking at the opportunities that voice messaging might offer. Ameritech, one of the regional Bell companies, had acquired Tigon Corp., the nation's largest voice messaging service bureau (with corporate clients like Ford Motor Co.) in late 1988. Bell Atlantic had recently contracted with Boston Technology, a small voice messaging company founded in 1986, for its newly introduced central office–based voice processing system. Although Boston Technology had first developed small, stand-alone systems, "from the beginning, we believed that there was a need for a huge voice processing system," said Greg Carr, the firm's president. "Their proposal got our attention immediately," commented Kathy Maier, Bell Atlantic's product manager for enhanced voice services. "Its size—1536 ports, 7000 hours of voice storage capacity, support of 104,000 voice mailboxes—is a major factor."[5]

Facsimile machines were the most recent addition to the electronic messaging segment. These machines, which were priced as low as $600 in 1989, used digital signal processing technology similar to that used in VSF to transmit images via telephone lines. Sales of facsimile machines in 1988 of $2.2 billion were projected to reach $6.6 billion by the early 1990s.[6]

Electronic mail involved computer-to-computer communication of data (rather than voice) messages. Although more expensive and not so easy to use as VSF or facsimile (because it required specialized training for each user), electronic mail had the great advantage of transmitting both messages and data in a format that could be understood and further manipulated by computer programs.

Distribution

The distribution system for information products and services was complex. For example, all the following were being used to distribute voice store and forward systems.

Local Exchange Operators Telephone companies purchased VSF equipment on an OEM basis, to build into the equipment they sold for their own telephone services, such as Centrex. GTE, for example, offered many services, including Telemessager (voice mail) and Telemail (electronic mail).

Telephone Equipment Manufacturers (OEMs) These firms purchased and incorporated VSF products into their own devices, such as PBXs. In some cases they would simply license the VSF technology and manufacture the actual products themselves. Many of these manufacturers would customize their VSF systems in order to differentiate their end products in the mind of the end user, even though the components might have a common origin. The identity of the VSF manufacturer was generally not revealed in the end product. Prominent among these original equipment manufacturers were AT&T, Rolm, TIE, and Iwatsu. The largest suppliers of VSF products to OEMs were Brooktrout, Genesis, and AT&E.

Telephone System Dealers Dealers were either independent or affiliated with an equipment manufacturer. Independent dealers generally carried multiple brands of business telephone systems, PBXs, and other telecommunications equipment. There had been an increasing trend for equipment manufacturers to integrate forward by purchasing independent dealers. As a result some of the dealers sold only one brand of equipment (e.g., Rolm or GTE), while others still represented multiple brands. Dealers generally provided complete installation and maintenance service.

Service Bureaus Service bureaus purchased large VSF systems to be time-shared by both small and large businesses.

Computer Stores Low-end VSF systems could be sold as add-on circuit boards for personal computers through computer stores.

Direct Sales Some firms, most notably Natural Microsystems, had promoted and sold their products directly to end users, using methods such as direct mail or advertising directed to the personal computer owner.

Historically PC-based VSF systems had been sold principally on an OEM basis to the telephone equipment manufacturers. Some two-thirds of VSF manufacturers' revenues were derived from OEMs. The remaining third was split between direct sales and computer and telephone system dealers.

Industry Trends

Several key trends were apparent in the telecommunications equipment industry at the end of the 1980s. Competition seemed likely to intensify. Worldwide markets were likely to appear as multinational firms spread their use of electronic messaging and overseas telephone companies upgraded their services. Prices were expected to decline as Asian manufacturers and new entrants brought lower costs into mainstream products. Continued reduction of the regulations on the Bell Operating Companies could translate to faster market expansion and larger shares for their OEM purchases. Rapid acceptance of new technologies, as exemplified by the history of the facsimile machine, could make any new product an overnight phenomenon. The appearance of new applications for electronic messaging products was likely, but what they would be was unknown.

In technology, customers and suppliers alike were pushing for adoption of industry-wide communications standards, rather than vendor-specific codes. This trend influenced the entire computer/software industry; it would eliminate the many difficulties that existed in 1989 in transferring information across networks containing hardware from many different makers. Information service providers stood to benefit directly from standardization, because their products could be used on a wider array of equipment.

In 1989 the information products and services industry was dynamic, complex, and highly unpredictable. A key phrase for the future of the telecommunications industry appeared to be system integration. One industry analyst stated:

> Computers can switch phone calls, and PBX's can do computing. [We can] predict a day, perhaps five or ten years away, when system integration for the business customer will include not only telephone service but word processing, commercial data processing, and facsimile data transmission.[7]

BROOKTROUT TECHNOLOGY, INC.: HISTORY

In 1984 Eric Giler, Dave Duehren, and Pat Hynes—a technical marketer and two design engineers—founded Brooktrout Technology to take advantage of the technical ideas they had begun to think about at their previous jobs. With their expertise in digital signal processing, they felt they could integrate voice messaging with text, graphics, image processing, and data communications, putting all the functions into a single piece of hardware.

Armed with a business plan projecting $3 million in sales the first year, they began to seek financing. Eric Giler reflected on the early efforts:

> We thought at first that raising capital would be easy. But when we tried, we found doors closing on us for two reasons. One, we were young. Second, the venture capitalists couldn't believe that

people would talk to machines, even if the systems worked perfectly. So for the first six months we operated the company out of an apartment.

Eric and his partners decided to seek money privately and in several private placements in the first two years raised $1.5 million from approximately 50 investors. In 1987 a major telephone equipment manufacturer injected $1 million in cash for a minority equity position. By 1989 Brooktrout had raised a total of $2.5 million to finance its growth and was anticipating its first profitable year (Exhibit C5.1 shows financial data and projections). The founders, equal owners from the beginning, still retained a 30-percent ownership stake in Brooktrout.

Eric Giler, Brooktrout's president, had received an undergraduate degree in management science from Carnegie-Mellon and an M.B.A. from Harvard in 1982. Pat Hynes (VP of engineering) and Dave Duehren (VP of R&D) were electrical engineers. Both had bachelor's degrees from M.I.T.; Duehren's M.S. was also from M.I.T., while Hynes's was from Columbia. Hynes, an avid trout fisherman, chose the name for the new company.

In 1987 Eric hired Stephen Ide, a twenty-year veteran in telecommunications and a former consultant to Brooktrout, as vice president of sales and marketing. Ide had founded and served as president of Computer Telephone Corp., a publicly held company with $14 million in sales. In 1988 Bob Leahy, former controller and treasurer of Cambridge Robotic Systems, was hired as treasurer. Leahy, holder of a B.S. in accounting from Bentley College, brought a diverse background in high-technology finance. Eric was comfortable with the progress they had made building the top management team as well as the technical organization; by mid-1989, six additional engineers—hired directly out of local colleges—supplemented the efforts of Hynes and Duehren. Another five worked in production and seven in marketing. "We have the team in place; now we have to figure out how to grow it," said Eric.

Brooktrout Products

The first products to be made by Brooktrout were for voice messaging. At the time, Eric Giler said, this seemed the most logical segment to enter: the technology was just beginning to take off, while the facsimile machine as an image communication device was not that far along. They then moved into the imaging segment with a circuit board facsimile messaging system ("Fax-Mail"), which enabled computer data to be translated electronically into facsimile images. With Fax-Mail, a PC user could send a computer file straight to the facsimile transmitter, without printing out the image first. (See Exhibit C5.8 for a description of Brooktrout's voice and fax products in mid-1989.)

In mid-1989, Fax-Mail was sold at retail to end users, for installation in their own personal computers, at a price of $499. The voice messaging products ranged in price from $5,000 to $20,000 retail. Most were sold to OEMs, at discounts up to 50 percent.

Brooktrout also did some design work under contract to specific customers. (Even AT&T had made inquiries about Brooktrout's capabilities.) A current contract with a major manufacturer was developing data transfer between modems and facsimile machines. A major advantage of designing under contract was avoiding the need to raise additional capital for the research effort. However, in the end Brooktrout might not have full rights to the products they developed.

Brooktrout Strategy

Traditionally individual companies specialized in voice, data, or image communication. Brooktrout believed these three modes of communication would become integrated in the near future, as the technology of digital signal processing became cheaper and better. Eric commented:

> Nobody does all three. Our goal over the long term is to provide solutions in all three areas, for

EXHIBIT C5.8
Brooktrout Products, as of Mid-1989

Voice Messaging

Operator Plus

- Advanced call processing systems for small and medium-sized companies
- Automated attendant, voice messaging, and voice response capabilities
- Digital Signal Processing technology to record, store, and play back digitized human voice
- Up to six ports capacity
- Up to 24 hours of stored messages

V-Mail 210/DID

- Allows outside callers to leave messages for individuals without dialing extensions, mailbox numbers, etc.
- Each user assigned an individual Direct Inward Dial number
- Ideal for answering services, voice mail service bureaus, and cellular telephone sites

Phoneware 470

- Development system
- Speeds creation of telephone-based speech processing applications software
- Ideal for voice-prompted order entry, voice bulletin boards, and information dissemination

Fax Messaging

Fax-Mail Systems

- Complete hardware/software systems
- Allows personal computers and fax machines to communicate worldwide over standard telephone lines
- Plugs into any IBM PC/XT/AT or compatible computer
- Permits PCs to receive transmissions from fax machines, store files on disk, display them on PC monitors, or print them out
- Compatible with CCITT Group III fax (machines that transmit a letter-sized page in less than one minute)

all the major telecommunications and computer manufacturers. We want to do something different from what other people are doing, based on our expertise in technology and our understanding of what makes electronic messaging possible.

Brooktrout estimated it had 5 to 10 percent of the voice segment market, selling against 30 to 40 competitors. Several of those were achieving success by selling further down the distribution channel, directly to dealers. Brooktrout, on the other hand, still sold its voice mail products mainly to OEMs. An advantage to selling to the OEMs, Eric said, was the ready access gained to certain segments of the industry. For instance, TIE Communications had developed a product using Brooktrout's technology that they sold to the Bell Operating Companies. TIE had access to the people in Nynex, Ameritech, etc., where Brooktrout did not.

Occasionally Brooktrout was called upon by their OEMs to assist in developing end-user applications for their products. Although this required additional effort, successful applications translated directly into more demand for Brooktrout's products.

Brooktrout had major OEM agreements for its voice and fax products with TIE, the second largest customer premise equipment (CPE) supplier of small business phone systems behind AT&T, and with the American division of Iwatsu, a major Japanese equipment manufacturer. Both TIE and Iwatsu built Brooktrout products into their own offerings; both also labeled the Brooktrout equipment with their own name and sold it separately. TIE's dealers sold only TIE products, whereas Iwatsu dealers also sold products made by other manufacturers.

Although Eric felt that selling to OEMs was the best bet for the future, his sales department saw things differently. They believed the company could grow more rapidly by promoting and selling through dealers. Eric reported:

> What the salespeople are saying is, "Here we have stuff we can sell now. We can make money. We can sell lots of them." The problem I have is

that our organization is not set up to deal directly with dealers.

All the sales department employees had either worked for dealers or owned their own dealerships. Eric felt, however, that the Brooktrout organization was not prepared to meet the needs of dealers or the dealers' customers. For example, operating manuals and instruction books would be required, along with 24-hour telephone and technical support. He said:

> We can sell to dealers to the extent it furthers our OEM goals. To the extent it isn't supporting those goals, I'm not sure it's worth it. Recently a potential investor complained about our selling to OEMs. He said, "Oh, that's the wrong way to do it. What you do is sell to users, then the users like it and they tell the dealers; the dealers like it and they tell the manufacturers, and the manufacturers have to have it."

> I never thought of it that way. The reason I never thought of it is simple: that's what you do when you have money!

Although distribution was an important consideration, many industry experts felt that market timing was also a critical success factor. The major task was to build a competitive product. Once the product was sold to an OEM and incorporated in its products, it became very difficult for competitors to dislodge it. Eric commented,

> The biggest competitive advantage I've seen in this business is what I call the first mover advantage. The guy who's first to do something kicks ass. It doesn't matter what anyone else does. Over the long haul, that's our best bet. And it probably doesn't matter where in the channel you sell as long as you're the first mover.

> Anyone can do anything—that's my premise. I have never seen anything in technology that is totally proprietary. You have to be careful though. There are also the pioneers with arrows in their backs; I've seen a bit of that also.

Sometimes being first was not that easy. The facsimile circuit board for personal computers was first introduced by a small California firm, Gamma Fax, while Brooktrout's similar product—fully designed and ready for production—sat on the shelf. Eric had felt the market wasn't ready: "Naw, fax for personal computers? Who understands that stuff?" Now Brooktrout had to make up for the first-to-market advantage that Gamma Fax had captured.

The Future

Eric and his partners aimed to be the first company to fully integrate voice, data, and image messaging—"tying all these things together; that's the long-term vision." Brooktrout would soon have the key technology they needed for that integrated product, as a result of one of their current development contracts. To exploit the new opportunity, however, would take more capital and other resources than Brooktrout had available in mid-1989.

> I have the product idea: a voice machine that will let a company handle requests for literature with no human intervention at all. The customers call in and the machine asks what they want. When it defines what literature they want, the machine faxes the stuff to them instantly. The customer should love it: he doesn't even have to wait for the mail, much less for some clerk to fill the request. There isn't any other product like that, anywhere. Eric said:

> If I had the money I would pursue it right now. I know it's going to hit. But I have to consider the effects of more stock dilution. I'd really prefer not to sell any stock.

> But people don't operate strategically on a day-to-day basis. If a venture capitalist called me right now and made the right kind of deal, I would take the dilution.

Eric was at a crossroads. He knew that the capital structure of Brooktrout, with fifty shareholders, was not very attractive to venture capitalists. It had actually scared some away. And he had other products, too, which had not been brought to market because of capital needs.

He wanted to bet on the new product where literature could be requested over the phone. That concept was very different. It would allow Brooktrout to diversify its customer base and, if successful, could possibly get them to the point of going public or being acquired by a larger company. But, he asked, what market channel would best reach all the potential users of such a product?

Eric also knew that there was some merit in selling directly to dealers as the salespeople wanted, and that being first was the "best possible thing to do":

Say we go out and raise more money and get diluted. Does the stock's value get pumped up? Some of the investors want out now. We have fifty investors and there's not a day that goes by that I don't talk to one of them.

If I had the capital resources right now, I would just be the best voice and fax company around. There is nobody there yet. We know it's going to be a big market; it doesn't take a rocket scientist to figure that out. It does take some thinking about how you want to position yourself, because it's a very fragmented set of business opportunities. Do you want a turnkey setup? Do you want to sell to OEMs? Do you want to build a system, or do you want to just sell components?

This is a very complex industry. There are people who spend their lives trying to figure this stuff out; they get paid a lot of money for being wrong. I've never seen so many consultants in all my life.

When asked where he thought Brooktrout would be in five years, Eric replied:

Five years is too long to project in a violent industry. I would probably like to see the harvest point before that. If your business is really hot, it's very hard to maintain your independence, because the thing grows and you get assimilated into something whether you want to or not. Ultimately you go public or you get acquired. We just want to keep playing the game—growing the beast as big as we can.

From a personal perspective, it will be fun at $10 million [in sales]. That's when it starts to get fun. You're not playing around as much, and you have enough mass to expect the bottom line to hit about 15 percent. That's what I'd like to see.

ENDNOTES

1. *Telephony,* May 16, 1988.
2. Ibid.
3 "Voice Mail Matures: Sales Boom as Applications Explode," *Teleconnect,* September 1988.
4. *Telephony,* November 14, 1988.
5. Ibid.
6. *Communications Week,* February 20, 1989.
7. G. R. Faulhaber, *Telecommunications in Turmoil: Technology and Public Policy* (Cambridge, Mass.: Ballinger, 1987), 129–30.

Sierra Research and Technology, Inc.

Raymond M. Kinnunen
Northeastern University

John A. Seeger
Bentley College

James F. Molloy, Jr.
Northeastern University

Don Spigarelli, founder and president of Sierra Research and Technology (Sierra), surveyed the crowd at his display booth. It was August 30, 1990, the last day of the "Surface Mount '90" conference and exposition at Boston's huge Bayside Exposition Center. Several thousand design engineers, purchasing agents, manufacturing executives, marketers, and salespeople strolled among the three hundred exhibits in the vast hall. Spigarelli's own display—an open island of some 500 square feet at the intersection of several aisles beside the cafeteria—dominated the back of the Exposition Center.

Eight Sierra people stood ready to demonstrate their machines and answer questions. At the moment, only four were occupied, and Don Spigarelli had a moment to talk:

How can you plan long range when you don't know how fast a new technology will be adopted? If our machines make it possible for the market to grow, and if design engineers recognize that it's now practical to use surface mount technology in applications where they couldn't use it before, then the market could explode. It's a chicken-and-egg problem, and at the moment we are the egg.

In the meantime we're adjusting our sights every month. Sales will reach approximately $4 million for 1990; next year's sales could be $8 million or $20 million. There are three "what if?" scenarios on my desk right now.

SURFACE MOUNT TECHNOLOGY

For decades electronic circuit boards had been manufactured in a traditional way. Automatic equipment picked up the electronic components, bent their wire leads, and placed them in position on the blank circuit board. The fully assembled board, containing perhaps hundreds of components, was then passed over a bath of molten solder, which would touch the heated leads on the underside of the board and rise into the holes, completing the electrical connections.

By the mid-1980s, as it became possible to make the components smaller and smaller, the wire leads themselves became cumbersome. Integrated "chips" were developed to combine the functions of many components within one device. Where most of the discrete components had two or three leads, the new chips might have a hundred or more; it was not practical to use wire. A new methodology called "surface mount technology" (SMT) eliminated the wire leads and holes in the circuit board by permitting delicate metal tabs of miniature components to be attached directly to the top surface of the board.

A high-speed automatic machine for assembling SMT circuit boards might be able to "pick and place" 6,000 to 8,000 standard components per hour. The machine might measure 25 feet long and cost some $250,000. By 1990 some 4,000 of these high-speed machines were installed and operating in the United States. In 1989 sales of this equipment had reached nearly 800 units, valued at $240 million. By 1990, however, more and more engineers were finding use for complex integrated chips, whose leads were too closely spaced to allow assembly with existing high-speed equipment.

FINE-PITCH DEVICES

Pick-and-place equipment worked well for miniature components and for simpler integrated chips—those with a small number of well-spaced leads. For example, a square chip measuring one inch per side and having ten leads per side, could easily be assembled with the high-speed equipment. But highly complex chips might have 20 or more leads per side of that one-inch square (a spacing of .025 inch on centers or smaller). These "fine-pitch" devices (FPDs) required extreme precision in placement, because if even one lead touched an edge of the wrong pad, the whole circuit board would be defective. Automated equipment available in 1990 could not reliably place these fine-pitch integrated circuit chips.

At the Surface Mount '90 show, Sierra Research and Technology was introducing one of the industry's first fully automated machines for placing and soldering FPDs. Don Spigarelli proudly showed off his new "Microplace" equipment:

> We say manufacturers should go ahead and use the production equipment they have, for all their surface mount components except the fine-pitch chips. Say they can produce one board per minute, with about one hundred components in place. If that board calls for a couple of fine-pitch devices, they would then bring it to the Microplace, which can automatically assemble the FPDs to finish off the board. Their production line is balanced, and the work is done at the highest possible quality.

The Microplace was priced at from $120,000–$250,000, depending on options, and could assemble two to four FPDs per minute. Although a number of high-volume electronics manufacturers had shown interest at the show, it was unknown how many had a current need for it or how many might begin to design fine-pitch chips into their circuits, now that assembly equipment was available.

For Sierra the Microplace represented an effort to establish itself in a new market niche. Since beginning its product development in 1985, the company had focused on the market for fine-pitch "rework and repair" equipment. This market served customers who needed to remove and replace defective or mismounted chips from finished circuit boards, usually on a one-at-a-time basis. Many low-priced techniques and machines serviced this niche, but most were low precision and laboriously slow. In the repair and rework segment, Sierra had brought in a full line of machines—from the "Low Sierra" manual rig at $9,000 each to the "Sierra FPD" at $23,000. The company had grown: sales of $22,000 in 1986 grew to just over $2 million in 1989, the first profitable year of operations (financial statements are shown in Exhibits C6.1 and C6.2).

THE FOUNDING OF SIERRA

Sierra Research and Technology was the second international firm founded by Don Spigarelli. His first company, HTC Corporation, was founded in 1974, when Spigarelli left BTU Engineering Corporation to develop soldering sys-

EXHIBIT C6.1 Sierra Research and Technology, Inc.
Balance Sheet
December 31, 1989 and 1988

	1989	1988
Assets		
Current assets:		
Cash	$ 225,443	$ (2,640)
Accounts receivable	312,443	195,474
Inventory (Note 1)	250,391	148,358
Prepaid expenses	44,010	11,842
Total current assets	$ 832,287	$ 353,034
Property, plant and equipment:		
Machinery and equipment	$ 38,727	$ 36,472
Furniture and fixtures	38,033	17,999
Computers	18,496	16,752
Less: Accumulated depreciation	(59,073)	(43,701)
Total property, plant and equipment	$ 36,183	$ 27,522
Other assets:		
Organizational costs (net)	$ 0	$ 44
Total assets	$ 868,470	$ 380,600
Liabilities and Owner's Equity		
Current liabilities:		
Accounts payable	$ 425,433	$ 343,514
Notes payable	232,393	205,069
Due to officer (Note 1)	78,099	395,864
Accrued expenses	69,059	219,630
Warranty reserve	20,000	20,333
Deferred revenue	23,999	9,000
Total liabilities	$ 848,983	$ 1,193,410
Owners' equity:		
Common stock, $.01 par value, 160,408 shares issued and outstanding	$ 1,604	$ 1,221
Paid-in capital in excess of par on common	1,851,644	1,352,027
Preferred stock subscribed, $.01 par, 188,800 shares subscribed, 0 issued	1,888	
Paid-in capital in excess of par on preferred	234,112	
Preferred stock warrants subscribed, 0 issued	472	
Retained earnings	(2,070,233)	(2,166,058)
Total owner's equity	$ 19,487	$ (812,810)
Total liabilities and owner's equity	$ 868,470	$ 380,600

continued

EXHIBIT C6.1 concluded

Notes to Financial Statements

Note 1: Amounts Due Officer

Amounts due officer are due D. J. Spigarelli. During 1989 Mr. Spigarelli loaned SRT $50,369. Accrued expenses of $89,506 due Mr. Spigarelli were converted to a note payable. On November 15, $500,000 of notes were converted to common stock. The conversion price was $13.05. During 1989, $34,966 in interest was accrued on the various notes. No interest was paid in 1989. At year end, the Amount Due Officer is:

Notes Payable	$ 3,761
Accrued Interest	74,338
	$ 78,099

It is anticipated that the notes and accrued interest will be paid in 1990.

Note 2: Legal Action

SRT is the defendant in a lawsuit brought by a former employee for wrongful termination. While SRT expects a favorable ruling, the loss potential is approximately $50,000.

tems for circuit boards, starting with a capital base of $60,000. HTC became a world leader in soldering equipment based on a new technology originally developed by AT&T, reaching $7.5 million in sales by 1984. In that year the company was sold to Emhart Corporation.

Don Spigarelli described the transition between HTC and Sierra:

> I actually incorporated Sierra about a month before we sold HTC, because I need a corporate form around me or else I just don't know what to do with myself. But we didn't do anything with the new company then.

> I had agreed with my wife to take a year off before I plunged into anything else. So I let the obligatory year go by. It was the most fruitless year I ever spent in my life. Not much fun—I didn't even play golf. For the first time, I didn't have a plan or a focus.

Sierra began product development in 1985 and shipped its first products the following year. By 1990 the company, located in a rural community 25 miles west of Boston, employed twenty people.

THE FOUNDER, DON SPIGARELLI

Don Spigarelli graduated in 1962 from University of California Berkeley, with a B.S. in mechanical engineering. He began his professional career in technical sales with Honeywell, Inc., and in 1964 had his first international exposure with Watkins-Johnson Company, where he established its worldwide sales operations. Spigarelli continued this international experience with BTU Engineering Corporation as manager of worldwide sales and marketing and as director of its Bruce Industrial Controls subsidiary.

Spigarelli had published numerous technical papers and had delivered many technical presentations (see Exhibit C6.3). He was also a member of numerous technical associations. Spigarelli held thirteen patents in thermal technology and machine design (the last three with Sierra Research and Technology). These patents were displayed prominently on silver plaques in Sierra's administrative offices.

Spigarelli's technological achievements had also added words to the dictionary. " 'Vapor-phase technology' is a term that did not exist before we used it at HTC," he said. "Now every-one uses it. People are starting to do the same thing with 'ballistic' and 'guided placement.' " "Ballistic placement" was Spigarelli's term for the traditional low-tolerance method of placing components where the operator could not see the actual contact between the component's leads and the circuit board. "It's like shooting the component at the board," said Don. "The operator prays it goes where it was pointed." "Guided placement," the Sierra technique, per-mitted an operator to adjust the chip's position right up to the point of contact.

Don Spigarelli was widely recognized in the surface mount engineering profession. He received a 1989 Technical Achievement Award from the International Society for Hybrid Microelectronics for his work in the field of surface mount technology, and he received the Exporter of the Year award from the U.S. Regional Small Business Administration in 1989 for his successful international management of both HTC and Sierra.

On a personal note, Spigarelli's ambitions for the long-range future were quite different:

> I want to be in the mountains. I'd like to be a cowboy. That's my alter ego. I have a ranch, north of Los Angeles in the California hills, with some horses and mules. That's where I'd like to be. That's living.

> I still want to be involved in the business in some sense, but without it controlling me as much. I want to be in control of my time and destiny.

MARKETS AND COMPETITION

In 1990 Sierra was targeting large, blue-chip firms, like IBM, in both the fine-pitch rework/repair and the FPD automated assembly markets. Don Spigarelli estimated the rework/

EXHIBIT   C6.2   Sierra Research and Technology, Inc.
Statement of Operations
For Years Ending December 31, 1989 and 1988

	1989	1988
Sales	$ 2,068,072	$ 1,217,262
Cost of sales	1,079,103	797,563
Gross profit	$ 988,969	$ 419,699
Operating expenses:		
Engineering & development	$ 411,960	$ 338,009
Sales and marketing	178,426	175,062
Administration	239,098	240,127
Total	$ 829,484	$ 753,198
Operating income (loss)	$ 159,485	$ (333,499)
Interest expense	63,660	64,721
Net income/(loss)	$ 95,825	$ (398,220)

repair market at under $10 million for "systems" sales worldwide in 1989. Many of these systems were noncommercial, in-house–built units. This market was expected to continue growing due to increased growth in the use of SMT (surface

mount technology), the ineffectiveness of reworking production volumes of FPDs by hand, and the lack of competitive products.

The FPD placement-with-soldering market, which was in its infancy in 1989, was estimated

EXHIBIT C6.3 Technical Papers and Presentations

Author	Presented	Title
Donald J. Spigarelli	Nepcon West 2/89	Development of highly accurate, entry-level systems for fine pitch and TAB placement
Donald J. Spigarelli	Nepcon West 2/89	Thermal separation in surface mount attachment and rework
Donald J. Spigarelli	China Lake 2/89	New hot-bar design addresses flatness and thermal uniformity issues for FPD and TAB soldering
Donald J. Spigarelli	SMTA 8/89	Thermal characterization for a surface mount rework system
Donald J. Spigarelli	ISHM 10/89	Development of convector technology for FPD and TAB soldering
Donald J. Spigarelli	Nepcon West 2/90	A comparative study of hot gas and hot-bar heating strategies for surface mount rework
Harold Hyman	Nepcon West 2/90	Fine-pitch placement with integral reflow; the logical cost-effective approach
Robert E. Cushman	SMT 4/90	Effects of preheating for surface mount attachment and rework
Donald J. Spigarelli	IMC 5/90	A system for fine-pitch device attachment incorporating lead-to-pad matching and integral reflow soldering
John M. DeCarlo	Nepcon East 6/90	A new technology for fine-pitch placement utilizing active lead-to-pad matching and integral reflow
John A. Romano	SMTA 8/90	Techniques for fine-pitch rework

Patents Issued

No:	SRT-001XX	
Entitled:	Programmable Electric Heater	
U. S. Pat Appl S/N:		Pat. No.: 4,775,775
Status:	Issued 4/10/88	COVERAGE: PMH
No:	SRT-002XX	
Entitled:	Programmable Circuit Board Rework and Repair System	
U. S. Pat Appl S/N:		Pat. No.: 4,832,250
Status:	Issued 5/23/89	Coverage: SRM-100
No:	SRT-003XX	
Entitled:	Component Centering Tool	
U. S. Pat Appl S/N:		Pat. No.: 4,821,393
Status:	Issued 4/1/89	Coverage: Centering Tool

at approximately $15 million/year. Substantial growth was expected here as well, due to an expected increase in the use of fine-pitch devices. There were no exact estimates of how much each market was expected to grow, since that would depend on the acceptance and integration of FPD technologies.

Sierra's competition in rework/repair came from over twenty companies already in the field. Although their products were less accurate, they were also lower in cost than Sierra's line.

Competitors in placement and soldering of fine-pitch devices included two Japanese, one Canadian, and three other American companies, all of which entered the market in 1990. Exhibit C6.4 lists these competitors; two were major makers of traditional SMT automated assembly equipment. By August of 1990 no company had successfully installed and run an automated FPD assembly machine in a production environment.

Geographically Sierra's markets were worldwide. Sierra shipped its rework/repair equipment internationally to England, France, Italy, Ireland, and Sweden. International sales were approximately 15 percent of 1989's total revenues and were projected to be 22 percent in 1990. Spigarelli viewed the overseas marketplace as a growth opportunity for Sierra:

> We went into international markets to increase orders. I don't understand why more small companies don't go overseas. To be timid seems so inconsistent with an entrepreneurial stance. I would think they would be excited by a virgin market. On the other hand, you have to produce a better product to market it internationally. It used to be, at least, that Americans were far more tolerant of low quality and performance than the Europeans were.
>
> I already had international experience with BTU and HTC, so it was no big deal with Sierra. Plus there's a well-kept secret: the International Trade Administration in the Department of Commerce is one of the most effective departments we've got. They teach you how to classify your product so you know what types of export licenses are

needed, and they help fill out the paperwork for export documentation.

EXHIBIT C6.4

Leading Competitors in Fine Pitch-Placement Equipment, 1990

Universal Instrument Corp., Binghamton, NY

subsidiary of Dover Corporation (ample resources)

major builder of automated electronic-assembly equipment

full line of through-hole and surface-mount capabilities

able to purchase and resell under own label

W. T. Automation, Florida

small, independent systems integrator

high-quality, high-price equipment

different heating technology, based on thermodes

Anorad, Texas

small, independent, custom-systems integrator

little presence at national shows

ATS, Kitchener, Ontario, Canada

builder of automated electronic-assembly equipment

sophisticated, efficient, high-price equipment

leader in SMT in 1990

strong in customized systems

Fuji
Panasonic

very large technology companies

exhibitors at national and international shows

little presence in direct competition

Nippon Avionics
Nitto Kogyo

leaders in Japanese home market

strong capabilities with small chips (28–40 leads)

little capability with large-scale chips (200+ leads)

little presence in U. S. markets

Source: Mr. Harold Hyman, Sierra Research and Technology, Inc.

PRODUCT PROMOTION AND SALES ORGANIZATION

Sierra promoted its products through a combination of trade shows, new-product releases, direct mail, and technical-paper presentations. Spigarelli himself wrote and presented many of those papers. Because of the emerging nature of the technology of placement and rework of surface-mounted devices, especially fine pitch, the company had placed a heavy emphasis on the presentation of technical papers. As a result, Sierra had become synonymous with the leading edge of technology and equipment for this field, according to many exhibitors at the Surface Mount '90 show.

Sierra marketed its products through eleven manufacturer's representatives in the United States and Canada and seven representatives/ distributors overseas. The company's representatives were supported by two in-house regional sales managers as well as Spigarelli himself. Exhibit C6.5 provides a partial listing of Sierra's U.S. customers.

In late 1986 Sierra sold its first repair/ rework units. By 1988 its product line was basically completed and sales totaled $1.2 million, more than doubling 1987's sales of $547,000. Sales doubled once again in 1989 to just over $2 million. Plans for 1990 were to double sales once again, to $4 million.

John DeCarlo, Sierra's director of engineering, believed that the market for Sierra's products presented a tremendous opportunity. Additionally he saw opportunities for Sierra to diversify within its markets. DeCarlo questioned, however, if the market was ready for Sierra's new robotic product:

> The question is, is the market ready for it now? This is why Don isn't sure how much we will sell in 1991. It's a Catch 22. Someone has to stick the stuff forward and bite the bullet. Once the equipment is out there, once it's a proven process, then it's embraced and it's like throwing a switch on. There's a technology curve and we're on the bottom.

EXHIBIT   C6.5
A Partial List of Current United States Customers

AT&T
Bendix Electronics
Boeing
Compaq Computer
Delco
Digital Equipment Corp.
E. Systems
Evans & Sutherland
Fairchild
General Electric
General Motors
GTE
Hewlett-Packard
Honeywell
Hughes Aircraft
ITT
IBM
Magnavox
Martin-Marietta
McDonnell Douglas
Motorola
NASA
Raytheon
U. S. Air Force
U. S. Navy
UNISYS
Westinghouse

CORPORATE STRUCTURE

Sierra employed twenty people, six of whom were former HTC employees. Spigarelli handled most of Sierra's hiring himself, relying on his personal assessment based on brief interviews.

He was very concerned with how potential employees might fit into the organization, both technically and personally. He commented on this in light of Sierra's retention rate:

> People come in fast, and they can go out just as fast. You have to pay attention to how they fit in the organization. Can they respond? Can they deal with pressures? I've learned as a manager that you have to act very quickly if a new person doesn't fit, or you get hurt and you're hurting everybody.

Sierra's organization included an operations manager, a production manager, a director of engineering, an international manager, and two regional sales managers. Additionally a board of directors had been assembled, and the formation of a technical advisory board was being considered. Spigarelli described his management philosophy in light of the establishment of Sierra's corporate structure:

> We just put together an operational board of directors, which consists of five members: three very successful career entrepreneurs, my wife, and myself. I could control the board, but I have chosen not to. I subject myself to the authority of the board for input into the overall direction of the company.
>
> I am very willing to share the management of the company. I don't demand to do my sales manager's job or my international manager's job, but I have to have the right people in place to do that. As little as two years ago I had none of the right people. I was doing it all. I have only gradually been able to build up competent management to do some of these things.

OPERATIONS

Sierra's products were assembled in a 1,000-square-foot area of the company's plant, from components made by outside vendors to SRT's specifications. Several workbenches contained partially built rework/repair machines; a six-foot-high steel frame for a Microplace machine stood by itself at one side of the room. Pat Cunningham, operations manager of SRT, commented:

> For the Microplace we place our vendor orders only when a customer order is in-house. The frame is custom-made, of course—welded and finished to our plans; it's our longest lead-time component, at about twelve weeks. Some thirty vendors supply about ninety-five percent of the parts for this machine.
>
> The unique things about the Microplace are its heating technology, its positioning algorithms— that's the way it looks at the chip and sees where it is in relation to the board—and the software that drives the process.

A small machine shop occupied one corner of the production area, but Cunningham indicated it was used only for small jobs, like relocating a hole in a purchased part. Sierra relied on its suppliers for all important fabrication.

FINANCING

Sierra had been financed through 1989 with Spigarelli's own personal investment of over $500,000, a bank-credit line secured by receivables, and a private placement totaling $260,000 secured in November of 1989. In order to ensure access to capital markets, Spigarelli required as a matter of policy that Sierra maintain a positive net worth. Since the accumulated expenses of product research and development very nearly equaled the total investment of stockholders, even a small loss in one month could tip the balance sheet into a negative net worth position. It was imperative that the company show a profit every month. Spigarelli mused:

> One of the biggest problems I have right now is the difficulty of spending developmental funds and/or increased marketing funds without hurt-

ing our profitability. Say you have, oh, $500K in the bank to plow into development, and you know that all of these developments are right on target and you can really achieve these things. And say you know that the more rapidly you spend it, the more rapidly you achieve the profitability. But if you spend the money, the next two years are going to show net worth at a deficit, and you can't permit that. What's the right answer? What do you do?

So one of the biggest problems facing me is the dedication to the bottom line. How do I do some of these things? I've got to figure out ingenious ways to utilize monetary resources to perform developments and marketing without hurting my bottom line. I've got a real conflict here, trying to balance all of these things out at the proper level. Because of the banks, I have been driven to be concerned with my immediate profitability, and I'm talking about month, by month, by month.

In September of 1990, Spigarelli was thinking about the need for additional financing. He had been talking to venture capitalists but was uncomfortable with that approach. On a fully diluted basis, he owned 74 percent of the company; twenty-six others owned approximately 19 percent, and the remainder represented warrants on the preferred stock. If he were to sell stock it would be at the same price as the private placement.

Operations manager Pat Cunningham estimated that additional financing of about $500,000 would be needed in 1991. That amount, however, would be influenced by the market's rate of acceptance of fine-pitch surface mount technologies and how aggressively Sierra pursued the market. Given the projected margins on the new product line, Don felt that it was possible to grow using internally generated funds. This approach, however, would take a lot of nailbiting on the part of Pat Cunningham, who had to balance available cash with vendors' needs for prompt payment.

INTERNATIONAL SALES

Harold Hyman, international manager, had spent the last twenty years in international sales management. He had worked with Spigarelli at HTC, staying on after the sale until October 1989, when he joined Sierra. He had grown up in London and spoke with a thoroughly British accent. Hyman described what it was like to work with Spigarelli:

> He's a very dynamic person—full of ideas, even pushy. But working with him is interesting and very challenging. It's not all roses, but I like it. It can be frustrating at times. Don has so much going on in his mind that you're never quite sure what the important thing of the day is.

> But we do have very developed plans. Those plans say what our objectives are and what certain things we have to do. We may change our minds about how we are going to achieve them, but our objectives are essentially the same all of the time. We're just dynamic and mobile in achieving them. You can't sit on your laurels. It's moving all the time.

Hyman's primary goal for 1990 was to reach $1 million in revenue from international markets; only $300,000 of 1989's revenue had been generated internationally, but no special effort was put into overseas business that year. Plans for the remainder of 1990 included cultivating markets individually, developing and training a network of representatives, and visiting territories. Those plans were in keeping with Hyman's approach to international success in a small company:

> I've worked internationally for many years, so I know the markets, the people, the companies. It was fairly easy to establish that we had a market. A lot of people use overseas markets as a dumping ground. I take the opposite view.

> You need a good—no, an excellent—product. You've got to be sure about what you ship. If

you've got a problem 3,000 miles away, it's a lot harder to deal with than if it's around the corner.

Depending on how the technology grows, I would like to see the company at $20 million by 1992.

MANAGEMENT PLANNING AND CONTROLS

Sierra's employees operated under a formal control structure that tied managers' compensation directly to their planning and performance. Spigarelli believed that setting specific targets was vital. Additionally he stressed timely resource utilization, since either under- or overusing resources would diminish Sierra's achievements. Sierra's plans were formally revised twice a year, but individual goals could be altered at any time by anyone. That, however, rarely happened, since any significant change in an individual department influenced all other operational heads and all their subordinates.

Don Spigarelli had once worked under a pay system that made bonuses totally dependent on meeting plan. In spite of a heroic performance in one period, he had not met his target—and he earned no bonus. The experience left an indelible impression on him:

If my bonus depends on your performance as well as my own, then I will work very hard to see that you perform well. Anything I can do to assure your success, I'll do. And I know you will expect the same of me, if your pay depends on my performance.

Spigarelli acknowledged the problems encountered in this system:

One of the difficulties with explaining this to new people and keeping it as an ongoing program is that it makes people responsible for things that are outside their own control. My salespeople are responsible for bringing in orders. Manufacturing is responsible for shipping. Sales can always say, "I would have done it but manufacturing was behind."

Getting over the initial barrier and developing interdepartmental trust and communication is a big issue. A person may not be totally in control. But the compensation rule is not optional. They are responsible for their plan regardless of what they can control. If the economy goes flat or if they get a windfall, they both count equally.

Compensation was based on both effective planning and achievement of the plan. According to Spigarelli:

It's good planning, commitment to measurement of achievement, and reward based on achievement that lets people know where they are. They don't even have to ask questions. They know if they're making it or not. Even though it's a stringent way to go, even though it's kind of a disciplinarian approach, it works. They're sort of like teenagers. They like to know where the boundaries are. They like to know if they're doing well.

People that have performed well regardless of the circumstances have been rewarded and people that have not performed well regardless of the circumstances have not. I'm strict as far as their reward is concerned, right from the beginning. They don't receive their reward unless they meet their plan within certain specifications that are set out in advance. I try to stress to them that their rewards are for a combination of good planning and good results; one without the other doesn't get it.

Cash bonuses were given to key personnel based on the achievement of objectives key to a particular position. For example, in production it was the shipment of a certain value of products. In addition, key personnel also participated in a stock option plan.

THE FUTURE

Sierra's financial objectives were to continue to double sales each year for the next few years. Spigarelli was confident that this was achievable in 1990, but he was uncertain of what would happen after that:

> I've got a two-year plan, but I'm not at all sure about the second year. In high tech, more than two years is a lifetime. I'm pretty confident that we'll go from $2 million to $4 million in 1990, but I'm not at all sure about going from $4 million to $8 million in 1991. We have yet to test the market in terms of real live revenues from the new Microplace system. I am uncertain about the upper limit. I have no qualms about the lower limit. My qualms are that it may not be big enough.

> We may not be able to go from 4 to 8. We may have to go from 4 to 20. To do this thing correctly, we may have to go faster, because by going slower we may not realize as much potential.

John DeCarlo was also concerned about the uncertainty surrounding Sierra's sales potential, particularly in its implications for engineering.

> If you're not properly prepared, you don't make the $20 million even if the demand is there. It's self-correcting. If you don't document your products and build them throug'h good engineering standards, then you can't support the first ones you ship. While you're trying to catch up, you suck all of the resources out of the company and you don't have the next generation product to satisfy the changing needs. So it kills itself. The company hits a plateau and declines from there.

> This is an important time for us because if we don't develop now, we won't be a part of the upswing.

Spigarelli commented further:

> My objective is to gain some personal liquidity by year end 1991. I want to realize a profit or at least to have the opportunity to create that profit. That doesn't necessarily mean that we'll sell the company or its shares, but we could if we wanted to. And I'm not hiding this from anyone. It's a stated objective with the board of directors.

> If I did intend to exercise that option, I would do so in such a way that I would still be with the company and everyone would benefit. Everybody participates in stock option programs and such so they really don't find this a distasteful goal.

Results for Sierra's first half of 1990 were close to plan (see Exhibits C6.6 and C6.7), in spite of the business downturn that plagued the Massachusetts high-technology community. Spigarelli was still uncertain, however, about the achievement of the second year of his two-year plan. Nobody could predict how quickly FPD technology would be received and integrated. This uncertainty further complicated the internal changes that would have to accompany Sierra's future growth:

> I saw it with HTC. After 125 employees all of a sudden things got harder to get done. I was very frustrated by that. It changes. I can't directly manage 125 people. I can't deal with every little thing and I shouldn't. I became uncomfortable with HTC when it got up to around seven or eight million dollars. I was uncomfortable with the fact that I was poor and all of my assets were riding on the company.

> I'm not sure that there is a size limitation now with Sierra. I'm past the point of looking at size being a limiting factor. I'm an engineer and there are issues that come with size that I don't want to deal with, but I've gotten beyond that. I understand now what my role is, and it's not to know everything that goes on with every UPS shipment. I've got to make things work by being creative.

SIERRA RESEARCH AND TECHNOLOGY, INC.: POSTSCRIPT

In 1990 Sierra had total revenues of approximately $3.2 million with profits of $36,000. International sales accounted for one-third of total revenues. The shortfall from the target of $4 million was partly attributed to the long sales cycle of the Microplace. Although there was considerable interest in the product, according to Spigarelli, no signed orders had been received by the end of the year.

In December of 1990 Spigarelli obtained $400,000 at $1.25 per share from the Venture Capital Fund of New England, a firm with capital under management of over $49 million. Having the new capital available helped reduce nervousness, Don said, but it did nothing to help answer the question of whether and when the market would materialize. A recent survey by CEERIS International, Inc., however, estimated the 1990 U.S. market for Ultra-Fine Pitch Assemblers (the class of equipment represented by Microplace) at $25 million to $30 million.

EXHIBIT   C6.6

SRT 1990 Revised Plan
Balance Sheet Variance Report
As of Month Ending June 1990

	Actual	Plan	Variance
Assets			
Cash	$ 58,749	$ 85,166	$ (26,417)
Accounts receivable	369,684	459,000	(89,316)
Inventory	448,325	425,000	23,325
Prepaid expenses	44,890	50,000	(5,110)
Fixed assets (net)	83,867	82,610	1,257
Other (software)	19,358	19,350	8
Total assets	$ 1,024,873	$ 1,121,126	$ (96,253)
Liabilities and Owners' Equity			
Notes payable	$ 289,364	$ 266,000	$ 23,364
Accounts payable	435,435	500,000	(64,565)
Accrued payroll	34,522	60,000	(25,478)
Accrued expenses	87,262	90,000	(2,738)
Warranty	21,488	21,000	488
Deferred income	0	0	0
Long-term liabilities	57,319	57,000	319
Total liabilities	$ 925,390	$ 994,000	$ (68,610)
Shareholders' equity	$ 2,086,765	$ 2,093,000	$ (6,235)
Retained earnings	(2,070,234)	(2,070,234)	0
Current year earnings	82,952	104,360	(21,408)
Total equity	$ 99,483	$ 127,126	$ (27,643)
Total liabilities & equity	$ 1,024,873	$ 1,121,126	$ (96,253)
Debt/equity ratio	9.3	7.8	

EXHIBIT C6.7

SRT 1990 Revised Plan
Income Statement Variance Report
For Period Ending June 30, 1990

	Current Month			Six Months Year to Date		
	Actual	**Plan**	**Variance**	**Actual**	**Plan**	**Variance**
Sales:						
STD System	$ 0	$ 121,025	$ (121,025)	$ 146,895	$ 146,895	$ 0
FPD Systems	114,100	100,000	14,100	724,006	826,396	(102,390)
TAB Systems	39,660	0	39,660	269,770	284,849	(15,079)
Auto	65,000	0	65,000	190,050	202,170	(12,120)
Low End Systems	0	46,000	(46,000)	0	0	0
Placement Systems ..	0	0	0	0	0	0
Options & Spares.....	36,414	45,860	(9,446)	256,538	225,124	31,414
Service....................	19,948	2,000	17,948	29,200	11,252	17,948
Sales Discounts........	(1,683)	0	(1,683)	(9,232)	(7,549)	(1,683)
Total Sales	$ 273,439	$ 314,885	$ (41,446)	$1,607,227	$1,689,137	$ (81,910)
Cost of Sales:						
STD Systems	$ 0	$ 65,836	$ (65,836)	$ 101,975	$ 101,974	$ 1
FPD Systems	50,281	47,511	2,770	355,889	403,462	(47,573)
TAB Systems	13,100	0	13,100	86,285	95,080	(8,795)
Auto	34,995	0	34,995	101,469	98,474	2,995
Low End Systems	0	19,264	(19,264)	0	(1)	1
Placement Systems ..	0	0	0	0	0	0
Options & Spares.....	10,168	18,809	(8,641)	53,574	45,407	8,167
Service....................	3,253	0	3,253	3,253	0	3,253
Total Cost of Sales ...	$ 111,797	$ 151,420	$ (39,623)	$ 702,445	$ 744,396	$ (41,951)
Gross Profit	$ 161,642	$ 163,465	$ (1,823)	$ 904,782	$ 944,741	$ (39,959)
Contribution..............	59.1%	51.9%	00.0%	56.3%	55.9%	0.4%
Net mfg.	4,183	12,970	(8,787)	23,732	19,435	4,297
Mfg. profit (loss)	$ 165,825	$ 176,435	$ (10,610)	$ 928,514	$ 964,176	$ (35,662)
	60.6%	56.0%	4.6%	57.8%	57.1%	0.7%
Operating Expenses:						
Development...........	$ 20,173	$ 22,342	$ (2,169)	$ 103,693	$ 112,366	$ (8,673)
Engineering.............	22,537	12,780	9,757	102,160	102,706	(546)
Sales Rework	30,568	39,941	(9,373)	218,264	219,209	(945)
Sales Replacement...	0	0	0	0	0	0
Marketing	14,086	10,321	3,765	38,318	30,265	8,053
Service....................	5,792	5,704	88	36,128	36,901	(773)
International	8,209	22,994	(14,785)	99,929	106,582	(6,653)
Administration	34,082	38,808	(4,726)	211,228	208,041	3,187
Total operating expenses..................	$ 135,447	$ 152,890	$ (17,443)	$ 809,720	$ 816,070	$ (6,350)
Operating Income	$ 30,378	$ 23,545	$ 6,833	$ 118,794	$ 148,106	$ (29,312)
Interest Income...........	537	0	537	4,521	4,500	21
Interest Expense...........	(1,884)	(5,189)	3,305	(15,035)	(16,000)	965
Federal Tax	(3,600)	(3,402)	(198)	(17,705)	(22,000)	4,295
State Tax	(1,400)	0	(1,400)	(7,623)	(10,000)	2,377
Net Income	$ 24,031	$ 14,954	$ 9,077	$ 82,952	$ 104,606	$ (21,654)

Clermont Builders Supply, Inc., and the Florida Concrete Products Association

Julian W. Vincze

Lawson (Speedy) Wolfe, president of Clermont Builders Supply, Inc., was enjoying his early Monday-morning coffee and planning his week's activities when a note he was reading triggered his ongoing concern for the viability of the concrete industry in Florida. He wondered if the industry could do more than eke out a marginal existence. He felt he had positioned his company satisfactorily to prosper regardless of what happened in the concrete business, but he hated to see the industry suffer so, as he felt it had in recent years.

Speedy was a very busy person. As president of Clermont Builders Supply (CBS), he had always practiced a hands-on style of management. All his employees were used to seeing Speedy several times each and every day. A desk jockey he was not. As a naturally high-energy person, Speedy liked to feel the pulse of his organization by "being involved." If things were happening in any aspect of the operations, Speedy would be there. Not constantly, necessarily—that is, unless there was an emergency—but there nevertheless, because he would drop by several times during the day just to "see that everything was all right." He had always been an active member and was past president of the Florida Concrete and Products Association, and he had used a similarly active style in that organization as well. He made a note to prepare his comments and position for the upcoming Concrete Block Committee meeting, where the industry's future was to be discussed. He decided that, more than that, he wanted to find out for himself what was happening in the industry, because no one seemed to know. He thought about his alternatives.

HISTORY OF CLERMONT BUILDERS SUPPLY, INC.

Clermont Builders Supply was founded by four investors in 1945. The majority stockholder was Fred Wolfe, who initially owned 70 percent of the stock. Within a short period, however, Fred Wolfe had purchased an additional 20 percent of the stock from two of the other investors. The remaining 10 percent of the stock belonged to John Lynn.

After World War II, building materials were hard to acquire. However, Fred Wolfe had made many friends and acquaintances during the war and so was able to get these scarce materials. At that time there was one machine in the concrete block plant, and that machine produced one block at a time (300 per day, using six people). These men did everything else, either by hand or by shovel. It is an understatement to say that after World War II the Florida concrete industry was very labor-intensive. If one were to compare the postwar production figures with what a three-man crew could do per machine today, the results would be rather surprising. Today three workers can produce 10,000 blocks per shift.

Labor costs have actually declined over the years because of the high volumes being produced with automated equipment.

CBS had no readily identifiable stages of growth; its growth was gradual and steady. In 1950 CBS had one ready-mix concrete truck, which represented an investment cost of $6,000, and one concrete block truck. CBS was involved primarily in commercial work. In 1957 CBS opened its preengineered roof trusses business. It was not profitable, however, and ceased operations in 1963. CBS seemed to be ahead of its time; the housing industry was not yet ready for preengineered roof trusses. In 1971 Fred Wolfe passed away, and his son, Lawson Wolfe, became president, having worked with the company since 1960. During 1971 CBS had sales totaling $800,000. In 1974 the present block plant was built in Clermont. In 1978 the preengineered roof trusses business was restarted. In 1980 CBS bought Eustis Block and Supply Company (EBSC). The EBSC plant manufactures both ready-mix concrete and concrete blocks. During 1980 CBS sales increased to $4 million. In August 1984 CBS opened a branch in Orlando. CBS's Orlando facility doesn't manufacture concrete blocks, concentrating instead on handling ready-mix concrete and building materials.

Currently CBS is divided into four separate divisions. Three of these divisions use ready-mix concrete products by CBS, such as prehung door units and roof trusses. These three divisions are organized around items that CBS manufactures and sells to contractors, and in total represent 60 percent of CBS's business. The fourth division includes building materials and supplies, which represent a resale situation. In general CBS buys these materials and supplies in large quantities and then sells them to contractors in smaller quantities. Approximately 10 percent of CBS's sales volume involves general retail sales mixed among the four strategic business units.

In 1982 CBS had $6.5 million in sales. In 1983 CBS had $9.5 million in sales, and in 1984 it had $12.5 million in sales. (Exhibits C7.1 and C7.2 show the details.) In fact, the last twenty-five years represent a huge growth period in the construction industry in Florida and for CBS. This growth is continuing as Florida leads the nation with a 3– to 5-percent annual increase in population. The Orlando metropolitan area is the major market area for CBS's products. About half of its 1983 and 1984 sales came from the sale of concrete block. In 1979 the concrete block industry was estimated to have an 80-percent market share for exterior wall construction in Florida. However, from 1979 to 1984 the concrete block industry experienced a dramatic decline in market share. Exact market share figures aren't available, but many operators guessed that it might have dropped to 50 percent by mid-1984.

In 1984 CBS had twenty-four ready-mix trucks, nine concrete block trucks, six building materials delivery trucks, and ten forklifts. To understand the changes that have taken place in concrete block production, one must realize that in 1945 a block machine represented an investment cost of $1,500 and could produce one block at a time, or 300 per day. By 1984 a block machine involved an investment cost of $135,000 but was capable of producing 1,200 blocks per hour. The investment cost for a complete plant is a minimum of $750,000, so today's Florida concrete industry is extremely capital-intensive.

CBS employs six outside salespeople. They call directly on contractors and really could be considered service people rather than salespeople. These salespeople write up and fill orders for a need that already exists; contractors have already decided they need concrete blocks, and the salesmen just write the orders and provide services for them. CBS's organization chart is shown in Exhibit C7.3.

CHANGES IN DIRECTION

After more than twenty years of being a manager, the last thirteen as president and CEO of CBS, Speedy had begun a new stage in his professional management career. He had enrolled in an executive M.B.A. (EMBA) program being offered by a local college. He knew this activity would place a real time constraint on his usual activity schedule. Speedy's dilemma was how to find time for all his usual activities and still have time and energy for this new commitment. He expected to learn better ways to manage his organization from this program and was looking forward to it. Becoming a student again after so many years was going to be quite a departure for Speedy. He was used to running his own organization and making most of the decisions (and all the really important ones). But Speedy had heard good things about this executive MBA program from several associates. He had even looked up a few of the program's recent graduates. They had all had both good and not-so-good things to say about the program. But

EXHIBIT   C7.1

Clermont Builders Supply, Inc.
Combined Balance Sheet
September 30, 1984

Assets

Current assets:			
Cash and bank accounts.......................		$ 64,037.47	
Notes receivable—current....................		35,419.06	
Accounts receivable		1,138,248.50	
Employee advances..............................		7,397.68	
Merchandise inventory[a].......................		1,068,370.13	
Gas and diesel fuel inventory		18,502.55	
Prepaid insurance................................		18,516.75	
Prepaid interest...................................		302,363.52	
Prepaid taxes and licenses...................		8,423.72	
Prepaid income tax..............................		75,793.00	
Total current assets			$ 2,737,072.38
Fixed assets:			
Land..		$ 492,432.32	
Buildings	$ 420,257.92		
Motor vehicles.....................................	2,187,114.45		
Store equipment	5,200.00		
Machinery and equipment....................	1,210,757.94		
Office furniture and fixtures.................	146,627.21		
Other fixed assets	266,739.51		
Less: Depreciation & allowance	(2,454,855.61)		
Depreciable assets...............................		1,781,841.42	
Total fixed assets...............................			2,274,273.74
Other assets:			
Notes receivable—long-term		$ 37,971.98	
Stock		411,557.61	
Deposit..		120.00	
Other investments		23,008.67	
Total other assets			472,658.26
Total assets...			$ 5,484,004.38

continued

[a] A LIFO inventory is used. LIFO reserve is $67,018.41.

EXHIBIT   C7.1   *concluded*

Liabilities

Current liabilities:

Notes payable—current	$ 516,949.82	
Accounts payable	727,147.91	
Employee accounts	(3,694.53)	
Coca Cola machines fund	2,102.61	
Accrued payroll	32,973.81	
Profit-sharing trust	45,980.00	
Accrued payroll taxes	1,033.63	
Accrued unemployment insurance	(6,887.72)	
Accrued property tax	14,636.84	
Accrued sales tax	20,096.78	
Accrued interest	15,027.69	
Accrued emergency excise tax	5,000.00	
Total current liabilities		$ 1,370,366.84
Long-term liabilities:		
Notes payable—long-term	$ 1,939,143.55	
Loans from officers	206,267.81	
D. Wolfe—annuity	63,426.75	
Total long-term liabilities		2,208,838.11
Net worth:		
Capital stock	$ 24,000.00	
Retained earnings	1,880,799.43	
Total net worth		1,904,799.43
Total liabilities and net worth		$ 5,484,004.38

EXHIBIT   C7.2

Clermont Builders Supply, Inc.
Combined Statement of Operations
Fiscal Year Ending September 30, 1984

Revenue:		
Sales	$12,538,713.58	
Discounts allowed	161,983.24	
Net sales		$12,376,730.34
Cost of materials sold:		
Beginning inventory	$ 699,466.98	
Purchases	7,977,952.78	
Less: discounts earned	(131,323.02)	
Direct labor	428,949.17	
Manufacturing overhead	424,220.57	
Less closing inventory	(1,068,370.13)	
Cost of sales		8,330,896.35
Gross profit		$ 4,045,833.99

continued

EXHIBIT   C7.2   *concluded*

Gross profit (brought forward)		$ 4,045,833.99
Expenses:		
Officers' salaries..	$ 278,595.22	
Wages and salaries...	1,359,965.65	
Payroll taxes...	124,808.91	
Group and workers' compensation insurance	137,787.86	
Employee benefits	30,266.36	
Office expense	58,024.24	
Small tools and supplies..	4,661.78	
Utilities	13,460.33	
Telephone	34,518.44	
Administrative expenses	90,000.00	
Repair/maintenance—property	15,473.53	
Repair/maintenance—vehicles	233,752.26	
Repair/maintenance—machinery	18,195.31	
Insurance	24,902.16	
Depreciation	383,310.88	
Taxes..	39,240.72	
Rentals	15,296.83	
Bad debts	163,758.92	
Gas, oil, and diesel fuel...	298,780.89	
Tires	49,880.21	
Travel and entertainment...	17,061.19	
Contributions	5,043.66	
Sales expenses..	2,671.36	
Errors and omissions..	703.35	
Dues and subscriptions	9,345.29	
Security expense	7,725.37	
Legal and promotional fees	39,466.61	
Deferred compensation	12,999.96	
Advertising	19,202.97	
Miscellaneous expense..	20,659.76	
Interest expense..	160,737.91	
Profit sharing	45,980.00	
Total expenses		3,716,277.93
Operating profit		$ 329,556.06
Add: Other income		84,268.25
Net profit before taxes..		$ 413,824.31

Note: LIFO method of accounting used.

the bottom line had always been the same: a firm recommendation that they had "learned a lot" and that most of it was "immediately usable" in day-to-day management. Each said he would "do it again," although it was a tough and time-consuming program.

Although favorably impressed, Speedy had reserved judgment until he had paid a visit to the college. He had talked to the coordinator of the EMBA program for a few hours and had taken away a full set of brochures. He liked what he had seen and heard, but he just didn't rush into things. Speedy didn't make commitments lightly. If he was going to enroll in the EMBA program, he was going to give it the time and energy to do it correctly—with a firm determination to do his best and get the most he could out of it.

EXHIBIT C7.3 Clermont Builders Supply Organization Chart

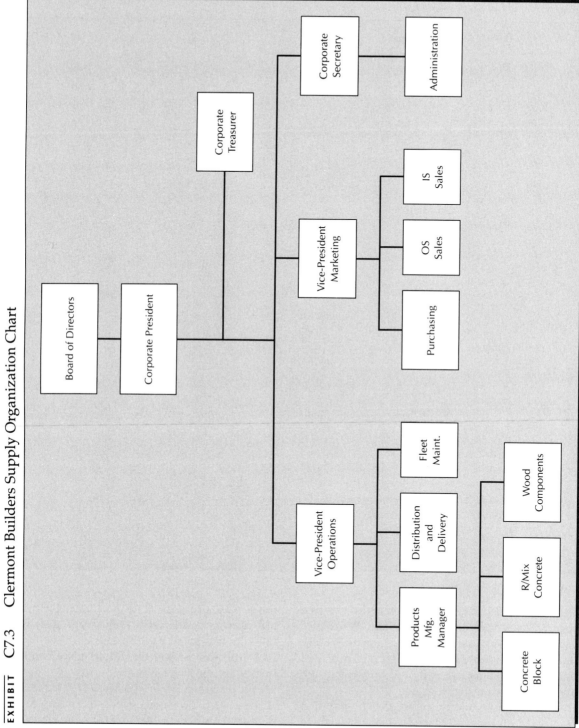

In fact this was a trait of Speedy's that was recognized by all his business associates. Speedy didn't do things in half-measure. When Speedy said he'd do the job, it was accomplished on time and in full measure. For example, his active role in Florida Concrete and Products Association affairs over the years had been recognized by his election as president for 1983–'84. In fact, it was his desire to continue his active role in the association, plus his responsibilities as president of CBS, that combined to make this morning's task of planning his week's activities calendar so meaningful. He felt the association was moving too slowly on its declining situation. He decided that maybe he needed to prod them a little bit as well as clarify the issues for himself.

FLORIDA CONCRETE AND PRODUCTS ASSOCIATION

The Florida Concrete and Products Association (FC&PA) was formed in 1955. Its membership numbers 150 companies that do business in Florida. The FC&PA was created to fulfill the needs and mutual interests of concrete and concrete products producers who chose to cooperate in creating an association. Examples of member firms are Rinker Masonry, which is said to have 25 percent of Florida's concrete block production capacity; Lone Star Florida, Inc., which employed over 1,400 people in Florida and was purchased in late 1984 by Tarmac PLC of Wolverhampton, England; and Tarmac PLC, already a member of FC&PA with a currently purported 30 percent of Florida's concrete block production capacity. Completing the list of the three largest (formerly four) producers of concrete block is Florida Mining. In total the FC&PA membership firms represent over 90 percent of all Florida producers and over 98 percent of production capacity.

The FC&PA organization structure is detailed in Exhibit C7.4. The association's charter and bylaws mandate the formation of fifteen permanent committees. The purpose of the Accounting and Credit Committee is to annually conduct a seminar for owners and/or accounting/credit personnel, to bring them up to date on current topics of general interest relating to accounting practices and credit policies. The Aggregates Committee is required to meet at least semiannually, or more often if necessary, to keep abreast of those activities that relate directly to aggregate producers. Another purpose is to coordinate activities of mutual concern with the Florida Department of Transportation.

The Associate Member Committee is expected to enhance the concrete industry in Florida and to ensure the maximum utilization of concrete and allied products and services. It also provides a liaison between all associate members and the FC&PA Board of Directors. The purpose of the Building Codes Committee is to meet and coordinate with the Florida Building Codes Commission in their determinations relating to the Florida code. During meetings with the commission the Building Codes Committee always attempts to make it known that in the opinion of FC&PA it is impossible for any single building code to satisfy all the needs in all the diverse areas of Florida. One of the purposes of the Education and Program Committee is to develop a program of education, short courses, meetings, and the like that will help owners, managers, supervisors, and other personnel of member organizations to do a better job. Another purpose is to determine the number of meetings, courses, and so on, to have each year. The educational liason–Florida of the FC&PA Joint Technical Committee is charged with the task of improving the quality of concrete and its inspection and testing and also to develop solutions to reconcile problems and complaints concerning concrete and its inspection.

Based on a decision made by the board of directors on October 4, 1968, the Finance and Audit Committee was formed and given the responsibilities of reviewing audits, preparing budgets, financing projects, and so forth, but not to override the treasurer or anyone else's

EXHIBIT **C7.4** Florida Concrete and Products Association Organization Chart

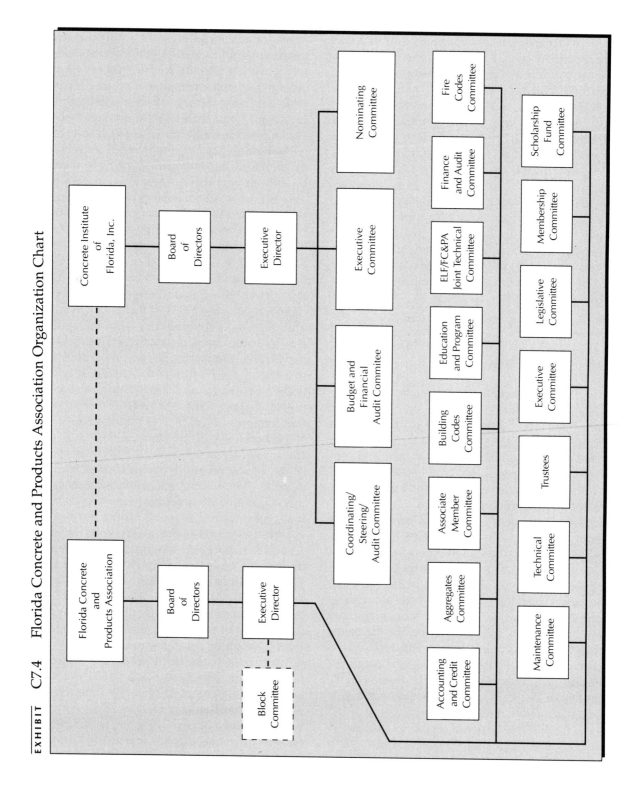

authority. The purpose of the Fire Codes Committee is to monitor the various building codes and to provide for coordination between the FC&PA and other masonry associations, for example, the Portland Cement Association (PCA), international associations, various fire marshals, and building officials. This coordination is to ensure that the fire-preventative qualities of concrete and concrete products are known, encouraged, and utilized in multifamily and commercial structures.

The purpose of the Maintenance Committee is to conduct semiannual seminars for the information and edification of all maintenance personnel in the concrete industry of Florida. The functions of the Technical Committee are to meet as a forum for discussion of industry developments, trends, and prospects of a technical nature and to bring to the board of directors recommendations for the benefit of the concrete and products industry. They are also expected to recommend to the board of directors any actions to be taken by the association regarding technical matters.

The remaining committees are the Trustees Committee, the Executive Committee, the Legislative Committee, the Membership Committee, and the Scholarship Fund Committee. Each of these committees has the responsibilities one would normally expect such committees to have. For example, the Legislative Committee is concerned about any legislative activity that is contemplated by any political entity in Florida and is charged with representing FC&PA's best interests in the political/legislative areas.

Executive Director of FC&PA

The executive director of FC&PA is Stanley Hand, who has held the position for more than fifteen years, since his retirement from the Air Force. Mr. Hand is responsible for the day-to-day operations of FC&PA and is its senior full-time employee. However, since Mr. Hand sits on all the FC&PA committees, his actual impact on FC&PA is very important. In many ways the continuity provided by the executive director is the basis of the momentum of the association, or the lack of momentum, as the case may be. Mr. Hand then could be described as one of the primary moving forces at FC&PA. In the fall of 1984 Mr. Hand informed FC&PA of his intention to step down in June 1985.

THE CONCRETE INSTITUTE OF FLORIDA

In 1970 the FC&PA realized that there was a need for promotional activities designed to help sell and spread the word on concrete. As a result the FC&PA formed the Concrete Institute of Florida, Inc. (CIF). It handles any and all promotional activities carried out on behalf of the association, such as supplying technical books and pamphlets on concrete to anyone requesting such information. CIF has four committees: the Coordinating/Steering/Audit Committee, the Executive Committee, the Budget and Financial Audit Committee, and the Nominating Committee. (See Exhibit C7.4.) The concrete industry has always been noted for not spending a great deal on promotion. In 1983, for example, the budget for promotion was only $100,000.

The promotion and advertising themes utilized by CIF concentrate on the advantages of using concrete and concrete products. These advantages include the following: the architect and the engineer have enormous versatility available to them because of the endless varieties, sizes, shapes, and strengths of concrete; the builder's job is made convenient because no unnecessary delays need occur to stop or delay construction (all the proper concrete materials are located locally in Florida); and the owner gets a structure that will provide a maximum return for the investment. Other advantages are that concrete withstands damage from weather, fire, termites, dry rot, and water; concrete affords the lowest possible insurance rates; concrete protects against noise from both outside sources and sources within the building; and the beauty of a concrete structure lasts indefinitely with no costly replacements required. Also, concrete walls slow the passage of heat from the inside out in the winter and from the outside in during the summer, providing for lower total energy consumption.

In 1983 the total construction dollar spent on cement use and production for residential and nonresidential building in Florida was estimated at $14.013 billion. This figure represented 4.8 million tons of cement, 15.5 million cubic yards of concrete, 300 million concrete blocks, 15 million tons of sand, and 25 million tons of aggregates.

Executive Director of CIF

The executive director of CIF is J. E. Paine, who has held the position for many years. Mr. Paine's position at CIF is virtually identical to Mr. Hand's at FC&PA. Even though CIF was formed by FC&PA, there were virtually no direct lines of responsibility or authority between the two entities. It seems that Mr. Paine's sole basis of responsibility and authority lies with the CIF board of directors. In fact, many members of FC&PA/CIF seem somewhat uncertain as to what, if any, accountability for results Mr. Paine may have.

DOWNTURN IN BLOCK UTILIZATION

As Speedy was grappling with his time dilemma caused by his commitments to CBS, FC&PA/CIF, and the EMBA program, that basic concern he had considered earlier kept interrupting his thoughts. It was during his tenure as president of FC&PA (1983–'84) that Speedy had become concerned about an apparent downturn in the utilization of concrete block for constructing exterior walls for the residential segment of the Florida construction industry. Speedy's concern had grown out of many conversations that had occurred over several months with a wide range of the membership of FC&PA.

Traditionally concrete block had been the dominant construction material utilized by Florida builders in virtually all exterior residential walls. This situation was consistent in all but the most northerly regions of Florida where wood-frame construction did have a small percentage of the residential exterior wall market. The residential segment of the construction industry was generally understood to include all noncommercial and non-high-rise multifamily buildings. As late as 1982 most of the members of FC&PA, in conversations, would estimate that concrete block held about 80 percent of the residential exterior wall market.

However, beginning in 1982 and by 1983 many FC&PA members were remarking that they had noticed a disturbing trend in tract housing developments. More and more of these developments seemed to be switching to wood-frame construction and away from concrete block. Also noticeable was the trend for the "prestige" residential market segment, which was the premium price market segment, to almost exclusively utilize wood-frame construction. Although these observations were not the same in reliability as a scientifically designed survey, Speedy's concerns stemmed from the frequency with which he heard these observations being voiced by block producers, and from the large increase in his lumber sales and little if any increase in his firm's concrete block sales.

Lack of Statistics

As Speedy's concerns had grown, he had turned to Mr. Hand, the FC&PA executive director, for help in understanding the situation. Mr. Hand seemed somewhat surprised by Speedy's concerns as he pointed out that the statistics gathered by FC&PA indicated the concrete block production levels for member firms had not shown any decreases. In fact, production of concrete block was increasing slightly according to FC&PA figures. (The concrete block production figures were reported to the FC&PA on a voluntary basis by the membership, and no efforts had ever been made to verify their accuracy.)

With this response from Mr. Hand, Speedy's concerns turned to puzzlement. How could concrete block production as reported by the membership be increasing while so many members were convinced a downturn in their use for residential exterior walls was occurring? The lack of anything but the most cursory of statistics on concrete block production was definitely a hindrance to really understanding the actual situation.

Because of his many presidential duties, Speedy didn't immediately do anything more about his concern regarding residential exterior wall construction trends. He did examine his own situation at CBS and found that he too had experienced a modest increase in concrete block production over the last few years. (See Exhibit C7.5.) However, what Speedy did discover was that the commercial use of concrete block he sold had increased dramatically while the residential use had declined. Thus, the slight overall increase was in effect hiding two trends in the use of concrete block: commercial use was increasing and residential use decreasing.

With this better understanding of his own situation, Speedy began to ask other producers if they were experiencing the same two trends. The answers he received were first of all a surprised "I'm not sure, I'll check on it" and then

later "You're right, Speedy, commercial is up and residential is down." Now Speedy had some general verification of these trends. But what remained an uncertainty was how much exactly had the use of concrete block in the residential market declined. If in 1980 it represented 80 percent of exterior wall residential construction, what had happened to this percentage in 1983 and 1984, and what did the future years hold for continuation of the trend?

Again Speedy approached Mr. Hand, the FC&PA executive director. Mr. Hand's response was once again a statement that total concrete block production as reported to FC&PA had increased over the years, and he wasn't at all certain how much of a decrease had occurred in the residential market. Mr. Hand again reiterated that he had no way of knowing what the current percentage had dropped to, although from conversations with members he thought that if the trends continued in 1984, the figures could be as low as 50 percent concrete block and 50 percent wood frame.

No one at FC&PA or CIF and no individual member seemed to know with any degree of accuracy what these relative market-use figures for wood frame and concrete block were. And perhaps of equal importance, no one seemed to know how to really find out what these figures were. Speedy knew that without accurate and reliable percentage-of-use figures, the seriousness of the situation was completely uncertain. Perhaps it was a serious trend or perhaps it was not.

After further deliberation about the situation Speedy, as one of his final acts as president of FC&PA (just prior to the end of his tenure), established a temporary Concrete Block Committee at FC&PA. Speedy felt that the FC&PA had a right to be concerned and perhaps to take some action.

EXHIBIT   C7.5
Clermont Builders Supply Inc. Block Sales

Fiscal Year	Eustis	Clermont	Total
1981	$ 815,270	$ 860,500	$1,675,770
1982	737,050	974,200	1,711,250
1983	938,370	1,138,500	2,076,870
1984	1,201,350	1,310,600	2,511,950

Concrete Block Committee

The Concrete Block Committee (not a standing committee at FC&PA) was formed to examine the concerns about downward trends of the concrete block industry and to take necessary actions to rectify them. Since there was a clear perception that existed among just about everyone in the industry that concrete block had lost a significant share of the residential market in the last few years, and since little valid and reliable information was available to substantiate this view, the committee was charged with examining the situation and recommending any action needed.

In order to fund any action that the block committee might recommend, a special concrete block production tariff had been established by FC&PA. This tariff, although on a voluntary basis, was suggested to be 1/10¢ on each block produced by all members who produced concrete blocks. An approximate figure of $150,000 per year was expected to be collected via this voluntary tariff. In this manner the block committee fully expected to be able to take specific actions. Another possible and additional basis of funding was being proposed by several members. This source would be to divert the dues currently paid by Florida cement/concrete producers and forwarded to the national Portland Cement Association. If this revenue source did in fact become reality, then an additional maximum of $400,000 per year could become available to the Concrete Block Committee.

The Concrete Block Committee examined two studies, one by the CIF and one commissioned by the Alabama Concrete Industries Association, in order to provide insights into general trends that existed in the nation and in Florida. The committee found that for the state the level of concrete block production was not as great in 1984 as it had been in 1973 and that production capacity had not increased during that time period. Some of the estimates and anecdotal evidence suggested to the committee repeatedly was that market share for concrete block was as low as 50 percent in 1984, while in previous years it was possibly as high as 90 percent. The Alabama study provided interesting evidence that nationwide there were trends of a current downturn in concrete block utilization. These findings and other statements made during the Concrete Block Committee's deliberation seemed to highlight the situation sufficiently that the committee became convinced that a potentially serious situation could arise shortly. However, the continuing lack of accurate statistical evidence of actual share percentages seemed to create a feeling of frustration that hindered the committee. This frustration appeared to cause the committee to do nothing but deliberate.

SPEEDY TAKES ACTION

Because these thoughts about the FC&PA Concrete Block Committee kept interrupting Speedy's attempt to plan his week's activities, he decided to take matters into his own hands. As a concrete block producer, Speedy felt that residential-use trends needed to be taken seriously, especially since for every dollar of blocks sold, he sold an additional 45 cents of accessory items. He was convinced that some action to verify the actual market percentages was necessary. He was concerned that the FC&PA Concrete Block Committee would continue to debate the situation and fail to act. He was certain Stan Hand at the FC&PA wouldn't act. Therefore, he telephoned two local consultants and asked them to examine the situation and prepare a brief report for him. Because of budget constraints, only a very brief and somewhat cursory examination was agreed upon. Speedy then settled down to finish planning his week's activities.

Examining the Situation

To find out about concrete block utilization, the consultants interviewed Lawson Wolfe, Stan Hand, and Jack Paine. They also examined related federal and state reference materials and those of the East Central Florida Planning Commission, the Regional and National Home Builders Associations, the CIF, and the FC&PA. While in the middle of this process, Jack Paine of CIF forwarded to Speedy some startling figures that had been prepared by Housing Industry Dynamics. Speedy asked the consultants to examine and verify those figures. Thereafter a discussion via telephone took place with a research staff member of the National Concrete Masonry Association in Washington and a research staff member of Housing Industry Dynamics. A very brief summary of the consultants' findings follows.

Consultants' Findings

The sheer absence of information upon which to make decisions was felt to be mind-boggling and in and of itself a major problem for the association. Everyone perceived a problem, but the data on which to make sound decisions were simply not available. For example, it was clear that in the major Florida cities, large developments produce most of the homes, but it was not known what percentage this was of total homes built. One interesting finding was that the National Concrete Masonry Association estimates of annual block production (apparently no state association keeps block data) are based on the application of a 20-year-old factor to Portland Cement Association production figures for that industry. These estimates then go into various federal information data bases. The factor was not originally accurate for any single state but was aggregate. It does not account for cycles, or for current conditions.

The CIF study pointed out several key factors: for example, who apparently makes sidewall building materials decisions in various situations and the factors influencing those choices. This study was found to not need replication, but it appeared advisable to obtain additional information to increase association knowledge of decision variables.

The Alabama Concrete Industries Association (ACIA) study raised issues related to:

1. Who makes decisions? The perception is that architects play the most important role, which is inconsistent with the CIF study.

2. Another issue is how important marketing is. A related issue involves determining the actual marketing activities of FC&PA members. Do these members' sales personnel sell or simply provide service? The implication is that, at best, they simply compete with other concrete block manufacturers and not with those in competitive industries (i.e., wood).

3. The ACIA study also indicates that technical and economic criteria are important in the decision process. The question raised is whether this is true in Florida, and if so, what are the perceptions involved and how can concrete producers utilize and/or change these perceptions.

4. The ACIA study suggests that members must increase their marketing efforts, and this is undoubtedly true for FC&PA members as well.

5. Additionally the ACIA study reveals the need for improved understanding and utilization of management techniques and the acquisition of the strategic ability to react to, and preferably anticipate, market changes.

The National Home Builders Association study, which provided figures of comparable use of wood frame versus concrete block in residential exterior wall construction, signals a dramatic trend. Those figures were verified by the consultants and indicated that whereas in 1979 almost 80 percent of residential exterior walls that were constructed in Florida utilized concrete block, by 1983 this figure had shown a startling decline to just over 30 percent. Although the rate of decline was less severe between 1982 and 1983 than it was previously, the question of future utilization trends remains. (See Exhibits C7.6, C7.7, C7.8, C7.9, and C7.10.)

This study was preliminary in nature and designed to determine the extent of available information, the crux of the problem, and future needed actions.

SPEEDY'S REACTION

Upon receiving the consultants' report in early November 1984, Speedy's worst fears were verified, but he still was surprised at the actual percentages and trends in concrete block utilization for residential exterior wall construction. He found it hard to believe that he and the other members of the FC&PA could have believed as late as the fall of 1984 that block still enjoyed at least 50 percent of the market when it actually had dropped below 50 percent in 1981 and was only about 30 percent in 1983. But he could find no reason to disbelieve the figures provided by Housing Industry Dynamics and verified by the consultants. Speedy asked the consultants to present their findings to a meeting of the FC&PA Concrete Block Committee and to also prepare some recommendations for action.

CONSULTANTS' RECOMMENDATIONS

A few weeks later the consultants did present their findings to the FC&PA Concrete Block Committee along with the following recommendations (paraphrased and abbreviated).

Several actions were perceived as being necessary to first of all obtain information so that appropriate decisions could be made:

EXHIBIT C7.6   Frame Trends

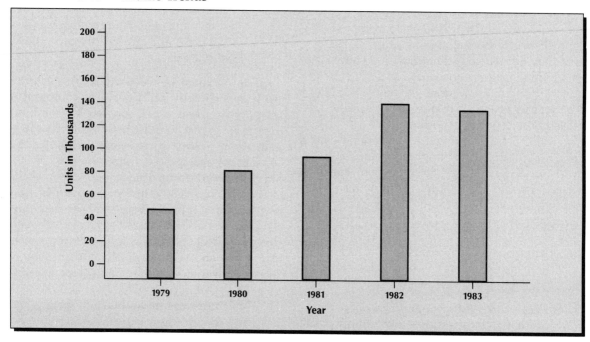

- Stage 1: Gather data. The consultants suggested that several types of data needed to be gathered from users of concrete block.
- Stage 2: Determine strategic alternatives in response to evidence provided by Stage 1. Strategic objectives and plans would result.

The consultants viewed the absence of decision information as a danger sign. The recommendations made were intended to focus on the major perceived problem areas. The tendency to make decisions without knowing precisely on what to base those decisions was noted by the consultants, who urged restraint until sufficient information could be gathered to determine sev-

eral key factors, such as affirming the CIF report regarding who makes the sidewall construction decisions, and very important, on what those decisions are based. Solving an ill-defined problem is really no solution at all, said the consultants. Stage 2 activities would be far more effective if Stage 1 was accomplished first. Information was needed to design the proper strategies, since the available evidence all seemed to indicate that a significant negative impact for concrete block producers had occurred.

Concrete Block Committee Reaction

After receiving the consultants' report, the Concrete Block Committee's meeting lasted several

EXHIBIT C7.7 Frame Trends

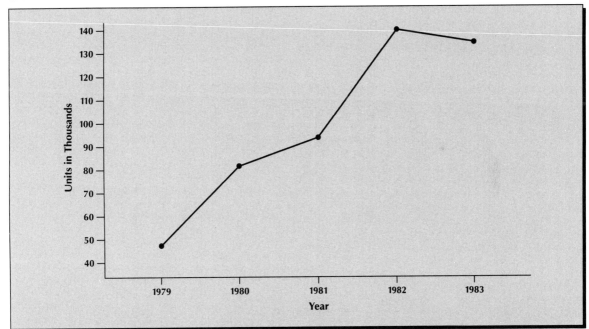

EXHIBIT   C7.8   Masonry Trends

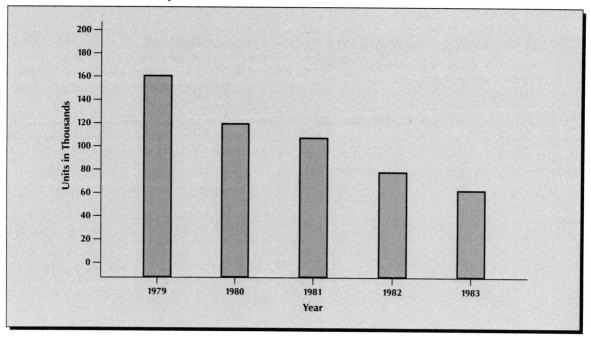

EXHIBIT   C7.9   Masonry Trends

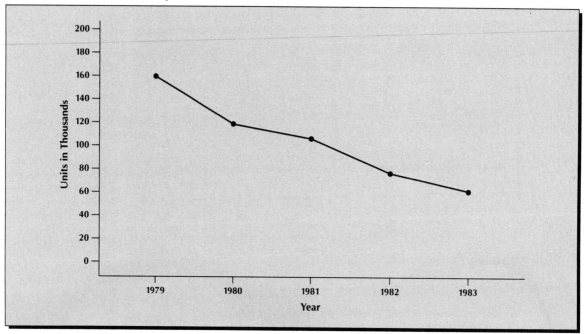

hours. Speedy later recalled that the members of the committee were shocked by the reported decline in concrete block utilization to only 30 percent of residential exterior wall construction. After the initial shock, the next reaction was to demand some action. But what exactly to do wasn't easily agreed to. Many members wanted to mount an immediate marketing pro-

gram to reverse the decline in block utilization. However, no one had an answer for who was going to design the marketing program or what role CIF personnel would have in such a program. In the end the committee decided to ask several consulting firms for proposals similar to the recommendations proposed by Speedy's consultants.

EXHIBIT   C7.10   Trends in Masonry and Wood

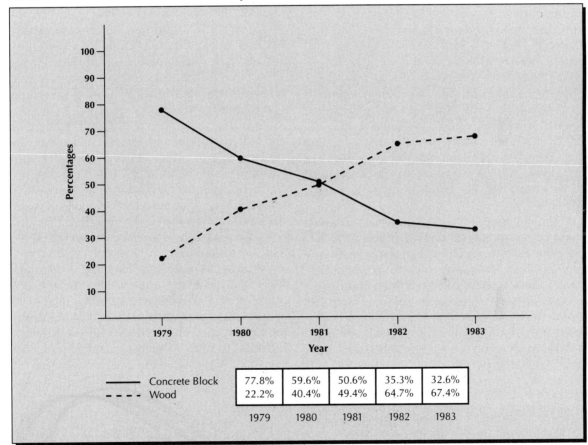

	1979	1980	1981	1982	1983
Concrete Block	77.8%	59.6%	50.6%	35.3%	32.6%
Wood	22.2%	40.4%	49.4%	64.7%	67.4%

Source: Figures provided by Housing Industry Dynamics.

Coastal Blind Company

**R. Dean Lewis, Keith A. Crow,
and Paul R. Reed**

Sam Houston State University

As the afternoon came to an end, Mark and his father were chatting about sagging profits and inadequate cash flow. "As much business as we have, you'd think we wouldn't have to worry about cash flow so much." Mark had said this a thousand times, but the fact was they just couldn't make ends meet anymore. Mark's father, Bill Benett, wished he could give his son an easy answer, but he was just as perplexed about their current financial status as was Mark. "Maybe we should raise our prices again?" Coastal was the only miniblind manufacturer/retailer in the county and had been able to raise prices as needed in the past without any significant change in sales volume. Mark nodded his approval and left the office to check on two of his employees who were completing a customer order.

The twenty-five-year-old owner of Coastal Blind Company had faced many problems in the past, but a lack of cash flow had not been a serious problem. Mark had worked for Mainland Craft Center, a well-established home improvement company, for five years before having the opportunity to purchase the business three years ago. Feeling that mini– and microblinds were going to be a popular alternative to

draperies and other window treatments for many years to come, he decided to purchase the company, change its name, and move exclusively into the interior blind business.

Bill Benett, age sixty, had started to work with Mark right after the acquisition. Having done some accounting work in the past and now being retired, he felt he could be of assistance to Mark in getting the business started. Bill's previous experience was in residential construction, and he believed his understanding of that industry and his numerous contacts could be converted into significant new business for Mark. Bill had no experience with the blind industry and had never taken part in any of the technical aspects of miniblind construction. His sole responsibility was financial management and cost control for the firm.

Initially Mark purchased blinds from other manufacturers sold to them with a lifetime warranty and provided "expert" installation. Because of product quality, extended product warranty, and personal service, he imposed a price mark-up of 52 percent. As the business initially grew, Mark and his father agreed that they should consider the manufacturing of the blinds they were retailing.

Equipment necessary for blind production was readily available and most equipment suppliers provided extensive training related to equipment use, maintenance, and manufacturing procedures. The needed equipment, which included two major pieces of machinery, cost $100,000. Ninety-percent dealer financing for the equipment was available with a ten-year payout period at a 13-percent interest rate. This was a slightly higher rate than bank financing, but Mark had already overextended his credit at his bank.

Along with the equipment, raw materials and supplies were then required to be carried in inventory. Slat material, used directly in blind construction, could be ordered and shipped within forty-eight hours. The metal rails that the blinds were mounted on had to be picked up in Houston, about fifty miles away. In the beginning this was not a problem, but as volume increased it was difficult to find time to drive to Houston to pick up materials every time an order was placed. Mark was faced with a new set of internal problems associated with manufacturing, inventory of material and finished goods, training, quality control, and additional costs.

THE COMPANY

Coastal Blind Company was located in Coastal, Texas. The town itself had a population of 21,000 and was located approximately midway between Galveston and Houston. Mark Benett was the sole owner and president of Coastal Blind Company, while Bill Benett, Mark's father, had no official title and had made no financial investment in the company.

Coastal Blind Company was located in the central business district of Coastal, with excellent access to the main traffic flow. The building was built in 1950 and had had several additions in the form of office and storage area, totaling 4,000 square feet. This had provided ample space even after the addition of the manufacturing equipment. The facility had been adequate to handle the manufacturing process and provided excellent retail exposure.

Company Philosophy

When Mark worked for Mainland Craft Center, the owner stressed product quality and the benefits that could be gained through impeccable customer service. Mark attempted to maintain these ideas as a guiding philosophy for his business. He believed that Coastal Blind Company could find a special niche in this somewhat new area of window-covering popularity. Special attention to customers' needs was what would enable Coastal Blind Company to fill that niche.

In terms of pricing Mark believed that if customers were treated fairly, courteously, and provided excellent service, that price could be on the upper end. Mark used a flexible pricing approach that depended on several factors. Prices were not firmly set and could be negotiated by customers. Pricing discounts are summarized below:

> **Commercial Accounts.** Construction companies, home builders, schools, and other commercial organizations were granted a 20-percent functional discount, with an additional 6-percent noncumulative quantity discount for orders over $1000. A 2/10, n/30 cash discount was also offered.

> **Retail Accounts.** A 10-percent discount was granted to customers who paid in full at the time an order was placed.

The breakdown of orders by type had been fairly consistent over the last two years. About 45 percent of all orders were placed by home builders; 35 percent were placed by schools, supermarkets, apartment complexes, and other local businesses and organizations; the remaining 20 percent of the orders were placed by individuals or home owners. The company had hoped to increase new accounts to home builders by 15 percent in the current year.

Management

Although Mark had not had any real management experience prior to purchasing the company, he had demonstrated leadership qualities. There had been numerous crisis situations in the past three years. Employees had worked double shifts with no extra pay and even continued at times when payroll could not be met. Besides Mark and Bill, there were four full-time employees and two part-time employees. They generally concentrated on manufacturing and product installation. Most of the employees had known Mark for some time prior to employment and agreed to accept reduced wages in anticipation of higher future profits and increased wages and benefits.

Mark functioned as owner-manager of the company and also played a key role in sales and production. It was not uncommon to see him trying to fill an order long after closing time. He was well experienced in equipment operation and was able to train employees effectively. He had proven to be an asset in sales as well and for the most part handled the larger commercial accounts. Many customers insisted on dealing directly with him.

Even though Mark was sole owner and manager, he tried to maintain a good rapport with all employees. Bill had little input on matters other than financial. However, Bill did not maintain good financial records and was not receptive to questions concerning financial affairs from Mark or other employees. This lack of communication had led to problems among all three parties: Bill, Mark, and the other employees.

Mark decided to pay his employees an hourly wage of $6.00. Since most of the employees were his friends, he didn't want to pay them too little. In an effort to increase production, Mark also initiated an incentive system to increase both speed and quantity of production. He found this system to be extremely effective since most orders were completed on time after the incentive plan was initiated. However, Bill resented Mark for implementing these employee concessions. He believed that the company could not afford these benefits and that Mark should be more demanding of his employees.

Promotion

One full-time commercial salesperson was employed by the company. The market area included Ball and Harris counties, with a combined population that exceeded 4 million people. The main focus of sales in the Houston area

consisted of residential construction firms. Almost 90 percent of the home-builder business was from the Houston area. Two large home builders, General and Pulte Homes, had placed several large orders with the company and had committed to more.

Retail or inside sales were handled by Mark, Bill, or whoever was available in the office. Retail sales had declined over the past two years due to inconsistency in retail personnel and operating hours.

Advertising was limited to local papers and direct mail pieces in the Coastal area. Retail sales came mainly from the local area, and most of this business resulted from local advertising and word of mouth. Commercial customers were called on directly by a salesperson and placed on a mailing list detailing merchandise and special promotions offered by the company.

The primary form of advertising for the company was via word of mouth. Product quality and service provided customers had proven to pay off. Many new customers had either seen or heard of Coastal Blind Company from satisfied customers.

The Product Line

Coastal Blind Company offered a variety of services, including manufacturing, retailing, installation, and repair of window blinds. The product line and description follow:

Miniblinds. Miniblinds were 1-inch-slat blinds. They could be manufactured in almost any shape or length to accommodate different size windows and could be ordered in thirty-eight different colors. These blinds rapidly became the major seller for the company and the industry as well.

Microblinds. These blinds featured slats approximately one-quarter inch smaller than mini blinds. Also, they could be produced in a wide variety of shapes and sizes, but available colors were limited to only twelve.

Vertical Blinds. These blinds were popular in homes and offices with large windows or glass doors. The equipment owned by Coastal Blind Company did not produce this type of blind; therefore, Mark purchased vertical blinds from other manufacturers. Customers were charged an installation fee and had the choice of a limited or a lifetime warranty. Vertical blinds accounted for only 10 percent of total sales.

THE MINIBLIND INDUSTRY

Mini- and microblinds became popular in the early '70s. Initially product acceptance was very slow, but their popularity as an alternative to curtains, venetian blinds, and drapes grew rapidly. Most of the people purchasing these blinds were between the ages of twenty and forty-five. In fact, many apartment complexes listed miniblinds as one of their amenities to attract customers.

The two major companies manufacturing miniblinds were Bally and Levolor. For the most part, these companies were manufacturing and wholesaling their blinds and had not entered the retail market.

Product success was attributed to low price, ease of operation, and convenience. Also, miniblinds offered increased security by screening outside vision and light better than draperies. These product benefits, coupled with modern and trendy appearance, allowed miniblinds to experience tremendous growth and market acceptance.

THE COMPETITION

As stated earlier, Coastal was the only manufacturer/retailer organization of mini blinds in the Coastal area. This enabled the company to not only service their market well but also penetrate surrounding markets. Department stores and home improvement stores sold miniblinds at retail prices in standard sizes and colors. These stores typically did not provide customer installation. By purchasing mini blinds wholesale and selling them at retail, as Coastal Blind Company had once done, the prices were kept highly competitive. High equipment and supply costs, as well as costs for labor, had forced Coastal to increase its prices above that of competition. This had not had an extreme impact since personalized service, quality, product warranties, and installation had enabled Coastal to maintain growth in sales volume.

The visibility of area department stores, coupled with availability of credit, had produced a major source of competition. In the Coastal area there were approximately six major department stores and four home improvement outlets that marketed miniblinds. The Houston area featured many more such stores that also provided these products.

FINANCIAL STATUS

Neither Mark nor his father had had any formal training or experience in financial management, which had resulted in their not having a good assessment of the company's financial status. Bill Benett maintained all the financial records of the company and attempted to develop an accurate balance sheet and income statement. Even though Bill was not officially employed by the company, he handled all financial matters with the approval of Mark. At times, however, Bill had been reluctant to share financial information with people he felt had no knowledge of finance. The financial records were all manually maintained, as the company did not own a computer or use an accounting service. Both Mark and Bill recognized the importance of automation, but neither was computer functional. As indicated by the income statement, net income had been erratic and dipped very low in 1987. It was this problem that puzzled the Benetts. Sales had been increasing steadily while income declined. It was impossible to accurately determine what was happening to revenues. The Benetts also noted that accounts receivable were becoming increasingly large. In 1987, total accounts receivable grew to $13,974. Financial statements are provided in Exhibits C8.1 and C8.2.

The most serious problem of the company was cash flow. The company, as of 1989, had only $599 in cash. Cash flow problems had led to difficulties in meeting salaries, operational costs, and debt service. Also, Mark and his wife had purchased a new home, and cash from the company was being used to meet monthly mortgage payments. Bill offered to invest capital in the company for a percentage of ownership, but

EXHIBIT C8.1

Coastal Blind Company
Comparative Balance Sheet
For Year Ended December 31, 1989

	1989	1988	1987
Assets			
Current assets:			
Cash	$ 599	$ 443	$ 4,635
Accounts receivable	13,974	10,161	2,460
Notes receivable	600	-0-	-0-
Inventory	140,140	108,000	54,300
Total current assets	$155,313	$118,604	$ 61,395
Property and equipment at cost:			
Machinery and equipment	$104,291	$104,291	$ 4,291
Fixtures and office equipment	6,479	5,287	3,287
Autos and trucks	12,843	12,843	12,843
Warehouse equipment	10,400	10,047	10,047
Leasehold improvements	3,635	3,635	3,635
Less accumulated depreciation	(30,390)	(29,096)	(27,802)
Total property and equipment	$107,258	$107,007	$ 7,321
Other assets:			
Utility deposits	$ -0-	$ 50	$ 50
Note receivable	2,254	3,203	3,603
Total other assets	$ 2,254	$ 3,253	$ 3,653
Total assets	$264,825	$228,864	$ 78,670
Liabilities and Owner's Equity			
Current liabilities:			
Accounts payable	$ 32,543	$ 24,720	$ -0-
Current portion of long-term debt	24,973	9,800	12,286
Accrued expenses	1,858	2,318	2,001
Income tax payable	-0-	-0-	-0-
Total current liabilities	$ 59,374	$ 36,838	$ 14,287
Long-term debt	148,130	147,033	30,131
Total liabilities	$207,504	$183,871	$ 44,418
Owner's equity	57,321	44,993	34,252
Total liabilities and owner's equity	$264,825	$228,864	$ 78,670

Mark had frowned on this alternative and hoped that profits would increase soon.

INVENTORY CONTROL

At the start of the business, Mark and Bill purchased small quantities of inventory as needed, but as demand increased they realized that they needed to stock more inventory. As the inventory grew, it was virtually impossible to keep track of what the company had in stock. Most of the inventory was stored in a room with virtually no plan or inventory system. Special orders or orders that involved materials that were not normally carried required the company to maintain a supply of these slow-moving materials. Mark tried to combat this problem by having customers prepay for orders, but most customers chose not to use this option.

Another materials problem dealt with waste. Due to construction that required exact and precise dimensions, the amount of waste materials had grown at an increasing rate. If measurements were not accurate or if construc-

tion deviated by a mere eighth of an inch, the blind was ruined and provided very little salvage value. Production errors were common, and Mark believed that he was losing a great deal of money in waste materials.

THE FUTURE

The future could hold many different scenarios for the Coastal Blind Company. There was a strong demand for miniblinds and, because they were a relatively new product, market demand was expected to be strong for several more years. The Houston and Coastal areas appeared to have adequate demand for the product, so the question was, "Can the Coastal Blind Company satisfy this demand and earn an acceptable profit?" Mark and Bill were quite confident they could. The company, however, seemed to be at a turning point. It was becoming increasingly more difficult to keep production rates high. It was apparent that the company must grow to keep up with demand. Mark and Bill were faced with a decision regarding this growth, but first they had to concentrate on survival.

EXHIBIT   C8.2

Coastal Blind Company
Comparative Income Statement
For Year Ended December 31, 1989

	1989	1988	1987
Sales	$171,493	$151,154	$119,735
Cost of sales:			
Beginning inventory	$107,140	$ 54,300	$ 49,800
Purchases	103,945	81,147	28,538
Ending inventory	140,140	108,000	54,300
Cost of sales	$ 77,322	$ 28,695	$ 28,538
Gross margin on sales	$ 94,171	$122,459	$ 91,197
Operating expenses	97,761	109,432	104,074
Income from operation	$ (3,590)	$ 13,027	$(12,877)
Other expenses	3,131	3,219	3,404
Net income	$ (6,721)	$ 9,808	$ (9,473)
Retained earnings, first of year	$ 23,592	$ 13,784	$ 23,527
Retained earnings, end of year	$ 16,971	$ 23,592	$ 13,784

Creative Dance Ensemble

Carla Litvany
Rollins College

On Thursday, November 5, 1990, a quorum of ten board members of the Creative Dance Ensemble (CDE) voted unanimously not to dissolve the dance company despite incredible odds against success. By 5:00 p.m. on Friday the company had to raise $14,000 to pay a visiting dance company and the salaries of all employees on contract. If successful, the company then had to raise a minimum of $75,000 by January 31, 1991, to erase most of the current deficit.

The company met the immediate crisis by securing an emergency grant of $10,000 from the Sarah James Foundation, given under the condition that no future funds would be available to the company until it eliminated its deficit. Another $4,000 was raised by contributions from three board members. It was now up to the board members to plan for the ultimate survival and future viability of the company.

HISTORY

The Creative Dance Ensemble grew out of Clark's School of Dance in Colorado Springs. It was founded by Ted and Laura Clark and Ted's sister, Sharon Geiger.

While Laura was interested only in teaching dance, Ted and Sharon wanted to choreograph works for performance. In 1984 all three became the founding directors of a newly incorporated nonprofit organization, the Creative Dance Ensemble.

During the next four years, the company performed locally, building audiences and developing dancers. An amateur company, it drew most of its dancers from Clark's School of Dance, and most of the board comprised their parents.

During this time, Ted and Sharon choreographed several pieces and experimented with new methods of expression. Two filmed dances were choreographed by Ted and shown on local public TV. One of these, *Mountain Dance*, was shown twice nationally on PBS.

In 1987 Sharon produced the ballet *Cinderella*, which was performed locally for a week to sellout crowds. This was the culmination of all their efforts of the past three years. Sharon and Ted felt that the enthusiasm of the audiences demonstrated a strong need for Colorado Springs to have its own professional dance company. The Creative Dance Ensemble was in a perfect position to fill this need.

Converting CDE into a professional dance company required an all-out effort. First they hired a business manager. Because of their limited budget, they could not afford to hire a professional, so they hired former actor Jerry Langley. For their first season (1988–1989) they hired six professional dancers (former students) and organized two other unpaid companies of younger dancers. To meet their objectives, they would present an annual subscription series of four productions. Each year they would include at least one well-known guest ballet company in the series, exposing Colorado Spring audiences to the many different styles of dance. To accommodate these companies and the full-scale ballet envisioned by Ted and Sharon, they decided to run the series in the 2,500-seat City Performing Arts Center. (See Exhibits C9.1 and C9.2.)

They did not consider the first season a success. The company performed in three productions. One was to feature two well-known dancers of the Oakland Ballet, Sally Michaels and John Toole, but they canceled at the last minute and had to be replaced by company dancers. The Cleveland Ballet was the one guest company for this series and received rave reviews. At the same time, arrangements were made with the Laredo County school system for fifty-two paid lecture/demonstrations.

During that year program expenses jumped over 200 percent and total income doubled, leaving a deficit of over $20,000 (see Exhibit C9.2). Other problems in adminstrative management led Jerry Langley to resign. Ellen Leland, a highly qualified nine-year veteran of a dance

company and an arts council member, replaced him. She encountered an exceptionally difficult situation. Jerry had left an inflated budget for the next fiscal year (FYE 1990) and had made commitments for the company that would be difficult to meet; the office records were poorly organized; and the company's credit record was very bad. Ellen set about correcting these problems, but others kept mounting.

Although the contract for the dancers had been reduced from forty weeks to thirty-six, the number of paid dancers had been increased by seven. This meant much higher production costs compared to the previous year. The season was to include three CDE productions plus one by the Houston Ballet. For the first fall performance, only one-quarter of the auditorium was filled for both presentations of the mixed repertory; the losses were high. Additionally, other sources of earned and unearned income were not productive. The costs of the second production, the ballet *Coppélia*, placed the company deeper in debt. Only an all-out campaign by the directors succeeded in raising sufficient

EXHIBIT C9.1　Creative Dance Ensemble—Company and Performances

	Projected FYE 1991	FYE 1990	FYE 1989	FYE 1988	FYE 1987	FYE 1986
Dancers' contracts						
Total weeks	22	36	40	—	—	—
Dancers						
Paid	14	13	6	—	—	—
Unpaid	—	15	15	32	27	30
Apprentices	14	20	17	—	—	—
Youth company	18	—	—	—	—	—
Performances						
Subscription	1	6	6	—	—	—
Lecture/demonstration	4	11	52	25	11	14
Other performances	28	17	13	24	19	8
National/state	5	—	1	1	1	1
Television, local	1	1	1	—	1	—
Television, national	—	1	—	—	1	—
Total performances	39	36	73	50	33	23
Total audience	40,000	38,000	67,756	27,925	22,000	9,850

funds to perform the ballet. This campaign also promoted the production, and large audiences attended.

Financially, however, the company was in difficulty. Forced to break its contracts and lay off the dancers for six weeks, the board and management tried to regroup. The available grant money was not enough to bring the dancers back after the six-week furlough. To meet the company's artistic obligations, the dancers were paid on a per performance basis for the remainder of the year. Several times the company was unable to meet its administrative payroll.

The guest production with the Houston Ballet and the final spring concert were presented.

This last concert was a mixed repertory of new works choreographed by Ted and Sharon. Thrown together on a low budget and performed without adequate rehearsal, the performance was lackluster.

After the 1989–1990 season, the board voted to continue the subscription series the following year, bring in two guest companies rather than one, tour the state to generate more revenue, and have a three-day home season in one of the smaller auditoriums in the area. It voted to increase the number of paid dancers to between fourteen and sixteen and add a ballet master. To accomplish these objectives, Ellen had to prepare a budget almost double the actual expenditures of the previous year (see Exhibit C9.3).

EXHIBIT   C9.2   Creative Dance Ensemble—Income Statement

	FYE 1990	FYE 1989	FYE 1988	FYE 1987	FYE 1986
Earned income:					
Ticket sales	$ 67,065	$ 94,164	$ 22,493	$ 8,710	$ 4,012
Nonseries	12,495	—	—	—	—
Total earned income	$ 79,560	$ 94,164	$ 22,493	$ 8,710	$ 4,012
Nonperformance earned income	9,196	—	6,865	—	3,647
Total earned income	$ 88,756	$ 94,164	$ 29,358	$ 8,710	$ 7,659
Unearned income:					
Tax support	$ 26,905	$ 46,662	$ 48,941	$ 31,016	$ 4,116
Private support	64,186	58,258	8,290	1,150	8,052
Total unearned income	$ 91,091	$104,920	$ 57,231	$ 32,166	$ 12,168
Total income	$179,847	$199,084	$ 86,589	$ 40,876	$ 19,827
Expenses:					
Programs	$149,213	$144,493	$ 43,181	$ 13,097	n.a.
Fund raising	3,887	13,647	3,071	—	—
General administration	41,172	61,198	42,033	24,398	—
Total expenses	$194,272	$219,338	$ 88,285	$ 37,495	$ 15,226
Net surplus (deficit)	$ (14,425)	$ (20,254)	$ (1,696)	$ 3,381	$ 4,601
Earnings gap (total expenses less earned income)	$105,516	$125,174	$ 58,927	$ 28,785	$ 7,567

By the beginning of the second performance of the 1990–1991 season, these plans had proved unrealistic. Financially the company was losing ground fast. These difficulties led to the November 5, 1990, board meeting.

OBJECTIVES

CDE's mission is to promote an understanding and appreciation of various forms of dance (including ballet, modern, and jazz) among cen-

EXHIBIT   C9.3   Creative Dance Ensemble—Statement of Income and Expenses as of October 31, 1990

	Actual 1989-1990	Actual 1990-1991	Budget 1990-1991	Budget (Under) Over
Income:				
Advertising	$ 6,756	$ 400	$ 8,000	$ (7,600)
United capital fund	—	—	3,250	(3,250)
Contributions:				
Corporate	10,433	7,749	50,000	(42,251)
Individual	19,904	16,987	50,000	(33,013)
Foundations	1,500		34,000	(34,000)
Sarah James: Challenge grant	25,000	10,000	10,000	—
Media grant	—	983	6,000	(5,017)
Grants:				
Colorado State	14,580		18,000	(18,000)
Colorado State NEA	6,075		—	—
City of Colorado Springs	4,000		—	—
County cultural committee	2,250		—	—
Balance of government grants, 1980–1981	2,000	750	2,370	(1,620)
Interest	277	474	1,000	(526)
Miscellaneous	651	2,667	500	2,167
Performance fees	3,196	2,050	50,000	(47,950)
"Raise"	3,424	16,381	20,000	(3,619)
Sales, retail	935	868	3,000	(2,132)
Sales, ticket:				
Home season	—	1,406	8,000	(6,594)
Series	67,065	9,238	85,000	(75,762)
School	—	2,210	25,000	(22,790)
Special events	9,298	131	15,000	(14,869)
Total income	$177,344	$ 72,294	$389,120	$ 316,826
Expenses:				
Administration	14,614	11,971	33,550	(21,579)
Payroll and benefits	78,779	49,047	186,456	(137,409)
Production:	60,204			
New		244	9,000	(8,756)
Repertory		3,827	28,900	(25,073)
Promotion	3,861	4,554	24,000	(19,446)
Series	33,144	15,545	76,300	(60,755)
Travel	1,641	496	21,050	(20,554)
Contingency fund	—	—	9,864	(9,846)
Total expenses	$192,243	$ 85,684	$389,120	$ 303,436
Net surplus (deficit)	$ (14,899)	$ 13,390	-0-	$ 13,390

tral Colorado residents by creating a resident professional dance company. This company would be a nonprofit organization and would provide a viable cultural institution offering works that were both entertaining and artistic and provide dancers the opportunity to live and work in their home state. The objectives as stated in the bylaws are "to produce programs stimulating public interest and involvement in dance, drama, theater and performing arts; to provide an opportunity for study and participation in dance, drama, theater and performing arts; to sponsor, produce and assist in the presentation of performances of all performing arts."

CDE promotes dance through various vehicles. The appendix to this case describes the primary liabilities and responsibilities for the board of directors of nonprofit organizations. It is one of three dance companies in Colorado to offer an annual subscription series at the City Performing Arts Center. The series normally includes four productions. Beginning in 1988 each production was performed twice, once in the evening and at one matinee, the latter to accommodate children and the elderly. Two performances also gave the dancers experience in consecutive appearance. The 1990-1991 season saw a reduction to one performance per concert.

CDE also presents lecture/demonstrations, miniperformances, and full concert performances to schools, festivals, civic and cultural organizations, and universities. A home season was added for the 1990–1991 year to include a series of three mixed repertory concerts to be held in January at the Santa Fe Auditorium. CDE plans to tour the state to generate more revenue and develop more audiences.

ORGANIZATIONAL STRUCTURE

CDE's organizational structure is shown in Exhibit C9.4. Ultimate authority for the operation of the company lies with the board of direc-

tors. Administrative and artistic management report directly to the executive committee.

Board of Directors

The 1989–1990 board of directors was composed of an administrative board with sixteen directors and an advisory board with eight directors. Carol Blackway was president and George Conover past president. Blackway had reluctantly agreed to take this position because no one else had expressed an interest. Board meetings during 1989–1990 were held frequently (sometimes twice a month) because of the repeated crises during the year. Normally about one-third of the directors attended each meeting. Although agendas were prepared, meetings were informal, with discussions frequently straying to other items.

The community was aware of the problems at CDE and occasionally an interested party would attend the meetings and offer advice. Blackway, interested in all possible help, would allow these visitors to take over even when other items were more pressing.

Traditionally board meetings had no time limits and lasted two or three hours. Because the company was plagued by so many problems, key issues frequently were glossed over and little was accomplished. Further, personality conflicts led board members to act independently on behalf of the board. The crisis often prevented either Ellen Leland or Carol Blackway from being fully prepared to discuss the topics on the agenda.

The nominating committee for the 1990–1991 board of directors consisted of Carol Blackway, president; Emily Briscoe, treasurer; George Conover, past president; and Bart Somers, director. According to the bylaws, the new board members of the following season are to be elected at the annual board meeting in May. Since there was none in 1981, the new members (Exhibit C9.5) were elected at the first board meeting of the next season.

Mike Chamberlin, the 1990–1991 president, knew very little about dance or fund raising but enjoyed leadership.

In general the board is responsible for setting policy for the company. The by-laws list the responsibilities and duties of the board. They were to:

a. hold meetings at such time and place as it thinks proper

b. admit members and suspend or expel them by ballot

c. recommend members of the company to the officers for appointment to committees on particular subjects

d. audit bills and disburse the funds of the company

e. print and circulate documents and advertisements to promote the purpose of the company

f. detail actions and decisions

g. devise and carry into execution such measures as are proper and legal to promote the objectives and purposes of the company and to best protect the interest and welfare of the company

The various committees include fund raising, long-range planning, finance, nominating, advertising, building and grounds, personnel,

EXHIBIT C9.4 Organizational Structure of the Creative Dance Ensemble

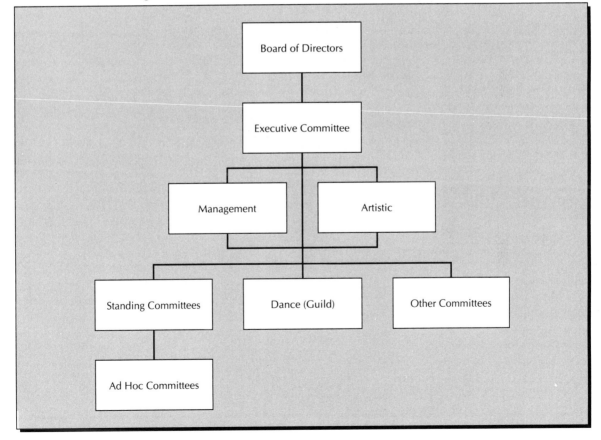

EXHIBIT C9.5 Board Members and Directors, Creative Dance Ensemble, 1990–1991

Board of Directors

* Mike Chamberlin, president
Assistant sales manager
KBCT Radio

* Dr. Morris Winekoff, vice-president
Chief of radiology
Mossinger Hospital

Lyle Clausen
Retired business executive
Arts consultant

* Leslie Porter
Travel consultant
Colorado Travel

* Charles Simwell
Executive director
Mossinger Hospital

* Paul Klein
Director of marketing and sales
Ski Magazine

* Sam Perkins
Textile representative
Cloth Manufacturers, Inc.

* Kathy Price
Sales representative
Mountain Beauty Supply

* Ralph Torrence
Public relations director
Smith, Blair & Marchman

* Lawrence Spears
Secretary/treasurer
Waldrop Enterprises

* Peter Maxwell
Vice-president
Western Liquors

* Darren Sycamore
President
Sycamore & Associates

* Pam Stearns
Realtor
Colorado Real Estate

Kirk Giovanni
Vice-president
Warren Ski Lift Services

* Martin LaPaz, Treasurer
Treasurer and comptroller
Colorado Springs Times

Carla Lopez
Colorado Springs

George Gardner
Attorney
Wassen, Wassen & Farmer

* Susan Larsen
Manager
High Point Apartments

* Sarah Barker
Colorado Springs

Founding Directors

Sharon Geiger
Artistic director
Creative Dance Ensemble

Ted Clark
Artistic director
Creative Dance Ensemble

Laura Clark
Owner
Clark's School of Dance

* New members of the board.

and dance (the volunteer organization). By the end of November 1990, none of the 1990–1991 committees had met.

Management

The administrative positions are filled by permanent staff, while the artistic positions, with the exception of the directors, are either contractual or paid on a performance basis.

General Manager

Ellen Leland, general manager of CDE, has nine years of experience in the arts. She has complete responsibility for the day-to-day administration of the company, assisted by a secretary and an administrative assistant (bookkeeper). She receives little assistance from the board. A complete list of her duties is given in Exhibit C9.6.

EXHIBIT   C9.6   Position Description

Position: General manager
                   Effective date: May 1, 1989
Reports to: Executive Committee

Description of position:

Responsible for overall administration of company's activities, including business and financial affairs, program planning and direction, public relations, and staff supervision

Duties:

1. Represents the company in all contractual and other business activities
2. Develops an annual budget in cooperation with the Executive Committee
3. Controls all expenditures in accordance with the operating budget and sound fiscal policies
4. Oversees the development and presentation of grant proposals
5. Coordinates all aspects of the performance schedule, including booking, touring, technical aspects, and production
6. Directs all public relations and promotion of company activities
7. Supervises the work of staff in accordance with effective management principles
8. Coordinates all volunteer activities
9. Reports regularly to the Executive Committee
10. Assumes other duties as assigned by the Executive Committee

Salary:

$24,000–$28,000 based on qualifications and experience

Qualifications:

1. Experience in arts management required
2. Degree relevant to arts management preferred
3. Demonstrated management skills
4. Grant-writing experience desirable
5. Willingness to adapt to irregular hours as required
6. Ability to work well with people

Artistic Directors

Ted Clark and Sharon Geiger choreograph for the company, teach the dancers, and serve as spokespeople. Their vision keeps the organization alive. Both are voting members of the board. When there is a cash flow problem, frequently they will arrange for a loan from friends or relatives. They first received a salary in the 1990–1991 season; after years of providing financial support, they can no longer support themselves without some income.

Artistic Staff

There are three dance companies in one. The core comprises fourteen paid dancers. In addition, there are fourteen talented young dancers in the apprentice company, most between the ages of fourteen and seventeen. The youth company is made up of eighteen younger dancers. Of the paid dancers, nine are new to the company and few come from central Colorado. CDE is considered a steppingstone to larger regional dance companies, such as might be found in Denver. The dancers are strong and enthusiastic, with good potential. In 1990–1991 the dancers' preparation has been greatly enhanced by the instruction of the new ballet master (a former dancer with American Ballet Theatre), who also has maintained high morale among the dancers. Exhibit C9.1 shows the progressive changes in dancers and performances for the company

Volunteers

The volunteer organization Dance has several responsibilities. Its only substantial contribution to the company, however, has been a boutique, which earned $935 in the 1989–1990 season. It is raising items to be sold at the Raise auction (a cultural fund-raising group). Many past volunteers have been parents of the dancers.

MARKETING

The Product

CDE presents classical and romantic ballet, modern dance, and American jazz. Sharon Geiger has selected such classical ballets as *Coppélia* and *Cinderella* and has choreographed several, including *Vermila*, to original and costly musical scores. Many pieces selected for concert require more technical strength than evidenced by the dancers in the company. Ted Clark favors modern dance and has choreographed many pieces for the company, including a 40-minute modern ballet. CDE also has contracted with outside choreographers to set dances for the company. Currently the company has thirteen pieces (between seven and 40 minutes long) and three full-length ballets in its repertory. Of these, eleven were choreographed in the 1989–1990 season at a low average cost of $2,000 each. (By contrast, the Cleveland Ballet recently presented *Coppélia* at a cost of $150,000.) Artistic selection and execution in the dance field require constant trade-offs between high artistic quality and cost.

Perhaps the performance that received the most audience exposure was *Mountain Dance*, choreographed by Ted Clark in 1986 and filmed for television. The film had an estimated viewing audience of more than 1 million. In 1988 Ted choreographed a second filmed piece, entitled *Perpetual Motion*.

In the 1990–1991 season both the Dan Wagoner Dancers and the Merce Cunningham Dance Company were scheduled in the series. Two CDE productions were scheduled—*Coppélia* and *Vermila*; however, the cost of reproducing the music was so high that *Vermila* was canceled and replaced by a guest company.

As a result of the "Help Our Dancers" campaign, CDE sold a record 2,258 tickets to its December 1990 *Coppélia*, with gross revenues of $25,135. For the fall 1990 concert, combined ticket sales for the performance and dress rehearsal were only 1,520, with a gross revenue of $10,386. Production costs amounted to $41,232. A total of 1,374 tickets were sold for the Dan Wagoner concert, grossing $13,742. Total production costs were $16,899. The next two productions were budgeted at $19,075 each. Most performing arts companies strive for 100-percent subscription sales; at 631 series tickets sold, CDE was only 25-percent subscribed for FYE 1991.

Several problems in recent years contributed to the disappointing attendance at CDE concerts. Performances conflicted with other scheduled major events; the arts center box office was uncooperative; and the quality of the performances varied. The 1989–1990 presentation of *Coppélia* was plagued by injuries, inadequate shipments of programs, and insufficient money and man-hours to promote the series. The company's financial struggles were well publicized; consequently, few people wanted to risk subscribing to the 1990–1991 series.

Price

Subscription prices for the 1990–1991 series ranged from $20 to $50, with 50-percent discounts given for senior citizens, students, and military personnel. Season tickets could be purchased by mail or phone, but hard-copy single tickets could be purchased only at the auditorium box office. Vouchers were available at various outlets. Because CDE personnel had no access to tickets, board members could take blocks of tickets to sell only if they paid for them in advance.

Publicity

A formal publicity program for CDE has been hampered by a lack of manpower and funds. The "Help Our Dancers" campaign was perhaps the most successful, having full cooperation and participation from the board. Because of arrangements of the local arts council, CDE receives a one-third discount off all advertisements placed in the local newspaper.

Occasionally just prior to a performance, one of the artistic directors or the general manager is interviewed on local radio or television. To announce an event, CDE relies primarily on posters distributed throughout the community.

Recently Ellen Leland decided to publish a monthly newsletter in a local cultural magazine. Each month she buys a page of advertising (with the help of a $3,000 media grant from the Sarah James Foundation) and prints current information about the company. The magazine has a circulation of 42,300, but few live in Colorado Springs.

FACILITIES

Since the 1988–1989 season, CDE has performed in the City Performing Arts Center, which has the only proscenium large enough to accommodate full-scale ballets. It seats 2,534 people. Exhibit C9.7 shows this and other possible locations.

The City Center is a city-run facility that also hosts the symphony, the opera, Broadway series, and big-name music concerts. Neither the opera nor the ballet may handle its own tickets. Except for season tickets, only vouchers may be sold, which allow the holder to pick up tickets at concert time. Regardless of discounts offered, City Center demands 10 percent of the full price of every ticket sold. Relations between the facility's manager and CDE are very strained.

At City Center, CDE must hire union stagehands, who receive 30 cents less an hour for nonprofit than for profit productions.

Until the summer of 1989, CDE offices were in the same building as Clark's School of Dance. Office and studio space were donated to the company temporarily. The donor was trying to sell the building and allowed CDE to use it until it was sold. One potential buyer wanted to use it as part of a major arts complex and would have allowed CDE to rent the space permanently; however, the purchaser defaulted. During the next five months, CDE staff had to be ready to move at a moment's notice but had no place to go. Also, there were two electrical fires and several power outages. Concomitantly, another closing was imminent, and building maintenance was being neglected, so CDE employees did all janitorial work. Minimal heat during the winter and no air conditioning in summer made conditions dangerous on the one hand and unbearable on the other. At the end of the summer of 1990, the Sarah James Foundation bought the building as a cultural complex to house offices of the ballet, visiting symphony, and opera. CDE will now have to pay an annual rent of $12,000 for its space.

FINANCIAL INFORMATION

The income statements, balance sheets, and relevant percentages are presented in Exhibits C9.2, C9.8, and C9.9, respectively. The deficits for the last three fiscal years were financed mainly with accounts payable and loans from friends.

The company suffered from severe cash flow problems in the 1989–1990 season. The dancers, initially on a 36-week contract starting in September, had to be laid off December 21.

The layoff was intended for six weeks, but when cash flow did not improve, the dancers were placed on a per performance basis for the remainder of the year. During the 1990-1991 season, the dancers were on a 22-week contract with a built-in three-week layoff. Although the contract had an extension clause to be implemented if the company were in a healthy financial position, the board chose not to use it.

Cash flow problems also prevented the company from meeting its administrative payroll several times during the spring and summer of 1990. Since December 1989 the board has been especially unresponsive to the critical cash needs of the members, who already have contributed to the limit both financially and emotionally. Just prior to the December 1989 production of *Coppélia*, it had appeared that the company would not survive. Only the "Help Our Dancers" campaign raised the amount required to keep the company going. Just prior to the 1990 Dan Wagoner production, the company was forced to take an emergency loan and received substantial assistance from several board members. Ellen has commented that "every time financial matters are brought up at board meetings, someone changes the subject."

EXHIBIT C9.7 Available Facilities in Central Colorado

	Number of Seats	Width of Proscenium Opening (ft.)	Rental Cost per Day
City Performing Arts Center	2,534	50	$500[a]
Sarah James Theatre	350	35	300
Santa Fe Auditorium	588	40	350
Steuben College Theatre	375	26	375
Rice Hotel Auditorium[b]	2,000	48	2,250

[a] The minimum stay for CDE in the City Center for one performance is four days. The fee is 10 percent of revenues or $500 per day, whichever is less and not to exceed $2,000.

[b] The Rice Auditorium is located about 11 miles south of Colorado Springs. The per-diem fee includes many benefits that are extra in the other facilities.

Comments made by a local museum administrator reflected the community's attitude toward the financial crisis: "Maybe this area is not ready for a professional ballet. There are a lot of large cities in this country that can't support a professional dance company."

There are several major sources of funds locally. The Sarah James Foundation contributes

EXHIBIT   C9.8   Creative Dance Ensemble—Balance Sheet

	FYE 1990	FYE 1989	FYE 1988	FYE 1987	FYE 1986
Assets					
Current assets:					
Cash	$ 2,795	$ 1,015	$ 2,574	$ 5,073	$ 1,196
Restricted funds[a]	2,640	6,552			
Accounts receivable	85	2,532	4,591		
Prepaid expenses		164			
Total current assets	$ 5,520	$ 10,263	$ 7,165	$ 5,073	$ 1,196
Other assets:					
Utility deposit	$ 1,130				
Fixed assets:					
Equipment	8,585	$ 5,339			
Less accumulated deposits	(3,104)	(992)			
Total fixed assets	$ 5,481	$ 4,347			
Total assets	$ 12,131	$ 14,610	$ 7,165	$ 5,073	$ 1,196
Liabilities and Funds					
Current liabilities:					
Notes payable (due within one year)	$ 18,237[b]	$ 20,112	$ 3,000	$ 496	
Accounts payable	13,380	2,770	122		
Accrued interest	2,197				
Accrued payables/receivables taxes	2,115	419	57		
Deferred income[a]	2,640	6,552			
Accrued salaries			1,105		
Total current liabilities	$ 38,569	$ 29,853	$ 4,284	$ 496	
Long-term liabilities:					
Notes payable	5,362	2,133			
Total liabilities	$ 43,931	$ 31,986	$ 4,284	$ 496	
Fund balance:					
Invested in equipment	3,924	1,751			
Unrestricted	(35,724)	(19,127)	2,881	4,577	1,196
Fund total	$(31,800)	$(17,376)	$ 2,881	$ 4,577	$ 1,196
Total liabilities and funds	$ 12,131	$ 14,610	$ 7,165	$ 5,073	$ 1,196

[a] Funds paid for next year's season.

[b] $13,500 is past due.

more than $200,000 annually to the arts in central Colorado, occasionally providing emergency funds to organizations. It does not anticipate any increased funding to the arts in the next several years. Corporations are another source that has been somewhat neglected by local arts organizations. Colorado Power and Light and Denver Oil have long supported the arts. Also, several major corporations have moved to Colorado Springs recently and may be looking for ways to enhance their public images.

CDE's fiscal year ends May 31; a preliminary budget for 1990–1991 was prepared in February 1990, totaling $470,050, but was never given final approval by the board, primarily

because it never took the time to review it. When, by July, it was obvious that some of the anticipated government funds would not be available, Ellen Leland began revising the budget. It was not ready for final approval by the first meeting of the new board in July, but was finally approved at the second meeting, in October 1990. Exhibit C9.3 compares this budget to actual expenditures and revenues for the previous year.

Several comments should be made about this budget. Each board member is required to contribute $1,000 annually, which was budgeted into the individual contributions. A single donor had already contributed $13,000. There were

EXHIBIT C9.9 Creative Dance Ensemble—Relevant Percentages

	FYE 1990	FYE 1989	FYE 1988	FYE 1987	FYE 1986
Percent distribution of earned income:					
Ticket sales	76%	100%	77%	100%	52%
Nonseries performance	14	—	—	—	—
Nonperformance	10	—	23	—	48
Total earned income	100%	100%	100%	100%	100%
Percent distribution of unearned income:					
Tax support	30	44	86	96	34
Private support	70	56	14	4	66
Total unearned income	100%	100%	100%	100%	100%
Percent distribution of total income:					
Earned income	49	47	34	21	39
Unearned income	51	53	66	79	61
Total income	100%	100%	100%	100%	100%
Percent distribution of expenses:					
Program expense	77	66	49	35	—
Fund-raising expenses	2	6	3	—	100
General and administrative	21	28	48	65	—
Total expenses	100%	100%	100%	100%	100%
Percent of total operating expenses met by income earned	46%	43%	25%	23%	26%
Percent of program expenses met by program income	53%	65%	52%	67%	26%
Percent of total expenses met by total income	92%	91%	98%	109%	130%

guaranteed funds from the Sarah James Foundation of $13,000. By July corporate contributions totaled $11,050. Raise is a local fund-raising organization from which $15,000 had been received already. Performance fees were budgeted for a state touring program; however, because of the constant attention required in the office and the lack of funds, no one had arranged it. As of August, not a single paid performance had been arranged. The fee for those performances was to have been $1,000 each.

THE FUTURE

The board now faces the awesome task of making the company financially stable. The Sarah James Foundation will not rescue the company again. While it is feasible for fifteen board members to raise $5,000 each by the end of January, past history makes this unlikely.

Several bright spots were on the horizon. Ted and Sharon planned to open a school of the Creative Dance Ensemble in January, which would be accessible to anyone interested in classes. Initial indications suggested considerable community interest. Because many of the costs involved as fixed costs would have been incurred anyway, the profit potential was quite high.

A local chapter of the Jaycettes has pledged to take on CDE as a project and raise $200,000 to pay the salaries and insurance for twenty dancers next year. The Jaycettes propose to mount a campaign from May to August 1991 to raise the first $100,000 for start-up salaries. The second half would be raised between September and December. However, since the dancers' contract should be signed by July 31, the company would be signing for contracts without the money in hand.

Ted (now divorced) is selling his interest in Clark's School of Dance and plans to loan the $40,000 proceeds to the company.

Ted and Sharon are planning to tour the state. Also, Sharon plans to stage *The Nutcracker Suite* next Christmas.

Colorado Springs has a rapidly growing cultural community with nine major nonprofit arts organizations and the Mountain Council of Arts and Sciences, which exists to provide support services to the cultural community. Exhibit C9.10 presents budget comparisons for these organizations. Exhibit C9.11 analyzes the sources of funds for the central Colorado cultural community.

EXHIBIT C9.10 Budget Comparisons

	1989-1990 Budget ($)	Surplus Deficit ($)	1989-1990 Earned Income %	1990-1991 Budget ($)	Change in Budget (%)
Mountain Civic Theatre	167,000	14,250	61%	201,000	20%
Mountain Art Center	155,000	(30,000)	50	212,000	37
Central Symphony	1,000,000	(17,000)	57	1,000,000	—
McCann Science Center	350,000	14,000	46	360,000	3
Laredo Art Center	463,000	46,000	n.a.	352,515	(24)
James Tyler Art Center	74,000	—	46	72,000	(3)
Western Opera	162,700	(5,000)	52	240,000	48
Community Center of the Arts	106,000	(7,000)	41	126,000	19
Creative Dance Ensemble	194,000	(14,000)	46	386,750	99

Fund raising is critical for nonprofit organizations because of the large gap between earned income and expenses. The national average of earned income as a percentage of total expenses for dance companies is between 55 percent and 60 percent. Baumol and Bower have theorized on the increasing gap. In industry, as costs have risen with inflation, so has productivity, that is, technology has made man-hours more productive. Consequently, more products are made and sold at higher prices to compensate for the higher costs. However, by their very nature the performing arts cannot increase productivity. While the same number of dancers and the same amount of time are required to perform *Coppélia* in 1990 as in 1951, production costs have since skyrocketed. Compensating increases in ticket prices have been restricted because of the risk of decreased demand. If the arts are considered overpriced, many consumers will find less expensive substitutes, such as television or movies.[1]

Although most organizations in central Colorado do not have sophisticated development programs, several of the nine organizations have well-organized fund-raising events. An analysis indicates that the most successful were those that have become traditional in the community. The most successful is the opera's fash-ion show, which has become a tradition in Colorado Springs and probably can be credited with the current financial stability of the opera. CDE never has had a very successful fund-raising campaign.

Until recently, it has been assumed that the very wealthy, older population provided the primary support for the arts. However, recent trends in the past several years indicate that the new audience comprises the younger, professional segment.

One market most culturals have not penetrated is the tourist market in central Colorado. The McCann Science Center is perhaps the only organization to solicit the tourists actively. In 1989 it attracted about 20,000 to the planetarium.

Underserved segments of the population are normally given exposure to the arts through outreach programs. All nine organizations purport to have them, but most are confined to school children. There are some notable exceptions. Mountain Art Center has its "Reach with Art" program, which provides art therapy to the elderly, the handicapped, and exceptional children. Community Center of the Arts has a special program for the blind. The Pre-Columbian Collection at the Laredo Art Center has attracted a large number of Hispanics, although it is not clear that this was by design. The Central Sym-

EXHIBIT C9.11 Income Sources for the Arts in Central Colorado, 1989–1990 Fiscal Year

	Estimated Dollar Amount	Percent of Total
Total expenditures of the arts	$3,187,500	100%
Total earned income	$1,346,672	42
Federal funds	58,903	2
State funds	62,774	2
County funds	91,000	3
City funds	35,950	1
Foundation funds	220,000	7
Ski resort funds	5,000	—
Corporate funds	170,000	5
Total income	$1,990,299	
Total individual contributions	$1,197,201	38

phony's chamber series was an unsuccessful attempt to reach the elderly. The mixed success of the outreach programs perhaps reflects the half-hearted attitude of some of the organizations because frequently they are obligated to promulgate them to comply with government and funding agency requirements. Substantively, however, most of these programs provide little exposure to the underserved segments of the population.

Competition permeates the cultural community of central Colorado on a number of levels, the most divisive being for local funding. The larger, older organizations resent the smaller, younger ones eating into their portion of locally available funds. The smaller organizations feel the larger organizations are trying to squeeze them out of the market. After recent budget cuts by the county commission, the three major organizations (each of which stood to lose $25,000) urged that all nine present a united front to the community; however, this arrangement lasted only as long as it benefited those major organizations.

Most performing arts groups are supportive of each other's programming rather than competitive. The symphony frequently accompanies the ballet and opera, and occasionally CDE's dancers perform in opera productions. Additionally, there appears to be substantial overlap of audiences. Interestingly, competition seems to exist among all nonprofit performing arts organizations and the profit-making entertainment industry in the community.

CDE competes not only with other professional organizations, but also with the local dance schools, which resent CDE, especially the Williams Ballet School, the oldest in central Colorado. The Clarks attended this school in their childhood. Bret and Joanne Williams, the owners, feel their position in the community has been usurped and refuse to cooperate with CDE. Their school presents *The Nutcracker Suite* annually at Christmas to provide a showcase for all their students and always performs to a full house at the City Performing Arts Center.

The economic environment for the arts in 1990 was grim, with President Reagan wanting to cut funding to the National Endowment for the Arts by more than 50 percent. While most of the cultural organizations in central Colorado are not direct beneficiaries of these funds, they are affected indirectly. State funding to the arts, partially funded by the federal government, has been cut back. Locally, city and county governments are trying not to raise taxes. This, combined with reduced federal revenues, is reducing the funding for the arts on a local level. Although CDE had received funds from the local government in the past, it was given no funds in 1990-1991 because of lower city revenues and because its stated emphasis was placed heavily on touring out of the area.

George Monihan, director of the Sarah James Foundation, summed up the future difficulties faced by the arts in obtaining private funds. He said that the foundation will be unable to take up the shortfall in federal monies as its revenues are generated from dividend income, which is not anticipated to increase in the next several years because of the current recession. Inflation has cut into the disposable income of most Americans, leaving people less willing to contribute to nonprofit organizations. While not all local corporate sources have been tapped, it is unlikely that current corporate supporters will increase their cultural contributions.

ENDNOTE

1. W. J. Baumol and W. G. Bower, *Performing Arts: The Economic Dilemma* (Cambridge: M. I. T. Press, 1986), 161–80.

APPENDIX TO CASE 9: PRIMARY LIABILITIES AND RESPONSIBILITIES FOR BOARDS OF DIRECTORS OF NONPROFIT ORGANIZATIONS

1. When an organization incorporates as a nonprofit agency:

    A. All profits must be reinvested in the corporation.

    B. The organization is entitled to received federal and state funding.

    C. The members individually take on the responsibility of the public good and can be sued individually, as they are individually liable for, among other things, the debts incurred by the organization and the failure of the organization to comply with the law.

2. The board of directors has ultimate responsibility for the success or failure of an organization. It makes top policy decisions within the framework of the stated mission and objectives of the organization. It is responsible for preparing and implementing long-range plans to achieve the stated objectives by either establishing committees within the board or delegating authority to the staff.

3. The most critical responsibility is fund raising. While the staff works toward maximizing the earned income, the board must close the income gap through fund raising.

4. The board is responsible for hiring and firing senior staff and for developing and maintaining an effective volunteer organization.

5. The board has ultimate responsibility for the marketing effort on two levels: effective marketing is essential for attracting audiences; and the organization must be marketed as a whole for fund-raising purposes. Members must advocate the arts in general and the organization specifically, creating a favorable image in the community.

6. The board must provide professional guidance and support to all staff, continuously balancing the artistic needs of the organization with financial considerations.

7. The board should control all fiscal matters. Each director on the executive committee should fully understand and review the budget before giving final approval and should closely monitor the organization's performance in relation to it. By approving a budget, members essentially are verifying that the budget is a realistic fiscal plan for the following year.

E. T. Blueberry Production, Inc.

R. Dean Lewis, Paul R. Reed, and J. Barry Teare

Sam Houston State University

Maxwell J. Johnson is sitting on the back porch of his double-wide mobile home, with his friend Bill, munching blueberries and drinking iced tea after a hard day's work on his farm. As the sun sets, he enjoys a beautiful, relaxing view as he gazes over a lush meadow and an irrigation lake at the rolling hills of neatly trimmed blueberry plants.

Maxwell admires his creation but voices great concern to his friend about the future of the farm. "Bill, I left the corporate life and moved my family from the city, which provided greater creature comforts, cultural, educational, and recreational benefits to this beautiful, but very basic and rural lifestyle. Debbie and the boys have adjusted well and we have worked very hard to develop the farm, but I have grave concerns about the future. This industry is new in Texas, and we are on the verge of starting commercial production. I am worried about the labor intensity of the farm, inherent risks of any agricultural venture, developing a marketing system for our product, and heavy financial needs of the farm. Bill, we have come a long way, but where and how do we go from here?"

THE TEXAS ECONOMY, 1980s

The Texas economy traditionally was based on oil exploration, production, refining, transmission, and marketing of petroleum products and derivatives. A continual rise in crude oil prices to over $40.00 per barrel resulted in near boom conditions in Texas in the 1970s. Expectations were high, and West Texas crude was expected to exceed $60.00 per barrel in the 1980s. This led to the development of numerous oil service enterprises and support businesses that were often developed with borrowed capital that was highly leveraged. Real estate prices across the state became highly inflated, and the commercial banking and savings and loan industries were eager to fund oil-related loans, often collateralized with single-purpose oil field equipment and overvalued real estate. In summary, the Texas economy became dependent on a healthy energy industry, and the financial institutions allowed their loan portfolios to become highly concentrated in energy-related loans, both foreign and domestic.

In the early 1980s, several events occurred that put the Texas economy and other energy-based states in an economic tailspin. Crude oil prices began to decline and reached a level of less than $10.00 per barrel. The banking industry moved into an area of deregulation, thereby allowing bank managements great latitude in lending policy, which in turn jeopardized capital structures. Another significant development was a change in tax legislation that reduced incentives for capital investments. These occurrences led to the failure or closing of numerous energy-related companies, a decline in economic activity, default on numerous loans, failure of real estate investment groups, and drastic reductions in real estate values that had been used to shore up energy loans. This economic domino effect, initiated by the decline in the oil industry, caused the financial failure of numerous individuals, and Texas suddenly led the nation in bank failures in the mid-1980s.

MAXWELL J. JOHNSON, PETROLEUM INDUSTRY, EXECUTIVE AND ENTREPRENEUR

Maxwell was raised and educated in the Gulf Coast region of Texas. He spent his early years in the oil field as a roustabout and roughneck. He earned a B.S. degree in biology in 1965 and later developed an interest in oil and gas accounting. Maxwell pursued graduate studies in accounting, earning an M.S. in accounting, and became a certified public accountant (C. P. A.). He served as vice president, chief financial officer, and director of Smith Oil & Gas Company from 1981 to 1983. He then became a comanaging general, founding partner of the S. J. Oil Interest in 1983. He had learned the oil business from the ground up, educated himself, worked in management of an oil and gas firm, and then established his own organization. He was ready to capitalize on his experience, education, and entrepreneurial spirit when external environmental changes would force him to leave the oil patch and search for a new career and livelihood.

DEVELOPMENT OF E. T. BLUEBERRY PRODUCTION, INC.

Maxwell and his brother, Benny, had purchased several tracts of land between 1970 and 1983 in east Texas, totaling 90 acres. The land was covered with timber, and the topography was rolling hills, covered with a rich, sandy loam soil. The land had been used over the years for a family weekend and holiday retreat from Houston. Timber had been sold off the land, and

approximately 80 acres were ready for cultivation. There was a lake that had been expanded, and with minimum excavation other water sources could be developed. Maxwell's dream was to utilize this land to develop a new career and earn a living. He initiated an extensive research effort in 1986 to discover how this limited acreage could be best utilized to produce revenue. He was ultimately introduced to blueberry production and was most impressed with a blueberry plant species known as the "rabbiteye," or *vaccivium ashei*. He then made the transition from the oil patch to the blueberry patch.

The rabbiteye plant is a perennial, long-life, deciduous, woody shrub, 8 to 20 feet tall at maturity and is considered the most vigorous (fastest growing) of all blueberry species. Compared to other varieties of blueberry plants, the rabbiteye is larger and more tolerant of heat, cold, and drought. Rabbiteye plants usually begin producing in commercial quantities in the third or fourth year and reach full production in six to eight years. If properly maintained, these plants can produce up to fifty years.

Maxwell became convinced that blueberry production was the best alternative for east Texas. However, it would require great capitalization, hard work, and pioneering a new crop production in Texas. Also, it required a lag time of four years before commercial production could be accomplished, and it assumed great financial and personal risk.

Additional partners were added to the venture to acquire needed capital. Ninety adjoining acres were purchased, farming equipment acquired, and work was initiated. See Exhibit C10.1 for projected costs and revenues for E. T. Blueberry Production.

THE BLUEBERRY INDUSTRY

Blueberry production has become a major fruit industry in the United States. The first wild blueberry was discovered in 1908 in the mountains of southern New Hampshire. In 1986 U.S.

EXHIBIT C10.1 Projected Cost and Revenues Per Acre for East Texas Blueberry Production

	Years							
	1	2	3	4	5	6	7	8
Yield in pounds	151.25	302.50	605.00	1510.00	2420.00	4840.00	7260.00	8470.00
Price per pound sold	$ 1.40	$ 1.40	$ 1.40	$ 1.40	$ 1.40	$ 1.40	$ 1.40	$ 1.40
Total revenue	$ 211.75	$ 423.50	$ 847.00	$2,114.00	$3,388.00	$6,776.00	$10,164.00	$11,858.00
Preharvest costs:								
Land preparation	$ 25.21							
Planting	$1,174.50							
Fertilizer	$ 58.20	$ 91.20	$ 124.20	$ 124.20	$ 157.20	$ 190.20	$ 190.20	$ 190.20
Weed control	$ 64.91	$ 72.66	$ 80.66	$ 80.66	$ 80.66	$ 80.66	$ 80.66	$ 80.66
Bees (pollination)	$ 15.00	$ 15.00	$ 15.00	$ 15.00	$ 15.00	$ 15.00	$ 15.00	$ 15.00
Fireant control	$ 11.56	$ 11.56	$ 11.56	$ 11.56	$ 11.56	$ 11.56	$ 11.56	$ 11.56
Pruning					$ 45.00	$ 45.00	$ 45.00	$ 45.00
Irrigation	$ 285.65	$ 287.10	$ 291.19	$ 303.15	$ 303.15	$ 303.15	$ 303.15	$ 303.15
Interest on operating capital	$ 149.15	$ 18.87	$ 21.96	$ 22.22	$ 23.91	$ 29.51	$ 29.51	$ 29.51
Total preharvest costs	$2,324.18	$ 496.38	$ 544.56	$ 556.78	$ 591.48	$ 675.07	$ 675.07	$ 675.07
Total harvest costs	$ 586.27	$ 409.27	$ 416.95	$ 424.77	$ 433.26	$ 443.10	$ 452.94	$ 461.44
Total variable costs	$2,910.44	$ 905.84	$ 961.51	$ 981.55	$1,024.74	$1,118.18	$ 1,128.02	$ 1,136.51
Returns over variable costs	($2,698.69)	($ 482.34)	($ 114.51)	$1,132.45	$2,363.26	$5,657.82	$ 9,035.98	$10,721.49
Fixed costs:								
Equipment:								
Depreciation	$ 144.05	$ 114.38	$ 114.38	$ 114.38	$ 114.38	$ 114.38	$ 114.38	$ 114.38
Interest	$ 166.52	$ 137.32	$ 137.32	$ 137.32	$ 137.32	$ 137.32	$ 137.32	$ 137.32
Insurance	$ 12.34	$ 10.17	$ 10.17	$ 10.17	$ 10.17	$ 10.17	$ 10.17	$ 10.17
Irrigation equipment:								
Depreciation	$ 15.71	$ 15.71	$ 15.71	$ 15.71	$ 15.71	$ 15.71	$ 15.71	$ 15.71
Interest	$ 7.15	$ 7.15	$ 7.15	$ 7.15	$ 7.15	$ 7.15	$ 7.15	$ 7.15
Land	$ 20.00	$ 20.00	$ 20.00	$ 20.00	$ 20.00	$ 20.00	$ 20.00	$ 20.00
Interest on established cost		$ 312.50	$ 434.55	$ 544.13	$ 606.17	$ 557.74	$ 271.80	$ 0.00
Total fixed costs	$ 365.77	$ 617.23	$ 739.28	$ 848.86	$ 910.90	$ 862.47	$ 576.53	$ 304.73
Total costs	$3,276.21	$1,523.07	$1,700.79	$1,830.41	$1,935.64	$1,980.64	$ 1,704.55	$ 1,441.24
Net revenue	($3,064.46)	($1,099.57)	($ 853.79)	$ 283.59	$1,452.36	$4,795.36	$ 8,459.45	$10,416.76

Source: Texas Agricultural Extension Service

growers produced 154 million pounds of blueberries valued at $94 million. Maine, Michigan, New Jersey, and North Carolina are the leading states in blueberry production. East Texas is particularly suitable for blueberry production, with fertile, high acid, sandy loam soils, quality (low saline) water supply, and annual rainfall of approximately 45 inches. The Texas Agricultural Research and Extension Center in Overton planted its first experimental plants in 1972. As the plants matured, it was determined that Texas varieties could yield 9,000 to 14,000 pounds per acre, which is among the highest in the nation. By 1980 it was evident that there was significant interest in blueberry production in Texas. In 1981 the first blueberry production meeting was held, and the Texas Blueberry Growers Association was created.

The Texas Department of Agriculture estimated in 1985 that market potential for blueberries in Texas alone was 40 million pounds. According to Texas average yields of 9,000 to 14,000 pounds per acre, this would require some 4,000 acres of mature producing plants. In 1989 Texas had approximately 900 acres in blueberry production.

In addition to a favorable climate, rainfall, and soil conditions, Texas has other advantages for blueberry production. Insect infestation problems are minimal and can be easily controlled. Plant disease problems have not been significant for fruit producers, such as peach growers. Texas also offers a longer growing season stretching from March to October. The early March blooming of plants result in Texas berries being ready to market six weeks earlier than Michigan, Maine, and New Jersey crops, thus providing Texas producers a tremendous marketing advantage.

MANAGEMENT

E. T. Blueberry Production, Inc., is in the development stage of growth and currently has no full-time employees other than Maxwell J. Johnson. The company uses consultants, attorneys, accountants, etc., as needed and does not anticipate a need to engage additional full-time employees until the farm goes into commercial production. Maxwell uses part-time laborers on a need basis. The company's officers, other than Maxwell, receive no salary; directors are paid $100 per meeting they attend.

The directors and executive officers currently serving the organization are as follows:

Name	Age	Position Held and Tenure
Maxwell J. Johnson	44	Director, chairman of the board of directors, chief executive officer, president since August 11, 1987
Benny E. Johnson	42	Executive vice president of the board of directors
Randy Q. Smith	37	Executive vice president, chief financial officer, and director since August 11, 1987
Augusto J. Garza	40	Director since August 11, 1987
Art B. Jones	45	Director since August 11, 1987
Richard B. Grant	42	Director since August 11, 1987
Eddie J. Smith	33	Secretary, treasurer since August 11, 1987

Directors are elected for one-year terms at the annual shareholders' meeting. Officers hold their positions at the pleasure of the board of directors. Only Maxwell had an employment agreement, and no other such agreements were contemplated. Maxwell devotes 100 percent of his time to the company's business, and the other directors and officers serve the corporation on an as needed basis. The board meets on a quarterly basis and more often if needed. All board members are very active concerning management decisions, and all are stockholders.

BIOGRAPHICAL INFORMATION OF DIRECTORS

Maxwell J. Johnson. Mr. Johnson has served as the corporation's president, and has been a director, chairman of the board of directors, and chief executive officer, since inception of the company. He has also served as an instructor at the College of Business Administration at two state universities, in the Department of Accounting and Taxation. Maxwell Johnson was the co-founder and comanaging general partner of S. J. Oil Interest in Longhorn, Texas. He served as vice president, chief financial officer, and a director of Smith Oil & Gas, Dallas, Texas, from October 1981 to October 1983. Mr. Johnson is a C.P.A. and received a master's degree in accounting from the University of Houston in 1974, and he received a bachelor's degree in biology from Lamar University in 1965. He performed post-baccalaureate work in biology but did not receive an advanced degree in that subject.

Benny E. Johnson. Mr. Johnson developed a major national sign company, sold the company, and maintains a lucrative management contract with the firm. He has also developed a redfish farm on the Texas Gulf Coast.

Randy Q. Smith. Mr. Smith has served as the company's executive vice president, chief financial officer, and a director since inception. Since February of 1980 he has served as vice president of Capital Investments, Austin, Texas. From April 1976 to February 1980, he served as treasurer for Tracy Construction Co., Ashville, Texas, and from June 1974 to March 1976 was employed as a staff accountant for Moore & Green, Houston, Texas. Mr. Smith is a C.P.A. He was awarded a master's degree in accounting from Rice University in 1976. He is the brother of Eddie J. Smith, the company's secretary and treasurer.

Augusto J. Garza. Mr. Garza has served as a director of the company since inception. He was employed by Garza & Sons, a produce company located in San Antonio, Texas, from June 1969 to August 1986 in varying capacities, including dispatcher, personnel manager, produce purchaser, and general manager. From August 1986 to the present he has served as president and general manager of the Garza Family Market, a wholesale, retail, and brokerage grocery company located in San Antonio, Texas.

Art B. Jones, Ph.D. Dr. Jones has served as a director of the company since inception. From July 1974 to the present he has served as a professor of accountancy and taxation at a major state university. He received a Ph.D. in business administration from the University of Minnesota in 1969 and a master's degree in business administration from Pennsylvania State University in 1965.

Richard B. Grant, M.D. Dr. Grant has served as a director of the company since inception. Since 1977 he has practiced medicine as an ophthalmologist as a partner in Clearwater Eye Associates and Southeast Texas Surgical Center, both located in Clearwater, Texas.

Eddie J. Smith, Ph.D. Dr. Smith has served as the company's secretary and treasurer since inception. From March 1981 to the present he has served as office manager and data processing manager of Capital Investments, Inc., of Austin, Texas. In 1977 he received a bachelor's degree in economics from Rice University. He is the brother of Randy Q. Smith, the company's executive vice president.

The company also has engaged the services of Ted S. Holmes, Ph.D., who will serve as an advisory director to the company. Dr. Holmes will attend all meetings of the board of directors and will advise the board during its proceedings and deliberations but will not have a director's vote. His biography is set forth below.

Ted S. Holmes, Ph.D. Since November 15, 1987, Dr. Holmes has served as an advisory director to the company. Since January of 1985 Dr. Holmes has served as professor in the Texas Agricultural Research and Extension Center in the field of fruit research. From January 1984 to January 1985 Dr. Holmes was a research associate and program coordinator for sweet cherry research at the Irrigated Agriculture Research and Extension Center of Washington State University. Dr. Holmes received a bachelor's degree in plant science from the University of California-Davis in 1977, an M.S. degree in horticulture from Iowa State University in 1980, and a Ph.D. in horticulture from Washington State University in 1983.

Directors were carefully selected because of their expertise, investment in the venture, and/or to facilitate the marketing and distribution of farm production. The board has been very supportive of Mr. Johnson and active in making management decisions.

Remuneration

None of the officers or directors has received any remuneration other than director fees, except Mr. Johnson. The following table represents the aggregate annual remuneration contemplated to be paid to the company's officers and directors after the completion of this offering.

Name	Title	Remuneration[a]
Maxwell J. Johnson	Chief executive officer, president	$50,000[b]
Ted S. Holmes, Ph.D.	Advisory director	6,000[b]
Total		$56,000

---

[a] In addition, each director and the advisory director will be paid $100 plus expenses per board meeting attended.

[b] This amount is subject to increase at the discretion of the board of directors.

The company has no retirement, pension, profit sharing, or insurance programs for the benefit of directors, officers, or other employees, but the board of directors may recommend adoption of one or more such programs in the future. The company also has in place an incentive stock option plan adopted pursuant to section 422a of the Internal Revenue Code of 1986.

PRODUCTION

E. T. Blueberry Production, Inc., specializes in growing, propagating, harvesting, packaging, and marketing blueberries. The farm currently has 40 acres of blueberries, covered with 16,000 rabbiteye plants and 8,000 southern highbush plants from one-and-a-half to four years old. The company owns 180 acres of land. Approximately 150 acres could be converted to blueberry production. The long-term plan is to have an additional 80 acres in production, for a total of 120 acres.

In addition to clearing and preparing more land for production, greater water supply must be developed. Due to potential drought conditions in east Texas, total irrigation for all plants must be available. Well and surface water is adequate for the existing eighty acres, but additional water supply will have to be developed to accommodate added acreage.

A "fertigation" system is in place to irrigate and fertilize the blueberry plants. The system consists of a pump and grid of plastic (PVC) pipe and polypipe, which will deliver a mixture of water and fertilizer to each plant by the drip method. A pressure-compensated emitter provides one gallon of solution to each plant per hour. The current system is made up of flexible polypipe lying on the ground adjacent to the plants. A future plan of Mr. Johnson's is to add an overhead irrigation system, which will minimize potential frost problems. However, this conversion will cost approximately $15,000 to cover existing acreage.

The industry planting standard is 605 plants per acre. However, E. T. Blueberry Production, Inc., has used a successful Florida practice of planting 726 rabbiteye plants per acre. The rabbiteye plant is predominantly being used, because it is particularly suitable for the Texas heat, drought, and limited winter chilling days.

MARKETING

Fresh blueberries are new to the Texas market and are considered a delicacy. It is believed that the demand for fresh berries will be much greater than the limited production (approximately 900 acres) in east Texas. The berries harvested by the company are being sold to the fresh fruit market primarily in Houston, Dallas, and San Antonio.

Some berries, because of size, color, or sugar content, will not be suitable for the fresh fruit market. The berries will be sorted by the company, and the lesser-quality berries will be sold as process berries, which are made into juices, concentrates, syrups, pie fillings, canned berries, candies, yogurts, frozen pies, and turnovers. The company is considering the development of a "private" brand identity for the fresh and process berries and products.

Since blueberry production is relatively new to the Texas market, distribution channels are not established. The Texas Blueberry Association is attempting to assist producers in establishing channels. The geographical production area is limited to northeast Texas, and producers are fragmented into small developing blueberry farms.

A significant challenge for Texas blueberry producers will be the development of a promotional mix to stimulate Texas blueberry demand. Individual producers will probably concentrate on local advertising to develop an identity and stimulate local demand.

Pricing will be market determined, and the producer will function much as a competitor in a perfectly or purely competitive market structure. The Texas market will have the advantages of excessive demand and a early production period relative to other producers.

In addition to the mass fresh fruit and process markets, the company plans to offer a "pick your own" market. Facilities would be provided for customers to come individually or in groups and pick blueberries. A picnic area will be provided next to the "pick your own" orchard.

CURRENT OPERATIONS

Mr. Johnson and his family have lived on the farm for a year. He has worked full time for the venture for the past two years. He commuted from Houston (eighty-five miles one-way) for one year prior to the move. He also has maintained a teaching position with a university during this time. Needless to say, Mr. Johnson is stretched tremendously timewise, working on the farm, teaching, and constantly trying to upgrade himself knowledge-wise concerning the blueberry industry. He reads and travels to seminars and other orchards to learn more. It is obvious when one talks to Mr. Johnson that his basic motivation is a "labor of love" as well as economic survival and success. Farm operations are very labor-intensive, which he and a few part-time laborers maintain. Blueberry production for the farm is provided in Exhibit C10.2.

Mr. Johnson and his wife, Debbie, are forced to wear many hats in an attempt to develop the farm and improve cash flow. The farm is located

EXHIBIT   C10.2   E. T. Blueberry Production, Inc.—Production Data

Year	Total Acres in Production	Total Number of Plants	Harvest Pounds	Average Price (/lb.)	Total Revenue
1987	5	4,000	—	—	—
1988	20	12,000	5,000	$ 1.40	$ 7,000
1989	40	24,000	20,000	$ 1.40	$28,000
1990*	40	24,000	60,000	$ 1.40	$84,000

* Estimated.

in a remote yet scenic area of rolling wooded hills. The enlarged lakes, developed for irrigation needs, have been generously stocked with bass and catfish. Picnic areas around the lakes are being landscaped and supplied with tables, chairs, and outdoor games. These recreational facilities will be promoted to individuals, groups, and businesses for retreats, picnics, and parties. Debbie will host and cater these parties. During berry season this segment of the enterprise will also enhance the "pick-your-own" business.

The Asian population has grown dramatically in the metropolitan areas in recent years, particularly since the Vietnam War. This development has derived a demand for Asian vegetables. Approximately four acres of the orchard have been committed to the growth and experimentation with these vegetables. This could develop a whole new market for the farm.

Floral plants and other varieties of berries are also being experimented with. Basically the land, water, and equipment are in place to produce numerous other products.

Debbie has finished a difficult week on the farm and feels very stressed trying to handle farm duties, family needs, getting the boys, ages 8 and 12, to and from school activities. She is busy in her cramped mobile home kitchen preparing food for two catering jobs for the weekend. She beckons Maxwell for help and asks, "Maxwell, are the picnic areas ready, have you paid the employees, scheduled laborers for next week, and called the cooperative for a truck to pick up berries next Friday? How are we going to get it all done?"

Merck: Strategy Making in "America's Most Admired Corporation"

Shaker A. Zahra

Georgia State University

Merck and Company is, perhaps, America's best kept corporate secret. Selected by Fortune 1,000 executives for four consecutive years as "America's Most Admired Corporation," Merck is hardly a household name. But Merck knows how to compete effectively and how to do the right things right. Merck is driven by an ambition to be on the cutting edge of research and development in its industry and by an obsession with building quality into its products. This dual goal pervades every aspect of the firm's culture, managerial decision making, and organizational structure. Guided by an innovative (or, more appropriately, a visionary) chief executive officer (CEO), Merck is determined to remain the U.S. leading pharmaceutical company.

What does it take to build "America's Most Admired Corporation"? This case provides some clues to the secret of one of the most successful companies in modern American history. This case shows how carefully crafted strategies orchestrated by a visionary and dedicated leader can pay off well. But to understand Merck's secrets, let us first examine how the company came into existence.

HISTORY

Merck's roots can be traced as far back as 1668, when the Merck family bought an apothecary in Darmstadt, Germany. More than 150 years later the Merck family decided to complement the apothecary by manufacturing its own drugs. In 1827 this decision became a reality when a manufacturing operation was opened also in Darmstadt, Germany. The Merck family brought its drug manufacturing expertise to the United States in 1887, when it opened a branch in New York. Shortly thereafter, in 1891, the Merck & Company partnership was formed in New York. Merck started manufacturing drugs and specialty chemicals in Rahway, New Jersey, in 1903. In 1908 Merck & Company incorporated in New York and later, in 1919, it sold stock to the public for the first time. By 1941 Merck & Company had established manufacturing facilities throughout the United States.

As Merck & Company was growing throughout the United States, another competitor, Sharp & Dohme, was following close behind. In 1845 Sharp opened an apothecary in Baltimore and later in 1860 formed a partnership with Dohme. While Merck was building expertise in manufacturing, Sharp and Dohme concentrated heavily on research. Today's Merck & Company was formed in 1953, when Merck merged with Sharp & Dohme. Other acquisitions and divestments would follow, but this merger represents what Merck stands for today, excellence in research and manufacturing of pharmaceuticals and specialty chemicals. Indeed, Merck defines its business as "a worldwide, research-intensive health products company that discovers, develops, produces, and markets human and animal health products and specialty chemicals" (annual report, 1988).

INDUSTRY SEGMENTS AND PRODUCTS

Merck competes primarily in two industry segments: human and animal health products and specialty chemicals. The contribution to sales for 1988 for each of these segments is presented in Exhibit C11.1.

Specialty Chemicals

The specialty chemicals group offers a wide variety of products that include xantham gum, a biogum with various uses, including growing oil field applications; Epi-Lock and Synthaderm, polyurethane wound dressings; and several water treatment–related products, including pHreeGUARD, BoilerGUARD, and POL-E-Z. In

EXHIBIT   C11.1
Merck Sales by Segment

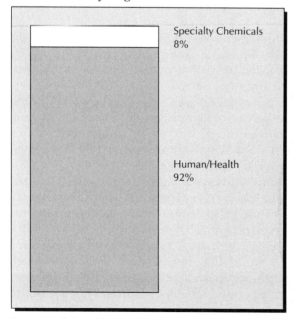

Specialty Chemicals
8%

Human/Health
92%

Source: Merck Annual Report, 1989.

addition, the group provides special software applications to maximize the efficiency of water treatment facilities.

Specialty-chemical products are used in a wide variety of applications. The most common uses are water treatment, food processing, and skin care. Merck entered the specialty chemicals market in 1968, when it acquired Calgon Corporation. Calgon's main business was the manufacturing of water treatment products and providing related services. In 1972 Merck strengthened its position in specialty chemicals by acquiring the Kelco company. Kelco mainly produced alginates and xantham gum. Today Merck's specialty chemical products come from the Kelco Division, Calgon Vestal Labs, and Calgon Water Management Division.

Sales of products and services from the specialty chemicals group are made in channels of trade, including industrial users, distributors, wholesalers, municipalities, and utilities. The group has been making steady gains in its segment, increasing sales over the last couple of years from slightly more than $350 million in 1986 to $450 million in 1988.

Human and Animal Health Products

Most of Merck's income comes from the human and animal health products segment. Within this segment Merck's products can be grouped into eight primary categories, as illustrated in Exhibit C11.2, which lists their contributions to company sales in 1988. The human health products that Merck offers include therapeutic and preventive preparations, generally sold by prescription. Merck sells prescription drugs through its professional representatives (called "detailmen") to drug wholesalers and retailers, physicians, veterinarians, hospitals, clinics, government agencies, and other institutions. Merck prides itself on the knowledge and competence of its detailmen. A new sales recruit can expect to be in training for two years, which includes technical training and is equivalent to that given at many medical schools.

The cardiovascular medications, particularly Vasotec, are the flagship products of the Merck line. Vasotec, originally developed as a blood pressure reducer, was approved in 1988 for treatment of congestive heart failure patients. Sales in 1988 for Vasotec alone were nearly $1 billion. Mevacor and Zocor (as yet to receive FDA approval) are two cardiovascular products with billion-dollar futures, also. Both are medications used to reduce cholesterol levels, and analysts expect these two drugs to be contributing in excess of a billion dollars a year by 1990.[1] Pepcid, a once-a-day treatment for peptic ulcers, has made great inroads on the once sacred grounds of SmithKline's Tagamet. Pepcid now contributes well over $100 million in annual sales, and is being prescribed more and more over Tagamet and Glaxo's Zantac.[2]

Antibiotic medications are another area where Merck's conviction to research is paying off. The product Primaxin currently has the broadest spectrum of antimicrobial activity of any antibiotic yet marketed.

Overall Merck has fifteen drugs currently producing annual revenues in excess of $100 million each.

EXHIBIT C11.2
Product Contribution to Human and Animal Segment Sales

Antihypertensive and cardiovasculars	34.2%
Antibiotics	14.6%
Anti-inflammatories/analgesics	13.8%
Ophthalmologicals	6.3%
Anti-ulcerants	5.2%
Vaccines	4.0%
Animal medicinals	8.9%
Other	1.3%

Source: Merck Annual Report, 1988.

FINANCIAL PERFORMANCE

The pharmaceutical industry tends to be somewhat immune to most economic conditions. Rather, demographics and public interest in health-related issues, such as cholesterol reduction, are more of an influence on the industry.

In the late 1970s and early '80s, Merck lost its number-one position in the industry to Bristol-Meyers, as the result of several of its drugs coming off patent protection.[3] Merck maintained a focus on long-term strategies, rather than managing for the short term, by spending a significant amount of time and money to develop new products. This long-term view is credited with bringing Merck through the difficult times of the early 1980s and back to the top of the pharmaceutical industry. Exhibit C11.3 presents selected financial data for the period 1983–'88.

In addition to excellent financial performance, Merck has managed to maintain an impressive rate of growth in sales in recent years, as shown in Exhibit C11.3. Between 1981 and 1985, as Merck's profits grew by an average of only 8 percent, the rest of the industry enjoyed rates in excess of 15 percent.[4] The reason for this gap between Merck and industry performance was simple: some of Merck's cash-cow drugs were coming off patent, and the company was losing sales due to increasing generic competition both domestically and abroad. Rather than seeking a quick fix, Merck stepped up R&D to protect its long-term survival. As a result, Merck's earnings have made a strong comeback and currently top the industry. Exhibit C11.3 shows Merck's progressive growth and recent surge in earnings. It should also be noted that Merck's return on investment (ROI) has far outpaced the industry average in recent years.

In addition to classic measures of performance, such as earnings growth, ROI, and net profit margin, Merck has been "America's Most Admired Corporation" four years running in *Fortune* magazine's annual feature of the same title. *Fortune* polls 8,000 top executives and financial analysts and asks them to rank companies in their industry in eight categories:

- Quality of management
- Quality of products or services
- Innovativeness
- Long-term investment value
- Financial soundness
- Community and environmental responsibility

- Use of corporate assets
- Ability to attract, develop, and keep talented people

For the fourth consecutive year, Merck has received the highest cumulative score out of the 300 largest corporations in America.

Foreign Trade Contribution

The pharmaceutical industry as a whole and Merck in particular have a favorable impact on

---

EXHIBIT C11.3 Selected Financial Data
($ millions, except per share amounts)

	1988	1987	1986	1985	1984	1983
Sales	5,939.5	5,061.3	4,128.9	3,547.5	3,559.7	3,246.1
Materials and production costs	1,526.1	1,443.3	1,338.0	1,272.4	1,424.5	1,263.4
Marketing/admin. expenses	1,877.8	1,682.1	1,269.9	1,009.0	945.5	905.1
R&D expenses	668.8	565.7	479.8	426.3	393.1	356.0
Other (income) expenses, net	(4.2)	(36.0)	(32.1)	(17.2)	9.8	25.6
Income before taxes	1,871.0	1,405.2	1,073.3	857.0	786.8	696.0
Taxes on income	664.2	498.8	397.6	317.1	293.8	245.1
Net income	1,206.8	906.4	675.7	539.9	493.0	450.9
Per share of common stock	$3.05	$2.23	$1.62	$1.26	$1.12	$1.02
Dividends on common stock:						
Declared	546.3	365.2	278.5	35.1	224.0	210.8
Paid per share	$1.28	$0.82	$0.63	$0.53	$0.50	$0.47
Capital expenditures	372.7	253.7	210.6	237.6	274.4	272.8
Depreciation	189.0	188.5	167.2	163.6	151.6	135.2
Year-end position:						
Working capital	1,480.3	798.3	1,094.3	1,106.6	1,076.5	734.9
Property, plant and equipment (net)	2,070.7	1,948.0	1,906.2	1,882.8	1,912.8	1,751.5
Total assets	6,127.5	5,680.0	5,105.2	4,902.2	4,590.6	4,214.7
Long-term debt	142.8	167.4	167.5	170.8	179.1	385.5
Stockholders equity	2,855.8	2,116.7	2,541.2	2,607.7	2,518.6	2,409.9
Year-end statistics:						
Average common shares outstanding	395,640	407,055	417,978	427,561	440,670	443,661
Number of stockholders	68,500	56,900	48,300	47,000	50,200	51,800
Number of employees	32,000	31,100	30,700	30,900	34,800	32,600
Financial ratios:						
Net income as a percent of:						
Sales	20.30	17.90	16.40	15.20	13.80	13.90
Total assets	20.40	16.80	13.50	11.40	11.20	11.50
Return on equity	42.26	42.82	26.59	20.70	19.57	18.71

the burgeoning U.S. trade deficit. Historically Merck has had large favorable trade balances and in 1988 Merck had a favorable balance of approximately $850 million. This can be attributed to Merck's aggressive global push for growth and the recent weakening of the dollar. Exhibit C11.4 shows both domestic and foreign sales for 1988.

MANAGEMENT

The current style and attitude of management at Merck & Company can be attributed directly to the efforts of the CEO, Dr. P. Roy Vagelos. Ironically, Vagelos grew up working at his parents' luncheonette that was located within walking distance from the Merck plant in Rahway. Listening to the scientists' discussions over lunch inspired Vagelos to seek a career in medicine.

EXHIBIT C11.4
Percentage of Sales Domestic and Foreign

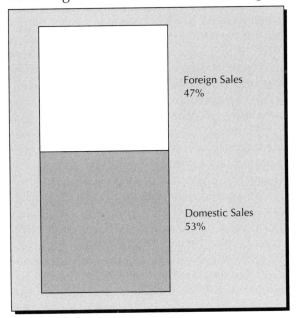

Foreign Sales
47%

Domestic Sales
53%

Source: Merck Annual Report, 1988.

Vagelos worked as an intern in Merck's labs while attending medical school at Columbia University. After completing medical school, he spent the next twenty years in basic research and teaching. In 1976 he joined Merck & Company as head of the research division. When Vagelos joined Merck, the research division was not productive, and "the company had not produced a big winner for a decade or more."[5] Vagelos determined that this lack of production was due to a lack of direction. Scrapping dubious projects, Vagelos began financing only major programs directed at discovering drugs that would cure known diseases.[6]

After pointing the research division in the right direction, he sought to perfect it by hiring the most talented people money could buy. He proceeded to recruit eminent university scientists. To entice these scientists, Vagelos created a "campus-like" atmosphere and offered outstanding salaries. His background as a scientist at Washington University and his other academic credentials made him credible to those he wanted to hire. Vagelos also made sure that researchers had first-rate facilities, which was often not the case in private industry. Vagelos sums up his recruiting philosophy as follows: "We don't always get our man, but we have never missed hiring someone we wanted because of money."[7]

Vagelos became the CEO of Merck in 1985. His management practices then spread from the research division to the entire company. Vagelos refuses to rest on his string of successes. For example, after the news on September 1, 1987, that the FDA approved the Merck drug Mevacor, Vagelos phoned the scientist that had headed up Mevacor to congratulate him. In the same conversation, he also asked the scientist how they were coming on possible substitutes. "Instead of running Merck defensively, avoiding risks and letting its current successes carry it along, he is driving the company just as hard today as he did when he became research chief twelve years ago. For all Merck's momentum, Vagelos is making sure it runs scared."[8]

The most significant feat that Vagelos has accomplished at Merck was gaining the respect of his employees. The employees realize that Vagelos is both a capable scientist and manager. As a result, they do not spend time second-guessing strategic decisions and instead concentrate their efforts on supporting and implementing the decisions. A significant indication of his appropriate style and capabilities as a CEO is the aforementioned fact that Merck has been "America's Most Admired Corporation" four years in a row. When the top executives from America's 300 largest corporations rate your quality of management at the top of all industries four years in a row, that indicates that you are doing something right![9]

RESOURCES

Excellence in management and development of its employees worldwide is of strategic importance to Merck. Vagelos's strategy is to "hire the best, provide the best training, and encourage professional growth."[10] Merck's managers and supervisors have the responsibility to establish and maintain work environments where people are given appropriate responsibility for their jobs, understand their objectives, and feel they are treated fairly.

Research is the lifeblood of Merck, and the recruiting and retaining of top researchers is key to the continuing success of Merck. Merck has worked very hard to set up its labs and research divisions in such a way as to erase the stigma most academics usually associate with moving from academia to industry.[11] Merck's research labs boast an excess of 3,320 employees, representing more than ten percent of the company's total work force. The researchers and scientists working in these labs enjoy a casual atmosphere, moving around the lab grounds in white coats and jeans, while having one of the best compensation packages in the industry. Vagelos places recruiting of top researchers at the top of his priority list. For example, to recruit Leslie Iversen, a

British biochemist and one of the world's leading researchers in Alzheimer's and other neurological diseases, Merck built a 122-person neuroscience research center in Harlowe, Essex, a short distance from Iversen's home.[12]

In addition to active pursuit of the best employees available, Merck also takes some progressive approaches to ensure its employees' job satisfaction. The turnover rate at Merck averages only five percent. Flexible schedules, daycare facilities, and work-at-home arrangements are a few examples of what Merck does to create a pleasant working environment for employees. In particular, Merck has adopted changes in policy to reflect the changing demographics of the work force, more specifically the two-worker family and the resulting need for quality daycare. For example, Merck will hold a position for new mothers and fathers who go on unpaid leave for up to eighteen months after the birth of a child, six times longer than most other companies. At the company's main facilities in Rahway, employees can get daycare for their infants at facilities started by Merck, for a price based on the employee's salary level.[13] Merck has also developed a fair performance appraisal system. In response to declining company performance during the early 1980s, Merck created a task force to identify factors responsible for these problems. The major conclusion of the task force was the overwhelming employee dissatisfaction with the company's current performance appraisal system and salary administration programs. In fact, the biggest single complaint was the lack of real reward distinction between the outstanding performers and those not performing as well.

To remedy the situation, Merck implemented a new appraisal system that evaluates employees' performance in three categories: specific job measures and ongoing duties, planned objectives, and management of people.[14] The third category, management of people, was added because employees and managers at all levels of the company felt that managers were primarily rewarded for their technical abilities, but that their managerial abilities were ignored, a common problem in technically driven companies run by technicians.

A distribution target for performance ratings was established to help managers rate the employees in relation to their peers. This essentially produced a two-step evaluation process; first, an employee's performance is measured against objectives and ongoing duties, and then his or her performance is compared with the performance of other employees in the same area of the company. Salary guidelines have also been established that define salary ranges for each position and the level and frequency of increase that may be given for each category of performance.

ORGANIZATION AND STRUCTURE

Merck and Company is divided into several divisions. Merck Sharp & Dohme (MSD) is responsible for the marketing and administration of Merck's human pharmaceuticals. This division employs approximately 2,500 people. The majority of these employees are Merck's "professional representatives," who present Merck's product line of human pharmaceuticals to physicians, pharmacists, and hospitals.

MSD's counterpart for the animal health markets is MSD AGVET. MSD AGVET is responsible for marketing and administration of agricultural products in addition to animal health products. Merck Sharp and Dohme Research Laboratories is the division responsible for the discovery and development of compounds for both MSD and MSD AGVET.

Merck Pharmaceutical Manufacturing Division (MPMD) is the manufacturing arm of Merck and Company. This is the largest division, employing 5,400 people. Merck and Company shows signs of backward integration in its Merck Chemical Manufacturing Division (MCMD), which produces bulk chemicals used by MPMD, in addition to making chemicals for sale to the public. Merck has a few smaller subsidiaries, such as Calgon Corporation, but the divisions outlined above represent the major business of Merck & Company.

Merck's divisions and departments interact frequently with each other. This is no accident. Because Merck's dedication to research is the gospel that Vagelos preaches, the company has a unique informal structure. Vagelos purposely instituted a free atmosphere so his scientists would not be restricted by formal authority. For example, a research team must sell its idea to those functional groups from whom it needs assistance on the projects. These functional groups, or units, are budgeted development money to invest in projects of their choice. "The idea is to gain greater collegiality and unity of purpose. As a consensus develops around a project, it gains support intellectually and financially from the team's members."[15] The flexibility and freedom of Merck's structure is what makes the research department, and thus the whole company, thrive.

A second important area that a research project must gain support from is marketing. In fact, marketing is second in importance only to research at Merck. With the advent of new products and the continued success of existing products, Merck has added sales personnel and restructured the sales force as well. Prior to 1988, Merck had 1,600 sales representatives divided into two groups. However, Merck soon realized that this organization was not adequately promoting the products. As a result, in 1988, it increased the sales force by one third and created three general groups of 550 representatives and a fourth group of 430 representatives to specialize in hospital products. Each representative in the general groups has one to three products to sell. This permits sales people to develop thorough knowledge of their products.

MANUFACTURING AND OPERATIONS

As mentioned earlier, Merck has two manufacturing divisions. The first is MCMD, which is responsible for producing specialty chemicals for the market and bulk chemicals used by the MPMD. Merck believes in quality. The MCMD facilities are "state of the art." For example, the Elkton, Virginia, plant uses robotics technology to ensure high quality. "This system guides a product sample through testing and returns the results electronically to the plant floor, minimizing response time and handling errors."[16] Safety is another big issue at Merck. The MCMD was recognized by the Chemical Manufacturing Association for having the best safety record of all firms having over 20 million hours of exposure.

This same commitment to quality and safety applies to the MPMD, as well. The MPMD produces products for direct human consumption, which makes a quality commitment a must. Since the MPMD receives almost all of its raw materials from the MCMD, management believes it is imperative that both divisions produce a quality product. The MPMD also ensures quality through state-of-the-art technology. As an example, Merck's plant at West Point, Pennsylvania, uses a unique Vision System. This system uses computer imaging to measure the accuracy of labeling. The MPMD is starting to design new packaging techniques to make them more consumer-oriented. Merck also has instituted modular designs into both manufacturing divisions so they can be used to produce more than one product.

Merck has consistently invested large amounts of capital into its manufacturing divisions, which has made them the model facilities that they are today. However, this financial commitment has seemingly peaked. Merck feels that its facilities are the best available and, therefore, is starting to turn its financial attention to its research laboratories and new administrative offices. The facilities are now completely modular and, therefore, can be more productive as well as adaptive to changes in the market. Also, the new high-potency medicines do not require the complex production facilities of the past, mainly because they do not require as many different raw materials. For these reasons, management believes that reductions are possible in capital expenditures on plant facilities without compromising their productive output.

Merck's manufacturing focus in the future will center on five objectives. First, Merck will still ensure that preventative maintenance occurs where necessary. Second, the company will provide expansion to support new products after careful review of existing plant capacities. Third, it will maintain its commitment to clean environment and employee safety. Fourth, it will continue to look for ways to increase productivity through advances in process technology. Last and most important, Merck will continue its dedication to producing the highest-quality products possible.

MAJOR COMPETITORS

The pharmaceutical industry is very competitive, with no single company holding a dominant market share position. In this industry it appears that gaining market share is not directly correlated to an increase in profitability. But gaining market share is the result of successful product differentiation.

Merck's major domestic competitors include Abbott Labs, American Home Products, Eli Lilly, Johnson & Johnson, Squibb, Warner-Lambert, Syntex, and Schering-Plough. In particular, Merck is currently engaged in a fierce competition with Squibb in the antihypertensive market. Merck's Vasotec competes head to head with Squibb's highly successful Capoten. Capoten sales continue to grow at about 26 percent per year, but Vasotec is growing faster and is expected to exceed Capoten's level of sales.[17] The outcome of this battle is particularly crucial for Squibb, since Capoten accounts for more than 40 percent of its sales. Both drugs have exceeded the billion-dollar mark in annual sales, a feat accomplished by only three other drugs.

The primary competition from outside the United States comes from Glaxo Holdings,

Hoscht, Ciba-Geigy, each with about 3 percent of the global market, and Sankyo, a Japanese firm. Merck's current goal is to expand its global market share, but each of the above firms uses Merck's same formula, plenty of R&D, and successful product differentiation, to compete.

In 1989 the pharmaceutical industry in which Merck competed was fiercely competitive. Between 1978 and 1987 the top four companies consistently accounted for nearly 25 percent of industry sales.

Instead of concentrating on building market shares within the pharmaceutical industry, key competitors opted to diversify into the related health care industry. Many of these companies believed that they could better serve "the changing health care industry as a diversified supplier of health aids, from drugs to equipment." The push for diversification among pharmaceutical companies began in the 1970s, intensified throughout the 1980s, and was expected to continue well into the 1990s.

In the 1970s pharmaceutical companies began purchasing companies that dealt with consumer products in an effort to diversify. For example, Warner-Lambert bought Entenmann's, a bakery products company, and American Optical, an eyeglass manufacturer, and Squibb purchased Lifesavers, a candy manufacturer. Toward the 80s, after displaying a dismal record of success with their consumer products acquisitions, many of the companies began shedding these units and investing in companies in other health-care types of businesses. For example, Warner-Lambert shed Entenmann's and used the proceeds to purchase IMED Corporation, a medical technology firm.[18]

Finally, in the mid 80s, the pharmaceutical companies began divesting their unprofitable attempts at diversification and funneling the proceeds back into their strengths, R&D and marketing new products. Divesting these units left many companies with some hefty cash reserves. A survey of estimated cash and liquid reserves of major pharmaceutical companies at the end of 1986 included Merck with $1.5 billion, Bristol-Meyers with $1.3 billion, Pfizer with $1.4 billion, and Eli Lilly with $800 million.[19] This enabled these companies to invest heavily in R&D and marketing. Yet these cash reserves, coupled with the industry's historically high profit margins, also made these companies targets for takeovers. As a result, many companies instituted stock repurchase plans as a defensive measure.

A summary of key acquisitions/divestitures in this time period is listed below.

1985
- GD Searle Corporation is bought by Monsanto.
- Sterling Drugs is bought by Eastman Kodak.
- Richardson Vicks is bought by Procter & Gamble.
- Bristol-Meyers buys Genetic Systems Corporation, a developer of diagnostic and therapeutic products.

1986
- Warner-Lambert sells off three medical equipment businesses.
- Squibb sells off its Charles of the Ritz cosmetic and fragrance unit.

1987
- Eli Lilly sells off its Elizabeth Arden cosmetics unit and announces stock repurchase plan.
- SmithKline Beckman repurchases 12.6 million of its outstanding shares.

What is the effect of these mergers, acquisitions, and divestments on the structure of the industry? Experts do not expect significant changes in the level of concentration in the industry. Rather, they predict that these companies will have to compete differently.

Product Differentiation

Fierce competition in the industry is in many ways a manifestation of product differentiation, through R&D spending and marketing activities.

R & D

A brief review of industry information shows there exists a strong positive association between R&D spending and corporate ROI. While not perfectly linear, the data show that spending on R&D is associated with superior corporate financial performance.

Exhibit C11.5 presents data on R&D spending by major companies in the industry. During the period 1985–87 Merck consistently ranked first among the sixteen leading companies in terms of R&D spending.

Statistics on R&D indicated that spending by pharmaceutical companies was one of the highest among U.S. major industries, rising from 11.3 percent as a percent of sales to 15.1 percent over the past decade. Statistics also show that about 70 percent of drug R&D in this country was funded directly by domestic pharmaceutical manufacturers, 10 percent by colleges and universities (often in conjunction with leading drug companies), and 20 percent by government and other sources.[20] These percentages translate to $5.4 billion spent in R&D in 1987, up from $1.4 billion in 1978.

Industry experts considered R&D spending to be essential for effective, sustainable product differentiation. Being the first to introduce new drugs resulted in very rewarding financial performance.

In addition, Ronald Bond and David Lean concluded that the original seller's "persistent dominance in the face of competition from

EXHIBIT   C11.5   R & D Expeditures ($=Millions)

	1987		1986		1985		Average	
	$	**Rank**	**$**	**Rank**	**$**	**Rank**	**$**	**Rank**
Merck	565.7	1	479.8	1	426.3	1	490.6	1
Eli Lilly	466.3	2	427.0	2	369.8	2	421.0	2
SmithKline Beckman	423.7	3	376.9	3	309.6	3	370.0	3
Pfizer	401.0	4	335.5	4	286.7	4	341.0	4
Abbott Labs	361.3	5	284.9	7	240.6	8	295.6	7
Upjohn	355.5	6	314.1	5	284.1	5	317.9	5
Bristol-Meyers	341.7	7	311.1	6	261.7	6	304.8	6
American Cyanamid	313.6	8	278.3	8	250.6	7	280.8	8
Schering-Plough	250.7	9	212.1	10	175.4	11	212.7	11
American Home Prods.	247.3	10	227.1	9	217.3	9	230.5	9
Warner-Lambert	231.8	11	202.3	11	208.2	10	214.1	10
Squibb	221.4	12	163.0	12	165.7	12	183.3	12
Rorer Group	81.8	13	69.7	13	17.9	16	56.4	14
Marion Labs	81.5	14	52.8	14	42.7	14	59.0	13
AH Robbins	58.4	15	51.8	15	52.4	13	54.2	15
Bausch & Lomb	26.5	16	25.7	16	21.5	15	24.5	16

cheaper, more highly promoted substitute drugs would suggest that the product differentiation advantage of being first with a 'breakthrough' is very substantial indeed."[21]

Exhibit C11.6 illustrates the number of new drugs that received FDA approval over the last thirteen years. These approvals represented a major milestone by companies achieving them and often served as a barrier to entry.[22]

EXHIBIT   C11.6
U. S. New Drug Approvals

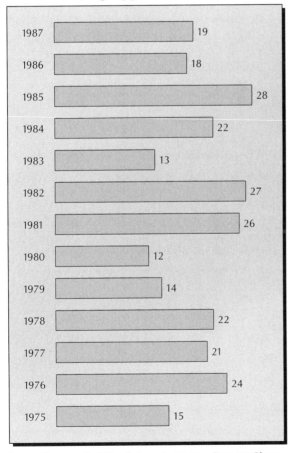

Year	Approvals
1987	19
1986	18
1985	28
1984	22
1983	13
1982	27
1981	26
1980	12
1979	14
1978	22
1977	21
1976	24
1975	15

Source: Pharmaceutical Manufacturers Association, *Facts at a Glance,* 1988.

Marketing and Advertising

Advertising is important in the pharmaceutical industry to build brand recognition with the public for proprietary drugs and to build brand recognition and loyalty with physicians for ethical drugs. In a study by Mier Statman (1981), he concluded that physicians had come to identify the drugs with specific brand names so that the original seller maintained most of his prior market position even after patent expiration.[23]

Pharmaceutical companies accomplished brand loyalty for ethical drugs mainly through direct selling, which built strong relationships with physicians. These salesmen, the "detailmen," were a valuable source of information for physicians. In fact, the Kefauver Committee challenged the pharmaceutical industry's selling expenses, claiming they were much too high and should be cut, which would result in savings for consumers. The industry replied that significant expenditures went into training the detailmen sufficiently to become a resource to the physicians. The physicians stood behind the industry by testifying that the detailmen were in fact an integral part of their information basis and relied heavily on them to keep up with the changes in the available drugs.

These marketing efforts comprise approximately 20 percent of sales.[24] "Traditional product advertising in scientific journals accounts for 24 percent of advertising efforts, direct mail about 6 percent, and detail staff for another 20 percent."[25]

Exhibit C11.7 presents data on advertising expenditures by the leading fifteen pharmaceutical companies during the 1985–87 period.

Industry Performance

During 1975–85 industry revenues grew at an annual average rate of 8 percent, and industry return of equity (ROE) was well above all other U.S. industries during the 1983–88 period. Using net profit margin as a measure of performance, the pharmaceutical industry also outperformed all other industries during the same time period.

Threats

Merck faces several major threats in the industry. First, as mentioned, the industry is fiercely competitive. In recent years foreign companies have posed the greatest threat to Merck. Foreign companies are not only active in marketing and distributing their products in the United States, but they are also increasingly involved in joint ventures that will solidify their competitive position.

Second, as of 1984, the government has undertaken many steps that may weaken industry innovativeness. The effect of government actions was to reduce the time span of patent protection, thus making it easier for other firms to manufacture generic drugs.

Third, the ever-rising growth of the generic drug industry is a major threat facing the industry. Firms in this industry (a few of which may also produce branded drugs) make copies of unpatented drugs and sell them under a generic name at a lower price than the branded drugs. The branded-only drug firms are vehemently opposed to generic drugs and claim that many of the generic drugs are not bioequivalent to the branded drug. In fact, "the FDA has acknowledged that, of the 6,000 marketed generic drugs listed in its Approved Drug Products with Therapeutic Equivalence Evaluations, about 20 percent have not been determined by the agency to be therapeutically equivalent to the pioneer products."[26] Despite the controversy, the generic drug industry is capturing an increas-

EXHIBIT C11.7 Advertising Expeditures ($=Millions)

	1987		1986		1985	
	$	% of sales	$	% of sales	$	% of sales
Abbott Labs	135.3	3.1	94.4	2.5	87.2	2.6
AH Robbins	109.7	12.8	95.5	12.1	86.8	12.3
American Home Prods.	447.3	8.9	441.3	9.0	408.1	8.7
Bausch & Lomb	77.3	9.2	40.1	5.7	36.5	6.2
Bristol-Meyers	918.7	17.0	820.4	17.0	775.9	17.5
Eli Lilly	29.9	0.8	49.4	1.3	47.6	1.5
Marion Labs	62.5	10.5	58.8	14.7	41.4	14.0
Merck	202.0	4.0	145.4	3.5	102.8	2.9
Pfizer	181.8	3.7	170.6	3.8	158.0	3.9
Rorer Group	49.4	5.3	40.0	4.7	19.3	5.7
Schering-Plough	321.9	11.9	262.4	10.9	224.5	11.6
SmithKline Beckman	250.8	5.8	236.5	6.3	176.0	5.4
Squibb	151.1	7.0	117.6	6.6	119.5	5.9
Upjohn	123.7	4.9	101.4	4.4	94.1	4.7
Warner-Lambert	797.5	22.9	692.8	22.3	630.8	19.7

ingly large share of the prescription drug market without having to spend any significant amount of money in research and development. Currently generic drugs account for about 23 percent of all prescriptions.[27]

Opportunities

The above threats notwithstanding, Merck is well positioned to explore many promising opportunities in the United States and abroad. Continuing its tradition of extensive R&D, Merck can target specific market groups, such as senior citizens, or continue its current strategy. Additionally, Merck's excellent reputation makes it an attractive candidate for strategic alliances in the United States or abroad. Opportunities appear limitless for Merck. Still, the question Merck must address in the 1990s is: How much emphasis should the firm give its pharmaceutical core business? Much depends on the preferences of Merck's senior executives, who so ably have created a great company.

| ENDNOTES

1. J. Byrne, "The Miracle Company," *Business Week,* October 19, 1987, 84–89.
2. Annual report, 28.
3. "Merck; admirable, but . . . ," *The Economist,* January 17, 1987, 61-62.
4. C. Eklund and C. Green, "A Research Whiz Steps Up from the Lab," *Business Week,* June 24, 1985, 87-88.
5. S. Quicker, "The Drug Culture," *Business Month,* December 1987, 36.
6. Ibid.
7. Ibid.
8. S. Quicker, "Merck & Company—Sheer Energy," *Business Month,* December 1988, 36.
9. E. Schultz, "America's Most Admired Corporations," *Fortune,* January 18, 1988, 36.
10. Annual report, 34.
11. "Giving Free Rein to Merck's Best and Brightest," *Business Week,* October 19, 1987, 90.
12. S. Quicker, "The Drug Culture," 36.
13. "The Flexible Work Force; What Organizations Think," *Personnel Administrator,* August 1986, 36-40.
14. W. H. Wagel, "Performance Appraisal with a Difference," *Personnel,* February 1987, 4-7.
15. Byrne, "The Miracle Company," 86.
16. Annual report, 22.
17. S. Benway, "Don't Look Back, Squibb—A Giant Is Gaining on You," *Business Week,* October 10, 1988, 68-71.
18. Ibid.
19. "Prospects Continue Strong," *Standard & Poor's Industry Surveys,* April 1987, H19.
20. "Industry Has Prescription for Success," *Standard & Poor's Industry Surveys,* June 1988, H19.
21. W. S. Comanor, "The Political Economy of the Pharmaceutical Industry," *Journal of Economic Literature,* XXIV (September 1986), 1188.
22. Pharmaceutical Manufacturers Association, "Pharmaceutical Research: Delivering Value in the Cost Containment Era," 1988, 27.
23. W. S. Comanor, "The Political Economy," 1189.
24. J. Kangilaski, "Drug Companies Reach into Mixed Marketing Bag," *Advertising Age,* October 24, 1985, 35.
25. Ibid.
26. G. J. Mossinghoff, "Generic Drugs," Pharmaceutical Manufacturers Association.
27. Ibid.

Pilkington Brothers P.L.C.

James Brian Quinn and Allie J. Quinn
Dartmouth College

In 1826 William Pilkington—son of a surgeon cum wine and spirit merchant cum apothecary—joined with two well-known glassmakers to form the St. Helens Crown Glass Company and later Pilkington Brothers, Ltd. (1894). The company remained privately held until 1970, when it offered some 5.7 million shares (10 percent) of its stock to the public. Then in 1973, after being honored as British Businessman of the Year, (Sir Harry) Lord Pilkington—the fourth-generation direct descendant of the founder to head the company—retired. From 1974–1981 the company's next chairman Sir Alastair Pilkington—scientist, inventor, professional manager, but not a lineal descendant of the ownership group—led the company's transition to a diversified worldwide, technology-leading glass company. In 1981, when Sir Alastair stepped down as CEO, Pilkington's new management team had to design its strategies for a vastly changed world.

This case is intended for classroom discussion only, not to depict effective or ineffective handling of administrative situations. All rights reserved to the authors. The generous support of the International Management Institute, Geneva, Switzerland, is gratefully acknowledged. The generous cooperation of Pilkington Brothers is gratefully acknowledged.

EARLY HISTORY

In 1894 Pilkington was the only British producer of both plate and sheet (window) glass, and it had diversified into other flat glasses. Because plate glass processes were so capital intensive, manufacturing was centralized at Pilkington's original St. Helens location, where all needed raw materials—coal, limestone, dolomite, alkali, and iron-free sand—were abundant within reasonable distance.

Flat Glass Technology

The basic processes for making flat glass had remained substantially the same from the 1700s to the early 1900s. *Sheet* glass was drawn into a ribbon through a (slotted) block floating on the surface of the melted glass inside a glass furnace. The ribbon passed vertically upward through asbestos rollers, a lehr which relieved stresses in the glass, and then into a cutting room where the cooled, hardened glass was cut and stacked. The process produced a good inexpensive window glass, but output was limited to relatively thin sheets of glass, subject to inhomogeneities and optical distortion.

These properties were unacceptable for mirrors, automobile windows, and the large windows increasingly used for retail displays and architectural effects. *Plate* glass was required to meet these demands. To make plate, molten glass was rolled into a plate with a waffled surface and then, in a discontinuous process, was ground and polished until both surfaces were smooth and parallel. Grinding required several stages using a series of very large grinding wheels—or disks—with successively finer abrasive surfaces. Polishing was done with buffers and various powdered rouges. Gigantic factories and huge process investments were required. Because of this, plate manufacture slowly became concentrated in the hands of a few producers. And even these could survive only in countries with large markets.

Then in the early 1920s Ford Motor Company began to develop a flow process for continuous rolling of plate. At the same time, and quite independently, Pilkington had developed a continuous grinding process to replace the disk process. Pilkington stepped in to provide the needed technical expertise, joined its development capabilities with Ford, and in 1923—combining continuous rolling with continuous grinding—installed the industry's first continuous plate manufacturing process (at St. Helens). Twelve years later Pilkington pioneered a machine (the "twin") to grind both sides of a plate glass ribbon simultaneously. The machine ranked as one of the world's finest examples of large-scale precision engineering and gave Pilkington world technological leadership in the manufacture of quality flat glass.

FLOAT GLASS DEVELOPMENT

Even the twin grinding process for making plate had substantial drawbacks. Tremendous equipment investments (of $30–$40 million) and sizable markets were required to support a single glass furnace and its associated plate line. Costs of operating and maintaining a grinding and polishing line were very high. Up to 800 people were necessary to keep a line operating continuously. Some 15–20 percent of the glass ribbon was ground away in the finishing processes. A plant discharged enough abrasives, polishing rouges, and glass to build waste mountains reminding one of the slag heaps of the steel industry. Plants were hundreds of yards long. The noise level of grinders, transfer machinery, and crashing cullet was formidable. And repairs often required costly shut-downs or

dangerous work in the grinding pits underneath the glass ribbon.

Many dreamed of combining the continuous flow, fire polish, and inexpensiveness of sheet with the distortion-free quality of polished plate. But the secret eluded the industry until the late 1950s when Lionel Alexander Bethune (Alastair) Pilkington[a] developed the float glass process. An intense and impatient but thoroughly gracious man, Alastair had joined the company in 1947 after graduation from Cambridge with a degree in mechanical engineering and service in the Royal Artillery in World War II. He started in the sheet works technical development group, moved into plate works technical development, and by 1949 was production manager at the Doncaster works. At Doncaster Sir Alastair started some original experimental work involving interactions of glass and molten metals.

The Invention

Sir Alastair later described how he arrived at the basic idea for float glass:

One quickly became aware that grinding and polishing was an extremely cumbersome way of making glass free from distortion. [You could see] that the window glass process produced a beautiful surface, which glass naturally has because it is a liquid. What you wanted to do was preserve the natural brilliance of molten glass and form it into a ribbon which was free from distortion. If you could do this you would have done something quite important. . . . A large part of innovation is, in fact, becoming aware of what is really desirable. [Then you] are ready in your mind to germinate the seed of a new idea. . . . You also must want to invent. This is terribly important. I don't know why, but I have always wanted to invent something.

[a] Later Sir Alastair Pilkington, F.R.S.

I was able to do some thinking about that time [June 1952] because I was bored. I had been very busy [in production operations at Doncaster and had been] brought back to work under the Technical Director. . . . I was actually consciously bored. This gave me time to think about the problem. . . . The idea came to me when I was helping my wife to wash up [dishes], but it had nothing to do with the act of washing up. It was just one of those moments when your mind is able to think and then it was sort of "bang"—like that. Indeed the final solution was very similar to the original idea, though it was an awful long journey from the concept to making salable glass.

Stage I—Experimentation

Alastair quickly drew up some sketches of the new process, which the Engineering Development Group converted into working drawings. The Board gave verbal approval to the project, and within three months a $70,000 pilot plan was built and operational. Fortunately some technical people were available for reassignment just then. Alastair—with a team of several engineers, a foreman, and workmen sworn to secrecy—essentially knocked a hole in the side of a remote rolled glass furnace and tried to pour molten glass onto a bed of molten tin. He described this stage as follows:

> We got the cheapest flow of glass we could find in the company. At the earliest possible moment we made a box for the molten tin. The first one leaked like a sieve because we heated the tin by immersed tubes. We had to make gland joints at the end, and I can tell you molten tin goes through any gland joint. It just poured all over the ground. But it showed you could take a ribbon of glass, pass it over tin, at a relatively high temperature, and produce bright parallel surfaces. [The only answer] we wanted out of Stage I was: did the process look promising? Or would we crash up against some basic chemical or physical laws which would prevent the process from operating.

The Pilkington Board decided to give the project the highest possible priority so that either success

or failure would be decided as early as possible. My own greatest fear was that float would drag on for years being a near success; interesting enough to justify further work but never quite achieving satisfactory results.

After some six months it appeared that it would be feasible to "fire finish" glass by floating it on a bath of molten tin. Once the process could be properly controlled, the bottom surface of the glass should be dead flat because it rested on the flat surface of the liquid tin. Natural forces of gravity and surface tension would tend to make the top surface flat too. And the glass should be of uniform thickness, with both surfaces completely parallel. There appeared to be no insurmountable barriers to achieving such results. But the process was far from producing commercial quality glass.

Still an important choice—that of tin as the support medium—had been made and was never changed. Only gallium, indium, and tin met the strict physical requirements for the process. The support medium had to be liquid from 1100 °F to over 1900 °F, the range necessary for melting and forming glass. The medium had to be more dense than glass. It needed a low vapor pressure at the 1900° end of the temperature range to avoid excess vaporization and contamination of the glass or the process. Finally the medium must not chemically combine with the glass during processing and had to be available at a reasonable price. Tin was the most attractive alternative on almost all counts. (See Exhibit C12.1a).

Stage II—Pilot Plants

Stage II was to make a ribbon 12 inches wide under controlled atmospheric conditions. The experimental team hoped to learn more about controlling the quality of the glass. A new pilot plant was built in early 1954 to allow long enough runs to analyze and hopefully correct faults in the process. But technological problems were formidable. Upon exposure to the atmosphere the tin oxidized and produced a crystalline scale on the glass' surface. A carefully selected and maintained inert atmosphere slowly began to alleviate this problem. But other technical challenges rose to take its place. Because of the company's expertise in forming a glass ribbon through rollers, the team initially chose this method to flow the molten glass onto the tin surface. (See Exhibit C12.1b.) But tin vapors condensed on the water-cooled rollers, which then imparted surface imperfections to the tin. Unless the tin was extremely pure it also reacted with the glass. Ultimately the team had to purify the tin well beyond the highest specifications for laboratory-quality tin. Finally, the glass source, a rolled glass furnace for making patterned glass, did not provide molten glass of sufficient quality to judge just how well the process was working. Some $46,000 was charged against revenues for the 12-inch experimental line, but no commercial-quality glass was produced.

EXHIBIT   C12.1a and b   Float Glass Process

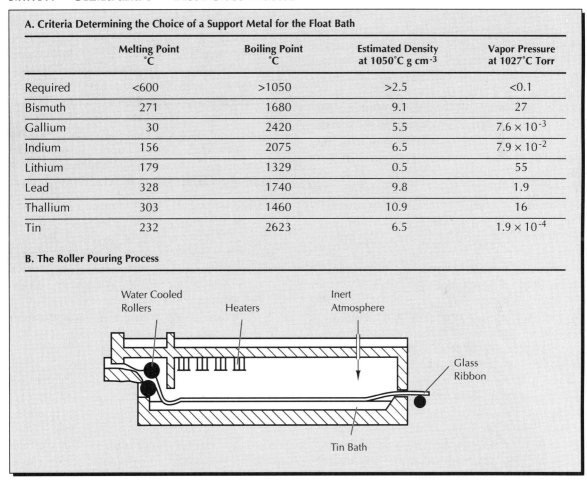

A. Criteria Determining the Choice of a Support Metal for the Float Bath

	Melting Point °C	Boiling Point °C	Estimated Density at 1050°C g cm^{-3}	Vapor Pressure at 1027°C Torr
Required	<600	>1050	>2.5	<0.1
Bismuth	271	1680	9.1	27
Gallium	30	2420	5.5	7.6×10^{-3}
Indium	156	2075	6.5	7.9×10^{-2}
Lithium	179	1329	0.5	55
Lead	328	1740	9.8	1.9
Thallium	303	1460	10.9	16
Tin	232	2623	6.5	1.9×10^{-4}

B. The Roller Pouring Process

Source: L. A. B. Pilkigton, "Review Lecture: The Float Glass Process," The Royal Society, February 13, 1969. Reproduced by special permission.

Still, progress was encouraging, and the team came upon one substantial bit of good fortune. When the glass was held for one minute at the 1900°F temperature needed to eliminate its surface irregularities, a combination of surface tension and gravity effects caused it to form at an equilibrium thickness of 7 mm (0.275 in.). By applying a tractive force from the annealing kiln (lehr) the glass might be thinned to 6.5 mm and sold as nominal ¼-inch glass. As Sir Alastair later said, "This was a fantastic stroke of luck." Some 60 percent of Pilkington's plate sales at that time were in the ¼-inch thickness.

In June 1953, upon the retirement of Mr. J. Meikle (former senior production director), Alastair Pilkington at age 33 became head of Pilkington's plate production and a subdirector of the company. He also continued to head the float glass experimental team. Despite the lack of progress in producing commercial quality glass, the board continued its confidence in the project, and in fall 1954 agreed to build a new pilot plant capable of producing a 30-inch ribbon of glass. This experimental line was designed and built in the incredibly short span of only three months at a cost of $140,000. Molten glass for the line came from the same rolled plate tank as before. The glass made by the process was better than sheet for distortion, but its bubble count would have made it unsalable as plate.

Although roller forming of the glass into a ribbon had appeared more favorable at the outset, the development team continued a parallel project on the alternative possibility of pouring the glass directly onto tin. This approach would avoid roller contamination, but in experimental work tin compounds formed to contaminate the glass. Other major problems of glass flow, ribbon formation, and oxygen and sulfur contamination also persisted. These and high bubble counts from the rolled plate source kept the glass from approaching commercial quality. Nevertheless, the technical team's enthusiasm and morale were very high. Sir Alastair said, "It was almost a crusade. Chaps were literally taken off on stretchers from heat exhaustion, yet came back for more. . . . We all thought the major faults in the glass were due to the glass source, not to the float process."

About this time the Board came to a very important decision. Float glass would only be launched on the world if it could replace plate glass. If float merely provided an improved sheet glass, it would occupy a peculiar position between two glasses with well-established positions, one of which (sheet) had very low margins. In describing this decision Sir Alastair said:

> The forum for the decision was the Executive Committee of the Board. I was clearly a party to the decision and remember the discussions, but it is difficult to locate an exact moment when the decision was made. It was sometime during the discussions about whether to put down a production scale plant. There were no detailed calculations of such things as the ultimate capital implications of the process or its effects on our overall capital structure. Nevertheless, over a period of time a consensus crystallized with great clarity. This evolved from a series of formal and informal discussions among the members of the Executive Committee and the Board.
>
> Once arrived at, I don't think anyone had any doubt this was the right decision. On the other hand, as technical director I was very disturbed to be expected to make such a tremendous jump forward in one enormous leap. It would have been easier for the technical group to learn about the process while making a better quality of sheet, then launch ourselves up the ladder from sheet to plate.

Stage III—The 100-Inch Line

By April 1955 the three small pilot facilities had cost the company some $1.5 million. At this time Alastair Pilkington presented the Board a requisition for another $1.96 million to modify a redundant plate glass furnace and go to a full-scale production line capable of producing a 100-inch ribbon. On it he hoped to achieve float glass of commercial quality. The cost of operating this full-scale line would be £100,000 ($280,000) per month.

At that time 3-mm sheet glass sold for 3.34 pence (3.9¢) per square foot, while 6-mm plate sold for 21.28 pence (24.9¢) per square foot. Calculations showed the cost of float, if successful, would be closer to sheet than to plate. Sir Alastair later recalled:

> The early tests had been encouraging on surface quality and parallelism. But we didn't draw up any PERT charts or statements of probability. Nor did we run out detailed financial figures other than project costs. We knew if we could bring it through it would certainly be a world beater. . . . I suppose one should be able to face reality about a major development. But the reality may be difficult to bear in the early stages. You have to live it a bit from year to year.

> In the case of float, the figures are intriguing. It eventually took float twelve years to break even on cash flows. At one time it had a negative cash flow of £7 million ($19.6 million). Yet float was a commercial success immediately after we had solved its process problems. That's just how long it takes. If you went to an accountant and said, "I've got a great idea to create a massive negative cash flow for certain, and it may—if it's a great success—break even on its cash flows in twelve years," you wouldn't find many accountants who'd say "that's exactly what I want."

> But you can't look at development only on the basis of cash flows. If your company never does undertake major projects, then your standing is much lower. Some companies make things happen. They take really strategic decisions. Others aren't prepared to take big risks to [possibly] achieve great rewards.

The Board approved the expenditure, and Alastair's team modified an existing plate glass line at the Cowley Hill works. Cowley Hill people were used to change. Many had seen continuous rolling, continuous grinding and polishing, and twin grinding introduced. But

the 100-inch line immediately encountered enormous troubles. Many of the faults the team had attributed to the poor-quality glass source on the 30-inch line were actually caused by the float process. The controlled atmosphere then in use still did not maintain a clean glass-tin interface. But the biggest problems occurred in transferring the molten glass onto the tin. Contamination and bubbles plagued the process. Tin oxide condensed on the water-cooled surfaces of the rollers metering the glass onto the tin, and this became imprinted on the glass surface. After some time the team made the momentous decision to move to direct pouring, even though this process was still unproved.

In the early experiments with direct pouring the refractory spout dipped into the tin to provide a smooth glass contact. (See Exhibit C12.1c.) The chemical erosion on the refractory spout at the glass-tin interface was very rapid and contaminated the process. Glass that had been in touch with the refractory spout and then touched the tin bath created optical distortions called "music lines" in the glass. Removing the spout from the tin and pouring with a "free fall" of glass cured the interface wear problem. (See Exhibit C12.1d.) But the "music lines" doggedly persisted. Finally the team understood the scientific problems involved and made some key inventions to keep glass that touched the spout from contaminating the whole ribbon.

The team attacked each problem one at a time even though the process might be producing unsalable glass for a half dozen reasons at once. While they slowly solved other contamination problems, bubbles continued to appear in the glass. For fourteen months the 100-inch line ran 24 hours per day producing useless glass. Every month Alastair had to go to the Board to request another £100,000 ($280,000) to continue. He says of this period, "One of my records which will never be beaten is that of making more continuously unsalable glass than anyone in the history of the glass industry."

As technical director Alastair discussed progress three times daily with the development team. Production executives in the plant were kept well informed. "We wanted the people who would operate the process to welcome it, not have it landed on them," said Sir Alastair. In addition, each morning Alastair would meet with the chief project engineer, Barradell Smith, to lay out strategy for the day:

> I took him away from the noise of crashing cullet so he could have a chance to think. A large pilot plant running 24 hours a day creates great stress and urgency. Glass making goes on around the

clock; it never lets up. The heat and crashing glass is unbelievably disconcerting. We would discuss results, what was needed ahead, how the morale of the people was holding up. Every month I would write up a project report for the Board and ask for another £100,000. For seven years it was an apologia as to why we weren't making salable glass, trying to explain the innumerable faults which occurred. But no single fault persisted. This is why we went ahead. When they would ask, "Can you make salable glass?" I would answer: "I don't know, but nothing has proved it's impossi-

EXHIBIT   C12.1c and d   Direct Pouring Processes

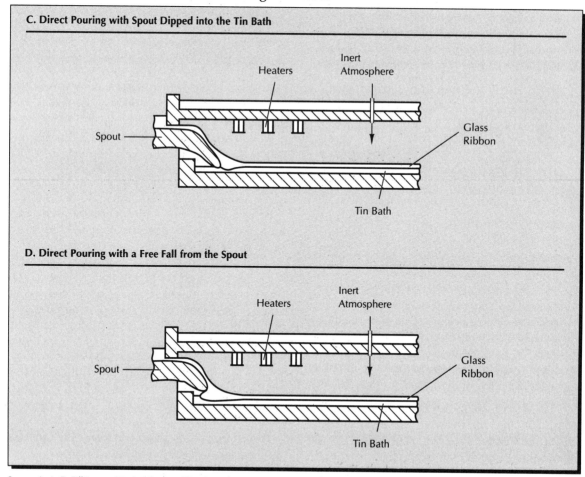

Source: L. A. B. Pilkington, "Review Lecture: The Float Glass Process," The Royal Society, February 13, 1969. Reproduced by special permission.

ble." I couldn't recommend that we stop, because we had no reason to stop.

The Board was remarkably understanding throughout all this. But it was very difficult for me at times. As the development leader I had to be an optimist and see problems as challenges to be overcome. I think this is crucial to the success of any development. As a Board member I had to be cold, analytical, and objective. It was hard to fulfill both roles.

Magic and Agony

Finally a magical day came. In mid-1958, the process suddenly made its first salable glass. Unknown to the development team an accident had gone the right way for them. The pouring spout structure was in poor condition. Finally the spout's back broke, and the structure sagged badly in the middle. The bubbles which had plagued the process for fourteen long months miraculously disappeared. The result was a beautiful plate of glass, which now came pouring off the line at the rate of roughly a thousand tons a week.

Fortunatly Pilkington could dispose of this vast outpouring. It quickly made arrangements with Triplex—in which Pilkington then owned a substantial interest—to sell the glass as windshields to British automotive companies. Triplex first tested the glass to ensure that it met their own strict standards. Then, because the surface characteristics of float plate differed slightly from those of ground plate, Triplex and Pilkington also let a few key procurement and quality control people in the automotive industry know that they were using "a new process." Otherwise the nature of the process was entirely secret. Pilkington actually sold over a million square feet of float glass before it publicly announced the process in January 1959. "One thing we were good at was security," said Sir Alastair. "People easily fail to understand that the greatest secret about a new process is not how to do it, but that it can be done." The process was a complete surprise to the industry.

Even after the announcement, there were skeptics in other companies who wouldn't believe what had been accomplished.

Later in 1959 the float line was shut down for long-overdue maintenance. The line was then carefully rebuilt with all that had been learned from the experimental line. There was agonizing disappointment when the new line was started up. The bubbles and crystals once again appeared. For several more months the team tracked down every possible cause of the problem. Using a model in which silicone oil represented the glass and lead nitrate took the place of tin, they identified certain factors associated with the broken spout as keys to success. With new knowledge of the process the development team both captured the good features of the broken spout and designed a way to feed any contaminated glass to the edges of the ribbon. Although much more work was necessary, the process ultimately became self-cleaning and could run continuously for years without a shutdown for repairs.

The company had spent some £7.5 million ($21 million) over seven years' time. And it had chewed up more than 100,000 tons of glass. But in late 1959 Pilkington could make a glass of quality suitable for the market.

A STRATEGY FOR FLOAT

In October 1958 when the 100-inch line was just beginning to produce salable plate, the Board formed a Directors Flat Glass Committee "to consider the broad issues of flat glass policy both in the present and the future." The committee[b] discussed all aspects of flat (rolled, sheet, wired, plate, etc.) glass strategy worldwide, but by far the most important issue was float.

---

[b] The Committee was composed of all the executive directors associated with float glass: Sir Harry (Lord) Pilkington, Arthur Pilkington, Alastair Pilkington, J. B. Watt, and D. V. Phelps.

The Directors Flat Glass Committee tried to raise all the key issues about float. How should Pilkington use its technological advantage? What would its impact be on existing lines, competition, investments? How would float affect exports, employment, facilities, depreciation and tax structures, and so on? Not many detailed staff or financial projections were involved at this stage. Instead the Committee dominantly tried to deal in broad concepts, to identify alternate routes, and think through the potential consequences of each route for some ten years ahead. Sir Alastair later said, "You would be surprised how it sharpens your mind to be told you are only to think about the future." Members consciously tried to bring out different sides of each issue. At one stage the Committee even hired a second patent attorney, gave him three of the people most knowledgeable about float, and invited him to attack the patent prepared (but not yet submitted) by the company's regular patent counsel. This helped sharpen and strengthen the ultimate application.

An interesting part of the deliberation was a series of process improvements made in the sheet glass division. Goaded by process on float, sheet glass engineers found a number of ways to improve the quality and lower the cost of their processes. In fact, for a while, the sheet and float glass teams were actively in competition with each other. The Directors Flat Glass Committee had to weigh the potential impact of these and future changes in sheet and plate technology.

They quickly agreed that float would surpass sheet's quality, but that it would not be sufficiently better than existing plate to demand a premium price because of its quality. On the other hand, a float line would ultimately more than halve labor requirements; it would lower energy costs by about 50 percent; the 15–20 percent of glass ground away in earlier processes would be saved, as would be the cost of abrasives and rouges; equipment investment would be about one-third the (then) $40 million cost of a conventional line; production space requirements would drop by over 50 percent; and

process interruption costs would virtually disappear. The Committee could not forecast the exact dimensions of these advantages. But it was clear that the process, if successful, would substantially lower existing plate costs. One director even predicted that float would be cost competitive with sheet by 1967–1968, but this opinion was not widely shared.

PATENTS AND LICENSING

Pilkington's goal was to see that float occupied its "right place" in the market place, to strengthen Pilkington's own position as a manufacturer, and to consolidate and extend Pilkington's own manufacturing interests throughout the world. Lord Pilkington later described certain key aspects of the resulting strategy as follows:

> We had the great benefit of time to decide upon our strategy. A great deal was said about ethics: that it was not our job to deliberately deny any existing glass competitor the opportunity of living in competition with us. I don't think we were shortsighted or rapacious. . . . There was a great deal of investment worldwide in plate, and people needed to have time to write off this plant or convert over. The alternative was chaotic disruption of a great industry.

Eventually Pilkington decided to license, and licensees quickly lined up, until by the mid-1960s substantially all plate manufacturers used the process and royalty income began to roll in to Pilkington. But licensing was not all a bed of roses. Sir Alastair described a chastening experience from this period:

> In the early sixties I was summoned with great urgency to a licensee's plant where an incredible thing was happening. The whole float bath was bubbling like a saucepan of boiling water. A unit which is normally calmer than a millpond was apparently on the verge of volcanic eruption! [The glass itself resembled swiss cheese.] . . . We were absolutely stumped. We had never seen

anything like it and had no immediate answer. ... Eventually we found that a thermal pump had been created in the bath because of the size of the pores in the refractory brick from which the bath was built. Once the refractory brick was replaced, the bath quieted down immediately.

After 1962, despite such temporary setbacks, *every new* plate glass facility built in the world used the float process. By 1968 float costs had become competitive with sheet glass in certain thicknesses. But float had much superior quality, and sheet manufacturers began to deluge the company with license applications. Since there were twenty to thirty times as many sheet manufacturers as there were plate producers, this created important policy dilemmas for Pilkington.

By 1974 the float glass process had virtually replaced polished plate glass worldwide. The plate glass industry had invested over £400 million (approximately $1 billion) in the process. Twenty-three manufacturers in thirteen countries (including Russia) operated some fifty-one float plants under Pilkington licenses, and float costs were very sensitive to scale of operations. Plants had to produce at least 2,000 tons of glass per week to be economical, and modern plants produced 5,000 tons per week. Many of the OPEC countries, possessing sand and fuel, wanted the process. But these and other developing countries did not have large enough national markets to support a plant.

Nevertheless, a long development process was required before float could make a full range of commercial thicknesses. By the mid-1970s float's thickness range was 2.3 mm to 25 mm, with other thicknesses being made experimentally. And float had become cost competitive with sheet in thinner sections. Through 1981 development and experimentation float continued. Sir Alastair noted,

Everytime you made a move, you needed to optimize the plant for that particular thickness, width, or speed. It was a long, long learning process. How does the tin flow? How does it return through the bath? How does the constantly

changing viscosity of the glass interact with the process? I don't know how many times I heard people over the years say, "We're just about on the limits of speed, or thickness, or something." Most times I said, "Rubbish! What you really mean is you've got to learn more or invent a new technique. You've reached the limits of your experience, not fundamental scientific limits."

Float opened new realms of chemical challenges to Pilkington's glass technologists. For example, they learned to introduce metal ions into the top surface of float glass. During the float process these ions were electrically attracted toward the tin bath. This penetration created a tinted plate extremely valuable in architectural and automotive uses. The technique, called Electrofloat, allowed the process to be switched from clear to tinted glass and back again in a fraction of the time needed for other processes. In 1967 Pilkington's Triplex subsidiary began work on its "Ten-Twenty" laminated glass for automobile windshields. This special plate made up from panels of thin float glass with a plastic interlayer was designed to greatly reduce laceration injuries in accidents. Pilkington hoped it would replace much of the "toughened" glass used for windshields throughout the world. A special high-strength, low-weight, Ten-Twenty (10/20) was developed for advanced aircraft. This led to Triplex receiving the Queen's Award for Industry in 1974.

CONSOLIDATION AND DIVERSIFICATION

In 1929 Pilkington and Triplex—the largest British safety glass producer—had formed a joint company, Triplex Northern, to produce laminate glass. In 1955 Pilkington and Triplex Safety Glass agreed that the latter should acquire Pilkington's 51-percent interest in Triplex (Northern), for which Pilkington received a block of Triplex Safety Glass shares. After 1955 Pilkington purchased Triplex stock at a steady rate as it came on the market, until in February 1965 Triplex became a subsidiary.

By 1967 Triplex controlled 85–90 percent of the English automotive safety glass market. Its main competitor was British IndesTructo Glass (BIG), which was controlled by four major auto companies. In early 1967 Triplex discussed with BIG's controlling owners the mutual advantages of a merger. Triplex took over BIG and terminated all production in BIG's works in July 1967. But Pilkington and Triplex agreed with the automobile companies and the British Board of Trade that they would at all times maintain adequate capacity to meet the users' forecast demands.

Optical and Specialty Glasses

Through its acquisition of Chance Brothers (1951) Pilkington had extended its entry into optical glass. In 1957 the optical business of both companies was merged into the Chance-Pilkington Optical Works. In 1966 a further company, Pilkington Perkin-Elmer (later Pilkington P.E., Ltd.) was set up to develop and produce electro-optical systems, including specialized glasses for laser optics.

Nineteen seventy-one saw the formation of the Chance-Propper Company to manufacture microscope slides and medical, surgical, and laboratory equipment. In addition to ophthalmic glasses and lens systems, Chance Brothers had also led the company into television tubes, decorative glassware, and glass tubing for the fluorescent and incandescent light fields. In 1974 Pilkington added the Michael Birch group—lens prescriptions, sunglasses, safety glasses, and a microfilm equipment company. In 1977–1978 it acquired Barr and Stroud, a U.K. maker of periscopes and precision defense products, and SOLA, an Australian-based maker of plastic ophthalmic lenses. But the Monopolies Commission blocked its bid for U.K. Optical, the dominant British supplier of spectacle frames and glass lenses. In 1980-1981, the electro-optical and ophthalmic businesses (including Pilking-

ton's successful light–sensitive Reactolite spectacle) were thought to each have revenues of over £30 million.

Fiberglass Products

Chance had been making glass fibers near Glasgow since the late 1920s. Pilkington acquired an interest in this activity in 1938 and eventually purchased the company from Chance Brothers. The company, reorganized as Fiberglass Ltd. in 1962–1963, extended its operations in the United Kingdom and abroad. In 1971 Fiberglass Ltd. announced the development of Cem-FIL fiber, the first glass fiber capable of enduring for any period as a reinforcement of portland cement. This product, jointly developed with the British National Research Development Corporation (NRDC), offered the possibility of lightweight, high-strength, concrete construction techniques not hitherto possible. The glass provided the tensile strength concrete lacked, and it avoided the weight, bulk, and chemical-oxidation problems inherent in steel reinforcing. As an alkali resistant fiber, Cem-FIL could replace asbestos in many of its uses. The development was a major breakthrough in glass chemistry, but in 1981 was only slowly working its way into a conservative marketplace.

Many of these successful diversifications became substantial businesses. But none compared in tonnage with the flat glass field. Here specialized glasses using float were developed for endless new uses: tinted windows, light-sensitive panes, special high-impact safety glass for vehicles, electroconducting glass for deicing, and specialized glass for air conditioning uses all entered the market. Perhaps the greatest potential impact lay in architectural glasses. Glass plates could be hung or suspended together to provide a wall with uninterrupted visibility. Pilkington's Armourplate glass was developed for high-impact uses like doors or squash court walls. And solar control or insulated glasses provided new opportunities for energy conservation in construction.

The company also had its failures, largely in the field of pressed glass operations. While some were relatively small—pavement lights, glass blocks for buildings, and battery boxes—in 1975 the company had to withdraw from the television tube glass market after considerable investment. A high level of Japanese tube imports and a U.K. recession were given as the primary causes for withdrawal.

But the biggest disappointment was the late 1970s commercial failure of 10/20 windshield glass. The glass removed about 98 percent of risk of lacerations or head injuries from automobile windshield accidents. When hit by an object, the glass broke into fine particles that literally did not cut. Yet the plastic interlayer was strong enough to prevent a body going through the screen and flexible enough to minimize brain injury. Still Pilkington could not get auto manufacturers to pay the 15-percent premium price over ordinary safety glass that made it economic to produce 10/20. Safety was not a great selling point, and the oil price increase put a premium on lightness and consequent fuel economy. The manufacturers said they could not pass costs on to consumers. Sir Alastair commented, "The program was one of those clear technical successes, but a commercial failure—most disappointing to all of us."

Geographical Expansion

In 1946 Pilkington had no glass production facilities outside the United Kingdom except a partly owned activity in Argentina. The 1950s and 1960s saw a great international expansion abroad. In 1951 Canada and South Africa started sheet production, followed by India (1965), Australia (1963), and New Zealand (1964). Vasa, in Argentina, became a subsidiary. Safety glass plants opened in New Zealand (1953), Australia (1965), and Rhodesia (1961). During the same period the company acquired interests in other companies in Nigeria (1964), Mexico (1965), South Africa (1965), Sweden (1968), and Venezuela (1973). By 1981 Pilkington had nine float plants in other countries. (See Exhibit C12.2.) It had 25,000 employees and £515 million in sales overseas versus 20,000 people and £377 million in sales in the United Kingdom. Approximately one-half of the company's net trading assets were outside the United Kingdom. Exhibit C12.2 summarizes Pilkington's production operations outside the United Kingdom.

MANAGEMENT STYLE CHANGES

Through the 1970s much of St. Helens depended on Pilkington for employment. And the Pilkington family was conscious of this trust. Young Pilkingtons were looked over carefully before they entered the company and, once in, were expected to work doubly hard. Family members developed personal contacts with employees by living in the town and visiting the works regularly. The company had provided pension funds and hospital services, long before these were common in industry. The family also built and endowed theaters and recreation clubs for its employees in St. Helens. There was a personal touch too. For a long while, retired employees had been given vegetable seeds for their gardens and coal to warm them during the harsh midland winters. The company threw an annual employee party complete with dog shows, parachute jumping, and the like, which someone described as "the finest blowout north of London."

A strong sense of morality and responsibility pervaded the company. As one director said,

> I think certainly the moral side does weigh with the company. If one runs a business one is to some extent one's brother's keeper. I think the company would still regard itself as being in business for something more than just money making, in the sense that it takes long-term views, and a long-term view is obviously that you have to look after your human capital as well as your money. It isn't just what you do this year that matters, but what you are working on that is going to bear fruit in ten years' time. It is impor-

tant that the company is not only profitable, but also has a "heart."

In the mid-1970s there were some 15,000 people in the St. Helens "family," many of them new members. General Board members were seen less regularly at the works. And lines of communication from shop floor to top management began to seem much longer. Diversification had led to anomalies between workers in different jobs and places.[7] And small incidents sometimes caused irritations. In a small community like St. Helens, one of these suddenly—a man's paycheck had been miscalculated, an error that was quickly corrected—amplified into a strike in early 1970. When management's hurt and shock subsided, the company recovered and learned from the strike. There were more formal procedures for negotiations and wage structures. Industrial relations professionals

were brought into the corporate offices of Pilkington. And both union and management groups said relations improved markedly after the confrontation.

Regimes Change

During this difficult period another matter which would vastly affect the company's future had been quietly resolved: Pilkington Brothers became a public company in 1970. As Lord Pilkington said, "Modern taxation makes it very difficult to either pass on the wealth you have accumulated or keep it in the company. And without a public market for the stock, death duties could place large individual shareholders in an impossible cash bind."

Lord Pilkington had originally intended to retire on his sixty-fifth birthday, which occurred

EXHIBIT C12.2 Pilkington Float Plants

Location		
Country	**City**	**Date of Start-Up***
United Kingdom	St. Helens	April 1962
	St. Helens	July 1963
	St. Helens	September 1972
	St. Helens	April 1981
Germany	Gladbeck	March 1974
	Gladbeck	December 1976
	Weiherhammer	October 1979
Sweden	Halmstad	July 1976
South Africa	Springs	April 1977
Canada (49% owned)	Scarborough	February 1967
		December 1970
Australia (50% owned)	Dandenong	February 1974
ICO (35% owned)	Mexico City, Villa de Garcia	November 1981

* Plants (owned in partnership with others) in Brazil, Venezuela, and Taiwan were scheduled to start up during 1982.

Source: Company records.

in April 1970, right in the middle of the strike. But it was agreed that he should stay in order to pilot the change from private to public status and should retire after the annual meeting in 1973, when Sir Alastair Pilkington became chairman for a period of distinguished leadership, ending in 1981.

Sir Alastair continued the important processes of professionalizing and decentralizing Pilkington's management. Of his era he said,

> I think the company started to take a much wider view of itself in the world—in processes, products, and geography. I think it moved much more consciously to feeling that it could think out the future it wished to have, define what it meant by success in the future, and then lay out a route toward it. The company moved from feeling that it would essentially deal with situations and opportunites as they arose. We felt that we should create the future, rather than react to external circumstances.
>
> I am very strong on people and on success definition. My own feeling is that unless you decide where you want to go, you never arrive there. I don't set goals for other people. That is one of their key jobs—to define their goals, define success. I set goals for myself. I will set goals for the company, but not for other people. I set the company goals in my own mind, and then they come out in discussions. But I don't sort of lay them down. I've never taken a major decision without consulting my colleagues. It would be unimaginable to me, unimaginable. I can't even see any point to it. Firstly, they help me make a better decision in most cases. But secondly, if they know about it and agree with it, they'll back it. Otherwise, they might challenge it, not openly, but subconsciously.

Throughout Alastair wanted to avoid diversifications or any other moves that led to mediocrity. He said, "I'm absolutely obsessional on the subject of excellence. If you are going to work on a worldwide basis, you must have excellence. One of our most important policy statements was that we would only take on things where we intended to match or lead the world's best performers."

The 1981 Situation

By 1981 the company had changed substantially. Like others in the industry, Pilkington's volume had grown throughout the world. Capacity expanded by a factor of three times from 1971 to 1981. (See Exhibits C12.3a and C12.3b.) Pilkington had large new facilities outside the United Kingdom, in Germany, Sweden, Australia, and Mexico. While other glass companies conglomerated and diversified into almost anything, in 1980 Pilkington bought Germany's Flachglas for £141M. *The Paper Clip* described how the new partners matched up: Pilkington had sales of £629M for 1980 and 35,000 employees, while Flachglas had sales (unconsolidated) of £219M for 1979 from raw glass (approximately 35 percent), insulating glass (25 percent), safety glass (25 percent), plastics and other (approximately 15 percent) with 7,900 employees. In justifying further acquisitions in the industry, Antony Pilkington, who took over as chairman from Sir Alastair said, "If you are technologically excellent, you can maintain your position in your chosen market. Glass is not as narrow a field as some imagine."

Both parties moved carefully into the merger, which had taken four years from concept to reality. The specific opportunity ultimately arose when BSN-Gervas-Danone, a French food company, decided to sell a large part of its glass-making operations. Many bizarre twists accompanied the purchase in which Pilkington could not—for competitive reasons—even investigate the facilities it was about to buy. For example, at the last moment due to legal considerations Pilkington had to come up with £28 million extra to up the percentage of stock bought from 55 to 62 percent. Then Pilkington had to learn to deal with the dual board and labor representation structures of German companies. But benefits accrued within a few months as Flachglas profits helped offset Pilkington's U.K. trading losses and Pilkington found new work practices to improve the productivity of its domestic plants. One special aspect of the merger was the fit between Pilkington's strength in process research and Flachglas' strength in product development. The acquisition made Pilkington the largest flat glass manufacturer in the world.

This degree of diversification had worked well. License fees and overseas operations—and importantly the Flachglas group's profits—had

bolstered Pilkington's lagging fortunes during the sharp downturn in Britain's 1981-1982 economy. The company's U.K. problems were compounded by a flood of glass imports from Europe and the worldwide recession of those years. Pilkington's share of the U.K. flat glass market plummeted from 80 percent to a little over two-thirds in 1981–1982.

The European market was rapidly being restructured. Guardian—one of the most efficient operators in the industry—built a new

EXHIBIT   C12.3a   Clear Flat Glass Salable Capacity, World, Excluding Communist Countries, 1971 versus 1981

('000 Tonnes per Annum)	1971			1981		
	Float/Plate	Sheet	Total	Float	Sheet	Total
North America	1,488	714	2,202	3,869		3,904
Europe	1,048	1,842	2,890	3,896	588	4,484
Australasia (including Japan and India)	280	1,058	1,388	1,301	793	2,094
Africa		68	68	115	37	152
Middle East		114	114		365	365
South America	45	263	308	94	505	599
Total	2,861	4,059	6,920	9,275	2,323	11,598

EXHIBIT   C12.3b   Two Years of Dramatic Changes in Europe

	Number of Float Lines		Capacity (Tons per Day)	
	1971	1981	1971	1981
Saint-Gobain	11.5	11.5	5,500	6,000
Pilkington	4	8	1,750	4,750
PPG	1	3	500	1,650
Asahi Glass	nil	2	nil	1,300
SIV (Italian government)	1.5	1.5	700	770
Luxguard	nil	1	nil	500
BSN-Gervais-Danone	7	nil	4,150	nil
Total	25	27	12,600	14,970

Source: La Compagnie de Saint-Gobain in *Financial Times,* January 25, 1982.

plant in Luxembourg, turning over its stocks ten times a year and reportedly making 20 percent on its capital before interest. Asahi Glass of Japan took over BSN's losing Belgium and Dutch plants, and PPG bought its French units. The new structure is outlined in Exhibit C12.3b. Much capacity was added while glass industry work forces plummeted—down 4,000 for St. Gobain and 3,000 for Pilkington in two years. Asahi controlled 50 percent of Japan's glass industry and was as efficient as Guardian. But the marketplace for flat glass in this period was over 50 percent in building and 20 percent in automobiles, both industries depressed by high interest rates. Overall demand was growing only 1 percent per year.

Although only 20 percent of Pilkington's flat glass output went to other divisions for processing, its optical business had moved steadily "down stream" through acquisitions. This division's growth rate led to its split into two divisions (ophthalmic and electro-optical) of some £30 million sales each in 1981. After fifteen years of technical work, fiber optics were slowly working their way into advanced technology applications, and Pilkington's sunlight-sensitive Reactolite spectacles were a great market success, especially in Japan. Many of these new high-technology businesses reported directly to Pilkington's technical board member, Dr. Oliver, who commented that "Pilkington is still as prepared as ever to commit itself to long

EXHIBIT   C12.4   Pilkington Brothers P.L.C., 1981

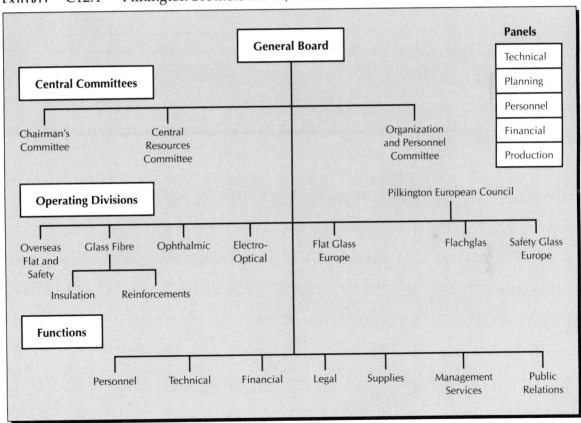

Source: Company records.

cycle developments like "integrated optics" which may some day provide an optical replacement for silicon chips. "Bread on the water for 1995," was the way he described such investments. "Waiting is the name of the game in high technology."

Against this background of great success and increasing pressures, Pilkington's new management team—under tall, elegant, and marketing experienced Antony Pilkington—had to arrive at its new strategies for the 1980s.

EXHIBIT   C12.5   Pilkington Brothers P.L.C.—Changes since 1961 (£ millions)

	1961	1971	1981
Group turnover			
Historical	58	123	786
In 1981 money terms	230	300, of which ⅔ U. K., ⅓ overseas	786, of which ⅓ U.K., ⅔ overseas
Group assets			
Historical	36	120	1,200
In 1981 money terms	150	300, of which ¾ U. K., ¼ overseas	1,200, of which ½ U. K., ½ overseas

Source: Compiled from company records.

EXHIBIT   C12.6   Group Financial Record for the Years Ended March 31, 1978–1982 (£ millions)

	1978	1979	1980	1981	1982
Sales					
Sales to outside customers	469.5	548.8	629.0	786.8	958.9
Profits					
Trading profit	42.6	50.5	49.0	48.2	26.7
Licensing income	32.8	37.9	37.0	35.3	39.4
Related companies and other income less interest	(3.7)	1.9	5.4	(2.5)	(12.7)
Group profit before taxation	71.7	90.3	91.4	81.0	53.4
Taxation	36.3	42.7	20.5	32.2	49.9
Group profit after taxation	35.4	47.6	70.9	48.8	3.5
Profit attributable to shareholders of Pilkington Brothers P.L.C.	34.1	45.7	68.8	36.3	10.7
Dividends (net of taxation)	7.2	9.8	14.8	17.6	17.6
Profit/(loss) retained in the business	26.9	35.9	54.0	18.7	(6.9)
Assets employed					
Land, buildings, plant and equipment, less depreciation	338.4	385.6	455.3	852.0	924.7
Investments in related and other companies	35.8	49.1	53.1	60.6	70.6
Net current assets (before deducting bank overdrafts)	162.8	193.6	263.4	239.5	262.3
Assets employed	537.0	628.3	771.8	1,152.1	1,257.6
Financed by					
Ordinary share capital	62.2	124.4	155.8	167.7	167.7
Retained profits and reserves	300.9	298.5	426.1	568.4	624.0
	363.1	422.9	581.9	736.1	791.7
Minority interests in subsidiary companies	21.6	20.8	29.5	138.2	120.0
Loan capital and bank overdrafts	129.3	156.2	136.0	235.0	300.5
Deferred taxation and deferred income	23.0	28.4	24.4	42.8	45.4
Total funds invested	537.0	628.3	771.8	1,152.1	1,257.6

13

Property Management

Paul R. Reed, James Prichard, and R. Dean Lewis
Sam Houston State University

The deadline for filing 1989 income taxes was two weeks away. Jay Price had just received his prepared tax forms from his accountant. As he read over the statements, he started recalling the past twelve months of his landscaping and lawn care business and all the changes that had taken place during that period. For a business that was started just to provide enough income to pay Jay's remaining years of college, the figures that appeared before him had far exceeded his expectations.

Graduation was six weeks away and Jay knew that he would soon be forced to make a decision in regards to the future of his business, Property Management. He also knew that any decisions made in favor of keeping the business would create further questions regarding growth, target markets, and inevitably more debt.

HISTORY

Property Management's main line of business was to provide landscaping services as well as commercial and residential lawn maintenance to Huntsville, Texas, and the immediate surrounding area. The business was started in

November of 1988, when Jay Price bought out a small lawn care operation from a group of local high school graduates.

Property Management was currently being operated out of a one-acre tract of land located six miles north of Huntsville. The property was purchased when Jay moved to Huntsville and was also serving as his residence. Due to the nature of the business, requiring no access by the public, the property had served as an ideal hideaway for business operations. Also due to its location outside the city limits, Jay had saved an estimated eighty dollars per month by burning trash and debris that were removed from his customers' properties rather than paying for disposal at the city landfill.

JAY'S BUSINESS EXPERIENCE

Prior to the founding of Property Management, Jay had accumulated six years' experience in the area of business management. The first three years were spent as a telecommunications inspector whose main responsibility was to oversee and supervise the installation of underground telephone systems throughout the southwestern areas of Texas. After deciding to move to Huntsville to obtain his bachelor's degree in business management, Jay accepted a job as a food/beverage manager at a nearby vacation resort. He spent his first two years of college employed at the resort before establishing Property Management. The work experience gained at his former jobs had enabled him to learn the importance of maintaining a good customer rapport and practicing efficient time management, both of which had played an integral part in the success of his new business.

LOCAL AREA

Huntsville is located on Interstate 45 some 60 miles north of Houston (Exhibit C13.1). Besides being a typical east Texas county seat, Huntsville enjoys the advantages of having Sam Houston State University and the headquarters of the Texas Department of Corrections (TDC) within its city limits. The university has approximately thirteen thousand students and one thousand faculty and staff members. TDC employs twelve hundred personnel to staff the headquarters and six nearby prison units. The majority of Huntsville's 25,000 population is supported by these two institutions or by the normal small service and light industry-type organizations. On the immediate west side of the city are three residential communities, the largest being that of Elkins Lake. "Elkins," as it is called, was developed in the early seventies to serve as a retirement community for those who wished to live in a rural setting but with all the amenities of big city life located in nearby Houston. Elkins contains about 550 homes and is centered around three lakes and an elegant

eighteen-hole golf course. The average home sells in the $150,000 range. The average age of the Elkins home owner is thought to be in the mid-50s. The other two communities, Spring Lake and Westridge, cater more to the younger professional who desires a country setting with lots varying in size from one-half to five acres. Both communities combined have approximately the same number of households as does Elkins. Home prices average slightly lower.

WEATHER/CLIMATE

The weather in this area of Texas usually requires lawn care ten months out of the year. The growing season usually begins in mid-March and extends through late November. December usually consists of clean-up jobs that are left over from the fall and also lawn grooming in preparation for the holiday activities. Traditionally January and February are the dismal months requiring little lawn maintenance. Tree trimming and pruning are carried out during this time. In late February all yards are dethatched (removal

EXHIBIT C13.1 Huntsville and Surrounding Area

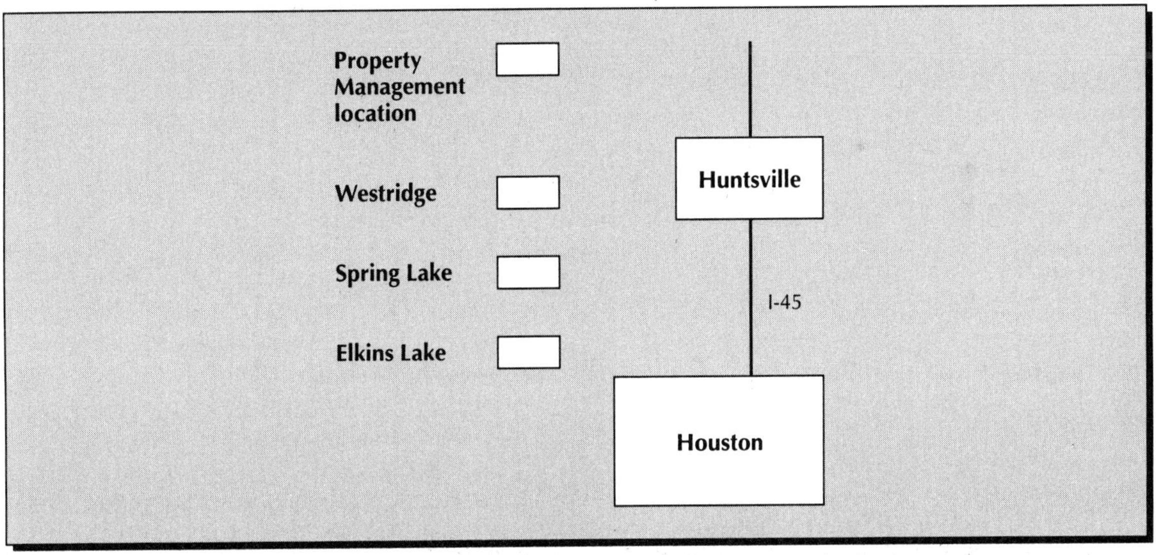

of decomposed matter from soil surface), in order to make ready for the upcoming fertilization process (see Exhibit C13.2).

SERVICES OFFERED

Property Management provided services in the following four areas: lawn maintenance, contract labor, tractor service, and landscaping.

- **Lawn Maintenance.** This area proved to be the "cash cow" for Property Management. Nearly 60 percent of all revenue has been generated by this service. Lawn maintenance can be broken down into the following categories.

  - *Contractual Services.* This area involved a year-round service with billing occurring at the end of each month. Maintenance was performed on a weekly

EXHIBIT   C13.2   Seasonal Demand Chart

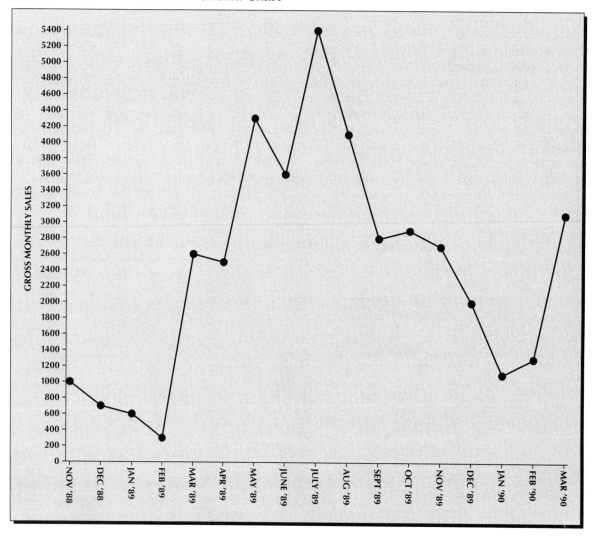

basis. Contract service covered all areas external to the structure (home or office) with the exception of tree removal and application of pesticides (see contract at Exhibit C13.3). It should be noted that payment for this service remained constant year round, regardless of external factors (example: rain or drought). Property Management had twelve yards under contract and total revenues averaged approximately $1,350 a month.

■ *Intermittent Services* were provided on a per unit basis with the customer paying for the services at the end of the month. (Example: Customer wants mowing services only twice a month and wishes to maintain all other areas himself (shrubs, fertilizer, rain gutters). Price

EXHIBIT   C13.3   Property Management Lawn Service Agreement

The following services will be included in the lawn maintenance program offered by Property Management:

1. remove weeds and miscellaneous grass from flowerbeds,
2. edge all sidewalks, driveways and patios,
3. trim all hedges and shrubs,
4. blow off any debris from decks, sidewalks, and patios,
5. clean out rain gutters,
6. blow off roof (high pitched roofs are not applicable),
7. fertilize during appropriate months,
8. perform minor repairs on underground sprinkler systems (parts and materials are to be furnished by home owner),
9. mow all grass,
10. haul off all grass, limbs, and other miscellaneous items upon completion of service.

The services listed above will be done for the price of $_____ per month, plus 8% sales tax.

NOTE: This price will be reduced 30% for hard-winter months.

At any time the property owner may hire J.P. Property Management to carry out any additional services that may be needed.*

PROPERTY OWNER _____

PROPERTY MANAGEMENT _____

DATE _____

* Additional services offered:
General contracting
Contract labor
Tree trimming and removal
Livestock care and hauling
Miscellaneous hauling
Tractor mowing

was based on estimated time—usually averaged $10.00 per man/per hour.

- **Contract Labor Crews.** This service was usually provided for major clean-up jobs, new lawn construction, and large-tract property owners. Price was established by the number of men assigned to the job and billed on a per-hour basis (example: three men/equipment @ $30.00 per hour).

- **Tractor Services.** In May of 1989 Jay and a local rancher teamed up to offer mower services for local banks and savings & loans that were holding large tracts of foreclosed property. The rancher supplied two Ford 5600 tractors, plus fuel and spare parts, while Property Management provided operators. The hourly rate was set at $40, with 50 percent going to each partner. Property Management held ten percent of the market for this service.

- **Landscaping Services.** Property Management offered only limited services in this area. All landscaping done at that time was priced on a cost plus 50 percent basis. At the present time revenue generated from this area amounted to around 5 percent of yearly sales. Jay also retailed various bark materials, landscape, timber, etc., used in landscaping projects. These materials were currently being purchased wholesale from a nearby Louisiana Pacific Lumber mill. Property Management retailed these products at an average markup of 300 percent. Finally, topsoil markup was cost plus 130 percent.

CUSTOMER DEMOGRAPHICS

Despite a relatively weak local economy, the demand for lawn care and landscaping had been on the increase. This was thought to be largely due to the number of retired and/or senior citizens that were moving into the local area. Age and accompanying infirmities, cou-pled with the hot, humid climate made these type services quite attractive. Property Management's customers reflected this phenomenon. See Exhibit C13.4.

Property Management's lack of customers in the Spring Lake and Westridge areas (see Exhibit C13.5) was attributed mainly to the large size of the individual lots. Tractors with 36- to 48-inch mowers would be required to economically ser-vice these one-half to five-acre properties. Jay figured that he would be forced to borrow between $15,000 and $20,000 to properly equip his business for this operation.

COMPETITION

Property Management's competition came from four sources:

EXHIBIT C13.4
Demand by Customer Category

Category	Percent of Total
Retired/senior citizens	70
Sam Houston faculty/staff	20
Commercial	5
Other	5

EXHIBIT C13.5
Demand by Geographic Area

Area	Percent of Total
Elkins Lake	75
Huntsville	15
Spring Lake	0
Westridge	0
Other	10

- **Champs Landscaping.** Champs' main line of business was to provide lawn care services in the Houston/Huntsville area. Champs had recently reduced its market share of residential lawn care accounts and had also withdrawn from the landscaping market altogether. Champs was currently centering most of its attention on commercial lawn accounts.

- **Neil's Nursery.** Neil owned and operated the largest nursery/garden supply in the city. In March of 1989 Property Management purchased all of Neil's residential lawn care accounts. Neil's, however, was the largest local competitor in the commercial field and in landscaping. Neil's policy of providing contract labor crews solely to tend to greenery purchased from his nursery had greatly lessened his firm's competitive position in the general contract labor market.

- **Plants & More.** Plants and More was Property Management's largest residential competitor in Elkins Lake. It specialized in landscaping and irrigation systems.

- **Others.** This category extended from the neighbor's son who earned spending money from mowing nearby yards to out-of-town individuals on business that provided service to the various lawn care target markets.

Jay estimated the market share held by Property Management and its competitors was as listed in Exhibit C13.6.

MARKETING MIX

Jay believed in the marketing four Ps of Product, Price, Place, and Promotion and felt he was therefore competitive.

- **Product.** Property Management differentiated its products, or more accurately services by offering fast, friendly, meticulous care. Workers were polite and willing to do that little "extra" for the customer. This author had on several occasions observed a worker walk clear across a yard to pick up an errant leaf or pluck a stray blade of glass.

- **Price.** Jay's prices were in line with the competition and were seen by many customers as a bargain when service quality was concerned.

- **Place.** Property Management's office location was rather unhandy, and daily round trips of 20 to 25 miles to reach some of the Elkins Lake accounts were expensive in both time and money. Jay had purposely avoided service to some areas because of lack of personnel or funds (Spring Lake and Westridge are examples).

- **Promotion.** During the first four months of operations, Property Management placed ads in the local daily newspaper. The firm soon discovered that its target markets relied on the "yellow pages" or word of mouth when seeking permanent and reputable lawn services. As a result, Jay placed a small advertisement under lawn maintenance in the 1989 and 1990 editions of the Huntsville phone directory yellow pages section. According to Jay, the business had recently been getting more requests for services than it could handle.

PERSONNEL

Property Management was organized as a "simple structure." Jay made all work schedules and prescribed the methods by which they were carried out.

At that time there were three other employees working for Property Management. Greg, also a graduating senior, had been with the business since its beginning. He received the highest compensation and was also perceived as the crew leader when Jay was not present on the job site. Should Jay decide to continue the business

EXHIBIT   C13.6   Percent Market Share by Competitors

	Property Management	Champs	Neil's	Plants & More	Others	Total
Commercial	3	20	30	7	40	100
Residential	30	—	—	20	50	100
Landscaping	5	—	60	30	5	100
Contract Labor	50	—	10	—	40	100
Tractor Mowing	10	10	—	—	80	100

after graduation, a replacement for Greg would have to be found.

The other two positions were also being held by college students. Turnovers in each of the positions had been high over the past year. The pay range for these three positions was $5.00 to $7.00 per hour. The majority of the jobs available to college students in this area paid $4.50 per hour.

At various times during the past year, additional employees had been hired for temporary lengths of time. But overall a four man crew (including Jay) had proven to be most effective.

EQUIPMENT

Property Management's equipment was mostly vintage but was well maintained. The three pick-up trucks ranged in age from six to seventeen years, and two of them would require replacement within a year. The four trailers were well-worn but would be serviceable for the foreseeable future. The firm's four push mowers, two weed eaters, three blowers, chain saw, riding mower, and various hand tools wore out or were misplaced during the year and were treated as expense items.

Equipment maintenance and repair was currently costing around 15 percent of gross monthly sales. At the current rate of use, new equipment would need to be purchased in the next few months. Estimated cost for the equipment would be around $1,500.00.

Jay had just received word that the Bryant Company, located in Huntsville, would be closing its shop in May. Bryant had been handling all repairs needed on Property Management's equipment since Jay started his business. Bryant's was the only repair shop in town that provided next-day service to commercial equipment owners. The closing of Bryant's would force Jay to take his equipment to Conroe, Texas, which was located thirty miles away.

FINANCIAL

Jay kept his own books, utilizing a journal and ledger. He backed up his entries with canceled checks and accompanying receipts and invoices. He penciled in monthly income and cash flow statements on a yellow legal pad. No formal balance sheet was maintained, but an asset list indicated the value of the equipment at $14,500. Jay owed a local bank $1,800 on a loan that enabled Property Management to purchase two new mowers plus lawn tools. The 1989 income statement at Exhibit C13.7 indicates that 41 cents of every dollar in sales ended up as net income. This high rate of return, coupled with skyrocketing demand for lawn services, made Property Management increasingly attractive as a viable, ongoing operation.

THE FUTURE

Property Management's future would obviously be governed by Jay's own personal aspirations. Jay had been too occupied with business to seriously get involved with interviewing, and as a result the immediate job market looked unpromising to him. Jay had given some thought to continuing on at Sam Houston State University in the M. B. A. program. He could use Property Management to pay for his continued education. This option also would give him more time to decide about his future and that of Property Management. On the other hand, Jay was tired of school and wondered if the business could be built up to support him in the style to which he would like to become accustomed, i.e., a yearly income of $35-40,000. Jay concluded that he would need to find answers to several questions before he could make a decision. The first few questions he jotted down included:

1. What was the size of the lawn care market, and where did Property Management fit?

2. What level of sales and customers would be needed to meet his desired level of income? How practical was this goal?

3. What marketing mix adjustments would Jay have to make to attain his aspirations?

EXHIBIT C13.7   Property Management Income Statement, 1989

Total Sales of 1989		$ 34,129.00
Sales Tax		2,730.32
		$ 36,859.32
Cost of Goods Sold		
Fertilizer	$ 560.24	
Landscape Material	487.14	
Grass (St. Augustine Pallets)	1,580.62	(2,628.00)
Gross Profit from Sales		$ 34,231.32
Operating Expenses		
Salaries	$ 1,129.56	
Payroll Taxes	750.48	
Insurance	1,500.96	
Gas/Oil	1,651.30	
Truck Repair	646.40	
Equipment Repair	1,202.30	
Equipment Replacement	2,283.84	
Equipment Rental	96.40	
Postage	60.00	
Telephone	93.62	
Bank Charges	35.00	
Accounting, Legal Fees	360.00	
Advertising	95.00	
Interest	156.14	
Texas Sales Tax	2,730.32	(18,791.32)
Net Income		$ 15,440.00

Turnaround at WTD Industries?

Stephen E. Barndt

Pacific Lutheran University

Through the mid– to late 1980s, Portland, Oregon–based WTD Industries was the fastest-growing forest products company in the United States, and at one time was the fourth largest. The company started with three sawmills in 1983 and by late 1990 had grown to own thirty-two sawmills and plants located in Oregon, Washington, Montana, South Dakota, California, Vermont, and New York, producing softwood lumber, hardwood lumber, plywood, and veneer. In addition WTD owns a relatively small acreage of timberlands in Oregon, most of which has been harvested.

Founder and president Bruce Engel directed WTD's growth through a consistent strategy that aimed at (1) maintaining a capital investment level that is low relative to competitors with comparable capacity and (2) the substitution of variable for fixed costs. The company received widespread recognition as a maverick among forest products companies through its unorthodox strategies, including:

1. Use of leverage for acquisitions.

2. Acquisition of new production capacity only when it is underpriced relative to its production potential.

3. Emphasis on improving employee productivity through nontraditional production incentives (rather than through facility/equipment technology changes).

4. Buying logs rather than harvesting its own and timing purchases so that inventories are kept very low and conversion into products occurs very quickly, before swings in either log prices or lumber prices squeeze profit margins.

The company's strategy was successful through most of 1989. However, beginning in late 1989 sales began a decline and worsened through 1990. Depressed sales were accompanied by increased raw materials costs as the supply of timber from public lands was reduced. As a result of these and other factors, WTD experienced losses every quarter in calendar 1990. WTD's inability to cover interest expenses and meet its debt covenants forced the company to file for protection under the provisions of Chapter 11 of the U.S. Bankruptcy Code in early 1991.

WOOD PRODUCTS INDUSTRY

Forest products industry companies compete in one or both of two basic product-market industry segments. One of these, the pulp, paper, and paper products industry, is largely restricted to larger companies because of the high capital investment required for mills and plants. The other segment, wood products, has varying capital requirements depending on technology employed, size of facilities, and level of timberland's self-sufficiency. The size of firms engaging in this type of forest products business varies from very large to very small.

Wood Products Industry: Products and Services

Firms engaging in the wood products business produce one or more of a number of products including: dimension lumber; beams; siding; hardwoods for furniture, cabinet, and other industrial uses; railroad ties; poles; plywood; decorative paneling; and composite panels for construction and industrial uses. Products used in residential and commercial construction are essentially undifferentiated and compete as commodities. Industrial products and special-dimension or proprietary products for the construction market are less vulnerable to direct competition from substitutes and can command a premium price. Special services to buyers, even among producers of commodity products can also allow those producers to command a higher price and/or a preferred supplier relationship. Services such as technical assistance on selecting the best type of product for particular applications, rapid order processing, assured delivery, shipments of assorted products, and split shipments are being offered increasingly, especially by larger firms, in the attempt to gain a competitive advantage.

Factors Affecting Profitability

Demand, prices, and profits in the wood products industry are tied to the national and international economy. Home building and commercial construction are primary markets for lumber. As a consequence, when housing and building starts decline, demand for lumber and other wood products also declines, placing competitive downward pressure on prices. In 1990 national housing starts were at their lowest level since the early 1980s but were expected to be marginally higher in 1991.

Demand for exports to and imports from foreign nations is directly impacted by the strength of the dollar relative to other currencies. A strong dollar adversely affects the domestic industry by both lowering demand for exports and encouraging imports of wood products, particularly from Canada.

The wood products industry is mature, with many firms producing and selling reasonably standardized products. Exit barriers are significant. Most owned timberlands can only yield a satisfactory return on investment through conversion of timber assets into lumber and other wood products. In addition specialized mills located in sparsely populated areas have few if any alternative uses. As a consequence, production does not decrease proportionately with demand during downturns. Often mills continue in operation as long as variable costs are covered. Independent mill operators tend to continue producing until insolvency forces them to close down. The overcapacity that results during periods of decreased demand intensifies price competition. On the other hand, increases in demand are readily matched with increased production through the addition of shifts, restarting closed facilities, and the addition of new mills.

In addition to price, cost is a major determinant of profit at the individual producing mill. Raw materials, that is, logs, are the largest single cost item. Therefore, the availability of a low-cost source of logs is critical to profitable operation. Some firms buy logs on the open market at competitive prices or purchase timber harvesting contracts from the state or federal government through competitive bidding. Others harvest timber on their owned timberlands. When open-market log prices are high, companies that harvest their own timber tend to have a cost advantage because of the typically lower costs of timber assets acquired in the past. On the other hand, when log prices are depressed, buying on the open market can provide an advantage over harvesting timber from owned land.

Environmental concerns and the export of logs have adversely affected the supply of timber available to processors. Where supplies are tight, log and timber prices have been driven upward regardless of lower prices for finished wood products.

The spotted owl gained threatened species status in the summer of 1990. Since the spotted owl prefers to nest in old-growth timber, the Federal government and environmentalist groups have taken actions to protect the owl's habitat. A U.S. Fish and Wildlife Service estimate indicates that when full owl protection restrictions are imposed in 1995, the harvest on Federal forest lands will be reduced from approximately 4.2 billion board feet to 2 billion board feet a year. California, Oregon, and Washington state governments have modified private woodland logging permit issuance to deny harvest of timber on the 70 acres of land surrounding a nest site and restrict harvest on another 500 to 1,900 acres around a site.[1] The harvest of timber on state-owned forestlands has likewise been reduced.

Foreign demand for logs has also cut into the supply available to domestic sawmills. Continuing high levels of log exports to Japan from state forests have come under criticism as a cause of mill shutdowns.

One estimate of the impact of timber supply shortages is a prediction that 20 percent of Oregon and Washington's processing capacity will be shut down in the next two years.[2]

Transportation cost is another important factor in the ability to profitably serve markets. Most wood products are bulky and costly to transport. As a result, marketing tends to be limited to the regional markets closest to a mill or plant, especially for commodity products. If there are many competing mills all vying for the same markets, competitive forces tend to reduce prices and profits. An exception to this dependence on immediate regional markets exists for firms with access to bulk ocean shipping. Firms with access to ocean-going shipping and with production sufficient to fill a ship or barge are able to serve other regions. For example, some Oregon and Washington coastal mills are able to cost effectively compete in the southern California and Gulf Coast markets.

The availability of substitutes is an additional factor that can impact the profitability of

wood products. Lower-cost (and price) composite wood panels are, for many uses, direct substitutes for plywood. Over a period of years, composite panels have been gaining user acceptance and making competitive inroads against plywood. Non-wood substitutes have also reduced demand for wood, for example, aluminum siding for wood siding, steel posts and beams for wood, and composite roofing for shingles and shakes.

Competitors

The United States' wood products industry comprises approximately fifteen large and mid-sized and a large number of small, localized companies. Although many of the larger firms have advantages in financial resources, research and engineering capabilities, and marketing, mills tend not to think of them as their direct competition. A mill sees its competition as other local mills, whether operated by a large company or independently owned, that compete with it directly for raw materials, labor, and sales.

International competition in the domestic United States markets comes primarily from Canada, which accounts for nearly 30 percent of U.S. sales. Significant competition in foreign markets comes from northern European, Asian, and Australian firms.

Virtually all the major U.S. competitors are involved in producing commodity products such as lumber. In addition all are striving to lower their costs of production. Owning or controlling timberlands for self-sufficiency and developing differentiated, higher-value-added products are other strategies being pursued by a majority of the larger firms. Two of the largest, Georgia Pacific and Weyerhaeuser, are seeking improved customer service and market penetration through use of extensive multiproduct sales and distribution systems.

Market segmentation strategies are being followed by several of the major competitors in an effort to better identify and respond to customer needs and shift production and marketing emphasis to capitalize on profit potential. The major movement has been to deemphasize residential and commercial segments and shift resources toward serving the do-it-yourself and industrial segments. The do-it-yourself segment is seen as particularly attractive because it is not directly tied to the housing cycle. The aging of residential structures indicates repair and remodel demand will continue to be strong. It even tends to increase during housing down cycles as owners try to make do with older structures by improving them. While the industrial segment demand is dependent on business conditions, it is not as sensitive to interest (mortgage) rates as are the residential and commercial construction segments. Thus, developing do-it-yourself and industrial markets is seen as a way of stabilizing revenues.

Typical major competitors include Boise Cascade, Champion International, Georgia Pacific, International Paper, Louisiana Pacific, Pope and Talbot, and Weyerhaeuser. These companies vary considerably with respect to their strategic thrust but all produce and sell commodity products that are similar to WTD's.

Boise Cascade is a large, integrated forest products company with significant operations in the Pacific Northwest, the Northeast, the South, and upper Midwest/Ontario. The company owns nearly three million acres of timberland that provides one-third of its wood needs. Additional timber resources are controlled through long-term leases. It engages in the production and marketing of pulp, paper, paper products, office products, lumber, plywood, hardboard, particleboard, and veneer. The building (wood) products business produces about one-fourth of the company's sales.

Boise Cascade has indicated its desire to grow in paper, paperboard, containerboard, and timberland ownership through acquisition; grow its office products distribution business internally; and maintain its position in pulp and wood products. The company has indicated it aims to:

1. Be a low-cost producer, stressing modernization, improved processes and cost reduction.

2. Continue as a producer and marketer of commodity products but move into higher value-added products and services. In the building products business, industrial particleboard, Ponderosa pine boards, and premium studs will be emphasized.

3. Pursue the remodeling (do-it-yourself) market.

4. Maximize the use of company-owned timber for higher margins.

5. Concentrate marketing in the Northwest, intermountain West, South Central, and Midwest regions.

6. Focus growth in paper and paper-related businesses with high, long-term growth potential and maintain position in building materials.

Champion International, with over 6.4 million acres of owned or controlled timberland, some eighteen lumber mills, seven plywood plants and numerous paper plants, is one of the largest integrated forest products companies. Its major business is the paper business, which commands a leading market position. The lumber and plywood business, which produces softwood plywood, lumber, particleboard, hardboard, and logs, accounted for approximately 19 percent of sales revenue in 1990. Champion also owns 85 percent of a Canadian forest products company.

Growth has been in paper, with the latest acquisition being the St. Regis Company. Recent divestitures or liquidations have affected the lumber and plywood business. These include the closing of sawmills that converted purchased timber and dismantling the company's building products distribution centers. Other thrusts in recent years have aimed at improving mill efficiency, reducing costs (mainly overhead), increasing employee responsibility for production, and paring down the product line.

Champion's principal strategy is to grow in pulp and paper sales through acquisition, update, and expansion of facilities. The lumber, plywood, and building products business has the role of supporting growth in paper by generating cash. The lumber, plywood, and building products business has the role of supporting growth in paper by generating cash. The basic strategy for the lumber and plywood business to meet cash generation objectives is to:

1. Produce commodity lumber, plywood, and other building products from company owned or controlled forests.

2. Supply building materials in bulk, keeping costs down by processing large orders and turning inventory over fast.

Georgia Pacific is a leading integrated forest products company producing a full line of building materials and paper products to serve markets throughout the United States. Approximately five million acres are under company control in the West, South, Northeast, and eastern Canada. The company is able to supply 50 percent of its wood needs from its own timberlands.

The company has been moving toward developing its pulp and paper business to a size equal to building products. At the same time, the building products business has been growing. This growth has been internal through market penetration and external through the acquisition of U.S. Plywood Corporation and smaller companies. The company is a leader in structural panels and lumber. Within the panels segment, Georgia Pacific has been moving toward developing markets for higher-value-added specialty products, especially in the remodel and replace and industrial segments.

Georgia Pacific has a strong distribution business that serves as a ready market for manufacturing operations. This has allowed plants and mills to run at or near capacity. The company has 143 distribution centers, the largest number in the industry. It adapts its overall distribution organization to fit emerging needs. For example, it created a new division in charge of manufacturing, marketing, and sales of prefinished panels in order to give focus and provide

better customer service. In addition, it opened a new pilot program distribution center to handle specialty products and has installed a computer network in its distribution division to speed up order processing and improve credit control, inventory control, and profitability analysis. A new sales group has been formed to market do-it-yourself products to major home center chains.

In wood products Georgia Pacific's strategic emphasis is on:

1. Continued backwood integration from distribution to products and production capability in growing remodel and replace markets, along with promising sectors of commercial and industrial markets while maintaining its position in residential construction markets.

2. Adding value to its lumber resource in general and its low-grade lumber in particular by producing specialty products. Specialty product lines will be expanded through internal growth and acquisition.

3. Capitalizing on its strong distribution system. Wide breath of coverage, personal selling or single point of contact selling, and a motivated sales force are key strengths to secure sales. Thorough planning, measurable and realistic sales objectives, constant communication of objectives, and pay incentives are supportive of sales productivity. Selling purchased as well as manufactured products helps to more fully use the distribution system and better serve customers.

4. Marketing emphasis on low price and fast delivery.

5. Running facilities at capacity with efficient processes to achieve low production costs.

International Paper, the largest producer of paper products, has control of some 6.3 million acres of timber through its greater than 90-percent ownership of International Paper Timberlands, Ltd. With such extensive holdings, the company engages in significant production of lumber and building products in order to extract the highest value from the timber and at the same time providing lower-value wood chips from the residual portions of logs for use in making pulp. About 9 percent of total sales is accounted for by timber, lumber, plywood, and other building materials.

Since the early 1980s, the company has committed to substantial investments for production rationalization, facility update, and modernization to get costs down and improve productivity. Within the company's wood products businesses, notable investment has been made in Southern lumber and plywood mills, opening four composite-panel plants, and in developing a network of distribution centers.

Improvements in International Paper lumber and building products are sought through:

1. Improving utilization of owned forests. This involves increasing the yield from timberlands by extending the harvest cycle and replanting with improved seedlings.

2. Modernizing mills to reduce labor content and waste.

3. Limited product line reshaping, e.g., a shift to higher value-added products such as laminates.

4. Improving customer responsiveness through quality, reliability, and product tailoring improvements and the development of distribution systems that support this responsiveness.

Louisiana Pacific is primarily a commodity-oriented firm that uses price and volume to its competitive advantage in markets where logistics are favorable. Most of its sales revenue is from lumber and structural panels. Its emphasis in growth and product development has been on waferboard and other fiber-composite-panel products. However, the company does own and operate two pulp mills, marketing domestically and abroad. Major capital investments in recent years have increased waferboard/oriented-strand board capacity, a fiber gypsum wallboard plant, Southern lumber production capacity, and the Southern lumber production base. The company has been generally shifting from the West to the South.

Marketing and sales are primarily aimed at construction (residential and commercial) and, to a lesser extent, repair and remodel uses with waferboard, lumber, and some specialty products. An increasing effort is aimed at selling industrial particleboard and medium-density fiberboard to industrial cabinet and furniture manufacturers. Geographically, Louisiana Pacific sees the world as their market, as evidenced by their investment in a mill in Alaska to produce lumber for Japan. However, U.S. domestic markets are clearly emphasized, particularly the South, West, and Northeast, in that order.

Louisiana Pacific has invested in modern physical and process technology in order to be a lowest-cost producer. These investments have included developing and operating small mills with lower depreciation expense, higher capacity use rates, and lower raw material transportation costs.

Pope and Talbot is a medium-sized forest products company that produces building materials, along with pulp and paper products. Its building materials are mostly commodity-type products. Five sawmills produce lumber, veneer, and chips. The pulp and paper businesses specialize in the production of private-label tissues and disposable diapers plus market pulp. The wood products segment of its business contributes roughly one-third of its sales revenue.

Building materials operations are located in Washington, Wyoming, South Dakota, and Canada. The company has spun off most of its timberlands to an independent limited partnership because of top management's view that owning and operating timberlands offers low returns. Virtually all required logs are purchased on the open market or through competitive bidding for the right to harvest government timberlands.

An overall objective of Pope and Talbot is to be a balanced forest products company. Highest priority goes to continued diversification and growth in pulp and paper businesses. In the wood products business, the company seeks to:

1. Maintain present size.

2. Be a low cost producer. This is accomplished by reducing costs through modernization of old mills and reducing manpower. Low labor costs and low production costs resulting from modernization have made Pope and Talbot's mills some of the most competitive in the industry.

3. Conduct sales by phone out of a central office with shipments direct from mill to customer.

Weyerhaeuser is a large, integrated forest resource company. Its nearly 5.6 million acres of owned timber in the Northwest and Southern states along with control over double that acreage in Canada provide a continuous presence near major markets and a substantial profit advantage during periods of high timber prices. Operations are conducted in every U.S. region, Canada, and the Far East. North America, Europe, the Middle East, and the Far East provide major markets for the company.

Weyerhaeuser's businesses include wood products, distribution, timberlands, pulp and paper, real estate, financial services, and other diversified businesses. Until 1988 forest products and paper were roughly equal in terms of sales and earnings. In 1990, a poor year for both paper products and lumber, forest products contributed 40 percent of their combined operating earnings. The wood products and distribution businesses that make up the forest products grouping produce and sell a wide range of tree-derived products, including logs, dimension lumber, plywood, composite fiber panels, and specialty cuts of lumber for industrial markets. The company has been moving toward higher-priced specialty application products at the expense of its traditional undifferentiated commodity-like lumber and panel products.

Heavy reliance is placed on owned-distribution and sales units for responsiveness and control. In addition to a large number of wholesale distribution centers, there are sales personnel colocated with and serving the individual mills and plants.

The Weyerhaeuser strategy is firmly anchored on managing its timberland yield and finding the best match between timber resources and market needs. Within the context of this driving need, the wood products and distribution businesses seek to assure profitability through:

1. Expanding the line of specialized products designed to meet customer needs in terms of form, fit, strength, appearance or other desired attributes.

2. Differentiating through superior sales, service, and quality of products.

3. Targeting sales growth in remodel and repair, industrial, and specialized markets with special-application and high-quality products and dedicated, service-oriented sales forces.

4. Pricing specialized products and services at a premium relative to competitors.

5. Developing export markets with offshore-based sales and distribution organizations.

6. Defensively investing at a level sufficient to maintain or slightly grow in market position and presence in commodity and most composite-fiber products. Invest to update mills and plants for efficiency. Limit offensive growth in capacity or capability to selected specialty products targeted at growing markets or unfilled niches.

Exhibits C14.1 through C14.7 reveal the magnitude of the wood products businesses and level of performance over the most recent five year period for each of the seven competitors discussed above. In addition Exhibits C14.1 through C14.7 provide selected company-wide debt posture information.

EXHIBIT C14.1 Boise Cascade ($=millions)

	1990	1989	1988	1987	1986
Net sales	$ 939	$ 993	$ 841	$1,031	$ 985
Oper. costs and exp.	$ 866	$ 858	$ 762	$ 903	$ 867
Depr., depl., amort.	$ 31	$ 28	$ 25	$ 32	$ 32
Oper. income	$ 42	$ 107	$ 54	$ 96	$ 86
Cap. expend.	$ 46	$ 59	$ 43	$ 37	$ 37
Ave. assets*	$ 768	$ 745	$ 744	$ 782	$ 805
Profit margin	4.5%	10.8%	6.4%	9.3%	8.7%
Asset turnover	1.2	1.3	1.1	1.3	1.2
RONA	5.5%	14.4%	7.3%	12.3%	10.7%
Cap. exp. to sales	4.9%	5.9%	5.1%	3.6%	3.8%
Net investment	$ 15	$ 31	$ 18	$ 5	$ 5
Co. working cap.	$ 239	$ 254	$ 186	$ 262	$ 313
Debt + equity/equity	3	2.6	2.2	2.2	2.4
LTD/equity	1.2	1	0.6	0.6	0.8

* Includes timber and timberlands assets

EXHIBIT C14.2 Champion ($=millions)

	1990	1989	1988	1987	1986
Net sales	$ 987	$1,126	$1,145	$1,185	$1,042
Oper. costs and exp.	$ 892	$ 944	$1,005	$ 953	$ 879
Depr., depl., amort.	$ 75	$ 67	$ 65	$ 67	$ 60
Oper. income	$ 20	$ 115	$ 75	$ 165	$ 103
Cap. expend.	$ 26	$ 53	$ 39	$ 50	$ 23
Ave. assets*	$2,512	$2,447	$2,063	$2,017	$2,000
Profit margin	2.0%	10.2%	6.6%	13.9%	9.9%
Asset turnover	0.4	0.5	0.6	0.6	0.5
RONA	0.8%	4.7%	3.6%	8.2%	5.2%
Cap. exp. to sales	2.6%	4.7%	3.4%	4.2%	2.2%
Net investment	$ −49	$ −14	$ −26	$ −17	$ −37
Co. working cap.	$ 303	$ 269	$ 232	$ 232	$ 71
Debt + equity/equity	2.3	2.1	2	2.1	2.3
LTD/equity	0.7	0.6	0.6	0.6	0.8

* Includes timber and timberlands assets

EXHIBIT C14.3 Georgia Pacific ($=millions)

	1990	1989	1988	1987	1986
Net sales	$5,923	$6,088	$6,029	$5,755	$5,088
Oper. costs and exp.	$5,259	$5,315	$5,386	$5,034	$4,118
Depr., depl., amort.	$ 241	$ 240	$ 215	$ 188	$ 153
Oper. income	$ 423	$ 533	$ 428	$ 533	$ 500
Cap. expend.	$ 102	$ 135	$ 653	$ 409	$ 248
Ave. assets*	$3,407	$3,469	$3,282	$2,794	$2,483
Profit margin	7.1%	8.8%	7.1%	9.3%	9.8%
Asset turnover	1.7	1.8	1.8	2.1	2.0
RONA	12.4%	15.4%	13.0%	19.1%	20.1%
Cap. exp. to sales	1.7%	2.2%	10.8%	7.1%	4.9%
Net investment	$ −139	$ −105	$ 438	$ 221	$ 95
Co. working cap.	$ −769	$ 905	$ 733	$ 733	$ 583
Debt + equity/equity	4.1	2.6	2.7	2.2	2.1
LTD/equity	1.9	1	1	0.5	0.4

* Includes timber and timberlands assets

EXHIBIT C14.4 International Paper ($=millions)

	1990	1989	1988	1987	1986
Net sales	$1,160	$1,224	$ 890	$ 790	$ 617
Oper. costs and exp.	$1,036	$ 979	$ 677	$ 585	$ 436
Depr., depl., amort.	$ 94	$ 89	$ 75	$ 66	$ 65
Oper. income	$ 30	$ 156	$ 138	$ 139	$ 116
Cap. expend.	$ 76	$ 68	$ 90	$ 65	$ 75
Ave. assets*	$1,629	$1,604	$1,333	$1,201	$1,248
Profit margin	2.6%	12.7%	15.5%	17.6%	18.8%
Asset turnover	0.7	0.8	0.7	0.7	0.5
RONA	1.8%	9.7%	10.4%	11.6%	9.3%
Cap. exp. to sales	6.6%	5.6%	10.1%	8.2%	12.2%
Net investment	$ −18	$ −21	$ 15	$ −1	$ 10
Co. working cap.	$ 784	$ 366	$ 781	$ 657	$ 296
Debt + equity/equity	2.4	2.3	2.1	2.1	2.1
LTD/equity	0.6	0.5	0.4	0.5	0.5

* Includes timber and timberlands assets

EXHIBIT   C14.5   Louisiana Pacific ($=millions)

	1990	1989	1988	1987	1986
Net sales	$1,604	$1,761	$1,572	$1,489	$1,183
Oper. costs and exp.	$1,334	$1,386	$1,279	$1,163	$ 964
Depr., depl., amort.	$ 131	$ 122	$ 126	$ 112	$ 91
Oper. income	$ 139	$ 253	$ 167	$ 214	$ 128
Cap. expend.	$ 214	$ 186	$ 159	$ 181	$ 527
Ave. assets*	$1,495	$1,430	$1,358	$1,314	$1,169
Profit margin	8.7%	14.4%	10.6%	14.4%	10.8%
Asset turnover	1.1	1.2	1.2	1.1	1.0
RONA	9.3%	17.7%	12.3%	16.3%	10.9%
Cap. exp. to sales	13.3%	10.6%	10.1%	12.2%	44.5%
Net investment	$ 83	$ 64	$ 33	$ 69	$ 436
Co. working cap.	$ 314	$ 474	$ 374	$ 132	$ 106
Debt + equity/equity	1.8	1.7	1.6	1.8	1.9
LTD/equity	0.5	0.5	0.3	0.5	0.6

* Includes timber and timberlands assets

EXHIBIT   C14.6   Pope and Talbot ($=millions)

	1990	1989	1988	1987	1986
Net sales	$ 192	$ 234	$ 223	$ 207	$ 163
Oper. costs and exp.	$ 188	$ 205	$ 199	$ 172	$ 136
Depr., depl., amort.	$ 7	$ 8	$ 8	$ 9	$ 9
Oper. income	$ -3	$ 21	$ 16	$ 26	$ 18
Cap. expend.	$ 11	$ 23	$ 14	$ 8	$ 7
Ave. assets*	$ 105	$ 111	$ 106	$ 98	$ 92
Profit margin	-1.6%	9.0%	7.2%	12.6%	11.0%
Asset turnover	1.8	2.1	2.1	2.1	1.8
RONA	-2.9%	18.9%	15.1%	26.5%	19.6%
Cap. exp. to sales	5.7%	9.8%	6.3%	3.9%	4.3%
Net investment	$ 4	$ 15	$ 6	$ -1	$ -2
Co. working cap.	$ 78	$ 61	$ 57	$ 45	$ 38
Debt + equity/equity	1.7	1.8	2	1.8	1.8
LTD/equity	0.4	0.3	0.5	0.4	0.3

* Includes timber and timberlands assets

EXHIBIT   C14.7   Weyerhaeuser ($=millions)

	1990	1989	1988	1987	1986
Net sales	$3,454	$4,026	$3,791	$3,462	$2,852
Oper. costs and exp.	$2,938	$3,520	$3,298	$2,927	$2,394
Depr., depl., amort.	$ 204	$ 199	$ 178	$ 180	$ 187
Oper. income	$ 312	$ 307	$ 315	$ 355	$ 271
Cap. expend.	$ 218	$ 231	$ 385	$ 250	$ 213
Ave. assets*	$2,405	$2,500	$2,454	$2,224	$2,006
Profit margin	9.0%	7.6%	8.3%	10.3%	9.5%
Asset turnover	1.4	1.6	1.5	1.6	1.4
RONA	13.0%	12.3%	12.8%	16.0%	13.5%
Cap. exp. to sales	6.3%	5.7%	10.2%	7.2%	7.5%
Net investment	$ 14	$ 32	$ 207	$ 70	$ 26
Co. working cap.	$ 666	$ 487	$ 755	$ 808	$ 482
Debt + equity/equity	2.2	2	1.9	1.9	2
LTD/equity	0.6	0.5	0.4	0.4	0.4

* Includes timber and timberlands assets

Source: Company annual reports

COMPANY HISTORY

WTD Industries is the creation of Bruce L. Engel, a Portland, Oregon, lawyer, educated at Reed College and the University of Chicago School of Law. In the early 1980s, Engel became involved in an effort to save a client's financially troubled sawmill business. Ultimately Engel and a partner acquired the bankrupt mill in exchange for assuming $2 million in debts. His original idea was to make changes necessary to achieve profitability, operate it until industry conditions improved, and then sell it. Subsequently success with the first sawmill and other opportunities for bargain acquisitions in a depressed industry caused Engel to shift to objectives of growth and profitable operation of wood products converting facilities. In pursuing these new objectives, during the eight years preceding the events that forced the company into bankruptcy, Bruce Engel built an original $3,000 investment into a company with $221,000,000 in assets and $460,000,000 in sales in the fiscal year ending April 30, 1990. In contrast, reduced demand, high costs, and plant shutdowns associated with the company's severe downturn in FY 1991 resulted in sales of only $244,000,000 and a reduction of total assets to $106,000,000.

The growth and profitability strategy of WTD are anchored on a low fixed cost—high variable cost structure with constant pressure to keep variable costs per unit of output low. Chad E. Brown, an investment analyst for Kidder, Peabody & Co., identified the following six key elements of the WTD strategy:[3]

1. Low acquisition cost. This has been achieved by buying mills and plants, most of which were financially distressed, at bargain prices. A result is that WTD's investment is at a level considerably below replacement cost. Increasing

output to capacity or near capacity allows WTD to operate at a fixed cost per unit of output well below many of its major competitors. In addition to concentrating on acquiring undervalued mills the company generally avoids investing in owned timberlands, preferring to buy its logs on the open market.

2. Substantially increase production at mills relative to levels achieved under prior ownership.

3. High labor productivity. Using bankruptcy and high unemployment in the depressed lumber industry as leverage points, hourly wages at newly acquired mills are lowered. However, workers are given the opportunity to earn compensation as high as or higher than paid by competing companies through the use of production bonuses. As a consequence, output per worker is high. None of WTD's mills are unionized.

4. Aggressively use debt leverage.

5. Aggressive management to keep working capital low compared to the rest of the industry. The major thrust is aimed at avoiding excessive inventories of logs.

6. Centralized financial controls and marketing that keep overhead low and provide advantages of scale and customer service.

Following acquisition of the original sawmill at Glide, Oregon, in 1981, a second mill at Silverton, Oregon, was acquired in 1982. In 1983 sawmills located at Philomath, Oregon, were acquired and the business was incorporated as WTD industries.

In 1984 the company added another softwood sawmill operation, this one near Corvallis, Oregon, and its first hardwood sawmill at Philomath, Oregon. The next year, 1985, WTD started operations in Washington with newly acquired softwood and hardwood mills at Sedro Woolley, Olympia, and South Bend. Three more mills were added in 1986—Valley and Aberdeen in

Washington and Tillamook in Oregon. Late in 1986, WTD went public with 1,850,000 shares of common stock. Net proceeds in excess of $15,000,000 fueled a major expansion in 1987.

Thirteen companies were acquired in 1987—seven in Oregon, five in Washington, and one in Montana. In addition to WTD's first geographic expansion outside of the Pacific Northwest, 1987 also marked the company's growth into non-sawmill production operations. Five of the 1987 acquisitions were plants producing veneer and one was a plywood plant. Growth in 1988 was modest by comparison, with only three acquisitions—sawmills in Washington and Oregon and a plywood plant in New York. Seven softwood lumber sawmills located at Alturas, California; Custer, South Dakota; West Burke, Vermont; Judith Gap, Montana; and Portland, Cottage Grove, and Central Point, Oregon, were acquired in 1989 and 1990. In addition the conversion of a hardwood mill at Tillamook, Oregon, to a higher-capacity softwood mill was completed in 1990. Partially offsetting acquisitions, four lumber or veneer mills were sold or otherwise liquidated in the period 1989, 1990, and 1991.

Most of WTD's acquisitions involved outright ownership. However, a number of the acquired companies operate as lessees of land or land and improvements. The company does have options to buy several of the properties.

Although it is contrary to company strategy to invest in timberlands, WTD does own 17,000 acres it obtained in 1987. The land located near the Philomath mills was acquired because open-market log prices in that area were considered too high. By mid-1991 most of the timber on this land had been harvested.

The cutback in home building in 1990 with its consequent reduction in demand for lumber resulted in 15-percent lower average lumber prices. At the same time log costs increased 7 percent because of export log demand and cutbacks in the harvest of timber from public lands.[4] Even with reductions in operating costs by curtailing operations in selected locations and a reduction of overhead, WTD's poor financial performance precluded its meeting all the covenants associated with debt agreements. When its bank line of credit was declared in default, the company and each of its subsidiaries filed for Chapter 11 bankruptcy (on January 30, 1991).

OPERATIONS

The forest products industry leaders are moving toward increased emphasis on specialized, differentiated wood products. In addition extensive capital investment in technologies that help extract maximum value from a log and investing in owned timberlands to assure a supply of known-cost logs are widely accepted as competitive necessities. WTD has rejected all of these as elements of its strategy.

Products and Product Strategy

The company produces and sells a variety of wood products, principally falling in the following categories: softwood lumber, hardwood lumber, softwood veneer, and wood chips. Softwood lumber is the major product, accounting for 72 percent of sales in fiscal 1991. Softwood lumber consists of studs and other dimension lumber in a wide range of widths, lengths, and thicknesses. The predominant species that are converted into softwood lumber are Douglas fir, hemlock, white fir, lodgepole pine, ponderosa pine, spruce, and larch. Although softwood lumber, along with all other products, is branded with the name of WTD's marketing organization and its logo, these products are basically commodities competing against similar, substitute products.

The second highest source of 1991 sales was chips, a residual product made from the parts of logs not suitable for conversion into lumber or veneer. Chips are used to make pulp for later conversion into paper products. Chips accounted for 13 percent of sales. Less important products include veneer, hardwood lumber,

and plywood. Veneer, a thin layer of wood peeled from logs, is used in the lay-up of plywood. Hardwood lumber is produced in sizes appropriate for cabinet and furniture manufacturers. The major species is alder although some maple is also cut. Plywood plants use veneers to produce sheathing, underlayment, sanded, and marine plywood in standard sizes. The company's plywood plants were closed during 1991.

With the minor exception of a few specialty or highly finished products such as special cuts of wood for furniture, WTD is a producer of undifferentiated products. The company aims to produce and move these commodity-like products in volume, relying on high per-worker output. In fact, labor productivity improvements in the company's existing mills were responsible for boosting their aggregate lumber production by about 50 percent.

Raw Materials Inventory Strategy

Inventories of raw materials, that is, logs, impact profitability in two ways. The first is that assured and continuous availability is necessary for an efficient conversion process and the satisfaction of customers' order delivery requirements. The second is that logs are a costly resource and can represent a substantial tie-up of working capital as well as a major factor in determining the profit margin. While lumber prices tend to slightly lead log prices, moving in the same direction, and maintaining a more or less constant relationship over the long term, short-term variations can and do occur. For example, increased foreign demand for logs, environmentalist special-interest group activities to restrict sale of government timber, and weather conditions unfavorable for logging have all decreased log supply and raised prices independent of domestic demand for lumber. With the cost of purchased logs at delivery accounting for two-thirds of finished product costs at WTD, such a supply-shortage induced rise in log prices not accompanied by a rise in lumber prices can turn a profitable operation into an unprofitable one. From 1987 to 1990 shortages of logs at reasonable prices were a major factor in the closing of forty-six less well managed or positioned Northwest sawmills. Since then the imbalance has intensified due to the continued high demand for high-quality export logs and severe cutbacks in government sales of timber harvest contracts associated with protecting the spotted owl.

Traditional industry response among its larger competitors to lessen risks associated with uncertain availability and the potential of high open-market log prices has been to line up inventories of standing timber sufficient for two years or more of production and stockpile substantial inventories of logs at the mills. These firms typically secure control over timberlands either through ownership or harvest rights. The timber-owning competitors are in a position to either (1) buy on the open market or through harvest contracts when log prices are low and harvest owned timber (presumably on the books at a lower, historical cost) when log prices are high or (2) give priority to filling their needs from owned timber on a continuing basis. In either strategy there is a potential to sustain higher operating margins. Competitors who lack their own timberlands usually contract with timberland owners or the government for the right to harvest timber over a number of years. Such contracts are subject to competitive bidding, and bid prices reflect the near-term profit potential of lumber-manufacturing operations and availability of timber. Companies that own timber contracts can be expected to do well during periods of rising lumber prices and poorly when lumber prices fall. In fact, WTD owes its start to the fact that in the late 1970s many sawmill owners committed themselves to high priced timber contracts prior to an industry downturn. When lumber prices fell they found themselves faced with bankruptcy because they were unable to operate profitably or break their contracts.

WTD purposely avoids holding large inventories of logs. The company has avoided speculating in logs, preferring to buy in the open market at prices that closely follow lumber market prices. Its intent is to buy its logs and convert them into lumber within a matter of weeks, before the profit margin can be eroded. The ability to follow this strategy provided consistent, although modest margins between materials costs and sales revenues through 1989.

In support of its low-inventory strategy, WTD has aimed to maintain log inventories equal to approximately three weeks operating requirements. Larger inventories are carried only when it is necessary to collect selected materials for specialty orders, weather or seasonal factors prevent regular deliveries, or open-market buying is not possible, necessitating purchasing timber-cutting contracts. The latter are primarily sold by government agencies and ordinarily require the cutting and removal of public timber within three years. WTD attempts to harvest timber under these contracts within one year and preferably within three to four months to minimize the risk of a reduced margin from falling lumber prices. WTD's preference toward the open market and away from timber contracts as its source of logs is reflected in Exhibit C14.8. In keeping with WTD's accep-

EXHIBIT   C14.8
WTD Sources of Logs

Fiscal Year	Open Market	Timber Contract	Owned Timberlands*
1987	78%	22%	0%
1988	73%	20%	7%
1989	70%	21%	9%
1990	69%	25%	6%
1991	75%	19%	6%

* By the end of FY1991 most company-owned timberlands had been harvested.

Source: WTD Industries 1991 Form 10K

tance of variable costs in place of fixed costs, all forest operations are contracted to logging companies. This includes road building, cutting, and delivery to the mills.

Reliance on a supply of reasonably priced logs has left the company vulnerable to imbalances between log supply and demand. Problems first arose in late 1987, when two softwood sawmills, both of which normally rely on timber-harvesting contracts with government agencies, were faced with a shortage of logs and unprofitably high prices created by foreign demand and forest fires. The company was forced to shut the two mills down temporarily until a supply of acceptably priced logs could be assured. In calendar years 1988 and 1989 several mills were temporarily closed from time to time because of log shortages. Unprofitable operations caused by shortage-induced high raw materials costs became more widespread in 1990 and resulted in the closure of twenty-one lumber and plywood mills in 1990 and 1991. In the first half of 1991 log costs and lumber prices came back into a more normal relationship but not before the cost-revenue imbalance had precipitated WTD's bankruptcy.[5]

Growing government recognition that the Northwest is experiencing a timber shortage has spurred government action. At one time pressure from organized environmentalist special-interest groups seeking to protect the habitat of the spotted owl had virtually stopped the sale of old-growth timber from federal lands in the West. In response to the spotted owl's endangered species status, environmentalists, and forestry pleas, the government has reached a compromise that reopened the sale of federal timber but at drastically reduced levels. The extent to which logging on federal, state, and private lands will be restricted to preserve the spotted owl at the expense of jobs has become a hotly contested political issue in the West Coast states. Further compromises are possible. For example, the federal government is considering use of its authority to place temporary bans on the export of logs from state lands in order to increase the supply of logs to domestic sawmills.

Technology Strategy

Many major competitors such as Weyerhaeuser have been investing in new technologies, some using computers and lasers, that increase the yield of higher value products by optimizing the way each log is cut. Other technologies are commonly being incorporated to reduce the labor content and increase capacity.

WTD has focused on employee productivity incentives rather than investing in expensive automated machinery to increase production. As stated in the company's 1987 report:

> We strive to avoid the capital costs of expensive high technology equipment that purports to eliminate production employees. We prefer to rely on the flexibility and productivity of our workers.[6]

Although the company purposely avoids investing in costly automated plants and machinery, it does invest in projects offering major savings or immediate production improvements that have paybacks of three years or less. For the most part this has meant modest capital expenditures, approximating annual depreciation costs, to replace and upgrade worn and inefficient equipment. As an example of the difference in WTD's approach to investment in technology, WTD invested a million dollars to replace old parts at its Glide, Oregon, mill while International Paper invested $90 million in a computer-driven mill process at its competing Gardiner, Oregon, mill.[7]

In FY 1989 the company began emphasizing recovery, increasing the volume of lumber produced from a log, and reduction of sawdust relative to chips as the major thrust of its modest capital improvements. This involves using thinner saws, re-layout of processes, modification of existing equipment and processes, and sometimes introduction of new equipment to optimize the way logs are cut.

Growth and Acquisition Strategy

WTD has evidenced a clear commitment to fast growth. The company's intent has been to grow both internally and externally when conditions are favorable. Internal growth in production at existing mills is a continuing goal that requires focused application of the company's human resource productivity strategy. One thrust of external growth is the acquisition of new lumber mills using cash generated from operations and leverage. Acquisitions are sought that:

1. Require reasonably low capital investment.

2. Are capable of increased productivity through incentive plans.

3. Are located in areas with an adequate supply of open-market logs.

4. In view of the above, offer an acceptable ROI.

5. Provide cash flow sufficient to service debt.

In the late 1980s the company started a second external growth thrust that was a departure from its past. WTD announced that it planned to enter the pulp and paper industry with the construction and operation of a market-pulp mill. Building a mill to produce pulp, although costly, is generally seen as an unusual opportunity for the company because of favorable foreign market conditions and synergy with WTD sawmill operations that provide the wood chips used in making pulp. Conditions favoring the project include:[8]

1. A current short supply of pulp.

2. A projected worldwide market-pulp capacity that is short of planned growth in paper capacity.

3. Expectations that the United States will be a low-cost producer of pulp in the foreseeable future.

4. Japanese (and other) market-pulp buyers prefer to own capacity to assure supply in a tight market.

5. WTD's mills produce the largest single supply of wood chips not controlled by an existing paper company in the Northwest. Demand for a new pulp mill can be expected to raise chip prices in the region. WTD expects the mill to provide a market for about half the wood chips it produces. WTD's revenue is expected to rise on the order of $10 million as a result of wood chip price rises alone.

WTD's plan has been to build a $450-million mill with a capacity of 300,000 metric tons per year of bleached softwood kraft market pulp. This type of market pulp is used in paper mills to produce newsprint. The mill would operate as Port Westwood Pulp Co. and export 95 percent of its production—75 percent of its exports going to Pacific Rim markets and 25 percent to Europe. The estimated annual market value of the output of this mill is $180 million.[9]

WTD's plan called for joint venturing the mill with foreign investors. Japanese, Chinese, and Korean firms have indicated interest in the project, and WTD does not anticipate trouble in finding partners. Discussions started with potential partners during 1989.

WTD planned to operate the mill and control the venture with majority ownership. Thus, the company would have needed to raise substantial capital for its share, possibly more than $200 million. Possible sources of funds considered by the company included a public stock offering, senior debentures, industrial revenue bonds and bank loans, alone or in combination.

In summer 1988 WTD subleased 250 acres of land owned by the Port of St. Helens, on the Columbia River, west of Portland, Oregon, from Portland General Electric Co. The location offers economical transportation from a large number of WTD mills and loading facilities for ocean-going ships. The lease option was for a two-year period, during which time WTD planned to arrange financing, secure permits, finalize engineering studies, and start construction. Originally production was expected to start in mid-1992.

WTD asked for state and federal approval to build the mill but encountered opposition from local residents and environmentalists who contend that the mill presents a danger to the public. Even with state-of-the-art emission-reduction technology the mill would still emit extremely small amounts of toxic dioxin, a cancer-causing byproduct, which would add to the already dangerous dioxin level in the Columbia River.

With its financial crisis, the company has abandoned its plan for a pulp mill indefinitely and has written off all start-up costs already incurred.

Operating Locations

WTD owns thirty-two manufacturing facilities in thirty different locations, mostly Oregon and Washington. Starting in western Oregon, the company expanded operation to western Washington in 1987, and in 1987, 1988, 1989, and 1990 to eastern Oregon, eastern Washington, Montana, New York, South Dakota, California, and Vermont. However, the majority of the facilities are located west of the Cascade Mountains. Exhibit C14.9 shows locations and production by product types.

SALES AND MARKETING

All marketing, sales, and distribution of WTD's products are the responsibility of Treesource, Inc., a wholly owned subsidiary. Treesource, with fifty-one sales, managerial, and clerical employees, is located at Portland, Oregon. Through this centralized sales and marketing unit, WTD gains economies of scale not available to independent mills. Treesource is able to coordinate production at various mills to satisfy customer orders, arrange lowest-cost production location–transportation cost alternatives, and fill orders for an assortment of products beyond the capability of any single mill. In addition centralized credit management offers economies in credit checking, monitoring, and collecting. Since each salesperson is responsible to do the marketing and sales for one or two of the company's mills, fewer salespersons are needed than if each mill is responsible for its own sales.

Treesource has targeted the construction, industrial, and remodel and replace (do-it-yourself) segments. Of these, the construction segment is the most active. Most sales are to distributors and wholesalers, industrial users, and retailers.[10] Products sold to distributors and wholesalers, the largest customer segment, include softwood lumber for the residential construction, commercial construction, and remodel and replace segments plus hardwood boards for the construction and remodel and replace segments. Major customers have included such large distributors as Georgia Pacific, Weyerhaeuser, and Dixieline. The second largest channel, sales to retailers, including chain merchandisers, provides softwood and hardwood lumber for the remodel and replace user. Sales to industrial buyers, the third-largest segment, includes hardwood for furniture and cabinet manufacturers. Direct sales of intermediate materials, including veneer plus products that are immediately usable by the customer, for example, railroad ties, are a minor market. The majority of WTD's sales are to buyers in the United States. Exports, primarily to Canada but also to Europe, Australia and the Far East, were expanding prior to the downturn.

Most sales are arranged through telephone contact between salesperson and buyer. The company offers competitive delivered prices, a variety of products, availability of products, and reliability as competitive advantages. In fact, Weyerhaeuser, a major customer, named WTD as its "supplier of the year" in 1987 for its reliability, cooperation, and quality. The company also offers a one-percent discount if an account is paid within ten days, providing an effective incentive for prompt payment. In addition WTD attempts to create a name familiarity

EXHIBIT C14.9 WTD Mills and Products

Mill/Plant Location	FY 1991 Production/Capacity (Millions)		
	Softwood Lumber	Hardwood Lumber	Veneer or Plywood
Aberdeen, WA		5/NA	
Alturas, CA	11.1/NA		
Central Point, OR	36.6/110		
Chiloquin, OR	38.7/NA		
Columbia Falls, MT	14.8/NA		
Corvallis, OR	25.6/75		
Cottage Grove, OR	0/NA		
Custer, SD	16.2/NA		
Eugene, OR	0/NA		
Glide, OR	90.2/125		
Goshen, OR			0/72
Halsey, OR			9.4/NA
Judith Gap, MT	17.5/NA		
Junction City, OR	0/NA		
Morten, WA	60.1/90		
	21.6/150		
North Powder, OR	51.2/90		
Orient, WA	0/NA		
Portland, OR	7.4/NA		
Philomath, OR	40.4/80		
Philomath, OR	159.9/245		
Ronald, WA			9.1/NA
Sedro Woolley, WA	45.3/105		
Silverton, OR	0/NA		
South Bend, WA			10.8/16
Spanaway, WA			34.2/NA
Tacoma, WA	31.1/60		
Tillamook, OR	6.7/120		
Tumwater, WA	37.9/50		
Valley, WA	14.6/NA		
West Burke, VT	30.6/45		
Whitehall, NY			16.6/NA

Notes: Softwood and hardwood production and capacity measured in board feet; veneer and plywood measured in square feet (3/8-inch basis).

NA means capacity is both not available and not applicable. Mills so marked have been shut down.

by identifying all product lots with the Treesource trademark and name of the producing mill after they are packaged or strapped.

Transportation is the third-highest cost component of a delivered product, exceeded only by logs and labor. Treesource arranges for the transportation of products from all WTD mills and, as a result, is able to secure volume discounts that help WTD to lower costs and be price competitive. Shipments of products are normally made direct from the mill to the buyer's destination via rail, truck, or barge.

HUMAN RESOURCES STRATEGY

WTD considers people to be the most important factor determining company profitability. This importance is operationalized in the human resource strategy and policies that support objectives of efficiency in the use of the total work force and high levels of individual and work team productivity. The issue of efficiency is addressed in the company's specialization of activities and locus of decision making. High productivity is motivated by programs that highlight the importance of individual contributions to the company through incentives based on those contributions.

Functional Specialization

Activities that benefit or apply to more than one mill are performed at a centralized location in order to gain advantages of functional specialization and scale. Sales, market development, engineering, finance, and legal services are the key activities that are centralized. Log-buying specialists are located at the individual mills because of their need to be familiar with and responsive to local conditions, suppliers, and mill needs. However, a vice president position was created in May of 1989 to be responsible for developing and overseeing log-procurement strategies. With most support functions performed elsewhere by others, local mill managers can concentrate on what is most important to them—effective and efficient production.

In May 1991 WTD employed approximately 1,200 employees, down from over 2,600 two years earlier.

Incentive Pay

To encourage flexibility and productivity, WTD has nonunion labor in all its mills and has substituted pay based partly on productivity for straight wages. As a nonunion employer, WTD has greater freedom in assigning duties and can require time lost from breakdowns to be made up on Saturday at weekday pay rates. However, it is a unique incentive pay system that underlies the company's labor cost advantage.

The industry norm is a straight hourly wage, often established in union-company labor contracts. Many firms in the industry recognize that under such a compensation system labor is essentially a fixed cost and their profits will be high or low depending solely on demand and price in the marketplace. However, they face stiff opposition in shifting to a system where labor cost varies with profitability. Several large companies have been moving in that direction but union opposition and tradition have presented formidable obstacles. Weyerhaeuser established a leading position in this slow movement in 1986 when it negotiated a wage reduction in exchange for an annual profit sharing bonus.

WTD has two incentive pay systems. One, applicable to salaried employees, is a profit sharing plan, like Weyerhaeuser's, but computed and paid monthly rather than annually. Bonuses are based on monthly pretax profits at the mill, region, or entire corporation, depending on the employee's level of involvement, and are allocated as a percent of base salary. In recent good years the bonus portion of total salary compensation has ranged from about 40 to 50 percent.[11]

The incentive pay system for hourly employees is based on production, safety, and attendance. Each mill sets weekly production goals. Each week a bonus is paid to all members of a work shift if the shift has met its production goals and minimum safety standards, with no worker losing more than three hours due to an on-the-job injury. In addition, for an individual shift member to be eligible for the weekly bonus he/she must not have been absent or late for work during the week. Although base wage levels are typically lower than prevailing wages in the local area, the addition of production bonuses makes overall compensation comparable or better. In 1988 WTD mill workers averaged $8.40 per hour in base wages and $3 per hour in bonuses.[12] In addition to the regular bonus system, when a shift sets a new production record, every member of the shift receives a cash bonus—a $50 bill handed out by Bruce Engel.

The bonus systems are significant contributors to the company's competitive advantage in low manufacturing costs. Profit-based bonuses for managers foster constant attention to cost control, while the production bonus system motivates teamwork, innovation, high levels of individual effort, improved safety, and attendance. By the time a new mill has completed implementation of WTD's operations and human resource strategies, production increases per shift typically have reached 50 percent. The result is a lower than average labor cost per thousand board feet. Chad Brown of Kidder, Peabody & Company estimated that WTD's higher than average labor productivity may account for a 4- to 5-percent profit margin on sales (out of its total 1989 6-percent profit margin).[13] In addition improvements in safety allowed the company to self-insure in Oregon and Washington, substantially reducing workers' compensation insurance costs.

WTD provides health insurance and a 401 (k) retirement savings plan where the company matches contributions of non-salaried employees. Vacation policies are in line with the industry and require a shorter period of employment for eligibility.

FINANCING GROWTH

The company has followed a two-step process of external growth through acquisition followed by internal growth of acquired mills. Capital required to support these two types of growth has been provided from three sources: debt, sale of ownership, and operations.

Acquisitions, modernizations, and working capital growth have been largely financed through assumption of existing debt and creation of new debt. The company's rapid growth in the last seven years through the use of debt leverage is reflected in $113,904,000 in long-term debt on April 30, 1991. This debt includes $70,000,000 in unsecured notes, due 1994, 1995, 1997, and 1999; various secured mortgage notes totalling $4,871,000; other notes totalling $12,395,000; $22,000,000 in sinking fund senior subordinated debentures, due 1997; $4,000,000 in secured economic development revenue bonds, due 2008; and $3,000,000 in unsecured economic development revenue bonds, granted for use on the company's Graham Plywood Company; all less total current maturities of $2,362,000. In addition, prior to bankruptcy WTD had a bank line of credit secured by accounts receivable and inventories. Certain covenants associated with its notes restrict the company from paying dividends and require a current ratio of at least 1.0, income-to-interest payments of at least 2 to 1, a tangible net worth of at least $30,000,000, and other restrictions.

The one-time 1986 public stock offering that netted over $15 million provided for working capital expansion and fueled much of the acquisition activity in 1987. A growing source of funds for capital projects until 1990 was current operations. The company has a policy of not paying cash dividends, leaving all net cash flow available for capital investment, working capital improvement, or long-term debt payment. In FY 1990 company operations provided over $17 million in cash to support such needs, and in FY 1989 it provided $24 million.

Acquisition criteria have been adapted to reflect greater availability of funds and changes in the industry environment. Initially the company targeted mills that were underproducing their potential and that were priced well below replacement cost. These tended to be firms that were in bankruptcy. The idea was to buy them with a minimum outlay of cash, fix them up, and implement the WTD system of human resource and operations management. A two-year start-up before reaching profit potential was not unexpected. A result was that low acquisition costs were offset to some degree by high costs of internal growth, for example, modernization costs and reduced income during start-up. More recently, reduced availability of bankrupt firms with profit potential and a greater ability to pay caused WTD to acquire efficient, already profitable plants at higher initial investment levels but with lower start-up costs. Total acquisition price has not been narrowly limited—prices ranged from less than $2 million to nearly $13 million. Most recent acquisitions have substantially exceeded the average book value of the company's subsidiary mills, which was roughly $2.8 million in FY 1989. For example, acquisitions in 1990 averaged $4.9 million each.

MANAGEMENT

WTD manages its operating locations using a decentralized-centralized structure. Individual production units (mills or plants) are profit centers under a manager who has overall responsibility for the profitability of his unit. Each production unit is incorporated as a wholly owned subsidiary under a name that identifies it as a local company, for example, Goshen Veneer Co., Sedro Woolley Lumber Co., and Morton Forest Products Co.

The company feels its use of a decentralized local mill management team concept provides operating flexibility to be responsive to local competitive conditions while maintaining tight control over costs. The local mill management team has responsibility for log procurement, log and chip sales, byproduct sales, log recovery projects, safety programs, workers' compensation claims, and accounts payable, as well as production scheduling and control. However, other key activities are not decentralized to the units. Where larger size, greater volume or other conditions favoring scale economies exist, activities are centralized. WTD currently centralizes marketing, sales, credit, mill-to-market transportation, and financing activities in order to capitalize on economies of scale.

With growth through the years, administrative and specialist support employment increased. Mill management and clerical staff were added for the administration of each new acquisition. Growth of WTD's centralized management and staff has occurred in spurts. The most recent such growth occurred in FY 1988 and 1989 coincident with the need to manage a larger-scale, more diverse company. Key additions to top management were experienced vice presidents of operations, acquisitions, timber, and pulp. The last was to be responsible for developing and implementing a proposed pulp mill. However, with the company's downturn in 1990, the executive officer ranks decreased to seven from thirteen. This included the loss of the officers in charge of operations, pulp, and acquisitions.

Bruce Engel, the president, along with wife, Teri, owns 2,254,952 shares, or 36.2 percent of the WTD common stock.[14] He has been the chief architect of WTD's growth. As indicated earlier, he added managers and staff capable of performing or assisting him perform most of the executive functions as the company grew. This did not diminish his involvement. He remained deeply involved in performing the duties of chief executive, including public relations, choosing and effecting acquisitions, integrating new units into the company, and guiding ongoing operations. With the scaleback in executive positions, his involvement has become more important. In addition to WTD, Bruce Engel is involved in other enterprises. In 1988 such outside interests were estimated to take five to ten percent of his time.[15] These included bowling alleys in three cities, a weekly newspaper, light manufacturing firms, and a clothing alteration and tailoring service. He also started a business publication aimed at executives in Washington state. Other outside interests may be added—recently he lost in a bid to buy the Seattle Mariners major league baseball club and in 1989 tried to negotiate a Portland, Oregon, franchise of a new professional baseball league.

FINANCIAL CONDITION

Through FY 1989 WTD showed a steady growth in net sales, operating income, and net income, reflecting both the addition of mills and plants and an increase in production in its mills, once acquired. In terms of efficiency and profit, as can be seen in Exhibit C14.10, from FY 1986 through 1989 WTD was a consistent performer without major variations from year to year. The only measure of profit performance that showed significant change was return on average equity, which was affected by the shift from private to public ownership in late 1986 (FY 1987) and subsequent growth in equity from increases in retained earnings.

Reflecting the strategy of rapid growth primarily financed with debt, long-term debt increased from $6.9 million in FY 1986 to $92 million in FY 1989, while interest charges increased from $1.5 million to $10.2 million in the same period. Except in FY 1987, times interest earned declined steadily to 2.1 in FY 1989. (See Exhibit C14.11.)

Expansion of capacity continued in FY 1990 and 1991 with investments of $49.3 million and $2.8 million, respectively. Long-term debt and interest grew to $114 million (FY 1991) and $11.3 million (FY 1990) to support the growth. This expansion did not result in further increases in profits. The profitability picture was sharply reversed. Log prices rose at the same time lumber prices were depressed. A continued high

demand for export logs accompanied by environmental pressures that caused closing of substantial acreages of public lands to harvest and the threat of further reductions in log supplies resulted in high log prices through all of calendar 1990. WTD expected declining interest rates to encourage demand for construction in the spring. This did not happen and the imbalance between log and lumber prices continued through the year.

WTD lost $10.1 million in its FY 1990 fourth quarter (February through April 1990), $7.3 million in first quarter FY 1991, $8.8 million in the second quarter, and $70.7 million in the third quarter. These losses included $8.3 million in fourth quarter FY 1990 and $58 million in third quarter FY 1991 in write-downs of asset values of facilities, write-offs of deferred costs incurred in the Port Westward project, and reorganization charges. Prices did not resume a more normal relationship until early in 1991, allowing the company to earn a modest profit of $1.7 million.

Losses in FY 1990 and continuing into FY 1991 caused WTD to default on substantially all of its debt agreements that required specific working capital, income to interest, and debt to total capitalization ratios. For example, Exhibit C14.11 shows the company's inability to generate enough income to cover its interest expense. Inability to meet its debt agreements resulted in a bank that had provided line of credit financing to call for an accelerated payback. WTD was unable to pay off the bank line of credit and so declared bankruptcy under the provisions of Chapter 11. Bankruptcy allows WTD to stop payment of interest on unsecured and undersecured debt and repayment of the underlying debt until conclusion of Chapter 11 proceedings. With its bank line of credit suspended, WTD must fund its operations solely with internally generated cash.

The company has shut down sixteen facilities and readjusted their asset value to estimated net realizable value—what they are expected to yield upon liquidation. With the substantial reduction in value of the company, most of

WTD's long-term debt and some of its current liabilities are only partially covered by assets, at best. All long-term and short-term debt that is unsecured or undersecured (value of collateral is less than debt) has been reclassified as a long-term debt titled "liabilities subject to compromise." Stock continues to be listed by the National Association of Securities Dealers' Automated Quotations System (NASDAQ) but at a very low price reflecting a negative book value and high risk. Recent prices have hovered at about a dollar a share or slightly below. Historical stock price ranges and comparative balance sheets are shown in Exhibits C14.12 and C14.13.

Although the industry generally suffered in 1990 because of low demand and prices, WTD performed the worst of those companies compared in Exhibit C14.14. The larger companies in the industry are diversified into other-industry businesses, such as paper.

EXHIBIT   C14.10   WTD Profitability ($=millions)

	1991	1990	1989	1988	1987	1986
Net sales	$243.9	$459.9	$359.6	$293.7	$176.2	$99.0
C of GS	$296.4	$404.3	$300.5	$246.5	$152.7	$85.2
S,G&A	$21.0	$29.7	$21.8	$20.0	$10.0	$6.6
Depr., depl., amort.	$12.0	$18.9	$15.4	$6.5	$3.3	$2.6
Oper. income	$-85.5	$7.0	$21.9	$20.7	$10.2	$4.6
Interest expense	$-10.2	$-11.3	$-10.2	$-7.7	$-1.7	$-1.5
Other, incl. taxes	$10.5	$2.8	$-2.9	$-4.6	$-3.8	$-1.1
Net income (A.T.)	$-85.2	$-1.5	$8.8	$8.4	$4.7	$2.0
Cap. expend.	$2.7	$49.3	$10.0	$16.8	$14.4	$4.5
Working cap.	$35.1	$43.2	$35.8	$18.3	$22.5	$-0.8
Ave. assets	$163.5	$202.9	$165.5	$125.0	$70.0	$29.0
Ave. owners equity	$-4.0	$39.7	$36.3	$27.5	$13.1	$2.4
Gross margin	-21.5%	12.1%	16.4%	16.1%	13.3%	13.9%
Profit margin	-35.1%	1.5%	6.1%	7.0%	5.8%	4.6%
Asset turn	1.5	2.3	2.2	2.3	2.5	3.4
Operating ROA	-52.3%	3.4%	13.2%	16.6%	14.6%	15.9%
Return on equity	NEG	NEG	24.2%	30.6%	35.9%	85.0%
Debt+equity/equity	NEG	5.7	4.5	4.6	4.5	11.5
LTD/equity	NEG	2.9	2.3	2.4	1.9	2.2
Net investment	$-9.3	$30.4	$-5.4	$10.3	$11.1	$1.9
Cap. exp. to sales	1.1%	10.7%	2.8%	5.7%	8.2%	4.5%
Prod. efficiency	121.5%	87.9%	83.6%	83.9%	86.7%	86.1%
Admin. efficiency	8.6%	6.5%	6.1%	6.8%	5.7%	6.7%

Notes: Fiscal year ends April 30.
    NEG indicates a loss or negative ratio.
Source: WTD 1991, 1989, 1988, and 1987 annual reports and 10Ks.

EXHIBIT C14.11 Long-Term Debt and Interest Burden

Fiscal Year Ending April 30						
	1991*	**1990**	**1989**	**1988**	**1987**	**1986**
Total long-term debt (millions)	$114.0	$112.0	$92.0	$75.7	$43.7	$6.9
Interest expense (millions)	$10.2	$11.3	$10.2	$7.7	$1.7	$1.5
Times interest earned (times)	−7.4	0.9	2.1	2.7	6.0	3.1

* LTD includes $106,447,000 in unsecured and undersecured bonds and contracts subject to
compromise.

Interest expense includes interest accrued up to Ch. 11 bankruptcy in January 1991. Interest expense
would have been $3 million higher had there been no need for bankruptcy.

Source: WTD Forms 10K.

EXHIBIT C14.12 WTD Stock Prices (Dollars)

	FY 1991	**FY 1990**	**FY 1989**	**FY 1988**	**FY 1987**
Low	1/4*	7 3/8	6 1/4	9 3/4	9
High	7 1/8	17 1/4	14	27 1/2	26
Shareholders (000s)	6229.5	6229.8	6322.8	6395.3	5466

* After Chapter 11 bankruptcy.

Source: WTD Forms 10K.

Because of this diversification and the difficulties in apportioning equity among business segments, return on equity is generally not attempted as a measure of performance. Commonly operating income is compared to the average net assets assigned for its generation. This operating return on assets measure of performance and its two components, operating profit margin on sales and asset turnover, are preferred by many managers of wood products businesses for comparison purposes. Using these measures, costs and assets beyond the businesses' control as well as income not attributable to its actions are eliminated.

Exhibit C14.14 shows the return on assets, underlying profit margins, and asset turnover earned by WTD and selected competitors for a five-year period. Through 1988 WTD was nei-

ther the best nor the worst performer with respect to return on assets but was the best in asset turnover and the worst in operating profit margin. This difference is indicative of a higher-variable-cost structure and lower-fixed-cost (asset) structure than the other companies. Normally a high-variable-cost and low-fixed-cost company will perform better when demand and prices are low because it can reduce the largest contributor to its costs and maintain modest but consistent margins. On the other hand, high cost–low variable cost competitors tend to experience high profit margins fixed in periods of attractive prices and high demand but low margins under the opposite conditions, when their fixed costs remain even through sales revenue declines. However, in 1990, when demand and prices were off but materials (logs) were high

EXHIBIT C14.13   WTD Consolidated Balance Sheet ($=thousands)

	April 30			
	1991	1990	1989	1988
Assets				
Current assets:				
Cash and near cash	$ 4,395	$ 3,128	$ 1,626	$ 2,019
Accounts receivable, net	9,384	26,675	36,958	20,181
Inventories	12,365	41,318	26,000	21,100
Prepaid expenses	4,173	1,961	1,662	2,285
Income tax receivable	6,252	5,951	0	0
Timber and timber related assets	15,078	30,241	19,276	10,885
Other	2,153	1,496	0	0
Total current assets	$ 53,800	$ 110,770	$ 85,522	$ 56,470
Notes and accounts receivable	$ 234	$ 0	$ 2,924	$ 1,346
Timber and timberlands	688	846	1,454	11,624
Marketable securities	0	0	6,505	0
Property, plant, and equipment	67,540	129,444	108,233	79,132
Less accumulated depreciation	(27,330)	(35,554)	(26,013)	(16,749)
Subtotal	$ 40,210	$ 93,890	$ 82,220	$ 62,383
Construction in progress	315	8,130	2,836	11,349
Subtotal	$ 40,525	$ 102,020	$ 85,056	$ 73,732
Idle assets	7,848	0	0	0
Other assets	2,943	6,990	3,439	2,910
Total assets	$ 106,030	$ 220,930	$ 184,900	$ 146,082
Liabilities and Stockholders' Equity				
Current liabilities:				
Notes and acceptances payable	$ 0	$ 16,400	$ 11,350	$ 11,025
Accounts payable	2,930	13,969	14,472	10,962
Accrued expenses	6,092	13,034	10,524	8,517
Income taxes payable	0	0	2,424	182
Timber contracts payable	7,347	16,603	8,336	5,132
Current maturities of long-term debt	2,362	7,611	2,606	2,329
Total current liabilities	$ 18,731	$ 67,617	$ 49,712	$ 38,147
Deferred income taxes payable	0	3,187	2,500	320
Long-term debt, less current maturities	7,457	89,519	64,964	48,721
Senior subordinated debentures	0	22,000	27,000	27,000
Liabilities subject to compromise	126,395	0	0	0
Stockholders' equity:				
Common stock	$ 15,205	$ 15,205	$ 15,835	$ 15,835
Paid-in capital	15	15	15	15
Retained earnings	(61,765)	23,387	24,874	16,044
Total equity	$ (46,545)	$ 38,607	$ 40,724	$ 31,894
Total liabilities and equity	$ 106,038	$ 220,930	$ 184,900	$ 146,082

Source: WTD annual reports and Forms 10K.

EXHIBIT   C14.14   Profitability Comparisons

	Year*				
	1990	**1989**	**1988**	**1987**	**1986**
Operating profit margins:					
Boise Cascade	4.5%	10.8%	6.4%	9.3%	8.7%
Champion International	2.0%	10.2%	6.6%	13.9%	9.9%
Georgia Pacific	7.1%	8.8%	7.1%	8.8%	9.8%
International Paper	2.6%	12.7%	15.6%	13.6%	14.7%
Louisiana Pacific	8.7%	14.4%	10.6%	13.5%	10.1%
Pope and Talbot	−1.6%	9.0%	7.2%	12.6%	11.1%
Weyerhaeuser	9.0%	7.6%	8.3%	11.3%	9.7%
WTD	−35.1%	1.5%	6.1%	7.0%	5.8%
Asset turnover:					
Boise Cascade	1.2	1.3	1.1	1.3	1.2
Champion International	0.4	0.5	0.6	0.6	0.5
Georgia Pacific	1.7	1.8	1.8	2.2	2.0
International Paper	0.7	0.8	0.6	0.8	0.7
Louisiana Pacific	1.1	1.2	1.2	1.1	1.1
Pope and Talbot	1.8	2.1	2.1	2.1	1.8
Weyerhaeuser	1.4	1.6	1.5	1.4	1.2
WTD	1.5	2.3	2.2	2.3	2.5
Return on assets:					
Boise Cascade	5.5%	14.4%	7.3%	12.3%	10.7%
Champion International	0.8%	4.7%	3.6%	8.2%	5.2%
Georgia Pacific	12.4%	15.4%	13.0%	19.1%	20.1%
International Paper	1.8%	9.7%	9.3%	11.4%	9.7%
Louisiana Pacific	9.3%	17.7%	12.3%	15.3%	11.1%
Pope and Talbot	−2.9%	18.9%	15.1%	26.5%	19.6%
Weyerhaeuser	13.0%	12.3%	12.8%	16.2%	11.8%
WTD	−52.3%	3.4%	13.2%	16.6%	14.6%

* Note: WTD figures are based on 8 months in the listed year plus the first 4 months of the following year.

Source: Author's calculations using company annual reports and 10K data.

priced, WTD's variable costs per unit of output rose while plant shutdowns resulted in unused assets and a low asset turnover. Consequently WTD suffered the worst profit margins, greatest reduction in asset turnover, and lowest return on assets. The second poorest performer in 1990 was Pope and Talbot, a company that also relies on purchased logs.

PLAN FOR TURNAROUND

WTD's approach to its turnaround involves drastic downsizing and restructuring its capitalization.

The company has taken action to reduce its scope of operation to only those mills that are profitable and provide cash flow given the log supply and cost situation. Mills that are not well positioned to be profitable in the future have been closed. These closings involved seventeen of WTD's thirty-one operating locations, including five of the seven 1989–1990 acquisitions and both plywood mills. Of the remaining fourteen operating locations, thirteen are producing and the fourteenth, a veneer mill at Goshen, Oregon, will reopen when conditions warrant. Other locations will be shut down if they prove to be unprofitable and the cost of closing is less than the cost of continued operation. Exhibit C14.9 notes WTD mills that have been closed (but not sold) and those currently remaining for operation.

High debt is another problem that WTD has targeted for correction. Its objective is to increase equity relative to debt by converting some of its prebankruptcy unsecured and undersecured debt to equity. The specifics of such conversion and treatment of creditors were expected to be proposed in a formal reorganization due at the end of September 1991. Any such provisions for conversion require agreement by WTD's creditors and shareholders.

Profitable operation, disposal of assets, and protection under bankruptcy laws will be used to improve liquidity and solvency. First, the reduced scale of operations to only those mills with attractive profitability is expected to be a primary source of cash to fund working capital needs. In addition, interest payments are not required for unsecured and undersecured debt. Although interest accrues on secured debt, payment is not required until the company is out of bankruptcy. Therefore, the company can avoid interest payments on both secured and un/undersecured debt, increasing cash for near-term needs. Further, losses in FY 1990 and 1991 provide offsets to future taxes. Operating loss carried forward totaled $38 million for federal income taxes and $35 million for state income taxes. A final potential source of cash for use in turnaround is the sale of assets: WTD intends to sell its 17,000 acres of (harvested) timberlands. This land has a cost basis of $1.4 million. Facilities that were shut down are also planned for divesting or liquidation. These idle facilities are listed at

a net realizable value of $7.8 million (after a $47.5 million reduction in their carrying values).

Of necessity, a hold has been placed on growth, and further commitment to the Port Westward pulp mill has been deferred indefinitely. Other aspects of the WTD strategy remain unaffected. The company will continue to buy its logs just prior to use and intensify its resolve to avoid buying high-priced logs. It will also continue to make investments for greater mill efficiency. The human resource strategy remains unchanged.

In a letter to WTD shareholders, the company's CPA firm, Moss Adams, cautioned that the operating plan for turnaround was based on the following three major assumptions with no assurance they will hold:

1. A supply of raw materials at prices that allow for reasonable margins to operate profitably.

2. The continued ability to utilize the cash collateral authorized by the bankruptcy court.

3. Acceptance by the company's creditors and shareholders of a reorganization plan that allows for the restoration of equity through the conversion of some debt to equity.[16]

ENDNOTES

1. T. Moore and D. Richardson, "Dissent Marks Owl Hearings," *Capital Press*, Salem, OR, September 20, 1991, 1–2.
2. L. Denne, "Forest Products: A Slump in Housing Spells Trouble," *Puget Sound Business Journal*, January 7, 1991, 19, 25.
3. C. E. Brown, "WTD Industries," company analysis, Kidder, Peabody & Co., August 18, 1987, 4.
4. WTD Industries, Inc. Form 10K, 1991.
5. WTD Industries 1988 and 1989 annual reports; 1991 Form 10K.
6. WTD Industries 1987 annual report, 12.
7. D. Arnold, "Risky Business," *Sunday Oregonian Magazine*, August 12, 1988.

8. C. E. Brown, "WTD Industries," company comment, Kidder, Peabody & Co. March 18, 1988, 2.

9. "Pulp Mills Proposed for Oregon," *The Oregonian,* August 25, 1988, and "Questions Asked About WTD's Funding of Mill," *Business Journal* (Portland, Oregon), September 11, 1988.

10. WTD Industries 1989 and 1991 annual reports and Forms 10K.

11. Brown, "WTD Industries," 1989 and Form 10K.

12. Arnold, "Risky Business."

13. Brown, "WTD Industries," 6.

14. WTD Industries, Inc., Form 10K, 1991.

15. Brown, "WTD Industries," 6.

16. WTD Industries, Inc., Form 10K, 1991.

Springboard Software, Inc.

Natalie Tabb Taylor

Babson College

Springboard produces and markets high-quality, high-value software products to satisfy the educational and productivity needs of consumers and students in the home and educational marketplaces.

The company has traditionally produced and continues to produce educational products characterized as aids to help children learn specific curriculums. We are now emphasizing, however, products which help people access data, organize data, understand data, and make wonderful, effective presentations of data.

Thus John Paulson, chairman and chief executive officer of Springboard Software, Inc., in January 1986, summarized his company's primary activities. Springboard had undergone many changes since its founding over three years earlier, as had the industry as a whole. The company had produced several educational products that had been or were currently on the industry's best-seller lists. Substantial growth did not begin for the company, however, until the February 1985 release of The Newsroom, software that made possible the creation of a small newspaper with a personal computer. The success of this product dramatically expanded

the options available to Springboard's management. The most intriguing choice facing John Paulson and Springboard Software early in January 1986 was whether to enter the business segment and, if so, how.

COMPANY BACKGROUND

Springboard Software, Inc. (formerly Counterpoint Software, Inc.), was engaged in the business of developing, marketing, and selling high-quality educational and productivity software products for the home and school marketplaces. Before founding the company, John Paulson had been a music teacher in the public school system of Wayzata, Minnesota. Paulson taught himself computer programming while he was still a teacher. His first computer program was written for his own children and was designed to help them learn basic skills through a series of nine activities. Paulson was careful to design the product so that it would give children a feeling of satisfaction and accomplishment, not frustration: "Young children are seldom in control of anything. A well-designed software program, however, can put them in charge of their computer activities. This helps them develop confidence in themselves and their ability to participate in the world."

The user interface and sound pedagogical principles of this first program made it very effective and popular with children. Paulson decided to market it under the name Early Games for Young Children and assigned it a retail price of $29.95. His first customer was Dayton's, Minneapolis' largest department store. Although the product was not professionally packaged, Dayton's made an initial purchase of twelve units. Sales to consumers were brisk, and Dayton's began a cycle of reordering.

Encouraged by similar experiences with other retail stores, Paulson decided to quit teaching, seek funding, and start an educational software company. The company was incorporated on August 24, 1982, with an initial capitalization of $40,000. Paulson repackaged Early Games, putting a color photo of his daughter on the front. Then he hired two telephone salesmen to follow up with telephone calls a few days later. Even though initial orders were small—between one and ten units—the company began shipping product in October. By December Early Games was the number-2 Apple educational software product in the country. The company broke even in 1982 with sales of $87,000.

In 1983 Springboard added IBM, Atari, Tandy, and Commodore versions of Early Games to its product line. Four new titles with translations for various machine formats were also added. New packaging was developed, and the company began a small advertising campaign. Sales for this first full year in operation reached $750,000.

In August 1983 Cherry Tree Ventures, a Minneapolis venture firm, invested approximately $250,000 in Springboard to help it with cash flow problems and to position it for additional venture capital investments in 1984. At this time the company's board of directors decided to hire a professional manager to function as CEO so that Paulson could focus his efforts on product development. An executive search was undertaken, and an individual with a strong marketing background was found; he became CEO in 1984.

The results of 1984 were not good, however. The company focused its efforts on developing relationships with the mass merchants at the expense of its established channels of distribution, the computer specialty stores. As part of this plan, a considerable amount of money was spent on advertising, packaging, and promoting the growing Springboard line of products to consumers. These expenditures were funded by an additional $2 million of venture capital. Even though five new programs were added to the company's product line in 1984, Springboard lost $1.6 million on roughly $1 million in sales. The company began to experience severe problems with cash flow.

In February 1985 Paulson's product-development team released The Newsroom. It was an immediate and unqualified success, even though it was launched without a single consumer ad or any promotion. Shortly thereafter, John Paulson resumed his position as chief executive officer.

INDUSTRY AND COMPETITION

The microcomputer software industry had experienced dramatic growth in its less than ten years of existence. During 1985, however, the rate of growth slowed. Software sales tended to track the activity of related hardware. Personal computer hardware sales had been in a slump throughout 1985. Industry experts attributed the slowdown to four factors:

- A glut of hardware suppliers and products
- Saturation in the business and home market segments
- Potential buyers waiting for new generations of machines
- The need for new applications software

The market for micro software was subject to rapid changes in technology. In order to succeed, a firm had to be able (1) to create innovative new products reflecting technological changes in hardware and software as well as customer needs, and (2) to translate current products into newly accepted hardware formats in order to gain and maintain market share. By 1986 the supply of software products exceeded demand. Retail shelf space was limited; hence competition intensified as increased emphasis was placed on price concessions, brand recognition, advertising, and dealer merchandising.

Rapid sales growth attracted a variety of players into the software industry. Such hardware manufacturers as IBM, Apple, Commodore, and Atari had integrated backward into software development. As hardware prices decreased and equipment became increasingly indistinguishable to consumers, software was becoming the primary means of adding value. Apple, for example, bundled a word-processing program and graphics program with every Macintosh it sold. Software helped manufacturers differentiate their hardware from competitors' offerings.

Some companies whose primary activities were in other industries had diversified into the software industry as well. Book publishers, for example, had entered the education market in order to capitalize on their established contacts and channels of distribution.

A separate group of companies competed in software only and were referred to as independents or third-party software houses. Independent software companies tended to be privately held and functioned as either developers or publishers. Developers wrote programs and licensed them to publishers. Most publishers licensed programs and provided the expertise and resources required to bring programs to market. Few were involved in both development and publishing. Most began as publishers, but increased competition forced them into development only or else drove them out of business altogether. The industry was currently undergoing a shakeout. Management believed more casualties would occur in the near future, creating potential opportunities for the surviving publishers.

While there were approximately 3,500 companies competing in the software industry, Springboard had roughly fifty direct competitors in the home and school market. No single company competed directly with Springboard's product line on a title-by-title basis. Sales figures for competitors were difficult to get, since the majority of these companies were privately owned. Competitor profiles, prepared by Springboard personnel, can be found in Exhibit C15.1.

PRODUCTS

In the first two years of its history, Springboard produced educational products for children. By 1986 the emphasis had shifted to products designed to help people of all ages become more productive in their lives at home and at school.

The cornerstone of Springboard's product-development philosophy was product usefulness. John Paulson explained:

Many of our competitors have entered this marketplace with a callous disregard for the consumer's wants and needs. They have often underestimated both the intelligence of the consumer and the importance of the technology. Humans are tool users, after all, and the computer is the most important, versatile tool ever created. To market products which exploit consumers' naiveté and superficial curiosity is counterproductive indeed. The quick sales may be made, but eventually the consumer will realize that money has been spent on something that is not useful. It will be some time before that consumer considers buying software again.

Furthermore, the growth of computer penetration is slowed considerably by those who market poorly conceptualized software that does not represent a real value to the consumer. When a potential computer buyer investigates the available software, he or she is often reassured that there is no persuasive reason to own a computer. It may be months, even years before that consumer bothers to investigate a computer purchase again. And when the consumer does return to the computer store, the first question will still be "Why do I need a computer?" It is up to the software developers and marketers to provide compelling reasons.

That is why each and every product Springboard produces is, first and foremost, very useful. Each product takes advantage of the computer's unique capabilities to help people do things they want to do in ways more efficient, more effective,

continued

EXHIBIT C15.1   Profiles of Springboard Software's Competitors

	Generic Strategy	Strengths	Weaknesses	General Information
Spinnaker	Low-cost producer; branding Breadth of line/access to shelf 60% in mass retail—first on the scene Price-sensitive Preemptive shelf-space managers	First mover/shelf control Strong marketing management Strong financing Diverse line Many offerings Big ad dollars = reviews Continuity in marketplace Slick marketeers Have executed a plan Video tape concept supports MVR strength	Defective disks and programs Lost First Software MVRs want hits, not full line Dependent on MVRs Working capital in channel (no controls) Weak quality image in schools especially Dependent on C64 base Inconsistent quality/appeal due to unrelated authors/sources; not highly thought of in traditional channels of distribution	
Broderbund	Focused on basic needs of less sophisticated users	"Hot" products—item merchants 30% MVR (C64 version of Print Shop), 70% specialty Product strategy = Apple hit to C64 Royalty strategy (reduced royalties as percent of revenues from 33% to 28%) Reduced administrative costs from 21% to 13%—talent spotters Probably attract freelance authors Not promotional or price oriented International dealings, good connection with Japan and MSX First move in "genres"—"good enough" product/user accessible: 20% tech→80% need of consumer	Marketing not POS Milk products Need items Lack of franchise on names Second-rate packaging Apple is 60% of sales, IBM only 16%	1984 sales of $11M, net income of $500 K Discount (55%); terms (30 days); freight (FOB headquarters); no coop; defective (return for replacement only); stock bal (10% of purchases over last 120 days) Policies set in stone, they do not bargain and are tough to work with Sales management left 3/85; company run by finance people Order fulfillment good but takes 3–5 weeks Support distributors, do not sell direct Produce home and personal productivity programs under $100 Games account for 20% of sales Planning product line based on hobbies and pursuits Bought Synapse in 1984 for $450K, may be looking for others

continued

EXHIBIT C15.1 *continued*

	Generic Strategy	Strengths	Weaknesses	General Information
Random House	Differentiated Educational (mostly), some productivity and entertainment High price	Strong financing Great licenses: Peanuts, Garfield, Potato Head Both in-house programming and external licensing 28 new programs in 1984; expect 18 new titles in 1985 Division for school market: internal sales staff and packaging Sell Handleman, two titles—is this a strength?	No major hits Not currently selling Softsel Heavy reliance on education (starting to do utilities/entertainment) Me-too packaging Me-too marketing Weak in IBM format	Division formed in 1982 Dominant format is Apple, some C64, weak in IBM PC
CBS Software	Differentiated Entertainment, education	Financial strength Offers extremely good terms Ability to market to the consumer (entertainment business) Name recognition @ 37 titles, breadth of line Strong distribution (retail service reps—good or bad?) Licensed famous characters (e.g., Big Bird) Ads in *Time, Newsweek, People* Promotions: Buy Felony and get another title free plus $5 refund Parent and associated companies	Trying to be all things to all people Maybe too big, not in tune with pulse of industry Service No big winners in product line Small presence at CES—are they getting out of business? Rumored to be losing money High return rate, low satisfaction MVR is 50% of business, schools 10% Specialty stores declining (40%) Me-too packaging Focus on C64 and Atari; changing to IBM, Apple Licenses are costly	Main sales team has been fired Planning ad shift toward schools Changing to S.A.T. types and home productivity Outside sales reps may start calling on large school districts

EXHIBIT C15.1 *continued*

	Generic Strategy	Strengths	Weaknesses	General Information
Davidson and Associates	Focused	Focused on basic skills (utility) All five products sell well (three on charts) Weak marketing works Little known about them	Only five products Original product is cash cow (3 years old) Questionable product-development capability Packaging/marketing *appears* weak	Founded 1982 1983 sales, $750,000 1984 sales, $2,500,000
EPYX	Differentiated Entertainment and utility products	Profitable in April and May Licenses: Barbie Dolls, G.I. Joe, Hotwheels, Olympics, etc. Have been able to choose their distribution channels Hot product (Fastload for C64)	Lost $500,000 in 1984 Computer specialty stores generate only 40% of revenue Mass merchants generate 60% Heavy reliance on entertainment software (starting to do utilities) Me-too packaging Me-too marketing Primarily C64 revenues (trying to change to Apple/IBM) Probably pay heavy fees for licenses and royalties Uphill battle to change image from entertainment to anything better	Founded 1978 as Automated Simulations, Inc. Name change to EPYX 1983 Product philosophy, according to Bob Botch, marketing director, is to slow down new product intros because of slower growth rate of home computer market: • New products require more planning • Increased support for products • Used to sell entertainment but now concentrating on utility products • Expanding line to include high-end machines Used to intro 25 titles per year, now down to 10–15; they will support only the best-selling titles Botch thinks Apple and IBM computers have more active users and longer life cycles Most successful product is Fast-load for C64 (retail of $30–$50): initially represented 50% of sales, now represents 15%; thus they plan to release more Hardware/software utilities as well as home productivity

continued

EXHIBIT C15.1 *continued*

	Generic Strategy	Strengths	Weaknesses	General Information
Houghton Mifflin	Focused "The 150-year-old software company" selling as an old established schoolbook publisher (*American Heritage Dictionary*, Iowa Test of Basic Skills)	Well recognized and highly regarded by its market (schools) Money Solid and deep penetration of the school market Good, consistent image in the product line; packaged by well-defined series Reasonable and stable pricing (c. $39.95) Established line of reps to schools Relatively alone in an unusual niche—business education (do more series; instructional aids to PFS, Lotus, Multiplan)	Limited distribution, almost 100% to schools through reps. SoftKat is an exclusive and their only access to the consumer market via retail. Very weak distribution at retail level No best-sellers Software such a nominal part of their business, may account for the relatively low profile in the industry and to the consumer Depends entirely on outside sources for software development and conversion Very limited promotional material; advertising restricted to school magazines Drill-and-practice-type software uninspired	
Hayden	"Throw a lot of titles at the wall and see what sticks" (50+ titles in a wide range of software categories; education, business, entertainment, productivity)	Diverse line going to the largest segments of the market (education, business, entertainment, productivity) Strong representation in the MAC world with five best-sellers: Ensemble, I Know It's Here Somewhere, Hayden Speller (all MAC only, business and productivity best-sellers); Sargon III, Music Works (MAC conversion from Apple) Eight bestsellers in all categories mentioned: Ensemble, I Know It's Here Somewhere, Hayden Speller, Sargon III, Music Works, Score Improvement System (Mac), Holy Grail Company name recognition Established channel through reps to retailers	Rely almost entirely on reps Lack of branding or consistent image throughout product line; confusing and weak packaging Maybe cash-poor; Consumer Electronics Show (CES) was financially hard on them and a "complete bust" Dependent on outside for virtually all software development/conversion Educational line is graphically dry and not at all their best performer; emphasizing productivity and business software	

continued

EXHIBIT C15.1 *concluded*

	Generic Strategy	Strengths	Weaknesses	General Information
Grolier Electronic Publishing, Inc.	Differentiated. Goal is to use electronic media to deliver information and educational programs in a timely, unique manner in ways that have never before been possible Currently participates in several market niches: • Productivity (spreadsheets, data base, graphs) • Interactive adult computer adventure programs • Educational (pre-elem levels) new 6/85	A subsidiary of Grolier, Inc., world's leading publisher of encyclopedias Good management team with emphasis on publishing and microcomputer software sales and marketing Strong financial backing from parent company Product line has 20 titles (Apple/IBM/Comm 64) Retail pricing mostly $30-$50 range Has comprehensive advertising plan to support sales Introduced Miss Mouse and Ryme Land reading-readiness software for kids (4-7) Can leverage Grolier name and reputation for quality educational materials	Staried in 1982; just entered software field in 1984 Majority of programs were just released and many are scheduled for release in next few months No products on the hit lists yet	

and more satisfying than they could possibly do without the computer. Every Springboard program provides an excellent reason for having a computer.

By year-end 1985 Springboard had a total of thirteen program titles, most of which were available in a variety of machine formats. Exhibit C15.2 provides information about Springboard's product line. Three of the titles listed were about to be discontinued because they did not represent the level of sophistication exhibited by the other products in terms of concept, design, or execution.

By September 1985 The Newsroom had become the best-selling home computer program in the United States, according to the *Softsel Hot List*, the industry's guide to best-selling software programs at the wholesale level. In October this program tied for places 9 through 14 at 2 percent in terms of unit market share of leading titles, regardless of category, as shown in the third graph in Exhibit C15.3. By year-end 1985 The Newsroom and related programs accounted for roughly three-quarters of Springboard's unit sales.

The second largest contributor to sales was Early Games for Young Children, Paulson's first program. Sold primarily in the home market for use by preschoolers, Early Games had been identified early in 1985 by *The Wall Street Journal* as the nation's fourth-best-seller in microcomputer educational software.

The company stood behind every title it sold with a guarantee that was rarely found in the industry: If a consumer was not satisfied for any reason, the product could be returned directly to Springboard for a full refund. To date, returns totaled less than 1 percent of sales.

EXHIBIT   C15.2   Springboard Product Series and Titles as of November 1985

Series and Titles	Date of Introduction	Suggested Age Group	Suggested Retail Price
Early Games Series			
Early Games for Young Children	September 1982	2 1/2–6	$ 34.95
Stickers	March 1984	4–12	34.95
Easy as ABC	June 1984	3–6	39.95
Music Maestro*	May 1983	4–10	34.95
Make a Match*	September 1983	2 1/2–6	29.95
Skill Builders Series			
Piece of Cake Math	September 1983	7–13	34.95
Fraction Factory	September 1983	8–14	29.95
Creative Paths Series			
Rainbow Painter	June 1984	4 and up	34.95
The Newsroom	February 1985		59.95
Clip Art Collection, Vol. 1	June 1985		29.95
Puzzle Master	September 1984	4 and up	34.95
Mask Parade	September 1984	4–12	39.95
Family Series			
Quizagon*	June 1984	Teens and adults	44.95

* Soon to be discontinued.

Source: Springboard Software, Inc.

EXHIBIT C15.3 Market Share of Software Publishers and Titles, October 1985

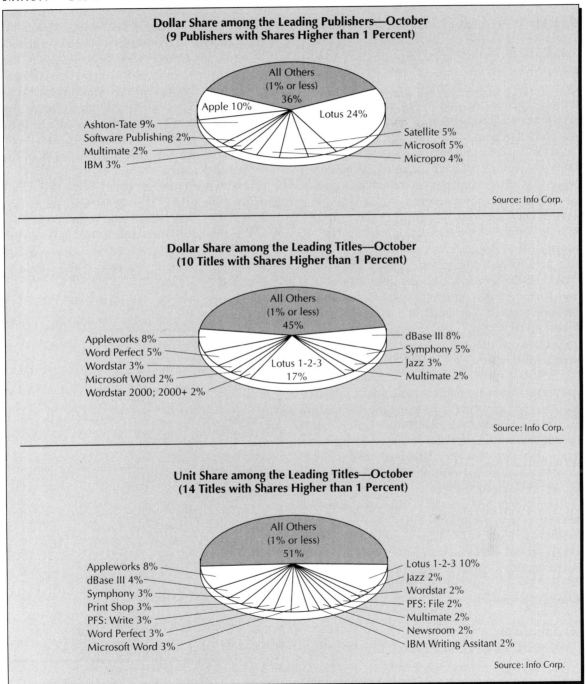

Dollar Share among the Leading Publishers—October
(9 Publishers with Shares Higher than 1 Percent)

All Others (1% or less) 36%
Apple 10%
Lotus 24%
Ashton-Tate 9%
Software Publishing 2%
Multimate 2%
IBM 3%
Satellite 5%
Microsoft 5%
Micropro 4%

Source: Info Corp.

Dollar Share among the Leading Titles—October
(10 Titles with Shares Higher than 1 Percent)

All Others (1% or less) 45%
Appleworks 8%
Word Perfect 5%
Wordstar 3%
Microsoft Word 2%
Wordstar 2000; 2000+ 2%
Lotus 1-2-3 17%
dBase III 8%
Symphony 5%
Jazz 3%
Multimate 2%

Source: Info Corp.

Unit Share among the Leading Titles—October
(14 Titles with Shares Higher than 1 Percent)

All Others (1% or less) 51%
Appleworks 8%
dBase III 4%
Symphony 3%
Print Shop 3%
PFS: Write 3%
Word Perfect 3%
Microsoft Word 3%
Lotus 1-2-3 10%
Jazz 2%
Wordstar 2%
PFS: File 2%
Multimate 2%
Newsroom 2%
IBM Writing Assitant 2%

Source: Info Corp.

Source: *Computer Retail News,* December 16, 1985, p.72. Copyright © 1985 by CMP Publications, Inc., 600 Community Drive, Manhasset, NY 11030. Reprinted with permission from *Computer Retail News.*

CUSTOMER MARKETS

Roughly 75 percent of Springboard's sales were made to the home market, primarily through computer specialty stores. Most of the remainder were to schools, through either educational distributors or local retail outlets. Approximately 5 percent of sales were through exclusive distribution agreements in countries other than the United States.

During 1985 management determined that Springboard did not have the resources to penetrate the education market effectively. As a result, the company entered into a licensing agreement with Scholastic Software, Inc., to distribute a special school edition of The Newsroom in the United States and Canada. Under this arrangement, Scholastic would produce a school package that included a teacher's guide and backup disks, capabilities that Springboard did not possess. Packaged in a Scholastic box, the program would be prominently identified as a Springboard product. Scholastic would sell the school edition for $75.

Scholastic had an excellent reputation in the industry. Other noted companies had entered into similar arrangements with the company. Intentional Educations, for instance, had licensed a Scholasticized version of its hit program Bank Street Writer. Scholastic had a large direct sales force that was already selling a variety of products to schools.

A potential drawback to this arrangement was that Springboard could not prevent Scholastic from selling the school edition to retail stores, where it would compete with Springboard's consumer version of The Newsroom. Management felt that this possibility represented a minor threat.

PRODUCT DEVELOPMENT

Springboard was unusual in the industry in that it developed its products in-house. Management believed that internal development facilitated control of product quality, expense, and schedule. The firm's recent experience with translations of The Newsroom had brought this point home clearly. When demand developed for an IBM version of the best-selling program, the translation had to be subcontracted because Springboard had no IBM programmers. Commissioned in February for March delivery, the translation was not completed until late July. Bringing this translation to market had taken much longer and had cost much more than the firm had anticipated.

The experience, coupled with the rapid growth in the IBM PC's installed base (shown in Exhibit C15.4), prompted management to augment its in-house programming staff with a team of IBM programmers. Management continued to explore outside sources for new products in order to:

EXHIBIT   C15.4

Installed Base of Home and Personal Computers, Year-End 1982–1984 (in thousands of units)

Computer Model	1982	1983	1984
Apple II/IIe/IIc	500	900	2,000
Apple Macintosh	—	—	265
IBM PC/XT/AT	700	1,300	2,200
IBM PCjr	—	275	275
Commodore 64	1,100	1,500	3,100
Commodore 128			
All others*	800	1,200	2,700
All models	3,100	5,175	10,540

* Includes Radio Shack TRS 80. Tandy 1000/1200/2000, Atari.

Source: *Marketing Technology,* January 1985.

- Expand its product line more rapidly
- Reduce product development risk
- Encourage cross-fertilization of ideas
- Develop specific expertise within certain organizations

Springboard was also unusual in the industry in that it had a proprietary code that allowed for the electronic transfer of graphics among incompatible IBM, Apple II, Macintosh, and Commodore computers. Since educational products tended to be graphics oriented, this capability dramatically reduced the resources required to translate programs from one machine to another. As Paulson explained:

Springboard has this unusual capability because it has an extraordinarily skilled and dedicated product-development team. State-of-the-art programmers are supported by a staff of experienced computer artists and child development specialists. The programmers have displayed a remarkable ability to adapt to different machines as required by the marketplace.

All Springboard products were written in assembly code. Although use of higher-level languages reduced product-development time, Springboard products tended to require an assembly code in order to maximize the limited capabilities of popular computers. A program as advanced as The Newsroom, for instance, could not be developed for a 64K Apple II computer in Pascal, C, Forth, or any other compiled language. While use of assembly language increased product-development time, it also made it more difficult for competitors to imitate Springboard's programs.

Another characteristic of the code developed for Springboard products was its evolutionary nature. Each product under development presented programming challenges that, when solved, provided a steppingstone to the next product. The programmers had methodically developed a library of software tools that could easily be adapted to specific program needs, thereby reducing development time for future

products. As a result, Springboard's existing product line represented a progression in programming capabilities that was marked by what was referred to internally as generations. In addition, current programs provided revenues to help fund programs under development.

In program development, Paulson placed top priority on developing families of products with the same relationship as a razor to razor blades:

The Newsroom, for example, is a powerful graphics/text presentation program that comes with over 600 wonderful, useful pieces of clip art. The number 600 is an interesting one in that it represents a real value to the consumer. Yet, after using The Newsroom for a while, the consumer realized that this amount of clip art has only whetted his or her appetite. That's why we are developing the Clip Art Collection. With our three outstanding computer artists we can create as many volumes of clip art as necessary to satisfy Newsroom users. To date, we have released Clip Art Collection Volume I and are thinking about releasing a Volume II featuring business clip art. Volume I sells very well, second only to The Newsroom.

Our ability to transfer graphics between incompatible computers electronically makes our razor blades very attractive. Once the art has been created, it takes only hours to make it available on all machine formats. Furthermore, as we continue to market high-quality applications programs which use clip art, a larger and larger installed based of users will be purchasing the Clip Art Collection.

Springboard created products for proven hardware only. New computer brands and models had to establish a user base before management would allocate resources to support them.

PRODUCTION

Springboard subcontracted disk duplication and product packaging. The company currently had several suppliers. Management preferred to pay a slight premium for duplication and packaging in order to work with local suppliers.

Management had evaluated and expected to continue to evaluate the benefits of integrating backware into disk duplication. Disk duplication was not considered to be technically difficult, but experienced individuals were required to oversee this kind of operation. Bulk disks, for instance, required special handling. Duplication had to take place in a climate-controlled room, equipped with special air purifiers. Although prices were dropping, duplication equipment was still very expensive. Packaging was a separate operation requiring specialized equipment and tended to be labor-intensive.

There appeared to be a trend toward in-house duplication among the larger software companies. Most of Springboard's direct competitors, however, did not perform their own disk duplication. Springboard's management felt that the economies of scale were not yet available to make backward integration superior to present supplier arrangements.

The company leased approximately 5,000 square feet of office space for an annual rental of approximately $96,000 in a Minneapolis suburb. The lease was to expire in 1988. The company's executive, marketing, product development, and operations were located at these facilities.

MARKETING AND DISTRIBUTION

A key conclusion of the early 1984 business plan was that Springboard should shift emphasis to the mass-volume retailer (MVR) channel of distribution. As a result, a mass-marketing strategy was developed. This strategy was fashioned after that of Spinnaker Software, the industry's fastest-growing educational software company at the time. Spinnaker was the first company to apply sophisticated consumer marketing techniques to the selling of micro software. This approach bought it a considerable amount of shelf space in such major U.S. MVRs as Sears, Kmart, and Toys R Us.

When Springboard adopted a similar strategy, it began to neglect the distributors and computer specialty stores that were its traditional channels of distribution. An example of this neglect was the manner in which the company changed its name from Counterpoint to Springboard. The change was not effectively communicated to retailers, and they mistakenly assumed that Counterpoint had gone out of business; Springboard was simply a new company they had never heard of. The result was a dramatic decrease in shelf space for Springboard's existing products and minimal access for its new products.

Financial results for 1984 did not meet expectations. Gross sales of well over $3 million were forecast for the year; actual sales barely reached $1 million. Paulson believed the shortfall was created primarily by the unwise and unsuccessful shift to the MVR channel of distribution as well as callous handling of existing accounts and ineffective use of resources. Springboard had considerably less distribution in the fourth quarter (the peak season) of 1984 than it had enjoyed in 1983.

Springboard's disappointing performance was masked somewhat by the problems suffered by the industry as a whole. Research firms had predicted a 100-percent increase in 1984 educational software sales, but they actually rose only 60 percent. Spinnaker, for example, posted $15 million in sales, a fraction of the $50+ million its management had projected for the year. As a result, the ability of mass merchants to sell software and the effectiveness of large ad budgets and mass-marketing techniques in general became topics of debate in the industry.

When Paulson took over again as CEO in 1985, he steered the company back to its original distribution channels: computer specialty stores that purchased from the company's wholesale distributor. Customers were once again the focus of Springboard's marketing and sales efforts. Paulson had not ruled out the Spinnaker strategy entirely, however. He explained:

At this time, the big-dollar marketing approach to consumer software is not leading to success. It can achieve moderate sales levels, but only at the sacrifice of profitability. Word of mouth from an army of satisfied customers is far more effective than a large ad budget. This may change in the future, however. It is important that we continue to evaluate just exactly what marketing techniques are effective and how much capital they require.

The company continued to support its dominant mode of distribution, wholesale distributors, as it attempted to expand into large chains of computer specialty stores. Management was cautiously testing distribution through certain MVRs as well as new forms of distribution, such as electronic distribution and direct marketing. Springboard's international distribution strategy was to expand through the use of agents and licensing agreements. The company's top four customers accounted for 18, 15, 14, and 12 percent of total gross sales volume during 1985.

FINANCE

Springboard had net sales of $889,750 and a $1.6 million net loss in 1984, the most recent fiscal year for which information was available. Unaudited financial results for the first nine months of fiscal 1985 indicated that the company was profitable on $3,066.000 in net sales. Exhibits C15.5 and C15.6 show historical and recent financial information on the company. While final results were not yet in, year-end 1985 sales were expected to approach the $6 million mark.

Springboard made a small public offering in Minnesota in 1983, which was exempt from SEC requirements for public financial reporting under Regulation A because of its small size and the limited number of shares sold. Roughly 8 percent of the 1.6 million shares currently outstanding were traded publicly through a second-tier Minneapolis broker who made a market in the stock. Shares had traded in the $2 to $3 range over the last year. As of January 1986 the company's major shareholders with their respective holdings were as follows:

Cherry Tree Venture Capital	30%
Former chairman and CEO	15%
V. Suarez, private investor	10%
John Paulson	4%

The company currently had $1 million credit line, consisting of a $150,000 term loan on fixed assets and a formula-based working capital loan of $850,000. Springboard had paid no dividends to date.

ORGANIZATIONAL STRUCTURE AND MANAGEMENT PHILOSOPHY

During 1985, three full-time employees were added to the company—two for the newly created Customer Support group and one for the Marketing Department. by January 1986, Springboard had twenty-four employees in all, as Exhibit C15.7 indicates. Contractors were hired to augment such capabilities as advertising, public relations, and production. Although the company had experienced a lot of change in its short history, Paulson felt confident about the personnel and Springboard's outlook:

> The most important, wonderful asset of Springboard is the people. The management team is experienced, competent, and dedicated. This is critical since Springboard is in a constant state of change. The growth rate of the company and of the industry in general requires that management respond appropriately to a variety of problems and opportunities.
>
> All of the employees are capable and share a common commitment. It is not unusual to hear people talking at lunch about ways they can improve efficiency or solve a problem. They know they can freely discuss their feelings about what the company is doing and share their ideas and suggestions with management.

It is my job to make certain that everyone understands and appreciates the importance of their unique roles within the company, how their responsibilities interrelate, and how much the company values their participation. From the very beginning I have insisted that all employees participate in the company's incentive stock option plan. I want all of our goals and hopes to

EXHIBIT   C15.5   Springboard Software, Inc., Balance Sheet, 1982–1984

	1984	1983	1982
Assets			
Current assets:			
Cash and cash equivalents	$ 408,469	$ 73,206	$ 14,372
Accounts receivable, less allowance for doubtful accounts: 1984, $23,953; 1983, $10,000	354,455	273,252	35,561
Inventories	153,605	112,505	7,387
Prepaid expenses	74,882	1,286	478
Total current assets	$ 991,411	$ 460,249	$ 54,798
Other assets:			
Certificate of deposit	$ 150,000	$ —	$ —
Property and equipment, at cost	227,849	30,737	1,333
Less accumulated depreciation	(39,635)	(4,904)	(45)
Product rights	—	1,229	2,364
Total other assets	$ 338,214	$ 27,062	$ 3,652
Total assets	$ 1,329,625	$ 487,311	$ 58,450
Liabilities and Shareholders' Equity			
Current liabilities:			
Accounts payable	$ 221,293	$ 154,438	$ 1,048
Working capital bank loan	154,608		
Current portion of long-term debt	37,500		
Accrued liabilities			
Payroll and taxes withheld	12,857	31,162	9,762
Vacation pay	10,732	2,515	
Other	56,230	2,423	
Total current liabilities	$ 493,220	$ 190,538	$ 10,810
Long-term debt less current portion	103,125		
Total liabilities	$ 596,345	$ 190,538	$ 10,810
Shareholders' equity:			
Convertible preferred	$ 83,737	$ 14,000	$ —
Common stock	7,850	5,350	4,100
Additional paid-in capital	2,363,490	384,654	43,400
Retained earnings (deficit)	(1,721,797)	(107,231)	140
Total equity	$ 733,280	$ 296,773	$ 47,640
Total liabilities and shareholders' equity	$ 1,329,625	$ 487,311	$ 58,450

Source: Springboard Software, Inc., *Annual Report*, 1985.

be harmonious. I will work hard to ensure that everyone who is contributing to our success will share fairly in its rewards.

Springboard is not, after all, a factory. It is not buildings or disks or cash flow. Our most important asset is our people. We depend upon them for the expertise, insight, and creativity that success demands. And they deliver. They are determined to transform programs into best-selling products, problems into worthwhile opportunities, and Springboard into one of the most respected leaders of this fascinating industry.

FUTURE EXPANSION PLANS

By January 1986, although home and school remained Springboard's primary markets, management was considering creating business editions of some titles. Paulson described the situation in this way:

Because productivity titles are more useful to a wider variety of people, they have the potential of being sold into the business marketplace. The Newsroom, for instance, is the most popular program currently being sold to schools in America as well as being a best-seller to the home market. We anticipated sales into each of these markets when we developed the program. The interest of the business world in The Newsroom, however, came as a surprise. It has many capabilities business people want to have.

Paulson felt that sales of this program into the business market would be inhibited by the following factors:

EXHIBIT C15.6 Springboard Software, Inc., Statement of Operations, Years Ended December 31, 1984 and 1983, and from August 24, 1982, through December 31, 1982

	1984	1983	1982
Gross revenue	$ 1,017,773	$ 766,100	$ 87,062
Less: Sales returns*	128,123	42,452	0
Net revenue	$ 889,650	$ 723,648	$ 87,062
Cost of sales	471,776	232,227	20,589
Gross profit*	$ 417,874	$ 491,311	$ 66,473
Percent of net sales	47.0%	67.9%	76.4%
Operating expenses			
Marketing	$ 816,967		
Sales	264,631	$ 282,062	$ 31,565
General and administrative	490,628	231,665	18,358
Research and development	411,967	92,290	16,645
Interest expense	35,473	0	0
Other	12,774	(7,335)	(235)
Total operating expenses	$ 2,032,440	$ 598,682	$ 66,333
Net profit (loss) before income tax	$(1,614,566)	$ (107,371)	$ 140
Income tax expense	0	0	0
Net profit (loss)	$(1,614,566)	$ (107,371)	$ 140
Net loss per common share	$ (2.92)	$ (0.22)	
Weighted average common shares outstanding	552,077	493,333	400,833

* Reflects one-time product line changes: write-off of Counterpoint inventory.

Source: Springboard Software, Inc.

- The packaging featured a picture of a high school newspaper
- The clip art included was not business-oriented
- The price point was too low to get the support of business retail outlets
- The program copy protection would be considered to be inconvenient

This situation required careful consideration, however, for it was likely to be repeated with other productivity programs currently under development, which, when completed, would represent a new generation of Springboard products.

A separate issue to be addressed was the disappointing sales performance of some of the company's other programs that Paulson perceived to be superior in quality to competitive offerings. In Paulson's words:

> Although Early Games continues to sell well and The Newsroom is a tremendous success, other titles are not reaching their sales potential. Mask Parade, Rainbow Painter, Stickers, and Puzzle Master are all outstanding products but they do not sell as well as they should. Easy as ABC, for instance, is often cited by dealers, teachers, and parents as the best alphabet program on the market, but it is consistently outsold by competing products which are nowhere near as good. Increasing the sales of these particular titles is one of the important challenges facing Springboard management.

> Our overall challenge is how to best use limited dollars to sell Springboard products. Is it possible to promote the company brand or is it safer to promote specific titles? How can management protect the strong growth of The Newsroom and related products and still develop sales for the titles which are not achieving their potential? What is the best way to release the new products? What role does trade advertising play? How should it be balanced with consumer ads? What monies should be dedicated to promotions, point-of-purchase displays, and other related tactics?

With these thoughts in mind, Paulson turned his attention to the 1986 report on the microcomputer applications software industry.

EXHIBIT C15.7 Springboard Software, Inc., Organizational Chart, November 1985

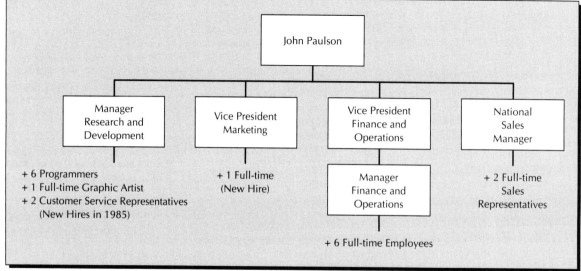

Source: Springboard Software, Inc.

STM Technology, Inc.

Raymond M. Kinnunen
Northeastern University

John A. Seeger
Bentley College

James F. Molloy, Jr.
Northeastern University

It was May of 1990, and Jerry Budinoff—founder, president and 80-percent owner of STM Technology, Inc., sat in his office, looking at the large framed print on the wall. It showed a C-130 military transport plane, the kind Jerry had navigated for two years in Vietnam. "That's what I want this company to be," he said. "A vehicle, capable of supporting large-scale projects in systems development. A rugged vehicle. The C-130 is exciting to fly and tough to shoot down."

Jerry grinned as he contrasted that vision for the future with the short-run plans facing his nine-person firm. "First, we have to develop the expanded system features demanded by our present customers. Then I have to rewrite the business plan in order to attract $900,000 in new capital. Then I'll switch back to my salesman role, to bring in the new business." He mused about the change in his thinking about the company's growth:

Originally I thought if you developed good software and supported it well, you would be successful. That was all you had to worry about. That got us up to this point, but we really won't go any further until I worry about the business stuff.

We're at $3–4 million a year in revenue now, but it isn't going to get any bigger without marketing, distribution, people, money—all of them. Just doing good software doesn't get it any bigger than this.

I just figured that out. It hit me like a club. It's that simple. We never had a business plan. We never had any long-range plan. The company just grew.

STM Technology, Inc., located near Boston in Acton, Massachusetts, was founded in 1983 to exploit Jerry Budinoff's skills in systems design and application. The first commercial customer was a small mental health center; STM had gone on to specialize in microcomputer-based management information systems for smaller health care providers and non-profit human service agencies. The product STM offered was more than just software. The company sold total systems: its customer support department provided training, software support, and consulting services, while its hardware and network department provided hardware, multi-user local area networks, and on-site maintenance services.

Since its founding, STM had installed some 129 systems in a wide variety of outpatient health care facilities. Revenues had grown steadily since 1983 and the company had been consistently profitable (see Exhibit C16.1). By 1989 the company had developed a hospital management system based on personal computers—the first to run on PCs, according to Budi-

EXHIBIT C16.1   STM Technology, Inc., Comparative Balance Sheet
For Years Ending December 31, 1985–1989 ($=thousands)

	1985	1986	1987	1988	1989
Assets					
Current assets:					
Cash	—	$ 55	$ 89	$ 83	$ 79
Accounts receivable	—	—	73	90	127
Supplies	—	—	1	2	7
Prepaid income taxes	—	—	—	15	3
Total current assets	—	$ 55	$ 163	$ 190	$ 216
Property and equipment, at cost:					
Equipment	$ 21	$ 26	$ 35	$ 47	$ 59
Motor vehicles	14	14	14	40	40
	$ 34	$ 39	$ 48	$ 86	$ 98
Less accumulated depreciation	14	22	32	45	59
Net property and equipment	$ 20	$ 17	$ 16	$ 41	$ 40
Miscellaneous costs	—	—	—	—	—
Organization costs	3	2	2	1	—
Total assets	$ 23	$ 74	$ 180	$ 232	$ 256
Liabilities and Stockholders' Equity					
Current liabilities:					
Accounts payable	$ 4	$ 5	$ 10	$ 12	$ 25
Accrued taxes	—	27	13	—	—
Deferred taxes	—	—	4	4	7
Deferred revenue	—	—	63	70	76
Total current liabilities	$ 4	$ 33	$ 90	$ 86	$ 108
Notes payable—stockholders	22	24	22	48	48
Total liabilities	$ 26	$ 57	$ 112	$ 134	$ 156
Stockholders' equity:					
Common stock, no par value;					
1,250 shares issued and outstanding	$ 4	$ 4	$ 4	$ 4	$ 4
Retained earnings	−7	14	64	94	96
Total stockholders' equity	$ −3	$ 18	$ 68	$ 98	$ 100
Total liabilities and stockholders' equity	$ 23	$ 74	$ 180	$ 232	$ 256

noff. This new product development prompted him to seek outside financing for STM, which had, until this point, financed its growth internally (see Exhibits C16.2a and C16.2b). Budinoff had concluded that proper exploitation of this new product and other systems required financial backing (see Exhibit C16.3).

THE MICROCOMPUTER SOFTWARE INDUSTRY

In the early 1980s, following the introduction of IBM's personal computer and wide market acceptance of microcomputers, demand for application software skyrocketed. Hundreds—

EXHIBIT   C16.2a   STM Technology, Inc., Comparative Statement of Income
For Years Ending December 31, 1985–1989 ($=thousands)

	1985	1986	1987	1988	1989
Sales and service	$ 93	$ 331	$ 555	$ 680	$ 700
Cost of sales and service	64	174	404	353	380
Gross profit	28	157	151	327	320
General and administrative costs	—	—	78	144	184
Product development costs	—	—	—	148	133
Total operating expenses	28	133	78	292	317
Income from operations	—	24	73	35	3
Interest income	1	1	4	3	3
Interest expense	—	—	3	5	5
Miscellaneous income	—	—	—	3	1
Miscellaneous expenses	—	1	—	—	—
Income before provision for income taxes	1	25	73	37	3
Provision for income taxes	—	4	23	7	1
Net income	$ 1	$ 21	$ 51	$ 30	$ 2

then thousands—of individual entrepreneurs founded businesses as designers, programmers, distributors, or retailers of computer software. By 1988 there were approximately 30,000 micro-computer software manufacturers in the United States, producing more than 70,000 products, according to the CIRR Index, 1989. In the Boston area alone, the "Business to Business" telephone directory listed 906 computer software and service firms and 555 computer systems designers and consultants.

This proliferation of entrants in the industry required firms to do more than just produce technologically sound products, if they wished to grow. By 1990 success in the industry called for brand development and firm name recognition, marketing and support, and product development and enhancement. Business expertise in marketing, sales, and support became increasingly more significant as prerequisites for success. Jerry Budinoff commented on the importance of providing service:

> Hardware and software require a lot of support. Technology changes quickly, and if you're not supporting the changes they just run by you.

We're small, but we try to provide all of the services. That's what really sells our products. It's not just the system; it's all of the training and support. A system is not just software. It's the whole human element and you have to concentrate on the people side with your service organization. Without that we'd be out of business.

THE HEALTH CARE INDUSTRY

For several decades expenditures on health care had represented the fastest growing sector of the American economy. The adoption of government payment programs (Medicare and Medicaid) in the mid-60s and growth in private insurance (such as Blue Cross/Blue Shield) encouraged the use of health care, since most people could pass their medical costs on to third-party payers. Estimated total U.S. health care expenditures for 1990 were 2.6 times the level of 1980, at $647 billion (see Exhibit C16.4).

As medical costs rose, governments and employers who were paying the bills came under increasing budget pressure. Repeated efforts to control costs showed little effect. In

October 1983 the federal government changed its Medicare payment policy from full reimbursement for hospital charges to reimbursement at predetermined rates for specific treatments. The government set rates for hospital services according to "Diagnostic Related Groups" (DRGs), resulting in standard reimbursements for medical treatments, regardless of how long the patient remained in the hospital. This new fixed-fee payment system provided strong incentives for health care facilities to control costs, since payment rates were nonnegotiable. Hospitals immediately began to send patients home to complete their recuperation.

Employers also responded to the ever-rising costs of employee health benefits. Some companies raised their employees' portion of health insurance premiums; some increased efforts to promote overall healthy living; still others encouraged employees to elect lower-cost plans like health maintenance organizations (HMOs).

These changes in health care payment did not, however, curtail national health care spending. Health care's portion of the gross national product grew steadily from 5.2 percent in 1960 to 11.5 percent in 1988. The increase, due partly to the aging population and partly to costly advances in medical technology, was expected

EXHIBIT   C16.2b   STM Technology, Inc., Expenses for 1988 and 1989 ($=thousands)

	Cost of Sales and Service		Product Development Expense		Selling, General, and Administration Expense	
	1989	1988	1989	1988	1989	1988
Purchases	$ 174	$ 189				
Salaries	141	118	$ 96	$ 113	$ 113	$ 90
Auto expense and travel	21	17			14	11
Payroll taxes	12	10	8	10	7	6
Consultants	9	3	2	—	3	
Employment benefits	8	1	7	4	5	4
Telephone	4	5	1	—	7	5
Depreciation	4	3	7	10	3	—
User meetings	2	1				
Insurance	2	3				
Equipment repair	1	1				
Printing	1	1			1	1
Recruiting expense			13	9	1	
Development supplies			—	1		
Rent					13	2
Acctg and legal					5	8
Commissions					3	5
Office expense					3	1
Sales exhibits					2	3
Sales expense					1	1
Miscellaneous expenses					3	3
Advertising					—	1
Seminar costs					—	2
Bad-debt expense					—	1
	$ 380	$ 353	$ 133	$ 148	$ 184	$ 144

Note: Totals may not add, due to rounding.

to continue. In 1989 the S&P Industry Survey "Health Care" showed that 11 percent of the total national population was over 65 years of age and generated 35 percent of the country's total health care bill. Older patients required more attention, thus increasing the labor costs of most health care facilities. Additionally, the number of diagnostic tests, medical treatments, and prescribed pharmaceuticals billed by hospitals to their patients increased greatly, even as hospital stays dropped under the pressure of the DRG payment system.

Except for outpatient services, hospital utilization declined steadily after 1983. Hospitals faced tighter margins, due to lower admissions and inadequate reimbursement. DRG rate increases lagged behind actual cost increases for health services, and under the Bush administration this condition was expected to continue: Medicare's fiscal 1990 budget was cut by more than $2 billion. Additionally hospitals had to contend with the high cost of preventing in-hospital contraction of infectious diseases such as AIDS along with increasing liability insurance.

EXHIBIT   C16.3   STM Technology, Inc., Restated Sales by Business Line ($=thousands)

	Actual			Estimated			
	1987	**1988**	**1989**	**1990**	**1991**	**1992**	**1993**
Hospitals and Clinics							
Software sales:							
New clients	$ 412	$ 248	$ 350				
Old clients	19	137[a]	20				
Subtotal	$ 431	$ 385	$ 370				
Hardware:							
Contracts	$ 61	$ 85	$ 101				
Equipment and labor[b]	66	103	110				
Subtotal	$ 127	$ 188	$ 211				
Total hospitals and clinics	$ 558	$ 573	$ 581	$ 1,125	$ 3,160	$ 5,305	$ 8,030
Support Software							
Contracts[c]	$ 36	$ 70	$ 94				
Training[d]	10	16	22				
Consulting	8	19	21				
Total support	$ 54	$ 105	$ 137	286	760	1,196	1,748
Tracking	—	—	—	45	200	300	400
Total revenues	$ 612	$ 678	$ 718	$ 1,456	$ 4,120	$ 6,081	$10,178

[a] Includes one special contract for $80,000.

[b] Labor for installation.

[c] Extended service contracts.

[d] Special training programs not associated with sales.

Source: Estimated by Jerry Budinoff

EXHIBIT   C16.4   U.S. Health Expenditures, by Type ($=millions)

Type of Expenditure	1980	1981	1982	1983	1984	R1985	R1986	R1987	1988	E1990
Health service and supplies	$237,100	$273,500	$308,300	$341,800	$375,400	$407.8	$443.0	$485.4	$535.7	$626,500
Personal health care	219,400	254,600	286,900	314,800	341,900	373.4	406.0	447.0	494.8	573,500
Hospital care	100,400	118,000	135,500	148,800	156,300	168.6	180.4	196.9	216.2	250,400
Physicians' services	46,800	54,800	61,800	68,400	75,400	79.3	89.2	100.1	112.9	132,600
Dentists' services	15,400	17,300	19,500	21,700	24,600	27.5	29.9	33.2	37.0	41,800
Other professional services	5,600	6,400	7,100	9,300	10,900	15.7	18.0	20.8	24.1	22,900
Drugs and medical sundries	19,300	21,300	22,400	24,500	26,500	32.1	34.1	36.5	39.0	42,100
Eyeglasses and appliances	5,100	5,700	5,700	6,200	7,000	7.7	8.5	9.4	10.5	11,200
Nursing home care	20,600	24,200	27,300	29,400	31,700	34.1	36.8	40.0	43.8	54,500
Other health services	6,000	6,900	7,600	8,400	9,400	8.3	9.1	10.1	11.3	18,000
Prepayment and administration	10,700	11,100	12,700	17,100	22,600	22.1	23.5	24.0	25.0	34,600
Government public health activities	7,000	7,700	8,600	10,000	11,000	12.3	13.5	14.4	15.9	18,500
Medical facilities	11,800	13,100	14,100	15,400	15,600	19.1	20.4	21.6	23.0	20,700
Research	5,300	5,700	5,900	6,200	6,800	11.0	12.3	13.4	14.6	11,500
Construction	8,500	7,500	8,200	9,200	8,900	8.1	8.0	8.3	8.4	9,300
Total health expenditures	$249,000	$286,600	$322,400	$357,200	$391,100	$426.9	$463.4	$507.0	$558.7	$647,300

R=revised; E=estimated.

Source: Health Care Financing Administration, reported in Standard and Poor's Industry Surveys, *Health Care*, p. H15, July 13, 1989.

Declining usage and tightening margins hit small public and rural hospitals (those having fewer than one hundred beds) especially hard. Many public and rural hospitals faced the threat of bankruptcy or closure. In addition to inadequate DRG rates, these hospitals were adversely affected by demographic changes and the distribution of federal health care funds. Increasing numbers of young rural residents moved away, reducing the tax base that supported community health care and shifting the balance of patients to an older, more Medicare-dependent base. Rural hospitals generally received 40 percent less in Medicare reimbursement per case than did urban hospitals, because government audits showed that rural hospitals had lower operating costs. A study by the University of Illinois Center for Health Services Research, quoted by S&P, found that 161 rural hospitals closed between 1980 and 1987, with 70 percent of those remaining losing money in 1987. And 600 more rural hospitals were expected to close before 1990.

Many hospitals attempted to compensate for declining revenues by shifting the weight of costs to private patients. Private and corporate consumers, however, reacted by seeking alternative means of health care. Outpatient services grew substantially in usage. In 1980 18 percent of all surgical procedures were performed on an outpatient or ambulatory basis. This increased to 28 percent in 1985 and was expected to be at 59 percent by 1990, according to Joyce Keithly, writing in *Nursing Economics* in 1989.

Health maintenance organizations first became a key component of health care in 1973 with a law requiring many corporations to include HMO coverage in their health care benefit menus. HMOs operate on fixed-cost contracts with health care providers, eliminating any fee for service. Although there was some concern that HMOs' protection might be discontinued, a Duff & Phelps HMO industry analysis expected annual membership growth to continue (see Exhibit C16.5) and revenue growth to remain near 20 percent.

In summary, health care providers felt intense pressure in 1990 to control costs. A prime area for their attention was administrative systems, where hospitals had automated many of their processes but smaller institutions had been unable to afford the high costs of modernizing systems to improve their efficiency.

STM'S COMPETITIVE SITUATION

A number of large competitors and a multitude of small ones served the medical market with computer systems, said Budinoff:

> Meditech, IDX, and Baxter are big in the hospital systems market, for example, but they don't bother with outpatient clinics. Baxter is huge. But their product sells for $250 to $300,000 to get the whole system in, including hardware. Baxter and IDX will both lease their systems at $75,000 per year. Clinics can't even look at that kind of money, and even a hospital of 100 to 125 beds can't afford it. They may pay it, but they're real unhappy.

Baxter International, a major supplier to large hospitals, was a manufacturer and distributor of health care products whose 1988 sales reached $6.8 billion. Baxter's products included intravenous solutions, dialysis and blood collection equipment, drugs, urological and diagnostic products, cardiovascular devices, and information systems. Additionally Baxter operated 120 of its own outpatient health care facilities.

> The big guys have had their systems out there for several years, and they're all based on minicomputers. We want to go in with a PC-based system that sells in the neighborhood of $75 to $90,000. We're the first ones to do it on PCs, and we have to get the financing so we can develop it properly and grow it before the others copy us. It's not easy to downsize a system from minis to micros, and the big guys have a minicomputer mindset. We have maybe a year's lead.

STM did not offer a lease plan to its customers. "I have no training in business," said Jerry, "and that kind of arrangement requires a lot of expertise."

Small hospitals and clinics, Jerry said, were "an everywhere market." Some 60 percent of hospitals tabulated in the 1989 American Hospital Association's data were below 200 beds in size (see Exhibit C16.6), and there was evidence that the smaller hospitals were having difficulty finding the systems they wanted. A survey of 3,000 hospitals with more than 100 beds, conducted by Modern Healthcare (see Exhibit C16.7), indicated a large number of small shoppers for systems, with many purchase plans cancelled or delayed for years.

The small institutions were served by a few small companies—Practice Management Systems, at about $5 million annual sales, was the largest—and by a legion of independent operators. Many of these, Jerry thought, were amateurs or programmers who had built a system for their own employers and were trying to peddle it to others. As "basement operators," they often quoted unrealistically low prices. Wise buyers in the market had come to demand evidence of a supplier's financial stability.

Every successful installation, Budinoff felt, would generate new sales through word-of-mouth contact from satisfied customers. Already, STM's development work in five hospitals was generating inquiries beyond the firm's capacity to service them. Jerry had just decided against pursuing a California hospital inquiry; the distance made installation and support unfeasible. Still, many hospital and clinic administrators desperately wanted economical systems. Budinoff had first-hand knowledge of their problem:

> I've had directors of facilities get a little annoyed with me because they wanted something like our system but didn't know we existed, so they bought something else. When they found out about us they'd call and say, "Where the hell were you when I needed you?"

STM TECHNOLOGY, INC.: CURRENT PRODUCTS

The success to date of STM was attributed to the sales of its Outpatient Billing and Administration System, with an installed base of 129 sys-

---

EXHIBIT   C16.5   Growth of HMOs, 1980 to 1988

Date	Number of Prepaid Plans	Enrollment (millions)	Percentage of Population Enrolled
June 1980	236	9.1	4.0
June 1981	243	10.2	4.4
June 1982	265	10.8	4.7
June 1983	280	12.5	5.3
June 1984	306	15.1	6.4
December 1984	337	16.7	7.1
December 1985	480	21.0	8.8
December 1986	593	25.0	10.4
December 1987	650	30.0	12.2
June 1988	643	NA	NA

Source: Adapted from Standard and Poor's Industry Surveys, p. H32, July 13, 1989.

tems in the fall of 1989. Jerry estimated the market to be approximately 2,500 clinics in New England; he was targeting an additional 335 installations over the next four years. This estimate was based on a significant upgrade to the present system, automating nearly the entire billing process. The new STM "Robotic" version would incorporate automatic scanning of services at the front end and electronic transmission and posting of receipts at the back end. Little or no hand data entry would be required. This new version could be marketable in four months with additional R&D funding, Jerry said.

Two additional products had been developed: a microcomputer Inpatient Billing and Administrative System targeted at small hospi-

EXHIBIT C16.6   1989 Health Facilities in Target Areas

Area	Hospitals[a] <50	<100	<200	Total	HMOs	Psychological Facilities	Substance Abuse Facilities	Total Facilities[b]
New England								
Connecticut	7	23	34	65	12	8	32	117
Maine	11	29	34	46	4	0	9	59
Massachusetts	12	52	98	173	26	4	34	237
New Hampshire	9	24	34	41	5	6	14	66
Rhode Island	2	11	15	19	4	1	6	30
Vermont	0	18	37	86	3	0	4	93
Total	41	157	252	430	54	19	99	602
Mid-Atlantic								
New Jersey	4	14	37	125	22	8	43	198
New York	25	72	138	322	30	23	119	494
Pennsylvania	19	72	160	302	26	5	90	423
Total	48	158	335	749	78	36	252	1,115
South Atlantic								
Florida	27	82	164	276	39	25	110	440
Washington, D.C.	0	2	4	18	8	0	7	33
Georgia	39	98	147	204	11	5	49	269
South Carolina	14	41	67	90	5	1	12	108
North Carolina	24	71	115	159	9	3	25	196
Maryland	8	18	40	85	22	6	51	164
Virginia	9	40	87	136	19	2	43	200
West Virginia	19	39	48	70	4	1	14	89
Delaware	1	4	8	13	7	1	4	25
Total	141	395	680	1,051	124	44	305	1,524
Miscellaneous								
Texas	184	313	437	553	47	31	139	770
California	91	233	386	566	119	21	163	869
Total	275	546	823	1,119	166	52	302	1,639

[a] Hospitals are grouped by bed number. Each category includes previous category's number.
  Total refers to all hospitals with unlimited bed size.

[b] Total facilities equal sum of total hospitals, HMOs, psychological & substance abuse.

Source: 1989 AHA Guide to the Health Care Field, American Hospital Association, Chicago, IL.

tals (under 150 beds), clinics, and HMOs; and a Patient Database, which provided a Medical Tracking and Analysis System linked with either the Hospital or the Clinic Systems. These programs formed an interrelated family of products that met the need for affordable, integrated medical systems. STM continued its market research in order to add to this family of products further through the development of new and follow-up software.

The Medical Tracking and Analysis System was a system to track the health care data of patients throughout their lifetimes. It could be integrated into the Billing and Accounting System but could also be available as a stand-alone product. The product needed six to nine months to complete, after funding came in. Jerry viewed the market as nationwide and potentially world-wide. He had targeted 245 sales within four years to employee assistance program providers, employers, government agencies, and health care practices.

STM TECHNOLOGY, INC.: HISTORY

Jerry Budinoff was an electrical and astronautical engineer by training (see Exhibit C16.8). He began working with computer systems shortly after leaving active duty with the Air Force and joined Procter and Gamble as a production manager. While working with computer professionals there, Budinoff discovered that he really enjoyed systems design. This would be his new profession.

EXHIBIT C16.7 Buying Plans for Patient Care and Patient Accounting Systems

Bed Size	Implemented Plans	Canceled Plans	Still Pending From 1986	From 1987	New Plans in 1988	Total
Outcome of 1987 Plans, as of End of 1988						
Patient Care Systems						
100–199	58	19	79	37	117	233
200–299	47	23	46	13	71	130
300–399	24	13	29	18	37	84
400–499	10	5	14	0	13	27
500 and over	21	5	33	10	27	68
Total	160	65	201	76	265	542
Patient Accounting Systems						
100–199	53	14	32	30	112	174
200–299	58	12	20	16	54	90
300–399	34	2	29	12	29	70
400–499	14	4	13	1	13	27
500 and over	25	2	13	10	28	51
Total	184	34	107	69	136	412

Source: *Modern Healthcare,* July 1989, p. 58.

EXHIBIT C16.8   Jerry Budinoff's Resumé

JEROLD E. BUDINOFF

Summary of Qualifications

- Six years president software development company
- Seventeen years' system development experience
- Designed and implemented systems in health care billing and administration, order processing, production control, bill of materials, MRP, receivables, and general ledger

Education

Purdue University—MS Astronautical Engineering, 1965

U.S. Air Force Academy—BS Engineering Science, Distinguished Graduate, 1964

Job History

1983 to present	President, STM Technology, Inc.
1981 to 1983	Senior Analyst, Raytheon Corporation
1975 to 1981	Manufacturing/MIS Manager, Digital Equipment Corporation
1972 to 1975	Systems Analyst, Keydata Corporation
1971 to 1972	Production Manager, Procter and Gamble
1964 to 1970	Officer, U.S. Air Force

8/83 to present   **STM Technology, Inc.,** Acton, MA
President

Founded company, which develops and installs a wide variety of software for the health care industry. STM's Health Care Office Management Systems are the most advanced Patient Registration, Billing, and Accounts Receivable systems available in Massachusetts.

Serve as STM's primary systems developer. Working with agency Executive Directors, Business Managers, and Administrative Personnel throughout Massachusetts, have designed all STM systems. Also serve as STM's only salesman. Responsible for all sales and marketing of STM's products. STM employs eight people.

12/81 to 8/83   **Raytheon Computer Services,** Wellesley, MA
Senior Analyst

Developed systems for Raytheon commercial customers. Responsibilities included client interface, project management, specification, design, test, and implementation. Produced systems in medical insurance and retail sales. IBM mainframes.

10/75 to 7/81   **Digital Equipment Corporation,** Maynard, MA
Group MIS Functional Manager, Headquarters, 4/80 to 7/81

Responsible for program management of all common systems in the areas of Manufacturing Engineering and Quality. Established strategies, business plans, and staffing. Coordinated system development between plants.

continued

Systems Development Manager, Westminster Plant, 2/78 to 4/80

Managed 15 analysts and programmers developing systems in materials, BOMs, quality assurance, and purchasing. Responsibilities included planning, budgeting, staffing, and project management. Successfully developed and implemented the first common Material Requirements Planning and BOM system in the Systems Manufacturing Group. DEC hardware.

Manufacturing Planning Manager, Westminster Plant, 2/77 to 2/78

Managed a group that accomplished long-range planning and developed tools for management analysis.

Systems Analysis Manager, Product Line Systems, 10/75 to 2/77

Built and managed team of analysts working in the Product Line Order Processing Group. Accomplished feasibility studies and functional specifications for order processing systems.

| 6/72 to 10/75 | **KeyData Corporation,** Watertown, MA |
| | **Manager of Communications,** Headquarters, 1/75 to 10/75 |

Managed 35 people responsible for Keydata's nationwide 1,000-terminal teleprocessing network. Department included communication customer services, line troubleshooting, contracts, and evaluation of new equipment.

Systems Analyst/Customer Rep, National Accounts Region, 6/72 to 1/75

Developed systems for Keydata's major national accounts. Worked closely with salesmen and customers in the sales phase and assumed full account responsibility after contract was signed. Designed and implemented systems in manufacturing, order processing, accounting, and electronic mail.

| 9/71 to 5/72 | **Plast-Alum Manufacturing Company,** North Hollywood, CA |
| | **Partner** |

Managed entire operation of a small (20 people) manufacturing business, including manufacturing operations, budgeting, inventory, and inside sales.

| 6/70 to 9/71 | **Procter and Gamble Corporation,** Cape Girardeau, MO |
| | **Production Manager** |

Managed 22-person crew operating four Pampers production lines. Responsibilities included personnel supervision, training, production, maintenance, and packaging.

| 6/64 to 6/70 | **U.S. Air Force** |
| | **Officer** |

Primarily a flyer with over three thousand hours flying time. Two years Viet Nam. Also an instructor at the U.S. Air Force Academy, in the Department of Engineering Mechanics.

After P&G, Budinoff worked for DEC and Raytheon, to gain management experience. Budinoff says, "I had a friend who thought you couldn't really run your own company unless you could be an executive in a large corporation. So I got to where I worked for a vice president. Then I said, 'Okay, I can do this,' and started this company."

In 1982 Budinoff left Raytheon to develop systems and start STM. He describes his entry into the health care market:

It was an accident. The first person I found who wanted a system developed happened to own a mental health center. That was it. There was no formal market research. It could have been a gas station. It didn't make a difference to me. I was a techie, and I just wanted to develop software.

After Budinoff incorporated the company in 1983 he brought in Evelyn Mittler (a Raytheon programming consultant) as a ten-percent stockholder and Richard Kelley (a software development administrator from Honeywell). It was with this limited staff that STM developed software products to enter the health care market, focusing on systems for nonphysician outpatient facilities. Budinoff saw STM's ability to serve a wide variety of outpatient clinics as his competitive advantage. He commented on this and the derivation of the company's name:

Mental health facilities, rehabilitation facilities, substance abuse facilities ... there are no other general-purpose systems out there that are right for all of them. Maybe 50 to 60 percent of them are nonprofit, and systems for them are much more difficult to do than for physicians. So there is much less competition for systems work for these facilities: everyone sees physicians as the big market, and these other things are much smaller.

There is no one who competes in all the different kinds of places we're in. We run into one set of competitors in mental health facilities, and another set in substance abuse companies. We're the only one with a generic product—one that serves all kinds of clinics. That is an advantage because when one of these guys gets aggressive and starts doing very well in some market, we can turn to another market. We're always going one direction or another within health care, while our competition is tied to one market and they go up and down as that market moves.

One thing all our customers have in common: they all want to save time and money. That's what STM stands for—"Save Time and Money." When I first went out to the market, I asked what people wanted. They said, "Anything that saves me time and money," so I put that right into the name. A panel at Harvard said it was a "harsh and nondescriptive" name for a company, where you want a name that's warm and friendly. But I want to tell you our customers and prospects remember it and identify with it. It always gets a smile. They greet me, "Here's the guy who'll save us time and money." Maybe that's why I haven't gone to Harvard.

In its first six years of operation, STM did not have an office facility; all employees operated out of their homes. In July 1989 Jerry leased a 1,400-square-foot, ranch-style building. A classroom for weekly training sessions and tastefully decorated offices for all the staff occupied the first floor. An equal-size basement, vacant but subject to rental, would provide expansion space when funding permitted the increased staff. STM at the time employed nine people who provided administration, hardware maintenance, customer support, training, and programming. Budinoff did most of the systems design work and was also the company's only salesperson. Evelyn Mittler, whose twenty-four years of systems and programming experience included extensive service with Raytheon, Varian, and Wang, assisted with design and was in charge of coding. All STM programs were written in COBOL. "It may not be the newest language, but it is much easier to find customer support people who understand COBOL," Mittler said.

STM had no affiliation or official status with the computer manufacturers whose hardware they selected for customer systems. Some years earlier, an IBM value added reseller had offered Jerry a System 36 minicomputer, hoping he would program the Outpatient Management System for their machine. "Even then, we thought the minis were dinosaurs, so we didn't do it," Jerry said. IBM itself was now showing interest—this time with the thought of selling STM's software along with their PCs and the new "6000 series" machines. Budinoff was hesitant, however; "I don't understand that kind of intercompany dealing," he said, "and it would take an immense amount of time to learn it."

As it became apparent during 1989 that the year would be profitable—so profitable that substantial taxes would be due—Jerry Budinoff decided to invest in additional marketing. He employed a salesperson for six months. Budinoff described him as "not having an in-depth knowledge of the product and the market. He tried to sell on personality and didn't get anywhere. This isn't like selling a car. And he didn't want to get the knowledge. We parted company." In 1990 STM's marketing still relied only on Budinoff's efforts, word of mouth between health care organizations, a couple of ads in the yellow pages, and past attendance at a few trade shows.

THE STM BUSINESS PLAN

In January of 1990, in order to solicit investments from venture capitalists, Jerry developed a business plan that aimed to take advantage of STM's innovative PC-based systems for small hospitals. The plan sought $900,000 in new capital (two-thirds in debt, one-third in equity), which would support the hiring of

> . . . a director of operations, who will relieve Mr. Budinoff's time for concentration on the key skill of systems design . . . immediate expansion of the programming and system analyst staff . . . a director of sales and marketing, who will hire the telemarketing and sales support staff . . . and a Chief Financial Officer. . . .

The new funds would be used, the plan said, in approximately the following amounts:

Research and development	$350,000
Extra marketing expenses in 1990-91	440,000
Hiring of new professional staffs	110,000

STM's business plan projected growth to 74 employees by the end of 1993, with sales just over $10 million (see Exhibits C16.9, C16.10, and C16.11). Jerry Budinoff commented on the opportunity:

> I never wanted to get financing before. I never understood the business side or the huge need for capital. But we've been in the health care market for six years now, and I do know what that market needs and how to design for it. We've got a real lock on it. I am positive that if we get the financing this thing is going to go through the roof like a rocket ship. There is just no doubt in my mind. So I'm not worried about the financing; it will be paid back. We just need the $900,000; that's the difference between total expenses and total income in the first year of the plan.
>
> But we have to take the new inpatient hospital system into the market the right way, not just dribble it in. Because as soon as we get visibility and prove to the market that 386s and 286s can do the job, then one of the big companies will come in. When we break the idea barrier, they'll get going with their resources and go right by us with marketing. We have maybe a year's lead, but if we don't get going we'll lose our real window.

Of the five hospitals with installed systems in 1990, two were in Massachusetts; one each were in Connecticut (at Yale University's infirmary), New Hampshire, and Maine. The business plan estimated the market as 3,000 small hospitals nationwide and 450 in New England. It targeted 235 installations in the next four years, representing a 12-percent market share nationwide.

The plan envisioned growth in STM's outpatient systems as well, based on selling the new "Robotic" integrated system to clinics throughout New England. Nineteen new sales in 1990 to Massachusetts facilities would bring that state's total to 143, representing 13 percent of its potential market. Twenty-six new sales were targeted for the five other New England states. For the first time in its history, a marketing campaign of mailings, trade journal advertising, and telemarketing would supplement the word-of-mouth networking which had so far carried STM.

The proposed marketing program began with direct sales by STM's own staff, expanding to branch offices in New York City and Tampa in 1991. California, Texas, Chicago, Denver, and St. Louis would follow in 1992. These remote sites would cultivate local vendors to provide hardware and maintenance and eventually distribution of STM software. New products—including some for diagnostics—would be sold through mail order and off the shelf through computer stores. By 1993 the plan called for

marketing outside the continental United States. To support these efforts, a variety of new promotional tools had to be developed, including new product packaging, advertisements, news releases, brochures, an exhibit booth for trade shows, a sales kit, sales training materials, professional videotapes, and telemarketing scripts. The business plan put the cost of these marketing and sales tools at $260,000.

STM AND THE FUTURE

To Jerry the new financing was absolutely critical. Without it he saw little point in continuing

EXHIBIT   C16.9   STM Technology, Inc., Estimated Profit and Loss Statement For Years Ending December 31, 1990–1993 ($=thousands)

	1990	1991	1992	1993
Revenues				
Hospitals	$ 675	$ 2,425	$ 4,345	$ 7,100
Clinics	450	735	960	930
Tracking	45	200	300	400
Support	286	760	1,196	1,748
Total	$ 1,456	$ 4,120	$ 6,801	$ 10,178
Less cost of sales and service	562	1,315	2,057	2,906
Gross profit	$ 894	$ 2,805	$ 4,744	$ 7,272
Operating expenses				
Product development	$ 346	$ 659	$ 931	$ 1,377
Marketing sales	665	1,169	1,874	2,455
General and administrative	311	452	768	1,025
Total	$ 1,322	$ 2,280	$ 3,573	$ 4,857
Operating profit	$ (428)	$ 525	$ 1,171	$ 2,415
Non-operating expense	27	63	66	45
Profit before tax	$ (455)	$ 462	$ 1,105	$ 2,370
Taxes	0	0	400	950
Profit after tax	$ (455)	$ 462	$ 705	$ 1,420

development work on the hospital system at all. In May of 1990 no new sales of the existing inpatient system were contemplated. The development work had to come first. Jerry commented:

> I deeply believe in the philosophy I learned at DEC: don't try to force a product onto an

unwilling market—let the market pull you in. Well, we were pulled into the hospital market, without knowing better. It is a very difficult system, and we might not have done it if we'd analyzed it first. We successfully automated what the hospitals were doing already. In the process we have learned what the market really wants,

EXHIBIT C16.10   STM Technology, Inc., Pro Forma Balance Sheet
For Years Ending December 31, 1990–1993 ($=thousands)

	1990	1991	1992	1993
Assets				
Current assets:				
Cash	$ 140	$ 254	$ 325	$ 1,114
Accounts receivable, net	260	517	830	1,213
Inventory	11	29	41	53
Prepaid deposits	3	6	11	21
Total current assets	$ 414	$ 806	$ 1,197	$ 2,401
Fixed assets:				
Equipment cost	$ 199	$ 299	$ 499	$ 699
Reserve for depreciation	89	141	201	261
Net	$ 110	$ 158	$ 298	$ 438
Other assets:				
Research and development	$ 150	$ 280	$ 390	$ 350
Miscellaneous	10	40	90	160
Total other assets	$ 160	$ 320	$ 480	$ 510
Total assets	$ 684	$ 1,284	$ 1,975	$ 3,349
Liabilities and Equity				
Current liabilities:				
Accounts payable/accruals	$ 58	$ 96	$ 132	$ 186
Deferred taxes	7	7	57	157
Deferred revenues	126	226	326	426
Notes payable—current	0	100	100	—
Total current liabilities	$ 191	$ 429	$ 615	$ 769
Long-term notes:				
New	500	400	200	0
Stockholders	48	48	48	48
Total liabilities	$ 739	$ 877	$ 863	$ 817
Equity:				
Common stocks	$ 304	$ 304	$ 304	$ 304
Earned surplus	(359)	103	808	2,228
Total equity	$ (55)	$ 407	$ 1,112	$ 2,532
Total liabilities and equity	$ 684	$ 1,284	$ 1,975	$ 3,349

and that would be a product that opens up the entire market.

But we ought to do it right. Without financial backing, we can't even begin to cope with that market. We would just make a little dent in it. I know how to "piecemeal" into these markets, and that's exactly what I don't want to do.

Budinoff and STM's two other equity holders were willing to relinquish 33 percent of the ownership for the $900,000 they sought. STM had already refused a $500,000 offer from one of its customers for 48 percent of the company. Jerry talked of his ideal investor:

Health care is a very parochial, localized market. And we've got an image problem because we're the little guy in the market and people worry

about us going out of business. My criterion for capital is credibility. I want someone who can give us credibility and who can give us second and third rounds. Ideally I would like a large computer-based company such as an insurance company to back us. That way they would have an interest in us. They could turn to us for consulting help. I'd be more comfortable with that.

I suppose one of our options, though, if the financing didn't come through, would be to shift into "retirement mode"—stay small and make a pile of money.

Evelyn Mittler, who had been quiet through much of the conversation, winced at this last suggestion. "Oh, no," she said.

Jerry continued:

EXHIBIT C16.11 STM Technology, Inc., Estimated Cash Flow
For Years Ending December 31, 1990–1993 ($=thousands)

	1990	1991	1992	1993
Beginning balance	$ 79	$ 140	$ 254	$ 325
Cash in:				
Profit and (loss)	$ (455)	$ 462	$ 705	$ 1,420
Depreciation	30	52	60	60
Amortization	0	70	190	340
Accounts receivable decr. (incr.)	(133)	(257)	(303)	(393)
Inventory decr. (incr.)	(4)	(18)	(12)	(12)
Prepaid decr. (incr.)	0	(3)	(5)	(10)
Research and develop decr. (incr.)	(150)	(200)	(300)	(300)
Loans/notes	500	100	0	0
Equity	300	0	0	0
Miscellaneous assets decr. (incr.)	0	10	10	10
Total in	$ 88	$ 216	$ 345	$ 1,115
Total cash available	$ 167	$ 356	$ 599	$ 1,440
Cash outgo:				
Accounts payable decr. (incr.)	$ (33)	$ (38)	$ (36)	$ (54)
Taxes decr. (incr.)	0	0	(50)	(100)
Deferred revenue decr. (incr.)	(50)	(100)	(100)	(100)
Equipment purchases	100	100	200	200
Note repayment	0	100	200	300
Miscellaneous purchases	10	40	60	80
Total out	$ 27	$ 102	$ 274	$ 326
Ending balance	$ 140	$ 254	$ 325	$ 1,114

Yeah, we could stay at about $750,000 a year, with a gross profit of maybe $300K. There are lots of other people who need systems work done, outside of the business. It's a never-ending market. I get calls all the time; it's hilarious. I was down in Washington [Jerry served one week per month as Reserve Assistant Division Chief for the Air Force Arms Control and International Negotiations Division, designing computer systems to comply with the Strategic Arms Reduction Treaty], and they wanted to know how to automate a whole Pentagon division of operations. I'm no expert in that, but it doesn't matter to them. I've got the reputation, and that's it. So we could turn away from growth in the medical systems.

"But none of us wants to," said Evelyn Mittler.

"We could cut back on the R&D and reap profits for the business. But we're not interested in just going along at a steady size," remarked Jerry.

"That would be boring," said Evelyn Mittler.

Jerry Budinoff concluded:

I view the Company as a vehicle—a resource base for the fabulous systems we'll develop next year and the year after that. That's what my core group of people like doing and we're very good at that. Now I have to get the company big enough to support what we come up with. I want to move it out of health care and into other markets too, eventually. In six years I would like us to be a $20-30 million company.

Yugo America, Inc.

Carolyn Silliman
Clemson University

Jeffrey Harrison
Clemson University

The five years that I invested in the Yugo project were rewarding and maturing for me, although I had a modest financial equity and a large amount of sweat equity invested in the company. In hindsight, there were areas where we failed, but I feel as though it all made a significant impact on the product and pricing aspect of the automobile industry.

William E. Prior, June 1989

William Prior, cofounder and former chief executive and president of Yugo America, Inc., collected his thoughts and reflected on the past five years as he glanced across a crowded airport. It was June 1989, only five months after his company had filed for Chapter 11 reorganization. Looking back, he noted that the privately held company had traveled a rocky road, yet had made a significant impact on the automobile industry in the 1980s.

It was 1983 when Prior and his two partners, Malcolm Bricklin and Ira Edelson, decided to form a company featuring a low-priced imported car. Bricklin, who was probably best

known for the flashy sports car prototype that bears his name, was heading up the project as its main financial backer. William Prior was the former president and general manager of Automobile Importers from Subaru, the nation's second-largest Subaru distributor, a company Bricklin had founded after the collapse of his sports car project. Ira Edelson was Bricklin's accountant and financial advisor. The three men had been researching the automobile industry, looking for a niche in the already crowded new-car market. From their research, the men came to the conclusion that there was no "entry-level car," that is, there was not a new automobile inexpensive enough for the average first-time buyer. Bricklin, Prior, and Edelson concluded that they had discovered "a market in search of a product."

Pursuing the concept for their business venture, the three entrepreneurs began a search for a low-priced, no-frills mode of basic transportation. They determined that production costs would be too high in the United States, so they began evaluating the possibility of importing. In selecting a foreign manufacturer whose car models could satisfy their business concept, they wanted to meet three requirements:

1. The foreign company should not be presently exporting to the United States, but should be desirous of gaining access to the U.S. market.

2. The overall quality of the car, even if inferior to American and Japanese cars, had to meet U.S. standards and consumer requirements.

3. The foreign company had to be able to supply the cars at a price low enough for their new company and the dealers they

recruited to make money retailing the car at a rock-bottom market price.

Bricklin, Prior, and Edelson spent four months investigating and traveling to foreign countries in pursuit of the right country and product that met the three requirements. They researched manufacturing plants in Brazil, Japan, Mexico, Poland, France, Rumania, Czechoslovakia, England, and the Soviet Union before they discovered the Zastava car factory in Yugoslavia. Zavodi Crvena Zastava, Yugoslavia's leading automobile manufacturer, had been producing the Yugo GV model for five years and was quite receptive to Bricklin's proposal. Bricklin, Prior, and Edelson toured the Yugoslavian plant in May 1984 and began discussing the terms of a contract that same month.

Yugoslavian officials were eager to hear of the Yugo America venture. The country's economy was weak, and it owed (in 1985) approximately $19 billion to the Western world. In order to purchase goods from the West, such as oil, steel, and electronics, Yugoslavia had to have "hard" currency (a universal currency of choice). The dinar, Yugoslavia's monetary unit, was generally not acceptable payment for firms shipping goods to Yugoslavia, so the country had to earn dollars by exporting. Yugoslavia's modest exports, including jewelry, tourism, furniture, leather, and sporting guns, did not contribute a significant sum toward reduction of the $19-billion foreign debt. Since car exports would generate lots of U.S. dollars (because the price of the car was so great in relation to other exported goods), Yugoslavian officials saw the venture as one of the biggest and best ways it could increase the supply of hard currency to finance imports into Yugoslavia.

Bricklin and Zastava agreed that 500 Yugos should be shipped to a Baltimore port in early August 1985, so that the cars would be in showrooms and ready to sell later that month. In addition, technicians would be trained at Zastava's plant prior to the launch in America, in order to guarantee customer satisfaction when the cars were sold and serviced. Bricklin and his partners returned to the United States in late May 1984 and began setting up operations.

COMPETITIVE STRATEGY

Competitive maneuvering among car manufacturers revolves around such factors as innovative options and styles, pricing, and brand name/reputation. Innovative options and styles were not considered important to the Yugo, since they would increase the price of the car. Also, the company could not rely on reputation, since the Yugo did not have an established name in the United States. Therefore, Yugo's strategy focused on pricing.

Yugo America took advantage of a pricing scheme that set it apart from other automobile manufacturers. At $3,990, it was the lowest-priced car in America. Because price is important to most car buyers, Yugo felt that its low-price strategy gave the company an advantage over other small cars. Major price competitors included the Chevrolet Sprint, Subaru hatchback, and Toyota Tercel; however, the Yugo GV was priced below all of these competitors (see Exhibit C17.1). Instead of targeting families or status-conscious individuals, Yugo America made its car appealing to the first-time buyer looking for an economical subcompact.

OPERATIONS BEGIN

Four strategic decisions were made at the onset of operations:

1. The cars would be sold through dual dealerships; that is, Yugo would be taken on as a second brand by established auto dealers looking for a low-priced model that could boost sales volume. In this manner, Yugo America's executives hoped the public would associate its

name with another successful manufacturer's name and reputation.

2. Prior, Bricklin, and Edelson decided that the company would market the Yugo regionally rather than nationally. Yugo America, based in Upper Saddle River, New Jersey, decided to focus on Northeastern dealers first. Approximately 23 percent of all import cars were sold in this region. Also, the Northeastern coast, being closest to Yugoslavia, would allow the company to minimize shipping costs.

3. There would be a small number of dealers selling a large number of Yugos. The idea behind this decision was that the dealers would be making a substantial profit from the large number of cars, which would motivate them and encourage them to sell more.

4. The price of the car would be low, but the company would stress the fact that the car was of acceptable quality.

The first task to accomplish before announcing the introduction of the Yugo GV in America was to set up a management hierarchy. As mentioned previously, Malcolm Bricklin was Yugo America's chief financial backer. As chairman, he owned 75 percent of the company. William Prior, who would act as president and head of operations, owned 1 percent. Ira Edelson owned 2 percent of the company and held the title of financial administrator. The remaining 22 percent was held by investors who were not involved in the management of the company.

In February 1985 the company began recruiting automobile dealers. (The company's founders had been reviewing dealers for over four months, but the actual signing did not take

EXHIBIT C17.1 Low-Priced Small Cars Available in the United States in 1986

	Price	Destination Charge	Engine Size[a]	Fuel Economy[b]	Predicted Reliability
Chevrolet Chevette	$5,645	$290	1.6	19 (32)	Below average
Chevrolet Sprint	5,380	190	1.0	37 (59)	Average
Dodge Colt	5,633	210	1.5	23 (45)	Above average
Ford Escort	6,052	308	1.9	21 (41)	Average
Honda Civic	5,649	189	1.5	22 (39)	Above average
Mazda 323	5,645	205	1.6	22 (42)	N/A
Mitsubishi Mirage	5,659	210	N/A	N/A	N/A
Nissan Sentra	5,649	210	1.6	24 (45)	Above average
Renault Alliance	5,999	358	1.4	21 (45)	Below average
Subaru Hatchback	4,989	N/A	1.8	21 (45)	Above average
Toyota Tercel	5,598	210	1.5	23 (46)	Above average
Yugo GV	3,990	299	1.1	24 (42)	N/A

Note: N/A = not available
[a] Engine size is in liters.
[b] Miles per gallon in city; highway miles per gallon in parentheses.
Source: *Consumer Reports,* April 1986, 230-34.

place until February.) Tony Cappadona was hired as dealer development manager and given the responsibility of locating established dealers who were interested in selling the Yugo. In addition extensive surveys helped Mr. Cappadona determine the best area placement of Yugo franchises. By the end of July the first fifty dealers were contracted in Pennsylvania, Massachusetts, New York, New Jersey, Connecticut, Rhode Island, Delaware, Maryland, and Washington, D.C.

Some dealers were hesitant to sign because of the financial commitment involved. Pressure from Manufacturers Hanover Trust Company required that Yugo America produce fifty letters of credit by December 1985. By the terms of agreement, all dealers had to produce a $400,000 standby letter of credit to cover at least two months of vehicle shipments. Each dealer also had to pay $37,000 to cover initial start-up costs and arrange financing for a floor plan. A floor plan is an agreement between a financial institution and an auto dealership to finance vehicles that are on the lot. The financial institution retains title to the automobiles until they are sold. A typical floor plan entailed a $600,000 line of credit. Dealers were reluctant to take on such debt and incur $37,000 in up-front costs to take on an unknown, unproven car model. Yugo executives countered such arguments with assurances that the Yugo GV would sell itself.

Bricklin contacted Leonard Sirowitz, a New York advertiser, to write and launch a $10-million media campaign to introduce the Yugo GV. Sirowitz, who helped to create the Volkswagen Beetle advertisements during the 1960s, expected the Yugo advertisements to reach a potential one million buyers via newspapers, magazines, and television. He hoped to convince Americans that, despite their views of communist Yugoslavia, the $3,990 car was of sound quality.[1] Yugo's first slogan intended to catch the consumer's eye by asking, "The Road Back to Sanity: Why Pay Higher Prices?"

In addition to trained technicians, Yugo's support system of quality parts and service was comprehensive. The company received 180 tons of spare parts to distribute among dealers during the summer of 1985. The company implemented the industry's first Universal Product Code inventory system, which enhanced the accuracy and efficiency of inventory processing. In addition, service schools were developed so that technicians would have no problems or questions when repairing the cars. For do-it-yourself consumers, Yugo America published its own repair manuals and included a toll-free telephone number for assistance.

THE YUGO ARRIVES IN AMERICA

The first shipment of 500 cars from the Zastava plant arrived in mid-August 1985 (Yugo features are listed in Exhibit C17.2). Ten cars were sent to each of the fifty dealers in the Northeast. Each dealer was asked to reserve two cars as demonstration vehicles and then to keep two demonstrators on hand at all times as further shipments and sales occurred.

Yugo's official entry into the automobile industry was announced on August 26, 1985. Consumers responded with enthusiasm. The Yugo frenzy spread so quickly that 33 dealerships were added and 3,000 orders were taken for cars by September 9. Customers paid deposits in order to reserve their cars, and by the end of 1985, a six-month waiting list was tallied. Indeed, Yugo America's founders had discovered "a market in search of a product."[2]

During its first year of operations, which ended July 31, 1986, Yugo America, Inc. grossed $122 million from the sale of 27,000 automobiles and parts and accessories (Exhibit C17.3 contains a sales breakdown by calendar year). The Yugo was hailed as "the fastest selling import car in the history of the U.S."[3] By mid-1986 Yugo had 220 dealers throughout the Southeast and East Coast. It was estimated that the consumer credit divisions of Chrysler, Ford, and General Motors financed one-third of the Yugo retail sales.[4] At the end of July, Prior announced the

EXHIBIT C17.2 Yugo GV Standard Features

Vehicle Type
Front-engine, front-wheel drive, 4-passenger, 3-door hatchback

Dimensions and Capacities
Wheelbase: 84.6 inches
Overall length: 139.0 inches
Overall height: 54.7 inches
Overall width: 60.7 inches
Headroom: Front: 37.0 inches
                    Rear: 36.0 inches
Legroom: Front: 39.0 inches
                 Rear: 39.0 inches
Ground clearance: 4.8 inches
Luggage capacity: 18.5 + 9.0 cubic feet
Fuel capacity: 8.4 gallons
Curb weight: 1,832 pounds

Engine
Type: Single overhead cam, 1.1 liter 4-cylinder with aluminum cylinder head; dual-barrel carburetor
Bore and stroke: 80 x 55.5 mm.
Displacement: 1116 cc.
Compression ratio: 9.2:1
Horsepower: 54 hp at 5,000 rpm
Torque: 52 lbs. at 4,000 rpm.

Drive Train
Transmission: 4-speed manual
Final drive ratio: 3.7
Gear ratios: 1st-3.5, 2nd-2.2, 3rd-1.4, 4th-1.0, reverse-3.7

Suspension
Front: Independent, MacPherson struts, anti-sway bar.
Rear: Independent, transverse leaf spring with lower control arms

Brakes
Front: 8.0" disc, power-assisted
Rear: 7.2" drum, power-assisted
Rear brake proportioning valve

Wheels and Tires
Wheels: Steel
Tires: Tigar 145SR-13, steel-belted radials with all-weather tread design

Electrical
Bosch electronic ignition
Alternator: 55 amp
Battery: 12 volt, 45 amp

Fuel Economy
City: 28 mpg
Highway: 31 mpg

Standard Equipment
1.1 liter 4-cylinder overhead cam engine
Front-wheel drive
4-wheel independent suspension
Power-assisted brakes, disc front, drum rear
Front anti-sway bar
Rack and pinion steering
Color-coordinated fabric upholstery
Full carpeting, including carpeted luggage compartment
Reclining front seats
Folding rear seats—27.5 cu. ft. luggage space
3 grab handles
2 dome lights
Visor-vanity mirror
Analog instrument gauges
Low-fuel warning light
Steel-belted radial tires
Lexan bumpers
Plastic inner-front fender shields
Bosch electronic ignition
Rear brake proportioning valve
Full-size spare tire
Front spoiler
Hood scoop
Hub caps
PVC undercoating
Opening rear-quarter windows
Rear-window electric defroster
Quartz halogen headlights
Body side molding
Special owner's tool kit
Cigarette lighter
Locking gas cap
Dual storage pockets
Concealed radio antenna
Spare fuse and bulb kit
Night/day rear-view mirror
Electric cooling fan
Console

Source: Yugo America, Inc. promotional materials

expansion of the New Jersey home office to include a corporate planning department. He also informed reporters of Yugo's new slogan, "Everybody Needs a Yugo Sometime."[5]

PROBLEMS BEGIN

In February 1986 *Consumer Reports* published the first of several articles criticizing the Yugo GV. Reporters criticized Malcolm Bricklin for his other car ventures (the Subaru 360 and the Fiat Spider) that had recently failed and pointed out that, after adding destination charges, dealer preparation fees, and a stereo, the price of the Yugo GV exceeded $4,600. The magazine's personal test evaluation was also published. It stated that the transmission was "sloppy," the steering was "heavy," the ride was "jerky," and the heating system was "weak and obtrusive."[6]

The writers continued by denigrating almost every aspect of the car, from seat coverings to the "not-so-spacious" trunk. The safety of the car was questioned but could not be verified by government crash tests. It was noted, however, that the impact of collisions at 3 and 5

Yugo GV Sales in the United States, by Calendar Year

Year	Unit Sales
1985	3,895
1986	35,959
1987	48,812
1988	31,545
1989	10,576
1990	6,359

Source: *Automotive News*, last January issue, 1986-1991.

miles per hours severely twisted and crushed the bumpers. It was estimated that repairing the damage to the front and rear bumpers was $620 and $461, respectively.[7] Twenty-one other defects were discovered, ranging from oil leaks to squealing brakes. A survey by J. D. Power and associates (included in the article) concerning customer satisfaction revealed that over 80 percent of Yugo buyers had reported problems. In short, *Consumer Reports* did not recommend the Yugo GV at *any* price.

The Yugo was facing increasing competition as well. Hyundai Motor America, a subsidiary of the giant South Korean industrial company, introduced the Hyundai Excel for $4,995. The Excel was a hatchback model that included standard features comparable to those of the Yugo GV. It posed a direct threat to the Yugo GV in the lower-priced automobile market.

By mid-October 1986 Yugo America responded to the *Consumer Reports* article and increasing consumer complaints by making 176 improvements to the car without raising its price.[8] William Prior stated that Yugo America spent between $2.5 and $3 million to improve its image thorough advertisements and national incentives. Independent dealers offered additional rebates as well in an effort to boost sagging sales.

Looking ahead, Yugo America planned to introduce some new models, all within the lower-price range. For 1987 the Yugo GV would be given a "face-lift" to take on an aerodynamic look, and a convertible GV was planned for later in the year. In order to meet the needs of couples and small families, Yugo anticipated the 1988 debut of a five-door hatchback, which would compete with the Honda Accord. A four-door sedan would be added to the line between 1989 and 1990, and a two-seater sports car named TCX would be the highlight of 1990.[9]

During 1986, Yugo America contemplated a move to go public by issuing common stock. The idea was abandoned for two reasons. First, Bricklin did not want to surrender any of his equity (75 percent). Second, the company was starting to feel the effects of negative publicity, and financial consultants felt that the stock would not bring a fair price.

MORE TROUBLE

In April 1987 *Consumer Reports* released its annual survey of the 1987 domestic and foreign car models and, once again, Yugo's image was tainted. The writers criticized the Yugo GV from bumper to bumper, stating that "the manual transmission was very imprecise . . . the worst we've tried in years." As for comfort, "small, insufficiently contoured front seats" contributed to an "awkward driving position." In addition, the ride of the car was described as "noisy" and "harsh."[10]

Besides the negative description of the car's driving performance, the article published the results of an independent crash test. This test, which was not mandated by law, disclosed the results of a crash at 35 miles per hour among domestic and foreign automobiles. (The National Highway Traffic Safety Administration requires that all cars pass the national standard impact at 30 miles per hour.) The Yugo GV was among the 40 percent that did not pass the test. In fact, it received the lowest possible ranking with respect to driver and passenger protection. The report indicated that the steering column "moved up and back into the path of the driver's head," and the seats "moved forward during the crash, increasing the load on occupants."[11]

Consumer Reports also reported that damage to the front and rear bumpers when hit at impacts of 3 and 5 miles per hour was $1,081, the highest in its class. This was particularly embarrassing to Yugo America because many of its foreign competitors (including Toyota, Mazda, and Saab) escaped the collisions without a scratch.[12]

Before the second *Consumer Reports* article, Yugo America sold every car coming into its ports every month. Sales in 1987 were the highest to date in number, but this proved to be sales peak. The negative press the Yugo received made car shoppers wary, and dealers were forced to offer $500–$750 rebates as an incentive to buy. In addition several new programs and extended warranties were offered to entice customers. Monthly sales levels started to decline, and waiting lists became virtually nonexistent.

Through all of these problems, William Prior remained enthusiastic, upbeat, and positive about the Yugo, thus providing a source of motivation for all of the employees. As Tony Cappadona stated, "Bill added a lot of charisma and dedication to the company. He let the employees know that everyone was working to achieve a mission. They (the employees) didn't mind working ten or twelve hours a day, because they saw Bill putting in twice as much."

CHANGES IN OWNERSHIP

In 1987, Yugo America, Inc., was acquired by Global Motors, Inc., a company founded by Malcolm Bricklin. Bricklin established Global Motors as an umbrella corporation for importing cars worldwide. Gaining 91 percent of Yugo America, Global became its parent, distributor, and holding company, and it helped with the coordination and distribution of Yugos as they arrived at the Baltimore port.

By 1988 Yugo America and Global Motors began contemplating the sale of a substantial portion of the company in an effort to avoid bankruptcy. In April Mabon Nugent and Company, a New York investment firm, purchased Global Motors for $40 million.[13] Bricklin sold 70 percent of his equity for $20 million, and a debenture was purchased from Global for an additional $20 million. A management group headed by Prior and Edelson agreed to contribute $2.1 million to obtain 5.5 percent of the company. The management group would be awarded stock options periodically over the following three years, bringing the group's total ownership to 22 percent. Prior was named chief executive officer during the acquisition.[14]

THE FINAL YEAR

By April 1988 the company's operating problems had also increased. Not only had a third *Consumer Reports* article on the 1988 models thrashed the Yugo GV again, but dealers were beginning to push potential Yugo buyers to consider their other models. To make things worse, buyers could only get 36-month financing toward the purchase of a Yugo, whereas they could get 48- and 60-month financing on many American models. The thought of lower monthly payments was incentive enough for many prospective Yugo buyers to change their decision in favor of an American-made automobile. If the former tactic did not persuade the buyer, salespeople would criticize the Yugo directly and accentuate the features of the other line the dealer carried. Higher commissions on more costly brands increased the motivation of salespeople to move away from the Yugo.

Even after deciding to buy a Yugo, many consumers ran into additional difficulties when they tried to obtain financing. Because the typical Yugo customer was a young, low-income, first-time buyer, lending institutions were hesitant to make high-risk loans to persons in this segment of the market. It was estimated that as many as 70 percent of all Yugo customers were turned down for credit, since the majority had no previous credit history and a debt-income ratio of over 50 percent. This common scenario was discouraging for both the customers and dealers. Enticing advertisements lured customers in, and yet many could not obtain financing. The dealers became frustrated because of the amount of time and effort it took to put the deal together. Mr. Prior described the situation as "an inefficiency in the market."

In an effort to hurdle these financing roadblocks, Yugo America announced in June 1988 that it would design its own program for financing. The first-time buyer plan was administered through Imperial Savings Association, a $10-billion institution based in San Diego. Yugo and Imperial intended to protect themselves by charging a higher annual percentage rate—as much as four percentage points higher than those of other finance companies. In doing so, Yugo America could establish a higher-than-average reserve for loan defaults. Though the annual percentage rate was higher, buyers could finance the loan over 60 months so that monthly payments remained low.[15]

Approximately fifty dealers were enrolled in the program. Imperial was hesitant to allow all of the dealers to take advantage of Yugo Credit, since there were still some bugs in the system. Also, each state required separate licensing, and Yugo did not have the time to wait for acceptance in each state.

The financing program was terminated after ninety days. One of the provisions of the plan required Yugo America to be in good standing financially. Unpaid bills were accumulating at Yugo America so fast that the company's debt was becoming unmanageable. Imperial Savings pulled out.

In November 1988 William Prior and seventy-one other employees were dismissed from the company, leaving a skeleton crew of seventy-one remaining. Mabon Nugent's intentions were to cut costs in an effort to relieve cash flow pressures and generate additional funds for product development. Marcel Kole, senior vice president and chief financial officer of Global Motors, temporarily replaced Prior as president and chief executive of Yugo America. Turnover within the company was high, and national advertising was brought to a halt.[16] Norauto LP of Ohio agreed to finance two shipments of Yugos backed by letters of credit. Norauto, a firm that aids bankrupt, terminated, or distressed companies, took possession of the cars until Yugo America could repay the $14.3 million letter of credit.[17]

Mabon Nugent and Company had written off $10.5 million as a loss in Global Motors by January 30, 1989. It was estimated that Global would need $10 million to get back on its feet, but Mabon Nugent did not feel that contributing more money to a dying company was a worthy investment. The firm's partners considered selling the company to Zastava or private investors, but neither of the ideas was pursued.[18] Global officially filed for Chapter 11 protection under the bankruptcy laws on January 30, 1989.[19] This provided Global with temporary protection from its creditors and some time to work out a plan of reorganization. Global's unaudited balance sheet reported in the petition for bankruptcy is contained in Exhibit C17.4.

ENDNOTES

1. J. Fierman, "Can a Beetle Brain Stir a Yearning for Yugos?" *Fortune,* May 13, 1985, 73.
2. "The Price Is Right," *Time,* September 9, 1985, 58.
3. J. L. Kovach, "We Don't Overpromise," *Industry Week,* October 13, 1986, 73.
4. Ibid.
5. J. A. Russell, "Yugo Grosses $122 Million in First Year," *Automotive News,* September 1, 1986, 42.
6. "How Much Car for $3990?" *Consumer Reports,* February 1986, 84–86.
7. Ibid.
8. Kovach, 73.
9. J. A. Russell, "Zastava to Construct Plant for U.S. Yugos," *Automotive News,* May 20, 1985, 2.
10. "The 1987 Cars," *Consumer Reports,* April 1987, 200–215.
11. Ibid., 200.
12. Ibid., 208.
13. J. A. Russell, "Bricklin's Import Firm Sold in $40 Million Deal," *Automotive News,* April 18, 1988, 1, 56.
14. Ibid.
15. J. Henry, " Low Finance: Yugo Offers Loans to Spur Buyers," *Automotive News,* August 1, 1988, 1, 51.
16. C. Thomas, "Prior Ousted: Shaky Global Trims Ranks," *Automotive News,* November 14, 1988, 1, 58.
17. J. Henry, "Yugo, Liquidator in Accord," *Automotive News,* March 27, 1989, 1.
18. J. Henry, "Global Struggles to Remain Afloat," *Automotive News,* January 30, 1989, 1, 257.
19. Henry, "Yugo, Liquidator," 1.

EXHIBIT   C17.4   Global Motors' Unaudited Balance Sheet, 1988 ($=thousands)

Assets	
Cash	$ 0
Due from subsidiaries	27,145
Due from manufacturer	15
Inventories	0
Prepaid and other current assets	48
	$ 27,208
Property, plant, and equipment (at cost)	8
Less: accumulated depreciation	(1)
	$ 7
Investment in subsidiaries	223
Total assets	$ 27,438
Liabilities and Shareholders' Equity	
Accounts payable and accrued expenses	$ 1,429
Notes payable	11,825
	13,254
Long-term debt	11,000
Shareholders' equity	3,184
Total liabilities and equity	$ 27,438

Source: Bankruptcy Docket Number 89 00680, filed January 30, 1989, United States Bankruptcy Court, District of New Jersey.

BIBLIOGRAPHY

Aiken, M., and Hage, J. (1971). "The Organic Organization and Innovation," *Sociology* 5: 63–82.

Aldrich, H., and Zimmer, C. (1986). "Entrepreneurship Through Social Networks," D. L. Sexton and R. W. Smilor (eds.). *The Art and Science of Entrepreneurship*. Cambridge, MA: Ballinger: 2–23.

Alexander, A. P. (1967). "The Supply of Industrial Entrepreneurship," *Explorations in Entrepreneurial History* 4: 136–49.

Allais, M. (1968). "Fisher, Irving," D. L. Sills (ed.). *International Encyclopedia of the Social Sciences—Vol. 5*. New York: Free Press.

Angle, H. L., and Van de Ven, A. H. (1989). "Suggestions for Managing the Innovation Journey," A. H. Van de Ven, H. L. Angle, and M. S. Poole (eds.). *Research on the Management of Innovation*. New York: Harper & Row.

Arrow, K. J. (1962). "Economic Welfare and the Allocation of Resources for Invention," *National Bureau of Economic Research*.

Arrow, K. J. (1974). "Limited Knowledge and Economic Analysis," *American Economics Review* 64: 1–10.

Astley, W. G. (1985). "The Two Ecologies: Population and Community Perspectives on Organizational Evolution," *Administrative Science Quarterly* 30: 224–41.

Baldrige, J. V., and Burnham, R. (1975). "Organizational Innovation: Industrial, Organizational, and Environmental Impact," *Administrative Science Quarterly* 20: 165–76.

Barney, J. B., Busenitz, L., Fiet, J. V., and Moesel, D. (1989). "The Structure of Venture Capital Governance: An Organizational Economic Analysis of Relations between Venture Capital Firms and New Ventures," *Proceedings—National Academy of Management*. Washington, DC.

Barreto, H. (1989). *The Entrepreneur In Microeconomic Theory: Disappearance and Explanation*. London: Routledge.

Bauer, P. T., and Yancey, B. S. (1957). *The Economics of Underdeveloped Countries*. Chicago: University of Chicago Press.

Baumol, W. (1968). "Entrepreneurship in Economic Theory," *American Economic Review* 58: 64–71.

Baumol, W. J. (1982). "Toward Operational Models of Entrepreneurship," J. Ronen (ed.). *Entrepreneurship*. Lexington, MA: Lexington Books: 29–48.

Becker, G. S. (1971). *Economic Theory*. New York: Alfred Knopf.

Becker, G. S. (1976). *The Economic Approach to Human Behavior*. Chicago: University of Chicago Press.

Begley, T. M., and Boyd, D. P. (1987). "Psychological Characteristics Associated with Performance in Entrepreneurial Firms and Smaller Businesses," *Journal of Business Venturing* 2: 79–93.

Bigelow, K. W. (1935). "Hawley, Frederick Barnard," E. R. A. Seligman and A. Johnson (eds.). *Encyclopaedia of the Social Sciences—Vol. 7*. New York: Macmillan.

Biggadike, R. (1979). "The Risky Business of Diversification," *Harvard Business Review* 59: 103–11.

Birch, D. L. (1979). *The Job Generation Process*. Cambridge, MA: MIT Program on Neighborhood and Regional Change.

Birley, S. (1985). "The Role of Networks in the Entrepreneurial Process," *Journal of Business Venturing* 1: 107–17.

Birley, S. (1987). "New Ventures and Employment Growth," *Journal of Business Venturing* 2: 155–65.

Bladen, V. W. (1968). "Mill, John Stuart: Economic Considerations," D. L. Sills (ed.). *International Encyclopedia of the Social Sciences—Vol. 10*. New York: Free Press.

Blaug, M., and Sturges, P. (1983). *Who's Who in Economics: A Biographical Dictionary of Major Economists 1700–1981*. Cambridge, MA: MIT Press.

Blaug, M. L. (1980). *The Methodology of Economics: Or How Economists Explain*. Cambridge: Cambridge University Press.

Block, Z. (1982). "Can Corporate Venturing Succeed?" *Journal of Business Strategy* 3: 21–33.

Block, Z., and MacMillan, I. C. (1985). "Milestones for Successful Venture Planning," *Harvard Business Review* 85: 184–88.

Boland, L. (1977). "Testability in Economic Science," *South African Journal of Economics* 45: 93–105.

Brenner, R. (1987). "National Policy and Entrepreneurship: The Statesman's Dilemma," *Journal of Business Venturing* 2: 95–101.

Brockhaus, R. H., Sr. (1980). "Risk Taking Propensity of Entrepreneurs," *Academy of Management Journal* 23: 509–20.

Brockhaus, R. H., Sr. (1982). "The Psychology of the Entrepreneur," C. A. Kent, D. L. Sexton, and K. H. Vesper (eds.). *The Art and Science of Entrepreneurship*. Cambridge, MA: Ballinger: 39–56.

Brockhaus, R. H., Sr., and Horwitz, P. S. (1986). "The Psychology of the Entrepreneur," D. L. Sexton and R. W. Smilor (eds.). *The Art and Science of Entrepreneurship*. Cambridge, MA: Ballinger.

Buchanan, J. M. (1968). "Knight, Frank Hyneman," D. L. Sills (ed.). *International Encyclopedia of the Social Sciences—Vol. 8*. New York: Free Press.

Burgelman, R. A. (1983). "A Process Model of Internal Corporate Venturing in the Major Diversified Firm," *Administrative Science Quarterly* 28: 223–44.

Burgelman, R. A. (1984). "Managing the Internal Corporate Venturing Process," *Sloan Management Review* 24: 33–48.

Burns, T., and Stalker, G. M. (1961). *The Management of Innovation*. London: Tavistock Publications.

Bygrave, W. (1989). "Micro-, Macro-, and Corporate Entrepreneurs: Can They All Fit in the Same Paradigm?" *Proceedings: National Academy of Management*, Washington, DC.

Cantillon, R. (1755). *Essai sur la Nature du Commerce en General*. London: Fletcher Gyles.

Cantillon, R. (1931). *Essay on the Nature of Commerce*. Translated and edited by H. Higgs. London, Macmillan.

Carland, J. W., Hoy, F., Boulton, W. R., and Carland, J. C. (1984). "Differentiating Entrepreneurs from Small Business Owners: A Conceptualization," *Academy of Management Review* 9: 354–59.

Carroll, G. R. (1984). "Organizational Ecology," *Annual Review Sociology* 10: 71–93.

Carsrud, A. L., Olm, K. W., and Eddy, G. G. (1986). "Entrepreneurship: Research in Quest of a Paradigm," D. L. Sexton and R. W. Smilor (eds.). *The Art and Science of Entrepreneurship*. Cambridge, MA: Ballinger: 153–68.

Casson, M. (1982). *The Entrepreneur, An Economic Theory*. Totowa, NJ: Barnes & Noble Books.

Christensen, C. R., and Hansen, A. J. (1987). *Teaching and the Case Method*. Boston: Harvard Business School Publishing Division.

Churchill, N. C., and Lewis, V. L. (1983). "The Five Stages of Small Business Growth," *Harvard Business Review* 83: 3–12.

Clark, J. M. (1938). *John Bates Clark: A Memorial*. New York: Columbia University Press.

Clark, J. M. (1968). "Clark, John Bates," D. L. Sills (ed.). *International Encyclopedia of the Social Sciences—Vol. 2*. New York: Free Press.

Clark, J. B. (1922). *Essentials of Economic Theory*. New York: Macmillan.

Coase, R. H. (1937). "The Nature of the Firm," *Economica* 4: 386–405.

Cochran, T. C. (1965). "The Entrepreneur in Economic Change," *Explorations in Entrepreneurial History* 3: 25–38.

Cochran, T. C. (1968). "Entrepreneurship" in *International Encyclopedia of the Social Sciences*. D. L. Sills (ed.). New York: Free Press: 87–91.

Cole, A. (1942). "Entrepreneurship as an Area of Research," *Journal of Economic History* 2: 118–26.

Collins, O. F., Moore, D. G., and Unwalla, D. B. (1964). *The Enterprising Man*. East Lansing, MI: Michigan State University Press.

Collins, O. F., and Moore, D. G. (1970). *The Organization Makers: A Behavioral Study of Independent Entrepreneurs*. New York: Meredith Press.

Collins, R. (1986). *Max Weber: A Skeleton Key*. Beverly Hills, CA: Sage Publications.

Cooper, A. C., and Dunkelberg, W. C. (1987). "Entrepreneurial Research: Old Questions, New Answers, and Methodological Issues," *American Journal of Small Business* 11: 1–20.

Cyert, R., and March, J. (1970). *A Behavioral Theory of the Firm.* Englewood Cliffs, NJ: Prentice-Hall.

Daft, R. L., and Becker, S. (1978). *Innovation in Organizations.* New York: Elsevier.

Daft, R. L. (1978). "A Dual-Core Model of Organizational Innovation," *Academy of Management Journal* 21: 193–210.

Damanpour, F. (1987). "The Adoption of Technological, Administrative, and Ancillary Innovations: Impact of Organizational Factors," *Journal of Management* 13: 675–88.

Dickson, P. R., and Giglierano, J. J. (1986). "Missing the Boat and Sinking the Boat: A Conceptual Model of Entrepreneurial Risk," *Journal of Marketing* 50: 58–70.

Dolan, E. G. (1976). "Austrian Economics as Extraordinary Science," E. G. Dolan (ed.). Kansas City, MO: Sheed & Ward.

Dolan, E. G., and Lindsey, D. E. (1988). "Entrepreneurship and the Market Process," *Economics,* 5th ed. New York: Dryden Press: 676.

Drucker, P. (1985). *Innovation and Entrepreneurship.* New York: Harper & Row.

Duncan, R. B. (1976). "The Ambidextrous Organization: Designing Dual Structures for Innovation," R. H. Killman, L. R. Pondy, and D. Slevins (eds.). New York: North Holland.

Ellis, B. (1975). *Entrepreneurship in Rough Seas.* Nashville: Vanderbilt University Press.

Fast, N. D., and Pratt, S. E. (1981). "Individual Entrepreneurship and the Large Firm," K. A. Vesper (ed.). *Frontiers of Entrepreneurial Research.* Wellesley, MA: Babson College.

Fisher, F. M., and Tamin, P. (1973). "Returns to Scale in Research and Development: What Does the Schumpeterian Hypothesis Imply?" *Journal of Political Economy* 81: 56–70.

Fried, V. H., and Hisrich, R. D. (1988). "Venture Capital Research: Past, Present, and Future," *Entrepreneurship Theory and Practice* 13: 15–28.

Gartner, W. B. (1985). "A Conceptual Framework for Describing the Phenomenon of New Venture Creation," *Academy of Management Review* 10: 696–706.

Gartner, W. B. (1989). "Who Is an Entrepreneur? Is the Wrong Question," *Entrepreneurship Theory and Practice* 13: 47–64.

Gatewood, E., Hoy, F., and Spindler, C. (1984). "Functionalist vs. Conflict Theories: Entrepreneurship Disrupts the Power Structure in a Small Southern Community," J. A. Hornaday, E. B. Shils, J. A. Timmons, and K. H. Vesper (eds.). *Frontiers of Entrepreneurial Research.* Wellesley, MA: Babson College Center for Entrepreneurial Research: 265–79.

Giddens, A. (1979). *Central Problems in Social Theory: Action, Structure and Contradictions in Social Analysis.* Berkeley, CA: University of California Press.

Glade, W. P. (1967). "Approaches to a Theory of Entrepreneurial Formation," *Explorations in Entrepreneurial History* 4: 245–59.

Gray, A. (1980). *The Development of Economic Doctrine,* 2nd ed. London: Longman.

Greenfield, S. M., and Strickon, A. (1981). "A New Paradigm for the Study of Entrepreneurship and Social Change," *Economic Development and Cultural Change* 29: 467–99.

Greenfield, S. M., and Strickon, A. (1986). *Entrepreneurship and Social Change.* Lanham, MD: University Press of America.

Greiner, L. E. (1972). "Evolution and Revolution as Organizations Grow," *Harvard Business Review* 72: 37–46.

Guth, W. D. (1991). "Research in Entrepreneurship," *The Entrepreneurship Forum.* New York: Center for Entrepreneurial Studies, New York University.

Hagen, E. E. (1960). "The Entrepreneur as Rebel Against Traditional Society," *Human Organization* 19: 185–87.

Hagen, E. E. (1962). *On the Theory of Social Change.* Homewood, IL: Dorsey Press.

Hambrick, D. C., and Crozier, L. M. (1985). "Stumblers and Stars in the Management of Rapid Growth," *Journal of Business Venturing* 1: 31–45.

Hannan, M. T., and Freeman, J. (1977). "The Population Ecology of Organizations," *American Journal of Sociology* 82: 929–64.

Hansen, A. H. (1964). *Business Cycles and National Income.* New York: Norton.

Harris, S. E. (1951). *Schumpeter: Social Scientist.* Boston: Harvard University Press.

Hebert, R. F., and Link, A. N. (1988). *The Entrepreneur: Mainstream Views and Radical Critiques,* 2nd ed. New York: Praeger.

Hebert, R. F., and Link, A. N. (1989). "In Search of the Meaning of Entrepreneurship," *Small Business Economics* 1: 39–49.

Higgins, J. M., and Vincze, J. W. (1993). *Strategic Management: Text and Cases,* 5th ed. New York: Dryden.

Hisrich, R. D., and Peters, M. P. (1989). *Entrepreneurship: Starting, Developing, and Managing a New Enterprise.* Homewood, IL: BPI-Irwin.

Hlavacek, J. D., and Thompson, V. A. (1978). "Bureaucracy and Venture Failure," *Academy of Management Review* 3: 242–48.

Hu, S. C. (1973). "On the Incentive to Invent: A Clarificatory Note," *Journal Law and Economics* 16: 169–77.

Hunt, E. K. (1979). *History of Economic Thought: A Critical Perspective.* Belmont, CA: Wadsworth.

Huntsman, B., and Hoban, J. P. Jr. (1980). "Investment in New Enterprise: Some Empirical Observations on Risk, Return, and Market Structure," *Financial Management* 9: 44–51.

Jennings, D. F., and Zeithaml, C. P. (1983). "Locus of Control: A Review and Directions for Entrepreneurial Research," *Proceedings—National Academy of Management:* Dallas.

Jennings, D. F., and Lumpkin, J. D. (1989). "Functionally Modeling Corporate Entrepreneurship: An Empirical Integrative Analysis," *Journal of Management* 15: 485–502.

Jennings, D. F., and Young, D. M. (1990). "An Empirical Comparison between Objective and Subjective Measures of the Product Innovation Domain of Corporate Entrepreneurship," *Entrepreneurship Theory and Practice* 15: 53–66.

Jennings, D. F., and Seaman, S. L. (1990). "Aggressiveness of Response to New Business Opportunities Following Deregulation: An Empirical Study of Established Financial Firms," *Journal of Business Venturing* 5: 177–89.

Jennings, D. F. (1986). "A Process Model of Organizational Entrepreneurship, Strategic Actions, and Performance," Unpublished doctoral dissertation. College Station, TX: Texas A&M University.

Jennings, D. F. (1993). *Effective Supervision: Frontline Management for the '90s.* St. Paul, MN: West.

Johnson, B. R. (1990). "Toward a Multidimensional Model of Entrepreneurship: The Case of Achievement Motivation and the Entrepreneur," *Entrepreneurship Theory and Practice* 14: 39–54.

Kaldor, N. (1934). "The Equilibrium of the Firm," *Economic Journal* 44: 60–76.

Kallenberg, A. (1989). "Defining Entrepreneurship," G. Libecap (ed.). *Advances in the Study of Entrepreneurship, Innovation, and Economic Growth.* Greenwich, CT: JAI Press: 158–61.

Kamien, M. I., and Schwartz, N. L. (1975). "Market Structure and Innovation: A Survey," *Journal of Economic Literature* 13: 1–37.

Kanter, R. M. (1983). *The Change Masters.* New York: Simon and Schuster.

Kanter, R. M. (1989). *When Giants Learn to Dance.* New York: Simon and Schuster.

Kaplan, A. (1946). "Definition and Specification of Meaning," *Journal of Philosophy* 43: 80–104.

Kaplan, A. (1954). "What Good Is 'Truth'?" *Journal of Philosophy and Phenomenological Research* 15: 151–70.

Kaplan, A. (1963). *The Conduct of Inquiry: Methodology for Behavioral Science.* New York: Chandler-Harper & Row.

Kauder, E. (1968). "Bohm-Bawerk, Eugen Von," D. L. Sills (ed.). *International Encyclopedia of the Social Sciences—Vol. 2.* New York: Free Press.

Kent, C. A. (1984). "The Rediscovery of the Entrepreneur," C. A. Kent (ed.). *The Environment for Entrepreneurship.* Lexington, MA: Lexington Books.

Kets de Vries, M. F. R. (1985). "The Dark Side of Entrepreneurship," *Harvard Business Review* 85: 160–67.

Kets de Vries, M. F. R., and Miller, D. (1984). "Neurotic Style and Organizational Pathology," *Strategic Management Journal* 5: 35–55.

Kets de Vries, M. F. R., and Miller, D. (1986). "Personality, Culture, and Organization," *Academy of Management Review* 2: 266–79.

Keynes, J. M. (1972). "Francis Ysidro Edgeworth," in *Essays in Biography.* New York: Macmillan.

Khan, A. M. (1987). "Assessing Venture Capital Investments with Noncompensatory Behavior Decision Models," *Journal of Business Venturing* 2: 193–205.

Kihlstrom, R. E., and Laffont, J. J. (1979). "A General Equilibrium Entrepreneurial Theory of Firm Formation Based on Risk Aversion," *Journal of Political Economy* 87: 719–48.

Kilby, P. (1971). *Entrepreneurship and Economic Development*. New York: Free Press.

Kim, L. (1980). "Organizational Innovation and Structure," *Journal of Business Research* 8: 225–45.

Kirzner, I. M. (1973). *Competition and Entrepreneurship*. Chicago: University of Chicago Press.

Knight, F. H. (1921). *Risk, Uncertainty and Profit*. Boston: Houghton Mifflin.

Knight, F. H. (1949). "Profit," W. Fellner and B. Haley (eds.). New York: Blakson.

Knight, F. H. (1956). *On the History and Method of Economics: Selected Essays*. Chicago: University of Chicago Press.

Koolman, G. (1971). "Say's Conception of the Role of the Entrepreneur," *Economica* 38: 269–86.

Kourilsky, M. (1980). "Predictors of Entrepreneurship in a Simulated Economy," *Journal of Creative Behavior* 14: 175–98.

Kuhn, T. (1970). *The Structure of Scientific Revolutions*, 2nd ed. Chicago: University of Chicago Press.

Kunkel, J. H. (1963). "Psychological Factors in the Analysis of Economic Development," *Journal of Social Issues* 19: 68–87.

Lakatos, I. (1978). "The Methodology of Scientific Research Programs," in *Philosophical Papers*. J. Worrall and G. Currie (eds.) Cambridge: Cambridge University Press.

Leigh, A. H. (1968). "Thunen, Johann Heinrich von," D. L. Sills (ed.). *International Encyclopedia of the Social Sciences—Vol. 16*. New York: Free Press.

Libecap, G. D. (1986). "Do Large Corporations Provide an Environment for Entrepreneurs?" G. Libecap (ed.). *Advances in the Study of Entrepreneurship, Innovation, and Economic Growth*. Greenwich, CT: JAI Press.

Link, A. N. (1980). "Firm Size and Efficient Entrepreneurial Activity: A Reformulation of the Schumpeter Hypothesis," *Journal of Political Economy* 88: 771–83.

Littlechild, S. C. (1979). *The Fallacy of the Mixed Economy*. San Francisco: Cato Institute.

Low, M. B., and MacMillan, I. C. (1988). "Entrepreneurship: Past Research and Future Challenges," *Journal of Management* 14: 139–61.

Lowry, S. T. (1987). *The Archaeology of Economic Ideas*. Durham, NC: Duke University Press.

MacMillan, I. C., Block, Z., and Subba Narasimha, P. N. (1986). "Corporate Venturing: Alternatives, Obstacles Encountered, and Experience Effects," *Journal of Business Venturing* 1: 177–92.

MacMillan, I. C., and Day, D. L. (1987). "Corporate Ventures into Industrial Markets: Dynamics of Aggressive Entry," *Journal of Business Venturing* 2: 29–39.

MacMillan, I. C. (1983). "The Politics of New Venture Management," *Harvard Business Review* 61: 8–16.

MacMillan, I. C. (1986). "Progress in Research on Corporate Venturing," D. L. Sexton, and R. A. Smilor (eds.). *The Art and Science of Entrepreneurship*. Cambridge, MA: Ballinger.

Macrae, N. (1976). "The Coming Entrepreneurial Revolution: A Survey," *The Economist* 11: 41–44.

Maidique, M. A. (1980). "Entrepreneurs, Champions, and Technological Innovation," *Sloan Management Review* 20: 59–76.

Maidique, M. A., and Zirger, B. J. (1985). "The New Product Learning Cycle," *Research Policy*: 299–313.

Mansfield, E., Rapoport, J., Romero, A., Villani, E., Wagner, S., and Husic, F. (1977). *The Production and Application of New Industrial Technology*. New York: Norton.

Markham, J. W. (1965). "Rates of Return from Industrial Research and Development," *American Economic Review—Papers and Proceedings* 55: 323–32.

Martin, M. J. C. (1984). *Managing Technological Innovation and Entrepreneurship*. Reston, VA: Reston.

McClelland, D. C. (1961). *The Achieving Society*. Princeton, NJ: Van Nostrand.

McClelland, D. C. (1962). "Business Drive and National Achievement," *Harvard Business Review* 40: 99–112.

McClelland, D. C. (1965). "Achievement and Entrepreneurship: A Longitudinal Study," *Journal of Personality and Social Psychology* 1: 389–92.

McGrath, J. E. (1964). "Toward A Theory or Method for Research in Organizations," W. W. Cooper, H. J. Leavitt, and M. W. Shelly (eds.). *New Perspectives in Organizational Research*. New York: Wiley.

Miles, R., and Snow, C. (1978). *Organizational Strategy, Structure, and Process.* New York: McGraw-Hill.

Mill, J. S. (1848). *Principles of Political Economy with Some of Their Applications to Social Philosophy.* London: John W. Parker.

Miller, D., and Friesen, P. H. (1980). "Archetypes of Organizational Transition," *Administrative Science Quarterly* 25: 268–99.

Miller, D., and Friesen, P. H. (1982). "Innovation in Conservative and Entrepreneurial Firms: Two Models of Strategic Momentum," *Strategic Management Journal* 3: 1–25.

Miller, D., and Friesen, P. H. (1984). *Organizations: A Quantum View.* Englewood Cliffs, NJ: Prentice-Hall.

Mintzberg, H. (1973). "Strategy Making in Three Modes," *California Management Review* 16: 44–58.

Mises, L. V. (1949). *Human Action.* New Haven, CT: Yale University Press.

Moore, D. G. (1970). *The Organization Makers.* New York: Appleton-Century-Crofts.

Moorhead, G., and Griffin, R. W. (1992). "Individual Differences," *Organizational Behavior*, 3rd ed. Boston: Houghton Mifflin: 72–101.

Morgan, G. (1980). "Paradigms, Metaphors, and Puzzle Solving in Organization Theory," *Administrative Science Quarterly* 25: 605–22.

Nerlove, M. (1972). "Lags in Economic Behavior," *Econometrica* 40: 221–51.

Nerlove, M. (1974). "Household and Economy: Toward a New Theory of Population and Economic Growth," *Journal of Political Economy* 82: 200–18.

Nielsen, R. P., Peters, M. P., and Hisrich, R. D. (1985). "Intrapreneurship Strategy for Internal Markets—Corporate, Non-Profit, and Government Institution Cases," *Strategic Management Journal* 6: 181–89.

Owens, R. L. (1978). "The Anthropological Study of Entrepreneurship," *The Eastern Anthropologist* 31: 65–80.

Palmer, M. (1971). "The Application of Psychological Testing to Entrepreneurial Potential," *California Management Review* 13: 36–54.

Paulin, W. L., Coffey, R. E., and Spaulding, M. E. (1982). "Entrepreneurship Research: Methods and Directions," C. A. Kent, D. L. Sexton, and K. A. Vesper (eds.). *Encyclopedia of Entrepreneurship.* Englewood Cliffs, NJ: Prentice-Hall.

Peterson, R. A., and Berger, D. G. (1971). "Entrepreneurship in Organizations: Evidence from the Popular Music Industry," *Administrative Science Quarterly* 16: 97–107.

Peterson, R. W. (1967). "New Venture Management in a Large Company," *Harvard Business Review* 45: 68–76.

Pfeffer, J. (1977). "The Ambiguity of Leadership," *Academy of Management Review* 2: 104–12.

Phillips, A. (1986). "Theory and the Analysis of Financial Markets," G. Libecap (ed.). *Advances in the Study of Entrepreneurship, Innovation, and Economic Growth.* Greenwich, CT: JAI Press: 80.

Pinchot, G. (1985). *Intrapreneuring, or Why You Don't Have to Leave the Corporation to Become an Entrepreneur.* New York: Harper & Row.

Quinn, J. B., Mintzberg, H., and James, R. (1988). *The Strategy Process.* Englewood Cliffs, NJ: Prentice-Hall.

Quinn, J. B. (1980). *Strategies for Change: Logical Incrementalism.* Homewood, IL: Irwin.

Reich, R. B. (1991). *The Work of Nations.* New York: Knopf.

Reynolds, P. D. (1987). "New Firms: Societal Contribution Versus Survival Potential," *Journal of Business Venturing* 2: 231–46.

Robbins, N. E. G. (1986). "Entrepreneurial Assessment: Characteristics Which Differentiate Entrepreneurs, Intrapreneurs, and Managers." Unpublished doctoral dissertation. University of Minnesota: Minneapolis, MN.

Roberts, E. B. (1980). "New Ventures for Corporate Growth," *Harvard Business Review* 60: 132–42.

Robinson, P. B. (1987). "Prediction of Entrepreneurship Based on an Attitude Consistency Model." Unpublished doctoral dissertation. Brigham Young University: Provo, UT.

Robinson, P. B., Stimpson, D. V., Huefner, J. C., and Hunt, H. K. (1991). "An Attitude Approach to the Prediction of Entrepreneurship," *Entrepreneurship Theory and Practice* 15: 13–32.

Robinson, R. B., Jr. (1982). "The Importance of Outsiders in Small Firm Strategic Planning," *Academy of Management Journal* 25: 80–93.

Robinson, R. B., Jr., and Pearce, J. A. II. (1986). "Product Life-cycle Considerations and the Nature of Strategic Activities in Entrepreneurial Firms," *Journal of Business Venturing* 1: 207–24.

Rule, E. G., and Irwin, D. W. (1988). "Fostering Intrapreneurship: The New Competitive Edge," *Journal of Business Strategy* (May–June): 44–47.

Sandberg, W. R., and Hofer, C. W. (1987). "Improving New Venture Performance: The Role of Strategy, Industry Structure, and the Entrepreneur," *Journal of Business Venturing* 2: 5–28.

Sathe, V. (1983). "Intrapreneurship: A New Form of Corporate Entrepreneurship," Cambridge, MA: Division of Research, Harvard Business School.

Sathe, V. (1989). "Fostering Entrepreneurship in the Large, Diversified Firm," *Organizational Dynamics* (Summer): 20–32.

Say, J. B. (1803). *Traite d'Economie Politique*. Paris: Caille Editeur.

Say, J. B. (1828). *Cours Complet d'Economie*. Paris: Secheresse.

Say, J. B. (1845). *A Treatise on Political Economy*, 5th ed. Translated by C. R. Prinsep. Philadelphia, PA: Wrightman and Franklin.

Schatz, S. P. (1971). "On Achievement and Economic Growth: A Critical Appraisal," P. Kilby (ed.). *Entreprenership and Economic Development*. New York: Free Press.

Schein, E. H. (1983). "The Role of the Founder in Creating Organizational Culture," *Organizational Dynamics* 12: 13–28.

Schere, J. L. (1982). "Tolerance of Ambiguity as a Discriminating Variable Between Entrepreneurs and Managers," *Proceedings—National Academy of Management*.

Scherer, F. M. (1972). *Industrial Market Structure and Economic Performance*, 2nd ed. Chicago: Rand McNally.

Scherer, F. M. (1992). "Competing for Comparative Advantage through Technological Innovation," *Business and Contemporary World* 4: 30–39.

Schneider, E. R. (1975). *Joseph A. Schumpeter*. Translated by W. E. Kuhn. Lincoln, NB: Bureau of Business Research.

Schultz, T. W. (1974). "The High Value of Human Time: Population Equilibrium," *Journal of Political Economy* 82: 2–10.

Schultz, T. W. (1975). "The Value of the Ability to Deal with Disequilibria," *Journal of Economic Literature* 13: 827–46.

Schultz, T. W. (1980). *Investing in People*. Berkeley, CA: University of California Press.

Schultz, T. W. (1990). "Demand and Supply," *Restoring Economic Equilibrium: Human Capital in the Modernizing Economy*. London: Basil Blackwell.

Schumpeter, J. (1934). *The Theory of Economic Development*. Cambridge: Harvard University Press.

Schumpeter, J. (1947). "The Creative Response In Economic History," *Journal of Economic History* 7: 149–59.

Schumpeter, J. A. (1950). *Capitalism, Socialism, and Democracy*, 3rd ed. New York: Harper.

Schumpeter, J. A. (1951). "Eugen Von Bohm-Bawerk," *Ten Great Economists from Marx to Keynes*. Oxford, UK: Oxford University Press.

Scott, W. A. (1933). *The Development of Economics*. New York: Appleton-Century.

Sexton, D. L. (1980). "Characteristics and Role Demands of Successful Entrepreneurs," *Proceedings—National Academy of Management*, Detroit.

Sexton, D. L., and Bowman, N. (1985). "The Entrepreneur: A Capable Executive and More," *Journal of Business Venturing* 1: 129–40.

Shapero, A. (1975). "Entrepreneurship and Economic Development," *Entrepreneurship and Enterprise Development: A Worldwide Perspective*. Milwaukee: Proceedings of Project ISEE.

Shapero, A. (1975). "The Displaced Uncomfortable Entrepreneur," *Psychology Today*: 83–89.

Shapero, A., and Sokol, L. (1982). "The Social Dimensions of Entrepreneurship," C. A. Kent, D. L. Sexton, and K. H. Vesper (eds.). *Encyclopedia of Entrepreneurship*. Englewood Cliffs, NJ: Prentice-Hall: 72–88.

Simon, H. A. (1947). *Administrative Behavior*. New York: Macmillan.

Sinetar, M. (1985). "Entrepreneurs, Chaos, and Creativity: Can Creative People Really Survive Large Company Structure?" *Sloan Management Review* 25: 57–62.

Smilor, R. W., and Gill, M. D., Jr. (1986). *The New Business Incubator*. Lexington, MA: Lexington Books.

Smith, Adam. (1776). *An Inquiry into the Nature and Causes of the Wealth of Nations.* London: Longmans. Republished by Modern Library (1937).

Smith, N. R., and Miner, J. B. (1983). "Type of Entrepreneur, Type of Firm, and Managerial Motivation: Implications for Organizational Life Cycle Theory," *Strategic Management Journal* 4: 325–40.

Sobel, R., and Sicilia, D. (1986). *The Entrepreneurs.* New York: Houghton Mifflin.

Spiegel, H. W. (1983). *The Growth of Economic Thought.* Durham, NC: Duke University Press.

Stevenson, H. H. (1983). "Entrepreneurship: A Process of Creating Value," Cambridge, MA: Division of Research, Harvard Business School.

Stevenson, H. H., Muzyka, D. F., and Timmons, J. A. (1987). "Venture Capital in Transition: A Monte-Carlo Simulation of Changes in Investment Patterns," *Journal of Business Venturing* 2: 103–21.

Stevenson, H. H., Roberts, M. J., and Grousbeck, H. I. (1989). *New Business Ventures and the Entrepreneur,* 3rd ed. Homewood, IL: Irwin.

Stolper, W. F. (1968). "Schumpeter, Joseph Alois," D. L. Sills (ed.) *International Encyclopedia of the Social Sciences—Vol. 14.* New York: Free Press.

Tansik, D. A., and Wolf, G. (1986). "Entrepreneurial Roles in the Process of Technological Innovation," G. Libecap (ed.). *Advances in the Study of Entrepreneurship, Innovation, and Economic Growth.* Greenwich, CT: JAI Press: 115–27.

Thomas, J., and Griffin, R. W. (1983). "The Social Information Processing Model of Task Design: A Review of the Literature," *Academy of Management Review* 8: 672–82.

Thompson, A. A., Jr., and Strickland, A. J. III. (1992). *Strategic Management: Concepts and Cases,* 6th ed. Homewood, IL: Irwin.

Thurow, L. (1992). *Head to Head: The Coming Economic Battle Among Japan, Europe, and America.* New York: Morrow.

Timmons, J. (1986). "Growing Up Big: Entrepreneurship and the Creation of High Potential Ventures," D. L. Sexton and R. W. Smilor (eds.). *The Art and Science of Entrepreneurship.* Cambridge, MA: Ballinger: 211–22.

Tushman, M. L., and Anderson, P. (1986). "Technological Discontinuities and Organizational Environments," *Administrative Science Quarterly* 31: 439–65.

Tushman, M. L., Virany, B., and Romanelli, E. (1986). "Executive Succession, Strategic Reorientation, and Organizational Evolution: The Minicomputer Industry as a Case in Point," *Technology in Society* 7: 297–313.

Tuttle, C. (1927). "The Entrepreneur Function in Economic Literature," *Journal of Political Economy* 35: 501–21.

Tyebjee, T. T., and Bruno, A. V. (1984). "A Model of Venture Capitalist Investment Activity," *Management Science* 30: 1051–66.

Van de Ven, A. H. (1986). "Central Problems in the Management of Innovation," *Management Science* 32: 590–607.

Van de Ven, A. H., Hudson, R., and Schroeder, D. M. (1984). "Designing New Business Startups: Entrepreneurial, Organizational, and Ecological Considerations," *Journal of Management* 10: 87–107.

VanderWerf, P., and Brush, C. (1989). "Toward Agreement on the Focus of Entrepreneurship Research: Progress Without Definition," *Proceedings: National Academy of Management,* Washington, DC.

Vesper, K. H. (1983). *Entrepreneurship and National Policy.* Pittsburgh, PA: Carnegie-Mellon University.

Vesper, K. H., and McMullan, W. E. (1988). "Entrepreneurship: Today Courses, Tomorrow Degrees?" *Entrepreneurship Theory and Practice* 13: 7–14.

Von Clausewitz, C. (1976). *On War.* Translated by M. Howard and P. Paret. Princeton, NJ: Princeton University Press.

von Hayek, F. A. (1945). "The Use of Knowledge in Society," *American Economic Review* 35: 519–30.

Weber, M. (1904). "Die Protestantische Ethik und der Geist des Kapitalismus," *Archiv fur Sozialwissenschaft und Sozialpolitik* 20: 52–89.

Weber, M. (1930). *The Protestant Ethic and the Spirit of Capitalism.* Translated by T. Parsons. New York: Scribner.

Weber, M. (1947). *The Theory of Social and Economic Organization.* Translated by A. M. Henderson and T. Parsons. New York: Free Press.

Weber, M. (1949). *The Methodology of the Social Sciences.* Translated by E. Kau. New York: Harper & Row.

Webster, F. A. (1977). "Entrepreneurs and Ventures: An Attempt of Classification and Clarification," *Academy of Management Review* 2: 54–61.

Weick, K. E. (1979). *The Social Psychology of Organizing,* 2nd ed. Reading, MA: Addison-Wesley.

Welch, F. (1970). "Education in Production," *Journal of Political Economy* 8: 35–59.

Weston, J. F. (1949). "Profit as the Payment for the Function of Uncertainty-Bearing," *Journal of Business* 22: 106–18.

Williamson, O. E. (1975). *Markets and Hierarchies.* New York: Free Press.

Wortman, M. S., Jr. (1987). "Entrepreneurship: An Integrating Typology and Evaluation of the Empirical Research in the Field," *Journal of Management* 13: 259–79.

Young, F. W. (1971). "A Macrosociological Interpretation of Entrepreneurship," P. Kilby (ed.). *Entrepreneurship and Economic Development.* New York: Free Press.

Zahra, S. A. (1986). "A Canonical Analysis of Corporate Entrepreneurship Antecedents and Impact on Performance," *Proceedings—National Academy of Management,* Chicago, IL.

Zahra, S. A. (1991). "Predictors and Financial Outcomes of Corporate Entrepreneurship: An Exploratory Study," *Journal of Business Venturing* 6: 259–85.

Zahra, S. A., Pearce, J. A. II, Jennings, D. F., and Covin, J. G. (1991). "Corporate Entrepreneurship and Innovation," *Proceedings—National Academy of Management,* Atlanta, GA.

NAME INDEX

SUBJECT
INDEX